Writers
on Artists

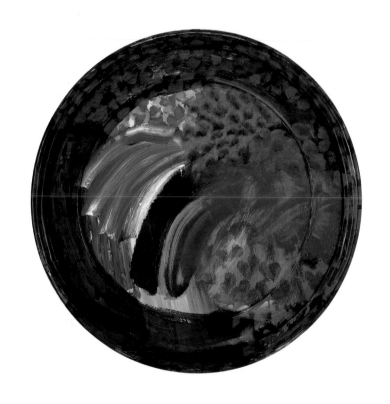

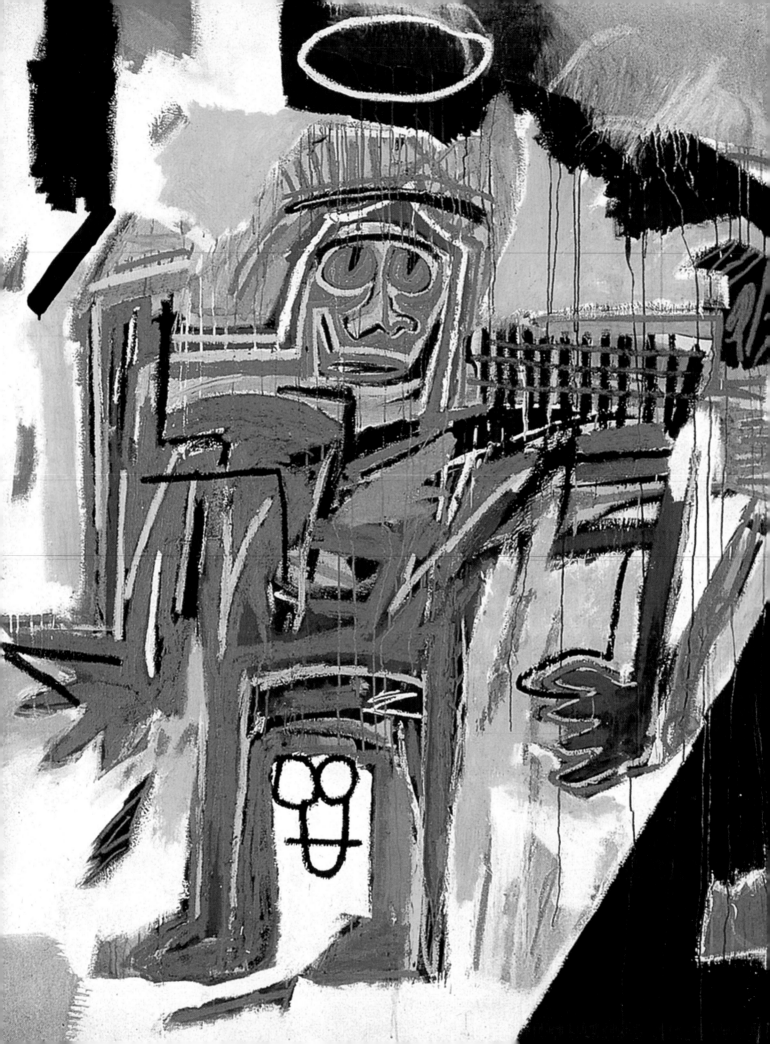

Writers
on Artists

In association with
Modern Painters

London, New York, Delhi, Sydney,
Munich, Paris and Johannesburg

LONDON, NEW YORK, DELHI, SYDNEY,
MUNICH, PARIS AND JOHANNESBURG

Project Editor Barbara Minton
US Designer Megan Clayton
Editorial Assistance Jane Perlmutter
Creative Director Tina Vaughan
Editorial Director Chuck Wills
DTP Russell Shaw
Publisher Sean Moore
Production Manager Chris Avgherinos

Modern Painters
Editor-in-Chief Karen Wright
Editor Craig Burnett
Managing Editor Anthony Jay
Copyright Coordinator Julie Bettridge
Editorial Assistance Kate Barrette, Shane Waltener, Maria David, Sarah Luddy, Litia Perta
Design Steve Hawes & Akio Morishima
Design Consultant Herman Lelie

Developed by
Cambridge Publishing Management

First American Edition, 2001

00 01 02 03 04 05 10 9 8 7 6 5 4 3 2 1

Published in the United States by
DK Publishing, Inc.
95 Madison Avenue
New York, NY 10016

DK Publishing offers special discounts for bulk purchases for sales promotions or premiums. Specific, large-quantity needs can be met with special editions, including personalized covers, excerpts of existing guides, and corporate imprints. For more information, contact Special Markets Department, DK Publishing, Inc., 95 Madison Avenue, New York, NY 10016 Fax: 800-600-9098.

Library of Congress Cataloging-in-Publication Data

Writers on artists / [essays by] A.S. Byatt... [et al.].
    p. cm.
    Includes index.
    ISBN 0-7894-8035-2 (alk. paper)
    1. Art, Modern--20th century. 2. Art, Modern--19th century.   I.
Byatt, A.S., 1936-   .
  N6490 .W755 2001
  709'.04--dc21
                                        2001042264

Color reproduction by Mullis Morgan, UK
Printed and bound in the United States by R.R. Donnelly & Sons Co.

See our complete catalog at
www.dk.com

Contents

• Foreword by A.S. Byatt 6 •

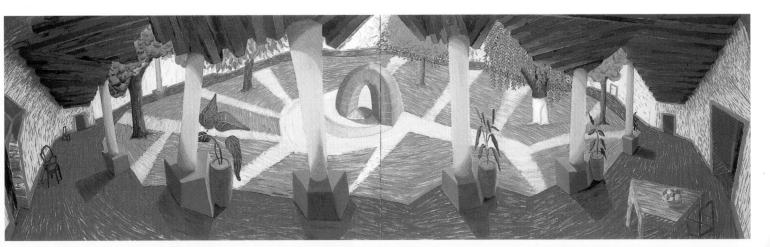

Foreword

by A.S. Byatt

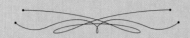

Writing about painting is peculiarly difficult. As Patrick Heron says "the flavour of words is intensely anti-visual. Strictly speaking, painting cannot be written about. Visual experience is *purely* visual…" A good novelist or poet, describing a place or person, knows that the words call up as many different mental images of that place or person as there are readers. Yet to write about painting requires unusual rigor and accuracy. A work of art is singular.

There are many ways of writing badly about painting. Most painters write badly, producing manifestos or vague lyrical afflatus. There is an "appreciative" language of threadbare, not inaccurate, but overexposed and irritating words- "tender," "delicate," "intense," "bold," and above all "vibrant." There is the language of the schools which "situates" works and artists in schools and movements and recently judges them with a remorseless innocent moralism, on political, social, and sexual grounds. Many novelists and poets write badly because they see paintings as allegories of writing, and make a beeline for any included verbal clue, including the signature, as a way in to a possible narrative or meaning.

Modern Painters puts good writing first. The contributions in this anthology are written by novelists and poets who can see, and describe accurately what they see, by painters who can write, and can make non-painters understand how a painter thinks about his or her work, and by those very rare writers on art who can explain how and why a work of art is as it is and strikes us as it does. It isn't a text-book – the pieces are chosen primarily for the quality of the writing. And they have in common the virtues of toughness, flexibility, delight in impossible accuracy, writerly modesty – and above all, putting curiosity before the need to judge and generosity before smartness or position-taking. There is little gallery-gossip though what there is is amusing, a bearable amount of jokiness, and almost no dated meta-language. Each piece is a revelation, both of artist and writer – and in the cases of Hockney, Riley, and Heron, indirectly of the art of the writer, as well of the artist discussed.

And the illustrations are plentiful, splendid, and indispensable. They bear out Patrick Heron's point. They are "strictly unamenable to words of any kind…But we can *hint* with any luck at the patently real realities of the eye." These writers do that. It is a truly civilized collection.

Introduction

by Karen Wright

Editor-in-Chief

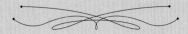

W*riters on Artists* has had a very long period of gestation—the fourteen years of the magazine's lifetime. *Modern Painters* was founded by the late writer and critic Peter Fuller: combative and idealistic, he issued a challenge to an art world he found devoid of spiritual values. Above all, he wished to make art writing both readable and enjoyable. Since his death in 1990, it has been my great pleasure to muster an extraordinary list of writers, from pop stars and poets to philosophers and novelists – as well, of course, as great critics. All of these writers share one vital quality, that of being visual: all of them relish the task of looking closely at art. Unfortunately, not all of them, or even a small proportion, could be fitted within these pages. The task of selection has been difficult, even painful, since so many more, as well as the artists they engaged with, deserve to be included here. And so this book is dedicated to all *Modern Painters'* contributors, and to all the artists who inspired them.

But there is one writer I want particularly to single out. David Sylvester, who died shortly before this book went to press, was one of a loyal band of contributors with whom I enjoyed an ongoing debate. Getting a piece from David entailed lively, often provocative, discussion about everything – from illustrations and presentation to the tone of an individual word or phrase. As a curator and critic, he cared passionately about being true to his subject, getting it right: he was a great example. Shortly before he died, I was anguishing over the order of contents in this book, and the risk of offending the more delicate egos of both writers and artists over their location in the book. David rebuked me: "There is only one solution," he said. "Place them chronologically, in order of publication." He was right—it was a simple solution and the best one. I should like to dedicate this book in gratitude to his memory. We will all miss his long silences.

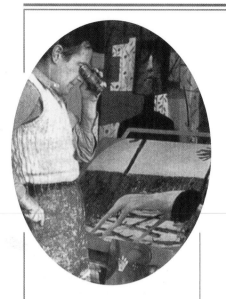

Sydney Nolan

by Peter Fuller

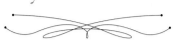

SYDNEY NOLAN
Australia's most widely known artist, Sir Sydney Nolan worked in a variety of media in his career as a painter, printmaker, draftsman, and set designer, using such varied materials as house paint and polyvinyl acetate on masonite, glass, paper, and canvas.

Born in Melbourne in 1917, Nolan had little formal art training. His first works, starting at about the age of 21, were abstract, and revealed the influence of Paul Klee. Typical of this period is Boy and the Moon *(1940) – a splash of yellow against a blue background. Later Nolan arrived at a more representational style, producing both landscapes and work that dealt with Australian folklore, history, and legend. The infamous Australian bushranger and outlaw, Ned Kelly, is featured in Nolan's work of this time.*

Nolan's work has been exhibited internationally; in the permanent collection of the Tate Gallery, London, and the Museum of Modern Art in New York. He was knighted in 1981 and became a member of the Order of Merit in 1983. Sir Sidney Nolan died in 1992.

PETER FULLER: *You once said, "My own history is involved in what I can probably call with truth a working class background." Your father was a streetcar-driver. How did you come to be a painter?*

Sydney Nolan: Well, I was always interested, from early days at school. I took up art classes as soon as I could, when I was twelve. Later, I went into the art department of a factory called Fayrefield Hats. It was our job to design displays to go in shop windows and exhibition stands for a big annual fair in some exhibition buildings in Melbourne. So I was working continuously throughout those years from fourteen to twenty-one on producing images of page-boys giving hats to visiting airmen who had flown out of Britain… That sort of thing. I also had tailor-made page-boy costumes, and I used to go to the various balls, with the advertising manager, and I'd be photographed giving a hat to some celebrity from overseas. I can remember one called Delysh, a French cabaret star, very beautiful. She was middle-aged by the time she got to Australia. I'd be dressed up and on stage. So I was not only designing page-boy posters and exhibition-stands; but I actually was one. So I intend to use the page-boy motif now, just as Beckmann did, to describe my own life during that

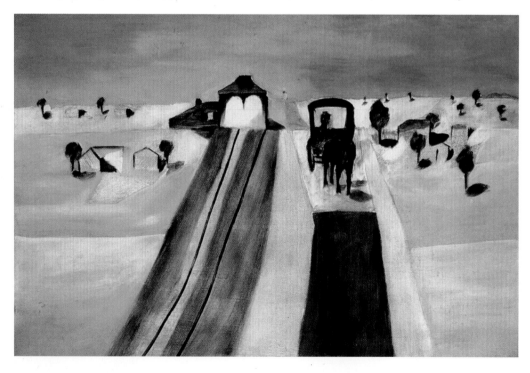

Kiata, *c1943, enamel on composition board, 24 x 36 in/61 x 92 cm. National Gallery of Australia.*

period: I was the living subject of the mythology of the hat factory.

Fuller: While you were working at the hat factory did you have another idea of what becoming an artist might mean?

Nolan: Yes, I got that from night classes. You see, I'd been through a technical school education: I'd been to jewelry classes, metal-work classes, and so on. I was well-trained in all the handicrafts. But I went to the night school at the Melbourne Gallery school, where they did charcoal studies from the antique; we had a marvelous collection of plaster casts. There was one of Ariadne, a Greek first century sculpture, which I now realize was a fantastic work of art; but then, of course, I didn't want to copy it in charcoal. That would have taken months! I thought it would be an awful thing to do, but I realize now I should have done that sort of thing. Anyway, I went upstairs and read, exhaustively, instead: Rimbaud, all the philosophers, Ouspensky, everybody. And so I started to base my life on a literary concept.

Fuller: Your early work was always very involved with abstraction, and in your most recent paintings, it seems, this abstract element has surfaced again. You once said, "I'm much more formal, and much less anecdotal than is sometimes imagined." Do you think that there is a sense in which the labels you have acquired as a painter of myth and of the Australian landscape have somehow obscured the preoccupations with abstraction and the formal dimensions which have run through your work since the beginning?

Nolan: Yes, it's been a kind of mirror-trick in a way. Recently, I had to do a painting for the Hall of Fame in Queensland, which is a big stockmen's (rancher) thing, almost like the Sydney Opera House; so I had to do something which would really be in line with

stockmen, or Australians' idea of themselves; but I could still turn away from that and, as I have been doing at home, do the abstract things. You see, my initial idea as a boy was that abstract painting was the way I wanted to express myself; the first exhibition I had, in 1940, was as abstract as I could make it. But then, in the situation that I was in in Australia, with things like Ned Kelly around, and all these lacunae in the mythology, or the history, of the place, I saw an opportunity to

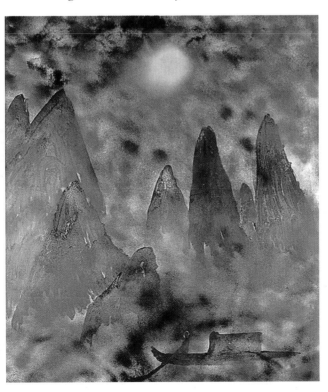

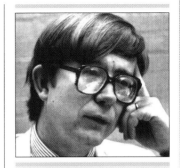

PETER FULLER
During his lifetime, Peter Fuller was widely considered among the most important art critics in Britain. Called 'the Ruskin of his time' by Sister Wendy Beckett, Fuller was born in Damascus, Syria, in 1947 and started as a staff writer at City Press in London in 1969 after studying at Cambridge.

His early fascination with psychoanalysis led to his first book in the field, The Psychology of Gambling, *and then,* Art and Psychoanalysis. *Other writings include* The Champions, The Crisis in the Fine Arts, Beyond the Crisis in Art, Seeing Berger, Robert Natkin, Images of God: The Consolations of Lost Illusions, Theoria *and the autobiographical* Marches Past. *Fuller considered himself a critic of the ideology and assumptions of later Modernism, and influenced by the writing of John Berger. Although he wrote as a "left" critic, he was opposed to those who "reduce art to ideology" and later abandoned a Marxist approach to art. In his later work, he argued for the importance of spiritual values in art, claiming that a materialistic approach was an impediment to perception.*

He founded Modern Painters magazine in 1987 as a polemical platform for these views. He was killed in a car crash in 1990.

Chinese Mountain Landscape with Boat, *c1982, acrylic lacquer spray on canvas,*
72 x 63 in /183 x 160 cm.
Estate of Sir Sidney Nolan.

use my knowledge of abstraction in that cause. And the Kelly paintings, really, are as abstract as they are anecdotal.

Fuller: I remember something Kenneth Clark said about your work: "I could not have accepted those upside-down birds and flying harvesters if my eye had not been led by the vivid communication of every touch, by the truth of tone, which is the surest sign of a natural painter." Well, he's not exactly talking about abstraction; but the sheer painterliness of your early pictures has perhaps been forgotten.

Nolan: Yes, it has, because the imagery was so tight and so localized that people missed the point. The other day I was reading in Richard Wollheim's book, *Painting as Art*, about the lure, the invitation in a picture.

Fuller: That's a great book!

Nolan: Yes, it's extremely interesting. Of course, he's using Adrian Stokes's theory about the invitation in art; but I have the impression that is where the secret lies, in that invitation or lure. That is the thing that grabs you from the end of a room and draws you to a painting; it doesn't really matter if it happens to be *Samson and Delilah*, or a Paul Klee abstraction, or if the dazzle of paint turns into a late Picasso

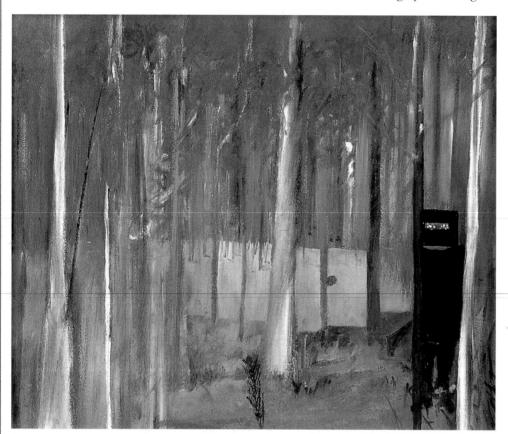

Kelly in the Bush, *1945, enamel on cardboard, 25 x 30 in/64 x 76 cm. Nolan Gallery, Cultural Facilities Corporation.*

nude, I really feel now that it doesn't matter much. It is a basic attraction. What are you going to say about Lascaux? Are you going to say that's representational art, or abstract art, or … how would you put it? What can you call that funny transition from certain fairy-tale or decorative painting: it just moves over a notch, and it's an abstract painting. But it's only a notch, isn't it?

So the battle fought on behalf of the Americans by Harold Rosenberg and, in particular, by Clement Greenberg was actually, like lots of conflicts, unnecessary and wasteful. Rosenberg said that abstraction was the art of the next three hundred years. Well, Martin Heidegger stood in front of his university and said that the Third Reich was going to last for a thousand years. So you've got to be very careful! Someone like Rothko who staked his all on doing what he did ended up rather puzzled. I think the same was true of Pollock. Toward the end, he started to want to paint heads and mythical figures that he could see emerging from his maze of paint; but everyone thumbs-downed on it. He just wasn't allowed any space to proceed in that direction.

Fuller: But when you did the Ned Kelly paintings you had already consciously rejected that kind of modernism, hadn't you?

Nolan: No, no, no … I wrote somewhere in my notes that it would be a good idea to take Picasso out of doors. The Ned Kelly paintings are ironic in their use of national mythology: Pharlap, Don Bradman, Ned Kelly, and all the rest of the things the Australians have thrown-up. I was trying to make an ironic comment on these clichés; the paintings, in themselves, in a formal sense, are ironic. They owe much to Matisse, in some cases, as anyone, with their tilted floors and wall-paper and all that. I was really nudging my way through what I felt was a false dilemma—it seemed that you had representational art, or you had abstract art; but, for me, that was a pointless battle. What you really had to look for were paintings that had this invitation or lure. That is where art has persisted; you can't pin it down to any of these categories. It's an

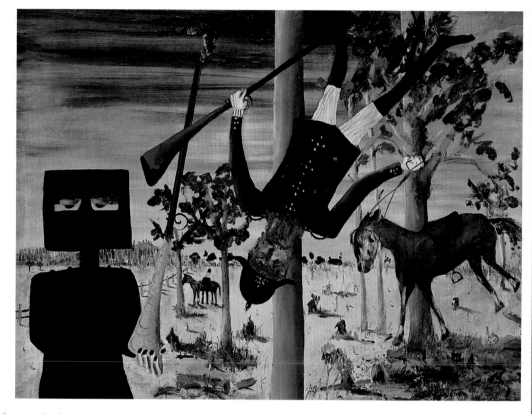

Death of Constable Scanlon, *1946, enamel on composition board, 36 x 48 in/90 x 121 cm. National Gallery of Australia.*

attraction of the thing in front of you which attracts you before you realize you are attracted. It's like some people you meet … Or like a word, or a phrase someone says suddenly, you're interested. And two seconds before you had no idea you were interested. Of course, sometimes, that momentary interest turns into your destiny; it becomes your thing. So you can put it two ways; in the negative sense, you could say that I've tried to back all the horses in the race, in the hope that I'd pick the winner. Well, my father was a bookmaker at one point; so I know that's a fatal thing to do. It's the way to lose all your money. But I could be accused of doing that, and I have been accused of doing that; people have said that I'm always changing styles, that I have a package of styles, or that I have no interest in style or consistency. But it's not really that. I just feel I'm trying to thread my way through this narrow gap which I can see in this century between these two opposing forces which stand in a highly theoretical and false dichotomy.

There's quattrocento art that looks the way it does; but, in two hundred year's time, what is 20th century art going to look like? Are people going to be lusting after Mondrian's *Boogie-Woogie*, or are they going to be tramping down to look at *Guernica* or are they going to be looking at the Blue Period of Picasso, or is Gauguin going to be seen as an extraordinary synthesizer? He's hardly this century I suppose; but nonetheless, he was in this century, just as G.F. Watts was. So I don't feel I have been wayward; I merely selected the only route I could find through a confused century. The one thing I didn't want to be in my painting life was confused. Artists are divided into two groups: the naive-spontaneous and the rest; I seemingly fall into the naive-spontaneous group. But I think, maybe, I'm the opposite; I've got a very strong will, and I've just kept on sticking to it since I was a boy.

Fuller: I wanted to task you about your first meeting with Kenneth Clark when he came to Australia in 1949. Did you know much about him before you met him? What was your first impression of him?

Nolan: Well, I didn't know very much. He was coming out to give some lectures on Cézanne; I'd read a couple of essays of his but that was all. I didn't go to a reception at the Sydney Art Gallery for him. But he saw a painting of mine there of an abandoned mine-

Pretty Polly Mine, *1948,*
ripol in on hardboard,
36 x 48 in/91 x 122 cm.
Art Gallery of New South Wales.

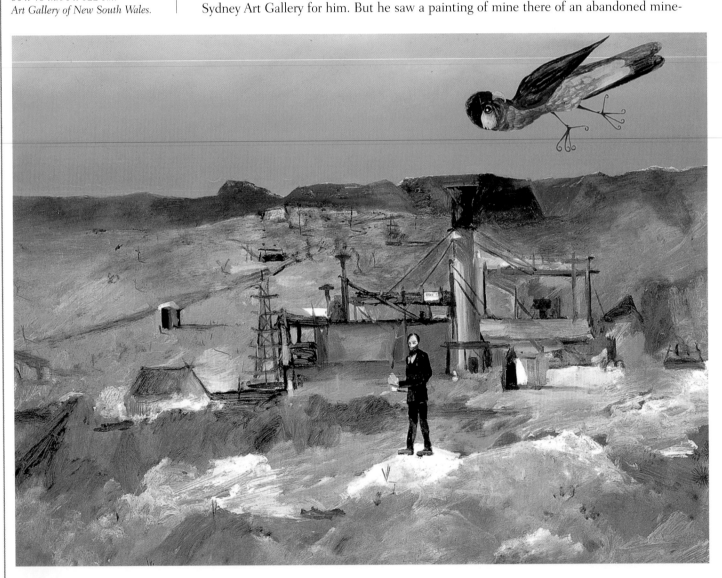

shaft. It was just a landscape and it had sort
of ochers and whites and the remains of a
kind of a wind-break structure. But it was
painted freely and tonally it was fairly precise,
even though it was full of color. And so he
asked if he could come and see me, and he
did. He was late because he had been visiting
a man who had a collection of Charles Keene
drawings. We had all the paintings around: the
central Australian paintings, the birds, and so
on. And then he behaved in a way that made
me feel a bit strange. He kept saying things
like, "That's jolly good!" And then he said
could he have the pictures out of that room,

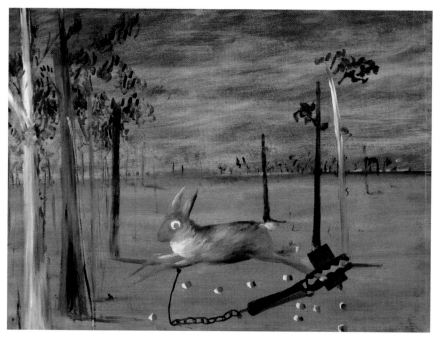

into the light, where he could see them better. He was with a chap called Professor Joseph
Burke, who wrote a book called *Hogarth and Reynolds* – an academic chap. And they talked
away like Englishmen about art and everything else. And, well, how can I put it, I thought,
"What the hell is he talking about! All his English stuff about, 'jolly good!', and so on."

But then it started to narrow down and he said, "You realize that if you leave Australia,
you might never come back." He told me that if I decided to leave, he would do everything

"I'M COMPELLED AND DEDICATED TO TRANSMITTING EMOTIONS AND I CARE FOR VERY LITTLE ELSE."

he could in London to facilitate my way. But he said, again, "You must think very seriously
about the fact that you might not come back. And you're in the middle of exploring all the
birds, flowers, and wonderful things to do with this continent. But when you get to Europe,
you'll find that there are other kinds of birds. And there's Florence … and there's this and
there's that." Of course, I didn't understand then that in Europe there was opera and
everything else that would draw me to it. But think of what it meant meeting a man like
that, fifteen miles out of Sydney, when I was twenty-eight and had been painting hard for
ten years. I was pretty deeply involved by that time of course; I'd done all the abstract
things, and the Wimmera pictures, in which there were quite a lot of innovations in relation
to Australian landscape. I'd done the Ned Kellys. I'd done some of the drought pictures, all
the Central Australian landscapes, the ones that are in the Tate now. So in a way I had
completed a decade of work; of course many people might perhaps say that that was the

"SYDNEY NOLAN…WAS INSPIRED LARGELY, THOUGH NOT EXCLUSIVELY, BY THE GREAT MYTHS OF THE AUSTRALIAN LANDSCAPES AND THE AUSTRALIAN PAST."

—*Russel Ward*

only decade in which I really succeeded in fulfilling my potential … I had been bred at the end of the world, but my mind was on the central experiences of Europe, you know, nature, Rimbaud, Schopenhaeur, and all the rest of it. So for a moment I felt a kind of twinge in myself. I knew that the man who was talking to me understood not only his own background, and Europe, but he'd picked up about me. He'd seen something about Australia, and something about me, which, as I say, I couldn't be conscious of. That's why he made the remark he did. Well, of course, it was quite prophetic.

Fuller: The commonest objection to your recent work is that it exhibits a certain fatal facility, which has led you to produce too much. Do you think this is true?

Nolan: An American once said to me, "Over here, we don't get blamed for working too hard." If a tennis player has "facility," well, then he's praised for it, isn't he? Public opinion and art criticism are both very unstable ground. A study was recently made of the art critics in *Le Monde* and *Figaro;* it showed they had a lamentable record.

Fuller: But this accusation of facility, it's not just a matter of how hard you work; it's a criticism of some of the techniques you use. Even an admirer of your work,

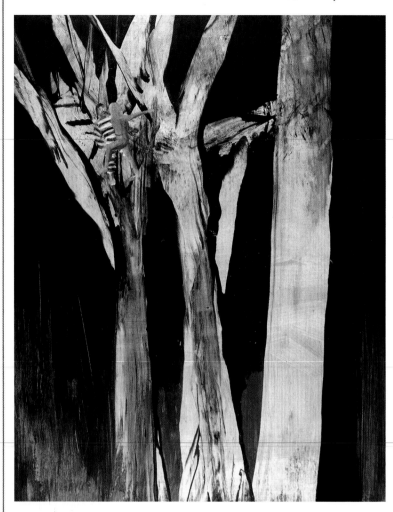

Figures in Tree, *1957, polyvinyl acetate on hardboard, 60 x 48 in/153 x 122 cm. Private collection.*

Kenneth Clark, hinted at this when he wrote, "There is in nearly all Nolan's work this preference for the insubstantial and the unphlegmatic. His pictures levitate with surprising ease; his dehydrated horses are so light that a man can pick one up." You have a fluid and insubstantial quality.

"PAINTING IS AN EXTENSION OF MAN'S MEANS OF COMMUNICATION. AS SUCH, IT'S PURE, DIFFICULT, AND WONDERFUL."

Nolan: These are considered rare qualities by the Chinese. And it would be difficult to do one of my paintings! Even when I was young, I had this feeling of transience. There is this sense of melancholy. And if what you are confronting is the decline of the West, how are you going to tackle it? Transience may be one aspect of this. It's like a relationship, one that you know is going to end. It is possible to enjoy that sense of transience. Everyone has their own stereotypes.

Fuller: So you are saying that your critics have not understood that your techniques are part of the meaning.

Nolan: I turn the criticism on its head, when I produced the Kelly paintings, nobody stood up for them. Now when they talk about my recent work negatively … it doesn't matter to me. Flattery will kill an artist. But I feel I am absolved from fulfilling other people's expectations.

Burke, *1964, ripolin on hardboard, 48 x 48 in/121 x 121 cm. Art Gallery of New South Wales.*

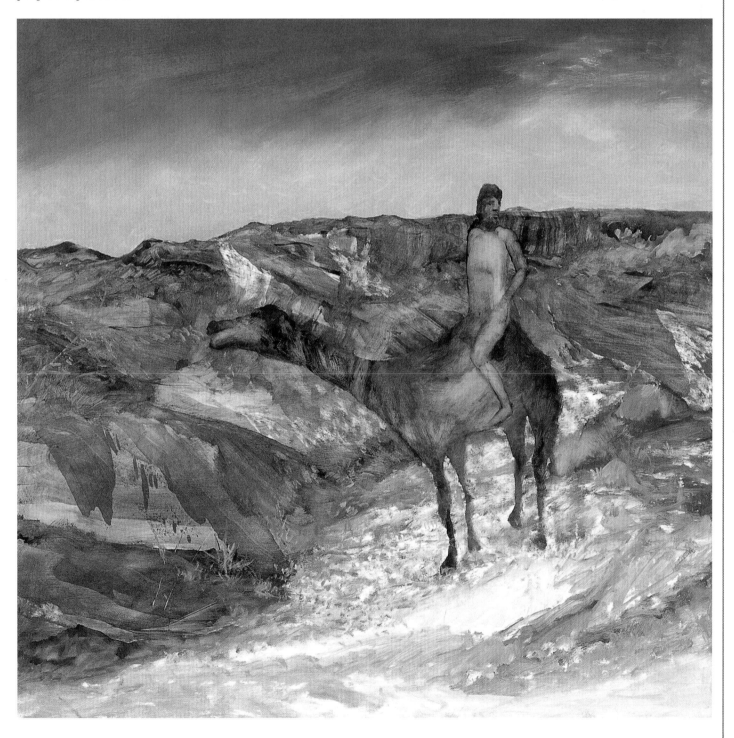

Pablo Picasso

by David Hockney

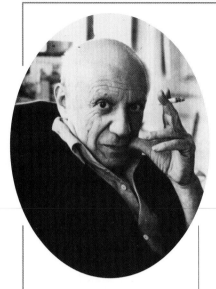

LATE LAST APRIL (1988), I decided on the spur of the moment to go to Paris for five days. It seemed worth the journey from Los Angeles as there was an exhibition of the late Picasso at the Centre Pompidou, Degas and Zurbáran at the Grand Palais, and Picasso again at the Musée Picasso. And then there was the new Musée d'Orsay which I still had not seen.

My first morning was spent in the Musée Picasso where there was a show of paintings and drawings relating to *Les Desmoiselles d'Avignon*; the picture itself was also on display. I had to queue for an hour to get in: but it was well worth it. It was a wonderful, insightful exhibition, about the origins of cubism really. And then in the afternoon, I went to see the exhibition of late Picassos. This was stunning!

But before I talk about that I want to say something about the Musée d'Orsay. I'd heard a lot of criticism of the museum. Friends of mine had suggested it was all wrong, that

> ## "IT'S NOT WHAT AN ARTIST DOES THAT COUNTS, BUT WHAT HE IS. CEZANNE'S ANXIETY IS WHAT INTERESTS US. THAT IS HIS LESSON."

the space wasn't right, and so on. I trusted their judgement so I wasn't particularly looking forward to going; in fact, I expected to dislike it.

My first glance at the massive space reminded me that a friend had said it made some of the masterpieces look like postcards. As I entered, I was still feeling antagonistic; but as soon as I went in the first small room with Daumier's marvelous clay heads of parliamentarians, I forgot all about the building itself. I had bought the guide which suggested a route and because I did not want to miss anything, I decided to follow it.

The guide explained that the museum was devoted to the 19th century beginning about 1840 and ending in 1907, the year that *Demoiselles d'Avingnon* was painted, just before the cubist revolution. So I looked at Ingres and progressed slowly and soon came to a room of paintings by Fantin-Latour; I had seen most of these pictures before. I knew the

Musée Jeu de Paume very well; I remembered exactly where all the pictures were. In their new setting at the Musée d'Orsay, they looked different and I became acutely aware that they were *tonal* pictures. The tones seemed almost photographic – there was not much color; the influence of the printed black-and-white photograph had made itself felt. I'm not just talking about the camera – Canaletto after all had that – but the *printed* photograph. I felt chiaroscuro dominated Fantin-Latour's pictures, the whole room in fact.

As I proceeded through the museum – the next rooms, I think, were orientalist painters, painters of North African scenes and so on – I became very conscious of the chiaroscuro in the pictures. I then came to the room with the Manet's. Here the hanging is not very good; they are not given suitable places. The two great masterpieces are hard to see especially if the room is a bit crowded. There were quite a few people, so I glanced around and thought, "Well, I'll walk through and see what else is here and then come back."

As you go upstairs, you begin to move into the impressionists. The first room is Sisley, Monet, Pissarro, and so on; I found myself becoming a little more aware of color in a different sort of way. Then I went into a Cézanne room which was somehow difficult to see; again, I knew the pictures. Next, I progressed into the Van Gogh room. It's not a very big room but it seemed to me just incredible! The pictures glowed; they jumped off the wall. I'd never seen them that way before. I noticed the painting of Van Gogh's bedroom, one of

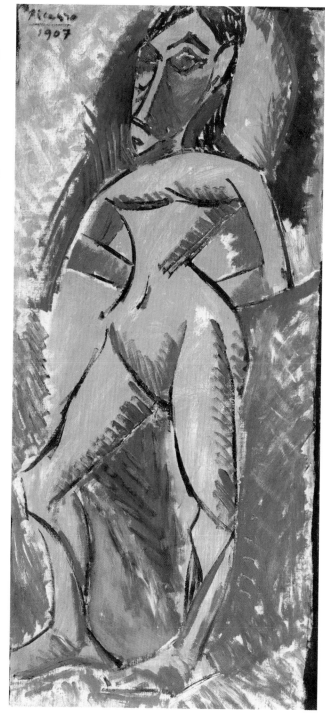

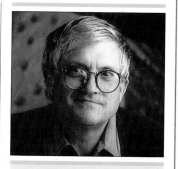

DAVID HOCKNEY
Born in Yorkshire in 1937, Hockney was a brilliant student at the Royal College of Art, where he experimented with broad-ranging styles and displayed influences by Picasso, Abstract Expressionism, and Pop Art in early work. As his painting matured, he expressed homage to the Italian master, Piero della Francesca, and gradually turned to representational paintings. In the early '60s, the California swimming pool – that icon of popular culture – became a favorite theme.

Awarded a graphics prize at the Paris Biennale, Hockney also became known as an outstanding draftsman and graphic artist. He produced several series of etchings and experimented with photography, combining many images of the same scene into multiple perspectives reminiscent of Cubism.

His work is collected internationally, and retrospectives have been presented at the Palau de la Virriena, Barcelona, and the Royal Academy of Arts, London. Major exhibitions include the Museum of Modern Art and the Metropolitan Museum of Art in New York; the Tate, London; and the Pompidou, Paris.

Female Nude (Study for Les Demoiselles d'Avignon), *1907, oil on canvas, 37 x 14 in/93 x 43 cm. Civico Museo d'Arte Contemporanea, Milan.*

three that he did and I think the best. Again, I knew the painting from the Jeu de Paume, but seeing it in the Musée d'Orsay, I realized for the first time what a marvellous picture it is. The orange bed just sings with life. While I was looking at it, I suddenly realized I had made a journey through the museum during which I had, in a sense, witnessed the disappearance of chiaroscuro.

I became intensely aware of this; and then I retraced my steps. I walked through the museum backwards to experience it again. Of course, when I did this, I knew what to look for; I was expecting it. And so I began to see it more clearly. I was excited; I'd never had this experience in a museum before. I had never seen pictures in this way.

I then realized that the curators at the Musée d'Orsay had missed something. Their scholarship can be criticized; on the way to the Van Gogh room there really ought to have been a room full of Japanese prints. They must have played an important part in the disappearance of chiaroscuro. This was a very big thing in European painting; but only in Europe. Oriental paintings don't really use chiaroscuro; there is very little in them about shadow. Occasionally they hint at volume that way; but shadows are never painted in. Perhaps they think that everything is a shadow, so it makes no difference. But I found it thrilling to be able to see this journey. No museum I had visited before had shown this. So I began to see the Musée d'Orsay in a different light; I went back the next day for

Girl With Bare Feet, La Corunna, *1895, oil on canvas, 30 x 20 in/75 x 50 cm. Musée Picasso, Paris.*

two hours. Again, I retraced my steps and again I saw things in the same way.

I was struck by how "Europe-centerd" the conception of the museum was: it is supposed to be a museum of 19th century art – not necessarily French, although most of the things in it are French. They do have some Japanese prints, of course. You can see them on the walls in a room devoted to ceramics at the turn of the century; this shows how designs from Japanese prints were used on plates made in Paris. But the rooms dealing with paintings and depictions don't do this; they don't illustrate the impact the Japanese prints had. I was struck by this. I have found myself getting more and more interested in oriental art; I now realize it is much more varied than I thought before. People are very often ignorant about oriental art. Even well educated art historians can know nothing about it.

I want to go back, now, to late Picasso. I've always been willing to give an artist like Picasso the benefit of the doubt. When people said to me, "Well, the late work is not very good," I used to think, "How do you know? How much have you really seen?" After all, the volumes of the Zervos catalog dealing with the last few years were not published until 1976 or 1977. I now have a complete set of Zervos: there are 32 volumes. It is a unique document covering about 75 years of Picasso's art. You can sit down, begin with volume one, and look through all his works singly and systematically. There are very few artists with whom you can do this at all and fewer who wouldn't bore you to death if you could! I've done this now with Picasso three times; each time, I deliberately set out to do it. And what I saw, of course, was an amazing journey. When you think of the first works in 1895, of what painting was in Europe then, and of the last one, 1973, it is incredible. I got the last ten volumes of Zervos to study

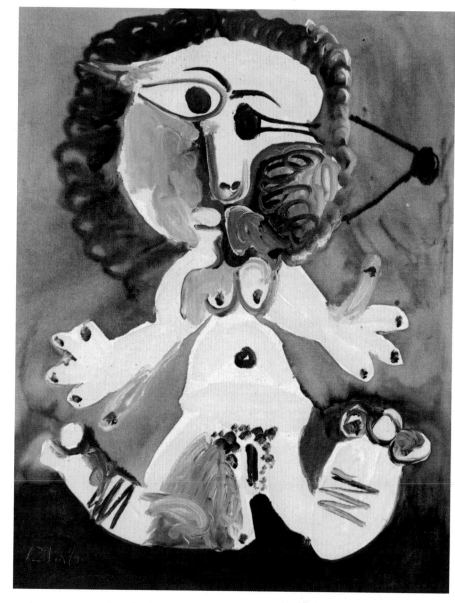

Reclining Nude, 1968,
oil on canvas,
58 x 45 in/146 x 114 cm.
Zervos – XXVII – 197.
Private collection.

about ten years ago. This is the only way you can begin to see what the late work is doing; and you are only seeing it in black-and-white after "decolorization." That's the only way you can see a lot of things!

I found that Picasso himself must have been very aware of what Mr. Zervos was doing, i.e. keeping a pretty good record of all the paintings and most of the drawings. Zervos printed them clearly. You can tell if Picasso did five paintings in a day; you can even tell which he did in the morning, which he did in the afternoon, and which he did in the evening. Everything like that is listed; so the catalog forms an incredible diary. This made a great impression on me. It led me to look at Van Gogh in a different way, too. If you add up all the time Van Gogh spent on his paintings and drawings and all his letters during the last three years of his life, you realize he had hardly any time left for anything else at all. All he could have done was to paint, write, eat, and sleep. What he left for us was in effect three years of his existence – an intense, human document.

Zervos' catalog of Picasso is also a remarkable and unique document in its own way. I am never bored with it. When I look through it, I don't start turning the pages quickly: every single page keeps my interest. And we are talking about a *catalogue raisone*. It's a mind blowing experience!

I am not that judgemental. I am not one to suggest the later work had all gone to cock. I saw these pictures for the first time in 1973, in the exhibition at the Palais des Papes, in Avignon. I was staying with Douglas Cooper at the time, and I went to the exhibition with him. He stormed around telling me that all the pictures were terrible. I said, "I'd like to look at them for myself if you don't mind." I thought that Douglas didn't want to understand because some of them were clearly about what it was like to be an old man; I told him this. Actually, they were marvelous as pictures of old age.

Anyway, I drove back with Douglas and discussed the paintings with him. He went ranting on, "No, no! He was just senile. He didn't know what he was doing." But I didn't believe it! I didn't think any artist of that caliber would spend twenty years just repeating himself: and I didn't think Picasso had done so. The paintings of the 1960s could not have been done in the 1950s. They are quite different: things get looser and looser. This happens in all marvelous painters. They get older. They seem to get unbelievable confidence – and they get looser. Think of Titian, Rembrandt, and Goya: it happened with all of them. And it happened with Picasso.

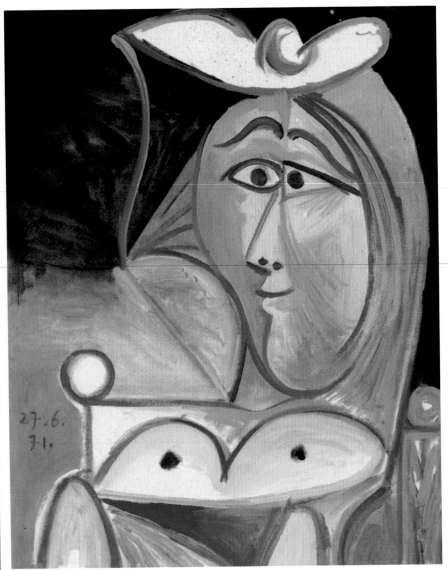

Bust of a Woman, *1971,*
oil on canvas,
39 x 32 in/100 x 80 cm.
Zervos XXXIII – 76.
Painting lost at sea.

I think he found another kind of cubism – different from the cubism of sixty years previously; but cubism nonetheless. There are many sorts of cubism. The cubism of the late Picasso depends on the brush: it seems to me that it relates to oriental art as well in that the brush did everything and nothing ever just covered itself up. You can see all the traces

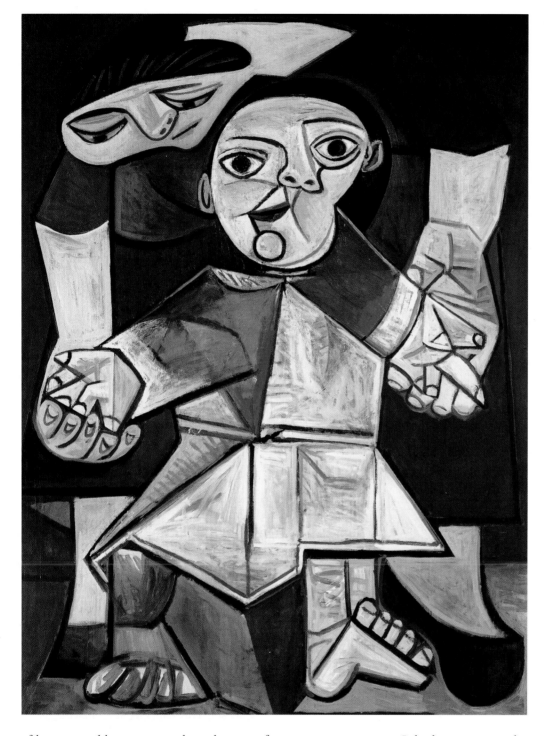

First Steps, *1943, oil on canvas, 51 x 38 in/130 x 97 cm. Museum of Modern Art, New York.*

"THE WHOLE STUDIO SEEMED TO BE BRISTLING WITH PICASSOS. ALL THE BITS OF WOOD AND FRAMES HAD BECOME LIKE HIS PICTURES... ONE GETS HARDLY ANY IDEA OF THEM FROM THE PHOTOGRAPHS, WHICH OFTEN DON'T SHOW WHAT IS PICTURE AND WHAT ISN'T... I CAME TO THE CONCLUSION THAT HE IS PROBABLY ONE OF THE GREATEST GENIUSES THAT HAS EVER LIVED."

—*Vanessa Bell*

of his arm and his energy in them: his way of seeing is just stunning. I think it is more real than what we call realist painting, *far* more real.

I found the exhibition fun on one level; but on other levels, it's deeply moving. For example, there is a painting of an old man, with a woman called *Homme et Femme Nus*, which Picasso painted in 1971. I recognized this as relating to *First Steps*, a picture of a mother teaching her child to talk, which Picasso painted almost thirty years previously. The mother is cupping her hands with the child's; her hands are very supple but the child's are stiff and angular. On the child's face, there is a kind of fear and thrill at what is happening

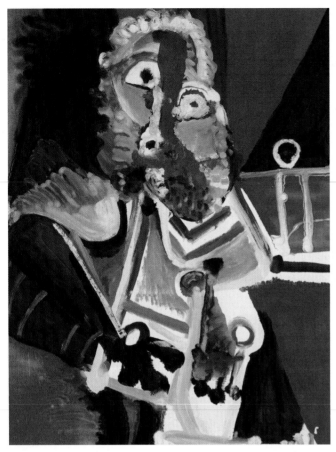

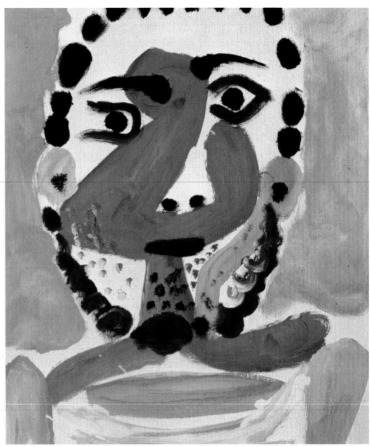

Left: Sitting Man, *1972, oil on canvas, 51 x 38 in/130 x 97 cm. Zervos XXXIII – 317. Private collection.*

Right: Head of a Man, *1972, oil on canvas, 22 x 18 in/55 x 46 cm. Zervos XXV – 146. Private collection.*

to him. The painting of the old man with the woman is very similar. He is bent at his knees; his knees are just circles. They are knobbly and he is bending down on his leg. His little balls are hanging down on the floor. The woman's hands are not cupping the old man's, as the mother's do the child's in *First Steps*; even so, in one way of looking at this picture, the women seems to be supporting the old man under his arms.

I think this is a marvelous and deeply moving painting. You can see how Picasso developed the language he was using: you can now see more in the pictures. And that, to me, is thrilling! I think there was so much to learn from the late Picasso exhibition. I really don't agree that Picasso found only an idiosyncratic way of doing things. His late pictures are the start of a new language, a more real way of depicting the world. And he does depict the world: with Picasso, depiction never stops. What he shows is recognizable; the visible world is there. I now think the pictures are more difficult to see than I once thought. I don't find them difficult, but they seem to be difficult for many other people. They seem to think there is still a lot of distortion there. This problem of "distortion" is one of the difficulties with Picasso; in fact, it has made modern art itself difficult for some people. But slowly you become aware that the Picasso's are not really distorted at all; and then they seem more and more real.

Much of the early antagonism to modern art had to do with the fact that it seemed to distort the world. The bottom line was, "It does not look like that." Until cubism, all art, all pictures, could be "read" by anybody. If this hadn't been so, the Christian message wouldn't have been seen by peasants and its importance would have been diminished. But after 1907, something new happened. The discoveries made then were very great; avant-garde art started with them. We don't seem to have an avant-garde, today. Or, if we do, it seems irrelevant. What would an avant-garde be about, today? If it is to have relevance, it must have a purpose, a noble purpose, the desire to lift the whole of humankind into a higher awareness. Such a higher awareness, when expressed in pictures, seems to me to be by definition spatial; space is also about our identity. It is obvious that this has not yet happened; perhaps the fact that the photograph is still seen as "real" has a lot to do with this.

I don't think that Picasso ever gave up cubism. You can't just give it up. As Juan Gris once said, "It's not a style, it's a way of life." Perhaps we have been misled by false divisions, like that between abstraction and representation. There can't be two things: there can only be one. Either it is all an abstraction or it is all a representation. The folly of where these false divisions can lead is wonderfully illustrated by Clement Greenberg's comment, "With an "advanced" artist, it's not now possible to make a portrait," and De Kooning's reply, "And it's not possible not to." De Kooning was so much wiser! If Greenberg's view had prevailed we would have had only photographic portraits. Similarly, the idea that painting was dead would have left the depiction of the visible world to the camera. What a horrible thought and what a dull idea!

In his old age, Picasso went on making discoveries. He just couldn't stop. About 1963 he made a whole lot of new discoveries. For example, the paintings he began to produce then can be seen from any distance. I sat, alone, in one of the rooms at the Centre Pompidou and I could see all the brush marks on the paintings even from the center of the room. Distance seemed to have been removed. Perhaps Picasso broke the European obsession with measurement. Scientists like Werner Heisenberg and Kurt Godel have suggested that we can't measure everything. These pictures may relate to an awareness that the journey to outer space is also the journey to inner space.

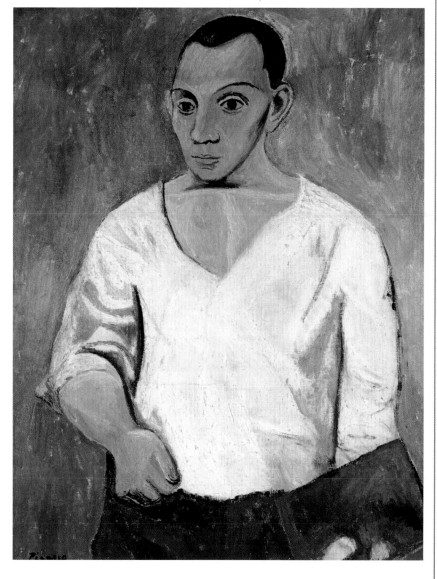

Self-Portrait with Palette, *1906, oil on canvas, 36 x 29 in/92 x 73 cm. Philadelphia Museum of Art, A. E. Gallatin Collection.*

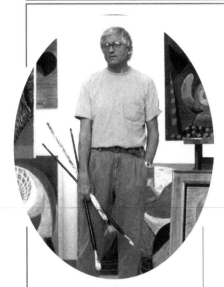

DAVID HOCKNEY
Born in Yorkshire, England, in 1937, Hockney is one of the best-known artists of his generation. A prize-winning student at the Royal College of Art between 1959 and 1962, he experimented with broad-ranging styles, displaying the influences of Picasso, Abstract Expressionism, and Pop Art. He later expressed his homage to the Italian master Piero della Francesca as his work matured.

In a visit to Los Angeles in the early '60s, he was inspired by the ubiquitous California swimming pool, an icon of popular culture, and made it one of his major themes.

Hockney was awarded a graphics prize at the Paris Biennale and is now internationally known as an outstanding draftsman and graphic artist. In the '80s, he experimented with photography, combining many images of the same scene or object into multiple perspectives reminiscent of Cubism.

Retrospectives of Hockney include the Palau de la Virriena, Barcelona, the Royal Academy of Arts; and the Los Angeles County Museum of Art. Major exhibitions have been held at the Museum of Modern Art, the Metropolitan Museum of Art, New York; the Tate, London; and the Pompidou, Paris.

David Hockney

by Richard Wollheim

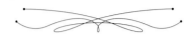

I SHALL PERMIT MYSELF TO QUOTE A LETTER . . . FROM ROME, in which George Santayana writes of Trivia: *"The whole makes a picture of the self-consciousness of the modern man which is not only delightfully vivid and humorous, but a document of importance . . . Men have always been the victims of trifles, but when they were uncomfortable and passionate, and in constant danger, they hardly had time to notice what the daily texture of their thoughts was in their calm intervals; whereas with us the intervals are all, and that is what you have painted."*

. . . When Robert Bridges said to him that I had written the most immoral book in the world, though every word could be read in the drawing room, he had replied that the book was not in his opinion at all immoral: it was meant to be light and irresponsible, not complete and ultimate. "And why," he asked, "should not things be largely absurd, futile, and transitory? They are so, and we are so, and we and they go very well together."

Logan Pearsall Smith, Unforgotten Years.

When I first had the privilege – and I count it a very high one – of meeting Mr. Walter Pater, he said to me, smiling, *"Why do you always write poetry? Why do you not write prose: Prose is so much more difficult."*

Oscar Wilde, review of Walter Pater, Appreciations.

In the last few years it has become a matter of general agreement among commentators on David Hockney, stemming doubtless from the most articulate and prolific of them all, Hockney himself, that the best way to discuss his work is to do so, or at any rate to start by doing so, in purely formalistic terms. Notions like one-point perspective, simultaneous perception, isomorphic projection, multiple viewpoint, illusionism, anti-illusionism, time, duration, movement, flatness, depth, come to the fore.

Personally, I feel this is a mistake. True, there are works of Hockney's to which a fundamentally formalistic approach is appropriate. But they are neither the best nor the most distinctive. Largely they are works in which Hockney seems to have been preoccupied with devising the kind of surface that a truly – truly as opposed to spuriously – modern picture should present to the world. Or they are those works on which Hockney, who by and large has understood so well the advice that Pater gave Wilde, has momentarily taken it rather too literally and has cultivated a new look for his painting because, simply because, the old look was something he had mastered. But in the best work, in the work where Hockney is most himself, an approach that is primarily formalistic will conceal as much as it reveals. It may show us what he has done, but only at the expense of making it harder for us to see why he has done it. And that is because, in the work itself, formal concerns have waited upon concerns of content. Content is primary, and it is so in an interesting way. For while formal concerns provide the dynamo of change in Hockney's work, this change is necessary only because content remains to recalcitrantly, so impregnably, constant. The changes in Hockney's work represent different assaults, using different techniques, upon different faces of an enduring subject matter. Content for Hockney is, like the highest mountain, there.

Two paintings, both early, establish the point I am making, if with a somewhat artificial clarity. The two pictures are *Bolton Junction, Eccleshire*, of 1957, and *Flight into Italy – Swiss Landscape*, of 1961. Hockney's very earliest paintings were painted in a manner that combined *intimisme* with the kind of indigenous English naturalism that can be found

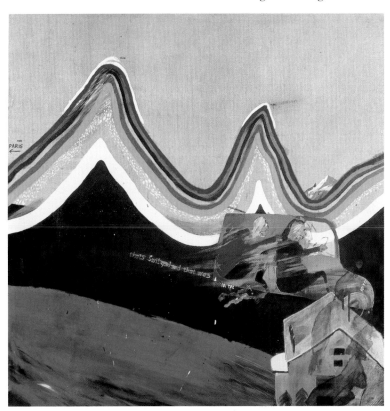

in Sickert, in the Euston Road School, and, closer in time to Hockney though not necessarily more accessible to him, in the art that in the course of the 50s radiated out from the Beaux-Arts Gallery, under the aegis of Helen Lessore, into the more advanced provincial art schools. If *Bolton Junction* is characteristic of this period, nothing is more natural than to explain the difference between it and *Flight into Italy* by citing the greater formal awareness and sophistication of a London art student: someone who had been influenced by the work of Jean Dubuffet and, almost certainly, by that of England's favorite transatlantic artist of the period, Larry Rivers, someone (in other words) who had been recently exposed not only to new ways of making a picture but also to new ideas about what making a picture is. Now certainly the second picture is inconceivable without this new sophistication having found

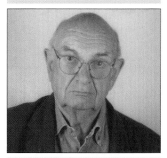

RICHARD WOLLHEIM
Philosopher Richrd Wollheim, one of the dominant figures in contemporary aesthetics, was born in London in 1923.

During the '60s and early '70s, Wollheim wrote a series of acclaimed essays on the visual arts. For over thirty years, he has taught philosophy at the University of London, and, since 1985, he has been a visiting professor at the University of California, Berkeley. He continues to write on aesthetics, and on the mind, ethics, political philosophy, and the history of philosophy.

Wollheim is the author of Freud, Art and its Objects, *and* Painting as an Art. *He also wrote a novel,* A Family Romance *and two volumes of essays, his latest of which is* On the Emotions. *He is currently writing on the idea of pictorial organization.*

Flight Into Italy, Swiss Landscape, *1962, oil on canvas, 72 x 62 in/183 x 158 cm. © David Hockney, Kunstmuseum, Dusseldorf.*

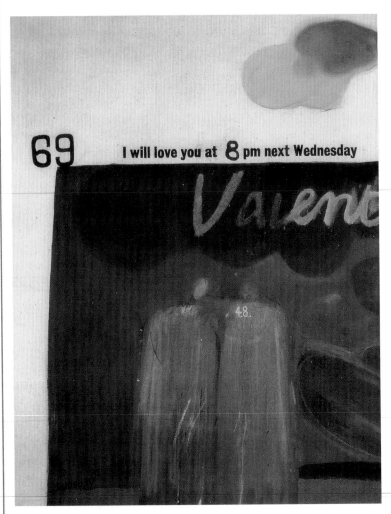

The Fourth Love Painting, *1961,*
acrylic and letraset on canvas,
36 x 28 in/91 x 72 cm.
© David Hockney, Private
collection.

its way into Hockney's head. But it doesn't explain the picture. For the prime fact about *Flight into Italy* is that it is the record of a holiday from which Hockney had hoped to return, as he himself explained, with magnificent views of the Alps, but in the course of which he saw little more than the inside of the van he was traveling in. Frustration, and imagination stimulated by frustration, led Hockney to find new and amusing uses for such resources as the raw unmarked canvas, streaking, smudging, graffiti; but these resources are not themselves the fundamentals of the painting. They are not what motivated the painter.

To grasp the motivating force of Hockney's art, even in its beginnings, we cannot do better, I think, than to turn to the very first item in the mammoth catalog, which has turned out to be one of the bestselling art books of the world. This is the prose-portrait of Hockney done by Hockney's old friend and fellow student, R. B. Kitaj, in his best Douanier manner. Central to Kitaj's portrait is the sense of someone determined to lead his own life; to lead his own life in his own way. As the whole world knows, this meant for Hockney leading a homosexual life is being free to do so. And the freedom that Hockney treasures, of which he will not be balked, is not just freedom from constraint; it is freedom from pressure, from censoriousness, from claims to ethical or ideological superiority; it is freedom from those who know better. Hockney is no anarchist; all his life – and I shall return to this later – he has been something of a student, he has thought it no weakness to admit that he can learn from others. But learning too is something that, he insists, can be done only in freedom.

This takes us halfway to the motiviating force, to the content, of Hockney's art. For it is no surprise that someone who was so desperately driven to discover a life for himself, and who felt this pressure at the very moment at which he was apprenticing himself to art, should take the next step and find it imperative that the art he made should take as its subject matter the life he led. At first he didn't know how to do this. He was at a loss. There was no precedent that art school provided. Hockney has recorded all this, and how he went for advice to the fellow student who, all these years later, was to write of Hockney's need to be himself:

The one student I kept talking to a lot was Ron Kitaj. Ron was slowly doing these strange pictures, and I talked to him about them and about my work. And I said, "Well I don't know, it seems pointless doing it." I'd talk to him about my interests; I was a keen vegetarian then, and interested in politics a bit, and he'd say to me why don't you paint those subjects? And I thought, it's quite right; that's what I'm complaining about. I'm not doing anything that's from me. So that was the way I broke it. I began to paint those subjects. But I still didn't have the nerve to paint figure pictures. The idea of painting figure pictures was considered really anti-modern, so my solution was to begin using words. I started writing on the pictures . . . And then Ron said "Yes, that's much more interesting."

"LOADS OF PEOPLE, PARTICULARLY ARTISTS, HATE PRETTY PICTURES. NOW I'VE NEVER MET ANYONE WHO DIDN'T LIKE A PRETTY FACE."

That Hockney's basic concern has been to incorporate his life into his art tells us how we should approach this art. But it tells us little about the art itself. For this we need to grasp how, in working out this concern, he has combined it with a very distinctive view of life. Then we have in full the content of his art.

It is not primarily the great dramas of life, nor even the great passions of life, that Hockney has tried to get into his art; in fact, barely them at all. The pleasures and delights of life – they certainly are recorded, and in such a recurrent way as to make their sources the most familiar part of Hockney's work – sunlight, boys' bodies, cherished faces and places, brilliant vegetation, curtains, and cushions, strong cast shadows, immortal music, and the activity, the discipline, of painting. But, even at his most hedonistic, Hockney has not tried to capture the core, the pure sensation (if there is such a thing), of pleasure, as, say, Matisse and Delacroix did. Hockney seeks the penumbra of pleasure, that which flickers round it. Small acuities of vision, brief valleities, funny juxtapositions of ideas,

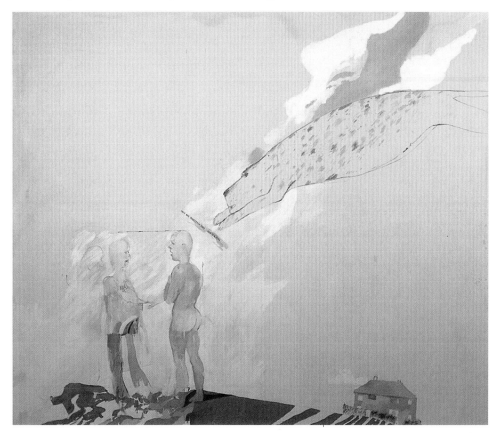

Picture Emphasizing Stillness, *1962, oil on canvas, 72 x 62 in/183 x 158 cm. © David Hockney, Private collection.*

momentary delusions of grandeur, sad, idle thoughts, memories of paintings once seen, boyish jokes, all these flutter around in the big, unoccupied spaces of Hockney's pictures, but they do so not so as to enrich or enliven the depicted scene after the fact, not so as to give it a significance that it never had at the time. They are there to convey the event as it really was; they are there to convey what Santayana, in the passage I have quoted, had in mind by the "texture" of experience. It is because of these fine webs of association which he spins around basically simple objects that Hockney's art at its best has a frank, quirky intimacy. On the face of it totally exoteric works, his paintings bear the full, precise imprint of psychological idiosyncracy which we have come, this century, to associate with extravagantly esoteric work – the boxes of Joseph Cornell, the novels of Firbank, the poems of John Ashbery, the autobiographical essays of Adrian Stokes, the late chamber music of Debussy, widely different though they are, all coming to mind.

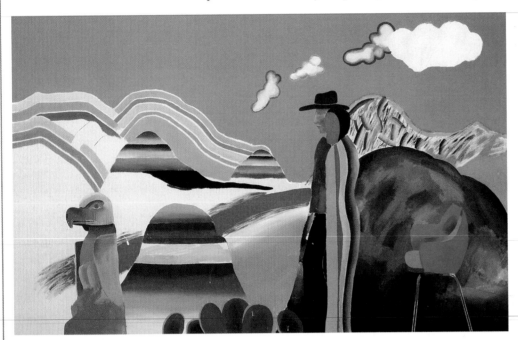

Rocky Mountains and Tired Indians, *1965, acrylic on canvas, 67 x 100 in/170 x 253 cm. © David Hockney, Scottish National Gallery of Modern Art Edinburgh.*

The purest example of this compulsion to capture, within the confines of a public, accessible picture, what is peripheral or auxiliary to experience, what is distinctive of one particular person's particular way of looking at things, is the painting called *Different Kinds of Water Pouring into a Swimming Pool, Santa Monica*, of 1965. Of this painting, and the splash paintings that follow it, Hockney says on the tape he prepared for the exhibition that they are studies in "dancing lines." That is Hockney emphasizing the formalistic approach to his work, and then he goes on to say, "I was fascinated with all the pools in California, and with the surface of the water . . . Many have talked of my swimming pools as hedonistic, but that was never particularly the way I thought about them myself." And he points out with amusement how he chose to devote two weeks of his life to painting an effect that in reality lasted only "fractions of a second." He calls it a paradox. He might equally well have pointed out how he chose to fill the body of the picture with something that lay on the periphery of the visual field. Neither is strictly a paradox, but both would be ways of pointing out how, in the cause of capturing how it really was, he privileges the transitory, the futile, the marginal: just because what accumulates at the margin is what carries the distinctiveness, the vividness, of life for each one of us.

Hockney's confidence in the marginal and the elusive was already well-established in the "love paintings" that he executed while at the Royal College of Art. The references, verbal and pictorial, to Walt Whitman, the bard of homoeroticism, prepare us for a bold statement, which is withheld. Take *The Cha-Cha that was Danced in the Early Hours of 24th March*. In this painting the painter paints a boy who attracts him because he looks like a girl, who, in turn, would not have attracted him if that was what she really was. If we now start to wonder what the boy must have looked like to be able to play this trick upon our biological affections, and we approach the picture to find out, we discover nothing. The boy is out of focus. We are face-to-face with a blur. This love-picture cleverly repeats the very equivocation with which in the early hours of the 24th March sight spoke to the artists' senses. Androgyny, and its allure, inevitably lies on the margin.

It is however no secret that, in time, ten years on, the pursuit of the texture of experience came to disappoint Hockney. The project encountered a reverse, and Hockney came to re-think it. He came to re-think it, not to abandon it, though it has not always been easy for spectators of Hockney's work to see this distinction clearly. And one obstacle that they have had to surmount in order to do so is, I am certain, the preference for talking about his work in formalistic terms.

Hockney himself has never had any doubt about which works of his it is where

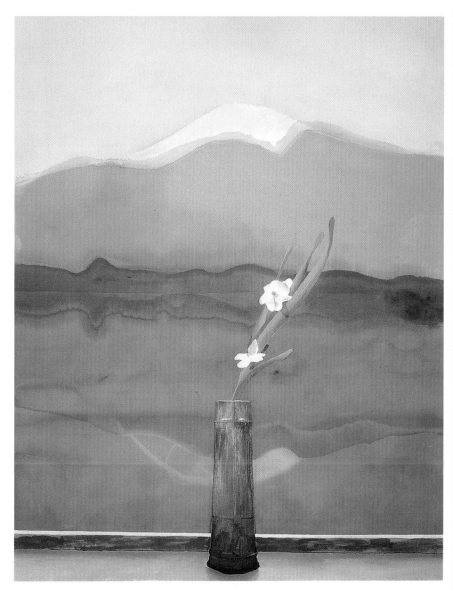

Mt. Fuji and Flowers, *1972, acrylic on canvas, 60 x 48 in/152 x 122 cm. © David Hockney Metropolitan Museum of Art, New York.*

his project, as it was originally conceived, ran into the ground. It is the series of vast double portraits which occupied him in the late 60s and early 70s and which culminated in two abandoned works. The finished pictures have come to represent for Hockney a kind of Pyrrhic victory over life, in which the element of victory and the element of defeat can be traced to the same source. This source, Hockney tells us, is the total commitment to single-point linear perspective. Perspective captures reality, but kills it in the process. From which it must follow that salvation lay in the use, in the selective use, of other projective systems: alternative systems of projection having been something that had always appealed to the student, the erudite, in Hockney.

However, as I looked at Hockney's assembled work, I became sceptical of this account, and another one suggested itself.

If we survey the first decade or so of Hockney's work, it is obvious that, though there is a wide range of material, without any corresponding hierarchy of genre, all of which suggests a democracy of interest, this suggestion is not really borne out by the pictures. For there is one topic that had a unique appeal, and represented a unique challenge, for Hockney. It is the representation of two human beings in relation with one another. The relationship may be to varying degrees erotic. There was nothing that seemed to Hockney so difficult and so worthwhile to capture – though, later, this was to find a rival in the relationship of one human being to his art.

However, as Hockney pursued this subject, he stumbled across – as I see it – one moment in the relationship of two human beings, one moment in time and one moment in the pattern of emotion, which came to engross him, almost certainly without his fully realizing it. It transfixed him, and he could not really escape it. The moment is one of stillness, and in this moment one person turns, turns in the direction of the other, and thinks, half-abstractedly or as if to himself, half as if trying to work something out, something really complicated, "What do we do now?" He thinks. "What next?" And next may mean next in life, or next in some erotic routine, or somewhere between the two. He thinks this and falls silent.

This becalmed moment may or may not have a sexual cast, but it is in an overtly sexual form that it appears in and appropriates the undoubted masterpiece of Hockney's early years: *Two Men in a Shower*, of 1963. The thought, What next? stirs in the mind of

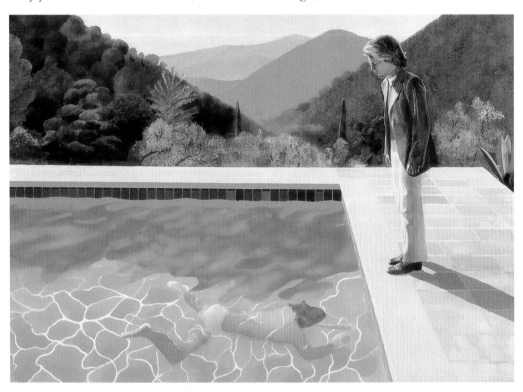

"HOCKNEY, BY TEMPERAMENT, IS ENTIRELY UNDISTURBED BY ANY CHARGE OF NAIVETY — AS AN ARTIST, HE BELIEVES THAT NOTHING CAN BE TAKEN FOR GRANTED."

—*Nikos Stangos*

Portrait of an Artist (Pool with Two Figures), *1972, acrylic on canvas, 84 x 120 in/213 x 305 cm. © David Hockney, Private collection.*

the bald, studious voluptuary who is its protagonist, and through the translucent shower curtain we sense the consternation and the mounting excitement that knowledge of this thought induces in the mind of the hidden partner. The exquisite tonal painting of the curtain rings and of the rod along which they slide heightens the quietness, the gravity, of this little domestic scene, filched (the artist tells us) from a photomagazine for men. Another work, equally shot through with the same suspension of time, and with the same sexual suggestiveness, is the painting called *Seated Woman Drinking Tea Being Served by a Standing Companion*, also of 1963, which exudes, self-consciously but nonetheless effectively for that, an updated variant of *fin-de-siècle* perversity.

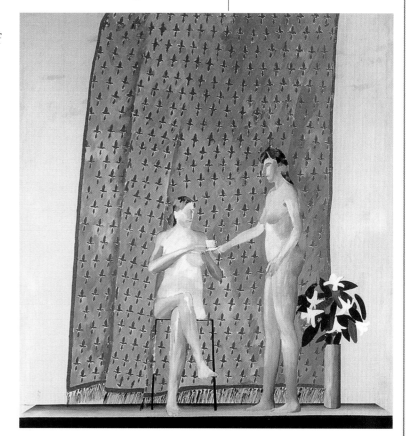

Seated Woman Drinking Tea, Being Served by a Standing Companion, *1963, oil on canvas, 78 x 84 in/198 x 213 cm. © David Hockney, Private collection.*

Then there are pictures like *Domestic Scene, Broadchalke*, in which stillness reigns supreme over innocent social situations. Nevertheless, it is tempting to think that for Hockney the fascination that the becalmed moment, the abstracted mood, held for him could never be totally detached from its sexual roots and for this reason it grew and grew until it gradually came to dominate the representation of the human figure, reaching its apogee in the monumental double portraits which it completely takes over. Of course it has much to offer. If it hadn't, it is certain that its dominance would have been challenged. By abolishing the dimension of time, it made composition easy, and it also provided a sure way of securing a unity of affect – something which Hockney in his earlier work had deliberately avoided, thinking it incompatible with capturing the "texture" of experience. At the same time, it demanded, if it was to be successfully realized, that the scene should be presented from a single viewpoint. Anything less static, more fidgety, could only break the heavy spell upon which the mood depends. I do not believe that it is utterly illuminating to say, as Hockney does, that these great Germanic machines are "about" perspective. They are about the abscinded moment, and it is the representation of the abscinded moment that necessitates perspective.

In point of fact, Hockney, as I see it, is unfair to the double portraits, these remarkable brainchildren of his, twice over. For not only is it incorrect to say that they derive from perspective, but it is unjust to hold that perspective has in each and every case the same baneful consequences. Both the Wiesmann and the Clark and Birtwell double portraits are ultimately claustrophobic works but for different reasons, though in both cases the reasons seem more to do with Hockney's own attitudes to the sitters than with strictly formal issues. Moreover, when we turn to the greatest work in this series, Christopher Isherwood and Don Bachardy, it becomes quite clear that the compositional structure of these pictures and the conscientious application of single-point perspective are as such perfectly compatible with the free flow of life through their parts. In the Clark and the Wiesmann portraits Hockney concentrated on the moment and what went on within it. In this picture Hockney relaxed his total control over the content, and allowed to pour back into it the significant trivialities, the little absurdities, the quiddities of two human beings together, that he vacuumed out of the other works in the series. It is not just a tableau that is before us, it is a drama, which comes alive as the older man, still carrying around inside himself an unruly boy, looks across at the younger man, who ripens under our eyes into an elegant duenna.

What is incontestably true of all these works is that they disclose mastery. Something, something in itself very difficult, has become eminently do-able, and it is hard not to feel that Hockney, who had come to realize that his art had to take a new turn if it was still to capture the texture of experience, as glad of the excuse to abandon something that no

Christopher Isherwood and Don Bachardy, *1968, acrylic on canvas, 84 x 120 in/212 x 304 cm. © David Hockney, Private collection.*

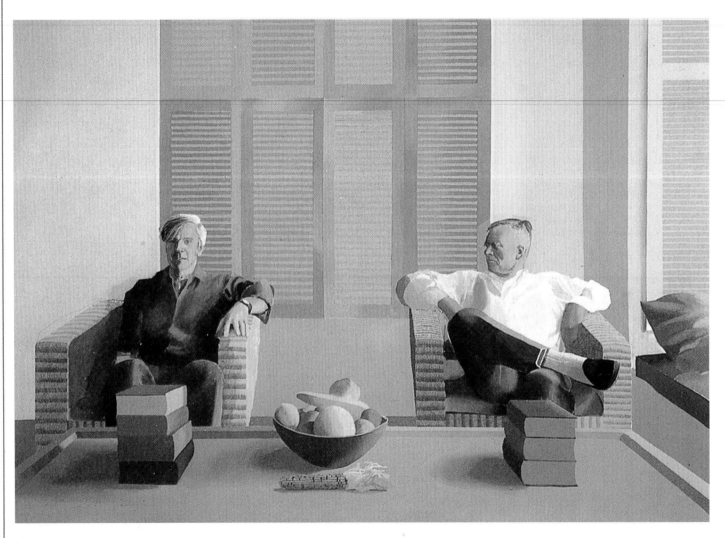

longer posed him a challenge. But which way to go, and why?

The last twenty or perhaps fifteen years of Hockney's art are, I believe clear only in outline. They present a broad pattern, but we are no longer able to plot his evolution year by year, grasping what came after what and seeing the reason. What can certainly be said is that his art is no longer just the diary of a singular eye. In two distinct ways Hockney has struggled to amplify its content – a struggle that his natural restlessness, his dissatisfaction with continuing to do something that he can (as the saying goes) do only too well, as well as his curiosity about the resources of art that he has left untried, have sometimes helped, sometimes hindered. In this whole period, Hockney's art has blended optimism and desperation in such a concoction that the former has often blinded his audience to the real, energizing presence of the latter.

The two ways in which Hockney has tried to extend his art are these: he has tried to enrich the visual findings of the eye with a depth of feeling to which he could not reach as a younger man, and he has also tried to implicate the eye, thus enriched, into the very scene that it seems to record.

At times the two aims pull apart. For instance, Hockney's most impressive attempt to increase the expressive power of his work is undoubtedly the *Paper Pools*, which he executed between August and October, 1978, in a technique invented by the east coast printmaker, Ken Tyler. The series is very well discussed in Marco Livingstone's admirable monograph on Hockney. What the technique in effect amounted to is that the sheet and the image are brought into existence simultaneously, in that the sheet comes about through pressing liquid color pulp into paper, which in turn calls the image into being. The series has an extraordinary emotional charge. But the emotions are solitary emotions: they are melancholy, loneliness, anxiety. In this respect, the *Paper Pools* form a path that leads away from the more involved, the more participatory, art that Hockney was simultaneously trying to construct.

It was in pursuit of this latter aim that Hockney was increasingly led not just to experiment with a variety of projective systems other than linear perspective, but also to present his art as fundamentally generated by such experimentation. I have already said that such a way of looking at Hockney's art inevitably obscures the dependence of these

Model with Unfinished Self-Portrait, *1977, oil on canvas, 60 x 60 in/152 x 152 cm. © David Hockney, Private collection.*

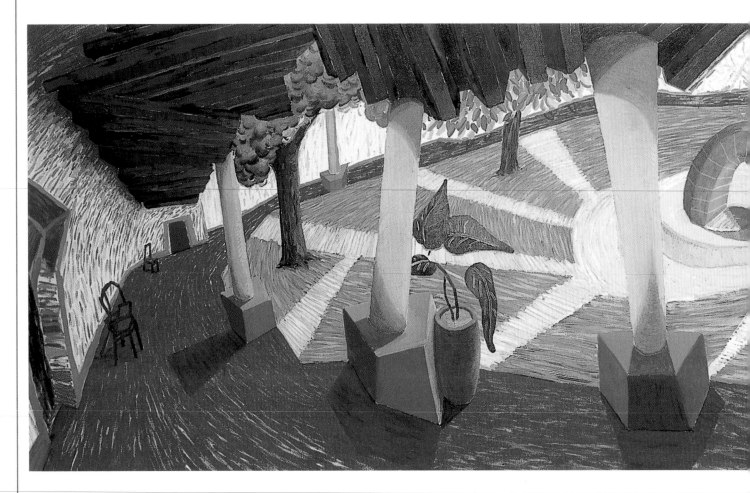

**A Walk around the Hotel
Courtyard, Acatlan**, *1985,
oil on two canvases,
72 x 240 in/183 x 610 cm.
© David Hockney, Andre
Emmerich Gallery, New York.*

formalistic concerns upon concerns, abiding concerns, of content. We have now to add to this the fact that Hockney's own characterization of the formal concerns in some measure misrepresents them.

The problem is this: In the more experimental works, which take off from the ingenious photo-collages, there are, in varying degrees, two very different kinds of experiment going on. On the one hand, there is experimentation with projective systems, that is to say with systems that supply methods for mapping a three-dimensional scene onto a two-dimensional surface. All such systems presuppose a point (or at least a direction) from which the scene is viewed. Each system determines for any particular scene the configuration that should appear on the surface, given the viewing-point. Linear perspective is only one projection, reverse projection, and Hockney had been interested in them all since his student days. On the other hand, there is experimentation with viewing-point. In other words, the projective system is kept constant, but a given scene gives rise to different configurations, through the employment of different viewing-points within the same picture.

Now it is obvious that there will be perhaps whole pictures, certainly large fragments of pictures, where the look of the picture can be accounted for equally well in terms of either kind of experiment. We have a configuration before us, which deviates from what

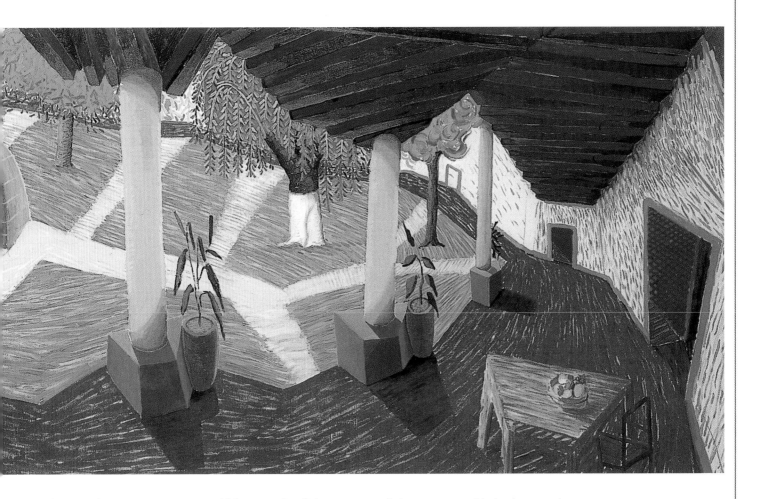

single-point linear perspective would have made of the scene, and this is compatible both with the use of an alternative projective system and with continuing to use (more or less) linear perspective but introducing a multiplicity of viewing-points. In Hockney's case, when such ambiguity arises, which of the two interpretations is to be preferred? We know which one Hockney tends to side with, but that ought not to be allowed to settle the matter beyond appeal. The question is: Which interpretation chimes with his deeper intentions?

Let us take *A Walk Around the Hotel Courtyard Acatlán*, a sumptuous work of 1985, and let us concentrate on one of the blue plinths on which the stumpy rustic columns stand. Now the configuration of the plinth as it lies on the canvas certainly conforms to the projective system called reverse perspective, on behalf of which Hockney has sometimes made bold metaphysical claims. The picture conforms to reverse perspective in that the orthogonals, or lines running back into space at right angles to the picture plane, in this picture furnished by the two sides of any at least of the near plinths, are represented as converging not at a vanishing point, as linear perspective requires, but at the viewing-point. However, there is another account that can be given of the way in which reality has been mapped on to the surface of the picture with which everything that we seen before us certainly conforms. To grasp this account, first take the left-hand side of any one of the near plinths, and this time pair it off, not with the right-hand side of the same plinth, but with the right-hand side of the neighboring plinth to the left. Then see these two sides as forming the two sides of a cone of vision with its own viewing-point. Then think of this cone of vision as one of several, ranged across the picture horizontally, and which collectively give the content of the picture. What falls within each cone is projected onto the surface in (more or less) linear perspective. On this account, the picture would be relatively conservative as far as projective systems are concerned, and what it experiments with is multiplicity of viewing-points. It lines them up across the picture.

Here then we have two accounts of one picture, and this can be extended to other pictures. Which should we adopt? And my suggestion is that we adopt the second, because, if it conflicts with Hockney's words, or some of them, it fits in with his broader pictorial aspirations. Multiplying viewpoints fits in with, it advances, it secures, his project of involving the eye in the scene it records, something which, as far as I can see, is not addressed by the adoption of alternative projective systems.

Above all, the kind of interpretation of the recent work that I favor allows the construction of the picture to be resolved where Hockney has always sought

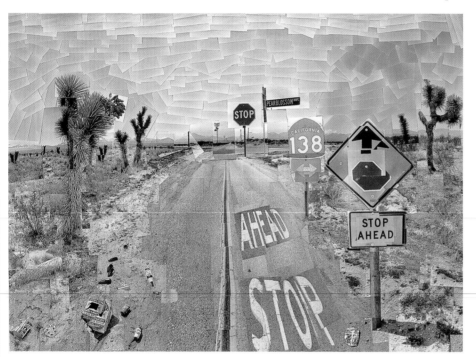

Pearblossom Highway,
11–18th April 1986 (second version), photographic collage, 72 x 107 in/182 x 272 cm.
© David Hockney, David Hockney collection.

arbitration. It would be settled by the minute judgments, but fine-grained sensibility, of the artist's eye, and not handed over to the once-for-all determination of his will. The superiority of such optical empiricism, at least for an art like Hockney's that blends life and art, was surely something that he learned on the verge of *Pearblossom Highway* in the spring of 1986. For the shimmering works, whose constituents he carefully amassed in the heat of the desert sun, is incandescent with life, not because it places the spectator at infinity – something Hockney links with reverse perspective – but because, with amazing fineness and intensity, it stockpiles the sensory input of the mind, it flutters in response to the many many saccadic movements of the eye. In a picture like this, the original project moves forward.

One of Hockney's most touching works – and also one of the most amusing – is an etching that he made in 1973–74, entitled *Artist and Model,* 1973 was the year of Picasso's death. The young Hockney, naked, sits at a table opposite the old Picasso, who is wearing the sailor's jersey familiar from photographs. It is hot, and Picasso examines a sheet of paper. Hockney has represented himself with that flat head which in his art is the sure sign of someone trying to learn from life.

Learning, where this includes wanting to learn, not being afraid to learn, not being afraid to show that one has something to learn, is a big theme in Hockney's life, and references to it, direct and oblique, are ubiquitous in his work. Learning appears as a way of staying young, perhaps of staying alive, and also as a way of growing up, perhaps of facing death. And since, as I have tried to bring out, for Hockney experience, in no matter what form, and curiosity, or the desire to learn from that experience, are never far apart, there is no sort of painting of his that does not have its overtone of learning. Even the so-called hedonistic pictures have it: they might be christened "studies in pleasure."

However, *The Artist and Model* not only is the most explicit depiction of the learning process in Hockney's work, it is also – if we exclude for the moment, though they must fit in somewhere here, the powerful slumped representations of the father – the one image that shows the process from the other end on. It addresses the question of how the teacher fares. And the answer seems to be that he thrives. In this picture he even returns from the grave.

The Artist and Model is a wonderfully unenvious work, and close examination of the detail of the scene reveals the lengths to which the young apprentice has gone to accommodate, to reassure, the old master. Naked though he is, he conceals the instrument of sex, the penis. He has left it outside with his clothes, though, as Henry Geldzahler points out in the catalog, it reappears in disguise at a point on the sheet directly above where we might have expected to find it. It is alive and well in the form of a knobbly palm tree, and it looks in on the scene from which it has been barred with a good-natured whimsicality. Sex is one way in which the young man might have aroused the ire of the older man, and art is another. Note, then, how Hockney, who freely places his left hand on the table in full view of the master, tenderly conceals the right hand, or the instrument of his art. But – the print is at pains to show – Hockney's attitude is polite, but it is certainly not placatory. His art, like his sexuality, is not annihilated, it is merely displaced. For we must believe that the sheet over which the older man pores is, if not by, then certainly of, his "model": either way round, the younger artist is reintegrated into the fold of art and his filial reticence is rewarded.

That a picture of Hockney and Picasso together should be the occasion of Hockney's most elaborate

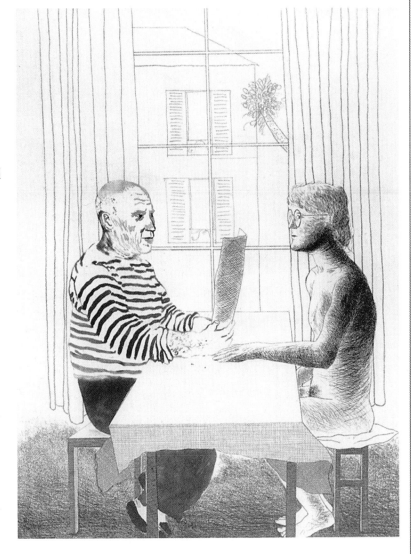

Artist and Model, *1974, etching in black, ed: 100, 23 x 17 in/57 x 44 cm. © David Hockney, Private collection.*

tribute to learning, and to teaching, has its own necessity. For, at least since Picasso's death, Picasso has been the major conscious source for Hockney's art, and for this too there are reasons.

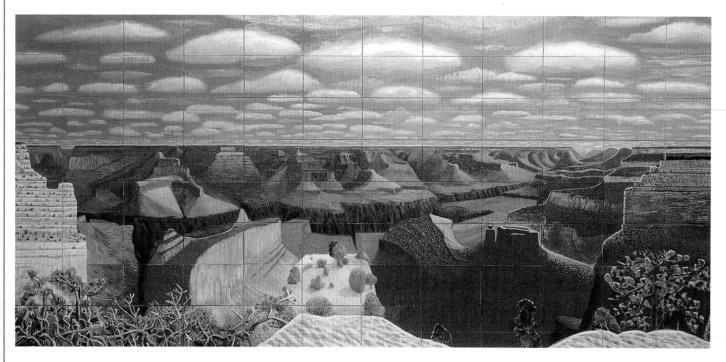

A Closer Grand Canyon, *1998,*
oil on 96 canvases,
130 x 293 in/330 x 744 cm.
© David Hockney, David Hockney
collection.

Several links bind the two artists together. In the first place, as John Richardson has done so much to show, Picasso too has been someone for whom his life has been the chosen content of his art: and, in his case, too, life has been given a broad reading so as to encompass the trivialities, the quirks, the little tricks, of existence. Secondly, Picasso and Hockney, whatever either may say, have both been artists for whom the represented figure has always been more significant than the space, or even the representation of the space, in which it stands. And thirdly – and the links are a mixed bag – both artists have injected into

> "IF WE ARE TO CHANGE OUR WORLD VIEW, IMAGES HAVE TO CHANGE. THE ARTIST NOW HAS A VERY IMPORTANT JOB TO DO. HE'S NOT A LITTLE PERIPHERAL FIGURE ENTERTAINING RICH PEOPLE, HE'S REALLY NEEDED."

their work a powerful, ambiguous sense of death. In Hockney's art there is none of the omnipotence that Picasso's work exudes, and instead there is a sensibility close to Watteau's, in which the trivial suddenly, abruptly, but still abjuring solemnity, stands for the transient.

But in the work of both men we from time to time find ourselves, quite unmistakably, in the presence of a somber power from which we thought ourselves a million miles away.

And then there are the great differences between the two artists, one of which Hockney has, I believe, disregarded to the detriment of some of his most recent work. Picasso is a carnal artist. He is one of the most carnal artists who ever worked. It is this fact that gives his massive transformations of the human face and the human body such terror and magnificence. Hockney is not a carnal artist. The boys, lying on crumpled beds or lilos, their buttocks provocatively arched, are for the most part cuddly toys. Without a doubt they have their own grace and sentiment, their own desirability, but it does not inspire Picasso's Jove-like rage for the human body. In consequence, when Hockney man-handles the human face or figure – as he does in the last portraits of Ishwerwood, or the images of Celia – the result altogether lacks terror and magnificence, it lacks power, basically it lacks interest. *It* lacks interest, though the artist never does.

An art-historical parallel irresponsibility comes to mind. It is not in all ways suitable. But the influence of Picasso upon Hockney recalls that of Michelangelo upon Titian. At its most direct it is disastrous, and it succeeds in doing what one would have judged impossible: throwing an artist with the most internalized of styles into stylistic disarray. But, mulled over, ingested, the influence is benign. It is fructifying, it presents a challenge, it is a spur to new things. The vitality of Hockney's art is what gives us genuine interest and reason to ask, not knowing the answer. What next?

> "(HOCKNEY WAS A) GREAT READER AND DAMN WELL KNEW THAT BOOKS AND ART ARE INSEPARABLE COMPANIONS IN MANY ARTISTS' LIVES."
> —R.B.Kitaj

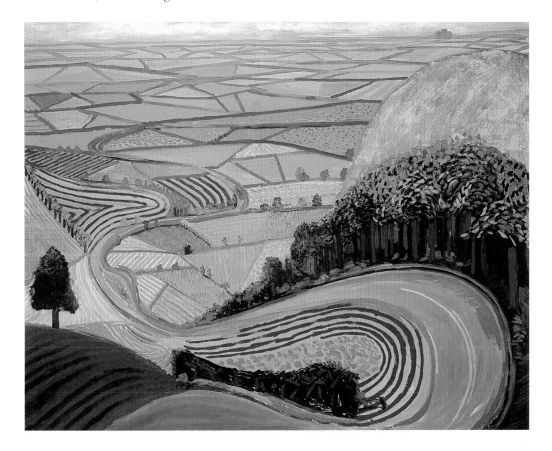

Garrowby Hill, *1998, oil on canvas, 60 x 76 in/152 x 193 cm. © David Hockney, David Hockney collection.*

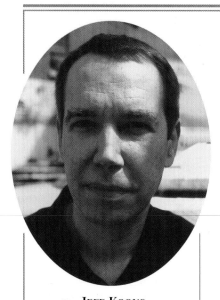

JEFF KOONS
Born in York, Pennsylvania, in 1955, Jeff Koons studied at the Art Institute of Chicago and moved to New York in 1977. He became a Wall Street broker in order to fund his artistic career.

In the 1980's, Koons used his sense of the absurd to promote his own brand of Pop Art. He focused on contemporary American consumer culture, especially kitsch, turning it into high art. His work displays a mass of contradictions: combining imagery of both sexuality and childhood. One of his best-known works, "Puppy" – a 50-foot-high topiary constructed of 17,000 flowers – emphasizes the transience of things.

Considered a genius by some, a charlatan by others, Koons produces work that exhibits the same spirit of audacity as that of Marcel Duchamp and Andy Warhol.

Although Koons persistently maintains he has a strong moral consciousness in his work, many critics dismiss him as a person devoid of substance and conscience. The art critic Robert Hughes wrote of him, "If Jeff Koons' work is about class struggle, I am Maria of Romania."

Jeff Koons

by Matthew Collings

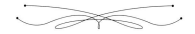

JEFF KOONS HAS A UNIQUELY MEMORABLE INTERVIEW STYLE, at once monstrous and evenly smiling and considerate, like a demented air hostess, or android. He is a conceptual artist, in the tradition of Marcel Duchamp and Andy Warhol. He thinks up ideas and has them made into objects by other people. He is different from his predecessors in that his objects are always immaculately presented, as near perfection as possible. He has been a constant presence in the art magazines for several years and has even made an appearance in the discerning *Modern Painters*. Before achieving fame on the international museum and gallery circuit – where his work now sells for extraordinary prices even by today's standards – he supported himself as an artist by working on Wall Street as a commodities broker. He caused a fuss in New York recently with his show of porcelain and wood sculptures of fluffy animals, big busted naked and semi-naked women, and a huge white-faced Michael Jackson holding a white-faced chimp. The exhibition was a big financial success but was called "racist" and "sexist" and "evil" and considered beyond the pale even for New Yorkers. Both conservatives and the liberal left pronounced themselves sickened. From the right, Hilton Kramer complained that this was a "new low" in an art world "already crowded with rotten art." Koons himself declared on BBC television that he had now taken the lead "at least in American art...." *M.C.*

After your "Late Show" debut the question most often asked was whether you really mean what you say.

I mean some of the things I say, and when I think about it the next day they still seem right. But other things I might just mean for the moment. These interview situations have a certain theatrical side. You're called upon to project an attitude. But having the freedom to take a completely different view the next day isn't just being frivolous. It's something that an artist really needs, otherwise you get too protective of yourself and fearful of making any new move. But there are things I restate again and again and these pretty much represent my position.

It's like a fairground spiel isn't it – the "Jeff Koons Show"?

Absolutely. This is "Jeff Koons Entertainment." I believe in art as a communicative device that's part of the entertainment world. It participates in "showtime." It just draws a slightly different audience than other entertainment vehicles.

Peter Fuller, the founding editor of Modern Painters, *said he disliked your art but he was impressed by this new work's effect on the liberal artworld's sensibilities. Do you really work at upsetting people?*

I never do anything just for shock value. I'm only interested in developing art and freeing it so that artists can be more liberated in what they do. I'm just showing what's necessary in order for the work to be really effective. It's like Michael Jackson's plastic surgery – I don't think he had it done just out of vanity, or because Michael is such a confused person. I think he's extremely realistic about what is necessary for him to do to be effective in his industry. For his photograph to be hanging on the walls of prepubescent and pubescent white middle-class girls, there were certain things he had to do. He had to make himself a mulatto, to make himself more white. That's radicality. That's abstraction. I'm much more interested in that kind of abstraction than in any formalist idea. I point to that sort of thing because it's an example of what everybody faces every day of their lives; when they have an opportunity to be really effective, that's exactly the moment when they back off. It's as plain as day. Effectiveness is power and the exercise of power. And that's what separates the men from the boys.

What else do you like about Michael Jackson?

He defends his territory – the territory of sexuality. He's able to express and to manipulate a very refined elegant sexuality.

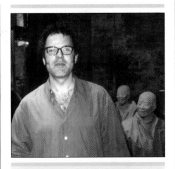

MATTHEW COLLINGS
Collings gained a reputation as an opinionated and humorous observer of the contemporary art scene through his television appearances and writings.

~

He was born in 1955 in London. After studying painting at the Byam Shaw School of Art and at Goldsmiths College, he edited the art magazine Artscribe International until being dismissed for an altercation. He then became the art critic for the BBC's The Late Show, and occasionally hosted the program.

~

He left the BBC in 1996 to write his first book Blimey! From Bohemia to Britpop for David Bowie's newly founded publishing company, 21. A critic described Collings' book as "hilarious and horrible, intelligent and frightening – the book the art world deserves." Collings also wrote a guide to contemporary art in New York called It Hurts: New York Art from Warhol to Now. This Modern Art, his book accompanying the UK television series, made Britain's 1999 nonfiction best-seller list.

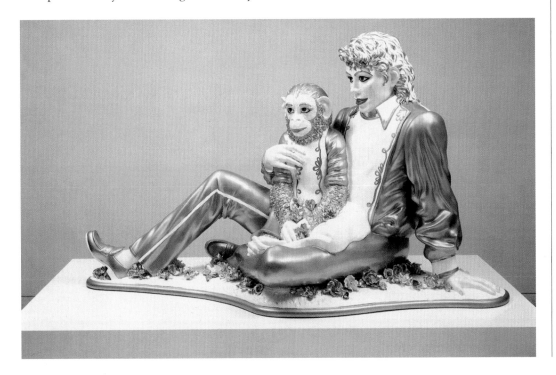

Michael Jackson and Bubbles, *1988, Porcelain, edition of 3, 42 x 70.5 x 32 in/107 x 179 x 81 cm. Sonnabend Gallery, New York.*

*And is that why you like Ciccolina, the
Italian porn star who was elected a member
of parliament?*

Actually Ciccolina represents innocence
and purity. Michael's kind of active – in motion,
whereas she projects a kind of pre-sex image.
It's all desire with her – like the eternal virgin.

I suppose Modern Painters *readers might
wonder what these sort of considerations might
have to do with art…*

Well my interest in art is that it should be
as effective a vehicle for communication as
possible. Other avenues have opened up, like
the electronic print industry, film, video, the
recording industry, and so on. But even though
the art market has grown enormously and
there's a much larger audience for art than
previously, as an effective communicating
device it hasn't really moved at all. If anything,
it's become completely lost in its own rhetoric.
It's an industry that thinks it carries so much
knowledge and virtue and of course it really
carries nothing at all. It's a self-protected
community that likes to think it deals with
these special levels of intelligence. But to me,
so long as something isn't really effective I
don't care what it's babbling about. It isn't real.

*And this perception of the artworld's limitations
has always been your central theme?*

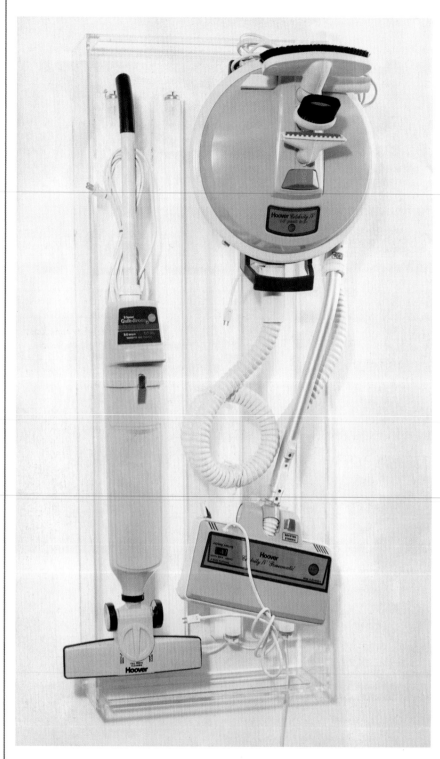

**New Hoover Celebrity IV, New
Hoover Quik –Broom**, *1980–86,
acrylic, fluorescent lights,
2 vacuum cleaners,
56 x 22 x 20 in/142 x 56 x 51 cm.
Saatchi Collection, London.*

It's one of the themes of the art I like. I always enjoyed Dada, and when I was a young child
I enjoyed Surrealism. What's great about Marcel Duchamp is that he frees you from the
masturbative aspects of art – this idea that says art is a very subjective activity where you can
learn about yourself. I mean, I live with myself everyday and that's one of the things I'm
most bored with. The world outside of myself, the objective world and relationships with
things in the world that we all share – that's what interesting in art. I know what I dreamed
yesterday – who cares? I'm interested in things that go way beyond that subjectivity.

Do you think Duchamp is really an "anti-art" artists?

On the contrary, I think he deals with the objective dimension and for me that's art. Everything that deals with the subjective should be called "anti-art." But that's just modern art. I think the last time art really dealt in a grand manner with the subjective was in the Baroque and Rococo periods. That's the last time it was really effective in that area.

"I'M MAKING SOME OF THE GREATEST ART BEING MADE NOW. IT'LL TAKE THE ART WORLD TEN YEARS TO GET AROUND TO IT."

Do you like to think of these new sculptures of yours as a bit like grand Baroque images?

I like that power of communication and that effectiveness in meeting the needs of people, yes. I would like to think that Jeff Koons is trying to meet the needs of the people, just as much as a Pop star meets people's sexual needs with that particular Pop star titillation. The way they have this "hook" – that's a wonderful thing to me. And I don't think it's just a short term effect. You can fake it for a moment but when it's really working it lasts because effective communication has a subversive aspect. You resist it at first, but somehow you're already hooked even before you realize you're actually enjoying it.

But to be so preoccupied with what you think other people need – aren't your detractors right when they say you're just a manipulator, always thinking "OK, what's the next step. I'd better do that now"?

I'm not interested in wondering what's the next step. I don't at all mind thinking of myself as totally absorbed in ideas of leadership. The reason I have this particular position in art right now is because I want it. I'm trying to exploit myself and to do everything that's possible within my limitations. And I think everybody should be doing that. I'm trying to be an example to others.

I expect when you explain your work you irritate those who feel uneasy with it even more.

I'm really very honest in what I say: If people listened they'd see I'm not saying anything just for sensationalism; I'm actually

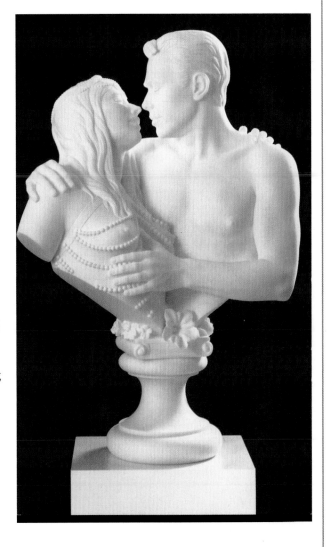

Bourgeouis Bust – Jeff and Ilona, *1991, Marble, edition of 3 and artist's proof, 45 x 28 x 21 in/113 x 71 x 53 cm Courtesy of the artist.*

describing the nuts and bolts of the work. In my exhibition of last year – that we looked at in "The Late Show" – the sculpture of St. John the Baptist, which was there to "baptize in banality," was suggesting that my art was really the starting point for a certain course of action. I was trying to present myself as an agent of salvation. Not so much Jeff Koons the person as what Jeff Koons stands for politically – this idea that you have to embrace other media, and industries other than "art," as the only way to be effective in contemporary society.

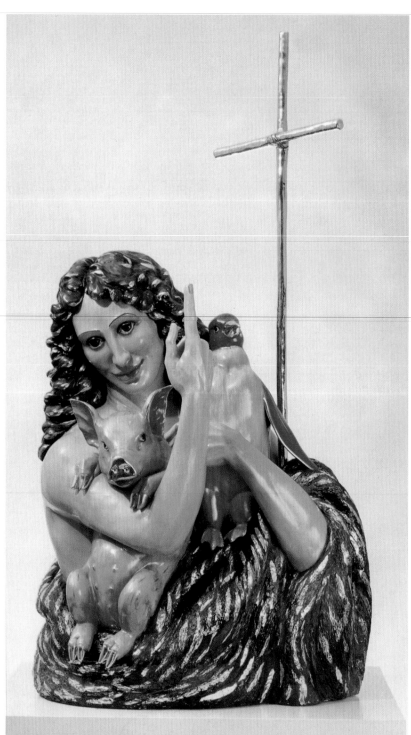

St. John the Baptist, *1988,*
porcelain, edition of three and
artist's proof,
57 x 30 x 25 in/144 x 76 x 62 cm.
Courtesy of the artist.

Well, this other media idea isn't so frightening. Sometimes you really sound like you're going off the rails though…

Well, I'm interested in freedom. Freedom is the commercial industry, where only effectiveness counts. You want to use tits and ass? It's effective – use it. And the people that'll say, "How dare you do that? That is a sexist statement" are the same people who are going out and buying perfume based on tits and ass ads in the magazines.

They don't know what they like?

They'll be motivated by and responsive to certain things and then appalled by the same things when they're faced with them directly. A lot of my exhibition was directed at this class of people, in as much as it was saying, "You're motivated by banality and the dislocated imagery you find in advertisements. Respect this aspect of yourself, remove the guilt and shame you have about it, and take a step forward." I used very simple ideas about guilt and shame. Like the sculpture with the pink panther, which is about the guilt and shame of masturbation. Here's a woman that's free of guilt and shame. Not everybody believes in original sin any more, but I think everyone knows about guilt and shame.

That's a lot of masturbation in one interview! You are so mild on the surface. What lies beneath?

Feelings of contempt for the art world? Of anger?

Well, it's funny you should ask that. I've been traveling a lot in Europe recently, and the other day I got back to New York, and I thought I'd go out that evening for a drink and whatever I wanted to say I was just going to say and not care what anyone else thought. I was really going to let rip. And all that hatred I had for the art world – if there was any hatred there – I was just going to let it out in one big explosion. Like: "Nothing can touch me now – I'm Jeff Koons and my art can defend me!" So I tried one little taste of it and I found that actually it wasn't me at all. I had no interest in it. I find I'm not angry at the art world. If anything disturbs me at all it's my own limitations. I want to be as liberated and free as possible. I'd like to think if I wanted to make films, for example, I could start tomorrow. I don't have to wake up in the morning and say,

"AS MORALITY SEEMS TO HAVE SUPPLANTED CIVILIZATION, I MOVE ON TO THE SPIRITUAL."

"Oh, I'm 34 and I'm an artist, not a film maker…" Or I might suddenly want to have a magazine but I don't know anything about writing – I read a maximum of maybe two books a year. So that's really the only thing I would be angry about: my own limitations that I face every day. Not the art world. The art world's a wonderful community. It's just that it's isolated and it's remained protected from any real power or effectiveness in the world.

You mean it isn't anything like Hollywood, as many people think?

Absolutely not. How effective are art stars? Their glamour is pretty limited. What have they

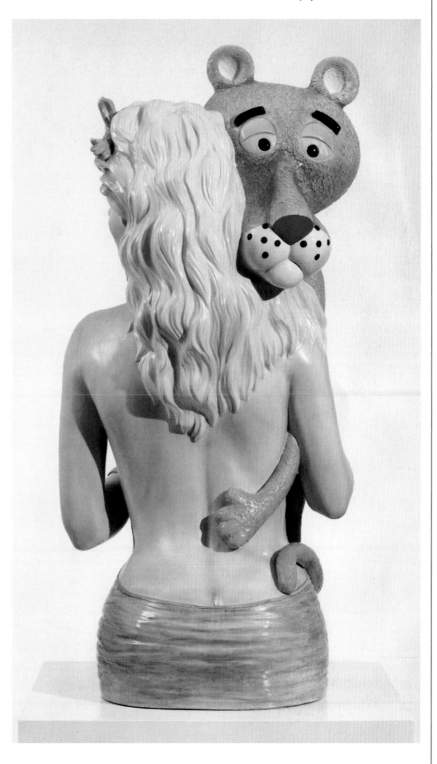

Pink Panther, *1988, Porcelain, edition of three and artist's proof, 41 x 21 x 19 in/104 x 52 x 48 cm. Courtesy of the artist.*

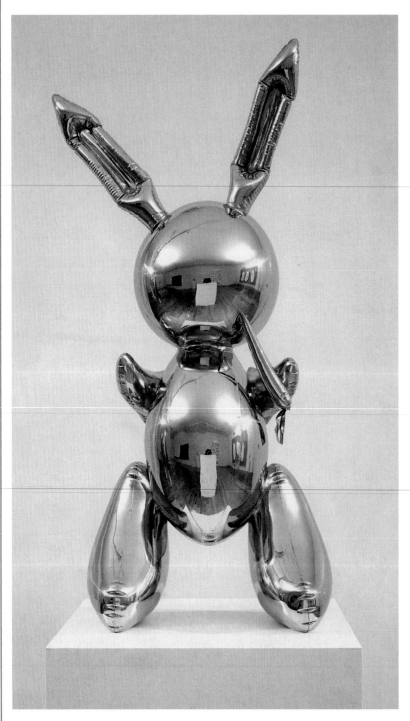

Rabbit, *1986, Stainless Steel,*
Edition of three and artist's proof,
41 x 19 x 12 in/104 x 48 x 30 cm.
Courtesy of the artist.

got to offer? The only way artists can find their own glamour is to incorporate aspects of systems other than "art" and to be creative and confident enough to really exploit what they have. And to bring out the primal artist in themselves. I'm not talking about some rough primal gesture but this idea of the real power of art – we should have a better understanding of it and a better sense of how to manipulate it. After all, we were the ones who put the marks on the caves. We were in charge of history, of the perception of what some asshole sitting beside you thought reality was. We told him what he did yesterday! And what he'd probably do tomorrow.

What about more old fashioned artists who just want to paint Nature and the model in the studio and so forth?

Well, if they weren't allowed to do that, then that's the thing we'd all want to start doing… there has to be this conservative aspect of course. If it was banned, then pretty soon radical artists would be moving into that void. Somebody's got to maintain it, otherwise we'd all be back in there fighting for Nature again.

You, think there's always an equilibrium in art, of radical and conservatives?

Absolutely. But do I believe these people who just maintain this area like it was a piece of property should be the leaders? Absolutely not. They are not courageous and I certainly wouldn't be on any front line with them.

Hilton Kramer said your sculptures represented a "new low" in art.

Yes, I find that difficult to understand. I know what I'm doing is very positive and I think I can have a positive effect on young artists and help them lead a better life where they can have more political power and have more of an effect. I would have thought anyone who'd been involved with the art dialogue for as long as Hilton has would know how suffocating and destructive it is. He's made all these statements over the years that make up his own territory, and he's probably fearful that if he opens up to something new then his whole world will fall apart. But you know, things like that don't deter me. I always know everything's OK when Hilton attacks me because in the same breath he always attacks my heroes. He says Jeff Koons had to occur since Jasper Johns painted his American flag. And the flag couldn't have occurred without Duchamp. And after Johns it was Andy… That sounds wonderful to me – Duchamp, Johns, Andy Warhol. Such good company!

Do you admire the image of himself that Jasper Johns projects – slightly sinister?

God, yes. I was watching this film about Warhol the other day that had Johns in it, and Johns back in the 60s was like a film star – this guy could really project! He is a tough motherfucker! Intellectually tough. Leo Castelli would sit down with him and say, "Jasper! So nice to see you." And Johns would say, "Why?" like it was a philosophical enquiry. What a guy! But this sort of thing is what brings about that seventeen million dollar market. That market doesn't just come out of nowhere. Whether this persona was consciously developed by Jasper, or is just elements of his personality coming out naturally, and he's really quite unaware of their impact… is irrelevant. Because in the end these are the building blocks toward making his market and his market is part of the total effectiveness. I'm really shocked he isn't in the Whitney Biennial this year. Getting seventeen million dollars for single painting – this is power. How can they not have that represented in the Biennial if it's supposed to be about who's been effective in art? To remove the market from the discussion in favor of this little critical dialogue and say, "Oh yes, but he handled paint so well…" and have everyone walking around New York saying, "Oh yes, what a good artist…" when everyone knows that the true political power, where the negotiating really takes place, is in the market. When you start throwing around seventeen million dollars, or fourteen million dollars for a painting, then the curators

"BRILLIANT, REFLECTIVE, CONTRADICTORY, JEFF KOONS'S WORK IS, AT ONE OF MANY LEVELS, AN ATTEMPT TO RECAPTURE THE LOST EDENIC 'NEWNESS' OF CHILDHOOD."

—*Nathan Kernan*

Balloon Dog 1995 – 8, *(installation of work in progress), high chromium stainless steel, 126 x 149 x 47 in/ 320 x 379 x 119 cm. Courtesy of the artist.*

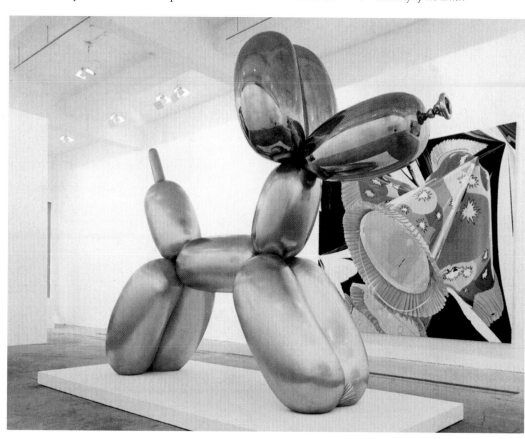

have to conserve their little bit of power and say, "Oh well, we don't know if the new *Four Seasons* series by Johns is really all that good." What they're really saying is that they're not going to let the market dictate the situation. When of course the market represents the only true power because it absorbs all their ideas and a lot of other ideas besides.

Don't you think collectors are boring on the whole? Don't you resent having to rely on them?

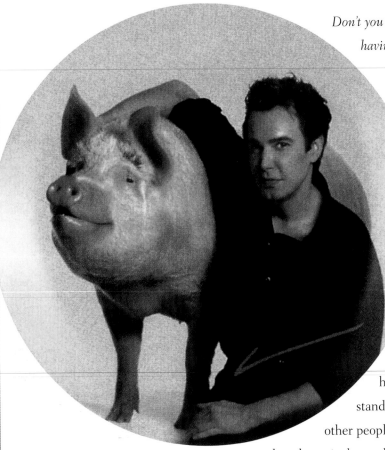

The first thing that any good artist has to develop is a sense of independence from the artworld. What really destroys a young artist is insecurity, the fear that everything could be taken away at any moment. The media, the galleries, the collectors – it's all very chaotic actually. The artworld doesn't have this defined corporate structure that people imagine. Of course there's a system of sorts. This person will talk to that person and somebody else will pass it on to somebody else… you can trace a line of power of some kind. But it's nothing like as clear and set as people think. And this chaos leads to a lot of insecurity. It's only after an artist has achieved some independence from it that he can really stand up to the collectors and the dealers and do his art. These other people all want to feel important and have their bit of power but the artist has to know he can survive without them. He may not be so visible for a while but he can still eat and provide for himself. You've always got to be ready to sacrifice what they're offering for what you truly want. You've always got to be winning at these negotiations.

Give me an example from your own career.

In the early years I had no political support. I wasn't getting it from the galleries I was working with, or from the collectors. I wasn't going to waste my time waiting for it, or for some kind of illusion of it, so I decided to go independent and achieve a better position from which to care for my work.

You became a commodities broker…

Yes, I achieved a better position by going to Wall Street. But I could have done any number of other things. I just know I can take care of myself, that I can support myself past the average level.

Signature plate (Parkett edition), *1989, Portfolio edition of fifty, diameter: 10 in/26 cm. Artist's proof.*

Opposite page, top to bottom:
Lips, *2000 (nearly finished state), oil on canvas, 10 x 13 ft/3 x 4 m. Courtesy Deutsche Guggenheim, Berlin.*
Grotto, *2000 (nearly finished state), oil on canvas, 10 x 13 ft/3 x 4 m. Courtesy Deutsche Guggenheim, Berlin.*
Mountains, *2000 (nearly finished state), oil on canvas, 10 x 13 ft/3 x 4 m. Courtesy Deutsche Guggenheim, Berlin.*

People assume that a commodities broker couldn't be an artist. That someone who deals with money can't have the spirit of an artist.

I was always an artist. I was a broker to earn a living, but I was always thinking about my art. Whether I was being a broker in the week and only making art at the weekends, or having other people make it for me – whatever – is irrelevant. What's important is the art itself and the passion and ambition that's involved. Not how many other activities you might be engaged in. I work with ideas. I'll think about things and let them resonate over a period of time and then I'll act – I'll go and execute those ideas. That's all I'm really interested in. Everything else is irrelevant.

Do you think there's a place in New York for Modern Painters, *which is quite a conservative magazine in many ways?*

I think because it *is* so self contained the New York artworld could probably absorb a more conservative stance without too much problem. I would like to think of myself actually as a radical conservative.

What are your conservative aspects?

I try to be realistic about the environment and to be rational and have an understanding of things. The radical aspect is actually to follow through and do what is necessary – to take action.

What do you think about this idea of Peter Fuller's that artists should get back to Nature? He says modern art has been too much concerned with abstractions and it would be better if there was a return to things like the natural environment and to the biological experience that is fundamental to everybody…

Well, I'm all for sex.

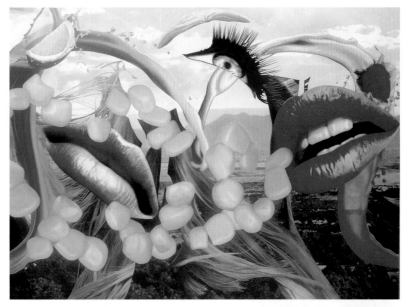

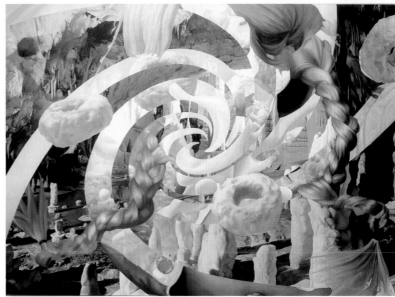

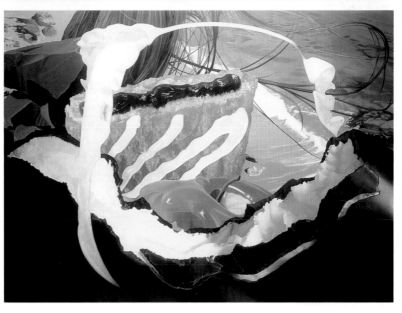

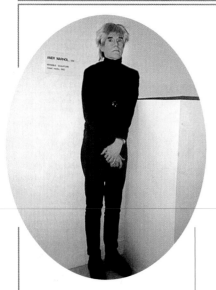

ANDY WARHOL
*Born Andrew Warhola of
Czechoslovak immigrant
parents in Pittsburgh in
1928, Warhol studied design
and art history at Carnegie
Institute of Technology in
Pittsburgh before moving to
New York City in 1949.
There, he became a
commercial illustrator for
Vogue and Harper's Bazaar
and did window displays,
later incorporating the
subjects of advertising into
paintings and prints. He had
his first one-man exhibition
at the Hugo Gallery in 1952.
Taking as subject matter
banal objects such as comic
strips and ketchup bottles, he
spearheaded the Pop Art
movement of the '60s,
culminating in his photo
silkscreens of Campbell's
soup cans and "Marilyn"
prints in 1962.*

*Warhol crossed media
boundaries producing films,
records – like the rock band
The Velvet Underground –
and the magazine Interview.
Most of his work was done
at his studio, an old silver
factory which was invariably
filled with other artists,
celebrities, and hangers-on.
Among this loose assemblage
was Valerie Solanis who, in
1968, shot and seriously
wounded Warhol.*

*Warhol died in 1987. In
1989 the Museum of
Modern Art organized the
largest retrospective
exhibition of his work.*

Andy Warhol

by Howard Jacobson

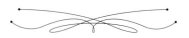

MINDING HIS OWN BUSINESS *outside the tradesmen's entrance to the Hayward Gallery last October, Howard Jacobson was accosted by a wraith-like, whey-faced figure in a skewed, peroxide wig, who thrust a manuscript into his hands, laughed spectrally, and vanished into the night. Realizing the value of this chance acquisition, and putting service to art history before personal gain, he sent it in a plain envelope (postage $2.50) to* Modern Painters. *Now read on…*

Saturday, August 26, 1989 – New York

Got up so late I missed the *Today Show*. Then realized it was the weekend and there was no *Today Show*. No one called all day, so I just sat and read the phone book. And I don't know, it was all so abstract. Found a number for George Bush and wondered if it connected to some hideout belonging to *the* George Bush. I started to call and then got scared in case he answered, and hung up.

"IF YOU WANT TO KNOW ALL ABOUT ANDY WARHOL,…JUST LOOK AT THE SURFACE OF MY PAINTINGS AND FILMS AND ME, AND THERE I AM. THERE'S NOTHING BEHIND IT."

Rang Chris and Victor and Bianca and Julian, but they were all out. Knew I was getting tired when I started to ring Marilyn. Would have been cute if she'd answered.

Still couldn't sleep, so I played with the telephone some more. Dialed U-P-Y-O-U-R-S and B-I-G-D-I-C-K to see what happened, and it was so exciting and so much fun.

Monday, August 28, 1989 – New York – London

Jean Michel, or was it Billy Boy, or was it Catherine, picked me up so early I missed the *Today Show*. I had my contacts in and really couldn't see too well. Bianca, or was it Jerry, went with me to the airport (limo $95, porter $20, magazines $60, mouth freshener

$15, presents for Anthony d'Offay $5). Got the Concorde. It was a starless fight. (*Laughs.*) The last time I said that to Sylvester Stallone he thought I was talking about the sky. He couldn't understand I meant it was a plane full of nobodies and kept saying how did I expect to see any stars if I traveled in daylight.

A hostess with a wide ass recognized me and handed me a sick bag to sign. Afterwards I wondered if she'd wanted me to be sick in it.

There was nobody to meet me when I arrived so I cabbed ($55) to the Savoy Hotel (doorman $10, porter $5, room probably $1,000,000). They looked at me really strangely when I checked in, like I was supposed to be dead or something, but they found me a great room, well more like a closet, overlooking some river. The bellboy hung around even after I'd given him a tip ($1). He had quite some bulge in his pants which was surprising considering he was about a hundred. So there you are kiddo, there's life after death.

Tuesday, August 29, 1989 – London

Got up early to catch the *Today Show*, then remembered I was in London. Watched something called *Good Morning Britain* instead, a couple of straight guys in cardigans

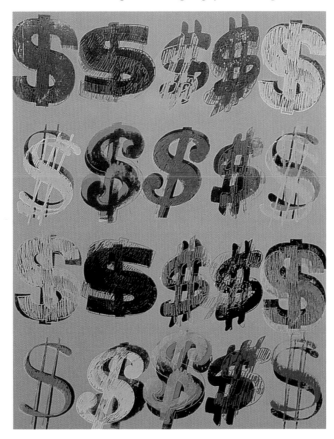

interviewing no ones. I waited for Fergie and the Queen Mother to be on but they weren't. How can you have a television show in London without Fergie and the Queen Mother being on?

Waited in all morning for a phone call but no one rang. That's the worst, when you sit there hoping for the phone to go and it just doesn't. Tried calling Zandra and Manolo and Rifat, but they were all out. Heard Dustin was in town, something to do with Venice and a moneylender, so I tried him, but he wasn't in either, unless his phone was on the wall and he couldn't reach it.

Did the usual thing – glued myself together and wandered around London (cabs $20). Went to the Hayward Gallery, where they were busy hanging me and worrying about some strike. It was kind of exciting, being hung, and also being ignored. Picked up a leaflet with

HOWARD JACOBSON
Jacobson was born in Manchester, England, in 1942, and educated at Cambridge University. He has taught in universities in England and Australia and now is a full-time novelist and critic.

Howard Jacobson's novels include Coming From Behind *(1983),* Peeping Tom *(1984),* The Very Model of a Man *(1992), and he has written four works of nonfiction, including* Seriously Funny: An Argument for Comedy *(1997). His most recent novel,* No More Mister Nice Guy, *is about a disillusioned youth coming of age in 1950s Manchester.*

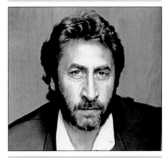

Dollar Signs, *1981, Silkscreen ink on synthetic polymer paint on canvas, 84 x 70 in/229 x 178 cm. Courtesy of Waddington Gallery, London and James Goodman Gallery, New York.*

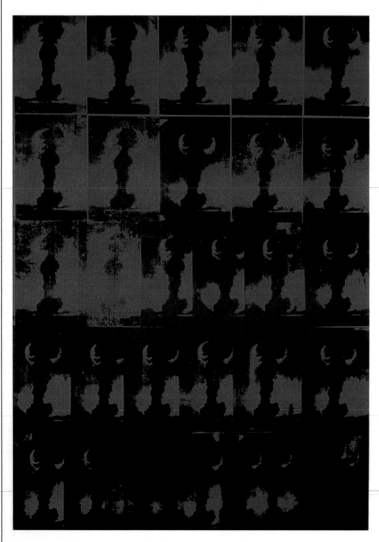

Atomic Bomb, *1965, Silkscreen ink on synthetic polymer paint on canvas, 104 x 81 in/264 x 205 cm. Saatchi Collection, London.*

that old Turquoise Marilyn on the front. Inside, it said I wasn't as "meretricious" as Dali. Went back to hotel and rang Bianca in New York, collect, to ask her what it meant. I'm talking like her: "Hellll-loooo." You call her and you get this whole low voice and Latino-Euromumble. I must have got her out of bed, or maybe she was wrestling on the floor with Alana. She was saying all these things to me like why didn't I give myself a blow job if I didn't have anything better to do, and what did I have against consulting the Oxford Fucking Dictionary. I asked her if that was what meretricious meant, being able to give yourself a blow job while reading the Oxford Fucking Dictionary, but she said how was she supposed to know, she was born in fucking Nicaragua.

Squeezed pustules and went to bed.

Wednesday, August 30, 1989 – London

Went sightseeing with my camera. Saw and photographed Big Ben. Seen and photographed bigger.

Thought the cab that was sitting behind me was like part of the whole set, but then it turned out it wasn't, so I got in and took it to the Savoy ($7).

Thursday, August 31, 1989 – London

Got up at 9 and went to get collagen. Cabbed to Buckingham Palace ($8), hoping to catch Fergie or the Queen Mother. Caught the eye of an adorable guardsman instead. Gee, he was so good-looking. Perfect chest and teeth. And a huge cock. You can always tell. The ones with the huge cocks have to stand very still, otherwise they overbalance.

Catherine will say things like, you don't want to bother with guardsmen, standing in the sun all day fries their brains. But I don't know – you could mold this one into anything you fancied, take him to the movies, give him books to read, teach him how to watch the *Today Show* (*laughs*) anything...

Went to McDonald's and got energized. Saw my picture on the cover of a freaky magazine. I don't remember doing any interview for them. It was all about how you could be Andy Warhol in ten easy stages. It didn't take me that many.

Friday, September 1, 1989 – London

Stayed in to dye my hair and eyebrows because of my surprise appearance at the

Serpentine the next day. An artist has to look the part, sweetheart.

Went back to bed to watch TV – still no Fergie – and read the papers. I was in most of them. But get this – I didn't bother to clip the articles. So you finally get past that.

Found a phoney baloney interview some creep did with Schnabel. All about the hundreds of thousands of dollars the guy gets for a canvas these days. Fischl, too. Don't know why. I guess they've both put their ice skates on in a new way. And so they're both like skating down easy street. Which is great.

Took sleeping pill and woke up at 10:30 at night, feeling depressed. I just missed the Queen Mother on the news, opening or closing something. I wish she'd get married again. If she could find someone, I'd feel more up about my chances.

Saturday, September 2, 1989 – London

Limoed to the Serpentine in time for the private view. "Success is a Job in New York."

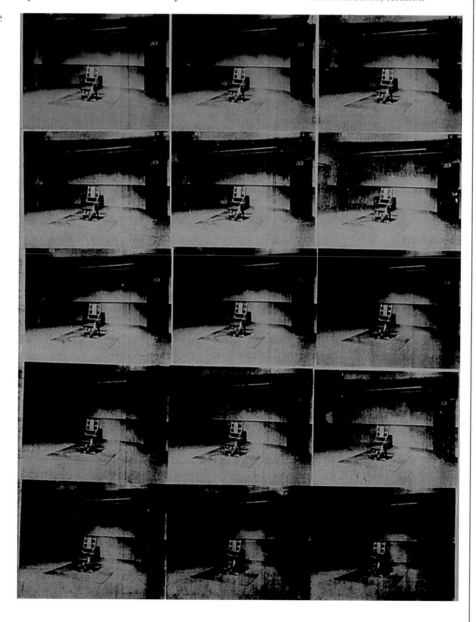

Lavender Disaster, *1963, silkscreen ink on synthetic polymer paint on canvas, 50 x 38 in/269 x 208 cm. Menil collection, Houston.*

It was the same show they had back home and in Pittsburgh earlier this year. Still can't decide if I think the idea is funky or junky. At the Pittsburgh opening I heard someone joke, "Success is a hand job in New York." It was so funny I had to leave and go to bed.

Hyde Park looked great. Like all these families were out walking. I got really thrilled seeing the poster for my exhibition. That old tacky Elvis Presley boot. It said private view, you know, you had to be somebody to get in, but anyone was allowed through which is great because the somebodies are everywhere and you're sick of them. You just looked artistic, ordered a mineral water from a trestle table set up in the middle of the gallery, like it was some kind of soup kitchen, and you were in.

A cute African guy in a knitted Afghan fez and tight cycling pants with more zips on him than I'd traced Mao Tse-tungs looked as though he thought he knew me, then shook his head and

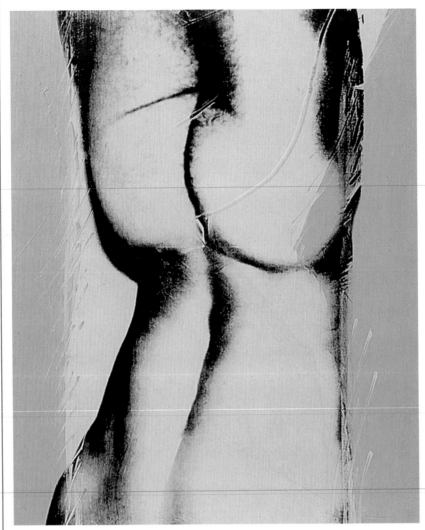

Torso, 1977, Silkscreen ink on synthetic polymer paint on canvas, 50 x 38 in/127 x 97 cm. Estate of Andy Warhol.

went back to concentrating on being looked at himself. He had an Islamic pattern on his shirt which from a distance looked like pairs of embroidered kisses and I thought that was sad. A few English girls in wrinkly black socks and thrift-store minis and baseball boots took hours inspecting everything on the walls, every nothing drawing and graphic design schtick, like they were in the Louvre or somewhere. I thought it was great, because their clothes were kind of go-to-hell don't-give-a-shit ironic but their faces were all serious and religious.

I get so confused looking at art. Even when it's my own. I don't know – one day you just want to do disasters and the next you just want to do cherubs sucking on tits. So who's to say what's a masterpiece? Anyway, I was really thrilled to see the Modess ads again – so funny. And the feet. I heard someone behind me reading out from the catalog: "The sensuous and expectant feet celebrate a youthful here-and-now, and the objects included embroider the moods of opportunity." I get so confused by catalogs.

Went across the street to the Polish Club in Princes Gate. I signed the book Warhola so that they would think I was Polish, but the little guy at the desk said, "Hey, that's a Czech name isn't it?" I wanted to say to him, "What does it matter? We're all American now. If you want to know what success is, it sure isn't a job in Gdansk." But he was so sad, and his face had that sunken Eastern look, as though the whole of Europe had marched across it, I just smiled at him. Which kind of made him sadder.

I ordered Bavarian knuckle of pig with meat dumplings which probably wasn't too good an idea. I must have put on a hundred pounds, in the wrong places as usual. Donna de Salvo – and don't tell me *that's* a Polish name – came in while I was eating. She curated the exhibition in New York and edited the catalog and uses funny intellectual words. She had this bunch of egghead types with her and someone called Alistair or Trevor – one of those fag English names. He was really pretty. Sort of smart but tousled, like a Wall Street banker wondering if he's a fairy. I wanted to invite him to come by and piss on some drawings for me if he was ever in New York. But by the time I got up the courage they were into their borscht.

I loved the waitresses. They were like from another age. They were wearing these flouncy black skirts and black stockings and cream sandals. *Cream*. There I go with my sensuous and expectant foot fetish again.

Sunday, September 2, 1989 – London

Went to church (collection $2). I was feeling so used and abused and lied to.

The priest looked so adorable in his surplice I wished I had brought my camera, and that's when I thought I had found the next idea I really wanted to work on – Ten Celebrated Celibates. I think it's a great subject, just so erotic.

Afterward I went to Trafalgar Square to feed the birds with this little package of seeds that you can buy, but they were standoffish, like the English, and took everybody's seeds but mine. I felt neglected. Maybe they thought I had some gay disease. It's almost comical; they'll eat shit off the sidewalk but they're particular who they take seeds off. People are the same. They give you their cheeks instead of their tongues but they'll still shake your hand before you've even finished peeing.

Thought about going into the National Gallery, then remembered it's only got old stuff in it.

"YOU'RE A KILLER OF ART, YOU'RE A KILLER OF BEAUTY,"
— *de Kooning told Warhol.*

Elvis I and II, *1964, Two panels: silkscreen ink on synthetic polymer paint on canvas, silkscreen ink on aluminium paint on canvas: each panel, 82 x 82 in/208 x 208 cm. Art Gallery of Ontario, Toronto. Gift from the Women's Committee Fund.*

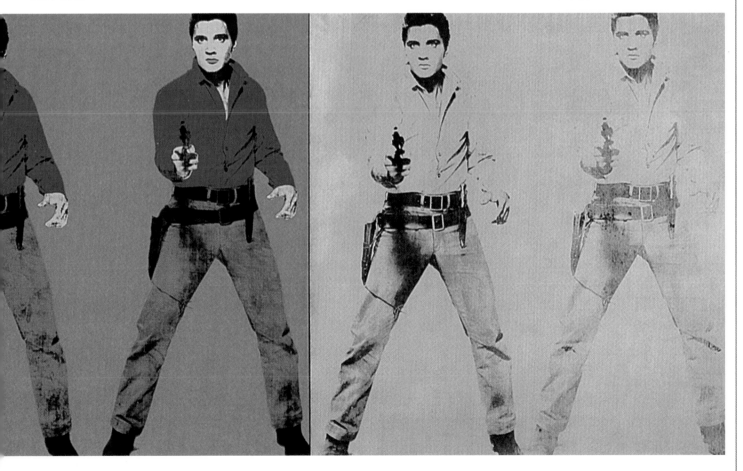

Tuesday, September 5, 1989 – London

Spent the last two days in the hotel squeezing pimples and looking for crabs and watching TV. I was really nervous about that reception to celebrate the opening of "Andy Warhol: A Retrospective" at the Hayward because some influential Arts Council hot shot who sounded as though he was high up in the Mafia was going to be there – Pietro Palabimbo or somebody – and I had this idea that Fergie might have been coming as well. But when it was all canceled because of the strike. I was so disappointed. I had gotten a new magic crystal to stop things like this from happening. I guess this one has now been invaded like the last, and I don't know where to get another until I'm back in New York. I'll just have to leave it out in the sun and hope it recharges.

Put on dark glasses and walked around Covent Garden. It reminded me of ten years ago when I went to Martha Graham's opening at the Opera House and then cabbed back to the hotel

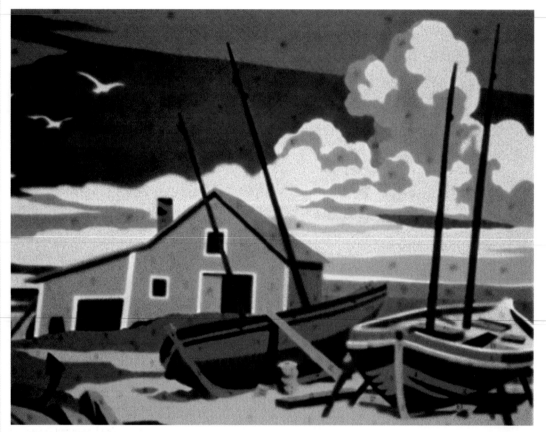

Paint By Number (Seascape), *1963, Synthetic polymer paint and Prestype on canvas, 54 x 72 in/138 x 183 cm. Private collection.*

with Halston and moved everyone's morning papers from in front of their doors to other places, so that like people who expected *The Times* got the *Daily Mirror*. The funniest thing I ever did. I felt like a different person this time. All alone.

Stepped in dog shit on the way back to the Savoy and had to throw myself in the bath with my shoes still on. I've read that the diseases you get from shit can eat their way through your shoes, so I stayed up all night burning leather ($295) and scrubbing the soles of my feet. If those intellectual nuts who say I've got a foot fetish had seen me you can imagine what they'd have thought.

Wednesday, September 6, 1989 – London

Cabbed ($10) to Alexander Roussos Gallery ($5) for preview of "Sexual Ambiguities." I half expected it to be called off by strikes so I only half glued myself together. I'd like to start wearing lipstick at night so my lips look wetter and fuller, but I'm afraid I'd get stuck under a bright light someplace. Anyway I was really thrilled the show was still going ahead, and I thought it was great that there was this notice outside the gallery warning that "This show contains imagery and subject matters that the general public may find offensive," because there was just this whole bunch of dicks on the wall. And that was so funny.

Some guy with a weird name – Robert or something – was standing in front of one of the cocks saying, New York would never have done this show and it was like actionable and it was really brave of Demis Roussos to put it on the for no profit or anything and the cops could be here at any minute. He seemed sort of shocked so I told him it was my come, but actually it was Victor's. Then I overheard the New Zealand waiter who was pouring the champagne say that he thought the drawings were tame and a bit short on penetration. Maybe in New Zealand they just penetrate before they're introduced because there's nothing else to do. But he was cute and had big muscles and he was grand.

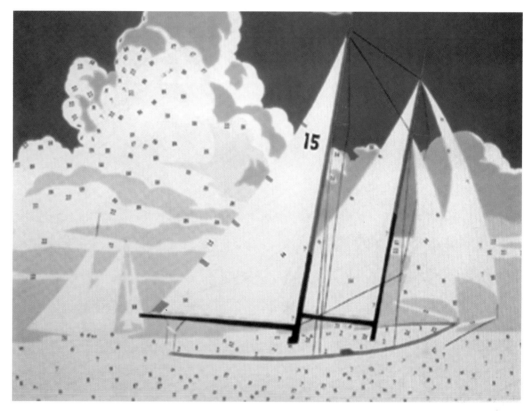

Paint By Number (Sailboats), 1962, *Synthetic polymer paint and Prestype on canvas, 72 x 100 in/183 x 254 cm. Private collection.*

And there was nobody really there. Just everybody you already knew, but nobody. Two Bananaramas. One Duran Duran. Oh, and Martin Taylor-Brown who manages some old has-been English group, the Beverley Sisters or Brothers, who all look like Marcel Duchamp in his wig. I hope they sing better than he did. And I said hello to Lady Edith Foxwell, the Disco Dowager, and she said hello to me and we chit-chatted but I don't think she recognized me. And Baroness Fiona von Thyssen was there, but I didn't go over. I had just seen her on TV. She said that her husband left her because she was the most beautiful woman in the world but also the most boring, and I didn't want to find out if he was right.

The best act was a black guy, kind of like Merce Cunningham only young, wearing a pink chenille bedspread and a matching turban and these silver high heels – about EIGHT inches – and the bedspread was slashed up one leg to the crotch. It was really romantic. But he kept touching the sandwiches before choosing one, so I couldn't eat any, and he kept putting his glass down and forgetting where, and ANYONE could have picked it up.

He asked me about my complexion so I just told him, "Listen, I haven't swallowed any sperm." He really put his foot in it.

And Chris Makos was running around in these long shorts and this kind of English tweed jacket like it was his cock on the wall, which it might have been, I just can't remember. And I was hurt because of what he'd said to this TV reporter at the Serpentine, that "Andy Warhol was a good friend of mine in New York and I never knew he did so many ugly paintings." Which just wasn't true because he helped me with some of those paintings himself. And he was so happy he depressed me. He kept charging up to everybody saying, "Hi, I'm the photographer, let me give you a souvenir of this special night." And it was a photograph of me looking unglued, the one Chris took in Paris about the time I offered him a reward if he could get Jon Gould to fall for me. That was before Christopher slapped Jon right in the face after the water pistol fight, and Jon just stood there taking it because he wanted to be slapped.

Chris left the party holding his camera above his head, sending off flashes like fireworks. It was like he was seeing himself off. He's still such a kid.

Went home and took some valium which didn't work. Thought about ringing that Saatchi guy who wanted to buy the Marilyn if he could pay for it over four years, but his number wasn't in the book.

Thursday, September 7, 1989 – London

Just lallied around, feeling blue.

Did a dog painting in 5 minutes. I had this picture and I used the tracing machine

"OH, I LOVE BEING PLASTIC, I'D LOVE TO BE A MACHINE, WOULDN'T YOU?"

that projects the image onto the wall and I put the paper where the image is and I trace. Five minutes. I timed myself. I'm really slowing down.

Friday, September 8, 1989 – London

Woke up feeling bad after seeing this creep on some news program saying how my paintings were devoid of spiritual values. How can something that you do by tracing machine have spiritual value?

Went off to the Hayward where Victor Bokris, that little guy in the suit who wrote my biography, was doing a guided tour thing. A whole crowd of kids was waiting for him to start, getting impatient like a mob scene. There are kids at all my shows in England, average age 17. Which is just great, because I thought I only got on with old people.

Victor said I was "the single most important artist in the world to appear since World War 2." Couldn't decide if that was better or worse than being "the greatest *American* artist of the twentieth century – and I mean that!" which was what this cute

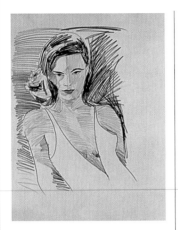

Untitled, *c. 1962, Pencil on Paper, 29 x 23 in/74 x 58 cm. Estate of Andy Warhol.*

"WARHOL'S INFLUENCE HAS BEEN SO STRONG THAT PICASSO AND EVEN POLLOCK TODAY APPEAR TO BE DISTANT, CHTHONIC GODS."

—*Bradley Bloch*

Norman Rosenthal guy said I was on television. He was sweet. I'd tried to ring him to give him the name of my wigmaker but he was out.

Then Victor led the kids into another room. And there were 3 fakes of mine there. Electric chairs. I didn't say anything. I don't know why I signed them. Victor said, "A great artist is a person able to confront images in his own mind that cause him great distress and then turn them into art." Like painting was, you know, like taking Quaalude. I'd forgotten how short Victor was. But he stands like he's a Colossus with his legs apart and tosses his quiff back. Maybe he thinks he's about six feet. But I think he's just got bongo drums in his pants.

He kept talking about how ill I was as a kid and how the first words I ever said were swear words. (*Laughs.*) You know – not "Mama" or "Papa," but "Blow job." Victor said I saw the world and cursed. I really don't remember that. Then he kept saying I suffered from "romantic fever." I didn't understand what he meant so I asked the girl standing next to me who was about 12, but sweet, with long legs and a boy's ass. And she said that Victor was

Five Coke Bottles, *1962,*
Silkscreen ink on synthetic polymer paint on canvas,
16 x 20 in/41 x 51 cm.
Private collection

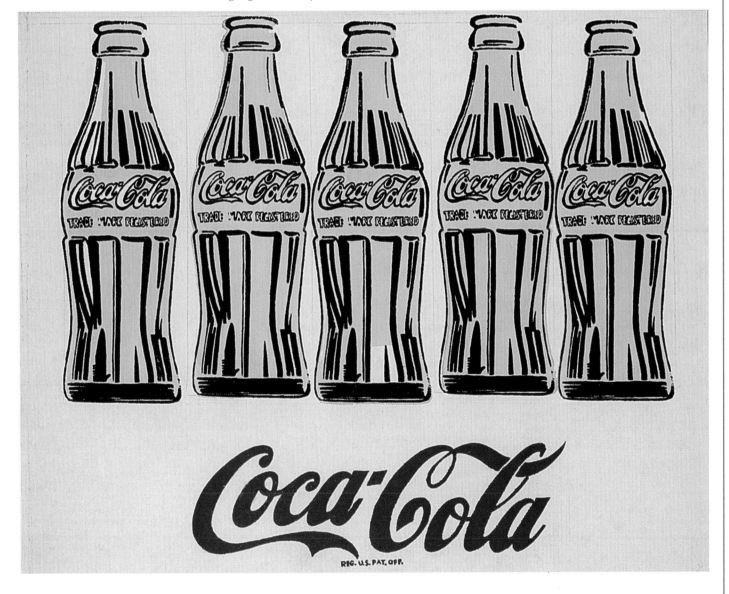

saying *rheumatic* fever." Then he said, "Now we're going to move upstairs to the CORE of Andy Warhol," like I was an apple or something.

Victor started to get hysterical, throwing his hands about and tossing his hair so hard I thought it would fly off. "The Atom Bomb was dropped on Hiroshima on Andy's 17th birthday… Andy was drenched in death… the American dream is the American death, this is Warhol's vision… These are religious paintings and of course political – they're everything." I mean such embarrassing stuff. He was just too goo-goo. A guy next to me was writing it all down. He'd written, "America dropped the Atom Bomb on Japan as a birthday present from Andy Warhol."

Then Victor started to talk about that program of TV last night. The one that discussed me. "When I hear these arseholes on telly saying Andy Warhol can't paint," Victor said, "I want to puke, because they look so stupid and sound so stupid." We all stood back a few steps because Victor looked as though he really was going to puke.

> ## "SOME CRITIC CALLED ME THE NOTHINGNESS HIMSELF…AND THAT DIDN'T HELP MY SENSE OF EXISTENCE ANY. THEN I REALIZED THAT EXISTENCE ITSELF IS NOTHING, AND I FELT BETTER."

He doubled up and let his head almost touch the ground, which fortunately was not too far down for him. Afterwards he signed copies of *Warhol: The Biography* ($26) in the foyer. *The* biography – meaning, you know, you wouldn't piss on the others. A lot of the kids he nearly puked over queued for his signature. "Andy gives himself completely to his art and to *us*," Victor said, but I don't remember giving myself to him. And anyway, it was himself – Victor Bockris – he was giving, that's if you call $26 a shot giving.

Every time he signed a book he looked at his watch as if he was a big hurry and couldn't stop thinking of all the busy places he had to be next, talking about romantic fever. Anyone would think I was an industry.

Saturday, September 9, 1989 – London

An abstract kind of day, the sort you want to block out. Rang everyone I'd ever known and left messages on all their answering machines. Stayed in waiting for someone to call back. The last time I was here I was mobbed. Truck drivers were usually the ones who were nice and recognized me and waved. Now nobody cares. It's funny, you think you have so much pizzazz and then no one calls and then you know you aren't anything.

Sunday, September 10, 1989 – London

Went to church. Then talked to priest. Not the young one with the bulge in his surplice but an older one. I worked hard for him to like me and talked about things I guessed he was interested in like Bianca and diet pills and Coke. Told him the best doctor to go to for collagen. He said God was the best doctor. I said yeah but sometimes he needed help, so I wrote to him an "I.O.U. One Art."

Wondering why I never painted God. Tried to ring Saatchi to say I'd do him God 72 times on monthly installments, but his number still wasn't in the book.

Tuesday, September 12, 1989 – London – New York

Watched the Late Show on TV. That guy who said I lacked spirituality was on. And Donna de Salvo who curated the Modess and Shoe Show, and Trevor Fairbrother who called me a *provocateur*, which was great, and Paul Taylor – he's hot – from Australia or New Guinea or somewhere, and someone called Ignatieff – he was moody – who was supposed to be the chairman but kept on interrupting and seemed to have this feud going with the spiritualist guy. He was intellectual, he laughed in all the right places.

I wished they'd got Fergie or the Queen Mother to talk instead. Anyway, the creep who was down on me kept saying I was trivial, empty, and banal, like as though he really knew me. And Donna de Salvo, who's a walking monologue, kept using this tool word, saying all artists use things as tools… but it was just dumb meets stupid.

Packed for Concorde ($3,000). And couldn't stop thinking how great it was that in a few hours I'd be back home, watching the *Today Show*.

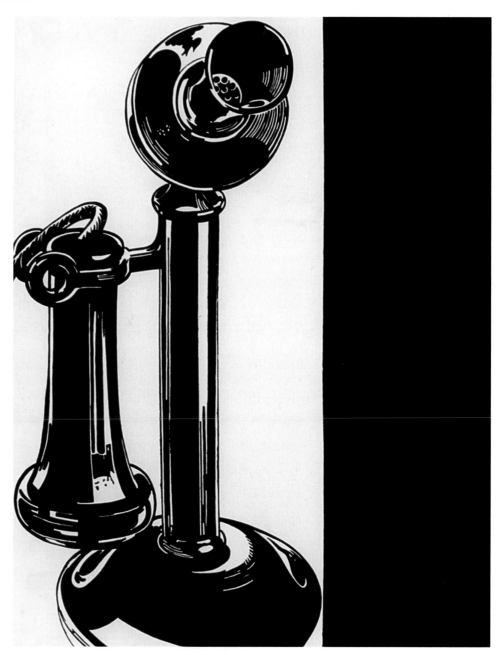

Telephone, *1961, Oil on Canvas, 70 x 54 in/177 x 137 cm. Estate of Andy Warhol.*

Paula Rego

by Germaine Greer

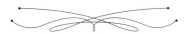

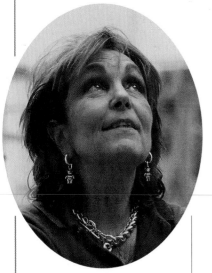

PAULA REGO

Born in Portugal in 1935, Rego left Lisbon in 1952 to study at London's Slade School of Art. She returned to Portugal with the British painter Victor Willing, and they lived together there before settling permanently in London in 1976, keeping strong ties to Portugal.

From the beginning, Rego's early drawings, paintings, and collages combined elements of fairy tales with images of women and animals, creating surrealistic scenes with strong psychological undercurrents. Because drawing has always been a fundamental part of her work, printmaking comes naturally to her, and she has produced several series of etchings – "Nursery Rhymes," "Peter Pan," and "Pendle Witches."

Rego's figurative paintings are exhibited in major museums and galleries. She has received many awards for her work, and both the Tate Gallery in London and the Centro Cultural de Belem in Lisbon have featured retrospectives of her work. Celebrated in her native Portugal and in Britain, she is considered among the finest of contemporary painters.

Aida, *1983, acrylic on paper, 94 x 80 in/240 x 203 cm. The Artist's Collection.*

WOMEN'S PAINTINGS ARE RARELY POWERFUL, for the culture of the west has no representational language to express the power of femaleness. Paula Rego is a painter of astonishing power, and that power is undeniably, obviously, triumphantly female. Her work is the first evidence that I have seen that something fundamental in our culture has changed; the carapace has cracked and something living, hot, and heavy is welling through. The process in Rego's work is so dramatic that one holds one's breath for fear that some cataclysm will prevent its full development.

Rego was born in Lisbon in 1935; from 1952 to 1956 she went to the Slade. Her first work is, as one expects, diffident, derivative, academic, self-conscious, but from the outset she demonstrates an engagement with the surface, a sensual interest in paint itself, which is belied by the tyranny of the palette knife and her later use of inscrutable collage. What may well have seemed to the young artist to be a struggle for control of her visual language seems to this observe, at any rate, to be an effort to present a violent and subversive

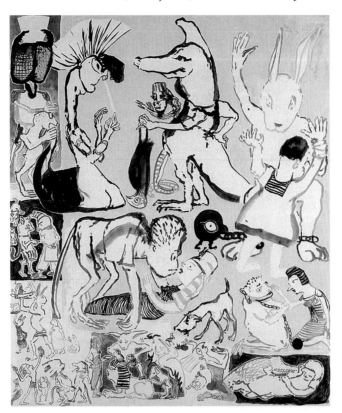

personal vision in acceptable decorative terms. For a technician as adroit as Rego nothing is easier than to create elegant hieroglyphs that seduce by the grace of their drawing. The range of line that she demonstrates once she escapes from the *faux-naif* straight jacket of *The Birthday Party*, 1953, and *Under Milkwood*, 1954, would be gratifying even without the full spectrum of color that Rego manipulates with a confidence rarely if ever found in British artists.

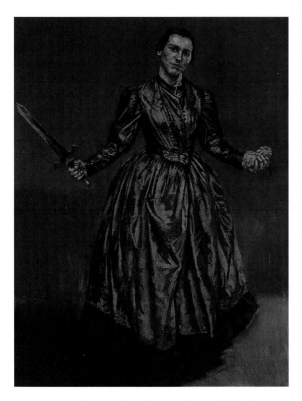

The affirmation that this sensuousness represents is the anchor of Rego's subversive perception; it is the justification for the astonishing icons of sparagmos, ritual dismemberment of the male god by the female visionaries, that proliferate, always in encoded form, in Rego's work of the sixties.

Rego is often discussed in the vocabulary of Freudian surrealism, and the overt content of her work encourages this kind of transliteration, but in fact her imaginative world is utterly unlike that of the Viennese middle class; Rego breathes the dangerous air of the region where species overlap; under the overhang of phallocentric culture she consorts with winged quadrupeds and eloquent birds. Her painting refuses to grow up and become discrete, self-knowing, genital and self-pleasuring; it rejects the superiority of mind on which all Freudian theory is based. *Centaur*, 1964, is at once a highly sophisticated pastiche of motifs drawn from Picasso and the Catalan primitives, invested with all the flattery that such imitation implies, and a mordant satire upon such pretension. The icon of man-horse, horseman, cabalero, cavalier, knight-thug is spread over the picture space like rabbits' guts on a dissecting table. What should be hard is soft and what should be soft is hard; scrotal shapes sag and mumble over gun barrels and battering rams. The beasts of burden, women among them, respond with passive aggression; the horse hind-quarters are jitterbugging or collapsing under towering absurdity. Similar contradictions are expressed in more headlong manner in *Warrior*, 1965, and less effectively in *Samurai*, 1982.

The essential character of Rego's work is already established. Invariably the subject involves interaction between sentient elements; the spatial context is theatrical, the background suffused with tender color laid on in interpenetrating strata, like the play of light upon a cyclorama. The light source is invisible, as if hidden in the flies. Living tableaux are erected on plinths and daises, standing clear of the artificially limitless background like creatures on a stage.

Of the hundred works in this year's exhibition organized by the *Centro de Arte Moderna*, with the collaboration of Ruth Rosengarten in Lisbon and Porto, only nine date from the seventies, six of them gouaches from the series *Contos Populares Portugeses*, 1974–75. These works, though in some ways related to Goya's *Proverbios*, are clearly

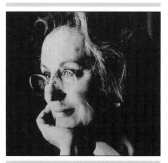

GERMAINE GREER
With the publication of The Female Eunuch *in 1970, Germaine Greer became one of the most important voices in the feminist movement.*

❧

Born in Melbourne in 1939, she moved to England to study at Cambridge. While writing for journals and teaching at the University of Warwick, she lectured on the sexual freedom of women. The Female Eunuch *established her career as a writer.*

❧

Her premise in The Female Eunuch *is that women are sexually repressed, deprived of the creative energy needed for achieving independence and full selfhood. This sexual passivity, a role foisted on women by history and by women themselves, is characteristically associated with castration, hence the title.*

❧

Greer's approach to feminism has evolved over the intervening thirty years of her life; her most recent book, The Whole Woman *(in 1999), states that women's success in a man's world is not progress since the price has been the denigration of female values.*

Above left: *Angel*, 1998, *pastel on paper mounted on aluminum, 71 x 51 in/180 x 130 cm. Marlborough Fine Art Ltd.*

influenced by English illustrators, most obviously (and lamentably in my opinion) by Arthur Rackham. The black line that Rego used sparingly as a defining and linking device in earlier work becomes a confining border, so that areas of vivid jewel-color are seen like *cloisonné* or stained glass in a chased grid. To perform this exercise in rigid self-censorship Rego's supple and expressive line is thickened, broadened, and flattened in pointless and self-defeating imitation of obsolete illustrative techniques. This period in Rego's artistic development

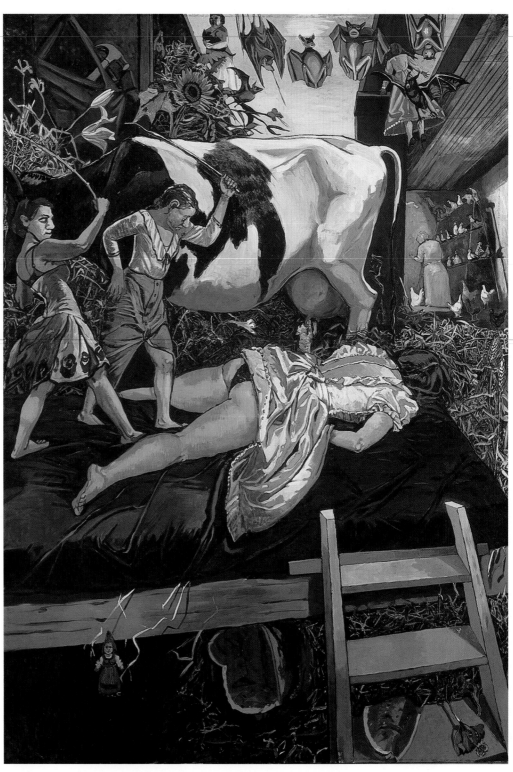

The Barn, *1994, acrylic on canvas, 106 x 75 in/270 x 190 cm. Marlborough Fine Art Ltd.*

seems to me at least a retreat from her own scale and preoccupations into something rather like embroidery. The disturbing imagery is still there but subordinated to so much embossing and diapering that its impact is all but frittered away.

It is possibly relevant here to point out that Paula Rego is the widow of Victor Willing whom she met, was immensely impressed by, and fell in love with while she was a student at the Slade, and lived with until his death in June this year (1988). For most of her career Willing's closeness has been evident in her painting. At first they lived in Portugal where she bore three children, of whom the youngest was born in 1961. In the first years of their relationship, despite Willing's generous encouragement and recognition of her talent, Rego found it very difficult to work at all. In 1962 she was given a grant by the Calouste Gulbenkian Foundation and from 1963 she divided her time between Portugal and London, becoming a member of the London Group in 1964. In 1976 she decided to

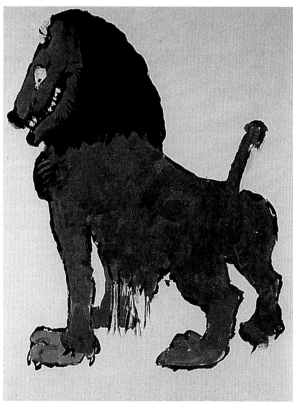

Criatura Encarnada, 1981, acrylic on paper, 30 x 22 in/76 x 56 cm. Private collection.

"WE INTERPRET THE WORLD THROUGH STORIES... EVERYBODY MAKES IN THEIR OWN WAY SENSE OF THINGS, BUT IF YOU HAVE STORIES IT HELPS."

make her home in London. Toward the end of the seventies, when her youngest child had reached relative self-sufficiency she began tentatively to work on her old defiant scale; the breakthrough is signalled in *Criatura Encarnada*, 1981. After a rather uncertain initial use of acrylic on canvas, Rego begins now to work on paper with all the speed and concentration that the medium makes possible. The brush that draws the defining line of the initial sketch vibrates like Goya's burin, skipping across the paper; layers and smudges of transparent color shimmer over each other with a frightening life of their own. The whole process is perfectly visible, the result is a new kind of rhetorical power; the images are extraordinarily engaging, moving, and unnerving.

"SHE HAS ALWAYS LIKED THE DIRECTNESS OF DRAWING, DISLIKING THE PAINTBRUSH BECAUSE IT PLACED HER AT ONE REMOVE FROM THE SURFACE; WITH PASTEL THE FINGERS THEMSELVES ARE THE BRUSH."

—*John McEwan*

It is usual when discussing Rego's work to inquire into the source of her vast fund of personal imagery, which turns out to be the same as everyone else's, her childhood. It is possible to press-gang Rego into the ranks of the Freudian surrealists but to my mind the fact that her motifs are closely related to a non-literary female tradition is much more exciting. Rego herself is acutely aware of the other culture, hence her long love-affair with popular fables and proverbs, but she might be surprised to know that her "carnival of the animals" theme is often encountered in such women's poetry as has survived. Like Rego who uses human female figures on the same ground and on the same scale as her animal characters,

Half Ant – Half Lion, *1981, acrylic on paper, 30 x 22 in/77 x 56 cm. Private collection.*

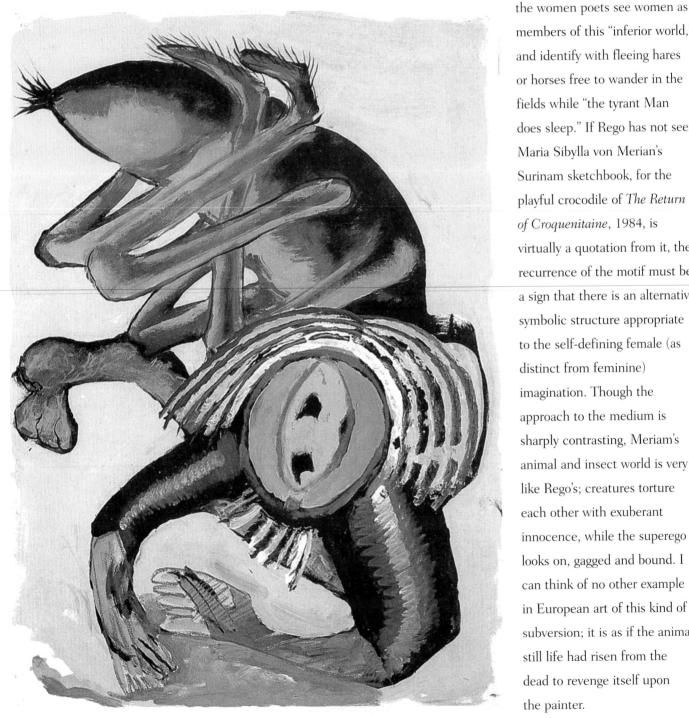

the women poets see women as members of this "inferior world," and identify with fleeing hares or horses free to wander in the fields while "the tyrant Man does sleep." If Rego has not seen Maria Sibylla von Merian's Surinam sketchbook, for the playful crocodile of *The Return of Croquenitaine*, 1984, is virtually a quotation from it, the recurrence of the motif must be a sign that there is an alternative symbolic structure appropriate to the self-defining female (as distinct from feminine) imagination. Though the approach to the medium is sharply contrasting, Meriam's animal and insect world is very like Rego's; creatures torture each other with exuberant innocence, while the superego looks on, gagged and bound. I can think of no other example in European art of this kind of subversion; it is as if the animal still life had risen from the dead to revenge itself upon the painter.

The most accessible sources of Rego's imagery are to be found in animal cartoons and commercial art, the *Vache qui rit*, the wicked bugs killed by the spray, and so on. Rego makes of the pulp culture by which housewives are daily confronted something new and phantasmagoric, sometimes as in *Half Ant Half Lion*, 1981, truly disquieting, even terrifying. The laughing flower face used to sell scented disinfectants and the like becomes a suffering cabbage, looking on in tears as a descendant of Bugs Bunny realizes with some surprise that carrots are alive. Once more Rego mounts her tableaux on an invisible stage. In *Little Girl Showing Off*, 1982 and *Going Out*, 1982, the picture plane is limited by an area of blackout as if the action was being carried out on an apron or on the sunny side of the bullring; in *Cabbage and Potato* and *The Sick Sparrow*, 1982, the dark element is suggested quite adequately by a single stroke of black at the margin of the picture.

In 1983 Rego undertook a series of large works, 94 x 82 in/240 x 208 cm, on paper, named after four operas. These, which remain in her possession, are compendia of her personal imagery, extraordinary collections of ideograms apparently drawn rapidly without *pentimenti* directly on the paper, using a brush loaded with a single color. The inspiration for these may come directly from a British Museum papyrus in which a similar technique is used to portray animals playing human roles, among them some of Rego's most often used characters, the striped cat, and the dog musician, for example. The papyrus was part of the "Animals in Art" exhibition at the Museum in 1977–78 which may have triggered the flow of unforgettable animal images that Rego began to produce in the eighties. More important probably are the *Caprichos* of Goya. *The Sandman*, 1985, contains a direct reference to Goya's *El Sueno de la Razon Produce Monstros*. The use of animal motifs as a way of saying the unsayable goes back in Rego's work at least to a major work of 1965, *Stray Dogs* (Dogs of Barcelona).

The germ of much future work is to be found in the opera series, in which for the first time there is no hint either in drawing, paint treatment or spatial organization of the closeness of Victor Willing. The bad girls make their first appearance, lifting their skirts to appall unwary passers-by, manipulating gravely attentive animals.

Paul Rego discovered Dubuffet and *l'art brut* as early as 1959, but it was a long time before her own work reflected the realization of what form anti-art could take for an artist who has already come through the indoctrination of conventional art school teaching. Rego

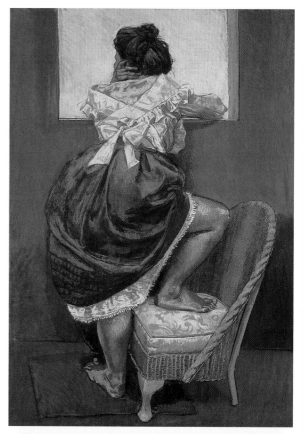

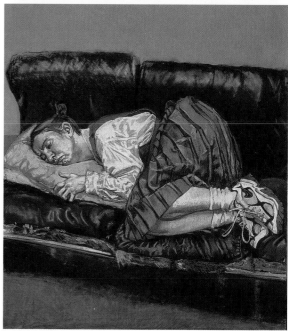

Top: **Looking Out**, *1997, pastel on paper mounted on aluminum, 71 x 51 in/180 x 130 cm. Marlborough Fine Art Ltd.*

Above: Untitled No.4, *1998, pastel on paper mounted on aluminum, 43 x 39 in/110 x 100 cm. Marlborough Fine Art Ltd.*

is virtually incapable of an ugly line or an inelegant juxtaposition, and too sane to work at the obsessive space-filling that is typical of most outsider art, although I would argue that the work of the seventies comes close at times to this kind of compulsiveness. By entering into the imagery of the bestiary of childhood, Rego discovered a new language in which to express her own status as unrepentant outsider and finally once and for all overcame the eclecticism of her artistic beginnings. In the *Vivian Girls* series of 1984–85 the bad girl's rebellion reaches its most strident expression; sensitive pigs and humorous birds tangle with insensitive female humans and lecherous vegetables in crammed works that read in episodes like medieval serial illustrations of religious legends. The quotations of the clever girl student are still there; motifs snatched from Bosch and Arcimboldo serve functions of which their inventors can hardly have dreamed.

No artist has made better use of acrylic on canvas than Rego in these four large, 95 x 70 in/242 x 179 cm, works, unless it be

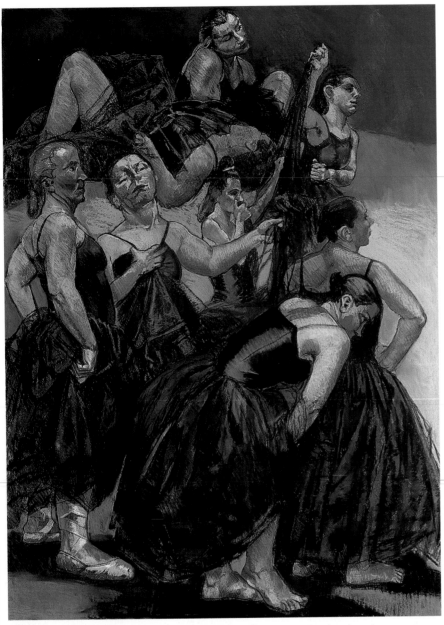

Dancing Ostriches from Disney's Fantasia, *1995, pastel on paper mounted on aluminum, 59 x 59 in/150 x 150 cm. Marlborough Fine Art Ltd.*

Rego herself in the works immediately following, *The Bride*, *At the Beach*, and *Paradise*, all of 1985. Never has the spontaneity and brilliance of the medium been better exploited than in these hymns of unholy glee. The bouncing figures dashed off in transparent blots are all the stereotypes of femininity tossed upon the white canvas as if it were a sheet. The holy phallus appears only as a limp, bad tempered sea serpent, a half peeled banana, a turkey neck, a green slow worm. One is reminded of the tallow effigies of dismembered limbs and isolated organs that the faithful offer for burning at Fatima, especially in Rego's use of the spiral, which for immolation purposes signifies the gut. This is not to say that Rego is making a conscious connection, by the way, but that she is drawing on the same stock of unselfconscious popular stereotypes. The striped cat who appears in the center of the foreground of *At the Beach*, can be seen by the un-innocent eye as the ultimate expression of the revolutionary conspiracy of the lower orders to replace man, proud man.

The possibilities of *l'art brut* are limited and by the end of 1985 Rego had already passed beyond them. The 1986 series of large images of single girls with single animals shows a new poise and candor. The monumental female type that Rego uses for this, and indeed for all the paintings of *meninas*, is very like the type favored by Artemisia Gentileschi. Like Gentileschi's *Esther, Judith, Susannah,* and her self-portrait above all, the *meninas* are stocky, heavy, swarthy, and filled with sleeping energy, in indirect commentary on the boneless collections of seductive surface planes that represent women as objects of aesthetic desire. Although the *meninas* all wear the insignia of little girlness, decorately patterned garments, little shoes, and colored gew-gaws in their hair, they are dangerous, intent, calculating, intelligent. The dogs they work on are subtle and moving icons of defenseless sincerity, whether they rest their paws on the knee of a girl with a cut-throat razor, or wait to be chained, or gaze impassively under a girl's lifted skirt. These works are less ambitious than the larger works that follow, but the energy and fierce concentration of their execution makes them if anything more impressive.

Dog Women – Waiting for Food, *1994, pastel on canvas, 47 x 63 in/120 x 160 cm. Marlborough Fine Art Ltd.*

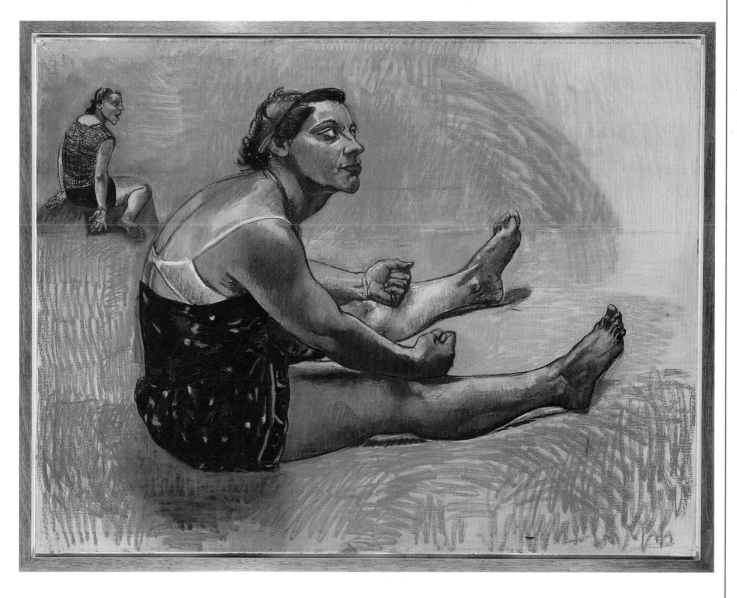

The Policeman's Daughter, *1987, acrylic on paper on canvas, 84 x 60 in/213 x 152 cm. Marlborough Fine Art Ltd.*

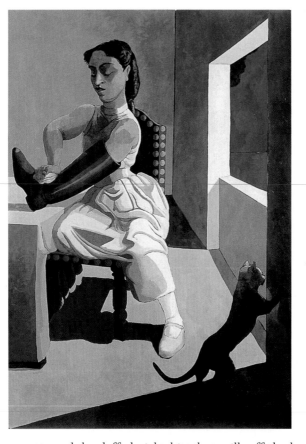

The eight most recent works are those which will make Rego's name a household word. If the magic realism of Gabriel Garcia Marquez could be transferred to paint, this is what it would look like. The imagery is apparently completely factual, except that scale is distorted in the interest of power and recognizable motifs appear in incomprehensible juxtaposition. *The Little Murderess* wears mistletoe in her hair; a tiny pelican stands on a painted chair behind her, and an ox-cart is half obscured by her skirt. The relevance of all these motifs is as easily explained as that of the green ribbon the girl is holding as a garrotte and the doffed nightshirt that spills off the bed in lieu of a corpse, but the solidity and directness of the technique here discourage pedantry. It seems ridiculous to point out that Gentileschi's great icon of *Judith* is about the same subject, the *giustiziamento* of the victim in his only vulnerable moment, naked and abed. The shock of the *menina's* intent gloating expression is projected by the massiveness of her dark dancing form.

The Policeman's Daughter does without the ideographic clues to be found in other paintings of this series, except for the silhouetted cat who checks the outdoor scene in the foreground; instead the setting carries the full force of the mystery. Outside is ultramarine night, but the only light falls aslant the window, as brilliant as a searchlight. Again the young woman's action is obvious; polishing a jackboot held at an angle as if it were goose-stepping. The ambiguity in the image derives from the light; the girl is either serving or mocking a Fascist order, or both. She, like the cat, must live in her master's house and eat his cream. The same ambiguity provides the tension in *Two Girls with Dog*; the girls are apparently playing but we cannot tell if they are dressing or undressing the unfortunate dog. They themselves are fussily accoutred in figured prints, smocking, bows, and pinnies (pinafores), and the tiny collars that Rego uses almost invariably, like stylized neck-irons. Emblems of the sado-masochistic order are used several times in this series, hammers of various kinds lie beside plucked flowers and fruit, here a daisy and an unbroken jug, elsewhere figs and tulips.

It is not often given to women to recognize themselves in painting, still less to see their private world, their dreams, the insides of their heads, projected on such a scale and so immodestly, with such depth and color. After the violation of Balthus' keyhole vision, feminists hardly dared to hope that a woman painter could reassert woman's mystery and restore her intactness. Rego's paintings are full of shuttered windows, closed doors, and vessels of ambiguous content. Her female types smile mirthlessly in a new version of the grin of the Maenads. Her paintings quiver with an anger and compassion of which we have sore need. Now that she has hit her stride, let us hope that she will run and run.

The Little Murderess, *1987, acrylic, 59 x 59 in/150 x 150 cm. Private collection.*

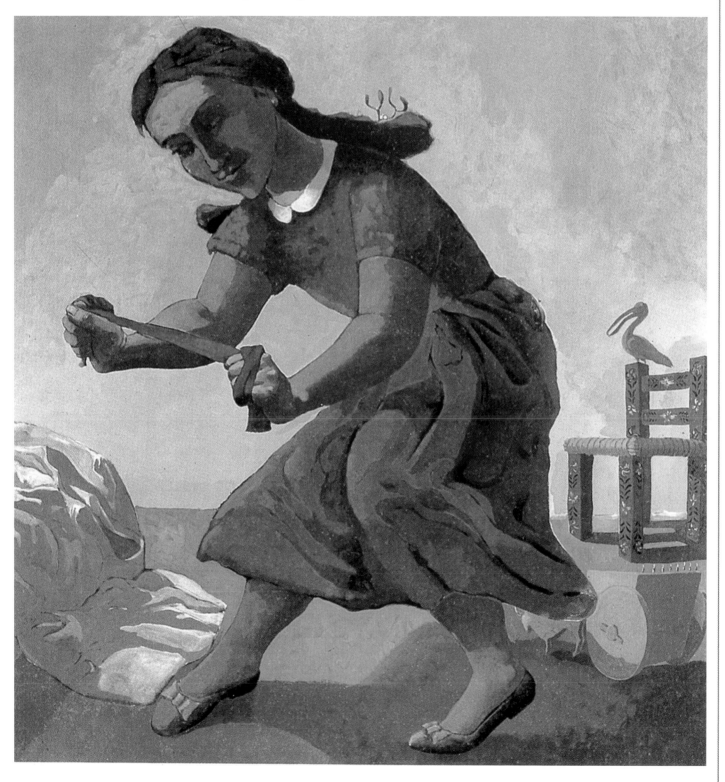

Larry Rivers

by Peter Jenkins

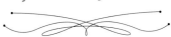

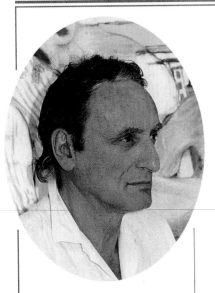

LARRY RIVERS

Born Larry Grossberg in the Bronx in 1923, painter and sculptor Larry Rivers began his career as a jazz saxophonist. He took up painting in 1945, studying at the Hans Hofmann School, and with William Baziotes at New York University.

Becoming a part of the New York City art scene in the early 1950s, Rivers shocked both the traditionalists and the pro-Abstract Expressionists with his figurative paintings that were freely Expressionistic in style. His subjects were cliched old-master paintings and banal objects from advertising, which were said to have paved the way toward the Pop Art movement. His stand-up treatment of the familiar painting Washington Crossing the Delaware *garnered him distinction in the art world.*

In the 1960's Rivers continued to explore, creating painted sculptures, collages, and prints, as well as working with theater set design, videotape, and multimedia. In the 1990s, he created a series of foam relief sculptures that used images from masters such as Matisse, Picasso, and Léger.

Rivers has exhibited extensively in the US and abroad.

LARRY RIVERS WAS A PRECURSOR OF POP ART. Jasper Johns' flag paintings were first shown by Leo Castelli in 1958. The Sidney Janis 1962 show, "The New Realists," was the first group exhibition of the Pop artists as, at about that time, they were becoming known. Rivers had painted his famous, and at the time notorious, *Washington Crossing the Delaware* in 1953. In 1960 he painted the menu at the Cedar Bar, the painters' Greenwich Village drinking haunt, and in the same year his *Buick Painting* which became influential among the British Pop artists such as Peter Blake and Allen Jones. In the early 1960s, Rivers was painting Camel cigarette and Dutch Masters cigar packs, and

"I GUESS I'VE ALWAYS LIKED THE IDEA OF BEING AN ARTIST."

had been using stenciled words in his pictures. According to his biographer, Professor Sam Hunter of Princeton, "He was undoubtedly the first American artist to use so-called 'vulgar' or vernacular objects in a larger artistic context." Yet Rivers was never a wholly paid-up member of the Pop movement, if movement it was, nor of any other school or movement. He seemed a good person to talk to about the history of New York's post-war art world, and so I visited him one Sunday in his studio in Southampton, Long Island, where he mostly lives, surrounded by family and retainers.

Rivers set out as a professional sax player, his hero Lester Young, and first took up painting when he was twenty in 1945. He was persuaded to study under Hans Hofmann, the émigré German painter who became the great mentor as well as a leading exponent of the New York School of Abstract Expressionists. I asked whether Hofmann had been disappointed in him as a pupil.

He guessed so, although Hofmann by then had lost the urge to bring a message to the world and was painting furiously against lost time. Teaching had become for him chiefly a way of making a living in order to paint. He didn't insist on his pupils painting abstractly, but Rivers had tried for a while "making rectangles and things" but found it absurd. "I was reading a lot of literature at the time, and didn't know how to square being interested in stories and just making shapes and lines and things like that."

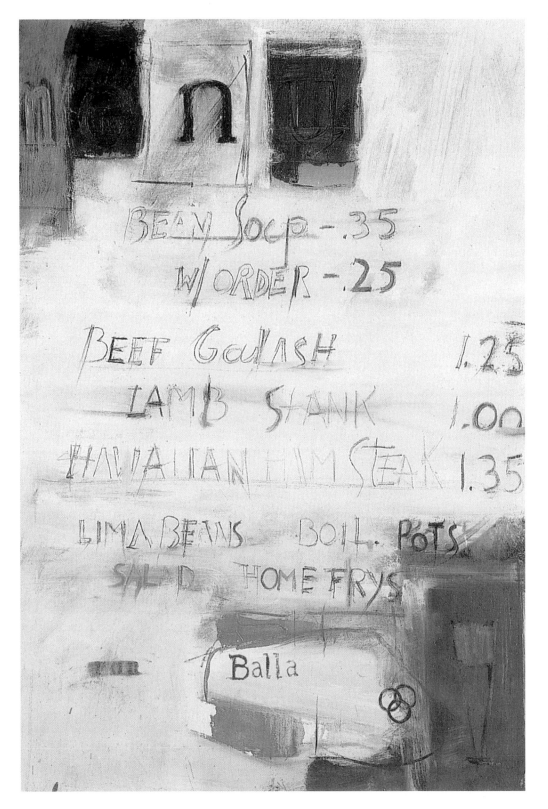

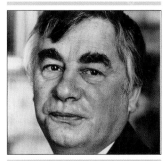

PETER JENKINS
Born in 1934 in Buckinghamshire, England, writer and broadcaster Peter Jenkins is best known for his political essays as political columnist and political editor for the Guardian *and* Independent *newspapers where, it is said, he gave an "insider's view of politics to those on the outside." He was educated at Cambridge University and at the University of Wisconsin.*

~

Jenkins is the author of The Battle of Downing Street *and* Mrs. Thatcher's Revolution: The Ending of the Socialist Era. *He also wrote for the theater – his political play* Illuminations, *was performed at London's Lyric Theatre in 1980. He was the drama critic for* Spectator *from 1980-83, and a writer for the UK television comedy series* Struggle *in 1984. Toward the end of his life, Jenkins began writing art criticism for* Modern Painters.

~

In the UK, he was designated "Columnist of the Year" for several years running, and named "Journalist of the Year," by Granada Television in 1978.

~

Jenkins died in 1992

All the same, he had taken a lot from the Abstract Expressionists. For example, size. "I loved the idea that they made big paintings. All-over paintings. That wherever they started they went right out to the edges. I remember that I had difficulties with paintings where I would be interested in the object – maybe a table or a person – and then wondered what you were supposed to do with what's behind them? Paint a wall?"

Cedar Bar Menu 1, *1960, oil on canvas, 48 x 35 in/121 x 89 cm. Collection of the Artists, Courtesy Marlborough Gallery, New York.*

"There were many things about the Abstract Expressionists I liked. I knew them. I admired several of them. I was actually friendly with de Kooning, and he was a very nice man, and he knew a lot about certain kinds of history, both of the United States and of painting. The only person I didn't like was Jackson Pollock, who was a mixture between a bully and a paranoid. When he was drunk, he was very loud and insulting, but when he was sober he sat with his head in his hands, bent over and sort of broody. So he wasn't very interesting but, otherwise, I liked them a lot: Philip Guston, Franz Kline – I knew all of those people."

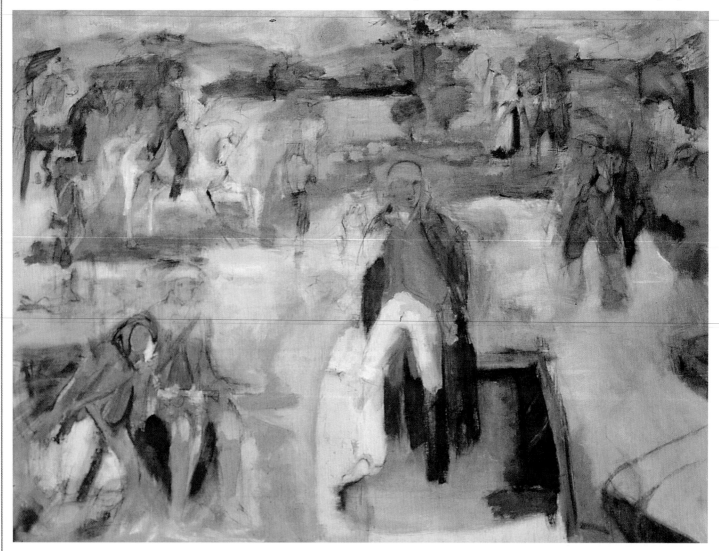

Washington Crossing Delaware, *1953, oil, graphite and charcoal on linen, 7 x 9 ft/212 x 284 cm. Museum of Modern Art, New York.*

We had begun by talking about Abstract Expressionism because it has been said so many times before that Pop Art was a reaction, a conscious reaction, against Abstract Expressionism by then grown decadent and effete.

"Not in his case," said Rivers. "Maybe later it dawned on me that it was possible that that was what I did, but, truthfully speaking, I had my own agenda. Don't forget I started doing things like *George Washington Crossing the Delaware* in 1953, and I was doing all sorts of things like Buicks and cigarettes in the late '50s. Sure, I didn't do it flat; my style – strangely enough – was still sort of Gorkyish or Abstract Expressionist, if you wanted to say that. I don't know if you'd call Gorky an Abstract Expressionist, would you? Anyway, I like Gorky with the smudges and everything like that. So you could say that there was a certain style, a way of painting on my part, that may have come out of Abstract Expressionism."

"But I didn't have a program. Sure, I felt that some people were getting attention and I wasn't getting attention – so maybe I was a little jealous or envious of the abstract painters – but the truth was I thought what they were doing was *boring*. They weren't saying anything about anything. They'd been telling me for ten years about how wonderful and interesting shapes were."

I wondered if, when Johns came upon the scene with the Castelli show, he saw himself, or was seen by others, as making a conscious break with the abstract school. "I don't know," said Rivers. "I think Jasper was very influenced by Duchamp. But he also studied under Franz Kline at Black Mountain College. So, I'm not sure, it's hard to know. He's a friend of mine; we saw each other – not so much now, but especially in the early days. At the time I was a little bit better known that he was – I'd been in New York longer – and he'd always wanted me to come over to his studio and see what he was doing. So he

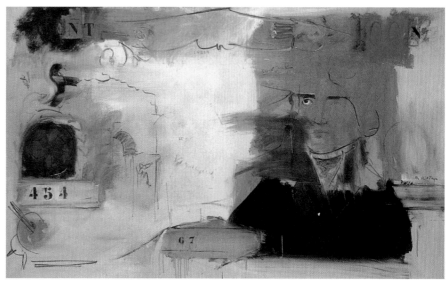

French Money, *1962, oil, charcoal and collage on canvas, 36 x 60 in/92 x 152 cm. Private collection, Courtesy Marlborough Gallery, New York.*

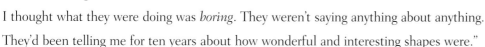

"... MAYBE I WAS A LITTLE JEALOUS OR ENVIOUS OF THE ABSTRACT PAINTERS – BUT THE TRUTH WAS I THOUGHT WHAT THEY WERE DOING WAS BORING."

obviously knew what *I* was doing. Now I don't know what influence I had. We never spoke about it, and it wouldn't have been very commercial for Jasper Johns and Leo Castelli to act as if Johns had been influenced by me. So I really don't know."

But what influence had the Johns show had on Rivers? None that he could remember, because he hadn't seen it. "I think Jasper got better as he went on. The American flag wasn't bad. But those targets and things like that, you couldn't get from them any notion of his hand – not yet. When he got into his numbers, then I began to see that he had something in his hand that was good, very good. Nowadays I don't think very much of what he does, because he's trying to combine certain things that have been

"I THOUGHT HE WAS CRAZY AND HE THOUGHT I WAS EVEN CRAZIER."
—*Frank O'Hara*

around for a very long time, and everything he adapts is something I've seen before. It's got something, but something's gone too."

Could he remember when the word Pop had entered the vocabulary of the New York art world?

"At the time of the Sidney Janis show in 1962. 'So that's Pop Art,' I heard people saying. Later I heard that Lawrence Alloway had invented it, and then I heard that he didn't invent it. I don't much care about those things."

And it was applied to him?

"Not right away. But we had gone to the show at Janis – I don't remember it very well, but we did go – and were having drinks afterwards and somebody said to me, 'And you did George Washington, of course,' and they started to talk about my paintings as if I'd been doing this kind of thing. And it made them very nervous because, don't forget, at that time the Abstract Expressionists were still very strong in New York. It took a few years for Pop Art to become the new art, a movement if you want to say, but already they were beginning to feel intimidated."

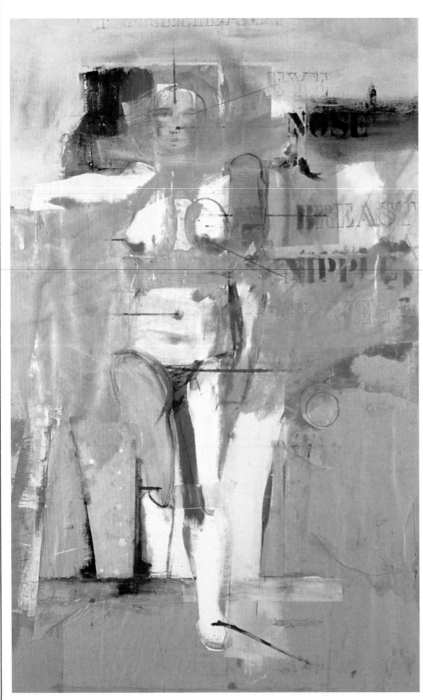

Parts of the Body: English Vocabulary, *1963, oil and collage on board,*
60 x 40 in/152 x 102 cm.
Private collection.

Had he identified himself with the Pop artists in the early '60s, did he consider himself a part of their movement?

"I kind of liked them. I thought they were humorous. They weren't creating a new world, they weren't knocking anything down; maybe they were directed against the Abstract Expressionists, but I don't think so; I think each of them had his own history of how he'd got to it. For example, Jasper's earlier works still looked more like Abstract Expressionism than Pop Art, and Rauschenberg never looked like a Pop artist, so I don't know how the hell he got in there."

Another critical commonplace was that Pop Art was inspired by a spirit of anti-materialism or anti-commercialism.

"You mean because they took commercial

things and made subject matter out of it? I think that was because it was part of people's experience. People know more about newspapers and ads and things like that than they know about a lot of other things. As I look back, I think that Hollywood had much more of an influence on me than anything else. The movies were just there, part of my existence, something you didn't even think consciously about. I don't think Pop Art was about anti-materialism. If people say that, they're full of shit, because they're Americans and none of them were monks."

"For instance, Roy Lichtenstein was really about something he'd been looking at in comic books. Are we including Lichtenstein in this anti-materialism? Roy lives down

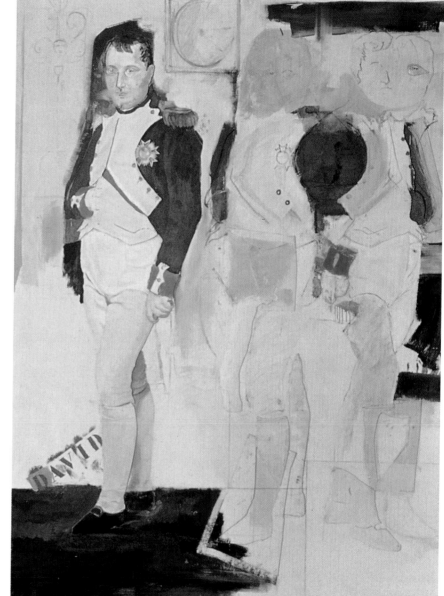

The Greatest Homosexual, *1964, oil on canvas, 80 x 61 in/203 x 155 cm. Hirshhorn Museum, Washington D.C.*

> ## "AS I LOOK BACK, I THINK THAT HOLLYWOOD HAD MUCH MORE OF AN INFLUENCE ON ME THAN ANYTHING ELSE."

the street here. He's got a big house, he's got a ranch in Scotland, cars. I don't want to hear any of that horse shit."

It has been often said also that Pop Art was a quintessential manifestation of the Sixties, the youth culture, drugs, the rapid obsolescence of fashion and ideas, and all the other clichés. Had he felt that he was living at an unusually heady moment?

Yes, he had, but he wasn't clear how it had affected his work. Did being interested in popular culture make you a Pop artist? He had painted *Washington Crossing the Delaware* after reading *War and Peace*. Tolstoy had made an extraordinary novel out of Napoleon invading Russia, and Rivers had tried to think of something comparable in American history.

"So, essentially, what I did was react to *War and Peace*. Later it gets to me that *Washington Crossing the Delaware* is part of some great Americana in which another guy does targets and another guy does comics.

"Take another example," he pointed to a large print of one of his Dutch Masters paintings on the wall of his studio. "Was that Pop Art? In the first ones I just did the cover of the box, but finally I got to do the cigars. I was making some comment about the use of Rembrandt in modern society. The painting is the *Syndics of the Drapery Guild* (*De Staalmeesters, The Sampling Officials at the Drapers' Guild at Amsterdam*). So they take something which has to do with drapery and put it on a cigar box and you're supposed to think that the kind of technical proficiency or perfection that these drapery guys had they're putting into our cigars. There was something really funny to me about that, really ironic, so that's what I did.

"But I had a copy of the Rembrandt, a fantastic reproduction I got from a guy in a secondhand furniture shop. So I used that to work from. The cigar box itself was much more "Pop." They'd scraped out all the color from around the figures and I could have done something like that. So where does that put me? In one way it's Pop because I'm

Dutch Masters I, *1963,*
oil on canvas,
40 x 50 in/102 x 127 cm.
Cheekwood Museum of Art,
Nashville, Tennessee.

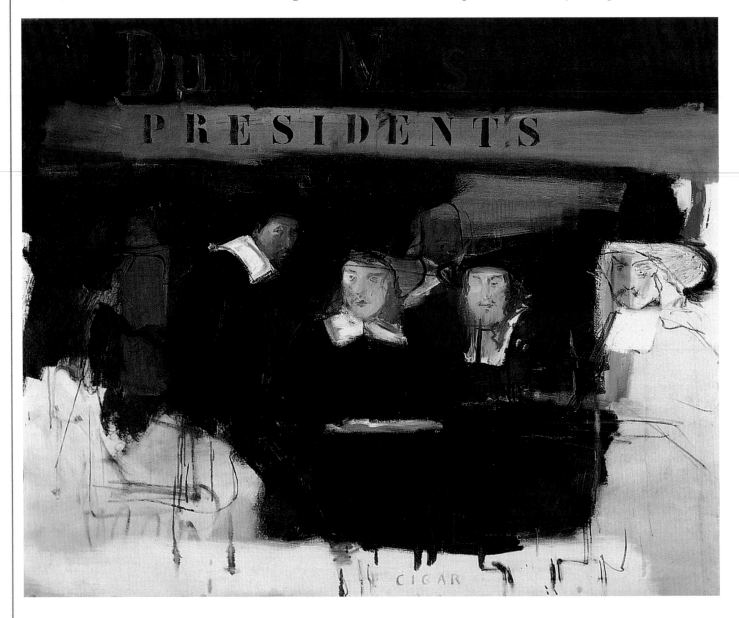

taking as a subject something that's definitely out there – a cigar box, one of the commercial aspects of society. Yet at the same time I'm investigating it in another way, thinking about Rembrandt. I feel I know that painting so I could practically do it by heart."

And then Pop Art was said at first to represent an anti-personality cult, a reaction against the artist as romantic hero. And yet Warhol had soon become the greatest personality cult of them all. What had he thought of Warhol? Was he a genuine artist or just a showman?

"Well, he stabbed at a lot of things and some of them were good. He got things done, and knew how to get them done fast and on a large scale. He was OK and I liked him. I still think his first thing was kind of stupid. People say what a shock it was, how influential, but I still don't think it meant anything. So, Barney Newman paints twenty feet of blue, and Andy Warhol comes along and says, 'I know what I can do – I can paint twenty feet of soup cans.'"

"He didn't seem to be that interested in painting with his hand, although I think he may actually have made some movement on some of those silk screens, although I know the guy who made the silk screens."

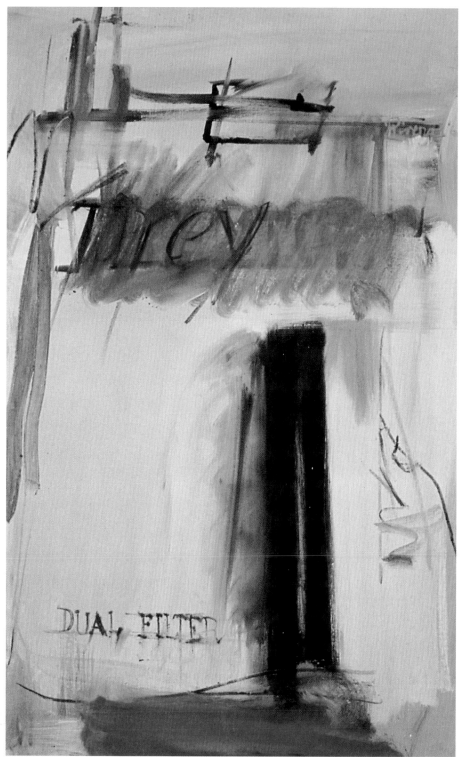

Dual Filter, 1961, oil on canvas, 38 x 25 in/96 x 63 cm. Private collection.

Then there had been the notion among the Pop artists that the painter should stay out of the painting.

"Yeah, well that's something else. A painter like Ad Reinhardt, he didn't want a story, no sort of narrative – just black. Step up to the painting and it clears your mind – of everything. It doesn't make mention of anything at all. And that's OK. It's like if you go over to Japan and see one of their gardens made of sand and stone, and it's wonderful to be there

History of Russian Revolution,
*1965. wood, oil, charcoal,
silkscreen, photomechanical
reproductions, and pencil on
canvas, paper, metal, plexiglass, and
fiberboard,
161 x 399 in/409 x 1014 cm.
Hirshhorn Museum, Washington
DC.*

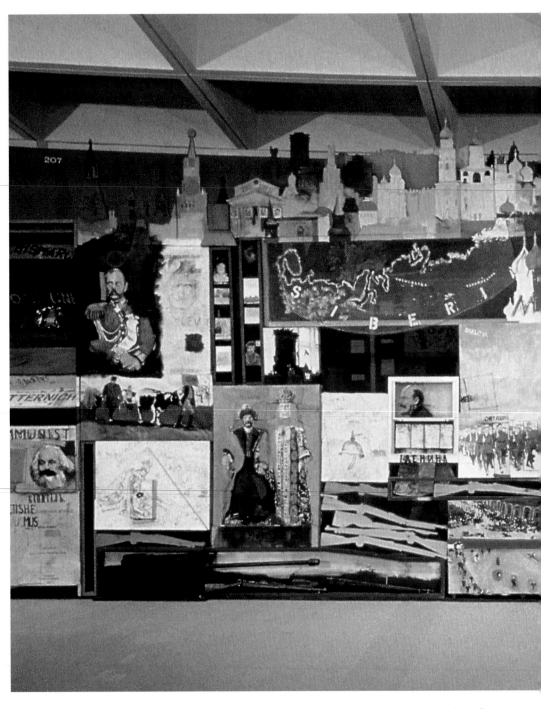

and suddenly not be thinking about sex or food or cars, and they have a special place for you to sit, and everybody's doing the same – contemplating nature or sand, very quietly and respectfully – and it's good. Well, some painters have that: Ad Reinhardt, maybe Mark Rothko, who – I'm beginning to understand why – would never show with other people."

It seemed to Rivers, on reflection, that the most important single trait the Pop artists had in common was that they painted flat. To be sure, Ellsworth Kelly had painted flat, but he hadn't wanted to be associated with the real world. The Abstract Expressionists had affected how people saw the things around them – lines, colors, and shapes forming some kind of intelligence. It became the same thing with Pop paintings: people started to

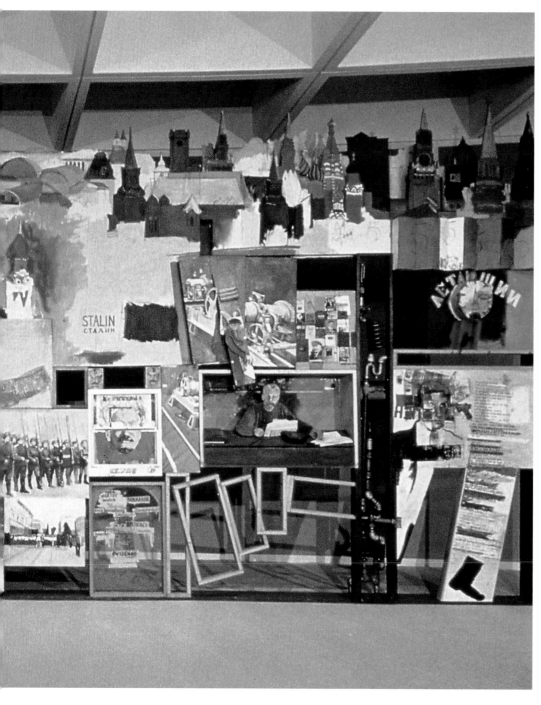

look at things in a different way.

"But this was chiefly because of *how* they painted. For some reason you're looking more at the painting. And I think today, when we look at it again, we're no longer going to look at what came through in the '60s and all that talk about it. We're really going to look at what people did on that flat surface. While at the time it made people see things a little differently, I don't think it will have much of that kind of effect today.

"Essentially it's as though the conceits of an age weren't available at that time. It's only when something else changes that you begin to look and see. I think it's clearer now what they were up to, those guys."

Otto Dix

by Michael Hofmann

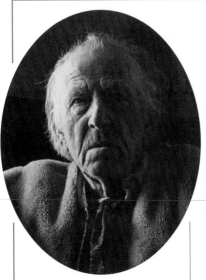

OTTO DIX

Painter/printmaker Otto Dix was born in Untermhaus in 1891 and later apprenticed in applied arts. While fighting in World War I, he drew a series of brutal scenes revealing his abhorrence of war. In attitude a moralist, Dix was influenced by early German Expressionism and by the Expressionism of the 20th century.

After the war, he attended the Dusseldorf Academy of Fine Arts, where he produced a series of etchings based on the war drawings. Later, he turned to masterfully painted depictions of German society, including Berlin's frantic nightlife, and became known for his bitter social/political criticism. The Nazi government declared him "degenerate" in 1933 and forbad him to teach. The Gestapo arrested and imprisoned him briefly.

In 1937, the Nazis, intending to show the public the "depravity of modern art," mounted an exhibition entitled "Degenerate Art" which showcased the confiscated work of 200 contemporary artists, including Dix. Later, the Nazis destroyed many of Dix's paintings.

From 1946 until his death in 1969, Dix exhibited internationally. The content of his work had became more mystical in its orientation.

"THE ENGLISH HAVE LONG DREADED GERMAN ART (*literature, painting and music*) as sure to be dreadfully ponderous, slow, involved, and pedestrian." Bertolt Brecht, to the members of the Berliner Ensemble, 5 August 1956.

UNSPARINGNESS, *SCHONUNGSLOSIGKEIT*, IS A GERMAN VIRTUE – though not all Germans appreciate it – and an English vice. It is probably a matter of geography as much as taste: an island begs to be spared, by definition. The blue movies on the Kurfürstendamm sell themselves as unsparing. The art of Otto Dix is unsparing, too, though not in a way the viewers of the blue movies would appreciate. Dix painted ugliness, and, being German, he did it unsparingly.

In the case of these big shows by great and distinctive artists – of which Dix, despite my initial doubts, is certainly one – not all the paintings are on the walls. Dix had two of

> "EVERYBODY THINKS THEY KNOW WHAT ART SHOULD BE. BUT VERY FEW OF THEM HAVE THE SENSE THAT IS NECESSARY TO EXPERIENCE PAINTING, THAT IS THE SENSE OF SIGHT, THAT SEES COLORS AND FORMS AS LIVING REALITY IN THE PICTURE."

his best years, 1925 to 1927, in this same Berlin; he painted the same human types you see on the streets now or looking at the paintings, and in a similar atmosphere. For at the beginning of 1992, Berlin seems to be just coming out of a war. The city is full of miles and miles of wasteland, beginning just outside the museum with the Potsdamer Platz, once the busiest square in Europe, now a derelict lot. In the damaged East, reconstruction is beginning. Commerce squats in the form of product names on top of reprieved concrete blocks. From their new premises the banks proclaim, incorrectly, "Investment is an art," and, unoriginally, "Money doesn't smell." Hundreds of thousands of Russian troops are still in the process of being withdrawn. You see their brown outsize caps and their coats and binoculars for sale. On the howling Stalinist expanse of the "Alex," the Alexanderplatz, there is pavement gambling and a spot of black market. The most superficial wants are also the deepest, and are attended to first: coffee, newspapers (especially the *Bild Zeitung*, fruit, posters, and pornography. The incredible scale of the Stasi's operations is becoming apparent; a quarter of the country tears itself up, the rest looks on, is concerned, gives advice. All this reflects on Dix, and he expresses it with his paintings of whores and cripples, his gray proles and louche portraits: social dislocation, impatience, submission, false glitter, and the inadequate healing powers of capitalism. The person who penned the hymn to lost opportunity on a BMW hoarding that began *Gestern abend stand hier 'ne knackige Alte* ("Last night there was this tasty old bird…") was Dix; and so was the Polish couple on the bus, mother and daughter, telling each other about the food, pulling out a tub of chocolate pudding as proof, a dark fake fur coat with white highlights, and the kind of golden ringlets Germans (and no doubt Poles, too) have painted, goldsmith-fashion, for hundreds of years, the latest and not the least of them "Otto Hans Baldung Dix," as his friend Grosz called him.

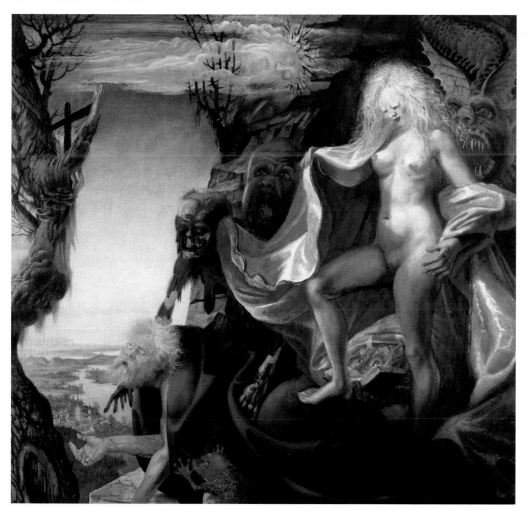

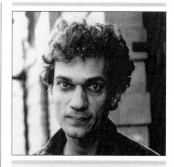

MICHAEL HOFMANN
Born in Germany in 1957, Hofmann was raised in England and in the US. Graduating from Cambridge in 1979, he moved to London to work as a freelance writer, reviewer, and translator. He published his first book of poetry, Nights in the Iron Hotel, *in 1983 followed by* Acrimony *and* Corona Corona. *The poems in his 1999 collection* Approximately Nowhere *deal with loss.*

Hofmann has also translated many works from the German, including a novel by his father Gert Hofmann, The Film Explainer, *and Kafka's* The Man Who Disappeared. *His poetry reviews and other writings have appeared in the* London Review of Books, The Times Literary Supplement, The New York Times, *and* The Times. Behind the Lines, *a collection of these essays, was published in 2000.*

His many honors include the Cholmondeley Award, the Geoffrey Faber Memorial Prize, the IMPAC Dublin Literary Award for translation, the PEN/Book of the Month Club Translation Prize, and the Independent's Foreign Fiction Prize. He was selected for promotion as one of Britain's "New Generation Poets."

Hofmann is married to the poet Lavinia Greenlaw and lives in London.

The Temptation of St. Anthony (with the head of Christ), *1937, mixed media on wood, 60 x 60 in/149 x 149 cm. Zeppelin-Museum, Friedrichshafen, on loan from a Private collection.*

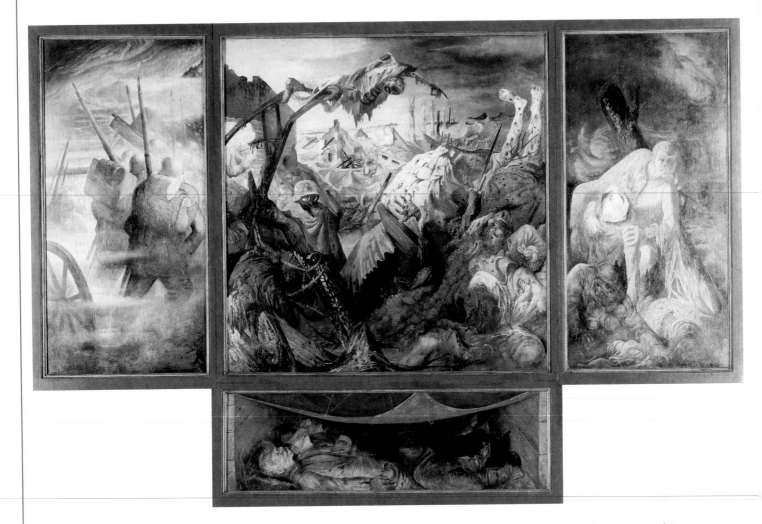

The War, 1932, Triptych with predella, mixed media on wood, left and right panels: 80 x 40 in/204 x 102 cm; center panel: 80 x 80 in/204 x 204 cm; predella: 24 x 80 in/60 x 204 cm. Staadliche Kunstsammlungen Dresden, Gemäldegalerie Neue Meister.

Otto Dix was an artist as protean as any this century, with the usual exception of Picasso; a man who got through the range of current -isms very early in his career, and in his thirties found himself painting in Old Master style, like the pupil of Cranach, Dürer, and Grünewald he occasionally claimed to be; an impressive, unsparing, and unlovable artist in the German tradition of accuracy, the sublime, and the unbeautiful. Dix was a member of no groupings of any significance for any length of time; he had no particular affiliation, no close associates (Grosz not very close); his name is not inevitably connected with that of any movement, unless it be that of Verism, a rather obscure offshoot of Neorealism, and *Neue Sachlichkeit*, coined largely to accommodate and account for Dix himself. His wilful and eccentric career was nevertheless almost wholly contingent, at the mercy of every passing political and economic change. German history shaped his output more than that of any other German artist this century; the lovely, rather decorative pen-and-ink field postcards he drew during the First World War; the watercolors that kept himself and his family fed during the German Inflation, when nothing more austere or expensive would have sold; his portraits in oils in the late '20s, when he was the most soughtafter and alarming of portraitists; a handful of brave and ambitious large-scale allegorical paintings (his triptych *The War, The Seven Deadly Sins, The Triumph of Death*) done before and immediately after 1933 and Hitler's coming to power; the landscapes he painted during the Nazi period as a form of emigration; and the Christs and Christophers and Lukes he did in Dresden after the War, in the Workers' and Peasants' State of East Germany. Each phase is chronologically distinct, and refers you to the political, social, and economic circumstances in which it was created.

And yet even this lightning summary of Dix's work raises certain questions about his effectiveness, his intentions, and his methods. At each stage, he seems to be in a kind of tacit opposition to what is going on, but he never elaborates on this. His contemporaries carried cards, sounded off, and explained themselves, but not Dix. There is the story of one of them trying to persuade him to join the Party, and Dix finally saying, I've had enough of this, let's go to the brothel. But the brothel, according to many commentators, is a highly politicized location: the painter, who sells his services for a living, identifies with the prostitute. Could Dix not in fact be proving himself to be *more* political than his would be recruiting sergeant? And so on. When Grosz draws and paints soldiers, industrialists, politicians, and priests, the intention is clear: to depict the enemy. His pictures are *Feindbilder*. Dix's, though, are *Zerrbilder*, distortions, an exaggerated, not an embattled reality. What they seem to say is not "These are the oppressors" but (as Goya wrote on some of his work) "I have seen it" and "This is how it was." Where Grosz uses caricature and metaphor, Dix refers you to the reality of what he depicts. The prostitute is not a metaphor for capitalism but an actual prostitute. If the pictures are political, they are so in a less narrow and less purposeful way. In particular, their relation to change is very questionable.

There is a kind of unwisdom, ambiguity, and perversity in many of Dix's attitudes and subjects. What made him settle on "the dead and the naked" (the title of one of the studies on him) as his preferred subjects in the '20s? How could he become a religious painter – though not personally religious – in godless East Germany in the '50s? What accounts for the rigorously uncontemporary appearance of so much of his work, like the tiny somber *Venus in Gloves* of 1932? The overwhelming tendency is for an over-literal interpretation of the subjects, to infer Dix's standpoint from them. Most famously, this is Carl Einstein's put-down of Dix as *malender*

> "(OTTO DIX IS) AN ESSENTIALLY REACTIONARY PAINTER OF LEFT-WING SUBJECT-MATTER."
>
> —*Carl Einstein*

Venus in Gloves, *1932, mixed media on wood, 10 x 8 in/25 x 20 cm. Private collection.*

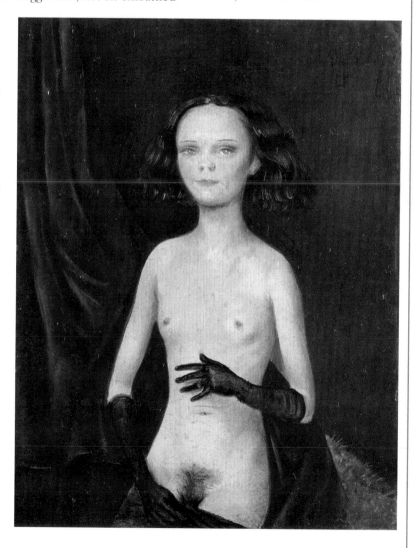

Reaktionär am linken Motiv, ("a reactionary painter of progressive subjects"); but it is just as true of political and religious interpretations of Dix. Late in his life, when Germany was still divided, he lent himself, wittingly or not, to splendid political-aesthetic wrangles between East and West. Neither side really had much use for him, but he did make a bitter bone of contention. In fact, but for the re-unification, there would not have been one, but two, Dix exhibitions!

I believe the arguments about him are too intellectual and too theoretical. At the root of Dix's art is a desire to abash or confront or be unfashionable. With his working-class background, his severe provincial training, and his four years in the War as a machine-gunner, he reached his thirtieth year in 1920, and no contemporary style or practice in art was unable to impress him. The Expressionists painted the world in primary colors; to him it seemed gray and he painted it accordingly (*Working Class Boys, Woman and Child*). He never gave anything for the French or for abstraction. His experiments with Dada, Cubo-Futurism and a merely photographic realism were all gifted and promising, but of short duration. In the way he worked later, he was almost always alone, away from the moderating influence of others, on terrain that was his own, often eccentric, and sometimes incommunicable. The artists with whom he had any relationship were his students, or they were local Dresden painters, or they had been dead for centuries.

The painting from which Dix generally said he took his beginnings is his 1912 *Self-Portrait with Carnation*, painted when he was just twenty-one and a student. It seems at once a beautifully solid and achieved work on which to found a career, and a complete anachronism, perhaps 400 years out of date, with nothing in common with any living style of the moment. And yet it is a real self-portrait, not an exercise or pastiche. In its accuracy and painstakingness and style, it proclaims its identification with the traditions of the past and its agnosticism toward the present. It could be a Martyr or a Saint or an Unknown Young Man of 1500 or so, but a twentieth-century

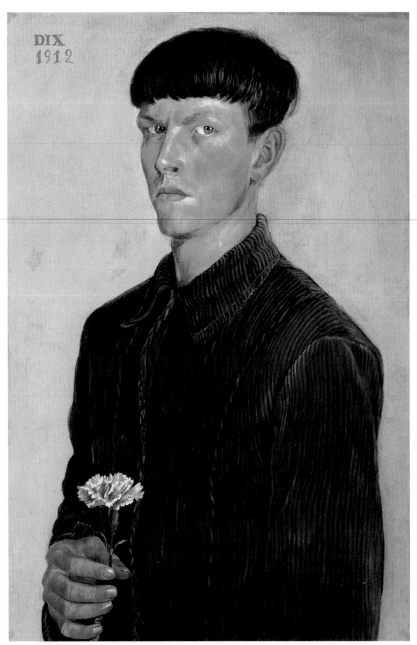

Left: Self Portrait with Carnation,
1912, oil and tempura on panel,
29 x 20 in/73 x 50 cm.
Detroit Institute of Arts.

self-portrait – never! Dix is standing half-sideways on, like a duellist presenting a small target to his opponent (in 1915, he painted a *Self-Portrait as Target*. He looks serious, glowering, watchful, a Henry at Hal's age. The eyes are deepset, the brow frowns, and the mouth is down-drawn: it is a picture of some sort of victory over a more generous and open self, an early maturity in the drab, armoring, magnificently painted corduroy. A helmet might go over the stringy fringe. You feel sympathy for the young man, putting on such a stern face to meet his portraitist – himself! The carnation (Nelke, also a clove, un clou, a nail), an emblem of pain, mortality, the Crucifixion (I don't know the exact iconography), has dropped into his hand from another century; he seems unaware of it even as he holds it, and is further characterized by it, as he is by the blue background – not a natural sky blue, but a heightened ethical blue, a rather sweet blue like a sugared almond.

This very early picture anticipates Dix's later practice: an unfashionable finish and perfection, both exaggerating and suggesting the use of props and one-color backgrounds

"Stop bothering me with your pathetic politics – I'd rather go to the whorehouse."

(Dix says somewhere that everyone has a personal color: Anita Berber's hot red; Sylvia von Harden's cool pink; the drapes, blue-green and German shepherd in *The Photographer Hugo Erfurth with Dog*), objectivity tending towards caricature (this last perhaps signalled by another portrait of Erfurth, this time holding a photo-lens – the German word for lens is *Objektiv*). Dix stressed the importance of first impressions – which seems to me odd for a portrait-painter, especially one with such long drawn-out processes as Dix used – and said he preferred to paint strangers. Where many twentieth-century portraitists seem to paint just one type of face – think of Schiele or Beckmann, among Dix's contemporaries – Dix's are all different. The human face is a terrible place, someone once sang, and that is the impression one has from Dix: a keen, instinctual, almost doggish sense of alienation from other breeds, faces like smells, different disturbing, unforgettable. Dix has obviously succeeded in capturing one's initial feelings of alarm, fascination, and repulsion, a sense of the disproportion and strangeness of other people's features, before habitual looking makes them acceptable. But he manages in his portraits to combine the vehemence of first impressions with a studied and permanent form (his *Lasurtechnik*, many thin layers of paint and varnish, if I understand it correctly, generally applied on wood, and demanding the making of full-scale cartoons beforehand). This is the basic tug or contradiction in his work: quick reactions or "low" caricatural subjects, executed in the most lavish, durable, and historically dignified way; the colossal – ironic – discrepancy

"... DIX'S USE OF DISTURBING OR OFFENSIVE SUBJECT MATTER, HIS USE OF DISTORTION AT TIMES BORDERING ON THE GROTESQUE, AND HIS OFTEN HARSH, STRIDENT COLORS MUST BE SEEN AS A NIETZSCHEAN-INSPIRED AESTHETIC STRATEGY, INTENDED TO FORCE THE VIEWER TO CONFRONT ISSUES AND FEELINGS IN A CRITICAL, DETACHED MANNER."

—*Sarah O'Brien Twohig*

between technique and content, the twentieth century through the eyes of the fifteenth or sixteenth. Take the painting *Nelly with Toys* of 1925. Dix paints his two-year-old daughter like an Infanta by Goya or Velazquez. His characteristic pink and green palette, often used to repulsive effect, is here kept pure. Nelly's outrageous ribbon is a crown, her ball an orb, her jumbled and anarchic tower (her stare challenges the viewer to say it's wrong) a scepter. Even her collar and cuffs might be ermine. Her fat fingers like carelessly on the sumptuously grained table like Botero trotters. Her dark eyes blaze from their blue whites; her chubby mouth is an imperious curl; her own curls are lovingly chased by the painter in the Old Master technique that Grosz witnessed. The portrait radiates the wilfulness, poise, beauty, and peremptoriness of the little girl. If she spoke, it would be to say, "Off with his head!"

The 1920s were Dix's decade: with his portraits, his pictures of prostitutes, his big set pieces like *To Beauty* and *The Metropolis*; he supplied many of the enduring images of those years. At the same time, in the 50 etchings that make up The *War series* (1924), he produced possibly his best work, and, with Goya, the strongest visual response to the subject. Again, the delay is characteristic, necessary for the finding of a medium and form with which to communicate his quick impressions. What he sent back from the Front at the time, in the form of his decorative field-postcards and the watermelon-pretty spatter of his watercolors must have dismayed him by its serenity and merriment. The titles are veiled apologies for this: *Concrete Trench with Flowers* (1916), *Shell Crater like Blossom* (1916). The same quality in Dix that made his early *Self-Portrait with Carnation* so austere and memorable, his will to create strong effects, his unsparingness, his aversion to color as

"THE WAR WAS A HORRIBLE THING, BUT THERE WAS SOMETHING TREMENDOUS ABOUT IT TOO. I DIDN'T WANT TO MISS IT AT ANY PRICE."

consolation, drove him to rework his wartime experience later, in black and white, with absolute technical mastery and freedom. The *War* series of etchings has an enormous range: from white to black, from fine, representational lines to an acid fuzz of pain and decomposition, from parodic sketching to papers that might have been stained by war itself. The 50 etchings seem to be in no particular order. Among the best in my opinion were I, 4, a pattern of white receding craters, II, 2, a gas attack by night, II, 9, a lovely patterning of corpses on wire, and III, 7, the dawn over a field of bodies. The *War* series was quickly recruited for the anti-war movements of the '20s – and Dix's main trouble with the Nazis was that his work was *wehrzersetzend*, or liable to weaken the instinct to self-defense; but I have more sympathy with the view that finds these images neutral, horrific, yes, but not

> "DIX COMBINED A THOROUGHLY 'REALISTIC' APPRAISAL OF THE BRUTALITY OF MANKIND WITH A CRITICAL AND ARTISTICALLY RADICAL ATTACK."
>
> —*Jill Lloyd*

evaluative, not condemning, not propagandistic. The tone is once again one of "I have seen it" and "These things took place."

Just as Dix's war art is not censorious, nor are his pictures of prostitutes; they are not prurient either. The fact that Dix was twice taken to court for obscenity is absurd; but just as absurd was his defense – which years later still made him burst out laughing – that these were deeply moral pictures, warning of the dangers of corruption and loose living. I simply cannot see Dix as such an infantile moralist. In his self-portraits and photographs, Dix always preserves a demeanor of the most tremendous earnestness. Even on the cover of a picture-book he made for his nephew "Muggeli," he draws himself in profile, smoking, hair slicked back, brows furrowed, mouth down – and you wish he would relax, just for once. In fact, though, the po-faced, puritanical image is misleading. Dix didn't spend the '20s glowering on the sidelines. Other photographs show him wearing make-up and a monocle for Carnival; he danced so well he thought of doing it for a living with Martha his wife; he was a dandy who sometimes took payment in the form of new shoes and a suit of clothes; he participated in the kind of scenes he depicted in *To Beauty* and *Metropolis*. When he painted his whores (many of whom were not), he didn't preach to them like Gladstone.

My point is that I don't think there is anything too considered, let alone too comprehensive, about Dix's subjects: his work doesn't add up to an anatomy of the society of the time, still less to an indictment of it. "It's what I do!" he said. "Say what you like. What it's good for I can't say myself. But I do it anyway. Because I know that's what it was like, and no different!" Dix was provocative artist: he liked to paint what he knew people wouldn't like to look at. Even among his watercolors – to which he looked to make his living – there were many that were unsaleable because of their subjects: old people, ugly faces,

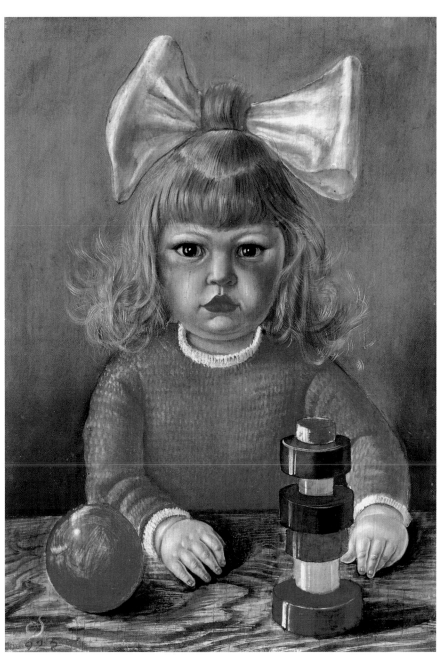

Nelly with Toys, *1925, oil and tempera on wood, 21 x 16 in/54 x 40 cm. Otto Dix Stiftung, Vaduz, on loan to the Galerie der Stadt, Stuttgart.*

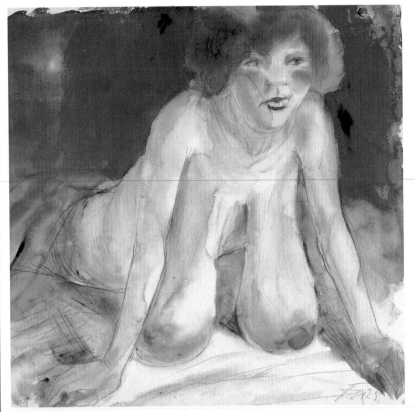

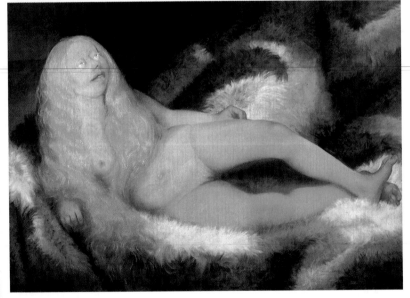

Top: Sphinx, *1925, watercolor, 20 x 21 in/51 x 52 cm. Otto Dix Stiftung, Vaduz, Liechtenstein.*

Above: Nude Lying on Fur, *1932, tempera and oil on canvas, mounted on wood, 39 x 56 in/99 x 143 cm. Scottish National Gallery of Modern Art, Edinburgh.*

Opposite page: Three Women, *1926, oil on wood, 71 x 42 in/181 x 106 cm. Galerie der Stadt, Stuttgart.*

suicides, murders, foul prostitutes. It's easy to pick out the ones that might have sold: slight and cynical skits on bourgeois happiness. What interested Dix was ugliness, which seems to him almost like a creed. When he said, later in his life, "I'm not that obsessed with making representations of ugliness. Everything I've seen is beautiful…;" he only succeeds in confirming its importance by suggesting a kind of *ésthetique du mal*, which I've argued is close to German art and writing anyway, in the poetry of Georg Trakl and Gottfried Benn. Many of Dix's paintings are truly horrible, vile, creepy: the first impression, under the many varnishing layers, like an insect trapped in amber. And yet they have a kind of beauty, too, beyond the skill with which they were painted. The watercolors are surprisingly messy and sloppy and spirited: *Mieze, abends im Café* with an ocelot round her shoulders, a lapdog burrowed into her crotch, toying with a green beaker with flame-red fingernails; the luscious red-on-red *Sphinx; The Suicide*, with his red tongue and loosened red tie (Dix's joke?) in his wan room.

In the oil-paintings, what is again and again arresting is the contradiction between a flawed or even disgusting face or scene and the perfection of its execution: *Still Life with Calf's Head* (like an illustration for some of Benn's *Morgue* poems), *Three Women, Elderly Couple, Three Prostitutes in the Street*, the disturbing *Nude lying on Fur*. These and other paintings can't be reduced to coded or simple statements. The ugliness in them is a continual and willed, yes, finely controlled vibration; the curtailed, minced-pork-and-parsley palettes; the opulent backgrounds; the heroic, classicizing postures and arrangements; the array of physical types and physiognomies; an airless glow in the painting, pallor and garishness together. It seems that the more there is in each painting – the more Dix puts in – the worse it gets. There is a kind of incremental nausea provoked by draperies, carpets, velvet, veils, marble balustrade, carpentry, jewelry, ribbons, hair, flesh in the *Three Women* of 1926. It is as though Dix had found a way of depicting *ars longa, vita brevis* in a tiny, annihilating glimpse. The "beautiful" – or at least the costly, the showy – is contaminated by the hideous human. It is as though one's nerves had become sated and couldn't bear to touch another gorgeous velvet or diaphanous silk, or see another piece of veined marble or porphyry. These props for cheap erotica become, in Dix's hands, the catalysts of disgust. Not the least disturbing part of this picture and others (say the *Nude Lying on Fur*, is the absense of any reciprocal thought on the part of the model, or any mutual awareness if there are more than one. Each figure – and this is true of all of Dix – exists solipsistically. The models for his portraits seem not to be aware of themselves, not to know what is happening to them; and so, at its very worst, the nude is assimilated to her fur, her hair dribbles blondly into it, her foreshortened wishbone legs beg to be cracked open, she becomes a stupid cow or a piece of meat (is that the "statement"); and in the eerie 1937 portrait of Jean-Jacques Bernauer, the model becomes an aristocratic wax mannikin between the carpet and the tapestry. Everything is texture, and texture in the end is inert, as *Still Life in the Atelier* shows, where a mouldering stuffed doll mimics a live and pregnant model.

Dix's biggest, most ambitious paintings tend to be the ones I am least impressed by: they dilute his ability as a portraitist, reality is diminished by

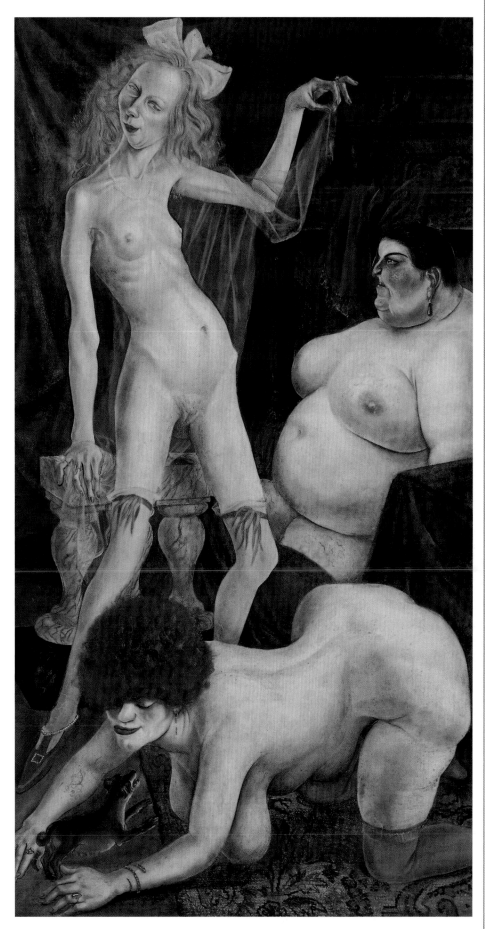

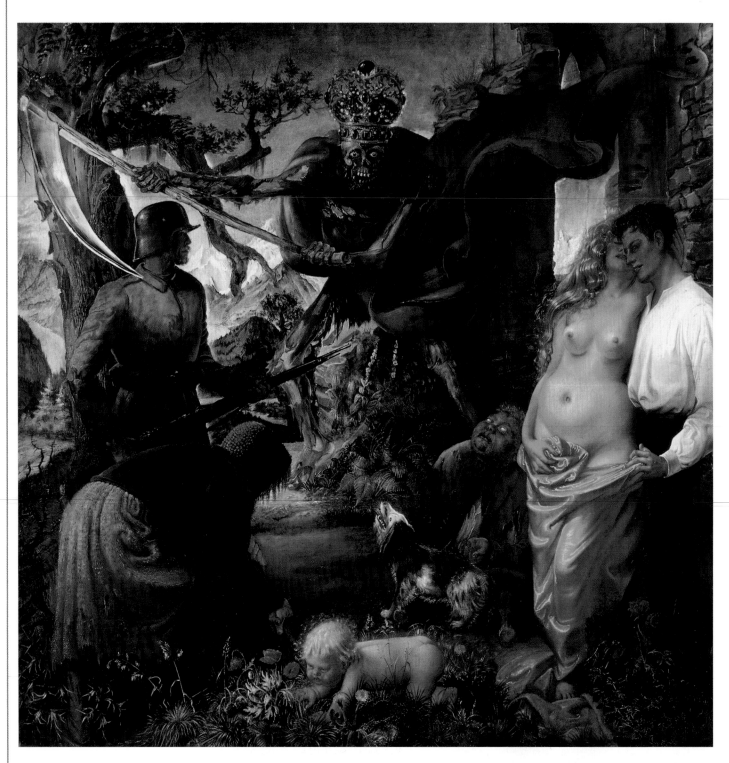

Triumph of Death, *1934,*
mixed media on wood,
71 x 70 in/ 180 x 178 cm.
Gallery der Stadt, Stuttgart.

allegory. *The Triumph of Death* is platitudinous; *Metropolis* is much less than the sum of its parts, and much less than something like Diego Rivera; *Flanders* and the other war paintings are better in their black and white versions in the *War* etchings. The religious paintings and landscapes of later years are fey and uninteresting, except perhaps in the way they extended Dix's range of creepiness. *St Luke Painting the Madonna* seems to contain more hidden birds each time you look at it; Dix himself as St Luke looks like a Florida dentist in the pink steam of some Everglades – an appalling picture. The landscapes are lurid, never-never landscapes under never-never meteorological conditions in the Northern European manner (out of Brueghel, etc.). Dix said somewhere that landscapes didn't interest him, and these have only the mildest historical interest, as war paintings by default.

If Dix's career had ended here, he would be seen as a brief, inexplicable, almost accidental phenomenon who lit up one decade, the 1920s, and did nothing else of note. Admittedly, the later work is not very well represented in the exhibition, but there is enough there to make a different case, in the form of three heavy, bold and expressionistically painted portraits: the *Self Portrait as Prisoner of War* of 1947, *Dr Fritz Perls* of 1966, and *Self Portrait with Marcella* of 1969. The first of these is the most moving – perhaps the only moving – painting I know of Dix's: dark wintry colors, green, blue, ocher, turquoise, but with black and gray breaking through everywhere, the paint applied in little flecks as though it wouldn't spread; three heads – or one in two mirrors – grizzled, numbered, in camouflage gear, with a suggestion fo camps and searchlights. It's a tragic painting, more Christian than any of his professed Christian work, perhaps with something of the *Odyssey* about it, too. The other two are lighter: Dr Perls with his curly Jewish face and curly body posture, purple suit, and mustard and cream background, a quick and wise piece of work – one survivor by another; and himself with Marcella, a granddaughter, the colors of youth and age, a light

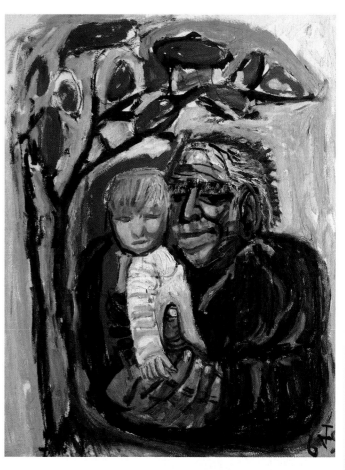

Self Portrait with Marcella, *1969, oil on plywood, 34 x 27 in/ 87 x 68 cm. Otto Dix Stiftung, Vaduz.*

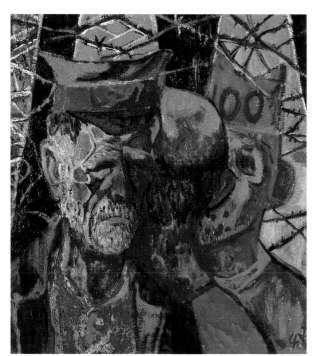

yellow and green to his own dark blue and maroon, the possessiveness of age, the old fingers holding this handful, a kind of crazy Bellovian joy in the eyes, the whole thing under a child's fantasy of a tree. All three seem to me great paintings, simple and sure, with a new and wonderful sense of color, "color no longer space, line no longer explanatory," giving a likeness and even preserving the element of mockery – can this be true? – that accompanied Dix all his life.

Self portrait as Prisoner of War, *1947, mixed media on hardboard, 24 x 21 in/60 x 54 cm. Otto Dix Stiftung, Vaduz on loan to the Galerie der Stadt, Stuttgart.*

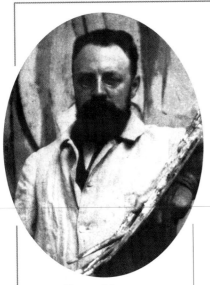

Henri Matisse

by Jed Perl

THE MATISSE RETROSPECTIVE WHICH OPENS THIS SEPTEMBER (1992) at New York City's Museum of Modern Art is an enormous undertaking. Some 300 paintings – plus large numbers of sculptures, drawings, prints, and paper cut-outs – are included in the show that has been organized by John Elderfield, who is director of the Modern's drawing department and a curator in the department of painting and sculpture. The Matisse show comes a little over a decade after the Modern devoted its entire space to a Picasso retrospective. That exhibition dominated the city during the long hot summer of

> "WHEN I STARTED TO PAINT, I FELT TRANSPORTED INTO A KIND OF PARADISE... IN EVERYDAY LIFE, I WAS USUALLY BORED AND VEXED BY THE THINGS THAT PEOPLE WERE ALWAYS TELLING ME I MUST DO. STARTING TO PAINT, I FELT GLORIOUSLY FREE, QUIET, AND ALONE."

1980; it left many of us feeling that we were living inside the fever dream that was Picasso's brain. The Matisse retrospective, which opens as the city enters its autumn glory, presents a cooler kind of imagination. It will doubtless have a very different but equally powerful impact on New York. These two artists dominated Parisian art in the first half of the century – their careers are humongous – and taken together the two giant retrospectives add up to a kind of double odyssey that defines the beginning of the artistic universe as we know it.

It's an adventure that begins in the nineteenth century: Matisse was born in 1869, Picasso in 1881. Regarded as pure narrative, it's the story of how art became abstract, and Fauvism and Cubism, coming before the century's first decade is over, are the odyssey's ultimate legendary episodes. In 1905, Matisse is pushing the colors that he sees in front of him to jangling extremes – on a face, patches of green and purple and blue and orange shove against one another startlingly, beautifully. Five years later, Picasso (along with Braque) is turning solid objects into mysterious, aerial traceries amidst which letters and bits of *trompe l'oeil* play hide and seek. Yet both heroes have rather complicated and even ambivalent relations to the advent of abstract art – they feel the birth pains as something traumatic – and this is part of what gives this double odyssey its psychological fascination. Even as Matisse and Picasso bring European art to the brink of abstraction, their work remains firmly grounded in the world around them.

Abstraction was the promised land of twentieth-century art. Matisse and Picasso discovered it and at moments defined it, but they never wanted to go all the way and take possession. They had arrived on the scene when the academies of nineteenth-century

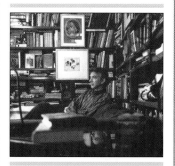

JED PERL
Essayist and art critic Jed Perl studied art and painting at Columbia University in New York, attended Skowhegan School of Painting and Sculpture, and graduate school at Brooklyn College. He now covers the contemporary art scene for The New Republic. *His books include* Paris Without End: On French Art Since World War I *and* Gallery Going: Four Seasons in the Art World.

Often critical of the "official" art world, Perl frequently champions less acclaimed artists, who, he believes, deserve more attention. These and other themes surface in his writing for Modern Painters, The Partisan Review, *and* The New York Times Book Review, *and in lectures at art schools, appearances on National Public Radio, and Public Television's Lehrer News Hour.*

Perl was awarded an Ingram Merrill Foundation Award in 1994 and serves on the Editorial Board of Modern Painters. *He has also taught art history at Pratt Institute, the Philadelphia College of Art, and at the Parson School of Design.*

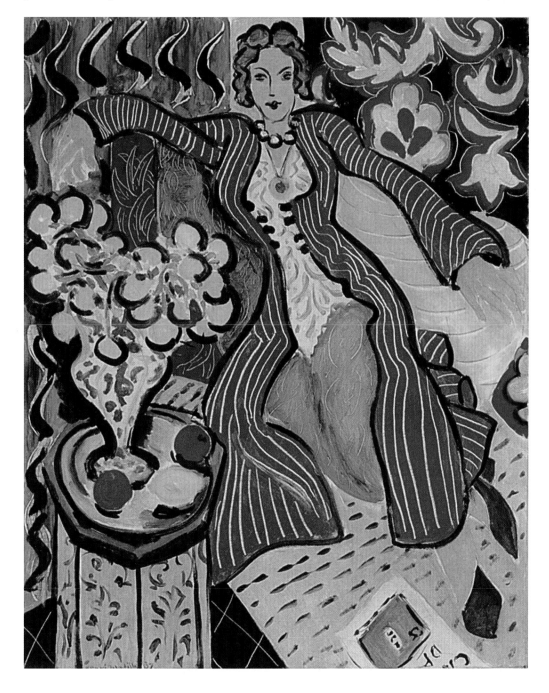

Woman in a Purple Robe with Ranunculi, *1937, oil on canvas, 32 x 24 in/81 x 62 cm. Museum of Fine Arts, Houston.*

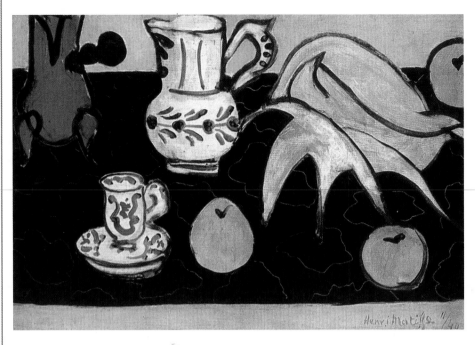

Still Life with a Sea Shell on Black Marble, *1940, oil on canvas, 22 x 32 in/55 x 81 cm. Pushkin Museum, Moscow.*

Europe were in their decadence, and perhaps because Matisse and Picasso were so conscious that things had to change, they also felt and immense responsibility toward the past. Their figure drawing can look like the last astonishing blossoming of the Western realist tradition: their draughtsmanship has an ease, an assurance, a variety that is rare in any century. These are men whose heroic achievements cannot be separated from the particularities of time and space, and in the retrospectives dedicated to their work, we go from room to room, regarding each gallery as an episode where our hero meets a new challenge. Some of the challenges are daunting, and there are moments in each odyssey when one wonders if the hero will know what to do next. The grandeur of these stories has something to do with the heroes' split allegiances – with their desire to understand the new world of abstraction even as they give a last glorious salute to the old world of appearances. Their slips and momentary failings often have to do with an unwillingness to take a clear enough stand. Their triumphs rest in many ways that, in the face of their divided allegiances, they manage to remain whole.

The Matisse retrospective will have a somewhat different kind of drama from that of the 1980 Picasso show. That Picasso retrospective, which opened less than a decade after the artist's death, was itself a part of his odyssey: it was the coda in which the friends and admirers gather to mourn the dead hero. The Matisse show celebrates an artist who died in 1954 – and almost 40 years ago; it represents a finished period and thus cannot impress itself upon us as quite so dramatic an event. But then again Mattisse has always seemed a rather more remote figure than Picasso – this was true even when both men were alive. After Fauvism was eclipsed by Cubism, Matisse was never again a star player within the Parisian avant-garde; he was always on people's minds, but as a man who'd gone his own way. By the end of World War I, Matisse was living in the south of France, at a considerable physical and psychological distance from Paris. While Picasso always endeavored to respond to the times – the Ballets Russes, Surrealism, Guernica – Matisse was relatively reclusive. This is by no means a bad thing. Far from it. Today many people believe that Picasso wasted his gifts trying to stay engaged, while Matisse, who kept to himself, was enlarging his art. Picasso was obsessed with self-promotion, both in art and in life; Matisse's desire for privacy was so great that even now, decades after his death, little has been revealed in print about his marriage and its troubles. Of the two heroes, one is intensely private, the other wildly exhibitionist; yet in the hugeness of their ambitions and the lengths of the journeys that they took out of the nineteenth century they are well matched. Their wary, admiring encounters – and their occasional exchanges of paintings – were acknowledgements, that despite all their differences, they were going the same way.

In a late poem, *Iceland Revisited*, W.H. Auden had this to say about his own fame: "He hears a loudspeaker/Call him well known:/But knows himself no better." This describes a paradox of fame as seen from the famous person's perspective, but those of us who contemplate an eminence can also find that although a person is called well-known we do not necessarily know him very well. The very nature of Matisse's art, which is rarely overtly autobiographical, gives an enigmatic quality. It is also in the nature of many long careers that, while we may see the main outlines easily, what lies beneath or beyond them can remain rather obscure. There are careers that are fairly consistent – Giacometti's or Morandi's, for example – and thus in some sense easier to know. But when we consider all the unpredictable things that life can do to a person, the homogeneous career may seem a stranger phenomenon than the career that is full of contradictions. Of course, the relative consistency of a career and its quality are not necessarily related: a genius like Piero impresses us as having a single, integrated vision. But when a huge career is highly complex, like Matisse's, and encompasses widely divergent manners – everything from rococo richness to iconic reduction – it is natural that people are tempted to choose among

The Sorrow of Kings, 1952, *gouache on cut-out and pasted paper, 115 x 156 in/292 x 396 cm. Musée National d'Art Moderne, Centre Georges Pompidou, Paris.*

the various aspects and argue that some of them are most characteristic, most important.

There has always been a tendency to explain Matisse's career in terms of a striving for simplicity. This is certainly the way we have been taught to regard Matisse in America. At the Museum of Modern Art the focus has generally been on the two stretches in Matisse's life: the period from about 1905 to the beginning of World War 1, a period beginning with

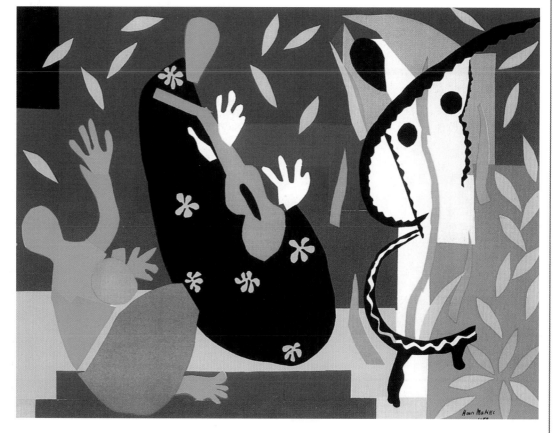

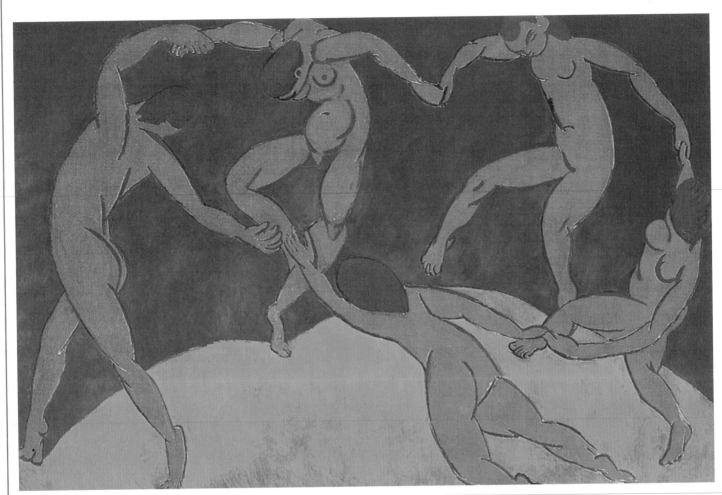

Dance (1), 1909, oil on canvas, 102 x 154 in/260 x 390 cm. Museum of Modern Art, New York.

Fauvism and ending with some of the most abstract works he ever did; and the period of the paper cut-outs, in the late 1940s and early 1950s. The man on the street's image of Matisse is of buoyant, simplified color shapes – the charged-up color of Fauvism, the bold arabesques of *The Dance*. More sophisticated viewers will think of Matisse in terms of the aspect of his achievement that has inspired Richard Diebenkorn's abstractions – the severity of such blue-green-gray images as *The Piano Lesson*. In both instances Matisse is the great exemplar of less-is-more; he's the artist who proves that nature is enhanced as it is distilled.

Nobody could love Matisse without loving this side of his personality; but there does at times seem to be a wilful refusal to see the other side of his personality, the side which glories in the overload of nuances and halftones and complications that meet him everywhere he turns. Matisse's most typical subject is a woman in an interior – an absolutely ordinary occasion that he regards with a penetrating attention to naturalistic detail – and many of the hundreds of works that he did on this theme went straight from his studio into private collections from which it seems they are fated never to emerge. The '20s were Matisse's decade for painting women day in and day out, and ever since then it has been well nigh impossible to see these paintings in New York City, save for occasional brief appearances in gallery shows. "Matisse in Nice" – the great show devoted to the work of the '20s that was mounted at the National Gallery in Washington, DC, in 1986–87 – made up, at least to some degree, for what we'd missed. But even that show (which was devoted to painting) did not include the fabulously detailed lithographs of nudes, lithographs that establish Matisse as among the transcendent figure draughtsmen of the Western tradition, right up there with Raphael. Matisse's considerable gifts as a landscape painter – another important aspect of the '20s – also remains unacknowledged.

And there are still, at this late date, whole periods that remain baffling. We may now have a fairly clear sense of the '20s, but as for the fifteen of so years between the beginning of the '30s and the final period of the paper cut-outs, this is a stretch of the career that has yet to be given its due. This is the period of Matisse's great book illustrations, of an increasingly freewheeling graphic style, and of paintings which, with their plethora of calligraphic black outlines setting off areas of acid, high-keyed color, stand (at least so far as I am concerned) as Matisse's most hard-to-understand works in oil. Many of them seem

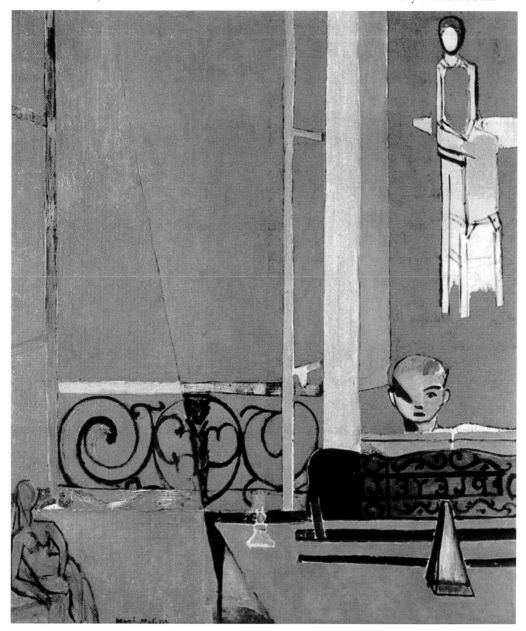

"HE'S ADMIRABLE. HE HAS A FORM OF EXTREMISM WHICH FORCES YOU TO EAT ROTTEN DUCK OR WILD CHEESES IN ORDER TO MAKE SURE YOUR PALATE IS EXPANDING ITSELF AND YOUR VISION IS GETTING MORE SOPHISTICATED."

—*Wayne Thiebaud*

The Piano Lesson, *1916, oil on canvas, 96 x 84 in/245 x 213 cm. Museum of Modern Art, New York.*

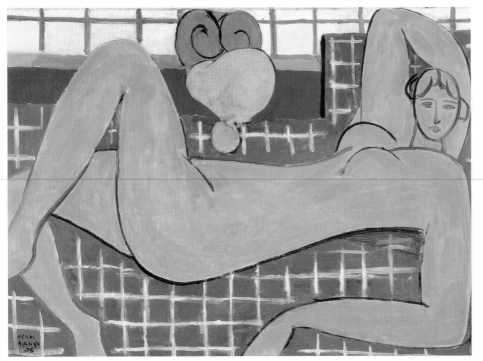

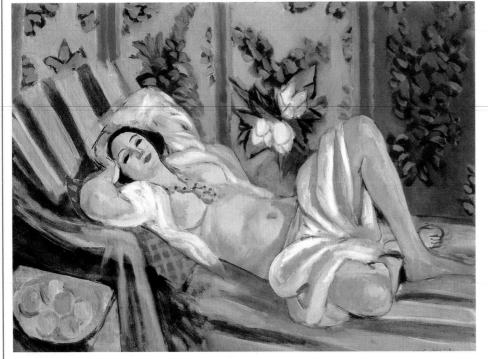

Top: Large Reclining Nude (The Pink Nude), *1935, oil on canvas, 26 x 36 in/66 x 92 cm. Baltimore Museum of Art, Cone Collection.*

Above: Odalisque with Magnolias, *1923–24, oil on canvas, 26 x 32 in/65 x 81 cm. Private Collection.*

almost too casual, too rapidly tossed off: that is, at least, my initial impression. But with Matisse one hesitates to accept initial negative impressions. So I ask questions: Is Matisse thinking about painting in a new way? Is he thinking of the full color painting as an extension of a drawing? Ought one to regard these paintings as a Western version of the Oriental brush painting?

I hope that the retrospective at the Museum of Modern Art will illuminate this shadowy decade-and-a-half. More than that, I want to see the celebrated early years and the equally celebrated late years as parts of a dynamic revolution. Ironically, John Elderfield's retrospective will only be a success to the degree that it illuminates precisely those periods of Matisse's career in which the Museum of Modern Art has, historically, taken very little interest. Everything that I know about Matisse suggests that this is a career in which reduction and complication function as pressure and counterpressure. Neither side of the equation is ever entirely absent. When reduction comes to the fore, it is the denial of complication that gives the simplicity its high-wire tension. And when complication comes to the fore, it is the underlying sense of simplicity that enables Matisse to fit everything together. If I were to diagram the entire career, I would say that its large movement is simplicity-complexity-simplicity. 1920–40, the period of complication, remains the stretch that our simplicity-obsessed age does not really want to know. The modern show will only be a complete triumph if it takes up the challenge of the middle years.

It's in the nature of a retrospective of the work of a great master that we arrive with many, many questions. A gathering of hundreds of works by Matisse cannot fail to hold our attention, but what makes such a show memorable (beyond the ability of the sponsoring institution to secure important loans) is the intuition of the curator – his ability to ask the questions that are on the audience's mind. The great retrospectives are shaped but not dogmatic; they give a form to a life in art, but they leave that form open enough for museum-goers to draw their own conclusions. William Rubin, who organized the Picasso retrospective, was a genius when it came to putting together a shaped but non-dogmatic picture of a great career. I hope – fervently – that John Elderfield has learned from Rubin's example.

At a time when the very concept of the blockbuster show is now under attack, one will nevertheless find very few people (or maybe none at all) who question why we need this much Matisse in one place at one time. While I am no lover of the blockbuster mentality, I think it makes a kind of sense in the case of Matisse or Picasso that it simply does not make in the case of many earlier masters. There is much more reason for our

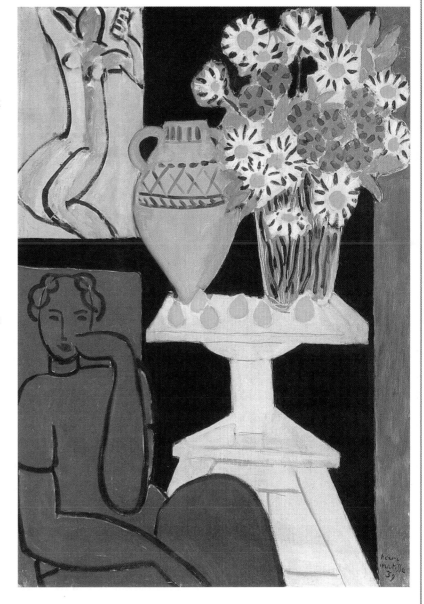

Daisies, 1939, oil on canvas, 39 x 28 in/98 x 72 cm. *Art Institute of Chicago.*

wanting to see all of Matisse than for our wanting to see, say all of Ingres or all of Breughel. The desire to see all of Matisse is somehow connected to our sense that he is, despite the 40 years that separate us from his death, still a part of our recent past. We're exploring our own attic.

If Picasso is our exhibitionist father-figure, Matisse is our withdrawn father-figure. The Picasso retrospective of 1980, with its carnival atmosphere, was perfectly tuned to the artist who was not above occasionally playing the clown or the buffoon. Now the Museum of Modern Art is giving the full treatment to the other father, the one who never quite wanted us to know his secrets. It is a far more difficult show to bring off, but if any institution is up to it, it must be the Museum of Modern Art. The museum that now proposes to tell us everything that we ever wanted to know about Matisse is, after all, the museum that, so far as many are concerned, taught us to love him in the first place. Here in New York we're getting ready for some primal experiences. That's a tall order, but we won't be satisfied with anything less. For the next couple of months we're planning to live inside Matisse's brain.

Marcel Duchamp

by David Sylvester

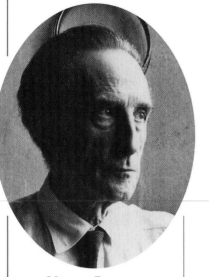

MARCEL DUCHAMP
After displaying his sensation-causing painting Nude Descending a Staircase *in 1912, Duchamp became both celebrated and reviled.*

Born in Normandy in 1887, into a family of artists, he experimented with Postimpressionism, Fauvism, and Cubism, before ultimately rejecting adherence to one particular style although he maintained a long-term connection with Parisian Surrealists.

After the uproar caused by the descending nude, Duchamp painted rarely, concentrating instead on assemblages. His most complex piece is the 1915 construction The Bride Stripped Bare by Her Bachelors *with its reference to sexuality, the occult, and to the artist's own life. The works* Bicycle Wheel *and* Pharmacy *were the beginning of so-called "ready-made" art, a concept whose importance was recognized decades later.*

When the Nazis occupied France, Duchamp emigrated to the US. The Museum of Modern Art exhibited The Large Glass, *and his art, always popular among the avant-garde, became celebrated by mainstream critics.*

Rrose Sélavy, *ca.1920-21, (Duchamp's alter ego), Photograph by Man Ray, 6 x 4 in/14 x 10 cm. Jederman Collection.*

PICASSO SAID THAT HE HOPED THE SCULPTURE OF A BULL'S HEAD which he made from parts of a bicycle might some day be found somewhere by a cyclist who would turn it back into a saddle and handlebars and that subsequently the reinstated bicycle would be transformed into a sculpture again and then into a bicycle again and so on, back and forth, for an eternity. That remark would mean little if sculptors using found parts almost invariably wanted us to remember that a piece of theirs was both, say, a bull's head and parts of a bicycle, but David Smith's avowal of unconcern that the spectator should be able to see from the finished sculpture where the parts had come from shows that there have been leading exponents of the found part for whom the parts, once transformed into art, are simply art.

Picasso's desire that we do recognize the source of the fragments of reality which he absorbed and transformed suggests that he would have felt the same about the existing art which he absorbed and transformed – that we should be conscious of the prototype

"DADA WAS AN EXTREME PROTEST AGAINST THE PHYSICAL SIDE OF PAINTING."

and thus of the extravagance of the adaptation. It is like a composer writing a set of variations on an existing tune: if we don't identify the original, part of the meaning is lost. Nothing was more central to Picasso's art than his obsession with metamorphosis, and the efficacy of a metamorphosis depends absolutely on our knowing what the thing was before it was changed. If we saw Cinderella's coach and six horses and did not realize that they had been a pumpkin and six mice, it would not be the same coach and horses. It is essential to the sense of the story that the meanest things from the kitchen have been turned into grandiose things: if the fairy godmother had turned, say, a Louis Quinze chair and six salukis into a coach and horses, the transformation would be less impressive. And Picasso went further than the fairy godmother. She made her horses out of mice, living beings out of living beings. Picasso wanted to make horses out of pumpkins when he said that it ought to be possible to take a bit of wood and suddenly it's a bird (*"on doit pouvoir prendre un bout de bois et que ce soit un oiseau"*). It is not just a question of making what is low and rejected into art; it is also a question of bringing dead matter to life.

Picasso's transformation of junk into human and animal images entered his work around 1930. In his early assemblages from junk of the period 1912–16, he didn't attempt to turn pumpkins into horses, only into coaches. He used the bits of wood and cardboard and string to make a representation of something which was also made of wood and string – a violin or a guitar. It is true that most of those constructions can also be read as masklike images of human heads, as can his modeled sculpture of the same period, *The Absinthe Glass*. Nevertheless, the suggestion of a human image – a suggestion which, after all, frequently occurs in his still lifes of that time on the flat – is secondary.

The essential and persistent aim when Picasso put junk together was to manipulate the material so as to bring it onto the plane of art.

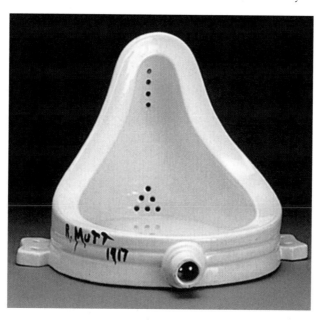

When Picasso started doing this in 1912, in collages as well as in constructions, it was one of the great moves in the modern artist's cult of poverty. Throughout the second half of the nineteenth century artists had been concerned to reject the traditional hierarchies of art, such as the idea that noble subjects were better than vulgar subjects. Then, at the turn of the century, there was a rejection of the idea that classical prototypes were superior to all other prototypes; exotic curiosities made by naked savages and collected in museums whose purpose was initially anthropological could now be accepted as art. But, whatever hierarchies had been rejected by 1912 as to subject matter and as to style, the idea still persisted that the art object itself was to be made of special materials produced specifically for the purpose of making art. Collage argued against this that art could be made out of the stuff of everyday life. When Cubism turned to collage – and, of course, any synthetic Cubist work, even when entirely painted, is conceptually a collage – it was turning away from refinement towards

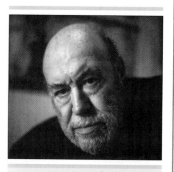

DAVID SYLVESTER
The influential British critic was born in London in 1924 and educated at University College in London. He went on to become a noted organizer of international contemporary art exhibitions.

In 1951, he curated exhibitions of sculpture by Henry Moore and drawings by Alberto Giacometti at the Tate Gallery, and he organized exhibitions including the work of René Magritte, Robert Morris, and Joan Miró.

After his first visit to New York in 1960, Sylvester's enthusiasm for American artists, including Jasper Johns, Willem de Kooning, Barnett Newman, and Mark Rothko resulted in a series on BBC radio supporting the New York School.

Sylvester's many books include The Brutality of Fact: Interviews with Francis Bacon. *He organized an exhibition of Bacon's work as Britain's contribution to the 1993 Venice Biennale, and was awarded the Biennale's Golden Lion Award – a first for a critic.*

Among his honors are Britain's Hawthornden Prize for art criticism, and, in France, the Commander in the Order of Arts and Letters. David Sylvester died in 2001.

Above: Fountain, *1917/1964, ready made, 14 x 19 x 24 in/36 x 48 x 61 cm. Private Collection.*

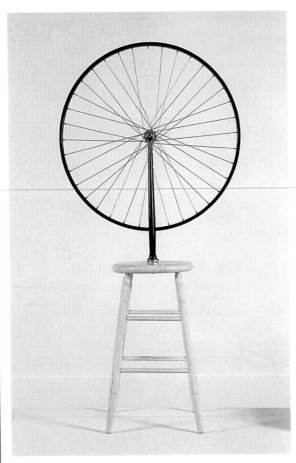

Bicycle Wheel, *1913/1964,*
ready made, height 50 in/126 cm.
Hessisches Landesmuseum,
Darmstad.

coarseness, away from the hermetic towards the common. Analytical Cubism had erected a delicate structure of transparent planes, one that became increasingly intricate, ethereal, arcane. And the language is a language the stuff of which is high art – an elaboration and systematization of Cézanne, a constant reminder of Cézanne's late style. But when the constituent parts of the structure become cut-out pieces of newspaper, cigarette packages, labels from bottles, and so forth, high refinement is replaced by the common touch, the solitary contemplation of the Montagne St. Victoire by sorties into Paris streets. The cut-out pieces of newspaper may represent a newspaper or they may be used to represent anything but a newspaper: all this is variable and uncertain. What is not uncertain is that the construction is being made out of something in daily use by ordinary people.

At the same time, whereas analytical Cubism imposes a homogeneity upon everything in the picture, a homogeneity something like that imposed by the brushmarks of, say, Seurat's sketches, collage often uses the strongest possible contrast between the pictorial elements, and this reinforces the idea of abruptness and plain-speaking as against the use of an even, measured tone of voice. Again, in place of analytical Cubism's exquisite splintering of reality, the fragments are now larger, broader, flat, frontal, bold, forthright. In every way the language is plainer. At the same time, the distinction between the two languages is very much more emphatic with Picasso than it is with Braque.

> ## "AND LATER, FOLLOWING THIS VIEW, I CAME TO FEEL AN ARTIST MIGHT USE ANYTHING — A DOT, A LINE, THE MOST CONVENTIONAL OR UNCONVENTIONAL SYMBOL — TO SAY WHAT HE WANTED TO SAY."

> "AND WHAT HOLDS TRUE FOR DUCHAMP'S WORK APPLIES AS WELL TO MOST OF THE ART AFTER HIM."
> —*Joseph Kosuth*

Picasso's synthetic Cubism began as a way out of late analytical Cubism, so-called hermetic Cubism, and it went on looking like a reaction against it; whereas Braque, in adopting synthetic Cubism, somehow made a much smoother transition to it, and his work in that manner preserved quite a lot of the rarefied atmosphere of late analytical Cubism. With Picasso, however, the change from analytical to synthetic was a resounding conversation from a mandarin language to a demotic language. Which does not mean that the works employing that demotic language did not turn out to be even more difficult and obscure than the works which are called hermetic.

The time when Picasso was making his first junk sculptures was also the time when Duchamp made his first sculpture from ready-made materials. It was a bicycle wheel placed upside down on a stool. Now, the two objects assembled here are the most basic objects in man's winning dominion over the earth and in distinguishing himself from the beasts of the field: the stool, which enables him to sit down off the ground at a height and a location of his choice; the wheel, which enables him to move himself and his objects around. The stool and the wheel are the origins of civilization, and Duchamp rendered them both useless. Picasso took junk and turned it into useful objects such as musical instruments; Duchamp took a useful stool and a useful wheel and made them useless. His stool is useless because there is no room to sit on it; his wheel is useless because, although it is still free to turn, it doesn't turn in contact with anything, and of course a wheel is only useful so long as it is in contact with the ground or some further mechanical component. But the dissociation from their normal context which makes the stool and the wheel useless also makes them more visible. One can't look at a stool while one is sitting on it, but if one can't sit on it, one can look at it. Moreover, the wheel raised on the stool can be seen far better than when it's on the ground: the beauty of the movement of the spokes is more visible near eye level, and that level is also an invitation to our fingers to put the wheel in motion. Also, it is made more important, like a statute mounted on a plinth. Duchamp renders the bicycle wheel and the stool useless, but neither more nor less useless than art is. He turns them into things that are there only to be looked at. Where Picasso seems to be saying that bicycle parts can become sculpture through the force of his personal magic, Duchamp seems to be saying that bicycle parts can become sculpture simply by being treated as sculpture.

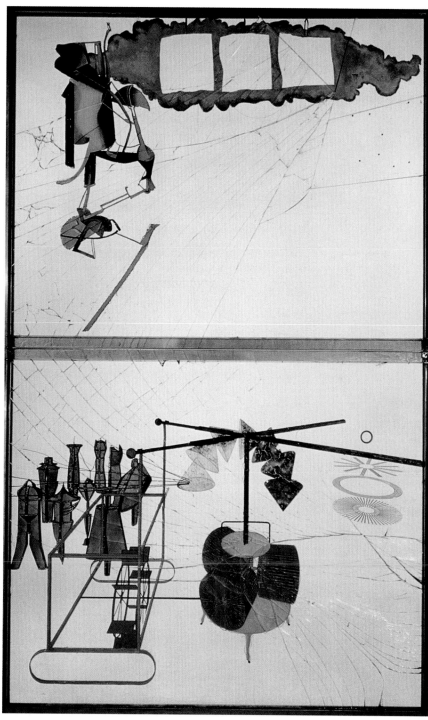

Bride Stripped Bare by Her Batchelors, Even, 1915–23, oil, varnish, lead foil, lead wire, and dust on two glass panels (cracked) each mounted between two glass panels and five glass strips, aluminum foil, and a wood and steel frame,
109 x 69 in/277 x 176 cm.
Philadelphia Museum of Art

The bicycle-wheel sculpture was an allegorical antithesis to Duchamp's morality as an artist (or simply his inclination as an artist): whereas the wheel went round and round, Duchamp, in noble contrast to practically every other professional artist in history, preferred inaction to repetition. At the same time, the piece involved an early instance of a gambit of his which was utterly typical – the separation of entities that are normally connected. The bicycle wheel is separated from the ground; in *The Bride Stripped Bare by Her Bachelors, Even*, the bachelors are separated from the bride. As Robert Lebel puts it, the male and female machines function separately and without any point of contact, man and woman act upon each other from a distance and on separate planes – onanism for two. That is to say, to act upon each other the bride and her bachelors act upon themselves. ("The bachelor," as Duchamp phrased it, "grinds his own chocolate.")

The composition is reminiscent of Titian's *Assumption of the Virgin*, where the Virgin on a nimbus above is clearly separated from the groping bachelor disciples. The separation can be seen as a paradigm of Duchamp's relationship with his public. He was the bride and we the bachelors from whom he kept his distance. Like the bride, Duchamp was never stripped bare. His audience were left like the masturbating bachelors, looking up at him and fantasizing about what he was up to but never coming to grips with him. He liked to observe that audience and how it reached, and he paid courteous attention to the interpretations it made.

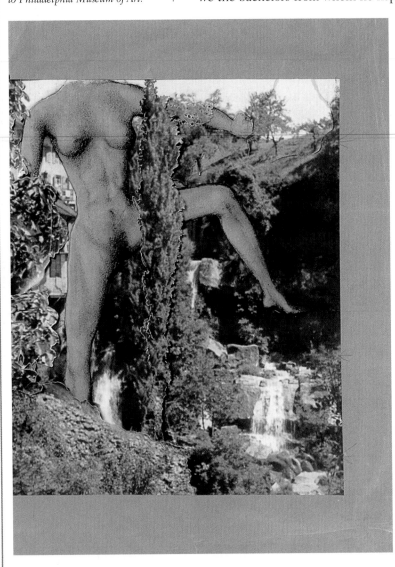

Etant Donnés; First – The Waterfall, Second – Gaslight, *1947, Private Collection, on loan to Philadelphia Museum of Art.*

Said the masochist to the sadist: "Hurt me!" Said the sadist to the masochist: "No." When Diaghilev said: *"Etonne-moi, Jean!"* Cocteau tried to oblige, but when the art world expected Duchamp to astonish it yet again, Duchamp said No. When we had been talking earnestly for nearly half a century about the implications of his having said No, he surprised us from beyond the grave, with the revelation that he had worked secretly from 1946 to 1966 on a piece as major as *The Large Glass: Etant Donnés; First – The Waterfall, Second – Gaslight*. It is a structure in which an antique wooden door has a pair of peepholes through which we are able to look at a *tableau vivant* realized with remarkable illusionism in a variety of media. What we see through the peepholes is a dilapidated wall with a very large hole in it revealing a landscape in the foreground of which a naked nubile girl is lying on a prickly bed of dead twigs and leaves, her legs spreadeagled, her outstretched hand holding up a lighted gas lamp. She, unlike the Bride, really is stripped bare, stripped to the skin, even on her prominent pubic mound – and the depilation is not that of academic statuary; it serves to provide and uninterrupted view of the display offered by the spreadeagling of the legs. The head, in contrast, is virtually concealed, through being excluded from the limited view we get of the scene. This *gesamkunstwerk* includes sound – the murmur of a distant fountain which apparently issues from a waterfall gushing and shimmering in the sylvan landscape beyond.

As *The Large Glass* is Duchamp's most complex and ambitious painting, *Etant Donnés* is his most complex and ambitious piece of assemblage. Halfway through the span of its long, secret realization, Picasso quickly put together his own most complex and ambitious piece of assemblage: *Les Baigneurs*, made in Cannes in the summer of 1956 almost entirely out of bits of wood. Now, *Les Baigneurs* belongs stylistically with a quantity of emphatically frontal wooden constructions looking like ethnographic art which the artist

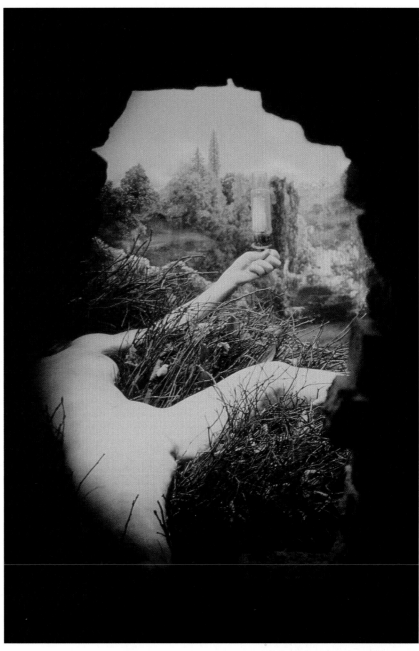

Etant Donnés; First – The Waterfall, Second – Gaslight, *detail, interior, 1946–66, twigs, pigskin, candle, and paint. Philadelphia Museum of Art.*

had been making for 40 years; it differs from its predecessors only in being far more expansive, with its six over-life-size figures spread across the scene, making large rhetorical gestures and broadly demonstrating principles of construction by presenting sizeable rectangular empty frames (redolent of the studio) among the irregular bits of driftwood (redolent of the beach): it's like many other Picasso assemblages except that it's on a much grander scale. *Etant Donnés*, on the other hand, is different in every conceivable way from the bicycle wheel and those other objects put in a place we walk about in: it is an elaborate piece of staging, it is unique, it is immovable, it occupies a place apart and beyond our reach, it can be seen by only one of us at a time.

What completes the analogy with *The Large Glass* is that *Etant Donnés* too evokes a major masterpiece of the Italian Renaissance. The painting has its affinity with Titian's painting of *The Assumption*; the assemblage has an affinity with sculpture – two separate similar sculptures – by Bernini. Duchamp's presentation of a reclining female figure in a place apart in which she seems to be undergoing, or to have just undergone, some searing crisis calls to mind Bernini's sculptures of St. Teresa and the Blessed Lodovica Albertoni, where a woman in a state of ecstasy is shown in a setting within a complicated marble frame. The latter work has the greater resemblance to *Etant Donnés* in that the figure is alone, the former in that it includes an element analogous to the flaming gas lamp held aloft – the flaming golden arrow held aloft by an angel. Now, these scenes of Bernini's are designed to be seen from one particular point of view: as Wittkower says of them, "the carefully contrived framing devices almost force upon the spectator the correct viewing position." And this is precisely, but without the "almost," the effect of Duchamp's peepholes. Duchamp's primary motive for having the peepholes, he told his wife, was to ensure that the work should have only one spectator at a time: he hated the thought of a work of art being viewed simultaneously by a mass of people, felt it degraded the experience of looking at it (felt this especially at the time the Metropolitan was showing the *Mona Lisa* – the very icon which he had virtually made his own). But an undeniable result of that strategy is the imposition, as with Bernini, of a viewpoint determined by the artist.

Wittkower sees Bernini's need to do this as a consequence of his insistence on

From or By Marcel Duchamp or Rrose Sélavy or The Box in a Valise, 1943, *leather and mixed media (containing hand-colored collotype of Vierge, 1938), 15 x 14 x 3 in/18 x 36 x 8 cm. (closed). Philadelphia Museum of Art, Louise and Walter Arensberg Collection.*

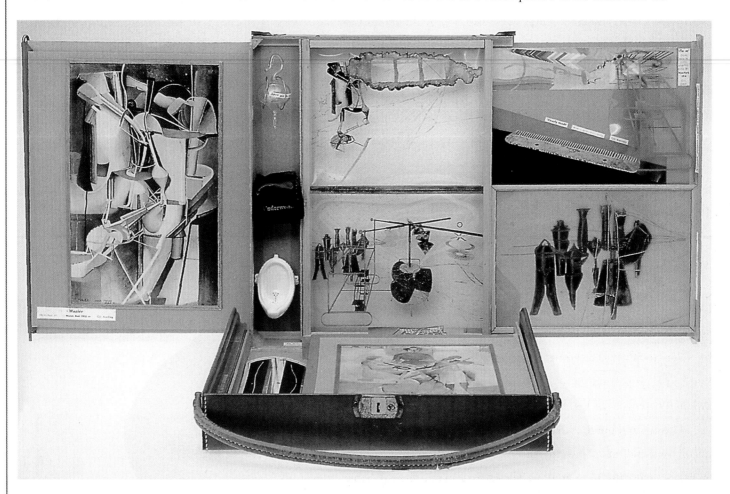

depicting moments of dramatic climax. And in *Etant-Donnés,* too, there is a sense of high drama, but with the difference that Duchamp, while revealing the secrets of his protagonist's body, declines to reveal what is happening or has happened to it. Bernini was giving enduring form to events in the lives of popular heroines which were totally known to his audience. They knew that these women in a state of utter abandon were feeling, as one of them wrote, a pain that made her scream loud but with it such infinite sweetness that she wished the pain to last eternally as the angel thrust the flaming arrow into her body again and again. But in *Etant Donnés* the story has to be guessed at. For example, has the figure herself been using the gas lamp in a fashion analogous to the angel's use of the flaming arrow? Duchamp withholds information mainly by his concealment of the

"I THOUGHT TO DISCOURAGE AESTHETICS . . . I THREW THE BOTTLERACK AND THE URINAL IN THEIR FACES AND NOW THEY ADMIRE THEM FOR THEIR AESTHETIC BEAUTY."

protagonist's face, and compounds our frustration by the tantalizing way in which that concealment is achieved. It suggests that there is surely a face there, behind the wall; it suggests the possibility of our getting a view of that face through altering our angle of vision so as to see around the corner; it denies that possibility by allowing the scene to be visible only through the peepholes (a reminder of the maddening boyhood experience of looking through the keyhole trying in vain to see one's sister or the maid undressed).

Since the onset of the romantic movement, artists have made a demand for total freedom. In our time freedom has come to be demanded of the artist by his public. The artist's position has become that of someone to whom we say: "Stand up over there and make a five-minute speech about anything you like and if I'm amused I'll give you a present." This approach, at once over-indulgent and uninvolved, has been an encouragement to the artist to develop an attitude of not taking responsibility for how he is read. It was an attitude totally repugnant to Picasso, who is quoted by Françoise Gilot as saying to Matisse while looking at some Pollock reproductions that it was all very well for Valéry to affirm that he wrote half the poem while the reader wrote the other half, but that he for his part did not want there to be three or four or a thousand possibilities of interpreting a work of his; he wanted there to be one.

Given the modern artist's freedom, Picasso gloried in the possibilities it opened for unconfined and unambiguous self-revelation; Duchamp handed on the freedom to the audience, and with it uncertainty. The Dionysian and the Apollonian.

"DUCHAMPIAN IRONY SANCTIFIED KITSCH AS A LEGITIMATE — PERHAPS THE ONLY LEGITIMATE — VEHICLE FOR ART, AND NOW THE POLITICAL ART-WORKERS ARE EXPLOITING KITSCH AS A PROPAGANDA MEDIUM. THIS, ABOVE ALL, IS WHAT MAKES DUCHAMP A PATRON SAINT OF THE POLITICAL ART MOVEMENT."

—*Hilton Kramer*

Stuart Davis

by Jamie McKendrick

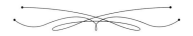

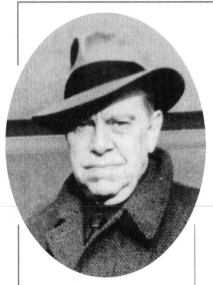

STUART DAVIS
Born in Philadelphia in 1894, Davis's artistic parents encouraged his interest in art. He began studying with Robert Henri, leader of the "Ash Can School," and exhibited five watercolors in this realist style in the 1913 Armory Show. Impressed by the avant-garde work of the show with its stylized form, objective order, and use of color, Davis radically changed his work.

After his first show in New York in 1917, he turned to synthetic cubism and to the geometric visual language of Mondrian. During the 1920s he moved toward minimal pictorial elements with boldly outlined objects. In the "Eggbeater" series, he focused on a less abstract approach and an increased clarity of form and color.

During the depression of the1930s, Davis painted murals for the WPA and edited for Art Front *magazine. Becoming politically active, he followed the communist line until the 1940s when he turned his enthusiasm to jazz. His work of this period is explosive with color and rhythm. For the next twenty years before his death in 1964, he incorporated jazz into lyrical paintings.*

Owh! In San Pao,
*1951, oil on canvas,
52 x 42 in/133 x 106 cm.
Whitney Museum of American Art,
New York.*

Taking a jab at Abstract Expressionism, Stuart Davis wrote of his 1951 painting *Owh! In San Pao*: "It has been scientifically established that the acoustics of Idealism give off the Human Sounds of Snoring, whereas Reality always says 'Ouch.'" The Owh and Ouch of his brash, abrasive colors, and of the jarring, strewn-about elements of his geometry have kept the sound of snoring safely at bay throughout his long career as a painter.

Davis not only overlapped themes, structures, and words in paintings which were made concurrently ("diads"), but also to a dramatic degree reworked images from his own art, sometimes over a period of decades. His basic egalitarian ethos regarding subject matter legitimized the use of commercial wrappers, labels, billboards, household utensils, storefronts, and, by extension, the recycling of the forms within his own paintings, as can be seen, for example, in the semi-abstracted *Percolator* of 1927, which reappears structurally unchanged though jazzily heightened in color and with the addition of words in *Owh! In San Pao* 24 years later. The premise that essentially nothing is unacceptable as material for the painting

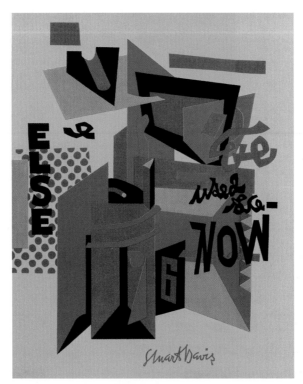

so long as it comes from the surrounding environment, obviously also includes his own paintings which have entered that environment. It was also Davis' nature to be reflective about his work as well as self-reflexive, and reabsorbing the structures of his own painting was a natural opportunity to explore and extend the frontiers of his art.

There are certainly lulls and dissatisfactions to be met with. The series of canvases, for example, set in Paris during the late '20s have a thin, decorative, Dufy-like quality, as though the creative air of the artistic capital had reached him pre-digested in the manner of London tap water. Léger, on an exchange of studio visits, found them "too realistic," but to Davis' delight commended his earlier, crucial "Egg Beater" series, abstracts grounded in the everyday, whose geometry has assumed a life of its own. It's odd that self-confessed exile in the "American Art Desert" should so deeply need the urban air of America to fire his imagination. Karen Wilkin begins her perceptive catalog essay with the claim that Davis is a "homegrown Cubist whose irreverent paints resemble no one else's." His early works do markedly resemble the paintings he saw at the Armory Show in 1913, displaying an initial predilection for Expressionism – van Gogh, even Munch – then proceed, as though in an accelerated

> ## "I DON'T WANT PEOPLE TO COPY MATISSE OR PICASSO, ALTHOUGH IT IS ENTIRELY PROPER TO ADMIT THEIR INFLUENCE. I DON'T MAKE PAINTINGS LIKE THEIRS. I MAKE PAINTINGS LIKE MINE."

learning curve through Cubism to Léger's tubular forms and Matisse's cut-outs. And yet by 1921, he was already producing work which was undeniably his own.

The so-called "Tobacco Still Lifes" of that year, including his famous canvas *Lucky Strike*, live up entirely to the latter title, representing one of the most fortuitous moments in his career, where he chances on a manner and subject way in advance of his own artistic certainties, as subsequent movements in his work expose his retreat from this radical and innovatory series which, with its emblazoning of brand names, predates Warhol's *Campbell Soup Cans* by some 40 years. Throughout his life as an artist and heavy smoker, tobacco brand names, cigarette packets, cigar adverts, etc. have a talismanic presence in his work, but never more centrally than in this 1921 series. Frontally addressed, these oil paintings on canvas give the impression of collages, though on an exaggerated scale. The strong color contrasts of *Lucky Strike*, the complementary red and green stripes broken by waves and circles to which the lettering conforms, have a dense rhythmic unity, and yet we simultaneously recognize the flattened packet become strangely and serendipitously monumental.

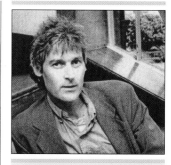

JAMIE McKENDRICK
Born in Liverpool, the poet/editor McKendrick has had a nomadic teaching career, including four years in Italy.

He writes poems that are sensitive questions of cause and effect on the nature of things. Recently published, Sky Nails Poems 1979-1997 is a selection from his three published books of poetry, The Sirocco Room, The Kiosk on the Brink, and The Marble Fly. "The marble fly" refers to an image on a Pompeian wall-relief that, to McKendrick, fuses the classical and natural worlds. His intricate poems involve both the natural and unnatural, the personal and impersonal. He uses references to transportation, such as Darwins' Voyage of the Beagle, the first airplane, and spiders sent into space on Skylab, to relate metaphorically with the natural world.

Lucky Strike, *1921, oil on canvas, 33 x 18 in/85 x 46 cm. Museum of Modern Art, New York.*

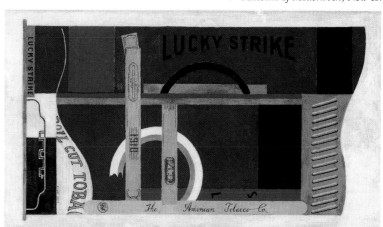

In the year following this series, Davis doubles back as if unsure of the underlying premises of his own lucky strike, and produces crude apprentice work in the manner of Synthetic Cubism, some ill-carpentered versions of Braque's *Guéridons*. It seems as though he was as yet unsure that he could give himself the go-ahead without securing the pictorial lessons of

"I PAINT WHAT I SEE IN AMERICA, IN OTHER WORDS I PAINT THE AMERICAN SCENE."

the European masters. And yet these experiments lead to the bold, black-outlined, bright-colored still lifes of 1923 and 1924, of utensils and light bulbs which look remarkably like Patrick Caulfield's canvases of the 1960s. These mundane household objects culminate in a

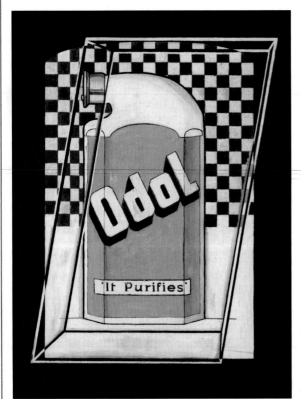

Odol, *1924, oil on canvas, 24 x 18 in/61 x 46 cm. Crispo Collection.*

repellent masterpiece, *Odol*, which depicts a product for oral hygiene ("It Purifies"), perhaps the remedy to a smoking habit and the Tobacco series. Framed by black and purple, the Odol flask with its squatly sloping top and nozzle is a mass-produced odalisque transposed from the Turkish bath to an all-American bathroom – or so we guess from the neat background of checkered white and green tiles and a slanted cube of lines (white against purple, black against white) which represents either a medicine cabinet or the beveled edges of a bathroom mirror. Never again would Davis be quite so uninhibitedly full-frontal in his approach to the picture-plane nor so joyfully vulgar in his color scheme.

This, like many other Davis paintings which feature labels and brand logotypes, raises the obvious but still perplexing question of what exactly the artist's relation was to the machine-age products his art is celebrating. Almost 40 years on, Davis took little pleasure in being seen as a precursor for Pop Art's deadpan reproductions of the industrially produced, insisting that his procedure and aims were entirely different. Is there in Davis a provocation which conflates high art and commercial design or is he asserting a belief that any subject is equally interesting (or for that matter equally boring) from an artist's standpoint? As a painter steeped in Marxist theory, and committed as an activist during the Depression, Davis undoubtedly felt these were questions that mattered:

An art of real order in the material of paint doesn't say "Workers of the World Unite." It doesn't say "Pasteur's theory has many beneficial results for the human race," and it doesn't say "Buy Camel cigarettes." It merely says "Look, here is a unique configuration in color-space."

Davis' *Visa* (1951) perhaps pushes his interest in brand names and his lifelong obsession with lettering to the extremest point. It reworks a canvas of the previous year called *Little Giant Still Life* which consists almost entirely of the word CHAMPION taken from a matchbook (smoking again) which advertises spark plugs. (There may be a buried allusion here to Picabia's *Jeune Fille Américaine* as spark plug, just as in the "Eggbeater" series there is a possible reference to Man Ray's *L'Homme* (1919) figured as an eggbeater). Why is Davis, who doesn't want to sell Camels, content to reproduce the lettering which the graphic designer has used to sell Champion Little Giant spark plugs? Davis claims that he used words "because they were part of urban subject matter… the design of this matchbook was singularly uninteresting and it was the

"FOR A NUMBER OF YEARS JAZZ HAD A TREMENDOUS INFLUENCE ON MY THOUGHTS ABOUT ART AND LIFE."

challenge of the lack of interest… rather than the direct stimulus of a subject" that spurred him. The catalog entry for *Visa* shrewdly speculates that Davis was aware of art (his own included) as a passport and commodity that crosses frontiers – *Visa* itself was intended for the São Paulo Bienal, and the next year Davis would represent America in the Venice Biennale. There's a smug glint to the painting in this respect, though clearly it also alludes to the American product destined for a global market. Does this mark a moment of self-doubt as well as self-satisfaction? What makes the artist so different from the graphic designer whose original (and boring) logotype he is content to exploit for his own not uncommercial ends? And how, given the above, is the artwork distinct from the commodity whose advertisement the artist appropriates when both pass into the international market place? The painting fabricates a teasing visual conundrum, with the self-referential phrase "The Amazing Contin-uity" (note the discontinuous hyphen) added to the right border in Davis' unique ribbony or crêpey script perhaps referring to the way his work is recycling with admirable parsimony the earlier canvas; but equally it draws attention

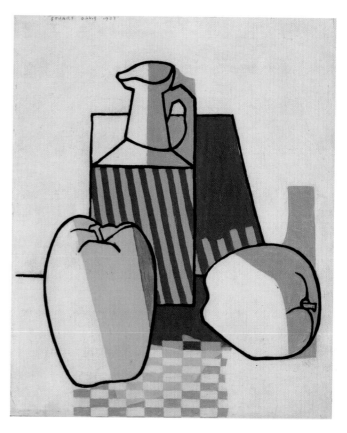

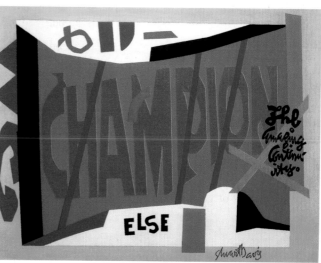

Top: Apples and Jug, *1923, oil on composition board, 21 x 18 in/54 x 45 cm. Museum of Fine Arts, Boston.*
Above: Visa, *1951, oil on canvas, 40 x 52 in/102 x 132 cm. Museum of Modern Art, New York.*

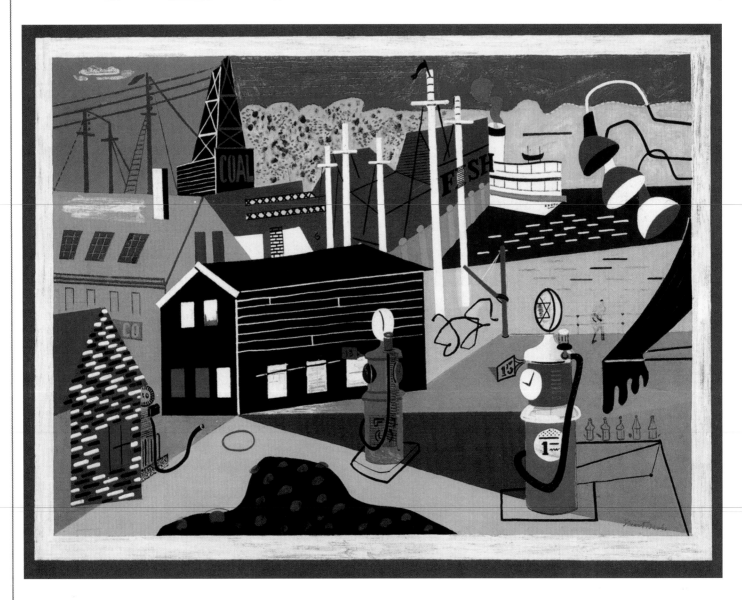

Landscape with Garage Lights,
1932, oil on canvas,
32 x 42 in/81 x 106 cm.
Memorial Art Gallery of the
University of Rochester, New York.

to the problematic continuity between the industrial product's advertising design and the artwork itself. Despite the knowing verve of this work, and of others from the '50s, there seems something schematic and over-determined about it, which makes me prefer the period through the '30s when, despite the demands of his political activism, he painted his great American cityscapes.

If the Parisian cityscapes are disappointing, they nevertheless helped Davis develop a pictorial language (and in his case the word is only partly metaphoric, since script – including the ever more conspicuous motif of his signature – continues to operate in his paintings as a key compositional effect) which was responsible for some of his finest paintings. *Landscape with Garage Lights* manages to make an intriguingly dissonantal harmony out of the maritime jumble of Gloucester, Massachusetts' industrial waterfront. Its childlike inclusiveness is astonishing – a fish-processing plant, a coal tower, factories and warehouses, boat, telegraph poles, petrol (gas) pumps with curly proboscuses and a café awning on the far right like a limp hand reaching for a row of bottles underneath. There's even (unusually for Davis) a faintly scumbled human figure at the railings looking out seawards. The large, flat, bright areas of color, broken up by angular sections of black and by parallel lines, curves, and crosses, delight in their angles and contingencies and toy with the actual, find a composite equivalent for it, rather than feeling obliged to *describe* it. The CO. of one sign echoes the COAL of another. The word FISH has a fishbone I, perhaps because it's occluded by a mast, while the last upright of the H seems to have slithered out beyond the wall it adorns as though leaping back into the black sea underneath. Although the exhibition is exclusively of paintings, it would have been interesting to see some of Davis' lithographs from this period, a

> "AN ARTIST WHO HAS TRAVELED ON A STEAM TRAIN, DRIVEN AN AUTOMOBILE, OR FLOWN IN AN AIRPLANE DOESN'T FEEL THE SAME WAY ABOUT FORM AND SPACE AS ONE WHO HAS NOT."

medium which must have assisted him greatly in this new and bolder use of black. The arrival of Abstract Expressionism would displace Davis somewhat from the vanguard of American painting. Although he found the Abstract Expressionists too introspective, nevertheless that period saw his own increasing commitment to abstraction. But it was during the '30s, when the plethora of urban life impelled him towards an abstraction which he both enjoyed and resisted, that he achieved some of his finest work. Perhaps most successful of all is *New York under Gaslight* (1941), which is like a summa of this stage of his career, putting together all his favorite urban elements in a gaudy stage set; though the colors are garish under a whitened chrome green sky, we understand that it is night time by the black hulk of one pier of Brooklyn Bridge in the background and by the white illumination from windows and shop-fronts, which compete for attention with their signs and (mainly smoking) advertisements. The lettering is as playful and varied as ever, the M in ROOM curtailed as if there wasn't enough room, the D in DENTI[ST] itself dented or chipped like a tooth. Its mood is valedictory, as if Davis sensed he was about to move on to the bold abstract variations of his final two decades. And yet the improvisatory, jazzlike quality of this painting, and the extraordinary classical intelligence that shapes an order from inner city clutter and from clashing non-representational color, is what makes Davis one of the finest twentieth-century painters of urban experience.

> "DAVIS BECAME THE MASTER OF THE BRIGHT, MULTICOLORED PICTURE...HE GAVE COLOR A MARVELOUS FREEDOM. THAT IS WHAT (DONALD) JUDD LIKED SO MUCH ABOUT DAVIS AND THAT IS WHY HE CONSIDERED HIM A GREAT PAINTER. I ENTIRELY AGREE."
>
> —*Rudi Fuchs*

New York under Gaslight, *1941, oil on canvas, 32 x 45 in/81 x 114 cm. Israel Museum, Jerusalem.*

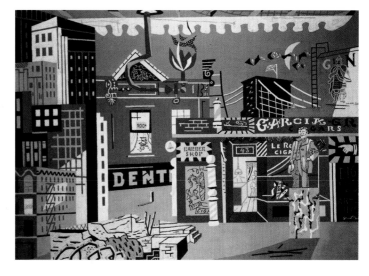

Salvador Dali

by Sister Wendy Beckett

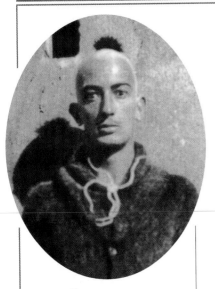

SALVADOR DALI
*The world's most famous
Surrealist painter, Salvador
Dali, was born in Spain in
1904. He attended the
Academy of Fine Arts in
Madrid where he formed
influential friendships with
the poet Federico Lorca and
the filmmaker Luis Buñuel.
Experimenting with various
Modernist styles in the 1920s,
became involved with
anarchist politics and the
Surrealist avant-garde, and he
discovered the work of Freud
which initiated him into the
world of the subconscious.
He then collaborated with
Buñuel on two Surrealistic
films – Un Chien Andalou
and L'age D'or.*

*In the '30s, Dali produced
paintings of deformed or
metamorphosed commonplace
objects placed within
landscapes reminiscent of his
Catalonian homeland. The
image of the melting watches
appearing in the painting
The Persistence of Memory
(1931) is the best known of
all Surrealism.*

*Dali's gradual indifference to
politics and his flamboyant
self-promotion led to a break
with the Surrealists. He went
to the US where he cultivated
his eccentric image.*

*From 1950 to 1970, Dali's
paintings focused on religious
themes. In the final years of
his life, he returned to Spain
where he died in 1989.*

PREJUDICE IS ALWAYS DANGEROUS. Equally dangerous are principles firmly asserted but in practice denied. A basic principle of art criticism, here firmly asserted, is that the personality of the artist and the quality of the art have no essential connection. We may warm to the mental balance and moral decency of a Rubens or a Corot; we may feel alienated by the self-obsessed anxieties of van Gogh or Guido Reni; yet these reactions are purely personal to ourselves. They can have no bearing on how we view the work (although this is to speak ideally). Fortunate Giotto and Vermeer about whom so little is known, and whom we can therefore see with untrammeled eyes. Where we do know some so-called facts about an artist, it is often hidden from our conscious mind how subtly our objective judgement may be skewed by prejudice, either for or against.

In Salvador Dali's case it is against. We have to strain to see him through a dense fog of gossipy incident, nearly all of it initiated by Dali himself and highly productive to his

> "AT THE AGE OF SIX I WANTED
> TO BE A COOK. AT SEVEN I WANTED TO
> BE NAPOLEON. AND MY AMBITION HAS
> BEEN GROWING STEADILY EVER SINCE."

career in terms of publicity and financial success. Before we can look at his work, we have actively to seek to become disentangled. Dali seems to have been like a small child who needs desperately to be noticed. He sought out the shocking: if spitting upon his dead mother's image would attract attention, he was a prolific and boastful spitter. Again, like an anxious child, he reveled in bodily fluids and the more lurid consequences of death. He mocked friendship and fidelity and clearly regarded himself as above all rules. If Franco was abhorrent to the right-thinking, Dali espoused his cause; he praised Hitler for the same show-off reasons. His famous remark to the effect that the only difference between himself and a madman was that he was "not mad," that it was "willed paranoia," has a sadly hollow ring. Jung, in his adolescence (like Dali, child of an autocratic father), also played the mad game, though never to such bizarre lengths. In his autobiography he recalls hearing himself discussed by his parents, and suddenly realizing that the game was a highly perilous one: he was slowly slipping into real madness, since we become what we pretend to be. Jung snapped out of his fantasies, but never forgot how near he had come to sliding over the edge of sanity. Dali, less fortunate, disappeared into his game-playing, and it is impossible not to feel that he was insane in the clinical sense.

Artistically, this should not matter at all. Richard Dadd is an example of an artist who created from within the painful recesses of homicidal mania; there is a neat, tight intensity in his work (think of *The Fairy Feller's Master Stroke* in the Tate) that is oddly reminiscent of Dali and his "instantaneous and hand-done color photography." This phrase, not inaptly describing his style, was, of course, meant to exasperate, color photography being considered a very lowly form of life, only a notch or two below the Salon art of Meissonier, another model to whom Dali smirkingly proclaimed allegiance. But something profoundly fearful, something escapist and, in the most literal meaning, sick, drew both artists to protect themselves against reality by cunningly perfecting their technique. Yet Dadd is an interesting artist. His fantasies have a genuinely intriguing validity. The game he played, he played in earnest. Dali's, however, hovers on the edge of falsehood, or so it seems. It is obvious that he is a deeply disturbed man, and that these disturbances are visible in his painting.

The same is true of Van Gogh, but with what a difference! Van Gogh reaches past his unbalance, incorporating it into his vision. He is communicating through his panics

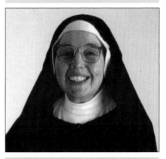

SISTER WENDY BECKETT
Born in South Africa in 1930, Beckett decided early to become a nun. Urged by her father to first get an education, she studied at Oxford, then went to teach in South Africa for 15 years. When her health became fragile, she returned to a Carmelite monastery in England, where she lives in a trailer and pursues a life of solitude.

In 1980, she began studying art reproductions on postcards and in books. Her down-to-earth observations were published in British journals, and in the mid-'80s she wrote her first book, Contemporary Women Artists. *Many titles have followed. Commenting on the pictures at an art exhibition, Beckett drew the attention of a BBC camera crew filming the feminist writer Germaine Greer. This lead to Beckett herself being filmed and, eventually, to a BBC program featuring her reflections on art.*

Despite the hugh success of her books and television programs, Beckett leads a disciplined and contemplative life. She wakes at 3 a.m., attends mass, and prays seven hours a day, allowing only two hours for her writing and studies. She writes prolifically about art, sometimes annoying the art establishment with her commentaries. Never shying from moralizing, in one program she stated, "You have a cold heart, Degas!"

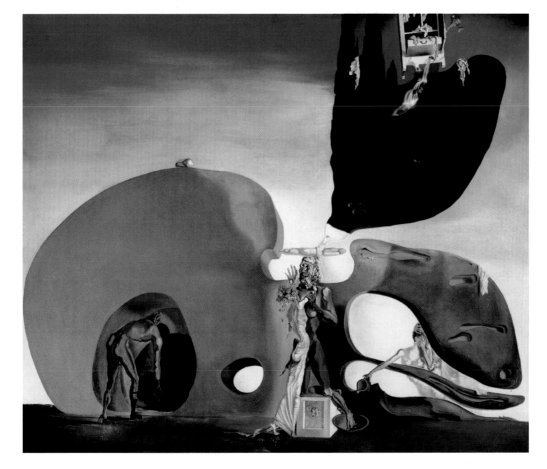

Birth of Liquid Desires, *1931–32, oil and collage on canvas, 38 x 44 in/96 x 112 cm. Guggenheim Collection, Venice.*

and delusions, passionately urging them into some sort of order. The brushstrokes leap and shudder, the shapes of tree, earth, and cloud swing with emotion, but the total effect is of a longing for integration that will not be denied. We are awed by van Gogh's courage, his persistence, his seriousness.

With Dali, there seems to be no fight at all. His delusions and fears are dear to him; he makes his art out of them, self-indulgently. It was not always so, and this is the great importance of the present exhibition. As he grew older, Dali slipped further and further into the self-pity and self-love of madness, and his art degenerated with him. The early work (a sinister parallel here with the far greater Miró) is incomparably his finest. Like Augustus John, Dali had all the gifts, but nothing to say with them.

An early work like the 1925 *Girl Standing at a Window* shows what might have been. Dali is barely twenty-one, as prodigious in his way as his compatriot Picasso. The girl has an objectivity, an attention to the world outside the artist's selfhood, that gives it unusual force. Dali had many problems with women, with his long-suffering sister (said to be the model here), with backsides, hair, illusions (there is something contrived about the scene outside the window and the cloth with its semi-transparency), but none of this is allowed to dominate. Rather, his secret difficulties are used to make the images functional, much as Picasso's tempestuous emotional relationships are invariably put to

"HE IS THE MODERN PAINTER BEST KNOWN TO THE GENERAL PUBLIC."

—*Jose Faerna*

Femme Couchée, *1926,*
oil on panel,
11 x 16 in/28 x 41 cm.
Salvador Dali Museum, St.
Petersburg, Florida.

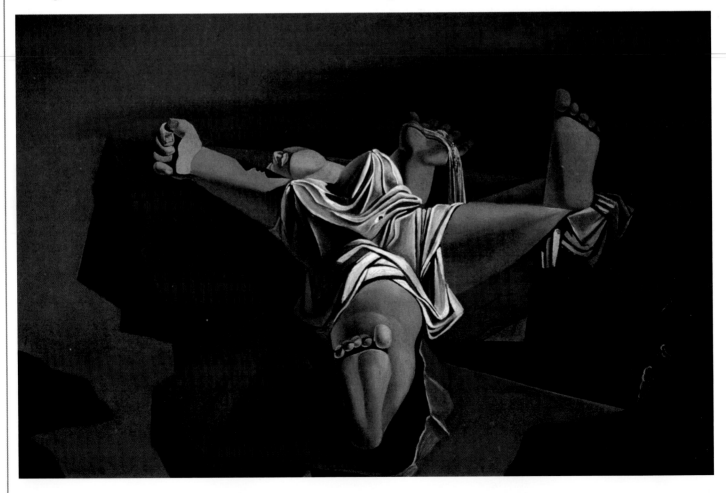

good artistic purpose. This exciting talent is even more evident in *Femme Couchée* of the following year. It makes one sigh for what Dali could have been. The image is not a likeable one: a young woman is spread-eagled on mountainous rocks, as if crucified. Her bulk and its sheer heft are reminiscent of the female giants through whose depictions Picasso distanced himself from what he considered a rapacious wife, yet the influence has been integrated. It is a very

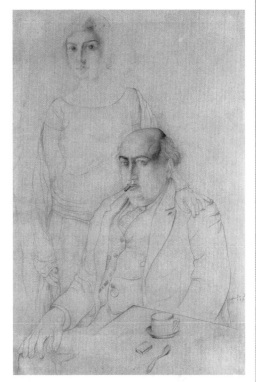

"Sometimes i spit on my mother's portrait for pleasure."

clever painting, the perspective as convincing as that of Mantegna's *Dead Christ*, to which it also vaguely alludes. (It seems to be impossible to write about Dali without art-historical references cropping up with annoying frequency). She is modestly concealed, in this strikingly unlike the images in which Dali later came to luxuriate. This girl is not meant to startle us, challenge our putative puritanism, or disgust us by her blatancy. She is merely there, splendidly lit by the steady light and ambivalent in her emotional condition. If one hand is clenched, the other is relaxed, and it is the great wedges of her feet, spotlessly clean, to which our attention is directed, not her half-averted face.

There is nothing surreal about *Femme Couchée*, nor about *Girl at the Window*, nor the limpid Le Corbusier-like *Still Life* of 1924, nor the magnificent pastiche of Ingres he drew in 1925, *Portrait of the Artist's Father and Sister*. Yet it is, of course, as a Surrealist, quintessentially so, that Dali is best known. The movement had immense attraction for him, and he employed all his verbal skills, far from inconsiderable, to explain why this was so. In the very first number of the Surrealist magazine, *La Révolution Surréaliste*, Breton, the movement's originator, and De Chirico, up to then its most famous visual practitioner, recounted their dreams, with the telling comment: Only the dream leaves man with all his rights to liberty. To Dali, harassed and obsessed by the menace of the

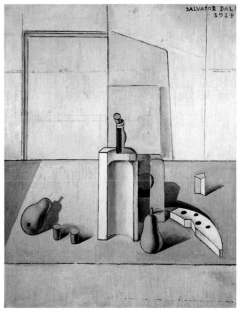

real, with its threatening responsibilities, this must have been irresistible. He set himself to enter the dream world and create solely from within its safeties. The irony is that the dream world, the true freedom of the imagination, does not open to self-conscious manipulation. This was at once evident to Freud, whom Dali, an avid reader of his texts, expected to fascinate, and in which, indeed, he succeeded. What interested Freud, however, was precisely the difference between the poetry of liberty and the manipulative fancies of the will: as he wrote to Dali, "It is not the unconscious I seek in your pictures but the conscious. While in the pictures of the Masters – Leonardo or Ingres – that which interests me, that which seems mysterious and troubling to me, is precisely the search

Top: Portrait of the Artist's Father and Sister, *1925, pencil on paper, 19 x 13 in/49 x 33 cm. Museu Nacional d'Art de Catalunya, Spain.*

Above: Still Life, *1924, oil on canvas, 49 x 39 in/125 x 99 cm. Fundacion Federico Garcia Lorca, Madrid.*

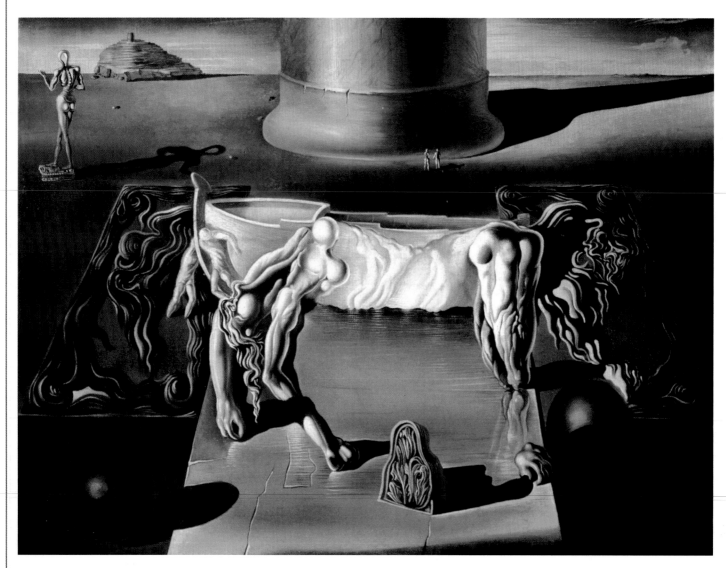

**Invisible Sleeping Woman,
Horse, Lion**, *1930, oil on canvas,
20 x 26 in/50 x 65 cm.
Musee National d'Art Moderne,
Centre Georges Pompidou, Paris.*

for unconscious ideas, of an enigmatic order, hidden in the picture. Your mystery is manifested outright. The picture is but a mechanism to reveal itself."

This is shrewd criticism. All in Dali is indeed contrived, a brilliant illustration of his own psyche as he understands it, as opposed to how it truly may have been.

The *Invisible Sleeping Woman, Horse, Lion* an image he painted more than once, shows his skill at this manipulation. The picture is about his own cleverness, how he can

"WHEN I PAINT, THE OCEAN ROARS. OTHERS MERELY PADDLE IN THEIR BATH."

play with shapes, etc. There is a multitude of concepts present, all doubtless of absorbing concern to Dali and his friends, but dull stuff to those who are not particularly interested in his thought processes. The connections between woman and lion, woman and horse, horse and lion (images arise from both Stubbs and Gericault's lion-attacked horses) seem to us to matter less than the superbly painted desert sands with the great central pillar, truncated but eery, and the strange blue ball and the other scatterings of the scene.

These things matter because, whatever their supposed significance psychically, they are lovely in themselves. Here, as from now on, Dali tried too hard, and the aesthetically important bits in his paintings are the extras, not the main actors. On occasion, he struck it lucky, coming across an image that is profoundly poetic. Even those who most dislike Dali find themselves haunted by the *Persistence of Memory* and those melting watches. This is an image that one can spin many theories round, explaining exactly why those limp and sagging circles so affect us. The theories may differ according to the writers' interests, and where one sees a fear of impotence, another sees a fear of mortality. But fear is strongly communicated, with its corollary, that whatever is communicated is to some degree controlled. It is a deeply disagreeable painting, and in that highly typical of this deeply disagreeable painter, but it is a marvelous work of art.

Dali wrote triumphantly, in "The Conquest of the Irrational," an essay that slightly postdates this exhibition (1935), that: "My whole ambition is to materialize the images of concrete irrationality with the most imperialist fury of precision… in order that the world of imagination and of concrete irrationality may be as objectively evident, of the same consistency, the same durability, of the same persuasive, cognitive, and communicable thickness as that of the exterior world of phenomenal reality. The important thing is what one wants to communicate: the concrete irrational subject."

It is in confusing imagination and irrationality that Dali comes to grief. What, we ponder sadly, is the actual point of what he so earnestly wishes to "communicate," this "concrete irrationality"?

The musings of the mentally sick are of value only to themselves. The tragedy is that Dali had, as his exhibition conclusively reveals, the talent necessary to communicate real imaginative truth, that which is at the center of all great art. But his self-absorption rarely lets him achieve what in theory should have been possible to him. We mourn the gifted who die young: Massaccio, Keats, Giorgione, Mozart. Someone like Dali who died young creatively, or at least, only half-lived, is sadder still. No artist ever needed a salvador more than Dali, but he was never fortunate enough to find one.

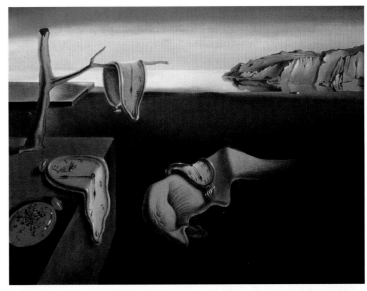

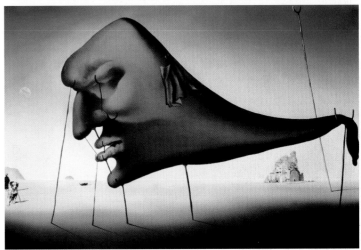

Top: The Persistence of Memory, *1931, oil on canvas, 9 x 13 in/24 x 33 cm. Museum of Modern Art, New York.*

Above: Le Someil/Sleep, *1937, oil on canvas, 20 x 31 in/51 x 78 cm. Private collection.*

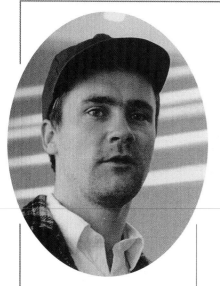

DAMIEN HIRST

Born in Bristol in 1965, Hirst came to London in 1986 to study at Goldsmiths College. While there, he organized and promoted "Freeze," an exhibition of students' work in a London warehouse. The independence, entrepreneurial spirit, and media savvy of the show became the starting point for the "Young British Artists Movement."

Internationally acclaimed, Hirst consistently interprets recurring themes of art – the meaning of life and the inevitability of death. He handles his explorations of mortality with originality and wit. Best known is his series of dead animals preserved in formaldehyde and enclosed in glass cases, the forms ironically similar to exhibits in natural history museums. In 1995, a New York gallery banned a Hirst piece of a dead cow and bull copulating by means of a hydraulic device. The New York City Health Department stated that gases from decay might explode if it were sealed or "prompt vomiting among the visitors" if it were not. In 1999 the Brooklyn Museum incurred the wrath of New York mayor Rudolph Giuliani when it presented the exhibition "Sensation" containing Hirst's work.

In 1995 he won Britain's Turner Prize.

Damien Hirst

by Will Self

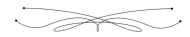

ABOUT TWENTY MINUTES BEFORE DAMIEN HIRST ARRIVES AT THE SERPENTINE GALLERY to talk to me, the susurration begins. The leavened minds of those-who-wait – gallery workers, a photographer, an editor, and me – are agitated by his pre-presence, the afflatus of what may – or may not – be his genius.

Calls are despatched to try and ascertain where the errant artist has got to. Pimpernel-like he has been sighted here, there, and everywhere. I imagine some sort of incident room map of Central London, with little colored lights moving about it, showing the relative

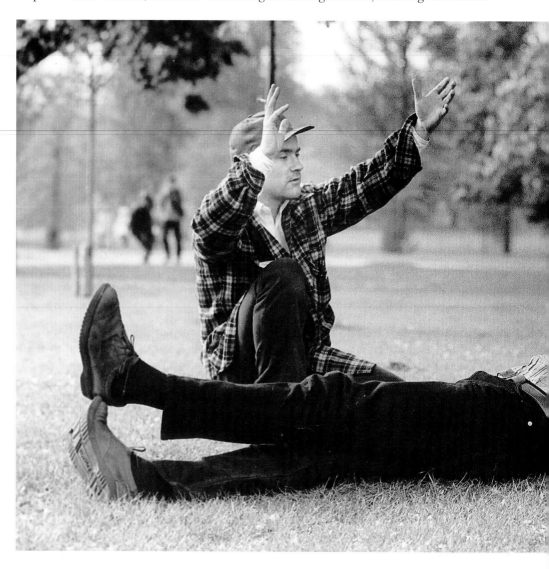

positions of Hirst, his critics, the buyers of his work. Possibly it could be entitled: *Moving Toward the Inevitable Impossibility of a Meaningful Encounter*. Or somesuch.

"He's definitely coming," reports a head, poked round – and apparently partially severed by – the door jamb of the staff kitchen where we wait. A new agitation is generated among the waiters. There is discussion of Hirst's antics, the put-ons that have been tried on him by his critics: "They asked him to draw a banana," says someone referring to a television appearance by Hirst, "and then he couldn't do it…" "That's not true!" counters another, "Damien is a brilliant draftsman."

I'm smoking moodily in a corner, and reflecting that this phenomenon is somewhat like J.G. Ballard's concept of the "Blastosphere," as described in his experimental work of fiction *The Atrocity Exhibition*. The Blastosphere is the implicit shape of the way matter is perturbed by an explosion. It is atemporal: it may just as well precede the fact of the explosion as follow from it. "We are all waiting in the Hirst Blastosphere, and as such it is inevitable that events, dialogue, thoughts even, should reflect the Hirst anti-aesthetic – a quotidian elision between the surreal and the banal.

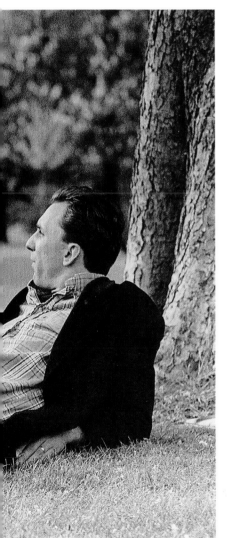

A gallery worker shows a suit-wearing man carrying a clipboard into the staff kitchen. She says, "Over there," pointing at a part of the room, and he replies "Mmm, mmm…" and notes something on his clipboard. They leave, without saying anything further, or even acknowledging the presence of the waiters. I wonder what the man with the clipboard would look like floating in a solution of formaldehyde.

And then he arrives. There's an almost audible thrumming that precedes the door being opened, an onanistic strumming, the essence of which is summed up by this proposition: It is better to masturbate over the image of the Emperor if he has no clothes on, or is it preferable to stimulate yourself discretely knowing that he is tightly sheathed?

In this sense Hirst's entrance to the kitchen is analogous to the way Ashley Bickerton's *Solomon Island Shark* – one of the exhibits in the current Serpentine Gallery show "Some went Mad, Some Ran Away" that Hirst has guest-curated – impinges on the viewer's sensibility. Hirst is hammerhead-down, tightly encased in PVC, rubber, and leather, and already garnished with the fatuities of those who observe and comment

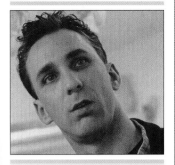

WILL SELF
Hailed by critics as a brilliant satirist in the vein of Swift, Will Self writes with a mixture of realism and absurdity on the spiritual emptiness in contemporary culture.

From his debut story collection The Quantity Theory of Insanity *in 1991, Self has used his wit "as a crowbar," one reviewer wrote, "to pry open the cracks in our culture." Self's subsequent novellas and novels include:* Cock and Bull, My Idea of Fun: A Cautionary Tale, Grey Area and Other Stories, Great Apes, Tough, Tough Toys for Tough, Tough Boys, The Sweet Smell of Psychosis, *and his latest,* How the Dead Live.

Winning awards and achieving recognition in both the UK and the US, Self's honors include the John Llewellyn Rhys Prize and the Geoffrey Faber Memorial Prize in Britain; My Idea of Fun *was named a New York Times "Notable Book of the Year." He also applies his outrageous imagination to journalism in his essays for the* The London Observer *and* The Independent, *and for* Esquire *magazine in the US. Born and raised in London, Self now resides there with his wife and children.*

All photographs of Will Self and Damien Hirst by Jon Mikol.

upon him. Fatuities that are as ordinary and perverse as the coconuts and plastic bags of Scope mouthwash that dangle from Bickerton's shark.

What's immediately apparent is that Hirst has a genuine charisma. Like many spatial artists he is concerned with the interplay between individual's senses of embodiment and their capacity for proprioception. He manifests this as an aspect of his being: his being-in-the-room acts on the flustered gaggle of waiters like an ultrasonic whine on a school of fish; and so they quit it.

We wander out into the gallery to look at the work. Conversation is desultory. We examine details of the various works rather than commenting on their totality. Hirst is annoyed that some of the myriad plastic tags that stipple the surface of Angus Fairhurst's

"I JUST HOPE THAT I CAN BE KIND OF LIKE THE BEATLES. I REALLY LIKE THAT KIND OF MODEL. I LIKE THE WAY THAT WITHOUT LOSING INTEGRITY THEY COULD CHANGE THROUGH FASHION AND NOT LOOK BACK AT THE '60S AND VOMIT WHEN THEY SAW WHAT THEY'D DONE."

Ultramarine Attaching (Laura Loves Fish), have been removed. I remark that it reminds me of my days as a shelf-stacker at Sam's Bargain Store in Burnt Oak.

Abigail Lane's *I Spy*, two glass eyes impaled on freestanding hanks of brass wire, calls forth from us both a warm recollection of the girder-impaling-eye sequence in Paul Verhoeven's film *The Fourth Man*, and we go on to bat back and forth anecdotes about other instances of bizarre discorporation, both real and filmic.

Another Lane – this time a full-size waxwork of a naked man crouching on the studio floor – calls forth a dialogue on the sense in which a sculpture can make the viewer aware of the distant provinces, the forgotten Datias and Hibernias of his own body. "Actually, you know," says Hirst, "the genitals of the sculpture are modeled on the real genitals off the subject." And we stand for a while, thinking a bout the sensation that the cold stone would make pressed against our own scrotal sacs.

Hirst talks about his interest in depicting "points of light moving in space." This he tells me, was most of the inspiration behind creating the spot paintings, where the aim is to set up a kind of visual humming, a titivation of the air above the surface of the canvas. This calls forth from me a lengthy effusion on "points of light in space," that runs all the way from the nature of the retinal after image, through Zeus appearing in a shower of gold, to the experiences of Terence McKenna, the Californian drug guru, on dimethyltriptamine. Hirst grunts noncommittally.

And indeed, as we tour the exhibition it becomes increasingly clear to me that not only does Hirst pay very little attention to the way that art critics are describing and categorizing his work, he doesn't even conceive of it in the same terms. For him the ascriptions of certain works as "gestural," "expressionistic," or "conceptual," are quite void.

What interests him are the details: the way that the butter curdles in Jane Simpson's terminal bird bath *In Between*, a brackish fusion of brass, butter, halogen bulb, and refrigeration unit; the implications of stress set up in Michael Joo's miscegenations of metal construction and Disney or scientific iconography; the way that Andreas Slominski's *Untitled* – a bicycle garlanded with bags of impedimenta – far from being difficult to assmble, in fact arrived at the gallery "ready to be wheeled out of its crate"; the exact ratio of formaldehyde to water that he uses for his own animal works. He seems most engaged when I remark on the way that little golden bubbles are trapped in the fleece of the lamb he incorporated into *Away from the Flock*.

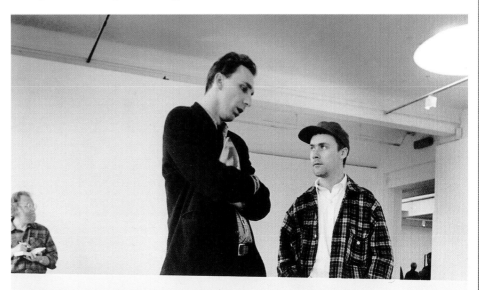

It's easy to see – talking to Hirst – why so many art critics should have seized upon him as grist to their word mills. They want his apparently gnomic comments on his work to be genuinely gnomic, evidence of a trickster mentality that teases the *cognoscenti*. The art critics who contemplate Hirst's work are like clever children playing with one of those stereoscopic post-cards: they flick it this way and that, to show that the Emperor alternately naked and adorned. Thus they get their kicks.

In fact, Hirst quite clearly thinks about his work in just the

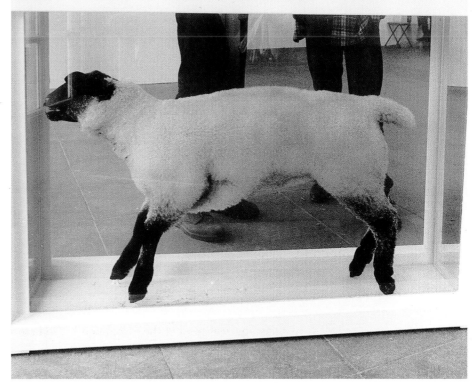

straightforward way that he says he does. Pace this transcription of our dialogue, which shows Self attempting to schematize, and Hirst quite properly resisting.

Self: What I thought was interesting about the way people are writing about you at the moment is that the art critics have to describe your work in their own arcane language – one which prettifies what you are doing. And that does for them for at least half an article.

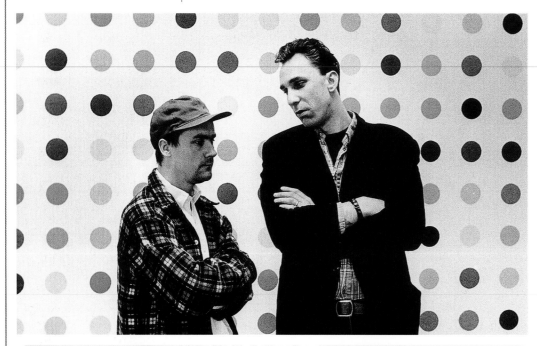

Hirst: They do it all the fucking time… they've been doing it for years… There's nothing more boring. They say: You go in, you see a thing… blah, blah, blah, just fucking describe it.

Self: But it seems to me that what you're really interested in is this dark side, this anima, the ingressability and internality of the body, and the way that culture refracts that experience. Your art is very kinaesthetic, it's about the internal sensibility of the body.

Hirst: I remember once getting really terrified that I could only see out of my eyes. Two little fucking holes. I got really terrified by it. I'm kind of trapped inside with these two little things…

Self: Pinhole camera?

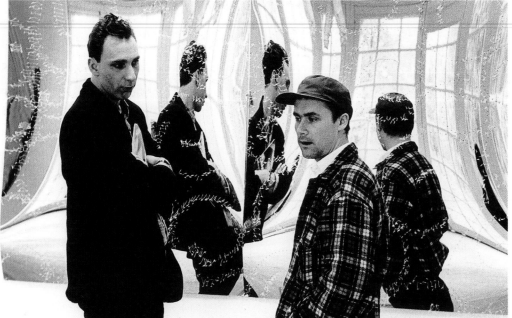

Hirst: Yeah, exactly.

When I attempt to outline some kind of epistemological development in his work, towards a more "visceral" approach, Hirst says, "I think I'm basically getting more yobbish. Yobbish is visceral. There's an idea of reality that you get from working with real animals … and I like formaldehyde."

And we go on to discuss the technicalities of suspending animal carcasses in formaldehyde: what the solution comprises, how he finds out about its properties, and so on.

Hirst tells me: "It's ridiculous what I do. I can't believe in it – but I have to." And this might reasonably stand as the motto of any serious contemporary artist. What the critic misunderstands is that the imaginative condition of an artist like Hirst is to be continually poised upon the fact of his own suspension of disbelief. The critic attempts to appropriate this queasiness as his own. This is because the critic, furthermore, wishes to appropriate the role of the artist for his own as well.

It's a mistake to be deceived by the ironic hall of mirrors that Hirst's work seems to present; to be distracted, like the waiters in the kitchen at the Serpentine Gallery, by the "phenomenon" of Hirst. While it's true that Hirst – like Warhol – is an artist who is as much sculpting in social attitudes as he is in physical materials, his approach to those attitudes is Myshkin-like in its lack of guile.

Hirst: I'd love to be a painter. I love those stories about Bacon going into a gallery where one of his paintings was being sold for £50,000 ($70,000), and buying it and just trashing it. But you can't really do that with a shark, it would take a whole gang of men with sledgehammers.

Self: That's why I brought up that Mach thing (the man who immolated himself trying to burn a sculpture by David Mach). Because what would you feel like if somebody came in and destroyed the work? Surely, it is part of a coherent vision and you would feel as if someone had hacked off your arm?

"IT'S RIDICULOUS WHAT I DO. I CAN'T BELIEVE IT – BUT I HAVE TO."

Hirst: I don't really mind, because I think the idea is more important than the object. The object can look after itself. It will probably last long after I'm dead. I'm more frightened of being stabbed myself. You can always get another shark.

In the course of our conversation Hirst describes many techniques that are explicitly Warholian: working with assistants who are inadvertently "pre-programmed"; attempting to generate "randomicity" in the spot paintings; the idea of a machine for producing "great art works." But while it may be too much to assume that he has stumbled upon these concepts wholly independently – they are, after all, very much part of the air we breathe – there's no doubt that his formulation of them is arrived at with a certain freshness. Hirst is a naïve rather than a sentimental artist in Schiller's formulation.

The comments that Hirst makes that are most interesting disavow his refusal to articulate a

"WHATEVER HE IS, I THINK THEY SEE CONTENT IN HIM THAT WE CAN'T. SOMETHING UNKNOWABLY, IRREVOCABLY BRITISH: FORMED IN THE PRIMORDIAL INTERSTICES BETWEEN JOHNNY ROTTEN'S GROUND-DOWN TEETH; STEEPED IN THATCHER AND CATHOLICISM; HAMMERED ON THE ANVIL OF ENGLAND'S DREAMING AND LOST EMPIRE."
—*Jerry Saltz*

coherent vision. Of fat people he remarks: "They just want to fill up more space." He opines that what really interests him about space is its purely formal properties: "I think it's all like collage … d'you know what I mean … that's why doing my own work and the group thing is basically the same. It's collage, shapes in space. As an artist you have these constrictions, when you make a work you have to decide whether it goes on the wall or the floor… Well, I hate that. My idea of a perfect art piece would be a perfect sphere in the center of a room. You would come in and walk around it and it would just be there… I love the refractions of light in the liquid pieces. With the shark I just love the reflections in the huge volume of liquid – you don't really need the shark at all."

We went on to discuss Hirst's new work, entitled *Couple Fucking Dead Twice*. He described it thus: "Just two tanks, with no formaldehyde in them, and there are four cows – two in one tank, two in the other – just stood upright, and the other one goes on its

"AND THEY'LL JUST ROT. BY THE END THERE'LL JUST BE A MESS OF PUTRID FLESH AND BONES."

back, giving it a really tragic, slow fuck. They're both cows, so it doesn't matter. And they'll just rot. By the end there'll just be a mess of putrid flesh and bones. I just want to find out about rotting."

There's an eloquence in this description that underscores his comments about the importance of the inspiration for him. He agrees readily enough when I suggest to him that the impetus for the creation of such works is the fact of their having arisen in the imagination in the first place. But this is as far as he can be driven toward intellectualising his own work or defining an aesthetic.

He is far more interested – both lying on the law outside the Serpentine Gallery, and much later drinking at the Groucho – in putting to me teasing choices: "Which do you hate more, serial killers or flab?;" "Are you an optimist or a pessimist?;" "Are you someone who sees the glass half-empty, or half-full?" I would hazard a guess that the need to throw up these niggling and trite queries is a dim reflection of the very real battle between appearance and reality that is always going on outside the cave of Hirst's mind, as the platonic forms of his sharks, cows and lambs, are carried by in the flickering firelight.

But I don't want to subside into the kind of waterbed of rhetoric that supports most art-critical speculation, any more than I want my prose to become a fancier description of a very ordinary accumulation of material objects ("They do it all the fucking time… they've been doing it for years… There's nothing more boring. They say: You go in, you see a thing … blah, blah, blah, just fucking describe it.") William Empson described the

(HIRST, IN HIS BEST WORK BRINGS THE)… "THE VISUAL AND THE MENTAL INTO PERFECT BALANCE."
— *Roberta Smith*

introductory copy that prefaces exhibition catalogs as: "A steady iron-hard jet of absolutely total nonsense."

The catalog copy for "Some Went Mad, Some Ran Away" is a perfect exemplar of this. Richard Shone's essay kicks off with a statement of mind-bogglingly discursive universality: "An urge to bring order to chaos – the search for meaning in the seemingly random flux of experience – has existed as a fundamental human motivation throughout history." What are we to gather from this? That this is an art show that somehow manages to bracket and contextualize the fundamental conundrums of all human experiences, for all space and all time?

I think not. Rather, this kind of bombast is an aspect of what I have alluded to above, just as Wittgenstein memorably remarked on the impossibility of a meaningful musical criticism, on the basis that it was otiose to describe one language in terms of another, completely alien language. So the excesses of contemporary art critics in attempting to define and fix the work of artists such as Hirst, reflects a wrong-headed and truly pretentious attempt by manipulators of language to reduce formaldehyde, flesh and bone, to some chintzy philosophic abstraction. In literary criticism we have seen the phenomenon of Deconstructionism – an attempt by critics to hijack the mantle of the metaphysician for their own scrawny shoulders; and this is what we are witnessing here as well.

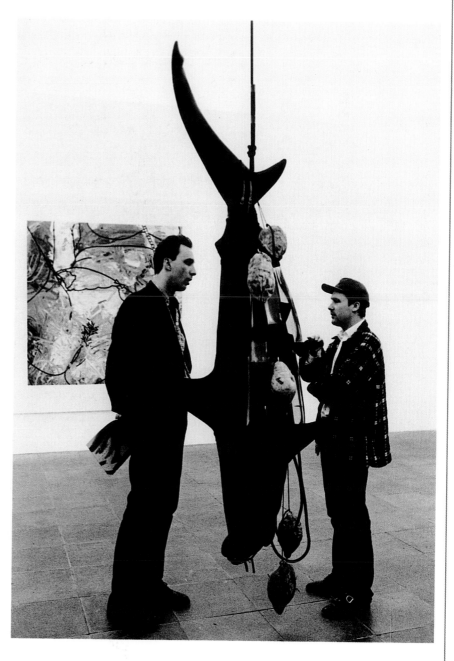

Shone goes on to characterize Hirst as "riding freely through the grasslands of art, finding nutrition in the company of his kind." I hope only one thing, that that "kind" continues to be artists as interested in the physicality of art as Hirst is himself, and not the pallid poetasters who see his enactments of tangible chutzpah as a springboard for their own aesthetic ambitions.

Empson's phrase is so correct in terms of Hirst's art because Hirst is creating "steady iron-hard jets," not uttering them.

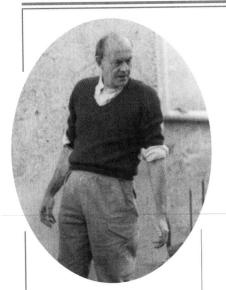

Cy Twombly

by Phillip Hensher

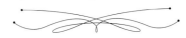

A PIECE OF CANVAS, SOME TEN FEET BY SIXTEEN. Over bare canvas, or a thin wash on canvas, some scribbles. An illegible word, perhaps in a scrawling hand; some circles, looking for all the world as if someone has taken fistfuls of paint and ground them into the canvas; great smears of red and pink and brown paint, poised in the empty space which might be sky, or earth, or just canvas, hanging on the wall. It might be random, a joke. It might be unfinished – though what painter starts a painting like this? – or unstarted. It's called *The Triumph of Galatea*.

I am writing this some time after the enormous retrospective of Cy Twombly's work has left Berlin and New York. The great canvases have left the basement in Berlin which, for a matter of months, they seemed to endow with new windows, new light. Wrapped protectively against ills and injuries, the accidents and disasters of their careless world they memorialize in their own happy accidents of paint, they have already journeyed back to their solicitous and well-insured owners. The radiant *Empire of Flora* is back on the walls, I suppose, of Dr. Erich Marx; the three canvases of *Hero and Leander* are conferring their beauty once again on the unimaginable drawing room of their anonymous private owner, whose luck has nothing to do with his undoubted wealth. I do not know what is now hanging on the walls of the Neue Staatsgalerie in their place; I do not care to imagine it.

But in writing about an exhibition which can no longer be visited, but only imagined, or remembered, I am not altogether indulging in critical perversity. Rather, there is a strange appropriateness in writing about these canvases in retrospect, and recommending them only to the imagination. Their subject is memory and imagination itself; they memorialize what has gone by taking on the appearance of ruins, of the graffiti and wreckage which time, unintending, visits on the monuments of men. It's right, then, to talk about them only when, for all normal purposes, they have disappeared, once more, from the view of everyone, and describe Twombly's work, not in a spirit of anticipation which could never reflect *their* spirit, but in a mood of memory and reflection.

Cy Twombly was born in 1928 in Virginia. His home town was dominated by two institutions of Washington and Lee University, where his father was an athletics coach, and the Virginia Military Institute. We may guess that the ancient virtues of honor and duty played some considerable part in his upbringing; we may care to speculate, still more wildly, on the part these values play in forming his stern and sybaritic masterpieces. Some time in the 1940s, Twombly came into contact with Jean Cassou's book on Picasso, and Sheldon Cheney's *A Primer of Modern Art*; the Sears Roebuck art kits were replaced by lessons from a Spanish artist in Virginia, Pierre Daura. The young Twombly was fired with enthusiasm for the modernist path. An admiration for Kurt Schwitters drove him to make assemblages; relocation to New York brought him the friendship of Robert Rauschenberg, and new horizons.

A period at the Black Mountain College in 1951 marked the end of Twombly's years of apprenticeship, and the first recognizable Twomblys. Painted under the influence of Dubuffet and of the art of American Indians, these canvases had a ferocity and instant energy which quickly made Twombly's reputation. In 1952, he and Rauschenberg traveled to Europe and to North Africa; there is a photograph of the 24-year-old Twombly, gaunt and handsome, facing a monumental Roman hand, its forefinger pointing heroically skywards. In North Africa he admired the Roman remains, and the geometrical art of simple tombstones. A joint exhibition of works with Rauschenberg in Florence – "tufted hanging pieces" – drew from their experiences; the pieces seem to have been dumped in the Arno at the end of the show. In 1953, the two artists held a major exhibition at Eleanor Ward's Stable Gallery in New York, and after a long-deferred stint of military

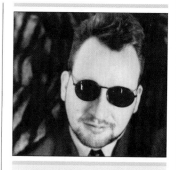

PHILLIP HENSHER
Hensher was born in London in 1965. He was educated at Oxford and then at Cambridge, where he wrote his PhD dissertation on eighteenth century painting and satire. From 1990 to 1996 he was a House of Commons clerk.

His books include the novels Other Lulus *(1994),* Kitchen Venom *(1996), which won the Somerset Maugham award,* Pleasured *(1998), and a collection of short stories,* The Bedroom of the Mister's Wife *(1999). He also wrote a libretto to Thomas Ades' 1995 opera,* Powder Her Face, *which has been performed around the world, recorded by EMI, and filmed by BBC Television. He is also a regular contributor to* The Spectator, The Independent, *and other British newspapers. Hensher was made a Fellow of the Royal Society of Literature in 1999, and serves on the Council of the society. He is the youngest writer to be included in A.S.Byatt's* Oxford Book of the English Short Story *and in Margaret Drabble's* Oxford Companion to English Literature.

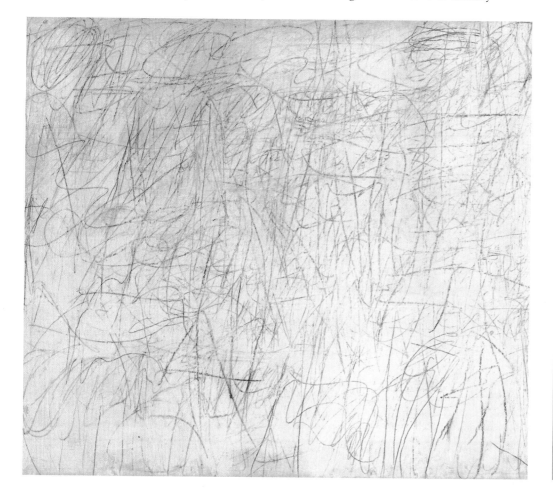

The Geeks, *1955, oil-based house paint, colored pencil, lead pencil and pastel on canvas, 43 x 50 in/108 x 127 cm. Daros Collection.*

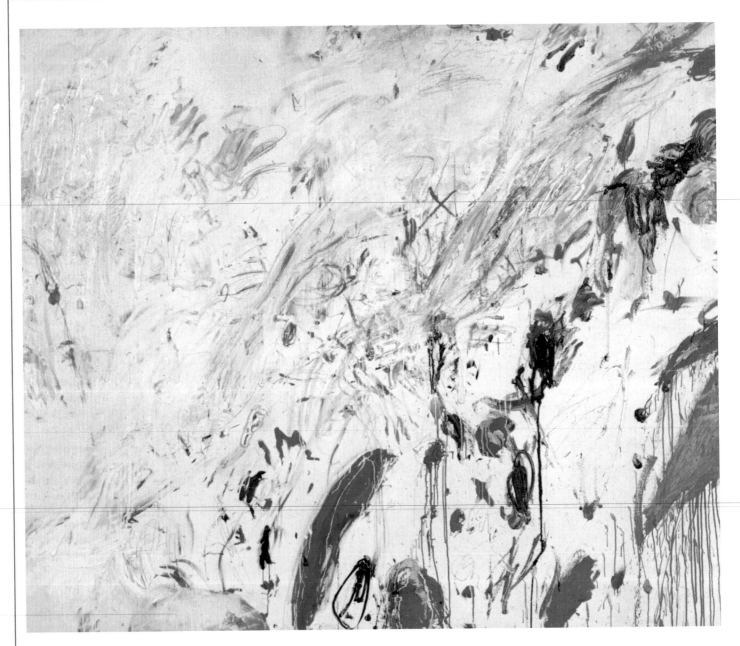

Ferragosto III, *1961, oil paint, wax crayon, and lead pencil on canvas, 65 x 79 in/165 x 200 cm. Daros Collection.*

service, and a job teaching in Virginia, Twombly left America for good. Since 1957, he has lived more or less permanently in Italy, painting, exhibiting, and accepting the honours and praise which rightly come his way.

That's one way of putting it; one biography. But a single life can have many biographies, and when we walk around the results of one man's work, as in the Berlin and New York retrospective, we may feel that there is another. This is another way of putting it. Cy Twombly was born; he began to paint; he learned nothing from anyone, or anything; and his work is what it is.

This may seem an unlikely account of a painter's life, and especially of this painter's life. Twombly, it might seem, is a painter who makes a definite appeal to a particular idea of the artist—a particular romantic idea. It may be tempting to compare him to a painter like Jackson Pollock, who, like Twombly, makes an apparently almost irresistible appeal to the viewer's interest in the artist. Looking at these paintings, we are drawn, it seems, into a contemplation of the artist's maneuvres in placing paint on canvas. We apparently follow a series of actions; we understand, we feel, how the paintings were put together, because we see, or can guess at, the order of brush-strokes; and having understood how the painting was physically produced, we are led, we suppose, to understand the painting itself. In other words, because the physical act of painting is explicit, the viewer is led to suppose that the metaphysical acts and decisions which precede and follow the movement of the brush must also be explicit.

In a 1961 untitled painting, for instance, the texture is so painterly that one can quite literally reconstruct the steps which led up to the final canvas. In an encrusted scrub of excremental brown in the bottom right, or a burst of purple in something approaching a heart shape in the center, placed with casual intensity over an intermediate cloud of tainted pale paint, the viewer imaginarily places himself in the position of the artist. It can be seen that, at the top of this beautiful painting, in executing one of his favorite motifs of this period, two red adjacent circles, Twombly painted the one on the left with a fully loaded brush – or perhaps fist – and the second, on the right with a meager scraping of paint; and because it can be seen *how*, it is tempting to assume that we can understand *why*.

> "TWOMBLY, UNLIKE MANY OF THE YOUNG TURKS WHO TAKE HIM FOR THEIR OLD MASTER, KNOWS HOW TO EXPRESS DISPASSION WITH A LITTLE PAINTERLY PASSION."
>
> —*Jed Perl*

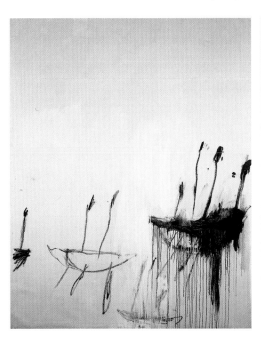 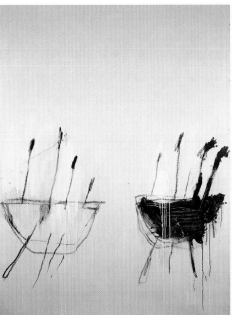 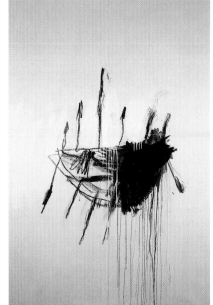

I said this appealed to a romantic idea of the artist. These canvases inevitably lead us back to the artist himself, and ask us to contemplate not just his brushstrokes, but his heroic endeavors. But in few painters is there such a gulf between the explicitness of the physical action and the hermeneutic mystery of the final work. The sense of the viewer is that he can understand such painting, because he can understand how it is made. But a moment more, and he will be left contemplating the gap in his understanding. Here the philistine comment on Twombly – "I could do that" – is not altogether absurd; the philistine might

Left to right: Three Studies from the *Temeraire*, *1998–99, oil on canvas, left: 100 x 80 in/253 x 202 cm, center: 103 x 80 in/261 x 202 cm, right: 102 x 77 in/260 x 195 cm. With permission of the Artist.*

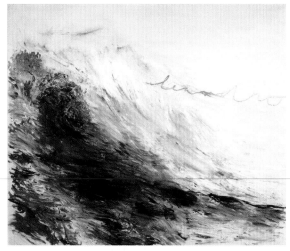

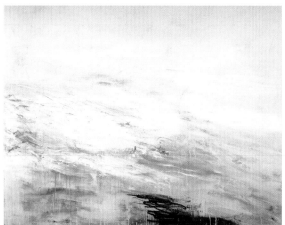

Above, top to bottom:
Hero and Leander (Part 1), *1984,*
oil paint, oil based house paint,
oil paint (paint stick) on canvas,
66 x 79 in/168 x 200 cm.

Hero and Leander (Part 2), *1984,*
oil paint, oil based house paint,
oil paint (paint stick) on canvas,
61 x 81 in/156 x 205 cm.

Hero and Leander (Part 3), *1984,*
oil paint, oil based house paint on
canvas, 62 x 81 in/156 x 205 cm.

All courtesy Gagosian Gallery.

very well be able to put together a Twombly-like canvas. He could not, however, understand it once made.

The unanswerable question "but what does it mean?" is central to Twombly's greatness, and when it can be answered, I think the art suffers as a consequence. *Hero and Leander* (1981–4) is a cycle of three canvases (or perhaps four: in Berlin a scrap of paper was appended on which Twombly's inimitable hand had scrawled the lines *He's gone: up in bubbles/All his amorous breath*). It is an exceptionally beautiful work. In the first canvas, we may assume, Leander drowns – and a great polychrome wave, like a shout, and the single word "Leandro." The two remaining canvases plot the after-events of the drowning. In the middle, the savage greens are muted; scrapings and drips are like the small ripples and collapses in the aftermath of a catastrophe; a black monolithic streak at the bottom of the canvas casts its pall over other, smaller events here. In the third canvas, the drowning is done, and the world resumes its calm course. I cannot think of many more perfectly beautiful paintings than this third one; it has something of the quality of Turner's Petworth landscapes. Both the scale of the brushstrokes and the spectrum are severely limited; but there is a ravishing evenness and serenity about it which transcends the self-imposed limitations of the means, the technique.

But, beautiful as it is, there is something slightly unsatisfactory about the *Hero and Leander* cycle; one knows a little too much about its meaning. The strength of it, again, lies in its inexplicable elements. Why is the painting a triptych; what lies between the separate panels? Are we looking at sea, or sky, or neither, in the last panel? These, and the inexplicable beauty of the almost blank last canvas, are the mysteries which make it profound; the story of Hero and Leander, I think, detracts from its value.

It's a typical Twombly paradox that the least eventful of his paintings is also the most explicit in its meaning. Most other paintings of his are almost over-emphatic in their imagery. Characteristic shapes recur from painting to painting. From the late 1950s onward, the tumble of imagery is frequently punctuated by rough suggestions of architecture – most frequently windows, as at the top of *Leda and the Swan* (1962). In *The School of Athens* (1961) the architectural imagery turns to arches; in a group of related works from 1969, the windows simplify into concatenations of boxes. Heart shapes are almost obsessively regular over a very long period; a radiantly playful, enormous, untitled canvas from 1968 has a flock of them, inscribed one on top of another, and all floating over a subtly modulated gray ground. The hearts in *Leda and the Swan* are much more aggressive, all pointing in the same direction, and inwards. Most striking is the *Olympia* of 1968, where the word MORTE seems to struggle towards becoming a heart; a struggle fulfilled in the distorted heart in red at the top right of the canvas. These heart shapes are related to the sexual iconography which, as has often been noted, recurs throughout the work, and to the other symbol of fecundity, flowers. Flowers are the theme of the marvelous *Kingdom of Flora*, but more recently, Twombly has returned to them in such paintings as *Summer Madness*.

Leda and the Swan, *1960, oil, crayon, pencil on canvas, 76 x 80 in/194 x 203 cm. Courtesy Gagosian Gallery, New York.*

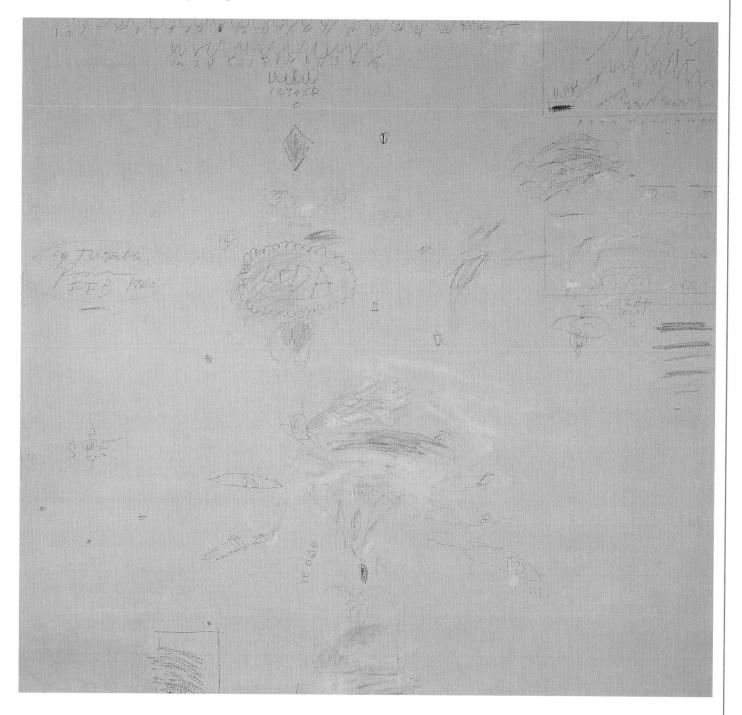

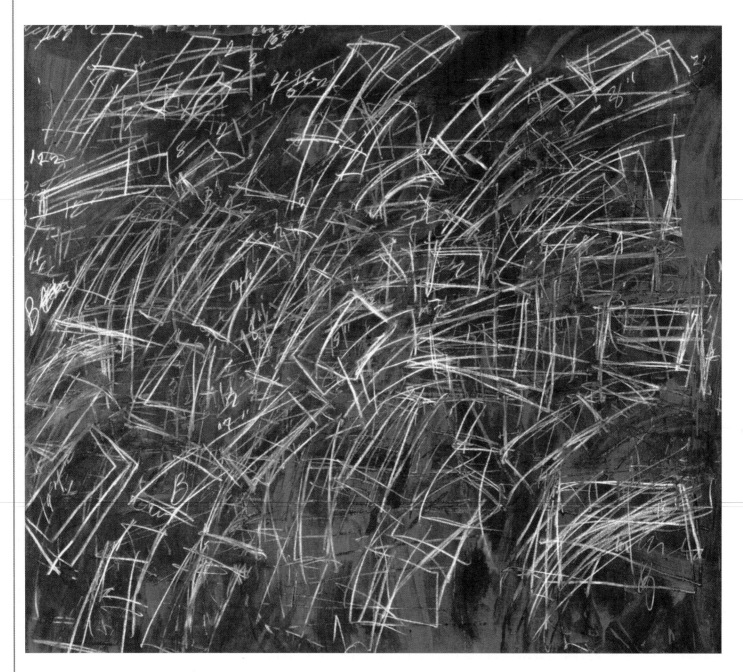

Untitled, *1967, oil-based house paint and wax crayon on canvas, 60 x 68 in/152 x 173 cm. Daros Collection.*

These recurrent icons have clear and often, specific meanings. But they only rarely endow a painting with a clear and single meaning. *Leda and the Swan* is filled with sexual images, but its apparently direct meaning is enriched, and, I think, veiled, by a wealth of other possible meanings. The window at the top, and the surprisingly Loony Tunes anarchic comedy of the great explosion of feathers are finely ambiguous. One might note that the absence, the uncovered blank at the top left-hand corner of the canvas, is just as much a motif in paintings of this period, in this particular position; one can note recurrence of this, just as with the hearts, penises and windows, but not ascribe meaning. More ambiguous still is the inscription of the title – or rather, the way the title is inscribed – at the bottom of the painting. And when we look at the writing in Twombly, we are led, I think, to the very heart of his mystery.

There are few paintings in Twombly's work without any writing in them, or which do not draw on the image of writing, without themselves including writing. *Leda and the Swan* is perhaps the clearest instance. The title – *Leda + the SWAN* has been written at the lower right hand corner of the painting, before two quick scrawls have nearly obliterate the last two words. Obliteration is always intimately connected with writing in Twombly; again, there is the word MORTE in *Olympia*, beginning its transformation into a pre-verbal symbol of death's opposite, love. Another canvas, *The Italians* (1961) neatly includes its title in a box, and, ringed repeatedly, the rest of the canvas is a riot of irrational imagery from which an individual letter occasionally struggles.

These are at the rational end of the writing in Twombly; other messages are much more baffling. The figures, somewhat resembling the marks of architects, which crop up increasingly from the 1960s, are a sort of writing which bears no meaning. Frequently, writing is thoroughly obliterated. As Kirk Varnedoe remarks of the paintings of 1955, the residual figuration now comes in the form of elemental signs, such as crosses, X marks, rectangles, grids, triangle, and circles, and especially in the emergent elements of written language. Letters, notably, A, E, K, N, V, U, H and I, alone or in words, appear on the teasing edge of legibility.

On the teasing edge of legibility; but falling off that edge, rather than clinging on. Twombly's apparent concern with writing is really a concern for the obliteration of writing. And his paintings, which use so recurrently the images of obliteration – the *Olympia*, the ancient and illegible graffiti on a monument – do not do so lightly , but in order to explore the subject of obliteration itself. One quite large group of Twombly's paintings is painted with white on black. They strikingly resemble the marks of chalk on a blackboard, but they are not the writing of a teacher communicating with his class; they are the loops and struck lines and smears which come before writing, or after. A number of times, Twombly returned, at low or difficult points in his career, to these paintings. The masterpieces in this manner which he painted at the end of the 1960s and early 1970s are, to borrow a phrase from Barthes, the degree zero of his paintings, which wipe out meaning like a classroom duster, which obliterate writing so thoroughly while evoking it, could be called, and overwhelmingly, they are called it: *Untitled*.

If one were to look for an analogy for Twombly's works, I don't think it could be found in Western painting. What they often resemble is the huge illustrations which, in Islamic countries, are painted on the façades of the houses of those who have carried out the pilgrimage to Mecca. With little obvious attempt at composition, the means of transport used in the journey is itemised and represented in individual icons. Like these, Twombly's works represent the steps on his journey in small, iconic form; like them, they represent the true, the metaphysical journey undertaken only by the brave inadequacy of their form, and in Twombly, their sceptical, heroic rejection of their own means.

TWOMBLY'S PAINTINGS... "SUGGEST A PRIMORDIAL, LIBIDINOUS MUMBLING, BUILT UP BY COUNTLESS GENERATIONS ON THE WALLS OF THE MEDITERRANEAN."
—*Martin Gayford*

Paul Cézanne

by Patrick Heron

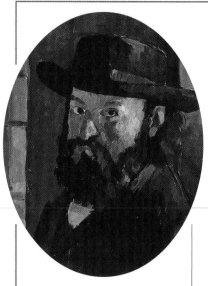

PAUL CÉZANNE
The evolution of Cubism was largely due to Cézanne, one of the most important of all modern painters.

Born to a prosperous family in Aix en Provence in 1839, Cézanne led a financially secure life. As a student, he formed a friendship with Zola that was to be his creative impetus. He studied at the Aix School of Design, at the same time satisfying his father by studying law. In 1861 his father consented for him to join Zola in Paris to enroll at the École des Beaux-Arts, but his application was rejected. Discouraged, he returned to Aix to work at his father's banking firm. Unhappy there, he went again to Paris, met Pissarro, and exhibited at the 1874 Impressionist exhibition.

Impressionism emphasized an immediate confrontation with the world, and the flatness of the picture plane. Cézanne created flatness and spatiality at the same time, a crucial step in the development of abstract art. After the dealer Ambroise Vollard exhibited his paintings, public interest in Cézanne's work began. The Salon d'Automne of 1904 devoted an entire exhibition room to his entries.

Never entirely comfortable in Paris, Cezanne periodically returned to Aix to work in isolation in nature. In the fall of 1906, he was overtaken by a storm while out painting, became ill, and died.

THE MOST PROFOUND EXPERIENCES OF WHICH WE ARE CAPABLE invariably burn into our consciousness a precise date, time, and place. I never visited Aix-en-Provence until the summer of 1962 – and then only for an hour, heading the family car in what I hoped was the direction of the sacred mountain. We were already outside the town when we swung round a corner to the left… and there it was, even more to the left, at the top of a slight valley and already framed by the boughs of three pines, exactly as Cézanne saw it in the sublime version at the Courtauld. Not pine needles, or bark-encrusted bending boughs, but separated, single, dry, square-tipped brushstrokes it was that hung in the air before one's eyes. In rhythmic ranks, vibrating gently in all directions, they formed strata of separated color which miraculously solidified there in front of one, in the so-recognizable opalescent atmosphere surrounding the mountain over there! Rose, ocher, violet, and cobalt… one already saw the paint embedded in the air!

I had slammed on the car brakes as we rounded that bend into the sudden full view of the breathtaking Cézanne subject I had known for so long. We'd even skidded, slightly, into the pine needles. A moment later, wandering a few feet above the road, I was confronted by a new-ish limestone marker which said, very simply, that Cézanne had painted the mountain from this spot – unnecessary as information; but excellently reverential as a salute. How

"DO NOT BE AN ART CRITIC, BUT PAINT, THEREIN LIES SALVATION."

good it would be if Aix would now remove the gigantic cross mistakenly added in recent years to the very crest of this most famous of all mountains in the history of painting.

I have always claimed that painting's prime function is to dictate to us what the world looks like. Each artistic generation recreates what it believes to be the natural appearances of the world, sometimes radically, sometimes only slightly, but nonetheless decisively. A given version is mandatory at a given time. What we imagine to be the "objective" look of everything and anything is largely a complex, a weave of textures, forms, and colors which we have learned, more or less unconsciously, from painting, and have superimposed upon external reality. The actual "objective" appearance of things (of anything and everything) is something that does not exist – or rather, it exists as data that is literally infinite in its complexity and subtlety, in the variety and multiplicity of its configurations. What assuredly floods in upon the retina from the outside world is an amorphous cloud of visual stimuli into which the human eye learns to inject a favored order of some sort or other. Historically, it is painting that supplies that order. It is painting that persuades the eyes of a generation to see swarms of ragged dots of disparate color overlying the entire scene, indoors or out, where none exists. It is painting that persuades another generation, elsewhere, that every solid object inhabiting the visual scene, in which we move, must have a black outline around it. It is painting, yet again, that licensed certain generations to believe that the entire landscape

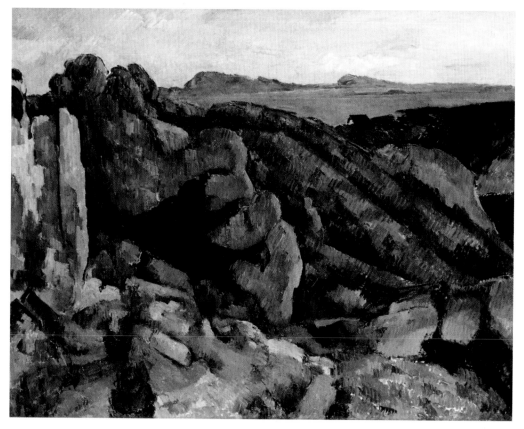

consisted of various browns. It is painting that cajoled the eyes of yet another age to see all solid objects, whether near or far, in terms of nothing more formally definite than a continuum of colored mists. Yet all these configurations nevertheless have been extracted out of the infinity of possibilities which comprise the visual scene.

So when Cézanne resolved visual realities into countless groups of delectably ordered *strata* of fragmented brushstrokes lying parallel to one another he was magnifying something *seen*. But the stacks and shelves and clusters of square-ended parallel brushstrokes are not an invented arbitrary abstraction: they are the intuitive magnification of fragmented stratifications which his remarkable eye saw hinted at absolutely everywhere in the visible world. And no one mistakes their origin and function. Seven short square-ended parallel brushstrokes stacked by a rapidly moving brush, side by side, do not for a moment allude to

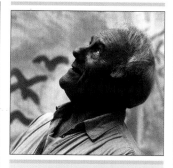

PATRICK HERON
One of the most prominent of Britain's post-World War II abstract painters and a leader of the St. Ives community of painters until his death in 1999, Patrick Heron also revealed his talent as an art critic. He wrote essays arguing against the need for pure abstraction in modern art in his writings for New Statesman *and* The Nation, *among other journals. From 1947 to 1950, he was the art critic for* New Statesman.

During this period, Heron's luminous still lifes and interior scenes show the influence of Matisse and, later, of the Abstract Expressionists. He was an innovator of the concept of denial of the picture plane, emphasizing the flatness of the surface by means of simple shapes and floating color. In his later work he used horizontal bands of intermingling color that still have reference to the traditional landscape. Simple forms dense with color appeared, and his color became richer and more organic.

Above left: Rocks at L'Estaque, *1879–82, oil on canvas, 29 x 36 in/73 x 91 cm. Museo de Arte de Sao Paolo, Brazil. Chateaubriand Collection.*

several separable *objects*, lying next to each other, for instance. No: the ubiquitous surface texture, in Cézanne, is almost always comprised of these clusters of quickly stated, dense stackings of separate brushstrokes; each group of strokes often largely consisting of one color. These strokes, these clusters, are not so much descriptive of the colors and textures of the forms they evoke as of the spatial position those forms occupy in the subject. The separate brushstrokes forming these clusters thus came into existence as a space-creating plastic device, and one of immense originality and power. They are frequently totally at variance in color and in texture with the color and texture of the actual surfaces of the natural forms they describe and evoke. It is as space-creators that the uniquely Cézannian hatchstrokes are so immensely powerful: so powerful, in fact, in their capacity to carve their way into the illusionistic spaces of the painting that they frequently seem to exist purely as space-creating devices, and almost, as I have been saying, to have relinquished the capacity to reveal specific colors or textures in the natural subject matter, which, nevertheless, they unfailingly evoke with unbelievable certainty.

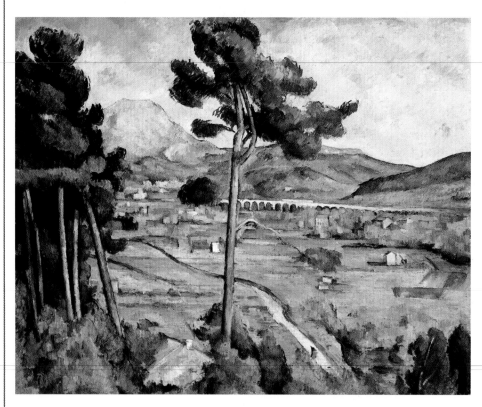

Mont Sainte-Victoire seen from Bellevue, *1882–85, oil on canvas, 26 x 33 in/65 x 82 cm. Metropolitan Museum of Art, New York.*

The most profoundly influential of all Cézanne's innovations has, of course, to do with the relation of the surface of a canvas to the myriad illusionistic depths into which all the sections, all the brushstrokes, however minute or large, lead the eye. "Space in color": an overwhelming sense of depth *through* surface color – depth of an apparently very precise and physical distance from the spectator's eye, back to a resistant plane sensed through and behind the equally palpable, physical plane of the brushstrokes on the surface of the canvas. It is *always* a double sensation everywhere, a double awareness of two distances, in depth, in every section of the painting: you know the physical distance from your eye to the physically painted gestures on the surface of the canvas. But at the *same instant*, you equally know the precise distance in illusionistic depth behind and through that flat statement to the forms which the painting evokes with such an overwhelming sensation of actuality. There is, therefore, a spatial counterpoint in Cézanne, and it too is of a revolutionary certainty: in every second of your eye's encounter with his surfaces your perception sinks through to a thousand different stops and planes of a thousand different sizes, each plane a different brushstroke, all these planes and strokes creating a mosaic – and each and every stroke or plane tending, of course, to lie *parallel* to the surface of the canvas. It is one of the profoundest sources of the overwhelming sense of visual harmony generated by Cézanne – this sinking of the eye through the surface-shape to the further stop deep in illusionistic space, each one of which exists at a *different* distance from the eye of the spectator. If one imagined a thread attached to each and every plane leading back to your eye, every thread would be of a different length; and a relationship between all these *differing lengths* of thread, these "eye-beams" of different lengths, assuredly exists; and these relationships between a thousand measured depths, away from the surface, to those planes deep in illusionistic space – these relationships between the different *depths* of recession are themselves a most potent source of the immense sense of harmony generated in any Cézanne. There is thus a counterpoint everywhere in a Cézanne canvas between measurements *across* the surface and measurements *into* the surface, measurements in depth, at right angles through that surface and into the illusionistic spaces of the painting.

But put like that, with some difficulty, in *words*, the impression is possibly created of a hyper-intellectual mode of consciousness? Nothing could be further from the truth.

"But I've gotta use words when I talk to you."

As Eliot's Sweeny said. And the flavor of words is intensely anti-visual. Strictly speaking, painting cannot be written about. Visual experience *is purely* visual; and strictly unamenable to words of any kind… But one can hint, with luck, at the patently real realities of the eye.

> "NO ONE WILL EVER PAINT LIKE CÉZANNE… BECAUSE NO ONE WILL EVER HAVE HIS PECULIAR VISUAL GIFTS."
> —*Marsden Hartley*

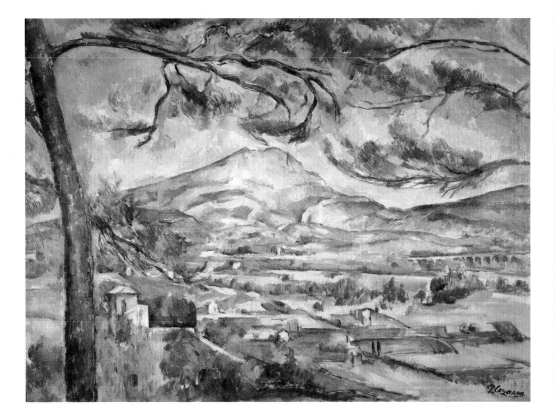

La Montagne Sainte-Victoire, *c.1885–87, oil on canvas, 26 x 36 in/67 x 92 cm. Courtauld Institute Galleries, London.*

The Gulf of Marseilles, seen from L'Estaque, *1886–90, oil on canvas, 32 x 40 in/80 x 101 cm. Art Institute of Chicago.*

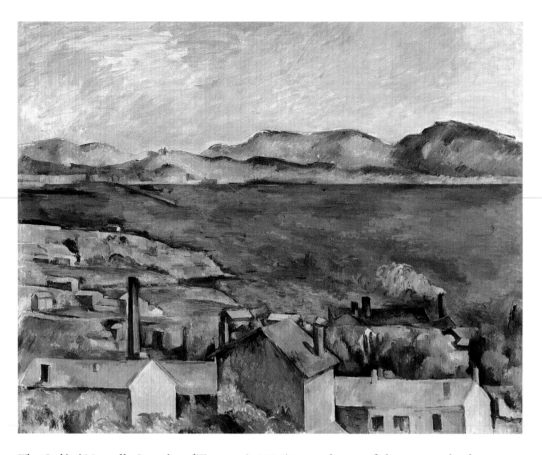

The Gulf of Marseille Seen from l'Estaque (c.1886) is surely one of the greatest landscapes involving the sea of all time. One could stare all day into that blue area of a hundred movements of the brush which is the sea, feeling again and again the tilt of its great surface below one, feeling panoramic distance in a plane of blue which nevertheless rises up into one's face – as do *all* areas in Cézanne. That "empty" blue of sea is an astonishing foil rising up above the consummately stated sharp geometries of the roofs of houses and factories below (below meaning nearer!): the wedges of ocher and pale red, which again and again form 45-degree angles, merge their sharpnesses so consummately into the olive and emerald softness of the trees between. And this whole band of immaculate complexities is so wonderfully conceived as lying horizontally "beneath" the great horizontal blue emptiness of the sea, which is both "nearer" and "above" and "behind" and "beyond"… all simultaneously. In painting there is a relativity about all spatial positions: no spatial relationships are fixed into a single rigid reading.

Now a still life – *The Blue Vase* (1889–90). If each object in a Cézanne landscape – houses, rocks, pines – has a form as carved and definite and weighty as the objects in his still lifes, so equally, perhaps, one can feel that the spaces between all objects in his still lifes are as tangibly definite – as defined spaces – as the open-air spaces which at the same instant separate and bind together a tree, a gable-end, a rock, a mountain in his *landscapes*. The subject of all Cézanne's paintings is space. And those solids which, by their presence, delimit and define the space between and surrounding them all – whether landscape or still-life objects – are not more solid, not more tangible than these shaped aerial spaces which separate them. The spaces between the solids in Cézanne's paintings are themselves solid! And these spaces between things are as solid and as individually shaped as those things themselves. This is the source of the unprecedented unity of design of which Cézanne is the discoverer and great exponent. It is the source of the overwhelming sense of alloverness, of the unprecedented awareness of the picture *surface*, of the altogether new *evenness* of emphasis, of the extraordinarily original equality of parts throughout their design which features from one end of his canvases to the other without a break. And here again is a paradox: the formal equality of all parts, the equality of spatial compositional pressure throughout his paintings, which has infected and dominated almost every single major painter coming after him, this allover-ness and evenness of emphasis did not in any way preclude his discovery of a whole range of utterly novel compositional arrangements. For instance, the compositional geometry of *The Blue Vase* could serve Braque or Picasso; even as late as Ben Nicholson, the wonderful asymmetric geometry of its distribution of rigid

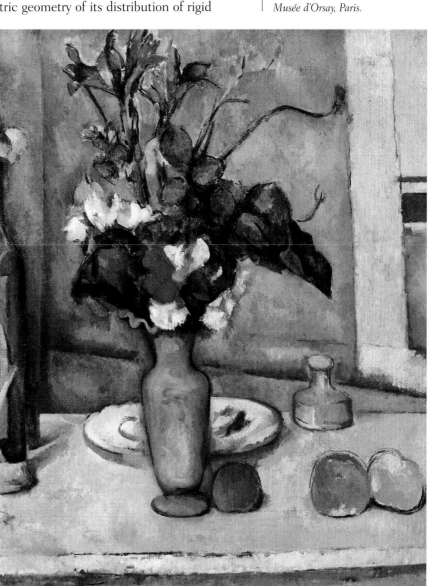

The Blue Vase, *1889–90, oil on canvas, 24 x 20 in/61 x 50 cm. Musée d'Orsay, Paris.*

learning verticals and horizontals had still not passed its "sell-by date." The half-bottle on the left-hand edge; the slightly leaning vertical of the pale rigid upright shape which turns off into the right hand edge two-thirds of the way down, making a tall cubist L; the two parallel horizontal bands which cross the very bottom of the canvas, running off it completely at both sides, but with their right-hand ends slightly higher than their left-hand ones, so that the darker ocher band is slightly wedge-like; the two halves of the whitish-blue plate, emerging on either side from behind the blue vase not quite matching in their position, right and left, as they pass behind the vase, thus perfectly preceding the famous Cubist device which fractured so many circular forms in just this way… in all these instances this great still life was the forerunner, by decades, of so many of the sensations at the heart of the Cubist movement.

But *The Blue Vase* also shows Cézanne developing a further great discovery, and one

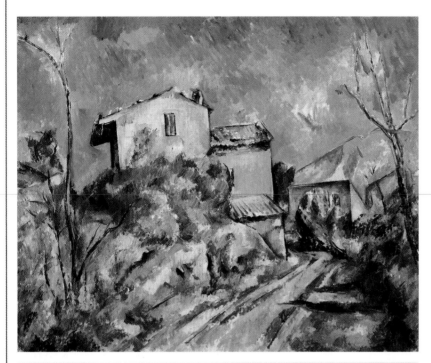

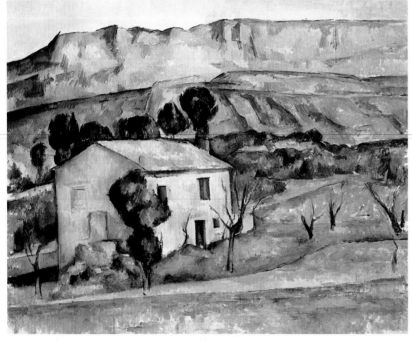

which has influenced all his greatest successors. One could call it the development of a *multi-directional perspective*, and the abandonment of that single perspective which had reigned from the Renaissance. It developed from a purely instinctive experience of the searching eye endlessly contemplating natural appearances: there was no theory. But the sort of intense visual contemplation of the scene, indoors and out, which allowed itself to be influenced equally by *everything* that displayed itself in the visual field – never limiting its interest to a single dominating form on a neutral ground, for instance – this wide ranging gaze was capable of savoring a new sensation of reality. It resulted in the final abandonment, as I have said, of that boring Renaissance perspective system which drew all receding lines towards a single "vanishing point" on the horizon. Instead, the moving eyes projected their own vanishing points wherever they focused; so that when, for instance, your eye dives off to the left of this blue vase, it projects or creates its own perspectival system; its own little avenue between objects which is slightly at variance with the avenues it finds to the right of the blue vase. It is as if the eye of the spectator itself projects separate avenues leading to separate vanishing points wherever it focuses, to the right and to the left and above and below all the objects in a

Top: The Maison Maria, *1895, oil on canvas, 26 x 32 in/ 65 x 81 cm. Kimbell Art Museum, Fort Worth, Texas.*

Above: House in Provence, Near Gardanne, *1886–90, oil on canvas, 26 x 32 in/65 x 81 cm. Henry and Rose Pearlman Foundation, Inc.*

composition. And it is one of the by-products of this roving eye, which projects so many variants of a perspectival system into various parts of a Cézanne painting, that it upends planes everywhere into positions which are more approximately parallel to the picture-surface. These multiple planes, which face the spectator frontally everywhere in Cézanne, were the brilliantly novel means for generating and entirely new pictorial space – Cézannian space! And, in passing, one should note *Still Life: Flowers in a Vase* (1885–88), a much starker forerunner not only of the Cubists but the Constructivists too, where a very similar blue vase holds a nest of extremely complex flower-forms, in a concentrated area, in the left-hand center of the painting. But apart from these very complex flowers, the painting consists solely of three wonderfully empty flat areas representing two sections of a wall and half a large bare tabletop. The straight edges of the visible corner of the empty tabletop are extremely sharp, and are met at right angles by an equally sharp vertical of the wall. That such razor-sharp geometry as the edges of this table and that wall could have emerged at a time when the world was still in love with Monet's soft clouds of color is a measure of Cézanne's amazingly advanced audacity – an audacity which Monet nonetheless himself revered.

Another great landscape painting, *Houses in Provence – The Riaux Valley near l'Estaque* (1879–82). In my youth I pored over a very bad black and white reproduction of this painting in Roger Fry's great pioneering book on Cézanne. I first saw the painting itself, 45 years later, at the National Gallery of Art in Washington; I remember a shock of surprise – surprise at its color, at what struck me as an extraordinary bleached paleness over all its surfaces, a paleness I described to myself as *silver* – a silvery lightness of tone permeating so many of those immensely weighty planal ridges in terms of which all the features of the hillside, the ridges of rock emerging everywhere through the dry grass, have been realized. To an extent perhaps unmatched in any other of his landscapes, this entire painting is realized in terms of those parallel ridges of parallel brushstrokes, all gathered at a leaning angle of 45 degrees - everything, that is, except the houses and the sky where, quite suddenly, very different brush-weavings obtain. *Their* surfaces materialize in very different terms: their brushstrokes are virtually disguised as such, merging in the flatter, smoother

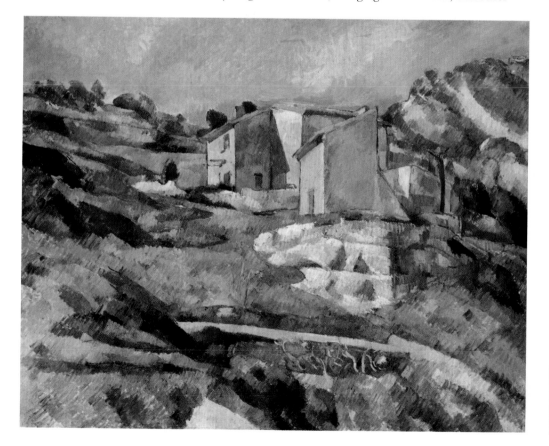

Houses in Provence – The Riaux Valley near L'Estaque, *1879–82, oil on canvas, 26 x 32 in/65 x 81 cm. National Gallery of Art, Washington D.C.*

"WILL ANYONE EVER APPEAR AGAIN WITH SO PECULIAR AND ALMOST UNBELIEVABLE A FACULTY FOR DIVIDING COLOR SENSATIONS AND MAKING LOGICAL REALIZATIONS OF THEM? HAS ANYONE EVER PLACED THIS COLOR MORE REASONABLE WITH MORE OF A SENSE OF TIME AND MEASURE THAN HE?"

—*Marsden Hartley*

evocation of the almost windowless walls, on the one hand, or in the atmospheric softness of vague clouds, on the other. The intense light of the Provençal or Mediterranean summer does tend to dazzle and bleach; and the heat of the day unquestionably radiates from this canvas. But its preeminence, as a pivotal work in Cézanne's development, lies in the almost total absence of the linear or the soft and feathery or the atmospheric from the vocabulary of its enormously emphatic and sure and plastically powerful diagonal brushstrokes. Almost all surfaces, evocative of the entire hillside, consist of these immensely emphatic and virtually parallel diagonals; only a very small group of curvilinear strokes, just right of center, towards the bottom edge of the canvas, is an exception. Certainly this painting represents a degree of abstraction that was entirely novel and one that was not repeated by any other artist until the floating rigid strokes of Braque's and Picasso's Cubism thirty years later.

Hardly ever does Cézanne repeat a theme – repeat a *subject*, yes, of course, many times, but composition is virtually never repeated; nor are the organisations of color. There are no cases of Cézanne imitating Cézanne. And almost every time, there are the most daring departures from what one had thought might prove to be habitual constructions of one kind or another. For instance, if one ever assumed that the "drawing" of all forms, all features, all profiles in a mature Cézanne would almost invariably consist of broken, *straight* lines, fractured stuttering lines, how utterly surprised one would be with *The Sea at l'Estaque* (1878–79), for in this painting an unbroken *curvilinear*, waving, snake-like treetrunk springs from the bottom right-hand corner of the canvas and curves its way right

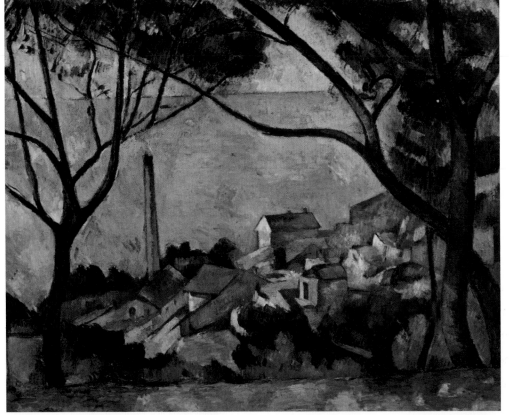

Sea at L'Estaque, *1883–86, oil on canvas, 29 x 36 in/73 x 92 cm. Musée Picasso, Paris.*

up and across to the very top left-hand corner – a continuous line of great elegence and tension. But no broken lines in its drawing; no planal facets to break up or disrupt the continuity and smoothness of this exquisitely undulating waving trunk-form. It is the sort of bare, swiftly drawn, upwardly curving treetrunk which Corot or Derain (forty-five years later!) would love. Yet here it is, combining with the equally curvilinear trunks of two other trees to form a great gateway through which we look down to the opaque blues of the uptilted

sea – and down to the
incredibly complicated
geometries of roofs, gable-ends,
and chimneys in l'Estaque,
there below. One could gaze
for a week into these
immensely complex yet totally
resolved geometries, both soft
and sharp, which are the roofs
and wall-ends and chimneys
and gables of l'Estaque – gaze,
that is, into the hundreds of
merging or differentiated tiny
brushstrokes, sharp or smooth,
wet or dry, which creates these
images on the canvas. And as
in all Cézanne's greatest
paintings – and this is a very

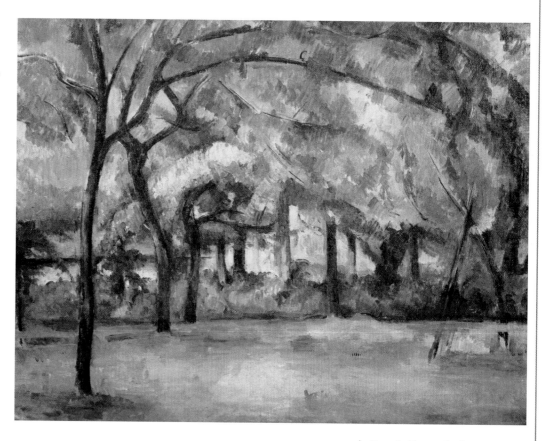

Farm in Normandy, Summer (Hattenville), *1882, oil on canvas, 20 x 25 in/50 x 66 cm. Courtauld Institute, London.*

great one indeed – there is a wonderful luminosity here. The richness of the dark grill of
boughs through which the multiple blues of the flat, flat sea shine upward, the pinks and
ochers and reds and violet-browns of the minutely geometrical sharpnesses of all those
buildings below – these form a nest of warm and sharp, cool and soft, advancing and

"WHEN A PICTURE ISN'T REALIZED, YOU PITCH IT IN THE FIRE AND START ANOTHER ONE!"

receding colors and forms, which lies at the lower center of this canvas, at a point which
one's roaming eyes visit and recross more than any other part of the painting.

I set out in this essay to try to present something of Cézanne's revolutionary awareness
of the visual realities of the world we inhabit. Spatial color generated out of flat surfaces of
an almost unparalleled richness and complexity, yet a complexity so organically unified in its
final presentation that each painting, in total, has an overwhelming simplified thrust and
naturalness. In pursuit of an attempted elucidation of, for instance, Cézanne's spatial color,
I find I have ignored completely the portraits and very considerably the still lifes, too. Yet
both these subjects provided Cézanne with challenges and inspiration – and success –
equal to those of the landscape.

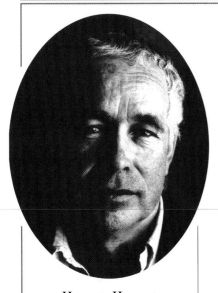

HOWARD HODGKIN

Born in London in 1932, Hodgkin studied at the Camberwell School of Art in London and the Academy of Art in Bath.

Visually stimulated by Italy, Morocco, and India, Hodgkin's paintings are combinations of memory, reality, and abstractions. Using asymmetrical patterns and strong, decorative colors. he incorporates remembered details – patterns, items of clothing, the light and space of a particular place – in his work. An Expressionist in that he blends psychological intensity with aesthetic considerations, Hodgkin is concerned with the surface quality of paint.

Hodgkin has taught at both the Slade and the Chelsea School of Art in London and was artist in residence at Oxford from 1976 to 1977. He served as trustee at the Tate Gallery from 1970 to 1976 and at the National Gallery, London, from 1978 to 1985. As well as receiving Britain's most prestigious award in art, the Turner Prize in 1985, Hodgkin was knighted in 1992. His work is part of permanent collections in museums throughout the world, including the Museum of Modern Art and the Metropolitan Museum in New York, the National Gallery in Washington, DC, and the Sao Paulo Museum, Brazil.

Howard Hodgkin

by William Boyd

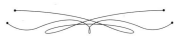

1906. February.

PAUL KLEE WRITES IN HIS DIARY: "My work in the studio will grow considerably more lively. I have succeeded in directly transposing 'nature' into my style. The notion of 'study' shall be a thing of the past. Everything shall be Klee, regardless of whether impression and representation are separated by days or moments."

I wonder if a similar revelation was ever experienced by Howard Hodgkin in about 1975, if he suddenly knew, instinctively, as Klee knew 69 years earlier, that henceforth "everything shall be Hodgkin." Certainly the marvelous exhibition that was in New York and moves to Fort Worth and then Düsseldorf later this year (1996) seems to imply that 1975 was the watershed.

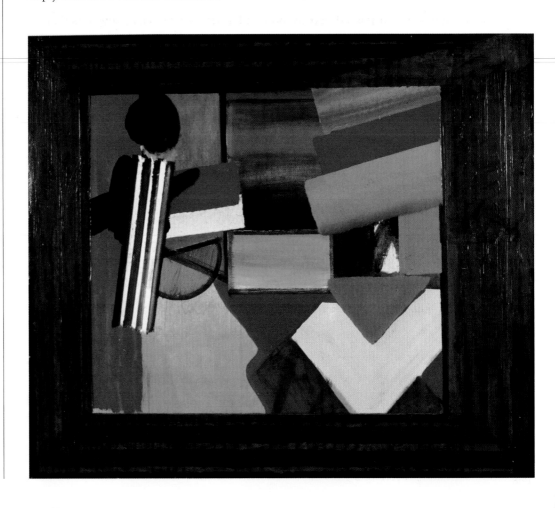

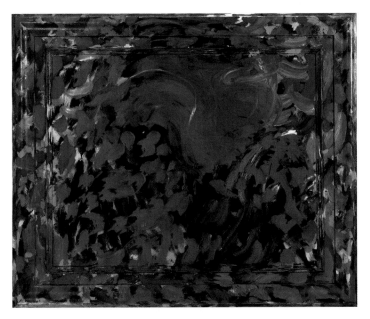

I was, serendipitously, reading Klee's diaries as I was visiting the exhibition and generally thinking about Hodgkin and his work. This happy accident provoked a series of parallel reactions and cross-fertilizations that wouldn't necessarily have been made otherwise. Klee and Hodgkin are not yoked together in the way that, say, Vuillard-Hodgkin and Bonnard-Hodgkin more commonly are. It proved an interesting way of looking at Hodgkin's work from a different angle, and in the light of a different exemplar. For simple instance, the idea Klee floats in the extract quoted above of "impression and representation" being separated by days or moments seems a succinct definition of the *modus operandi* that Hodgkin also avows. The impression – the private event, the memory – is transfigured in paint on wood as representation, although its final

> ## "I THINK A LOT OF PEOPLE IN ENGLAND ARE AFRAID OF PICTURES WHICH HAVE VISIBLE EMOTIONS IN THEM. THEY FEEL CALMER IN FRONT OF PICTURES WHICH ARE PLACID."

"representation" may take years, rather than days or moments, to be finalized. In Hodgkin's case the original afflatus may be entirely lost on the viewer, or is so enigmatic as to have an identical effect, or may – simply – have been rendered in shapes and color tones. Klee can often be quite as oblique as Hodgkin and, set beside his, Klee's titles possess a similar hazy allusiveness – are oddly Hodgkinian – and hint at a hidden meaning rather than describing the painted image. Klee: (examples taken at random) *Contemplating, Blossoming, Uplift and Direction (Glider Flight)*. Hodgkin: *Self-pity, Writing, Talking about Art*.

Klee's remarkable diaries prove salutary and humbling reading in this the day and age of the artist on fast track, the artist as snake-oil salesman, the hype-master with limited or nugatory formal skills, the one-smart-idea peddler. We see in these candid and beguiling pages the fascinating record of a great artist's growth: its almost unbearable deliberation, full

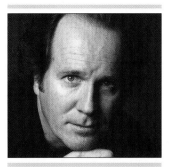

WILLIAM BOYD
Born in Ghana in 1952, the novelist, critic, journalist, and screenwriter William Boyd was educated in Nice and Glasgow, and at Oxford, where he later taught from 1980 to 1983.

His darkly humorous fiction, which critics describe as "a fine balance of satire, black comedy, and horror," reflects his view that life is completely unpredictable, that even the most banal people are challenged by fate. He draws from recent culture, science, and politics, and writes imaginatively about the conflict of cultures. The novels –
A Good Man in Africa, Stars and Bars, Brazzaville Beach, The Blue Afternoon, *and* Armadillo *– deal with destiny and how his characters cope with it.*

Boyd writes for newspapers and journals, he reviews fiction for the London Sunday Times. *Among the major literary prizes he has won are the Whitbread and the Somerset Maugham awards. He now lives in London, and is on the editorial board of* Modern Painters.

Above: Writing, *1991–93, oil on wood, 46 x 55 in/116 x 138 cm. Private collection.*

Left: Talking about art, *1975, oil on wood, 42 x 50 in/106 x 127 cm. Private collection.*

of struggle, laborious self-education, moments of despair and doubt, of inspiration provided by other arts – literature and music – and we are reminded of the old definition of "genius" as being the infinite capacity for taking pains. Klee's sheer diligence, his doggedness, his search for that moment when "everything shall be Klee," are powerfully reminiscent of Hodgkin's own slow and steady development, of its learned and scholarly undertones; there is a further parallel in Hodgkin's comparatively late flowering.

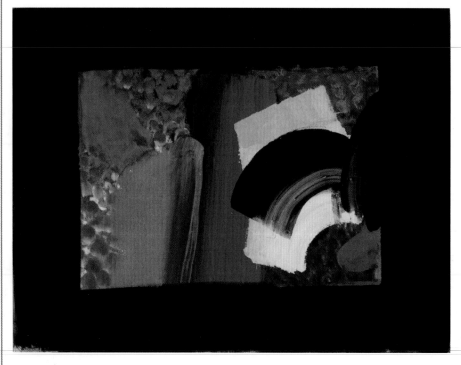

Left: Patrick Caulfield in Italy,
1987–92, oil on wood,
44 x 58 in/110.5 x 146 cm.
Private collection.

That it has indeed flowered is clearly evidenced in this collection of paintings spanning two decades – two decades of work, moreover, that display an astonishing homogeneity and occupy a near perfect plateau of success. The nature and extent of this consistency is quite clearly revealed in two similar paintings: *The Hopes at Home* and *Patrick Caulfield in Italy*. The first was painted in 1973–77, the second in 1987–92. In both pictures we see gathered together what we might call Hodgkin's painterly vocabulary, the key Hodgkinian tropes. Two things strike the viewer immediately: the framing effect, a dark inky green in *The Hopes*, black in *Caulfield*, and the glowing lambency of the colors the frames surround. The frame, of course, achieves several ends. It "offers" the painting; it defines its edges; its color offsets and complements the colors in the frames space. It creates, too, a *trompe l'oeil* effect of, as it were, setting back the painted area. These visual consequences are commonplace and were doubtless understood by the first artist who painted a border around his picture or set it within a wooden frame. Hodgkin, however, has made it almost his trademark: the painted frame itself and the painted framed surface are integral to the whole effect of the composition and not a decorative afterthought. Almost without exception we view Hodgkin's pictures through a painted framing device.

Klee too, interestingly enough, was very conscious of where his picture ended – took pains pointedly to establish the picture edge (often achieved in his case by a form of mounting). In both Klee and Hodgkin the rationale behind this practice can be summed up thus: the more evident the frame – the more "edged" the picture – so the more discrete the image becomes. The concomitant idea of a cinema frame is entirely wrong here. These pictures are resolutely bounded, hemmed in. Nothing is implicit beyond the picture's border. The gaze may not wander, it is precisely focused.

And within that frame Hodgkin spreads or stipples his refulgent color tones. The effect, it has to be said, is highly seductive. These are paintings you covet, that boldly change your mood, that – to put it very crudely – you want to steal (no higher praise?). Many artists achieve this effect from time to time, but few can sustain it over a whole body of work: Matisse, Braque, Sam Francis are some modern artists that come to mind, but it is a tribute to Hodgkin's mastery of color that time and again one finds oneself entranced, ravished by the intensity of contrast, of counter-posing, and harmonizing color and hue.

"MY PICTURES REALLY FINISH THEMSELVES."

This is, I would claim, the initial response to a Hodgkin painting: immediate and instinctive, almost physical, I find, provoking an interior shout or laugh of recognition that this sorcery has worked so swiftly upon you. It is not simply a question of electric ultramarines offset by Naples yellows. Hodgkin can work his magic with a limited palette, too. A picture like *After Degas* is completely beguiling, playing with a pistachio green and a chestnut brown and yet managing to glow as if it were lit from within.

The paint is applied in certain basic modes. There is the splodge, or dotted, or stippled effect and then there is what might be termed the smear, or swathe, often a gentle ogee or section of a curve in which the history of the painted gesture can be read. The loaded brush passing over the wooden ground, releasing its thinning paint to reveal colors beneath. This apparent spontaneity is, we now know, the product of possible years of reflection and afterthought and is far removed from the aleatoric frenzy of the abstract expressionist. However, like the abstract expressionist, Hodgkin's painting can often be described as "gestural," but it is important to establish that the individual

> "HE DOESN'T 'BELONG' TO ANY ARTISTIC MOVEMENT, HE IS UNTAMED BY CONVENTION, HE IS UNAFRAID OF FEELING — HE HAS THE 'GIFT OF TEARS.'"
>
> —*Julian Mitchell*

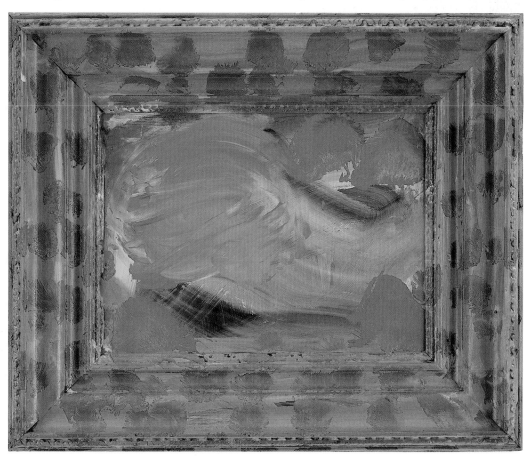

Afterwards, *2000, oil on wood, 30 x 37 in/76 x 91 cm. Anthony d'Offay Gallery, London.*

gesture has been studied, rejected, and reapplied many times and is not the impromptu slashing of some tormented id.

Klee, 1908: "By using patches of color and tone it is possible to capture every natural impression in the simplest way, freshly and immediately."

This was Klee documenting his slow shift from a heavy reliance on the graphic to a greater confidence with color. By 1975, the graphic element in Hodgkin's work is almost entirely subsumed by the process Klee describes above. The drawn object – a figure, a window, a tree – is at most blurrily present or is hugely stylized in the paintings of the last two decades. But Hodgkin does not rely only on color and tone to achieve all his ends. There is no doubt – whatever protestations to the contrary – that the titles he appends to his paintings are designed to have an effect on the whole. Otherwise why not call them *Composition no. 168* or some such, if it were simply a matter of designation? But in almost every Hodgkin the totality of the "impression" the painting conveys is adulterated, sometimes significantly, sometimes in a minor way, by the title the artist gives to it.

Haven't we met? *1985–88,*
oil on wood,
19 x 25 in/49 x 64 cm.
Saatchi Collection, London.

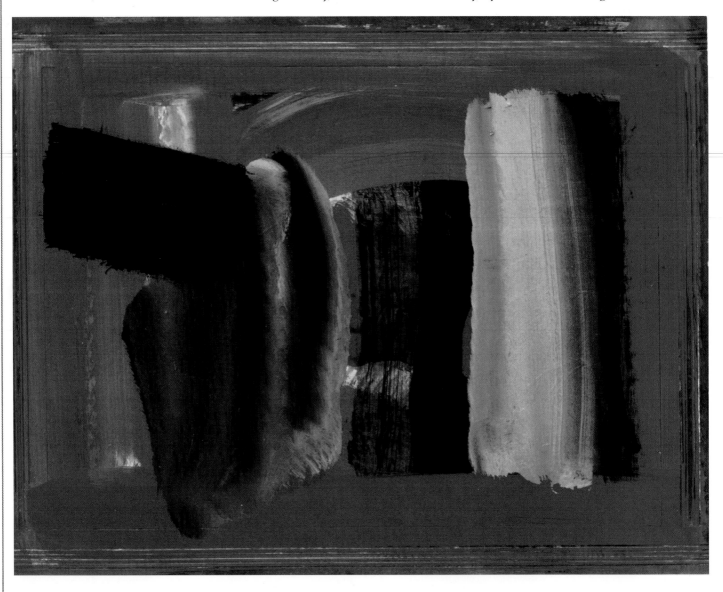

(Again, this is an old trick – even the banal can be rendered portentous by a suitable title, as both Marcel Duchamp and Joseph Beuys were aware.) Hodgkin has consistently individualized his paintings by the titles he bestows on them. Sometimes this has the effect of a lens twitched into focus. In *Red Bermudas*, for example, crude columns of beige and red suddenly become the bottom half of a sunbather. The title *In Bed in Venice* makes the painting immediately semi-figurative. Whereas *Haven't We Met? Of Course We Have* or *Burning the Candle at Both Ends* remain impenetrably private references. This form of titling can also, it must be said, be an irritating affectation. The innocently ignorant viewer is stymied, redoutably bogged down in his ignorance, denied the significance that the painting clearly holds for the artist and a few privileged others. A sense of exclusion is fostered, and nobody likes to be left out.

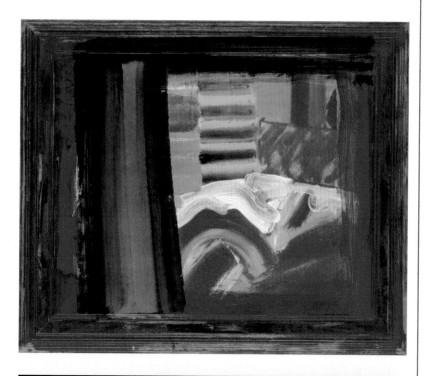

The late Bruce Chatwin was the subject of a Hodgkin painting (of the 1960s and not exhibited) and explained its genesis and key *points de repère*. The inspiration was a dinner in Chatwin's minimalist flat decorated only by a Japanese screen and "the arse of an archaic Greek marble kouros." Mr. and Mrs. Hodgkin and a couple called the Welches were the other guests. "The result of that dinner," Chatwin wrote, "was a painting called *Japanese Screen* in which the screen itself appears as a rectangle of pointillist dots, the Welches as a pair of gun turrets, while I am the acid green smear on the left turning away in disgust."

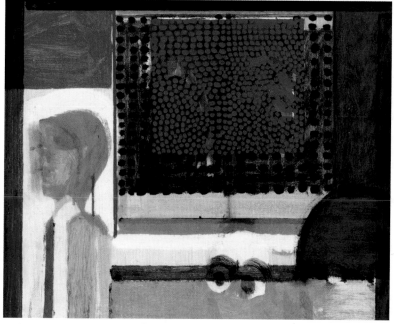

Top: In Bed in Venice, *1984–88, oil on wood, 39 x 47 in/98 x 119 cm. Private collection.*

Above: Small Japanese Screen *or* **Japanese Screen**, *1962–63, oil on hardboard, 16 x 20 in/41 x 51 cm. Private collection.*

Chatwin gives a further insight into Hodgkin's approach: I remember Howard shambling round the room, fixing it in his memory with the stare I came to know so well.

Chatwin also elucidates another painting called *Tea*, which he explains as "a seedy flat in Paddington where a male hustler is telling the story of his life."

Hodgkin may not encourage us to attempt an interpretation or to try to seek out a figurative element in his paintings, but there is no doubt that an important side effect of the titles is to make us do exactly this. In fact I think this tendency is a distinct advantage even though we are frequently balked and defeated. There is a figurative undercurrent in Hodgkin's work, sometimes strong, sometimes subtle, and the paintings, even the most seemingly abstract, benefit from this potential urge to investigate and decode.

It is an instinctive and natural process, in any event. The eye and the mind unconsciously seek to arrange and interpret the phenomena they encounter, and particularly those things deliberately presented to them, a category that includes abstract paintings hanging in art galleries. This natural human urge has to be curbed voluntarily or by some formal element in the painting, if we are to respond to it, judge, and appreciate it solely, purely, in terms of shape, color, and composition.

Hodgkin's paintings – with their knowing allusiveness, their *taquineries*, and their representational shadowings – encourage us to look deeper, to go beyond the initial aesthetic thrill and try to see if there are more profound chords to be struck. What we are talking about here is a particular stimulus common to certain works of art where visceral delight cohabits with analytical curiosity or even analytical imperatives. The two responses are not mutually exclusive, they can exist separately and can be present *fortissimo* or *piano*. But in Hodgkin's case I find that what I have described as the aesthetic thrill generates a potent need to understand how this thrill was brought about. Vladimir Nabokov said that the first response to a work of art should be with the nape of the neck, but there is more going on in a Hodgkin painting than mere spine tingling. There is a complexity of reaction that functions on deeper, more cerebral levels, too, and that demands further deliberation. The best of Hodgkin's paintings, and there are many of them, provoke this

Chez Max, *1996–97, oil on wood, diamerte: 70 in/177 cm. Private collection.*

response, and this explains, I think, both the unique frisson his work delivers – it's sheer pleasure quotient – and its ultimate seriousness.

Klee's art functions in the same way, it seems to me: it both delights on a simple level and reveals complexities of more profound and complex tenor. I don't want to push the Klee-Hodgkin thesis too far. I'm reluctant to posit Hodgkin as a late twentieth-century Klee; there are marked differences on the graphic level, for example. But time and again the

"THE ONLY WAY AN ARTIST CAN COMMUNICATE WITH THE WORLD AT LARGE IS ON THE LEVEL OF FEELING."

correspondences illuminate and odd affinities elide harmoniously; reasons for admiring Klee will be found to be similar to the reasons for admiring Hodgkin.

For example, Klee, in 1915: "I have long had this war inside me… And to work my way out of my ruins, I had to fly. And I flew. I remain in this ruined world only in memory, as one occasionally does in retrospect. Thus, I am 'abstract with memories.'"

Abstrakt mit Erinnerungen: it could be the cipher to unlock almost all of Hodgkin's work. That combination of private event, recalled and eventually transfigured (with words, with music, with paint), is the deep source of much artistic endeavor in many art forms. One thinks of Wordsworth's definition of poetry as "emotion recollected in tranquillity," and, indeed, it is to poetry that one can go, in my opinion, to find a key to Hodgkin's particular alchemy.

After visiting David Hockney, *1991–92, oil on wood, 19 x 24 in/49 x 62 cm. Barclays Bank Collection.*

Klee and Hodgkin choose memory as that function of the mind which provides the motor for their art. The American poet Wallace Stevens was obsessed with another transforming power of the human mind – imagination – and, in many respects, his entire oeuvre is a sustained meditation of this unique power and how it reshapes, irradiates, and adds value to the world of appearance. Stevens's poetry is a combination of a highly seductive word-mongering and manipulation ("the aesthetic thrill") coupled with this basic concern, this serious contemplation of the faculty that lies behind all art and, as

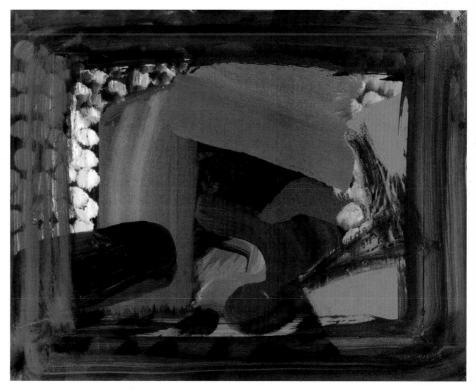

Stevens would have it, all meaningful human existence. There is a short, not very well known Stevens poem called *Bouquet of Roses in Sunlight* (it is one of many that could be chosen) which analyses the emotional charge that comes with seeing something beautiful, that tries to establish "what exactly is going on" in that moment (his *Ode to a Grecian Urn*, if you like). Taking the sunlit vision of the roses as its starting point it begins:

> Say that it is a crude effect, black, reds
>
> Pink yellows, orange whites, too much as they are
>
> To be anything else in the sunlight of the room…
>
> And yet this effect is a consequence of the way
>
> We feel and, therefore, is not real except
>
> In our sense of it, our sense of the fertilest red,
>
> Of yellow as first color and of white,
>
> In which the sense lies still…

I can't think of a better description of the effect of looking at a Howard Hodgkin painting – one can almost imagine the Hodgkin version of *Bouquet of Roses in Sunlight* – but what lifts the poem beyond mere apt description is the awareness of the defining interaction of the human mind. And of course the very experience itself has in turn been distilled and reconstructed in a work of art. Life, Stevens says – to put it very straightforwardly – is not truly real "except in our sense of it." And this is what great art both understands and acknowledges when it tries to make sense of our sense

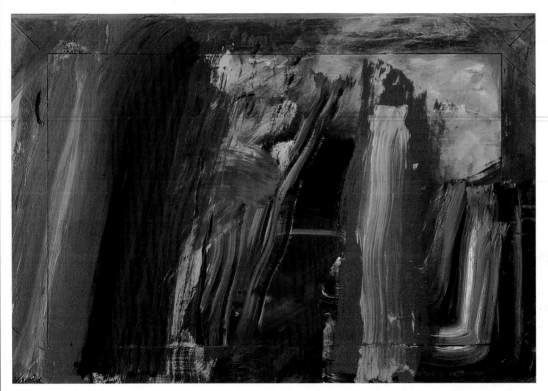

Memories, *1997–99, oil on wood, 47 x 69 in/120 x 175 cm. Private collection.*

of life. A similar process to the one that Stevens elucidates – a highly conscious one, it seems to me – is going on in Howard Hodgkin's work: an attempt to fix the quiddity of an event – or a view or a moment or an emotion – rendered significant by "a consequence of the way we feel" through the manipulation of pigment upon a flat ground. "The move," as Klee describes it, from "impression to representation) The finished result, when it works, provides an elemental and intense pleasure but is also, as Stevens says later in the poem,

Like a flow of meanings with no speech

And of as many meanings as of men…

…this is what makes them seem

So far beyond the rhetorician's touch.

At the risk of sounding like a rhetorician I would claim that Hodgkin's paintings are, in their own way, a contemplation of what it is to be human – a celebration of all the complexities accruing in the act of being alive, sentient, and conscious. Of course these are ancient – not to say timeless – concerns of all serious artists, but art that can do this is exceptionally rare: it deserves to be richly celebrated.

In a Darkened Room, *1999-2001, oil on wood, 12 x 13 in/ 31 x 33 cm. Anthony d'Offay Gallery, London.*

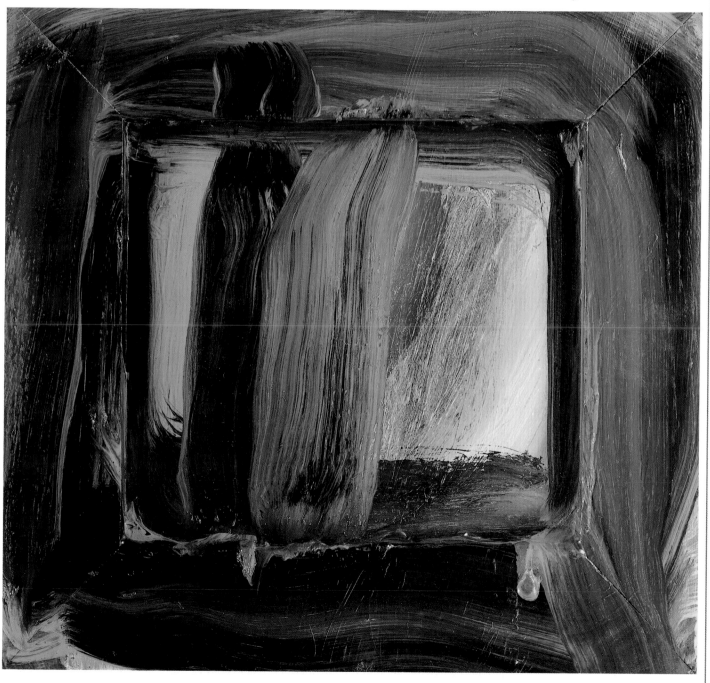

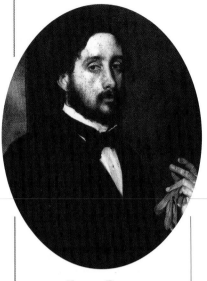

EDGAR DEGAS
*Although frequently
categorized as an
Impressionist – his paintings
were shown in several of the
first Impressionist exhibitions
– Edgar Degas stands apart.
His work reflects his interest
in interior light and studio
work, and in compositions
that took advantage of
the advances of the time
in photography.*

*He was born into a wealthy
Parisian banking family in
1834. At age 21, he attended
the Ecole des Beaux-Arts,
but dropped out to study the
work of the Renaissance
masters in Italy. His early
work was historical, based
on the style of Mantegna,
Bellini, and Ingres. In 1865,
after meeting Manet in Paris,
Degas abandoned historical
painting and turned to more
contemporary images – the
ballet, opera, the races at
Longchamps, brothels, cafes,
boudoirs, and prostitutes.*

*He continued these themes
throughout the 1870s and
1880s. In oils, watercolor,
gouache, pastels, charcoals,
monotypes, and sculptures,
his figures appear to be seen
as if "through the keyhole"
from a voyeur's standpoint,
captured in natural
poses with an emphasis
on the way they relate
to interior settings.*

*After 1890, his eyesight
failing, Degas worked almost
exclusively in pastel. He died
in Paris in 1917.*

Edgar Degas

by Julian Barnes

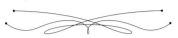

GREAT ARTISTS ATTRACT BASE PREJUDICES; BASE BUT INSTRUCTIVE. Jean-François Raffaelli, 1880–1924, painter of the Parisian suburbs, claimed in 1894 that Degas was an artist "seeking to render ignoble the secret forms of Woman"; he was someone who "must dislike women"; and in evidence Raffaelli reported the words of one of Degas' models: "He's a strange gentleman – he spent the whole four hours of the sitting combing my hair." Edmond de Goncourt (who had his own sarcastic doubts about Degas, as about everybody else) noted down these charges in his journal and added, as a

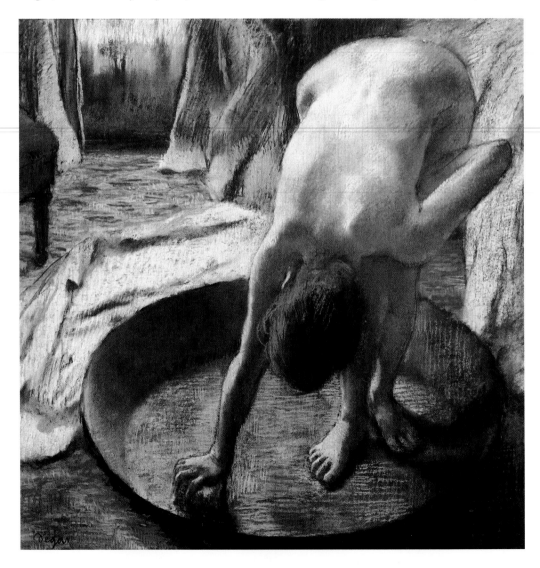

clincher, a story told him by the writer Léon Hennique, who at one time had shared with Degas a pair of sisters as mistresses. Hennique's "sister-in-law" had apparently complained of Degas' "lack of amorous means."

Could anything be plainer? Can't get it up; hates women; behaves oddly with models; rubbishes women in his art. Case closed, defendant guilty. Nor should we laugh knowingly at such century-old crassness and envy (Raffaelli was at the time announcing his intention to address the subject of Woman, which perhaps makes his motivation easier to read). Here is a critic of our time, Tobia Bezzola:

> "It is not known whether Degas had sexual relationships with women; at any rate there is no evidence that he did….[His] series of monotypes depicting brothel scenes is the most extreme example of the mixture of voyeurism and abhorrence with which he reacted to female sexuality."

"TRUTH IS NEVER UGLY WHEN ONE CAN FIND IN IT WHAT ONE NEEDS."

Or, if you prefer an even more catchall version, listen to our own Tom Paulin on *The Late Show*. Paulin went to the Degas exhibition at the National Gallery with the foreknowledge that the artist was anti-Semitic and anti-Dreyfusard:

> "I wondered how this would affect the paintings. You can't see it in the paintings, and I thought, Well, I should be admiring their beauty, but then I realized from reading this study of Eliot [by Anthony Julius] that misogyny and anti-Semitism are closely connected, so that what we have in this exhibition are women in contorted poses… They're like performing animals; they're like animals in the zoo. There's some deep, deep hatred of women, and I thought what does this remind me of, and I thought something like a concentration camp doctor has created these figures… I'm inside the head of someone who's a deeply, deeply hateful person…"

This is a masterly application of the biographical fallacy; "admiring beauty" is obviously a suspect business best got out of by discovering that beauty's creator was someone you wouldn't employ as a childminder. The show which provoked this outburst of effervescing Puritanism was at London's National Gallery in 1996. As an exhibition it is wise in its theming of work, resourceful in its assembly (late Degas is widely scattered, and rarely shown), and of exactly the right size. All this is to one end: to show a great and aging painter working obsessively at that border-crossing between Truth to Life and Truth to Art, pushing constantly at and against form and color and technique. Most single-artist shows tend to be cherry-picking jobs: the best example of this or that particular phase of the artist's

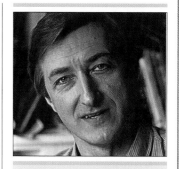

JULIAN BARNES
Born in 1946 in England, and educated at Oxford, Barnes worked as a lexicographer for the Oxford English Dictionary *for several years before becoming a reviewer and literary editor for the British newspapers* The New Statesmen *and* The Sunday Times. *For the* New Review, *he wrote "The" infamous gossip column, "Edward Pygge," and from 1979 to 1986, he was the television critic for the* London Observer.

In 1980, Barnes published his first novel, Metroland, *and, in 1984,* Flaubert's Parrot, *which was shortlisted for the Booker Prize. Treating the themes of history, reality, and truth, his present oeuvre consists of eight novels, a book of short stories, and an essay collection. Among the awards he has received in his career are the Somerset Maugham Award, the Prix Medicis, the E.M. Forster Award, and the Shakespeare Prize. His most recent novel,* Love, etc. *continues the theme of his 1991 novel* Talking It Over. *Under the pseudonym Dan Kavanagh, Barnes also writes crime novels, and he is currently at work on a collection of essays.*

The Tub, *1886, pastel on cardboard, 24 x 33 in/60 x 83 cm. Louvre, Paris.*

"development," the canvases in which the painter plays our favorite tunes. Such shows are not actively misleading, but they are subtly deceptive if we therefore view the artist's life as a succession of lottery numbers, of wins and losses – masterpiece, dud, dud, semi-masterpiece, dud, masterpiece. The artist's life, as Richard Kendall's exhibition cleverly demonstrates, is more likely to be a matter of obsessional overlap, of ferrying back and forth, of process rather than result, journey rather than arrival.

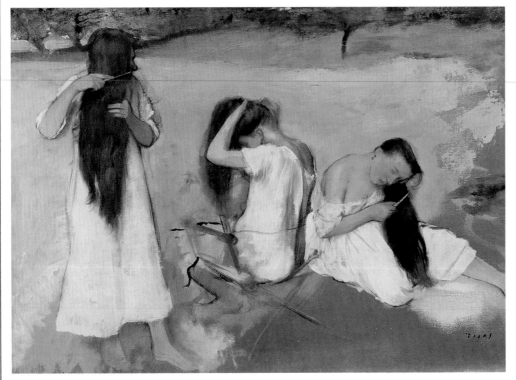

Women Combing Their Hair,
1875–76, oil on paper mounted on canvas, 13 x 18 in/32 x 46 cm. The Phillips Collection, Washington, D.C.

Many of the works are on tracing paper, for reasons both aesthetic – tracing paper takes pastel particularly well – and practical: the image proposed (rather than arrived at) can be copied again and again. Copied, that is, in order to be reused and redeveloped, or even reintegrated into an entirely different composition. That twist of the hip, throw of the head, splay of the feet may turn up again sometimes on the same wall, sometimes two rooms away. The pose or gesture segues from charcoal to pastel to oil to sculpture (the role of the sculptures – not cast until after Degas' death – is nicely enigmatic:

"OH! WOMEN CAN NEVER FORGIVE ME; THEY HATE ME, THEY CAN FEEL THAT I AM DISARMING THEM. I SHOW THEM WITHOUT THEIR COQUETRY, IN THE STATE OF ANIMALS CLEANING THEMSELVES!"

were they sufficient unto themselves, made to help the paintings, developments of the paintings, or all three?). Is it sentimental to sense an anger behind such fretful and unceasing investigation of certain forms? An artistic anger, that is, fury that time is running out, that light (given Degas' encroaching blindness) is running out, and still there is more to be seen, still forms to be pushed further.

Time. Degas spent four hours combing a model's hair. What a strange gentleman, when the norm might have been – get your kit off, hop on that pedestal, and how about a quick drink afterwards. The "strange gentleman" was always looking. There is a story of Degas coming out of a party one evening and turning to his companion with the complaint that

you never saw sloping shoulders in society any more. It's the tiny aside of a great artist. Goncourt reports the remark, confirms its justice, and seeks its explanation habits of physical breeding over several generations; but it is Degas – the artist, rather than the novelist, social observer and art critic – who has seen it. Degas' tone, it's worth noticing, is one of complaint. The story remains unannotated by Goncourt, but the complaint is presumably an artistic one; a realization that the great and fundamental shape which was the subject of so many of his paintings was changing, if not exactly before his eyes, then within his lifetime – and would continue to change thereafter.

Four hours (and this was only one four hours among many); this show is full of moments which hair is "seen." Intimate, informal hair – hair with its hair down.

Degas knows how a woman holds her hair to comb it, how she supports it when another is combing it, how she alleviates scalp-strain with a flattened palm a the tuggingest moments of the business. But (truth to life melting into truth to art) hair is also so malleable and metamorphic that it seems eager to take on abstract form. In many of the after-the-bath pictures, it echoes and plans against the twists and cascades of the towel, sometimes appearing to trade places. There is even a kind of jokey visual misleading, in one image, where the maid's water-jug – posing as a bunched up hair – occupies the space of the head, while the head itself is ducked down forwards.

The modern female body represented in a state of intimacy by and observing male. A century on, we have become more self-conscious spectators; queasiness and correct

Seated Nude from behind, combing her hair, *c. 1897, charcoal and pastel, 28 x 28/71 x 71 cm. Kunsthaus, Zurich.*

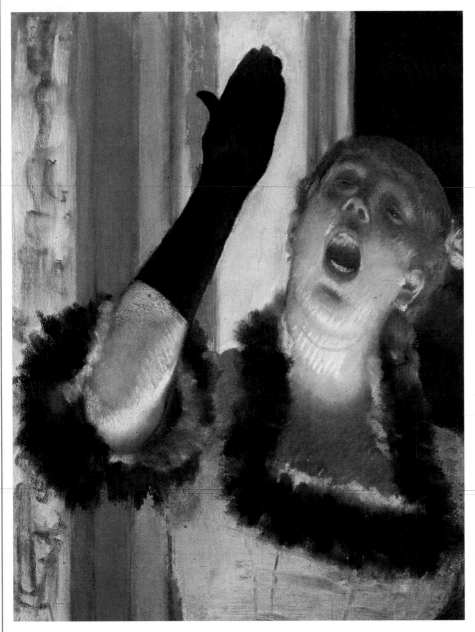

thinking have entered the equation for some. The artist also helped things along with his much-quoted statement that: "Women can never forgive me; they hate me, they feel I am disarming them. I show them without their coquetry." Perhaps extremely coquettish women hated him for his art; perhaps the models he shouted at (but whom he also treated with "enormous patience") felt they had earned their corn. On the other hand, as Richard Kendall acutely demonstrates, it was often women who were the first purchasers of these scenes of private grooming. It is a strange coincidence that two of the finest recent exhibitions in London have both had female self-absorption as a central theme: the other being the Vermeer.

This isn't an easy area: we all import our prejudices. At the National Gallery press view I ran into a museum director who said he thought the pictures were all about "the decay of the flesh"; whereas it seemed to me that Degas was

Singer with a Glove, 1878, *pastel on canvas, 21 x 16 in/53 x 41 cm. Fogg Art Museum, Harvard University, Cambridge, Massachusetts. Bequest Collection of Maurice Wertheim.*

portraying flesh at its most robust. His ballet dancers are no longer sylphs and nymphets; but even their states of exhausted resting (that hands-on-waist, backstrainy, can't-wait-for-it-to-end pose) are predicated upon a vital physical life. Is this just my prejudice? As it's my prejudice to differentiate between the life, in which Degas may or may not have been misogynistic, and the art, in which it seems to me that Degas, plainly loved women. That remark needs immediate qualification, of course (when he painted he wasn't "loving women," he was painting a picture, and the picture was doubtless what filled his mind), but otherwise let it stand. Do you constantly and obsessively fret at the representation of something you dislike or despise? "For each man draws the thing he loathes"? On the whole, not. Would Degas' "lack of amorous means" (if true – and there is recent evidence of condom buying to dispute it) have made him a misogynist? Not necessarily: it might even make him the more attending observer.

The artist as "voyeur"? But that is exactly what the artist should be: one who sees (and voyeur can also carry the sense of hallucinatory visionary). The painter who tortures his models by forcing them into uncomfortable poses? Except that he also used photography, and memory; besides, if the body could get there, it had clearly got there before in its history. The brothel-depictor who thus let slip his "abhorrence" of female sexuality? Yet these monotypes seem to me to reflect all the jollity, boredom, absorption, professionalism,

"WOMEN THINK IN LITTLE PACKAGES. I UNDERSTAND NOTHING ABOUT THE WAY THEIR MINDS WORK. THEY PUT EVERY SUBJECT INTO AN ENVELOPE, LABEL IT AND IT'S FINISHED…LITTLE PACKAGES…LITTLE PACKAGES."

and "work" of those engaged in this assembly line trade, the tone no more abhorring than it is in Lautrec's brothel work. Perhaps Lautrec's reputation as a merry figure marginalized by dwarfism – and thus on a moral level with the marginalized prostitutes – works for him, whereas Degas' reputation works against him here. The graphic output remains the same either way. But if you can look at, say, Degas' *La Fête de la Patronne* and see only

"HIS BATHERS ALWAYS SEEM TO HAVE BEEN CAUGHT IN MOMENTS OF NO IMPORTANCE, CHOSEN APPARENTLY AT RANDOM FROM AN INFINITY OF GESTURES AND MOTIONS, WHILE HIS DANCERS ARE POSED IN ATTITUDES OF TRANSITION, NEITHER THE ALERT STANCE OF PREPARATION NOR THE TRIUMPHANT ACHIEVEMENT OF A FULLY EXTENDED ARABESQUE."
—*Karen Wilkin*

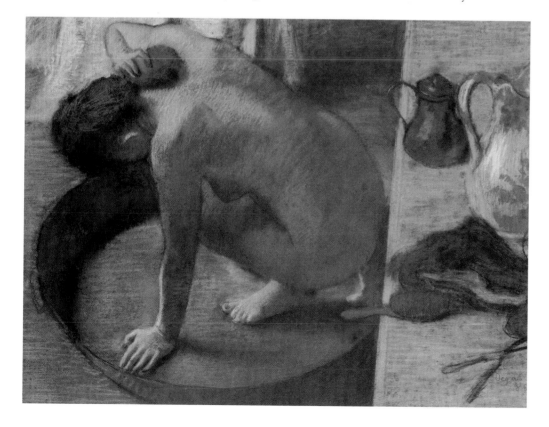

The Tub, 1886, *pastel on paper, 28 x 28 in/70 x 70 cm. Hillstead Museum, Farmington, Connecticut.*

abhorrence of female sexuality, then I suspect you are in deep critical trouble.

Another line of reproach is to suggest that the frequent averting of the face in the later paintings indicates quasi-pornographic intent. All arguments imply their reverse: you might equally argue (if you wanted to) that the averted face is that of a woman ignoring the painter/spectator, aloof in her privacy and self-involvement. More to the point, this is not portraiture; or at least, not portraiture as the depiction of revealed character. It is portraiture of the body as form, the end of a lifetime's search which had begun with a devotion to Ingres, and with Ingres' instruction to the young Degas, "Draw lines, young man, draw lines." Degas at one point owned Ingres' *Angelica Saved by Ruggiero*, as well as a pencil study for *La Grande Odalisque*. How far Degas' art took the representation of the female

The Millinery Shop, *1879-84, oil on canvas,*
39 x 43 in/100 x 110 cm.
Art Institute of Chicago.
Mr. and Mrs. Lewis L. Coburn
Memorial Collection.

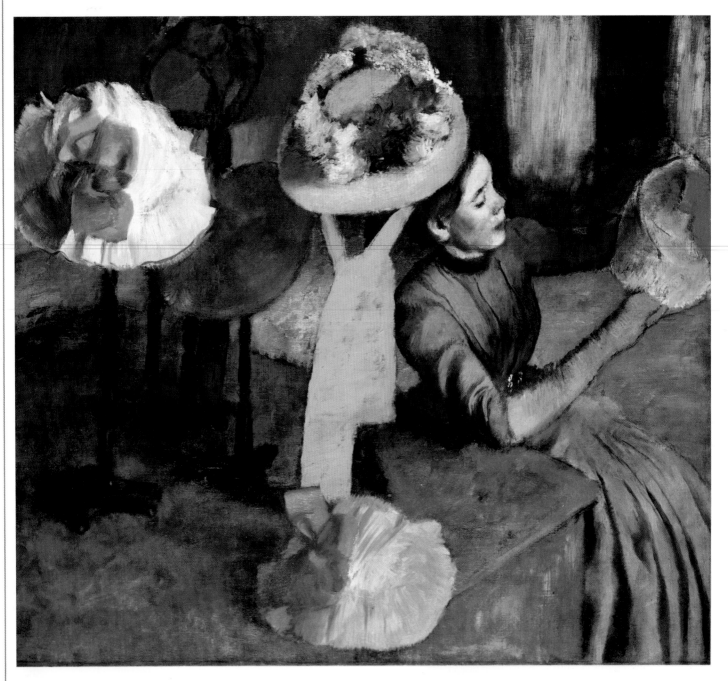

body can be seen by looking at these two works in the (London) National Gallery's concurrent "Degas as a Collector." There we have the nude as line and finish, depicted in exalted splendor even when suffering. In the pencil study we see a spine as architectural as the keel of a Viking ship, a svelte bum, and a breast which, despite what the turning-away posture ought to have done for it, keeps its silicone splendor. Chez Ingres, that mammarial is marmoreal; chez Degas, the breast has the mobility, slope, and fall of real life. Of course, male artists depicting the female nude are bound to get it in the neck nowadays from someone or other (Lucian Freud had probably better start wearing a neck protector). Idealization or naturalism? "Should poets bicycle-pump the human heart/Or squash it flat?" The same goes for artists and the body; we have our current preferences and principles – though they are, of course, only current.

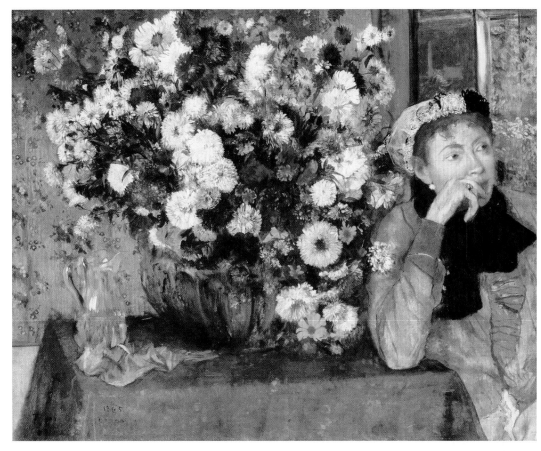

A Woman with Chrysanthemums, *1865, oil on canvas, 28 x 36in/71 x 92 cm. Metropolitan Museum of Art, New York. Bequest of Mrs. H. O. Havemeyer, The H.O. Havemeyer collection.*

The early section of Kendall's show includes *The Millinery Shop* (of 1879–84). You could, if you were plodding, see it as another example of the "averted-face" approach; for yes, here is the milliner with her face half turned away. But that's because this is a painting about hats. It's not a portrait, it's not about work, it's about hats; here fabric is the equivalent of flesh. And in its plain boldness of design it recalls Degas' great portrait *Woman with Chrysanthemums*. This is, more properly, *Chrysanthemums with Woman*: the sunburst of flowers occupies the center of the canvas, while the woman looks out of frame to the spectator's right. Whenever I see this painting I hear a challenge and an implicit question: you think you know what a portrait is? There are more ways to paint a woman and a bunch of flowers than you or I have even dreamed of, this picture whispers. And in this respect it foreshadows what we see more vividly and hauntingly in late Degas: the artist pushing at form, at color, at the still expandable possibilities of human form and movement. If he was unforgiving of his models, he was no less forgiving in his expectations of himself, and of what art could see and show.

"HE IS AT ONCE UTTERLY FAMILIAR AND REMARKABLY ENIGMATIC."

—Karen Wilkin

Jasper Johns

by Trevor Winkfield

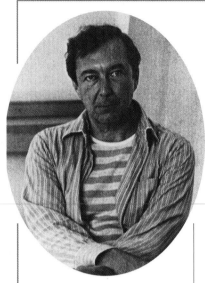

JASPER JOHNS
*One of the most influential
of the Abstract Expressionists,
Jasper Johns ultimately
rejected the form to create
images that were simple and
commonplace, while at the
same time ironic.*

*Born in 1930 in Augusta,
Georgia, he left for New
York in 1949, but was soon
drafted into military service.
Returning to New York,
he established friendships
with Rauschenburg, the
choreographer Merce
Cunningham, and the
composer John Cage.*

*He painted his first flag
picture in 1954, and
exhibited more of these flags
– along with paintings of
targets, numbers, and letters
– at his first one-man show.
This Castelli Gallery show,
many believe, marked the
beginning of the Pop Art,
which eventually Johns
developed into Minimalism.
His reductive images of
familiar symbols and objects
focus on the painting as an
object in and of itself rather
than a representation
of an object.*

*Johns' major exhibitions
include a retrospective at
the Whitney Museum in
New York, the Museum
Ludwig in Cologne, Musée
National d'Art Moderne in
Paris, the Hayward Gallery,
London, and the Seibu
Museum of Art, Tokyo.*

THERE APPEARS TO BE NEITHER RHYME NOR REASON why good art is produced at any given time. Take Russia in 1915: who would have suspected that in the midst of war, in one of the most conservative and repressive societies then existing, a society disintegrating from its own lack of imagination, Kasimir Malevich could have wrenched himself free, ignored his freezing apartment, his dire poverty, his meager food rations, and settled down to paint the first Suprematist compositions? On the other hand, when all the elements are in place nothing seems to happen. Japan, after 1950, blessed with unparalleled wealth and a curious, acquisitive middle-class lusting after wallcoverings, failed miserably to initiate any contemporary art of value (to the extent of having to import it). All the power of Victorian England, too, only squeaked forth the Pre-Raphaelites and the Royal Academy.

Jasper Johns, who rose to prominence after his first show at Leo Castelli's in New York in 1958, has had a career which at first glance seems a product of the perfected version of the Japanese model. A country (the United States) at the height of its mercantile and military power (1947–65), secure in its material achievements, with a small but influential and extremely knowledgeable intelligentsia, seeks to legitimize its new wealth by patronizing

"ONE WORKS WITHOUT THINKING HOW TO WORK."

the arts. Of course, it helps when there's a bushel of talent awaiting patronage, a bushel moreover firmly ensconced in a city affordable to artists (as New York then was, and alas no longer is). A generation of Abstract Expressionists had somehow managed to survive and fabricate its finest paintings prior to this upsurge of patronage, but it is Johns' generation which reaped its full benefits, and ultimately its poisoned chalice. For around the mid-1960s a new bevy of wealthy collectors (as opposed to middle-class art lovers) muscled into the American art world, their eyes formed by film and television rather than the old masters, and for the most part unable to differentiate good from bad art. For them, Pop Art was an easily assimilated movement, as Bauhaus abstraction had been for an earlier generation. While one doesn't want to denigrate the simplistic liberating effusions of Pop, its legacy (and that of its successor, Minimalism) forms part and parcel of one of the most paradoxical of recent American achievements: the ascent of proletarian taste by purely capitalist means.

Stylistically, Pop represented a massive surrender of complexity in favor of numskull homogeneity, signaling that great ennui of the imagination now trudging through the West. Financially, the reckless throwing around of huge sums of money which Pop ushered in usurped the old art world and imposed an art market mentality where the relationship between dealer and artist shifted to one between dealer and collector. Art became just another capitalist industry, with aesthetics more or less thrown out of the window. Simultaneously, criticism suffered a massive loss of nerve, refused to take the lead, and degenerated into bad journalism, or worse, pseudo-esoteric twaddle. Once this had happened, it was only a matter of time before contemporary art, following on from modern art, could itself be gobbled up by that strange commercial hybrid "gallery art." Under this rubric more bad art was churned out – and sold – during the 1980s than at any time since the reign of the nineteenth-century salons. Artists by and large were reduced to mere purveyors to the trade and any art managing to escape its homogenization tended to be buried by the dross. Thus, by the early 1990s, New York, its eyeballs exhausted, found itself in the parlous state in which Paris had found itself in the mid-1950s: a plenitude of galleries with nothing much of interest to display and the glum realization that American art's Golden Age was well and truly a thing of the past.

Through all this dissolution and venal mayhem, Jasper Johns has sailed apparently unscathed, a bemused survivor, perhaps the only one, of that gifted slew of explorers gravitating around the Abstract Expressionist/Pop axis. Some had died, still others took early mental retirement, content to endlessly recycle their early formulas (which *were* formidable – nobody can dismiss the sheer visceral impact of early Warhol and Lichtenstein). Those still alive more or less spent their later

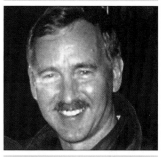

TREVOR WINKFIELD
A British painter living in New York City since the 1960s, Winkfield was born in Leeds in 1944. He attended the Leeds College of Art and received his M.A. from the Royal College of Art in London. He has long been associated with writers, and his idiosyncratic works of art have appeared on book covers for the poet John Ashbery.

Winkfield's intensely hued, collage-like paintings are made up of seemingly odd personal allusions to events and objects, but a persistent viewer can find narrative in them. Fragmented images of people, animals, objects, and patterns form a kaleidoscope on the canvases, and the effect is a distinctive melding of formalism, surrealism, and Pop Art.

Winkfield has won the Award in Art from the American Academy of Arts and Letters and a Pollock-Krasner Award. He continues to live, paint, and write in New York while exhibiting his paintings in the US and in England.

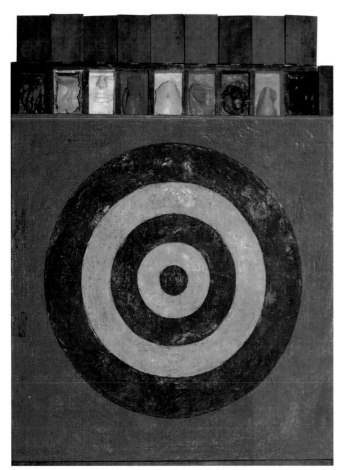

Target with Plaster Casts, *1955, encaustic and collage on canvas with objects, 51 x 44 in/130 x 112 cm. Private collection, New York.*

careers wasting their oxygen. Johns alone has cleaved to his self-imposed role of research painter, one of that endangered band whose password might be Kant's "I no longer know where I am," and whose first requisite is to be perpetually dissatisfied by the direction their work is taking at any given time.

This discontent is one reason why so many American artists have dedicated a special niche to Johns in their pantheons. He's remained, despite his commercial success, a quintessential artists' artist, on a par with Marsden Hartley and Willem de Kooning, admired at the same time as they are plundered by artists of widely divergent tastes. He is, in fact, one of the least imitated but most influential of American artists (Pollock's work, by contrast, has had little to offer later generations beyond a concept of what "greatness" can look like). It's this aspect of Johns' work – the solitary's dedication to research despite all that's going on around him – which brings us back full circle to Malevich.

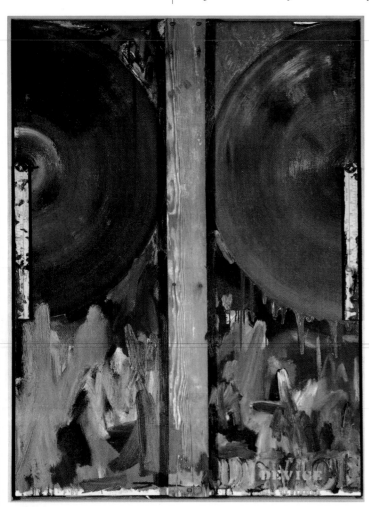

Device Circle, *1962, oil on canvas, 40 x 30 in/102 x 76 cm. The Baltimore Museum of Art; Purchased with funds provided by The Dexter M. Ferry Jr. Trustee Corporation Fund and by Edith Ferry Hooper (BMA 1976.1).*

Johns' early work – the flags, targets, and numerals – were hatched in the same mood of defiant solitude as Malevich's white fields. Few saw them while they were being painted. Only when they emerged as a group in Johns' first show in 1958 did they enter public discourse, and then with alarming rapidity. Johns was obviously the right painter at the right time (unlike all those who emerged in the 1980s, who were the wrong painters at the right time). This ready acceptance was due in no small measure to Johns' ability to render the achievements of Abstract Expressionism comprehensible to an audience more amenable to figuration. This coming together of figurative subject matter with an abstract handling of paint marked a historic breakthrough, and still seems one of Johns' most memorable reforms.

Forty years later, these early emblems have only increased their magnetic luster. One can easily reconstitute their original appeal, a paradoxical union of opposites. Their flat, banal imagery (whose iconic starkness bespeaks America) married to a sensuous, idiosyncratic handling of pigment – a melding of public and private faces – still strikes one as a terrific accomplishment for a young painter. The works vibrate with all the giddy arrogance of early Seurat and Picasso, when those painters knew they too could and would change the way people looked at the world.

Shorn of their weeping veils of encaustic droplets, the flags and targets might be cast as forerunners of Warhol's masterpieces for morons of the following decade. But retaining the veils signaled Johns' rejection of reductive modernism, which in turn allowed him to bypass the dead-end of Pop and continue along that visionary road he's spent the rest of his life traversing, albeit with many a feint and stumble.

This repudiation of his early success – a triumph based on monolithic imagery confining autobiographical intrusions to the action of the painter's wrist – erupted in 1959 with *Device Circle* and *Out the Window*. In these paintings, the confines of the canvas for once seem too restrictive. The patient, contemplative brush-strokes are ushered away to make room for vociferous pattering wind-bursts looking to spill over onto the wall. The paintings stop being monologues and become conversations, as though

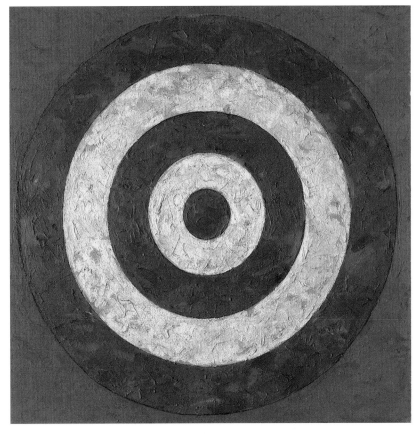

Johns had taken to heart Duchamp's insight that it's the viewers, replete with personal histories and their own interpretative skills, who complete the painting. Johns' target surfaces had looked as though they were guarding the images beneath, not only clamping them down but trying to hide them – subsumed violence personified.

Target. *1958, oil and collage on canvas, 36 x 36 in/92 x 92 cm. Collection of the artist; on loan to the National Gallery of Art, Washington, DC.*

Three Flags, *1958, encaustic on canvas, 31 x 46 in/78 x 116 cm. Whitney Museum of American Art, New York.*

From the early 1960s the images bubble to the surface, break free, and start parading around, beckoning the viewer to follow. It's little wonder that Alfred Barr, who'd purchased three of Johns' paintings for the Museum of Modern Art from the first show, blanched when he saw the second show in 1960. In place of the secular altarpieces he'd lionized, he found *tableaux* which had the quality of bins (trash cans) into which everything had been tumbled. Many of these later paintings, executed at a time when Johns was claiming "I don't want my work to be an exposure of my feelings," have literal intrusions: spoons, cups, brooms – a whole pantry of images. They're still bedecked with petrified wax, evoking troops of nerves circulating beneath, as though the paintings' real lives, as ever, took place out of sight. Here Johns (a ravenous reader of poetry, whose work contains numerous references to

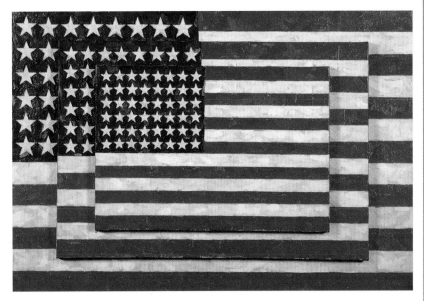

Right: Savarin, *1977, color lithograph, (sheet) 45 x 35in/114 x 89 cm. (sheet) Published by Universal Limited Art Editions.*

Opposite page, top: Periscope (Hart Crane), *1963, oil on canvas, 67 x 48 in/170 x 122 cm. Collection of the artist; courtesy of the National Museum of American Art, Smithsonian Institution, Washington, DC.*

Opposite page, bottom: Voice 2 (detail), *1971, oil and collage on canvas, three panels, each 72 x 50 in/183 x 127 cm. Kunstmuseum, Basel.*

"JASPER JOHNS USUALLY LOCATES THE BEGINNING OF HIS CAREER AS AN ARTIST IN THE YEARS 1953 AND 1954, WHEN HE WAS IN HIS EARLY TWENTIES, AND WHEN, HE HAD DECIDED TO STOP 'BECOMING' AN ARTIST AND 'BE ONE.'"

—Nan Rosenthal

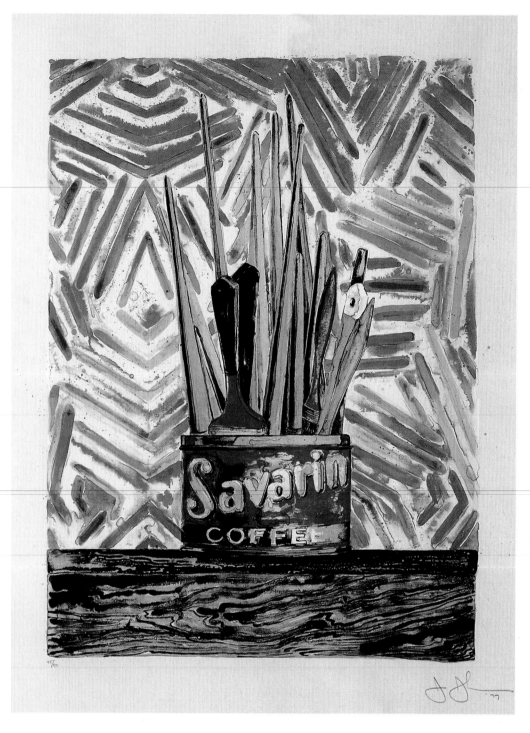

poets such as Frank O'Hara, Hart Crane, Ted Berrigan, and Tennyson) consciously or unconsciously succumbed to that well-worn but still potent Mallarméan notion of painting not the thing itself but the effect which it produces. Seen in this light, are the targets surrogate self-portraits, as some have hinted? Are the body parts, corpses, skulls, sleeping soldiers, wooden beams, and bloodied bandages evidence of the strangest religious painter of our time? Has Johns' life work been a struggle to erect a crucifixion without painting one?

Johns' own intentions have remained skilfully shrouded in ambiguity. In the interviews and remarkable sketchbook notes, we're supplied with elliptical clues rather than the hard facts that lazy-bones crave. There's no simple "Yes" or "No" to Jasper Johns, it's always overlaid with "Either/Or." He himself asserts: "I don't put any value on a kind of thinking that puts limits on things." His mercifully reticent biography offers few clues as to how to approach the work. At one point in the chronology running through the Museum of Modern Art catalog (one of those unnecessary rib-crushers so beloved of contemporary curators) the compilers are so stumped for interesting tidbits they're reduced to such small potatoes as the entry for October 7, 1983:

> *From Stony Point, Johns writes to Castleman denying rumors he he has broken his leg. He adds that the monotypes are being cleaned by Bill Goldston, and that he will soon decide on how to tear these prints' margins.*

One can, I suppose, dismiss these non-events. But reading between their lines we can detect that the important part of Johns' life has been lived on the canvas, not in the world outside – which gives his inert slabs of encaustic a terrible poignancy.

A problem which such a devotion creates is the sheer boredom and loneliness many artists experience when confined to their studios for hours at a time, day in and day out, decade after decade. It's the main reason so many abandon the task, or start talking to themselves.

"I THINK A PAINTING SHOULD CONTAIN MORE EXPERIENCE THAN SIMPLY INTENDED STATEMENT."

Johns, about the time his paintings stopped being monologues and became conversations (1960), with studio fever mounting, adopted the clever strategem of taking up a team activity in the form of printmaking. The revivifying impact apart – maneuvring raw lithographic ink jolted his paint into chromatic overdrive – it led, by the end of the decade, to an increased flattening of the paint surface.

With his passionless "Screen Pieces" of 1967–8 one suspects he no longer meant what he painted. As their titles suggest, the "Screen Pieces" were more about flatness than hidden depths, more about print than paint. By the time he came to paint *Decoy* in 1971 he'd become a moody topographer of atmosphere, but little else.

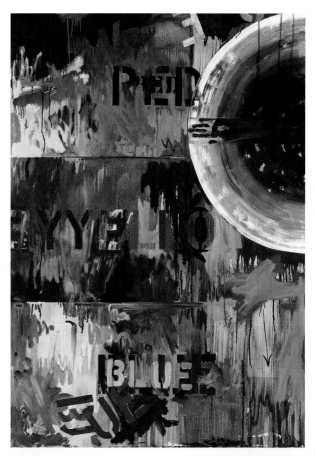

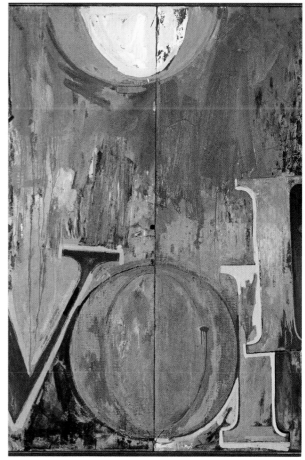

It's clear he'd simultaneously run out of ideas of what to paint and how to paint. The three interchangeable panels of *Voice 2* (1968–71) illustrate the color crisis he was experiencing at the same time. It's often been said – Johns has tacitly agreed – that he has at best a rudimentary grasp of color. I beg to differ. He's a wonderful colorist. While it's true he rarely puts us in a lather with cunning arrays of tints the way Matisse does,

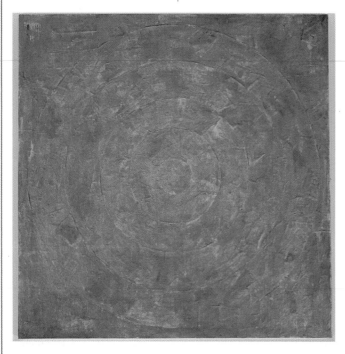

Green Target, *1955, encaustic on newspaper and cloth over canvas, 60 x 60 in/152 x 152 cm. Museum of Modern Art, New York. Richard S. Zeisler Fund.*

he's always used color so it doesn't overpower his ideas. When we leave Matisse, on the other hand, often we're left with a stunning crimson glow, and an empty head. *Voice 2* does, however, betray Johns' lack of self-confidence in his innate color sense to an alarming degree. Originally, each panel was painted primary red, yellow, and blue (remnants of these colors act as *mementi mori* along the edges of the canvases). In this primal state – still visible in slides taken in 1970 – the whole ensemble was a prismatic riot. Alas, Johns lost his nerve and felt compelled to tone it down by reverting to his usual monochromatic gray overlays; so what we perceive now is very much a shadow of its former self, still a masterpiece, not ruined but muted.

At this impasse (impasses occur regularly at the turn of each decade in his career), Johns was driving on Long Island and saw a car coming towards him. Covered in cross-hatchings and glimpsed only for a second, its fortuitous dazzle supplied subject matter sufficient for a decade's mining. This ability to capitalize on apparently trivial occurrences (witness his dream of painting the stars and stripes, or the casual suggestion by a friend that he paint a pet) marks him not only as a willing sponge but draws attention also to his relative lack of imagination. Not that there's anything wrong with that – many find Picasso too overpoweringly protean. And besides, painters by and large aren't the most imaginative creators; compared to musicians and poets, they come pretty low on the imaginative totem. Mainly it's a matter of finding and refining a few subjects, and Johns slots into this scheme of things perfectly.

The range of his subject matter may be narrow but it runs deep, sparking endless shufflings and myriad interpretations. Just as Cézanne's apples, contemplated long enough, take on the gravity of planets in their orbits, so Johns can transform a green target into a whirlpool, one which becomes a bird's-eye view of the roof of a tower, its multiple floors receding into the wall behind. This awareness that what we are seeing is not all that we can get (*Voice 2*'s buried spectrum being this concept's most tangible archaeological evidence) is made explicit in the works from 1980 onward. Thanks to paint's ability to depict and disguise at the same time, previously secret layers are hauled to the surface yet retain their unfathomable ambiguities. Autobiographical elements such as the floor plan of his grandfather's house are carpeted by ladders, body shadows, segments of sidereal space, stick men, and Picassoid eyeballs. It's as though Johns is finally declaring his life to be an open book … if only we can find him on the shelf.

Laboring under the label *Greatest Living American Painter* (a burden which should be returned to the *Guinness Book of Records*) cannot have been easy for Johns. He must

> "IN PART IT CONNECTS WITH DUCHAMP'S IDEA THAT AN ARTIST HAS ONLY A FEW IDEAS AND HE'S PROBABLY RIGHT. ONE'S RANGE IS LIMITED BY ONE'S INTERESTS AND IMAGINATION AND BY ONE'S PASSION."

often have felt he'd been transformed into one of his alleged self-portraits, a target. Certainly he's received more than his fair share of brickbats when he's failed to deliver a Great Painting. Much better to think of him as a Remarkable Painter, a maverick isolationist who has never stopped painting his best work.

Map, *1961, oil on canvas, 78 x 123 in/198 x 315 cm. Museum of Modern Art, New York.*

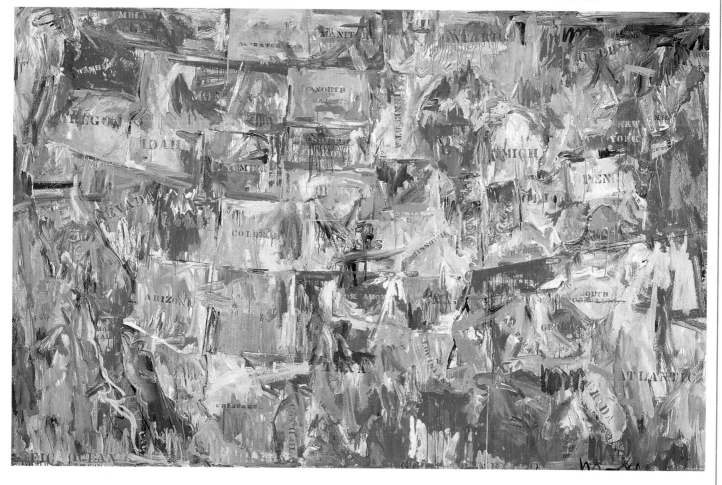

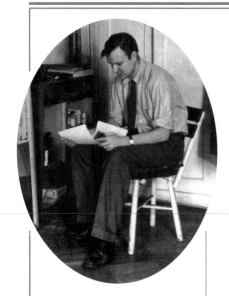

Robert Motherwell

by Norbert Lynton

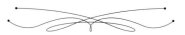

"Every picture one paints involves not painting others." Robert Motherwell to Frank O'Hara, 1965.

SHOWING A MAJOR MOTHERWELL EXHIBITION IN SPAIN MAKES GOOD SENSE. Dore Ashton curated it for the Tàpies Foundation in Barcelona and there, carefully, sparsely hung, it looked both strong and enticing, especially in the main gallery whose atrium allows it air and space and light, coming down from a new ceiling above a gallery supported on unusually slender, modern, cast-iron columns. One could glimpse a few Tàpies up there, and go up to see them. Motherwell was never a "matter painter" building images out of heavy, dense materials – he usually works thinly, even when paint

> **"REGARDLESS OF THE MEDIUM, WHETHER IT IS IN ELIOT OR PICASSO OR A TV THIRTY-SECOND ADVERTISEMENT, I THINK COLLAGE IS THE TWENTIETH CENTURY'S GREATEST CREATIVE INNOVATION."**

goes over paint – but there is a real kinship between the two artists. Both use blacks powerfully, and ochers and white, and sometimes inscribe ancient signs in compositions we call abstract. Both have a vivid sense of scale. For Tàpies, very much alive, to welcome Motherwell, who died in 1991, to his Foundation is a fine act of collegiate homage. From March to May the exhibition will be in the Reina Sofia Museum in Madrid, in beautiful but more impersonal spaces. The dozen or so paintings that were omitted in Barcelona will find room there and the result must be an even more persuasive show.

Many of Motherwell's best paintings refer to Spain. We tend to think more of his links with France, his deep and somehow essential regard for French Symbolist poetry and literary theory as well as French painting. He wrote his art history thesis on Delacroix's Journals in Paris, Grenoble, and Oxford. From 1944 on he edited that famous series of source books, "The Documents of Modern Art," inevitably looking first to French material. He wrote several introductions for it, of exactly the sensitive, slightly chancy, entirely stimulating sort one hopes to get from spirited artists who are good with words. Marcel Raymond's *From Baudelaire to Surrealism* appeared in the series too, a surprising choice because it was not about art, yet altogether right and timely for the light it throws on the principles of modern art. Historically the most important book in the series is the exceptionally large one dealing not with resonances and silences but with "anti-art," as it was called in the 1950s: *The Dadaist Painters and Poets*, published in 1951 when the Dada movement had all but disappeared from modern art history, perhaps to leave what we could call Modernist "pro-art" unchallenged.

The exhibition's multilingual catalog includes an important essay by Professor Ashton who knew Motherwell over many years, witnessed his activity as part of the New York School, and is the most multicultured of American critics. She writes about his attachments to many things, stressing his enduring regard for Spain. He heard André Malraux speak on the Civil War in San Francisco in 1937. He soon discovered Spanish poetry. Just when he was beginning to paint seriously, in 1941, he spent some months in Mexico, where he fell in love with and married a Mexican actress, met various sorts and degrees of Spanishness but also had contact with Spanish refugees from Fascism. Young Motherwell, of partly Scottish stock and born in Aberdeen, Washington (his father was Robert Burns Motherwell II), a

student of philosophy, psychology, and art history – unavoidably international subjects – had settled in New York in 1940 to pursue art history further under Meyer Schapiro. He was painting part-time and Schapiro introduced him to the Surrealists sheltering from the war in and near New York. Motherwell said he spoke pidgin French with them; they found him young and eager, responsive and helpful. It was the un-French Surrealist Matta, from Chile officially but from just about everywhere in effect, who told him about automatism and drew him down to Mexico

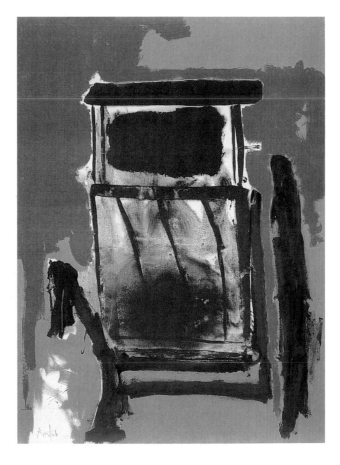

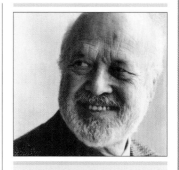

NORBERT LYNTON
The art historian and writer was born in 1927 and educated in London at Birkbeck College and at the Courtauld Institute. He has taught at several colleges and universities, including Leeds College of Art, Chelsea School of Art, and the University of Sussex, where he is now Professor Emeritus of the History of Art.

During the 1960s, Lynton was the London correspondent for Art International, *and from 1965 to 1970, the art critic for London's The Guardian. From 1970 to 1975, he worked for the Arts Council of Great Britain as the Director of Exhibitions. He has written widely on art of the twentieth century, and recently co-authored* The Yale Dictionary of Art and Artists *with Erika Langmuir. He is on the editorial board of* Modern Painters.

He now lives and writes in Brighton, England.

Personnage (**Self-Portrait**), *1943, collage of Japanese and Western Papers with Gouache, oil, and ink on paperboard, 41 x 26 in/104 x 65 cm. Guggenheim Collection, Venice (Solomon R. Guggeheim Foundation, New York).*

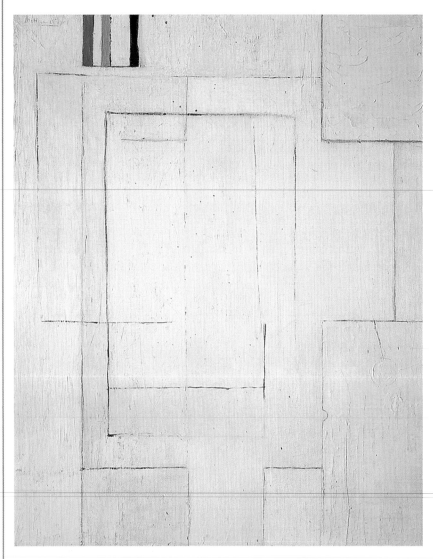

Spanish Picture with Window,
1941, oil on canvas,
42 x 34 in/107 x 86 cm.
Modern Art Museum of
Fort Worth, Texas.

in 1941, to black, reds, and ocher in sunshine and popular celebrations of death. The visit unsettled and resettled him. He returned to New York with the first item in the exhibition, *Spanish Picture with Window*, and began painting *Little Spanish Prison* (1941–44; MOMA, New York).

Dore Ashton touches only lightly on Motherwell's isolation among the leading Abstract Expressionists, even once he was exhibiting mature work and was paraded as one of them. She refers to Harold Rosenberg's words about "coonskins" and "redcoats," identifying the new painters of New York with those un-uniformed guerillas and the traditionalists, practicing European maneuvers, with the square-bashing English soldiers, useless in the wilds. That was a useful and entertaining image then. She also mentions Philip Rahv's distinction with American literature between palefaces, the family of Henry James and of Eliot, and redskins, descended from Emerson and Whitman. How did Motherwell, aware of these tropes, see himself?

Beginning in 1960, David Sylvester's interviews with the major New York painters were broadcast by the Third Programme, including one with Motherwell. Sylvester titled it "Painting as Self-Discovery," aptly enough according to the general image of the new American painting and Motherwell's particular interest in automatism etc. When *Metro* wanted to publish the text, Motherwell wanted it retitled, to "Painting as Experience." He also stopped speaking of automatism preferring the "free association" to refer to the way of drawing on his unconscious. At the risk of oversimplifying the situation, alone among the heroes of Abstract Expressionism, Motherwell stood for peripatetic, experience-gathering activity, in the studio and outside it. Motherwell's colleagues, Rothko, Pollock, Still, Gottlieb, de Kooning, Guston, etc. accepted the role of pioneers. Pollock's and de Kooning's paintings fitted the coonskin/redskin image. Rothko's, Still's, and Gottlieb's did not, though they adopted, and Still amplified, the associated cliché about venturing into the unknown and risking all while focusing their work on one kind of image. That Rothko could do so more brilliantly than Still while Gottlieb became boring is another matter. They were serious, thinking, learned painters, ambitious for art as well as for themselves.

Motherwell associated with them in 1948 in forming and running the short-lived but famous school they entitled "The Subjects of the Artists." I suspect Motherwell did most of the running; he certainly organized the lectures, by John Cage and others, that people remembered long after it closed in 1949.

Motherwell was youngest of the group – eleven to twelve years younger than Rothko, Still, de Kooning, and Gottlieb, and at university a university student while they worked for the WPA, developing a new awareness of each other and wondering about the place of high art in modern society. Pollock and Guston were merely two or three years older than Motherwell but painting professionally from the mid-1930s. Motherwell was better off,

"IT IS TRUE THAT EVERY ARTIST HAS HIS OWN RELIGION."

and perhaps too eager to join in producing new journals and be a spokesman for them all, not out of playboyish self-regard but out of missionary zeal. We have forgotten how reluctant America was to see any virtue in the new art. A lot of basic teaching was needed, and young Motherwell volunteered to do it. I suspect the others used him while not taking him entirely seriously.

It would have been wholly against his nature and desire to set close limits for his work – even, or especially, highbrow ones. Not "self-discovery" but "experience": he wanted an art fully related to life as lived. Motherwell worked out many of these ideas and developed some of the imagery for the Spanish Elegy series in *Possibilities* (1947–8), one of the sequence of avant-garde journals he helped edit. Ashton also quotes a passage in *From Baudelaire to Surrealism* in which Marcel Raymond speaks of experience in terms that seem echoed in Motherwell's art:

> "Experience becomes a sense of certainty that penetrates one's whole being and stirs one like a revelation—a state of euphoria that seems to give the world to man and persuades him that he 'possesses' it."

For this to happen, Raymond goes on, one has to accept the free play of received sensations and "not to place them in a logical framework." John Dewey, developing William James's thoughts on pragmatism, in 1934 published *Art as Experience*. Its title alone must have stirred

"FOR MOTHERWELL, ART WAS AN AESTHETIC, ETHICAL, AND ULTIMATELY SPIRITUAL FORCE."

—*Stephen Aldiss*

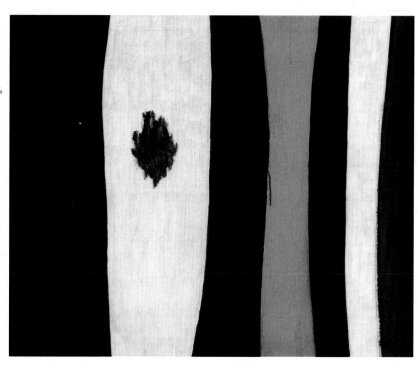

The Guillotine, 1966, oil and acrylic on canvas, 66 x 50 in/168 x 127 cm. Israel Museum, Jerusalem.

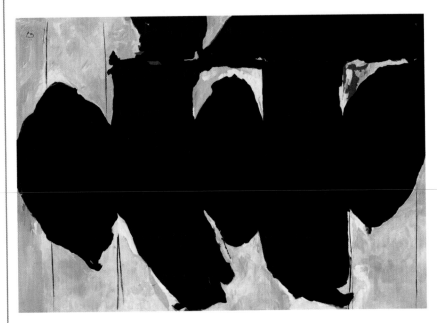

Elegy to the Spanish Republic No. 172 (With Blood), *1989–90,
Acrylic on canvas,
84 x 120 in/213 x 305 cm.
Denver Art Museum, Denver.*

young Motherwell, as Ashton implies; perhaps also Dewey's notorious statement, "the true is that which works."

Our habit of identifying him with the "Elegy" series – images that do imprint themselves readily in our memories – runs counter to the man himself and to his inclusive way with art. Masterful though it is, the series was neither his goal nor the culmination of his career. There are other series: the "Open" series, quite as dramatic on occasion but involving another kind of exploration; the series of "Je t'aime" paintings, explosions of lyricism that stand up well to those epic statements; more than one series of collages, many of them displaying his attachment to scraps of France (Gauloises packets, envelopes from the Nouvell Revue Française, printed and written words in French such as Eluard's "Jour la maison/nuit la rue," on a collage and a large painting, references to Mallarmé, and so on); paintings incorporating figures in varying degrees of directness; the "Iberia" series of primarily black paintings; discrete series of calligraphic paintings on paper and of images drawn in response to favorite pieces of writing brilliantly represented here by ten pages

Iberia No. 17, *1958,
oil on paperboard, 11 x 14 in /
27 x 35 cm. Walker Art Center,
Minneapolis.*

A La Pintura No. 12, *1971–74,
acrylic and charcoal on canvas,
108 x 120 in/274 x 305 cm.
Albright-Knox Art Gallery, Buffalo,
New York State.*

from his Dedalus Sketchbooks of 1982; a large range of print series, usually done in spurts between major painting campaigns and including a fine suite of etchings done during 1968–72 in response to Raffael Alberti's poems *A La Pintura*. The Spanish poet, who had thought of being a painter, wrote delicately but also with hypnotic rhythmical insistence about paintings, about colors, especially black, in ways that Motherwell found confirming on a good day and a stimulus to action when his spirits were low.

This list could go on and probably should. Trying to see Motherwell's work whole, one is overcome by its variety over a ground bass of challenges yet to be met, preferences to be indulged. "Here is God's plenty," as Dryden said of Chaucer. In a New York where freedom of search and expression was associated with one path per artist he must have looked open, directionless even, to a fault. Rothko kept his earlier work secret. Some of the lesser Abstract Expressionists (as they seemed to me then, and still do) were content to repeat patented brand-images, Gottlieb, Still, Kline, particularly Pollock, we know, felt trapped by his own best work. The 1959 Tate show made Francis and Guston look as though they had settled on their brand-images, but they soon moved on. The horrified response to Guston's radical redirection of his work in 1970 was an amplified version of the dismay that had greeted de Kooning's "Woman" series in 1953. Both were sinning

"FOR YEARS THE
ARTIST AND
THE COLOR HAD
KEPT GRAVE
COMPANY."

—*Mary Ann Caws*

against the "my way" convention. New York had on hand prominent examples of such constancy in the work of Mondrian, and then found it again, by focussing only on what seemed relevant, in Monet's *Waterlilies* and Kandinsky's apocalyptic "abstracts" of 1913–14. American references to European art contracted and hardened. Cubism was the essential European modernism, and it was Cubism that had to be overcome.

Some of Motherwell's paintings acknowledge Cubism; others are rooted in Matisse. Many belong to the new world of expansive, neither centered nor episodic, painting. If his collages adhere to European ways, his large quasi-monochrome paintings do not. Both sorts are intensely personal, the lyrical and the epic. They are his *Eine kleine Nachtmusik* and the *Jupiter Symphony*. No one complains of Mozart's range, we don't associate authenticity in music with one tune or one form. And the Motherwells are not all "Masterpieces." Someone should study the rise of this obsession, that every work by a major artist has to be a "masterpiece" (forget the true meaning of the word). In this exhibition one is knocked breathless by the most august paintings, including the "Elegy" and the "Open" series, and some of the almost entirely black paintings referring to Spain (including a tiny, intimate one, a superb little thing a more self-important artist might well have been embarrassed by).

Figure in Black (Girl With Stripes), *1947, oil with paper collage fragment on painting board,*
24 x 19 in/61 x 48 cm.
National Museum of American Art,
Smithsonian Institution,
Washington, D.C.

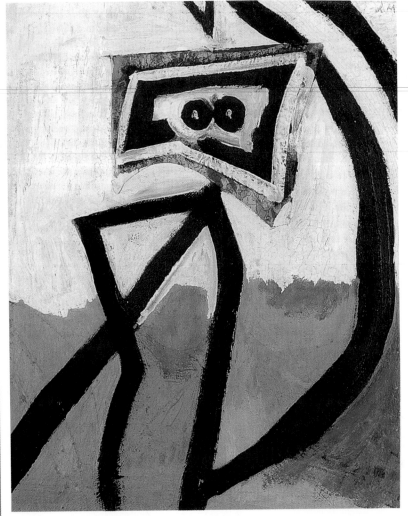

There are also large singletons, such as *The Voyage: Ten Years After* (1961), *Chi Ama, Crede* (1962) and *Threatening Presence* (1976) – real adventures, reaching well beyond the artist's range at that time. They involve more color – there is always more color in a Motherwell than reproductions allow one to see – and they show him at his most aggressive, furthest from what we begin to think his particular territory. He called some of them monsters. Between the two extremes come radiant interventions, neither lyrical nor epic, but responses, it would seem, to a sight and a moment, and in that sense more out-turned. *Summertime in Italy No.7 (In Golden Ocher)* (1961) is such a one. The title overburdens it, making us imagine a specific source. Also, there is not one ocher but variations on ocher, and with them come glimpses of red.

The most surprising painting was his *The Hollow Men (From T.S. Eliot)* (1983). I know I have seen it reproduced, but it hadn't registered. Now it haunts me. Motherwell had always included references to figures in his armory, with Picasso and Klee in mind. His *Figure in Black*

(Girl with Stripes) (1947) is indicated by black bands that may have come from Klee's late work; his *Doorway with Figure* (1953) makes me think of *Las Meninas* as mediated by Picasso. But *Orange Figure with Interior* (1953) suggests other stimuli. Here the figure, a truncated torso reduced to midriff, abdomen and thighs, is unmistakably female and painted with lust as well as awe. Her fleshiness and date point to de Kooning's "Woman" series, first seen in 1953. She pre-echoes a heavy pink figure on a larger scale and a much larger canvas in *The Feminine II* (1988–9), her form defined and divided by black lines which summarize the body almost beyond recognition yet catch its sexual appeal. We are left uncertain exactly what is presented, shoulders and arms, or legs and groin, or some of both, and hints of breasts. The interior brusquely

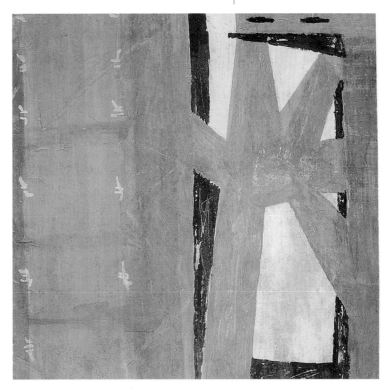

Doorway with Figure, *1951, casein on tan wrapping paper mounted on masonite, 48 x 40 in/122 x 75 cm. Denver Art Museum, Colorado.*

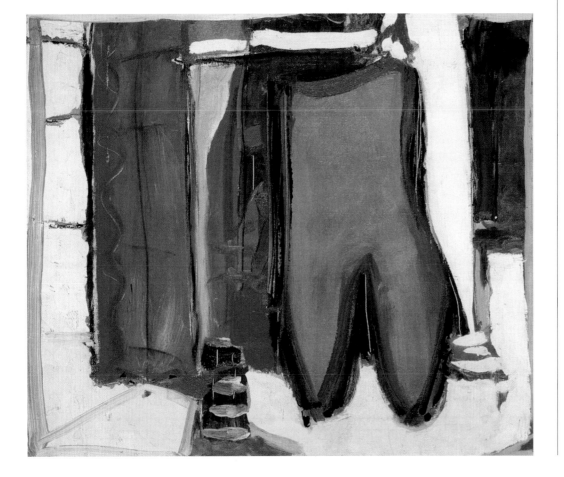

Orange Figure with Interior, *1953, oil on canvas, 20 x 24 in/51 x 61 cm. Modern Art Museum of Fort Worth, Texas.*

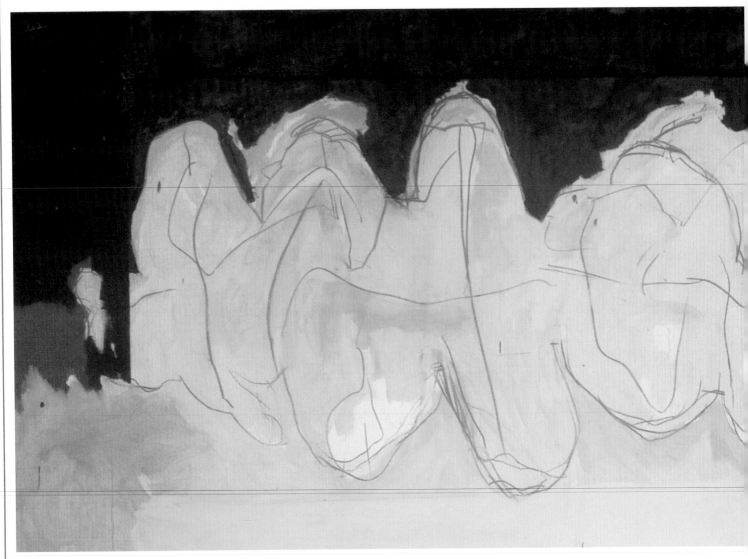

The Hollow Men (From T.S. Eliot), *1983, acrylic, charcoal and pencil on canvas, 88 x 176 in/224 x 447 cm. Private Collection.*

supplied in the 1953 painting, perhaps derived from Matisse, is here replaced by an entirely Motherwell expansive firmament of blacks and off-whites.

With *The Hollow Men (From T.S.Eliot)* we are in another world. As often, the title surfaced as the image developed. Motherwell kept poetry and other books in the studio, to read between bouts of painting. He painted with reading in his head where others work

> **"ONE OF THE MOST STRIKING OF ABSTRACT ART'S APPEARANCES IS HER NAKEDNESS, AN ART STRIPPED BARE."**

accompanied by music. He always valued American-English poetry, especially Eliot and Stevens; Eliot perhaps became more important to him as the years passed. But of course the painting, in alluding to Eliot's 1925 poem, refers also to the situation Eliot addresses: this is

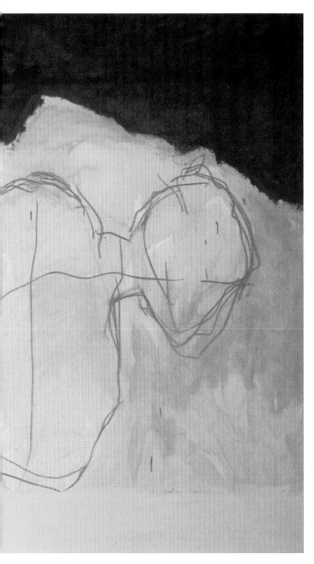

a political painting more than an act of homage to a piece of writing, though perhaps we should see it as both. The "men" occupy much of this painting, nearly fifteen feet across, yet are its weakest element, swiftly, almost dismissively outlined in thick charcoal and brushed in cursorily with diluted ocher acrylic. There are denser areas on the left, in black and red, and there is a band of yellow at the bottom. These underline the slightness of the rest, including the thin black overpainting at the top which lets us glimpse the red continuing under it. This repressed red is part of the message, the context in which these wobbly figures dominate the scene. In front of the painting my main response was to them, to those hate-filled lines and their conjunctions. Weightless, gutless, the "men" hang in the nightmare space of the painting. It is now that I can name the memory they stirred: they are Motherwell's perhaps unconscious answer, by very different means, to Duchamp's Nine Malic Molds in *The Large Glass*. Eliot's early poems and Duchamp's elaborately crafted painting confront the same world.

The Royal Academy's panoptic American show of 1993, "devised from a European standpoint," excluded Motherwell even while emphasizing the quarter-century from Abstract Expressionism to Conceptual Art as defining the US's "essential contribution to the art of our time." To identify that contribution with what can now seem and adolescent rhetoric of leaving home seems in itself immature. The exhibition found room, in some instances a lot of room, for Haring, Holzer, Peter Kelley, Koons, Sherman, and others, clever professionals working their chosen seams without finding much in them and looking slight, to use no harsher word, in the company of the best Abstract Expressionist painters and such artists as Johns, Ellsworth Kelley, Nauman, and Twombly. The only excuse for excluding Motherwell would have been that three or four canvasses could not have done justice to this profound as well as mobile artist. I suspect his European connection kept him out – which seems odd, almost obscene, in this little would-be great world of ours.

"MORE THAN ANY OTHER ARTIST SINCE VASARI, I THINK, ROBERT MOTHERWELL UNDERTOOK TO SITUATE THE ART MOVEMENT IN WHICH HE PARTICIPATED IN THE LARGER STRUCTURES OF HISTORY. HE PLAYED A TRIPLE ROLE, AS THINKER, AS MAKER AND AS INTERMEDIARY, IN THE TRANSFORMATION OF MODERNISM THAT TOOK PLACE IN NEW YORK IN THE 1940S AND '50S."

—*Arthur Danto*

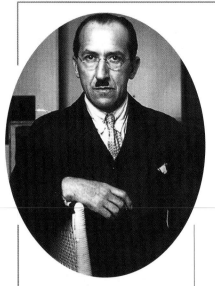

PIET MONDRIAN

Born in the Netherlands in 1872, Mondrian took an early interest in art. To please his family, he earned a degree in education, but after beginning a career as a teacher, he soon left the profession to pursue painting.

His first exhibited works were in the Dutch traditional style – landscapes and still lifes in subdued colors with attention to light. He then exhibited with the Postimpressionists in Amsterdam's 1907 Quadrennial Exhibition, afterward producing "The Red Cloud," a rapidly sketched drawing dense with color.

Mondrian moved to Paris in 1912, where he was influenced by the early Cubism of Picasso and Braque. Mondrian experimented with his own approach to Cubism. Along with three other painters, he founded the art movement and journal, De Stijl. The movement strove for purity and rejected external subject matter; it restricted pictorial language to the straight line and right angle, and color to the three primaries and to the noncolors white, gray, and black. Mondrian called the style "Neoplasticism."

Leaving Paris in 1938, Mondrian lived for two years in London before settling in New York, where he continued to develop his Neoplasticism style until his death in 1944.

Piet Mondrian

by Bridget Riley

AN ARTIST'S EARLY WORK IS INEVITABLY MADE UP OF A MIXTURE of tendencies and interests, some of which are compatible and some of which are in conflict. As the artist picks his way, rejecting and accepting as he goes, certain patterns of enquiry emerge. His failures are as valuable as his successes: by misjudging one thing he confirms something else, even if at the time he does not know what that something else is. In that sense, although Mondrian may sometimes fail, he never makes mistakes, everything in his development is of use and contributes to that development.

There are two conflicting traits in his temperament, in the sense given to the word by Baudelaire and Cézanne – "temperament" as an artist's own particular and ineradicable nature. One is a feeling for rhythm, which quickens to the pulse of life and seems somehow to be connected with his positive sense of the new; and the other is a love of order and balance, which is at the root of his search for unity and fullness. Both these traits can also

> "ART IS NOT MADE FOR ANYBODY AND IS, AT THE SAME TIME, FOR EVERYBODY."

have an obverse side: the lively quality may lead to an extreme dynamism and fragmentation, while the insistence on order can sometimes turn into a bland and almost schematic statement. These two temperamental qualities ebb and flow throughout the various preoccupations and styles of his development – now one in ascendancy, and then the other, until they slowly find a resolution in the late abstract works.

The early landscapes painted in Holland are predominantly tonal in treatment and have a low-key, moody character. Trees and buildings reflected in water produce self-contained symmetrical images which cut the recession short and pull the field of vision up close. Evening light is frequently chosen and there is a marked interest in visual phenomena bordering on the apparitional. The tree in *Evening on the Gein with Isolated Tree* (1908), far from calling on natural similitude, looms over the dark shape of the river bank and its reflection like some ominous sign; and in *Trees on the Gein: Moonrise* (1908) the five trees are treated as a spectral frieze spread flat against the light of the moon.

This up closeness is carried further in a choice of subjects in which the sense of an unencompassable presence and an overpowering scale dominate. In his *Trialogue* (1910–12) Mondrian, under the guise of the "abstract realist painter," says about the *The Mill at Domburg (The Red Mill)* (1910):

"Indeed I find this windmill very beautiful, particularly now that we are too close to view it in *normal perspective* and therefore cannot see it or draw it normally. From here, it is very difficult merely to reproduce what one sees."

The final painting conveys the sensation of something grand towering up above the spectator's viewpoint.

The recurrent subject of sea and dunes provides a theme of vast, uncentered openness. The lack of differentiation in such motifs gives a singular prominence to the horizon line and its reverberations. By stacking and interlocking horizontal divisions of different weights and differences, Mondrian creates a fluctuating, inpalpable envelope of space.

From very early on there seems to have been a special attraction to trees and to the pictorial problem of how branches, sky, and foliage or blossom interact and interpenetrate. Being essentially a subject that cannot be treated "realistically," the tree offers a marvelous pretext for the

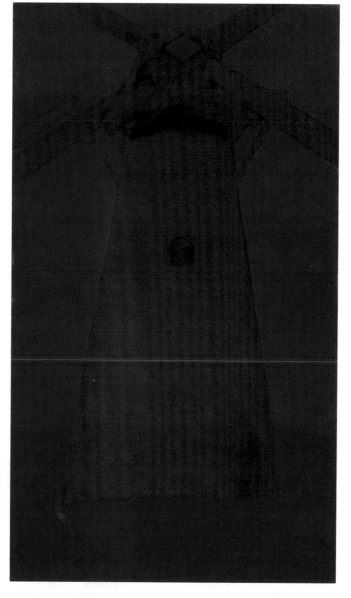

fabrication of a rhythmic structure of shallow recessions and advances that have little or nothing to do with the void and solid of the original motif. The potential of this subject was to be fully realized in Mondrian's Cubist work.

But before that Mondrian discovered color. It first entered his world through van Gogh and Divisionism. Both the vibrancy of autonomous brushwork and the abstract intensity of

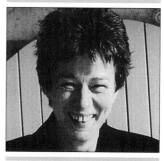

BRIDGET RILEY
One of the few British artists to have won the Premio award at the Venice Biennale, Riley, a pioneer of Op Art, enjoys an international reputation. She was born in London in 1931 and educated at Goldsmiths College of Art and the Royal College of Art in London. Her first solo exhibition was in London in 1962, after which she began to exhibit widely.

Riley's best-known paintings capture the intensity of light and color, creating the visual equivalent of energy. Works from the early '60s feature small triangles, ovals, and curved, verticle, and horizontal lines, painted in black and white. In the late '60s, she began working in colors, adding rich coloration to the black and white.

Riley's recent work includes an installation of a large-scale sculpture comissioned by Citibank for its offices at Canary Wharf in London. Her work has been exhibited in Europe, Japan, Australia, and recently in New York at the Dia Center.

Riley currently lives and works in London, Cornwall, and France.

The Mill at Domburg (The Red Mill), 1910, oil on canvas, 59 x 34 in/150 x 86 cm. *Gemeentemuseum, Slijper Collection, The Hague.*

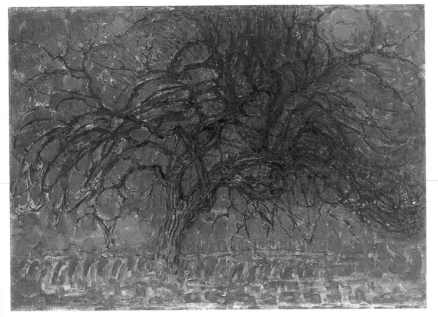

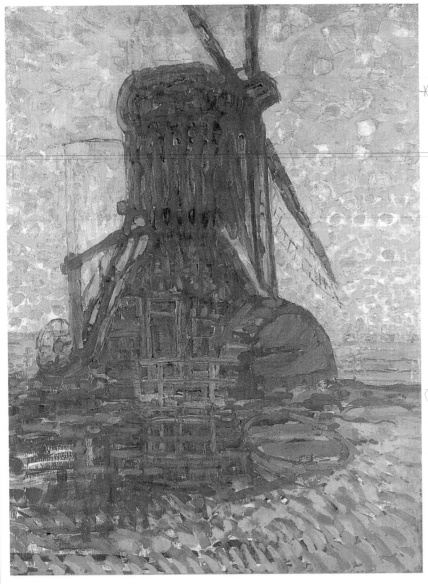

color contrast must have appealed to his feeling for rhythm and dynamism. In *Evening; Red Tree* (1908) the sensation of evening light has shed its moody aura, and Mondrian fairly crackles the painting into life with equivalents of red and blue and short energetic brushmarks. From there it is only a small shift to the liberating of color from any descriptive or representational function. This Fauvist approach can be seen in *Mill in Sunlight* of the same year. The dazzling heat and light of a midsummer day is recast in stabbing strokes and blotches of red and yellow shot through with pale blue and violet.

But Mondrian's development is not simply one of a young painter finding out what to paint and how to paint it. Like van Gogh, he comes from a Dutch background deeply involved with religious matters, and in a similar way his fulfillment as an artist is inseparably connected with transforming these roots. The parallel is striking because it shows that even a cultural basis as alien and unsympathetic to artistic aspiration as fervent Protestantism is not necessarily an obstacle. It is a question of whether an artist is strong enough to turn this predicament to advantage. Van Gogh was able to transform his religious zeal and empathy with the people working in the coal mines into preaching a virtual gospel of the power of the sun. Whereas Mondrian, who initially engaged in theosophy and all sorts of attempts to reconcile philosophical speculation with Christianity, had to discover in the basic properties of painting the means that allowed him to fulfill his spiritual quest.

The crucial painting in this context is *Evolution* (1910–11). It is something of an embarrassment to many people who love Mondrian as an abstract purist; and for those who claim that Mondrian is a symbolist and not really an abstract artist at all, this painting serves as the basic reference point. In fact it deserves neither of these responses. It is a unique and revealing failure on an imaginative scale only comparable to Cézanne's early expressive works such as the *Eternal Feminine* and the *New Olympia*. No fashionable or well-behaved artist would ever dare risk something like this; it takes an unselfconscious and

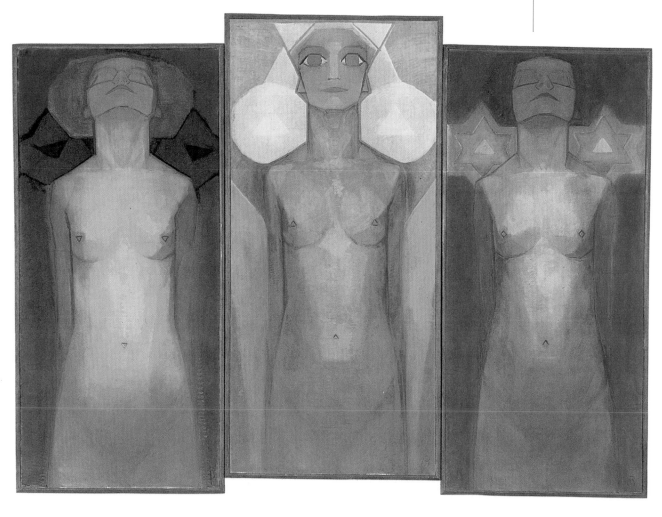

uncompromising imagination to go to such awkward lengths. Over and above its obvious pictorial shortcomings, the failure of the work is objective. In *Evolution* Mondrian attempts to make a universal statement about life – a task of dimension traditionally only accomplished through the agency of Biblical subjects and Antique mythology. The fact that this whole sphere of representation was no longer available had been an essential mainspring in the formation of Modern art in the nineteenth century. Mondrian had to discover for himself that literary symbolism and personal invention could not make up for this loss. The creation of a common social language does not lie within the scope of an individual and the lack of such a basis has to be accepted by Modern Painting.

It would have been almost impossible for a young artist to deal with this gigantic

Above: Evolution, *1910–11, oil on canvas, triptych: side panels 70 x 34 in/178 x 85 cm, center panel 72 x 34 in/183 x 88 cm. Gemeentemuseum, Slijper Collection, The Hague.*

Top Left: The Red Tree, *1908 –10, oil on canvas, 28 x 40 in/70 x 99 cm. Gemeentemuseum, The Hague.*

Bottom Left: Mill in Sunlight, *1908, oil on canvas, 17 x 14 in/44 x 34 cm. Gemeentemuseum, The Hague.*

problem on his own, particularly when living in a provincial context. Soon after *Evolution* was completed, Mondrian left for Paris where, through the daring and brilliance of its pioneers, the Modern movement had already begun to make its response to this crisis. Just as van Gogh had found liberation in the Divisionist approach to color that nineteenth-century Paris offered him, so Mondrian, following a similar pattern of emancipation, found a key to spatial organization through Cubism in twentieth-century Paris. However, as some contemporary critics observed, his interpretation of Cubism was clearly very much his own. His work was recognized for being "extremely original in conception" (Leo Faust) and for the mark that it bore if temperamental distinction, while his complete indifference to the Cubist "laws of volume" (André Salmon) – that is to say the remarkable flatness of his paintings – drew the criticism of other reviewers.

In Paris Mondrian worked first from the latticelike drawings of trees done previously in Holland and then from small, diagrammatic notes he made of the planes of interior walls exposed in the demolition of large houses near his studio. These walls bore the remnants of

"INTELLECT CONFUSES INTUITION."

the wallpaper and paint that had once decorated rooms on each floor and presented patches of color placed haphazardly on a flat surface. Both motifs were treated close up, filling the visual field, and provided Mondrian with a loose, informal grid within which he could articulate planes of subdued colors: the warm-cold binaries of classic Cubism, his own lightly colored grays, or muted shades of red, yellow, and blue. Ultimately the two aspects of his Cubist paintings that were to prove most important to the development of his later abstract work were the dynamic relationships of these areas within the picture plane and the new role assigned to the spectator in assessing these relationships. That is to say, the way in which we "read" the paintings is a constituent part of their formation.

Within a few years Mondrian had absorbed influences from three seminal movements of Modern art – Divisionism, Fauvism, and Cubism. The impact was clearly very strong. To sort out this experience he needed time and reduced exposure to the Parisian art scene. He returned to Holland for the summer of 1914, and when the War broke out in August was unable to return to Paris until 1919 when it was over. This enforced break enabled him to take stock, to reflect on the various phases and changes that had taken place in his work, and gradually to find his own footing with greater certainty. In 1915 he made a distinction between the human spirit in its role as a builder within the realities of an artistic medium and the "moody" quality of emotion with its expressive dependence on external reality.

Emotion is more outward than spirit. Spirit constructs, composes; emotion expresses mood and the like. Spirit constructs most purely, with the simplest line and the most basic color.

> "A MONDRIAN IS WITHOUT TOLERANCE. NO ELEMENT CAN BE CHANGED, MOVED, ADDED, OR SUBTRACTED WITHOUT REFORMING THE WHOLE."
> —*Tom Lubbock*

In Holland Mondrian at first continued with the façade motifs, now based on the church at Domburg, but the dunes and the sea soon exerted their pull. We have a friend's account of strolling with Mondrian on the beach:

"On a walk beside the ocean, late in the evening, under a radiant, starry sky, he took a tiny sketchbook out of his pocket and made a scribbled drawing of a starry night. For days he worked over that suggestive little scribble. Every day he took a tiny step further away from reality and came a tiny step nearer to the spiritual evocation of it." (Autumn 1914)

This gradual shift from an emotional response to a spiritual realization gave rise to the beautiful series of preparatory drawings leading up to *Pier and Ocean* (1915). In the final painting an immensity of sensation opens up; one feels oneself surrounded by the sparkling stillness and the rhythmic movement of some boundless continuum. Here Mondrian's lines take on a wider range of functions, they act as breaks, points, and accents. At one stage in the development of *Pier and Ocean* Mondrian thought of adding color, but in the end he

Pier and Ocean, *1914, charcoal and white watercolor on buff paper, 35 x 44 in/88 x 111 cm. Museum of Modern Art, Mrs. Simon Guggenheim Fund, New York.*

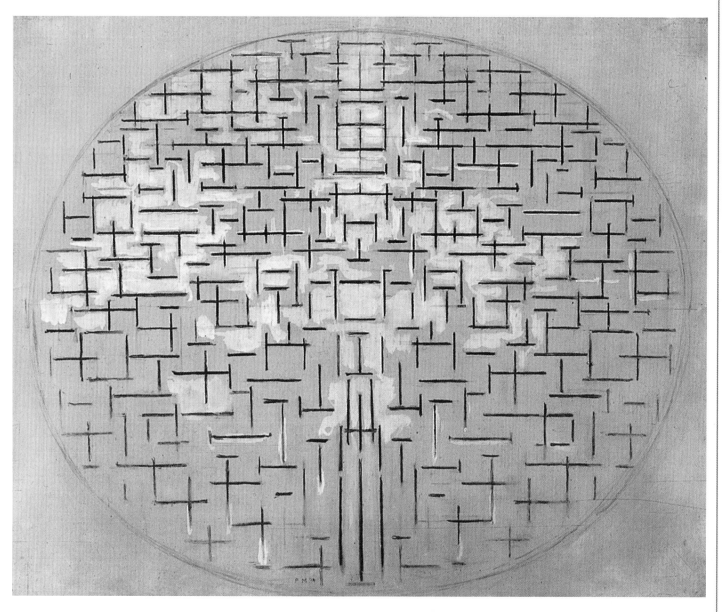

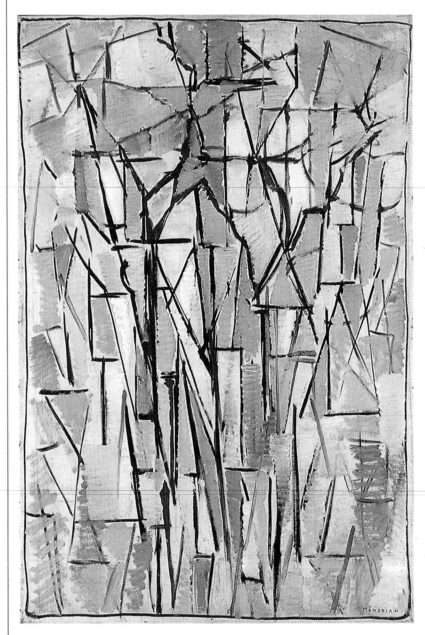

Composition with Trees II, *1912,*
oil on canvas,
39 x 26 in/98 x 65 cm.
Gemeentemuseum, The Hague.

decided against it. However, in the very next painting, *Composition 16*, he did precisely that. A pervasive gray with red, yellow, and blue patches – sometimes light, sometimes darker, but always adjusted – support and contradict the beats, crosses, and intervals of the lines.

Slowly the work loosens its moorings in what Mondrian refers to as a "given in Nature" and begins to make its way autonomously. Color planes are simply arranged on a white ground, gray lines are added to provide a context for the spatial movement of these planes without destroying the dynamism. The introduction of regular grids was strongly objected to by friends such as van Doesburg for being repetitious and denying composition; but Mondrian defended them on the grounds that he reworks the regular division considerably, and in the case of the "Checkerboard" paintings he maintained that he achieved contrast through the weight and disposition of his color planes. However, he also had reservations about his direction, as he later admitted, for being too "vague": "The verticals and horizontals cancelled each other; the result was confused; the structure was lost."

During this period in Holland Mondrian wrote and published *The New Plastic in Painting* (1917) in which he sets forth his criteria. Part speculative thinking, part soliloquy and part reverie, this book has done almost as much to confuse as to enlighten his followers. However, although it does not provide a complete framework with all its reference points in place, the expression and definitions Mondrian uses offer important clues in themselves. One gets nearer to the nature of his endeavor by starting from these basic terms than by trying to grasp an overall system or find a comprehensive theory.

On his return to Paris in June 1919 the effects of this reflective and withdrawn period in Holland soon became apparent. Of *Composition A; Composition with Black, Red, Gray, Yellow, and Blue* (1920), on which he worked for the best part of a year, he said: "I have now made a painting that pleases me more than all my previous work… It has been a long quest." Although, in the light of his classic period in the '20s this work can be seen as transitional, it is more revealing in many ways than those highly accomplished paintings. The peculiar flatness of his pictorial space that had already been observed in his Cubist work is now developed and clarified. The color planes take up different positions in space – some advance, some recede; and this is not a simple matter of a particular hue always taking up the same spatial position wherever present. It is a question of context. Take the three yellows, for example: the yellow in the top right corner is on a different plane from the yellow in the center, and both of these are again on different planes from the yellow in the lower right. Although one customarily thinks of yellow as a light color, these three yellows have varying visual *weights* – that is to say, the block in the top right appears slightly heavier than the central yellow, which in turn weighs visually more than the yellow rectangle in the lower right. These three yellows, therefore, do two principal things simultaneously: they

explain

take up different spatial planes and they exert pressure through their different weights. The same applies to the reds, the blues, and the blacks, and of course to the grays and whites (although there it is perhaps less easy to see). This brings about a field of forces in which the various weights and planes are building up dynamic relationships and tensions.

Such dynamism could easily lead to a sort of visual anarchy. But Mondrian practices a form of ordering that he later referred to as "the equivalence of the dissimilar." The disparate visual qualities – each in itself completely "real," or as he would say "determinate" – are balanced in such a way that they both build a whole and yet

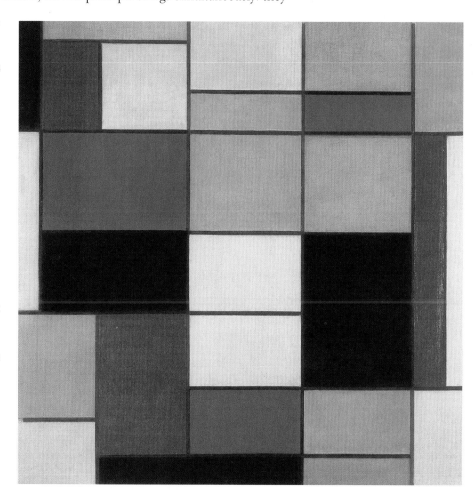

Composition A: Composition with Black, Red, Gray, Yellow, and Blue, *1920, oil on canvas, 36 x 36 in/92 x 92 cm. Galleria Nazionale d'Arte Moderna, Rome*

retain their individuality. "I have just got that large work right," he writes to van Doesburg about *Composition A* "I made that blue square on the right and changed that yellow one on the left to white; I painted over the gray, the black, and the white; I wish you could have seen it like this." And as the final result shows, he altered the painting again. In this way an "equilibriated relationship" is achieved which, in his words, "most purely expresses the universal, the harmony, the unity that are proper to the spirit." So anxious was he to preserve the individual characteristics within this unity that he worried for quite a while about the intensity of the large red in the lower left of the painting: "I am not absolutely sure that it ought to be so totally homogeneous. In theory it should be, but in practice…?" Eventually he decided to leave it alone.

Gradually it becomes clear that this abstract way of ordering forms the content of Mondrian's work. His paintings are not symbolic or transcendental, but perceptually accessible and plastic in the sense that he builds up a structure of relationships that places us, as spectators, in an analogous "equilibrium." We are invited to participate in a visual interplay between weights, forces, and tensions held together by a balance that is neither symmetrical nor systematic. In a remarkable essay of 1923, "No Axiom but the Plastic Principle." Mondrian describes this balancing between the individual elements and their dynamic unity as the plastic principle and purpose of his art in a period when "everything is seen 'relatively' … Moreover the relativity, the mutability, of things creates in us a desire for the absolute, the immutable." Far from resolving this conflict by offering a new "absolute," he turns the in-built contradiction into a dynamic relationship that becomes something of an absolute in itself and which has to be re-discovered and re-established: in each particular instance; that is to say: painting by painting.

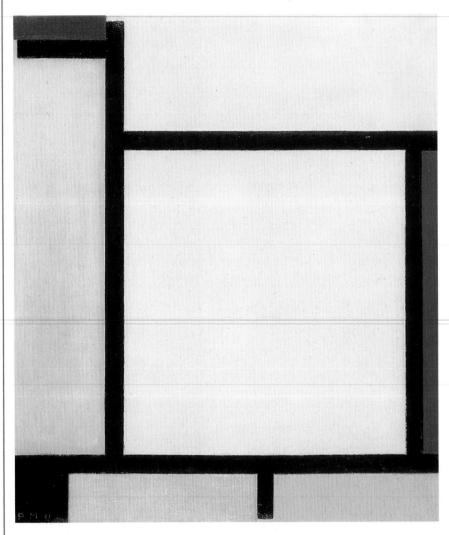

**Composition with Red, Blue,
Black, Yellow, and Gray**, *1921,
oil on canvas,
16 x 14 in/40 x 35 cm.
Gemeenemuseum, The Hague*

Composition with Red, Blue, Black, Yellow, and Gray (1921) shows with what awesomely simple means Mondrian can achieve his objective. There is no explicit center to the painting, and yet the peripheral events do not drift apart. With their differing characteristics they form a correlation of forces that hold the square in tension, being both open and defined at the same time.

As the body of Mondrian's mature work grew throughout the 1920s this plastic principle gave rise to a tremendous richness and variety. Quite apart from changes in the proportion of the rectangular canvases and the dramatic shift in orientation of the lozenge paintings, Mondrian pursues, alongside these changes, a number of themes in the almost serial manner he had sometimes employed in the past. He may explore the weights and tensions that can hold an empty center as in the painting just described; or the reverse, as in *Tablou I; Composition with Red, Black, Blue, and Yellow* (1921), where the linear divisions cut across the central area and the visual forces are turned inside out, as it were. As a result the color weights and planes, being well within the pictorial field, provoke relationships that concentrate or diffuse attention. Other areas of investigation include an even greater reduction of his already simplified means, such as the black bands of varying width with

just white planes of varying proportion; or compositions with only one or two color planes occupying the spatial compartments provided by the linear divisions.

For a long time this period was regarded as the zenith of Mondrian's achievement. Certainly the monumental stability and grandeur reflects one side of his temperament. However, the other, the lively feeling for rhythm, was soon to assert itself and to increase dramatically the dynamic element in his work. In 1932 he made his first "double line" paintings, among them *Composition with Yellow and Double Line*. The rapid repetition of the horizontal line adds a new and different quality

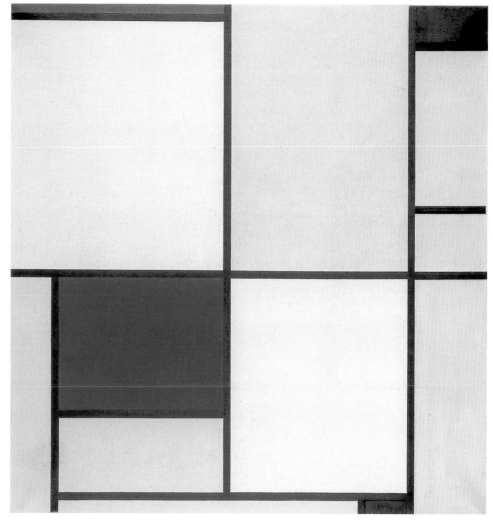

Composition with Red, Black, Blue, and Yellow, *1921,*
oil on canvas,
41 x 39 in/103 x 100 cm.
Gemeenemuseum, The Hague

of plane, a kind of outlined band, to the relationships in the painting – and one so subversive that it puts the stability and coherence of the painting at risk. But when, as in *Composition C (No. III; Composition with Red, Yellow, and Blue* 1935), he widens the interval between the two lines, the ambiguous duality of this new relationship is reduced and the plane thus created sits more easily with others in the painting. However, the friction of the "double line" is there to stay, as Mondrian is obviously fascinated by its rhythmic potential and repetitive insistence. In the following year, 1936, he painted *Composition C; Composition in Blue and Yellow*. There a centralized black vertical cuts the pictorial field in half and is repeated to the left to form a "double line," while a pair of

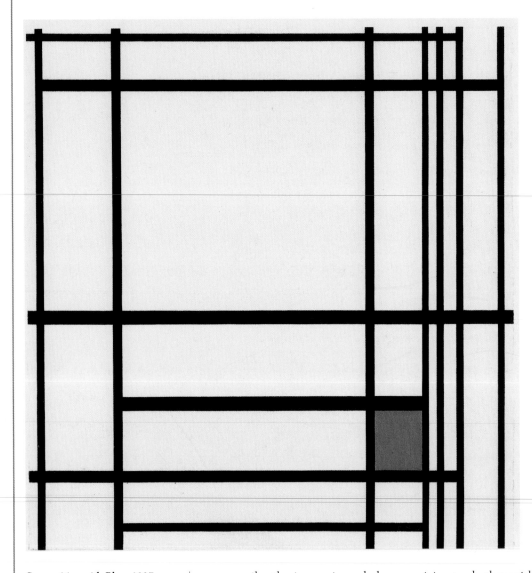

horizontal "double lines" (with slightly wider but equal intervals) crosses these verticals, setting up virtual flashing points at the intersections. But now Mondrian tackles directly those aspects of repetition that perhaps seemed most problematic to him: the accumulated intensity of the overall dynamism which threatens to diminish the "particular" at the expense of the "universal." By adding a large yellow plane and a small blue one he introduces a strong asymmetrical bias that checks the evenness of the rhythm.

In 1937 – the year before he left France for England and New York – he made *Composition of Lines and Color, III (Composition with blue)*, a most beautiful painting that

Composition with Blue, *1937,*
oil on canvas,
32 x 30 in/80 x 77 cm.
Gemeentemuseum, The Hague.

reconciles the increasing role he was giving to rhythm with a new sense of scale and tectonic strength. Generated by various black verticals and their intervals, the movement

"THE COLORED PLANES, AS MUCH BY POSITION AND DIMENSION AS BY THE GREATER VALUE GIVEN TO COLOR, PLASTICALLY EXPRESS ONLY *RELATIONSHIPS* AND NOT FORMS."

sweeps across the painting and is brought to a complex rhythmic close on the right. A subtle counter-movement of horizontal intervals modifies and harmonizes the drive and tempo of the painting. As a finishing stroke an implied diagonal descending from the top left is pulled up for attention by the deep blue rectangle it carries, the only color plane in the painting.

During the last few years of his life, spent in New York, Mondrian carried on with his explorations which more and more amounted to a reversal of the priorities that had governed his work in the '20s. In his writings and in conversation he insisted repeatedly on "dynamic rhythm" and "creative destruction" by which he meant the transformation of the actual elements – the basic colors and lines – into the "purely plastic" agents of an expressive dynamism. His last completed painting, *Broadway Boogie-Woogie* (1942–43), seems to sum up his entire endeavor in one amazing statement. Earlier tendencies such as those revealed in *Pier and Ocean*, the "Lozenge," and the "Checkerboard" paintings are integrated with interests which previously seemed to contradict and exclude them. The striving for constancy and immutability coexists with the love of rhythm and movement. It can be taken as a proof of Mondrian's rigorous and somewhat antiquated effort to achieve the "equilibrium of the universal and the particular" that his paintings have not been rendered obsolete by history. However frail and modest their physical appearance may be, they shine among the best work of this century with a unique vitality and mysterious timelessness.

"THE STRONGEST IMPRESSION IS OF HOW STRAIGHT HE WAS AS AN ARTIST, ONCE HE'D FOUND HIS PATH, AND HOW HE MADE STRAIGHTNESS SEEM RICH AND ENDLESS, WHICH IS A HARD THING TO ACHIEVE."
—*Matthew Collings*

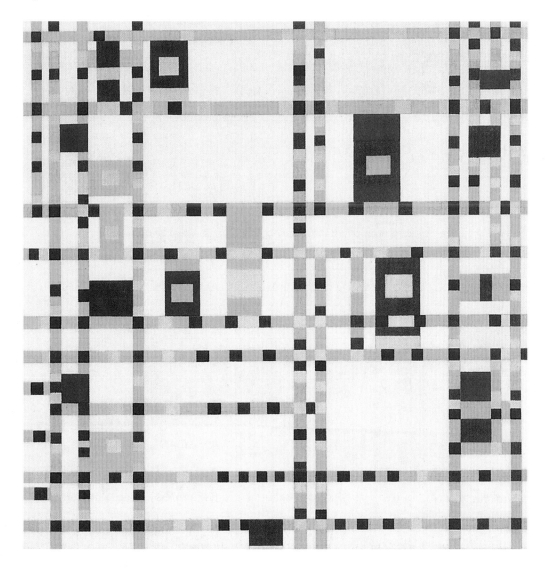

Broadway Boogie-Woogie, *1942–43, oil on canvas, 50 x 50 in/127 x 127 cm. Museum of Modern Art, New York.*

Georges Seurat

by Craig Raine

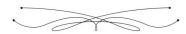

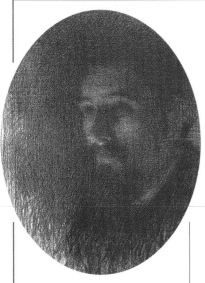

GEORGES SEURAT
Born into a well-off Parisian family in 1859, Seurat was able to pursue an artistic career free of material worry. After studying at the Ecole des Beaux-Arts, he spent his entire, brief life in Paris, except for summers painting on the Normandy coast.

Rejecting the formlessness of Impressionism, Seurat combined certain elements of the movement with the structure of Classicism. He became the leader of the Neo-Impressionist group that included Pissarro, Signac, Gauguin, and Toulouse-Lautrec. Upon entering his first major painting, Une Baignade, Asnieres, *in the Paris Salon of 1883, the jury's rejection of it caused him to ally himself with the young independent painters who later formed the Societe des Artistes Independents. During the next two years, he laboriously, almost fanatically, painted* A Sunday Afternoon on the Island of The Grande Jatte, *in which solid masses emerge from infinite fine points of color. This painting, when it was displayed at the Independents show in 1886, brought the attention of critics to Seurat.*

When he died very young at the age of thirty-one, Seurat left only seven major paintings.

Bathers at Asnières, *1884, oil on canvas, 79 x 118 in/201 x 300 cm. National Gallery, London.*

TWO METERS BY THREE METERS, *BATHERS AT ASNIÈRES* FILLS ONE WALL – a silent, still, difficult, ironic masterpiece. Its hazy colors recall the faded pigments of a Piero della Francesca fresco, as do its vivid yet flat figures. The scene is monumental enough to hint at higher things; it gestures towards the contemplative, it is composed and quasi-meditative – and then it insists on what Matthew Arnold called the object as in itself it really is. *Bathers at Asnières* is the suburban scene in a trance of torpor. Its figures are not spiritually naked but nearer a banal vacancy. Seurat evokes the idea of epiphany, a transfiguration of the ordinary, then settles for a mildly hedonistic vapidity. He was too intelligent a painter to exaggerate or sentimentalize his subject matter. He was a painter of modern life, but one who ignored Baudelaire's stipulation to heroize the stove-pipe hat and the pipe-clayed spats. Seurat's preferred note was tougher, ugly, accurate, secular, ironic.

In Fellini's film *La Strada* (1954), the Clown is killed by Zampano, when the Strongman meets his teasing rival by chance on a deserted road. The Clown, in mufti, is repairing a flat tire. The two men exchange a few blows in a ragged, realistic fight. The Clown dies only because he bangs his head against the metal corner of his car: the two men separate, the Clown looks at his wrist and complains that the Strongman has broken his watch, then he lies down and dies. That watch. Bizarre, less symbolic than comically incongruous, a pedestrian interpolation at the moment of pathos, it is also a perfect example of modernism. Modernism refuses to edit in the interests of afflatus. The process begins with Flaubert, its first uncompromising practitioner.

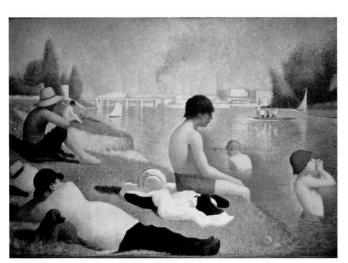

When Emma Bovary's arsenic poisoning enters its final phase, her daughter Berthe is brought to the bedroom. The burning candles remind the little girl of New Year's Day, of being woken early, of gifts. Her eyes cast about, looking for

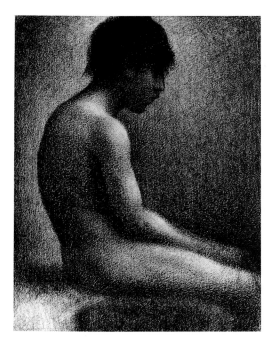

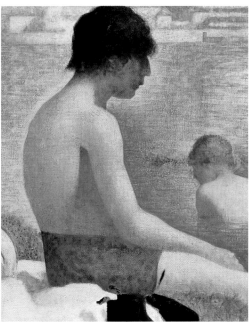

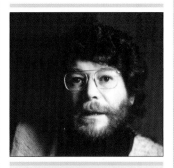

CRAIG RAINE
Raine was born in England in 1944 and educated at Oxford. He became editor of Quarto *in 1979 and was the poetry editor at Faber from 1981 to 1991.*

His works include the poetry collections The Onion, Memory, *and* Rich; *a libretto for an opera* The Electrification of the Soviet; *a verse drama* 1953: A Version of Racine's Andromaque; *and a collection of essays,* Haydn and the Valve Trumpet. A Martian Sends a Postcard Home, *perhaps Raine's best-known collection of poetry, is written from the perspective of an alien, describing the lives of Earthlings. This work established him as the founder of a group dubbed "The Martian School of poets." The title poem is described as "ingenious," inviting "a certain element of self-congratulation in the reader who unravels them."*

Raine currently teaches English literature at Oxford, and is the editor for the literary magazine Areté.

her stocking, cubist with presents, depending from the mantelpiece. Her innocent, infantile egotism takes its place with the other infantile egotisms gathered around the deathbed. Pathos is stayed, impurities are unflinchingly reported, the grotesque is given its due. Ironies are treasured.

"SOME SAY THEY SEE POETRY IN MY PAINTINGS; I SEE ONLY SCIENCE."

Philip Larkin thought that photography epitomized this tendency to embrace the awkward and inconvenient: "But o, photography! as no art is, / Faithful and disappointing! that records / Dull days as dull, and hold-it smiles as frauds, / And will not censor blemishes / Like washing lines, and Hall's-Distemper boards…" And will not censor blemishes. My argument is that, to the heartbreaking beauty of the preparatory drawings, Seurat, in the finished picture, brought blemishes. Deliberately.

The magic of the drawings is cognate with photography, though far from photography's vaunted accuracy of finish. In a dozen or so early drawings we can see Seurat's technique mature rapidly. When it arrives it is incomparable. Let me try to describe it. Using the texture of the paper as a central part of the process, Seurat's conté crayon develops its image as if the paper were light-sensitive. The results look like a photographic detail enlarged to a grainy shimmer. More than usually, the process of drawing seems to be preserved in the finished drawing. And the process is also akin to brass-rubbing: it is sculptural in its emphasis on shape, on outline rather than line. And its textures summon up the surface of polished granite – not a high, machined polish, but a worn patina, still preserving its precious irregularities.

Top Left: Seated Nude Boy: Study for *Bathers at Asnières*, 1883–4, *conté crayon on paper, 13 x 10 in/32 x 25 cm. National Gallery of Scotland, Edinburgh.*
Top Right: Detail from *Bathers at Asnières*, 1883–4.

A good chalk drawing of Seurat by his art-school contemporary Ernest-Joseph Laurent shows us, by contrast, how little store Seurat set by the line. Seurat's *Woman Reading* has already moved beyond convention, where what is captured is aura, as though drawing were a species of spiritualism. The woman is there in outline, granite, granular, her one distinguishing feature a downcast eyelid – a detail which is indistinct, almost an accident of the paper, yet utterly authoritative and precise. That eye is reading, not resting. The drawing is a record of discovery. Seurat finds what is there within the paper. He doesn't seem to draw on the paper. This sense of finding images is reinforced by the presence of the MICHALLET watermark in several drawings. In the portrait of Aman-Jean it is picked out vertically in the top left of the drawing.

Not all the early drawings are uniformly successful. *Locomotive*, for example, tries to make conté crayon work like charcoal. The enlargement effect is in abeyance and in spite of the conveniently obnubilated subject, the texture is curiously perfunctory and the stylized smoke a particular failure. In *Two Men Walking in a Field*, Seurat addresses the problem of total texture – background, middle-ground, foreground. He favors overlaid wispy lines, a little like fiberglass, which can stand for cracked earth, scrubby vegetation, brambles, in a non-representational way. As texture it fails, because it is so clearly a device – clever, relatively versatile, but without the inevitability of the granites conjured out of the paper by his conté crayon.

These granites are at once monumental, particularly where the human figure is in question, and capable of the subtlest inflections – as when, for instance, Seurat manages to specify a heavy twill material for the cloak of *The Nanny*. As a technique, it is perfect for textures, and eventually it marginalized other interesting stylistic experiments – like the penciled ur-Cubist, Gris-like rendition of *Woman Seated on a Bench*, or the worn dry-point quality of the charcoal sketch, *The Seamstress: A Painting on the Wall*. These explorations are broken off in

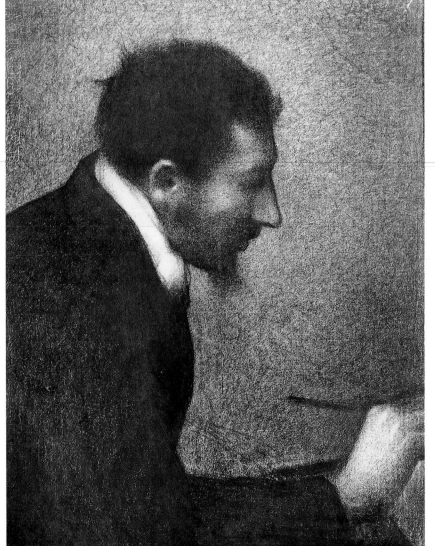

Portrait of Aman-Jean, *1883, conté crayon on paper, 25 x 19 in/62 x 48 cm. Metropolitan Museum of Art, New York.*

favor of the sculpted conté crayon, where the image seems to seep out of the paper like the legendary veronica.

The technique has its limitations. It can make for some difficulty with a thing as intricate as the ear. Aman-Jean's portrait has wonderful spikes of hair in his back crown and a linen cravat whose white weave is almost palpable – and yet his earlobe is the size of a small mastoid. Seurat has given his fellow-artist a thick ear. Apart from that, it is a marvelous drawing, whose effect is at first

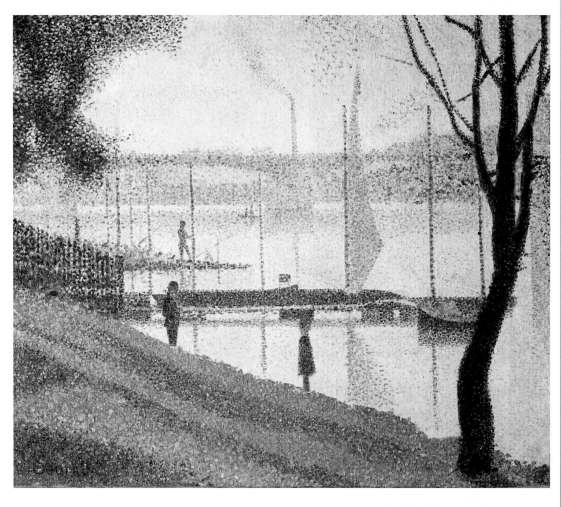

The Bridge at Courbevoie, *1886–7, oil on canvas, 18 x 22 in/46 x 56 cm. Courtauld Institute Galleries, London.*

academic – though a glance at Seurat's early charcoal study, *Standing Man, Hands Outstretched*, merely emphasizes the extraordinary distance between the earlier, meticulous work (with its graphic, ragged prepuce and its cock and balls the dark shade of furniture stain) and the essentially suggestive later piece. The *Portrait of Aman-Jean* is deliciously granular and shimmers in a way that anticipates Seurat's pointillism – though pointillism is,

"PAINTING IS THE ART OF HOLLOWING A SURFACE."

of course, a theory of color. Here the dots are created by the surface of the paper. They are brought out rather than brought there by the crayon. Later the dots are put there by the point of the brush: Seurat's *Bridge at Courbevoie* is fully-fledged pointillism, whereas *Bathers at Asnières* has a single pocket of touches to the hat of Echo. Pointillism, for all its laborious application, can create a permanent spontaneity of effect because, as viewer, you are as aware of the representation as of the scene represented. In *Bridge at Courbevoie*, smoke emerges from a background chimney like a gyre of midges. In fact, the whole picture is so minutely speckled, you half feel that the marks may just take off like a host of insects.

"WHEREAS OTHERS PAINTED COHESIVE FRAGMENTS OF A COMPLEX SOCIETY, SEURAT PAINTED SOCIETY FRAGMENTED INTO DISPARATE INDIVIDUALS."

—*Richard Thomson*

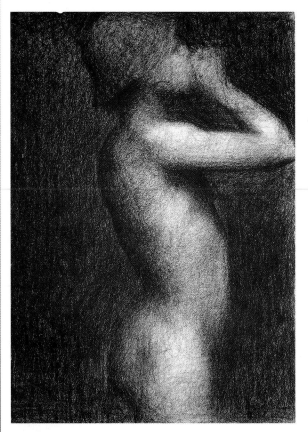

The Echo: Study for Bathers at Asnières, *1883–4, conté crayon on paper, 12 x 9 in/31 x 24 cm. Yale University Art Gallery, New Haven.*

Detail from Bathers at Asnières, *1883–4.*

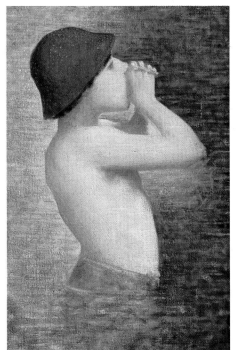

The nine drawings for *Bathers at Asnières* are a miracle of obvious, unsurpassed, immediate beauty, classical and perfect. They are unforgettable and flawless. In particular, there is a previously unknown drawing, *Study for "Bathers at Asnières,"* which materialized (the *mot juste* for Seurat's technique) recently. The drawing is crucial for a proper understanding of Seurat's final grand oil, though it is possible to deduce the same argument from *Seated Nude Boy* which is part of the holdings

"ORIGINALITY DEPENDS ONLY ON THE CHARACTER OF THE DRAWING AND THE VISION PECULIAR TO EACH ARTIST."

of the National Gallery of Scotland. One thinks of Michelangelo's idealized heads. Very little else can begin to compare with Seurat's frank pursuit of balance and beauty, poise and perfection. In the drawings, both figures are naked, more boyish, slighter, vulnerable – and edited for effect, idealized. The genitalia of the standing boy are invisible. Instead, the emphasis is on his tilted, boyishly sturdy waist and one prominent buttock, muscular and pleasingly scalloped. Adolescence on the cusp of manhood. The seated nude, on the other hand, is more fragile – curved shoulders, narrow neck, a long slim thigh. Knee, calf, and complicated hands have been silently censored to keep the simplicity and balance. Not that you notice until you look at the final oil.

One argument suggests that Seurat effects an elision of this classicism with the realities of contemporary Asnières. I think this idea is wrong. What takes place is not an accommodation, but rather a repudiation of the idea of classical perfection – in favor of the task of painting modern life. In the final picture, both these figures are clothed. The swimming costumes make an enormous difference. The seated figure is deliberately and systematically deprived of beauty – his profile coarsened, the nose enlarged, the upper lip an ungainly flap. The hands reappear. The knee turns down into an amputated calf, a stump. Beauty, texture, intricacy have gone. In their place is a pair of cotton swimming trunks and a hairstyle like a ginger wig. Echo's buttocks are out of sight underwater and clad in a costume too. The figure from Ovid has been metamorphosed into an ordinary urchin. These decisions show exemplary artistic courage.

To forgo obvious beauty, irresistible beauty, is never easy. Matthew Arnold wrote that poetry should be a criticism of life. Oscar Wilde misinterpreted this to mean that art was a series of cosmetic improvements on life in the interests of beauty. What Arnold really meant by "criticism," whether of an artwork or life, was that it should not remake the object under scrutiny, but describe it accurately – as it really is. The greatest artists take their stand with Arnold, even if this involves uglinesses of every kind. It isn't the business of art to flatter reality. Seurat's conté crayon confers a twilit charisma on *Hats, Shoes and Undergarments*, not to mention a pair of elasticated boots. But he could also see these items as

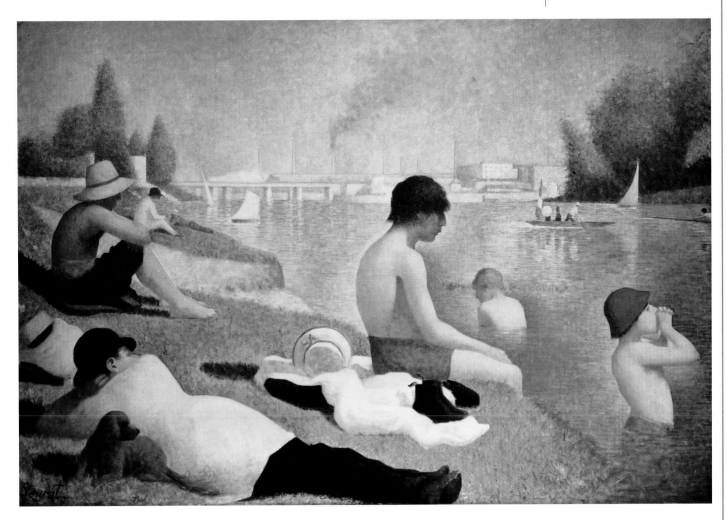

Bathers at Asnières, *1884, oil on canvas, 79 x 118 in/201 x 300 cm. National Gallery, London.*

in fact they really were – banal, obvious, devoid of poetry, but redeemed by their irrefutable reality, the truth of their ordinary ugliness. In the final oil, the boots have their loops restored and they move, with that one touch, from the abstract world of shape into the welter of seams, stitching, shoe-horns, polish, and welts.

When Claudio Abbado had been with the Berlin Philharmonic for a year, the BBC screened a documentary in which the conductor rehearsed a young violinist *protégée*. At one point, he interrupted her playing to tell her she was making a particular passage too beautiful. "It should be an ugly sound," he advised. Seurat's great picture is a similar discovery – that great art is not necessarily synonymous with beauty. There is love and there is sex. There are other, less obvious satisfactions. Think how powerful the idea of obscenity is.

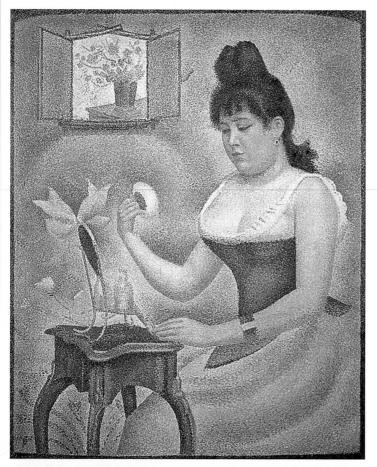

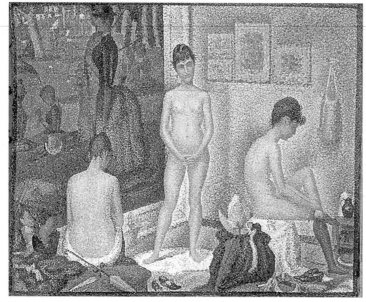

Bathers at Asnières offers immense formal satisfactions, all of them orchestrated by the figure of Echo, who is a self-conscious synecdoche in a picture where so many things are echoes of other things. Those loops on the boots, for example, mimic the flick of red hair at the base of their owner's neck. His half-visible straw boater parallels the submerged figure with his back to us. Then there is the

"ORIGINALITY DEPENDS ONLY ON THE CHARACTER OF THE DRAWING AND THE VISION PECULIAR TO EACH ARTIST."

reclining, bowler-hatted figure in the foreground, whose little spaniel mirrors its master: both are looking over their shoulders and presenting a profile. The dog's long tail picks up on its master's long brown trousers.

This figure is also the lynch-pin of one of the picture's two compositional templates. He is the apex of a triangle which runs (echoically) from the background triangle of sail on the left to the other triangle of sail to the right. The left-hand side of the triangle runs from the sail to the bowler-hatted figure, through a series of echoing intermediate figures – a stretched-out figure in a pink shirt, then two figures both with raised knees, then the stretched figure of the bowler-hatted dog-owner. The right-hand side of the triangle runs from the bowler-hat to the right-hand triangular sail, via the bather on the bank, the submerged figure whose back is turned, and the wherry with its two passengers. The river itself forms a further, overlapping triangle, whose apex is the bottom right-hand corner of the painting. The base of both triangles is the background bridge of Clichy, which is a shared horizontal. These two triangles echo each other as they overlap like an old-fashioned W, which was a double V.

In addition there is a second compositional shape which counters the picture's

Top: Young Woman Powdering Herself, *1888–9, oil on canvas, 37 x 32 in/95 x 79 cm. Courtauld Institute Galleries, University of London.*

Above: The Posers (small version), *1887, oil on canvas, 16 x 19 in/39 x 48 cm. Berggruen Collection.*

tendency to tilt to the right. The figure of Echo has raised hands and his bent elbows bring us back into the picture. The controlling shape here is the ellipse, like a ring of Saturn. We see this shape in the wherry, in the skiff, in the elongated green (of rushes? of grass?) in the river, as well as in the sandy shape of the riverbank. The figures make a flattened ellipse, too. From Echo the eye moves to the figure with his back to us, to the figure in the straw hat with raised knees, to the man in the "wig," and back to Echo. The man in the

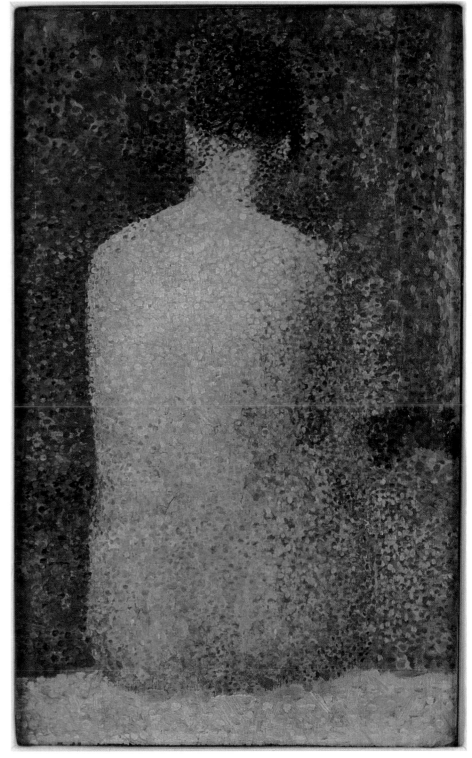

Study for The Posers, 1887-1888, *oil on canvas, 6 x 9 in/16 x 24 cm, Musee d'Orsay, Paris.*

bowler-hat is partly co-opted to this template and partly an echo of it – an entire ellipse in himself. The rim of his bowler is a further, echoic, mini-ellipse. Echo, then, is internalized, formal, silent and central to the composition.

The key to Seurat's attitude lies in *The Posers: Small Version*. Here the models are clearly intended to invoke the *Three Graces*, but the models (equally clearly) exist also in relation to *La Grande Jatte*, which apparently forms a whole wall in this painting. *La Grande Jatte* looks, in fact, like a window – a picture window – through which we can see the fully-clothed, parasol-bearing Parisian public. Alongside there are these nude women who are surrounded by the clothes they have taken off, their shoes and their parasols. These models, then, are not the *Three Graces*, Seurat insists; they are ordinary women like those at the edge of the Seine, ordinary women who just happen to have taken their clothes off. The classical is present in *Les Poseuses* but it is present only to be ironized by a great painter of modern life. Seurat was capable of classicism's easy, familiar "poetry," but he preferred the more arduous task of depicting the truth, the whole truth, and nothing but the truth.

Tracey Emin

by David Bowie

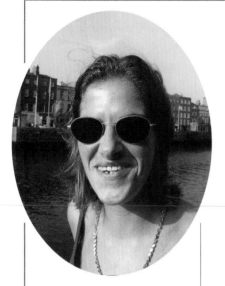

TRACEY EMIN
Emin's installations, drawings, paintings, sculptures, videos, and photography, inspired from personal experience, generate attention and controversy on both sides of the Atlantic. Born in London in 1963, Emin grew up in Margate, a town on the south coast of England, with her twin brother Paul. She studied painting at the Royal College of Art.

Emin's work is confessional in nature. Her disclosure is evident in works such as Everyone I have Ever Slept With 1963-1995, *which features a tent embroidered with a list of 102 names, including her brother Paul with whom she "slept" while in the womb. The work was included in the group exhibition* Sensation *that provoked the ire of New York Mayor Guiliani when shown at the Brooklyn Museum in the Fall of 1999.*

Every Part of Me's Bleeding, (1998), was her first solo show in the US. It contained the piece My Bed *Emin exhibited at Britain's Turner prize in 2000. Emin has exhibited in Germany, Japan, Great Britain, and the US and continues to work in London.*

Photos of Tracey Emin and David Bowie by Iman.

SHE CAME TO DUBLIN DID TRACEY EMIN. We walked around the library at Trinity and loved the smell of old leather. We lined up with ten thousand others to get a ten-second squint at the *Book of Kells*. A handful of patients from a nearby psychiatric hospital helped create an atmosphere of benign hysteria. One tall skinny gentleman stood by a fifteenth-century harp, alternately rocking backwards and forwards then revolving slowly all the while intoning his mantra of "NAAW-peer-NAAW."

She came to the gig at the Olympia did Tracey. She rocked backwards and forwards and shimmied like a disco-queen (which she nearly was once). Possibly screaming her mantra "Write this; Draw this." If she wanted, she could travel the length and breadth of the land with me and my band. Everyone from stage hands to musicians immediately fall in love with her. She's so charismatic, she sends off sparks.

We stay at the U2-owned Clarence Hotel on the River Liffey. Iman takes some photos of us looking out to the far side of the water and two small girls throw themselves into the shot.

"Are you a model?," asks the smaller one, of Tracey. Tracey laughs. "Make your mouth do this," orders the girl and makes a grimace. Tracey obliges."Naw, you're no model. Now send me copies of them pictures to me house will ya,"

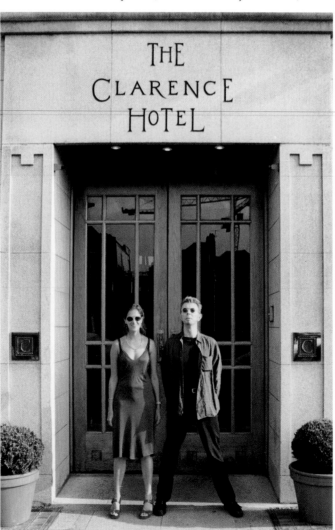

and they nonchalantly wander off picking up their previous conversation. Back inside the hotel, Tracey and I talk.

There is a childlike excitement that at last people will show, in a gallery, all the nooks, crannies, and fag-ends of her life. I never knew her before this year, but who I see in front of me now is someone highly charged with solipsistic overdrive. Within 30 minutes of meeting her I have a full run-down on her newest intimate relationships, her hopes and dreams for her personal life as well as proffered opinions on Balthus ("a dirty old man, a pervert"), my interviews with Damien Hirst ("You're obsessed by him") and her sponsorship contract with a rather exotic alcohol brand. The latter it seems is extremely important to her as booze is a 24-hour companion to her life.

I love her fractured energy and could sit and listen to her for hours. Although her viewpoints, tastes, and interests are standard and unvaryingly those of any eighteen-year-old art student, it slowly dawns on me that she is in fact a 34-year-old woman. Her natural youthfulness is exhilarating. She is also extraordinarily sexy. The elastic lips, famous broken teeth, and half-closed eyes, deliver one of the more seductively interesting faces in British art. I think I can look at her face for even longer than I can listen to her talk. She wants very much to be firmly identified in this modern world, but time and again she reveals a deep fascination with passions from another time – Munch, Schiele, Rembrandt, Vermeer, Giotto, narrative painting.

She says her work has been compared to Joseph Beuys and Andy Warhol. I don't buy into this at all. If anyone springs to mind it's William Blake as a woman, written by Mike Leigh. There is little sarcasm, cynicism, or even intended irony in her work. It has little of the mystic hippiness of Kiki Smith or the Fuck You diffidence of her best friend Sarah Lucas. It has more of the construct of the self. The dawning of late eighteenth-century self-conciousness, that first realization of self you find in early nineteenth-century self-portraits. Or maybe, even, a Mary Shelley of Margate.

There's also the smashed glass-splinter effect echoing the deeply dysfunctional work found at Gugging Hospital in Vienna, the bastion of working "Outside" artists, or at L'art Brut, Lausanne, the Vatican of fringe.

Her little museum in Waterloo is not so much a '90s absurdity, but more an updated reflection of the nineteenth century "I am" reverberations of the John Soane house and museum.

A few others, but only a few, also have an ambivalence toward her work. Charles Saatchi, in curating his upcoming "Masterworks at the Royal Academy," belatedly acquired a single 1995 Emin piece, her tent with lovers' names, only a few weeks ago. This doesn't seem to imply a passion for her work, but rather a need to make up a full set of Mod-Brit Artists. Amusingly, this piece having acquired an almost iconic status set Charles back considerably more than he is used to shelling out. Having said all that, there is an earnest and serious folk-story telling quality to her work that pulls an audience in completely. When I saw a recent show of hers in Toronto, two girls in their early twenties were sitting mesmerized in front of one of Tracey's video monologues. There were tears running down their cheeks. Now that's art, Jim, but as we know it.

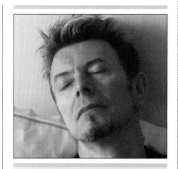

DAVID BOWIE
David Bowie's talent and ever-evolving musical and personal style secured his status as a rock/pop icon. Born in London in 1947, he fronted various bands in the 1960s achieving success as a solo singer-songwriter with 1969's Space Oddity, *an eerily modern science fiction single, unique among the music of that time.*

His postmodern personas of the '70s began with the futuristic rock-star martyr concept The Rise and Fall of Ziggy Stardust and the Spiders from Mars. *Other early '70s releases include* Diamond Dogs *and* Young Americans.

By the late seventies, Bowie joined the avant garde, collaborating with Brian Eno to produce Low, Heroes, *and* Lodger, *and he ventured into acting with his noted debut in Nicholas Roeg's* The Man Who Fell to Earth. *Bowie's films of the early '80s produced three Top 20 hits. He continues to release albums, and in 1996, was inducted into the Rock and Roll Hall of Fame.*

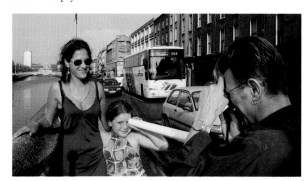

DB: So, how does only knowing half the alphabet feel? Which half do you prefer anyway?

TE: Only knowing half the alphabet. Well, I do know the whole alphabet except I can't actually put it in the right order. I can see this going into "Pseuds Corner" immediately.

DB: You don't feel wanted unless you're in there once in a while. Is there any dyslexia involved?

TE: When I was seventeen they said I was dyslexic, but I don't actually think I in fact was. I just never went to school basically. And they had to come up with some theory like that because I obviously was quite clever. Except if you leave school at thirteen there's a certain… I mean most people leave school at eighteen. And do "A" levels. But I didn't.

DB: I was out at sixteen.

TE: You're older than me.

DB: Am I? Not much!

TE: Not much, no.

The Tracey Emin Museum, London, 1996.

DB: Much of the time I feel a little bit like Tom Hanks. Did you ever see *Big*? Well, Tom Hanks in this film wakes up one day – he's thirteen years old – and he makes a wish at a fair ground at this very strange wishing machine, and he wishes that he was a grown-up, and he wakes up a grown-up the next morning. I often feel like that.

TE: I think that's what happened to me. That's probably what happened to me when I was thirteen, yeah. I'm the happiest I've ever been in the whole of my life now at 34 and I really like things about being a woman.

DB: Is it a sense of contentment or do you still have strong ambition?

TE: Oh God no, fuck, I, well – I wouldn't actually say I was that ambitious, but other people might think very differently. But my ambition is not a problem – whatever I really want, I find a way of being able to achieve it, so I don't actually think – especially with art, my art is just part of me and it's just what I do. My idea of success is being able to do what you want to do, and if that's being ambitious then I am. And the thing about being happier than I've ever been now, it's the first time in my life that I've come to terms with who I am, and I seem to be accepted for who I am, and I have a good group of friends around me and that makes me feel good. So, it's got quite meaningful really.

DB: But those friends that seem to gravitate toward you, are they friends that you've acquired since you've become popular as an artist, or were they friends that you were amassing before you became popular?

TE: Some of them were before, like Sarah Lucas, Carl Freedman, Gillian Wearing. I knew them before. I mean they knew me when people just thought I was completely mad.

DB: But all three of you were thrust into friendship, no? – more by the circumstances of your art?

TE: Yeah.

DB: So what about prior to you becoming an artist? Do you have friends from that period?

TE: Well, my best friend Maria, since I was four really. But she's like my sister. It's almost like we have the same blood.

DB: What does she do?

TE: She's antiques – well not antiques, like art nouveau, art deco, pre-war artefacts – bits of furniture and stuff.

DB: So she lives by her eye as well. How does she read?

TE: You mean read as a person…?

DB: Does she know the whole alphabet?

TE: Yes, she knows the whole alphabet, yeah. She reads a lot actually. She probably reads a book a week or something. But then she's just sitting there, isn't she, with all her antiques and stuff about her, reading books. But I'm – you shouldn't say about me not reading. I didn't read a book till I was about seventeen.

DB: I didn't say you didn't read.

TE: You did, last night, you said, "You don't read."

DB: I was just being provocative.

TE: I didn't read until I was seventeen. And then from seventeen I read a book a week till 1989, and the last big major bulk reading that I did was esoterics, and then after that I stopped reading basically. But I read occasionally.

DB: '89 – would that be the period when you really started to discover your own style of work?

TE: No, 1989 to '90 was when I was pregnant and I had an abortion and I stopped everything. I stopped art, I stopped reading, I stopped living. I smashed all my paintings up in 1988, and then I just threw a load in the skip (trash) in 1989, and then I destroyed everything in 1990.

DB: And when did you start working within an autobiographical genre?

TE: I've always worked in an autobiographical way.

DB: OK, but when it became more literary, like using your writing in your work.

TE: When I realized that I had some value, you mean?

DB: Yes.

TE: Well, first of all I've always written. I've always kept a diary since I was fourteen. I'm a prolific letter writer – the most obsessive letter writer – and in 1992 I did a philosophy course for two years, and that really sorted out a lot of things in my head regarding contemporary art, because previously all I could think about was like Edvard Munch and like I said Byzantine frescoes, Giotto, and early Renaissance. My head had stopped working. There was nothing artistically that filled it up, and then after doing the philosophy course – modern philosophy – it kinda opened up a part of my mind which hadn't been explored before… It's like when I started looking at early Renaissance paintings, I started to understand classical music a lot more, and when I did the philosophy course, I started to understand contemporary art, so it opened up a big space and I realized that anything could be art. It's the conviction and the belief behind what you do – the essence of where it's coming from so it's more like a conceptual idea, even though I don't make conceptual looking work. And in 1992, I asked people to invest in my creative potential, which I found…

DB: Very modern.

TE: That wasn't supposed to be a piece of

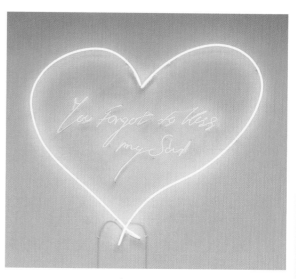

You Forgot to Kiss My Soul, *2001, Neon, 46 x 55 in/116 x 141 cm. Courtesy Jay Jopling/White Cube, London.*

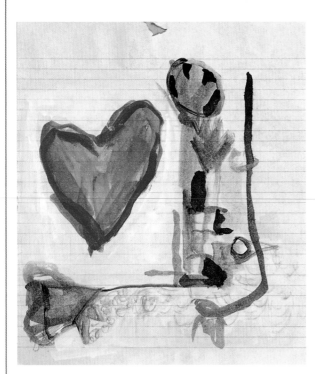

After My Abortion (XIV), *1990.*
watercolor on paper,
8 x 10 in/20 x 26 cm.
Courtesy Jay Jopling/White Cube,
London.

art, that was out of desperation. (Long pause.) I mean you must have had it. A time in your life when you've been so low, when everything is just so terrible that given the choice you think that either you're going to die or that this is what death feels like, and then you just carry on. And at certain times in my life that's happened to me quite profoundly, and it's at those moments when everything gets shook up and everything gets rediscovered. It's almost like a new me or something.

like illustration.

DB: Well I see – you're not going to like this – I see Schiele more as an illustrator. His pencil and ink work is extraordinarily strong. He has a fantastic eye for layout and design. I find his painting really murky.

TE: He was only 28 when he died.

DB: It doesn't matter. Shall we go through a list of great painters that were dead by the age of 28? It doesn't demean the work he did do and does it really matter, if it puts it into any kind of perspective? Probably not, because the hold he has on people seems to be essentially some of what art now embraces. The hard image. The cult of personality.

TE: Yeah, but I think with Egon Schiele you've got this problem. Because his work's reproduced so often, the general public take it as a…

DB: A graphic logo almost?

"WHAT'S REALLY GOOD ABOUT THE WORD 'ART' IS THAT 'ART' IS A WORD LIKE 'LOVE,' OR 'GOD,' OR WHATEVER. IT TRANSCENDS SO MANY THINGS… IT'S TAKEN ME A LONG TIME TO COME TO TERMS WITH THAT."

DB: I felt very much like that in the late '70s. I probably felt every day was intolerable and that living itself was a burden that I wasn't prepared to continue hoisting upon my small frail shoulders. Yeah. Do you see what you're doing as a trade or…? You like early Renaissance, and also, to a certain extent, Expressionism.

TE: Yeah, a lot. Especially Schiele and Munch. Not all Expressionism. Some of it I think is a bit almost passé kind of, almost

TE: … As opposed to… Yeah, it's like Munch's *Scream*, for example, it's used even in cartoons.

DB: Oh, shall I tell you something interesting about that – not many people know this?

TE: Yeah, go on.

DB: What do you think of when you see that picture?

TE: A noise coming from the hills and it's coming from the fields.

DB: That's interesting, because not many

people would say that. Most people would say, and wrongly, that the figure in the painting is doing the scream. But he's not, he's reacting to a scream.

TE: Yeah.

DB: Munch made notes prior to making the painting, suggesting that he wanted to capture the reaction to a scream, so the guy is reacting to a scream. He's not the screamer, in a manner of speaking he's the screamee!

TE: Yes, but it's also like the scream that you hear in your head. I've got a love poem for Carl [Freedman] and it's:

> *"You put your hand across my mouth,*
> *But still the noise continues.*
> *Every part of my body is screaming. I'm lost,*
> *About to be smashed into a thousand*
>   *million pieces.*
> *Each part forever belonging to you."*

And that's about *The Scream*.

DB: A thousand million little screamers.

TE: It's about having sex, but a love poem. Don't you think that when your whole body's screaming? And it's terrible when it happens, but when it goes away it's like a loss and you want it to come back again.

DB: Staying on your influences for a second. Do you shun the more technically aspiring styles of work, like high Renaissance or, to come up to today, somebody who's technically pretty sound, such as Freud, who one could feel dismissive of just because technique seems to be pre-eminent in what that work represents?

TE: Yeah, at least in Freud I think like that, yeah.

DB: Is it a feeling of vulnerability?

TE: The thing is, to start with, Expressionism I do not like, the majority of Expressionism, when I think about it, I don't like. I saw a really big showing of it in Brussels last year,

and I just don't like loads of people like Heckel and people like that, I find them quite – just too base or something.

DB: I love Heckel.

TE: Yeah, whatever, but…

DB: I love his woodblock prints. Again, I'm not keen on his paintings.

TE: Well, maybe that's also why I relate to them, I'm not a very good painter. I don't mind saying it. I get accused of being naive, but I don't see anything naive about what I do.

DB: I would take it as a compliment.

TE: My drawings actually can be quite sophisticated now, I mean I've been drawing since 1982.

DB: What about the word "Art?" Botticelli against Manzoni's shit in a tin-can. Is the "Art" word big enough to encompass both works?

TE: But you can talk about the alchemy of both of those things. You could wax lyrical as much as you like, yeah.

DB: Does alchemy apply as much as the word art?

TE: Yes, but I wouldn't use the word alchemy, you see, what's really good about the word "art" is that "art" is a word like "love," or "god," or whatever. It transcends so many things.

DB: So you're content with the word.

TE: Yeah, definitely, but it's taken me a long time to come to terms with that.

DB: Do you not think that the word "art" is so offputting to the majority of people?

TE: No, I don't think so, not any more. I

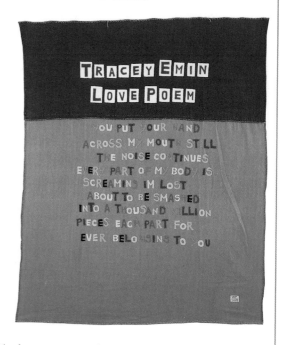

Love Poem, *1996, applique blanket, 96 x 96 in/244 x 244 cm. Courtesy Jay Jopling/White Cube, London.*

"YOU ARE THE UNRIVALED BEARER OF YOUR OWN GIFTS. YOU DO THIS WITH A HEART AND A GREATNESS THAT CONQUERS MY NORMAL DISTASTE FOR SUCH CONFESSIONS."

—*Gary Hume*

think that's changing. Definitely. If someone asked me what I do, I say I'm an artist, without any hesitation. Art's for everyone.

DB: I saw a recent statistic that suggested

Mad Tracey From Margate, Everyone's Been There, 1997, *applique blanket (from clothing provided by friends), 85 x 105 in/215 x 267 cm. Courtesy Jay Jopling/White Cube, London.*

that as many people go to galleries and art museums as go to rock shows and clubs.

TE: Yes, but also with art it's such a recent thing that – Britain's more literary based, but now it's becoming visually based as well. It's becoming more aesthetic with everything, from furniture to fashion to nice looking, for example.

DB: I don't agree with you there. We are

not primarily a literary based nation. I think that's a cliché that's been thrown around far too much. I think we're incredibly visually aware actually. We always have been. I think that the history of British painting is extraordinary. Every century a great fist of brilliance has thrust through the old sixteenth-century repression. Always there has been a great painter.

TE: Turner for one.

DB: Do you know where the word "Impressionism" came from?

TE: Tell me.

DB: After Monet's gang's efforts at capturing the spirit or impression of Turner's light on water, Monet did a little manifesto signed by the others which said something like: "Our intention is to create form in movement and the phenomena of light, knowing we have been preceded by the illustrious Monsieur Turner." Hey, it's not fucking French – the seed of modern art, mate!

TE: What's so brilliant about Turner is the fact that it was through experience of living so…

DB: Yeah, he was a randy old bugger…

TE: Yeah he was, but apparently, I heard this and I really believed it, that he had a house, three-story house in Chelsea, and the bottom bit was a pub, the middle of it was a brothel and at the top was his studios. And when he died Ruskin came and destroyed all of his erotic drawings and…

DB: Yes, Ruskin certainly did that, but Turner also lived down in Margate as Admiral Puggy Booth. He had, of course, a masked life, he was living with the widow Mrs. Booth down on the coast. I mean he was quite a strange, randy little guy. Working class and a bit insecure.

TE: Margate. Another great connection

there. Me and Turner.

DB: Wilde said, "Those who want a mask have to wear it. That is their punishment." Ironically, by becoming the anonymous Admiral Booth, Turner gave himself the freedom to create some of his most seriously breakthrough paintings.

TE: Yeah, but imagine tying yourself to a mast to know what it feels like to be in the head of a storm. I mean, that to me is what art is about really. It's like this risk thing; it's like pushing yourself to a limit which is beyond your own notion of existence.

DB: So that's art for you?

TE: Yeah.

DB: How about artists who don't use a life/experience approach. Would you dismiss it?

TE: No, because if I did that, I'd waste a lot of time and a lot of energy looking over my shoulder. What's more important to me is to look forward to what I'm doing, not start complaining about what other people are doing.

DB: Because, say, you get somebody like Ken Curry, for instance. Do you know his work – the Scots painter? Well, he's very technically accomplished. Incredibly proficient. Now let's be really corny. Tintoretto, no, even better, Titian – who was not exactly, you know, he had parties and everything, quite a socialite, but he had a serious approach to painting and doing a good job. Not so much about expressing himself or…

TE: Yes, but I've got friends who do that. They get up, they go to the studio, they do their work but they…

DB: They do extraordinarily accomplished paintings.

TE: Yes, and then they go home again. But it's not like that for me, and it never has been. Basically, I don't think there's any point

in making something which has already been made before.

DB: So you put high value on originality?

TE: Yeah.

DB: Why?

TE: Because it's the moment of something.

DB: Is a more traditional artist not creating another kind of moment in his own work?

TE: For themselves, yeah, but not for the rest of the world.

DB: That's very general isn't it, because there is a world that also appreciates that kind of work, no? [I want to suggest that more people flock to see a Turner or Vermeer show than say a Gilbert & George, but Tracey's off and running!]

TE: No, I'm talking for the whole world. I'm not talking about the people who happen to be patting me on the back at the moment. The thing is that if you've got a message and you want it to be heard, you have to find a way of communicating which excites people, and for me it wouldn't be worth doing what I did if I just re-created something which was done fifty… I can paint really good Edvard Munch paintings. I can do really good Heckel woodcuts, 'cause I did it as a student. But I'm not a student any more – well, we're all a student of life if you want to put it like that –

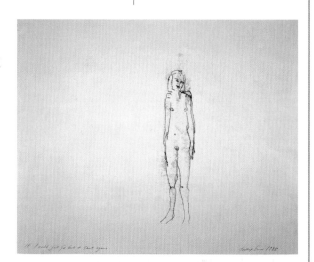

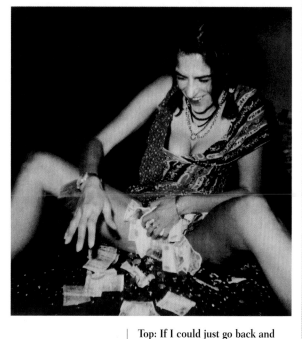

Top: If I could just go back and start again, *1995, monoprint, 26 x 32 in/65 x 82 cm. Courtesy Jay Jopling/White Cube, London.*
Bottom: Good Smile Great Come, 2000, *C-print, 30 x 31 in/76 x 78 cm. Courtesy Jay Jopling/White Cube, London.*

but for me I have be excited about what I'm doing, I have to reinvent, re-create.

DB: So it comes back to the same question. You sound a little bit dismissive of artists who don't work in what would be called "the original."

TE: I'm sure a lot more of them are a lot more dismissive toward me.

DB: Rembrandt doesn't care.

TE: Yes, Rembrandt's fucking brilliant.

DB: But he was working in a very traditional style.

one person and that's me.

DB: Yes, I understand. That's good then isn't it?

TE: Yes.

DB: I don't want to argue about it (chuckles).

TE: We're not going to get into a fight or anything.

(Long pause.)

No but the biggest influence in my life is my life, like my experiences – not what I do from day to day but how I make sense of the world or whatever.

"I HAD TO COME TO TERMS WITH MY FAILURE AS AN ARTIST... I HAD TO FIND A WAY FOR MYSELF."

TE: But he had a fantastic sense of humor. Look at his etchings, all the ones with him dressing up and everything. What was going through his mind when he was doing that? Other people weren't doing those kind of things at that time. Also, I really really like Flemish and Dutch Master painting... I like the narrative and I like looking at the paintings and working out exactly what was going on.

DB: Yes. So there is something in it for you, in a traditional narrative way?

TE: Yes, of course. I mean a lot of my work can actually have the appearance of traditional work – my drawings or whatever. Things for me are quite personal. I had to come to terms with my failure as an artist. And the artist that I was trying to be was that traditional type artist, and I was just crap at it. I was just not very good at it. I had to find a way for myself. So what I'm talking about is personal experience. I'm not being judgmental about other people, I'm being judgmental on

DB: Fame in a frame.

TE: Fame in a frame (laughs).

DB: Because – what your work is becoming, whether you like it or not, is a celebration of personality, because of its autobiographical hub, and because of its literary pursuit. Your work has been dragged out of the library, almost out of the area of memorabilia and autobiography into an art context or gallery-showing context, which is quite interesting. It doesn't have what some critics would call deeper context, it has a what-you-see-is-what-you-get kind of honesty to it – it's not for instance like Beuys or whatever. His thing, I feel, works in a different way because there is much more of a sense of what you called alchemy, or complex symbolism, about his work. With you it's not like that, so it becomes much more of a personality based subject. Anyone can empathize with your strong life-story line.

TE: Yeah, but there's been loads of people who've had... Gilbert & George...

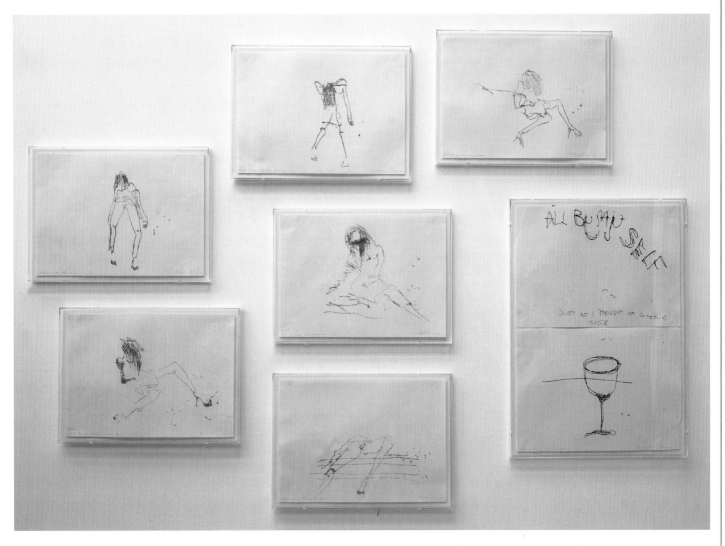

Installation: You Forgot to Kiss My Soul, *27 April – 26 May 2001, monoprints. Courtesy Jay Jopling/White Cube, London.*

DB: I'm not attacking you.

TE: Gilbert & George, Andy Warhol, let's say van Gogh. More people know that van Gogh cut his ear off than know the titles of his paintings.

DB: Of course they do yes, yeah – yes, but they're not quite so obviously the subject of their own work. Gilbert & George nearly, but even in their work they themselves are only cyphers standing in for themselves.

TE: People, critics…

DB: Forget critics.

TE: I don't forget them because I like to listen to what people have got to say, and if people have a derogatory point of view about what I do then I want to hear why. I'm interested. And if, you know, "How long can she keep churning this sort of stuff out for?" – it's obvious.

DB: (chuckles) Yes, the longevity bit.

TE: Yeah, it's obvious, I'll keep doing it until I die. Cause my life keeps, you know – and the other thing is, oh well she made all this work about how hard life was, now what's she going to do, make work about jumping into rich people's swimming pools with bottles of champagne?

DB: What they're saying is how long will her work have currency.

TE: Yeah.

DB: I understand that. I could go off at a tangent here, because it is an interesting point. I think you're not the only one that this happens to, I think there are a lot of your particular generation who are now getting what "we in the rock industry" call a backlash. There's a feeling that you sit on laurels, you haven't got much more to give apart from the first statement, the first shock or whatever, that there is no real ambition or desire among the YBAs to make art. It's more about going to

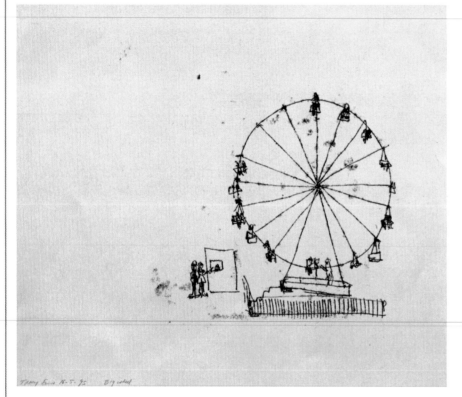

Big Wheel, *1995, monoprint,*
23 x 30 in/58 x 75 cm.
Courtesy Jay Jopling/White Cube,
London.

parties and being seen.

TE: I think that comes through ignorance, because if people knew how fucking hard we worked and the fact that I'm 34. This YBA thing is stupid. I'm a 34-year-old woman. And I haven't actually ever sacrificed anything in

my life, but I've worked really hard at what I believe in, to do what I believe in. It's not a whim. It isn't just a little bit of a fashion thing. And when my work ceases to have currency, I'm not gonna stop doing it. But that's just me actually, I can – I'm in a

privileged position because I'd like to write novels. At the moment I'd like to have a radio show – that's what I'm interested in doing. I don't see art as just a visual thing.

DB: That's an interesting point though, Tracey. If you go ahead and do a radio show, is it very important to you that the word art is attached to it?

TE: Yeah, Tracey Emin, the artist, has her radio show.

DB: Yes, but the thing itself, the event, is it important that it's considered art? Is it not enough that Tracey Emin gets a radio show?

TE: If I did a radio show I would actually say how the format of the radio show is and the radio show would be more like a kind of sound piece.

DB: So there's not going to be a sense of you doing a radio show like – "I'm doing a radio show," like in the "ironic event."

TE: No, it wouldn't be ironic. It would be really sincere. Everything that I do is totally sincere.

DB: So it would be OK if people down the road said, "Oh that artist is doing a radio show" and didn't say, "Have you heard of her latest art project – it's a radio show?"

TE: It would be that artist doing a radio show, yeah.

DB: But it would be OK if it was thought it was merely a radio show? That they didn't

"EVERYTHING THAT I DO IS TOTALLY SINCERE."

know it was art. That's OK, right?

TE: Yes, it's absolutely fine by me. It's like that piece in *Time Out. Time Out* did the seaside issue and sent me down to Margate or whatever, and there it is –

DB: – nice little picture.

TE: Tracey in her bikini with the donkeys at Margate beach and a yes I've come home kind of thing.

DB: I thought that was lovely actually, it was very nice.

TE: Yes, and that two pages that I had was like a piece of art to me, because it was something fantastic to me.

DB: So it's more important that you know it's art?

TE: Yes.

DB: It's not important that nobody else does?

TE: No. It's like my birthday party, the Karaoke party. It got written about in the press like it was the art event of the year. And it's just my fuckin' birthday party. But just the way in which I do things, and my belief behind things, the event of something happening, for me it feels like a fantastic piece of art. The art of existence. The art of living, the art of being. And everyone can do that.

DB: Yeah.

TE: And I think a lot of people in life have problems because they don't have a door. They don't have a place to go and think freely and be true to themselves.

DB: [I'm completely lost now as I'm not sure if the birthday party being written up as an art event is a good thing or a bad thing.] It's much easier to be an artist in Italy or France or even Germany, because the windows and doors thing was broken down a lot earlier than it was in England.

TE: Yes.

DB: I think the idea of doors as being a way into new perceptions was accepted a lot earlier on the continent than it was in Britain. That's the one place where we really lagged behind.

TE: But I'm not Anglo-Saxon. I think part of the problem is – this is going to sound so terrible – but it's a bit of a class thing really. You know. Is that I've had to battle hard to get into college and do the things I've done and be taken seriously.

DB: Well, it seemed it was only in the '60s that a few working class lads were allowed to be artists. It's a recent phenomenon.

TE: That's because of the conscription thing. "What would you have done if you hadn't been conscripted?" "Oh, I would have gone to art school."

DB: Where do you see yourself in ten years?

TE: Ooh, I've changed my mind about that because I used to imagine that I wouldn't be here and be quite romantic about it.

DB: The Baudelaire gag?

TE: Something like that – become part of the sun or something. But now I'm feeling pretty good, that I've never been very good at conforming and becoming part of society

DB: NO!! Oh really?

TE: Yeah, really!! I've always felt that I was somehow outside of it. Well, I don't really want this to be in print, but +++++++++++ +++++++++++++++++++++++++++++++

DB: OK – we'll leave that alone.

TE: They were asking me questions like: "Is it art?" And I was saying, "Well, if it isn't art what are you doing sitting talking to me about it for?" It's obvious that it's art. If it's not art what the hell is it doing in an art gallery and why are people coming to look at it? I mean

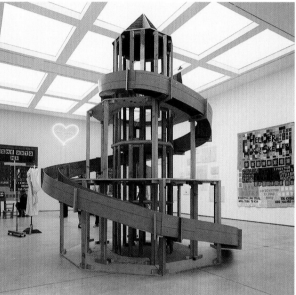

Self-portrait, 2001, *reclaimed wood and sparrow,*
144 x 140 in/366 x 356 cm.
Courtesy Jay Jopling/White Cube, London.

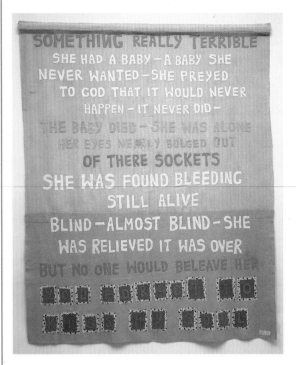

SOMETHING REALLY TERRIBLE
SHE HAD A BABY — A BABY SHE
NEVER WANTED — SHE PREYED
TO GOD THAT IT WOULD NEVER
HAPPEN — IT NEVER DID —
THE BABY DIED — SHE WAS ALONE
HER EYES NEARLY BULGED OUT
OF THERE SOCKETS
SHE WAS FOUND BLEEDING
STILL ALIVE
BLIND — ALMOST BLIND — SHE
WAS RELIEVED IT WAS OVER
BUT NO ONE WOULD BELEAVE HER

Something Really Terrible, *2001,*
appliqué blanket,
95 x 80 in/240 x 202 cm.
Courtesy Jay Jopling/White Cube,
London.

"SPECIALIZATION
HAS NEVER BEEN
HER FORTE; HER
ART CROSSES
BOUNDARIES OF
AGE AND CLASS
AND DEALS WITH
LIFE IN GENERAL:
LOVE, DEATH,
THE WHOLE DAMN
THING..."

—*Stuart Morgan*

people don't sit around and say to Jarvis [Cocker, lead singer of the band *Pulp*] "Is it music?"

DB: Let's think of somebody else. I know what you mean, but you need somebody…

TE: Well, let's think of somebody experimental.

DB: John Cage is a perfect example. Or even early *Velvet Underground* when they were just making noises [taps cutlery!]… but is it music?

TE: Well is it art? Music is art anyway. Music's the highest form of art, isn't it?

DB: It'll make a grown man swoon.

TE: But there're people who spend all their lives in the New Forest painting horses. They're not artists. They're picture makers. It's more like a craft, or a trade or whatever, it's an industry of sorts.

DB: You're saying facility with technique produces craftsmen rather than artists.

TE: Brilliant example here. *Finnegans Wake.*

DB: Yeah! Um. Art, as far as I'm concerned.

TE: William Burroughs.

DB: Both.

TE: Those were the great ones. But, you get others and they write books and novels all their lives and they don't actually create absolute masterpieces.

Iman: Joan Collins (chuckles).

TE: Joan Collins, yeah.

Iman: She wrote a book and was sued. They wanted the money back because they said it was so bad. But she won. They didn't say it had to be good. (all laugh)

TE: Going back to the idea of alchemy in the

true sense of art, something magical happens between the mind and hand in the presence of the making of it.

DB: And that's what Turner touched on because he did something else other than just – his so called realistic paintings were imbued with a metaphysical subtext that gave them… that made them much more than what they were. I mean those things actually struggle to free themselves from their frames. They're so powerful.

TE: View it with a magnifying glass as well.

DB: It's quite touching that there is still a spiritual fetishism attached to owning art. All art. Everything – there's something about it, even the real superstitious act of some collectors I know who will kind of buy stuff hoping that if they stand close enough to it some of the transcendent perception will rub off on them. You know there's that feeling when people go and see the *Book of Kells*, or the *Mona Lisa*, and get near it, that something special will happen to them. It's the martyrs-relic syndrome.

TE: Well, I know definitely with my work it's the experience the viewer goes through looking at it that's important. And I once had this idea that things, visually, were important, but not as important as the essence of where it's coming from in the first place. Loads of people can make work that looks like mine, but it won't be the same will it?

DB: Well I should hope not. Would you allow that people would follow in your tradition?

TE: Teaching. I teach at colleges and there's a lot of people who are doing my kind of thing.

DB: How do you feel about that?

TE: Uhm. OK. 'Cause they'll grow out of it, won't they, and get their own style.

DB: I'll see to them.

TE: I'll sort that one out.

DB: Just leave that one to me. Isn't it rather nice to think that you've contributed to what they'll become?

TE: Yeah, well when I went into colleges I'd remember that I'm talking to someone who's fifteen years younger than me and there's quite a lot of difference at that age. Can't even talk about art, we're talking about shoes and things.

DB: Frequently I'm talking to kids 30 years younger! Can you imagine that? You know it's quite astonishing. Some bands I've talked to think of *Scary Monsters* [1980] as my first album. Mostly young American bands though. But it's satisfying… it's a different feeling to be older and to have actually kind of created a certain environment with your work.

TE: Well, it's still some years away, but I'd quite like to be an old woman and have students come in for tea in the afternoon.

DB: I can tell you who you could do that with right now, the next time you go to the States, but you'd better be fast because she's getting up there. Louise Bourgeois, down in The Village.

TE: I was being interviewed and I was saying that I would like to meet her. I just bet she's – have you met her?

DB: It's one of the things Iman and I are going to do when we get back to New York next time. She's very old now. Her last show in Milan was stunning. Absolutely fantastic.

TE: When you look at her work, you don't think that this has been made by somebody who's 90, you've got no idea. Even in her old work you have no idea when she made it.

DB: The guns of the twentieth century. The Duchamps, the Burroughses, the Louise Bourgeoises, Picassos.

TE: I don't like Picasso.

DB: Oh, come on. His adventurousness and his pure playfulness, right up to the day he died, that aspect of him – it was phenomenal.

TE: Yeah.

DB: You're probably a Duchamp school person if any…

TE: Well not really, I'm more into…

DB: I know. Munch.

TE: I'm Munch. My man Munch.

DB: You're more Munch than Duchamp. My man Munch. There's a book for you.

TE: Yves Klein.

DB: Yeah, he's great. I love his work.

TE: He died when he was twenty-eight.

DB: What is it about twenty-eight-year-old dead artists? That was kind of sad. I mean

Automatic Orgasm, 2001, *appliqué blanket*, *104 x 84 in/263 x 214 cm.* *Courtesy Jay Jopling/White Cube, London.*

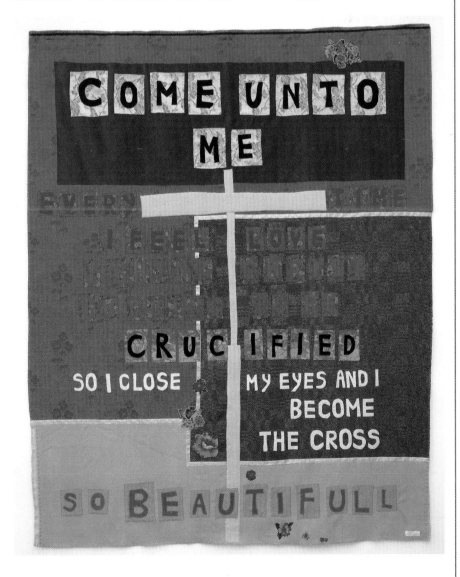

he really should have carried on working and not given up the ghost, because he was terrifically talented.

TE: Maybe he thought he'd gone as far as he could go. But when it's time to go it's time to go.

DB: I don't know.

TE: Don't you think so?

DB: Not for me. It's so fickle, Tracey. I'm so glad that I survived any of those things myself. I'm having such a great time now. And when I think how long ago it was that I was twenty-eight.

TE: So how old were you in '73?

DB: About twenty-six.

TE: Twenty-six – wow.

DB: We've covered a lot of ground actually. Oh, you said one thing last night – going back to something we've already talked about to a certain extent. One of the reasons that you destroyed your work was that your painting would never get you sitting down talking to me or being on the television.

TE: What I said to you was if I hadn't destroyed the paintings then I wouldn't be here sitting talking to you now, would I?

DB: And I meant to follow that up with, is what you do, therefore, a means to an end?

TE: Yeah, definitely.

DB: So it's anything for the result?

TE: No, because I'm doing it for genuine reasons. I don't know what the end is, do I? But I know that what I've done in the past makes sense to the point where I am now, because otherwise

I would have always been surrounded by these not very good paintings. I'd go to the studio, I'd just walk in and would want to make something beautiful by the end of the day, and I would have failed all the time and I'd feel depressed and depressed and feeling like a failure. So I decided to stop because I didn't really have the heart in me, but if I hadn't done that seven years ago, you know, eight years ago, I swear I wouldn't be doing all the things that I do now. I wouldn't have valued… it's almost like denying in life what you're naturally good at.

DB: Yes (laughs). I'll stick with Expressionism then – I'm good at that. I can tell you "Oh, I can do you any number of Heckels."

TE: Yeah, I'll knock off a Heckel for you.

DB: I did knock off a Kirchner for somebody, they wanted a…

TE: Oh, I like Kirchner.

DB: Yeah, he's good, he's fun to paint as well. I did a couple actually. For somebody who really loved him. I did them as a present one Christmas.

TE: But people like you with your painting, it's for your pleasure kind of thing, whereas with your music it's like you're always pushing, pushing, pushing, pushing, never satisfied. Whereas with the painting it's just a really personal thing. It's like you having a dialogue with yourself.

DB: Not proper art? And shouldn't be shown? I'm very into the visual stuff that I make. I'm quite purposeful about the stuff that I make and do. I've got another show coming up in March. My ninth in two years.

TE: Where?

DB: Oh, Marconi in Milan. Three or four floors of it.

TE: It's not – is that his dad? Is it Joe Marconi?

The Baliff, *2001, wooden cabinet, DVD (40 mins 30 secs), monitor, 103 x 33 x 36 in/261 x 83 x 91 cm. Courtesy Jay Jopling/White Cube, London.*

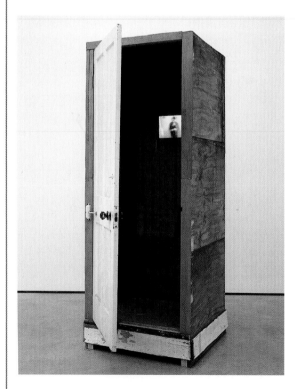

DB: Yeah. It's the same gallery.

TE: Joe Marconi?

DB: Yeah, Joe Marconi.

TE: Oh, 'cause I met him.

DB: Yes, he's lovely.

TE: He's got a swimming pool as well.

DB: Uh?

TE: He's got a swimming pool.

DB: Yeah. Well, whatever.

TE: In Milan. Yes this is really interesting because when I met him, he said, "If you'd be interested in doing something with me..." And I said, "Well I'm interested in going shopping in Milan" – let's get our priorities sorted out. So the idea is like go to Milan and go shopping and stay over and use his pool.

DB: Yes, well, I'm more interested in his gallery. Milan's a long way for a swim isn't it? Give me some quick one-liners. You don't have to if you don't want to.

TE: Good, I like one-liners.

DB: Bridget Riley.

TE: Appears to be a good woman.

DB: Glenn Brown and appropriation, I suppose.

TE: I think he's probably one of the best in his field.

DB: These are very personal I suppose. Gillian and Sarah. Shall I separate the two? Is it unfair to put the two…

TE: Yes, it's unfair.

DB: Gillian.

TE: Exceptionally close good friend whom I've been friends with for years and years and she became friends with me at a time when people wouldn't touch me with a barge-pole.

DB: Wyndham Lewis.

TE: I always thought he was a bit of a fascist.

DB: Chapman brothers (laughs).

TE: Individually, they're really crap artists but together they do pretty good, I think.

DB: Do they now? Not as morally repugnant as Balthus for instance?

TE: They don't – their work to me is like fun really. I know you like their thing, their *Devils at Wars* – when they did their Goya stuff – but now I just think they have a lot of fun together.

DB: Children with mutant genitals?

TE: I actually don't really want to think about that too much. But I'll tell you one thing about them. Exceptionally generous, when it came to the ICA auction. Yes. Generous people. Generous spirited.

DB: (Laughs) Mark Quinn.

TE: I respect him immensely for giving up drinking, and I really, really like Mark. I think he's a great person.

DB: What do you think of the work?

TE: Some of Mark's work I like. I really liked his exploding bread pieces that he cast in bronze – baroque and crazy. I was in Amsterdam when he was showing those in

> "TRACEY IS AMAZINGLY LIKE THE MYTH OF HERSELF IN REAL LIFE."
>
> —*Matthew Collings*

Conversation with My Mum, *2001, two children's chairs, DVD, TV and table, 40 x 16 x 13 in/101 x 41 x 32 cm. Courtesy Jay Jopling/White Cube, London.*

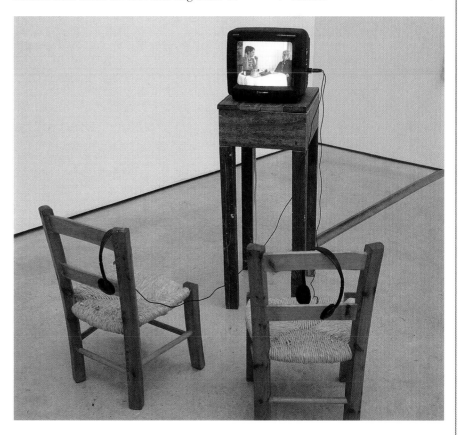

"SHE CAN SEEM NAIVE ABOUT THE PITFALLS OF EXPRESSIONISM TO A DEGREE THAT BRINGS HER TO THE BRINK OF BEING A REALLY BAD ARTIST."

—*Jonathan Jones*

The Perfect Place to Grow, *2001, wooden birdhouse, DVD, monitor, trestle, plants, wooden ladder, 103 x 33 x 64 in/261 x 83 x 162 cm. Courtesy Jay Jopling/White Cube, London.*

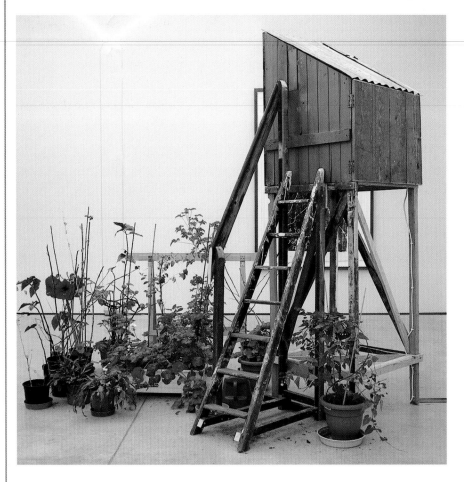

the Hilton, I thought they were really good. I don't like all Mark's work, but I think…

DB: I'm also an admirer. I think it's looking fairly conservative, his work, recently.

TE: I think in a way Mark's work always has been.

DB: Antony Gormley.

TE: Antony is the most loveliest, generous talk-a-holic person I've ever met in my fucking life. And I like his concrete castings best.

DB: What do you think of – I personally think that it's one of the most spiritually uplifting sculptures produced this decade – *Case for an Angel*? Do you know that one?

TE: Oh, that one. No, I much prefer things when they're not so figurative. When they're much more… actually like the concrete cube things.

DB: Don't you think they're a bit '60s Nauman. Knees of Five Famous Artists, for instance. Nauman stuff?

TE: Well, I…

DB: I mean, I'd say that piece of work and most of Rachel Whiteread's stuff is no more than Bruce Nauman, but bigger. Whiteread's *Oasis* to Nauman's *Beatles*. It was already there in *Cast of the Space under My Chair* [a 1965 Nauman sculpture].

TE: Why don't you ask me what I think of Bruce Nauman then?

DB: What do you think of Bruce Nauman then?

TE: Fucking brilliant.

DB: True.

TE: Yeah. One of the top artists…

DB: Top man.

TE: Top man, yes – no, brilliant artist. Fantastic. He's influenced so many people… and I bet he's really good fun as well.

DB: He's great fun.

TE: Yeah, I've never met him, but I bet he's great fun.

DB: I met him last year. He's "Stetsony" – you know, jeans and jacket with fringes. Yeah, he's a cowboy. He's like a… Clint Eastwoody kinda guy. A very down to earth guy.

TE: I like cowboys. Sarah Lucas? Partner in crime.

DB: Yeah, Sarah Lucas. Partner in crime. Is that it?

TE: Yeah.

DB: Hume?

TE: Gary's a fucking good painter. Gary Hume is the only art I have up in my home. A Gary Hume painting. It's the only thing I've got. I've got nothing else on the walls.

DB: That's interesting. Which one?

TE: It's a small one. It's really small, it looks like a really weird flower.

DB: I thought it might be.

TE: But it's not a flower, but it looks like a

flower. And it's the only thing I've got up on the wall. When Gary gave it to me I started crying I was so touched. I have a piece of work by Mat Collishaw which is on the floor which is a mirror with… scratched beneath the mirror is the face of a Neanderthal man which really looks like Mat. That's good. I've got work, but I've got videos as well – I've got a video by Lisa Maypost, one by Georgina – and videos are easier for me to collect, because I don't have to have them up on the walls or anything.

DB: Clive Barker.

TE: I don't know who Clive Barker is.

DB: Colin Self.

TE: I don't know who Colin Self is either. Is that the right answers?

DB: Oh no, it's fine (laughs)… they're interesting people. They might be people you'd like to look at. Clive Barker and Colin Self are two guys who came out of the '60s. Clive Barker cast six hand-grenades in bronze and then tried to take them through customs.

TE: I came through customs the other week from Nuremberg with my tent, and they said, "What've you got there?" They said, "Where did you come from, did you come from Egypt?" And I said, "No I've come from Nuremberg." They went, "Oh!, and what've you got there?" I said, "A tent." They said, "What kind of tent?" I said, "It's my art, it's my tent." They said, "Do you want to show it to us?" And I said, "Well no, not really, but I'll tell you exactly what's on it. It's the names of everyone I've ever slept with from 1963–1995. If you want me to open it up I will."

DB: They must have loved that.

TE: It was funny, yeah.

DB: But, Barker actually had his hand-grenades in his case and they were going through and it comes up on the television

screen… there's guns everywhere. Angus Fairhurst.

TE: I love Angus… I like his band *Low Expectations*, and I love his drawings.

DB: How are they, *Low Expectations*?

TE: They're pretty low. Don't have any expectations about them.

DB: Is this his band?

TE: Yeah, but once me and Angus were talking about bringing a fish – a live fish, in a bag, and taking it through customs. And they go, "What's that in your bag?" and you say, "It's a fish," and when you take the fish out all you have is a bone. I don't know why we found it so amusing.

[My wife re-enters the room. It's my siesta time. A pre-show habit I've adopted since being with Iman.]

DB: Well I'm off for a kip then.

TE: Can you fall asleep? It's terrible when you're excited and you can't fall asleep. Do you take anything?

DB: No, I seem to have that together. Well, young Tracey, I expect you to be able to write perfectly in Celt the next time I see you. You know one of the first things Iman made for me – the first time that I did something with Damien? She did his lamb in a box. She needlepointed it from a drawing that I made and I've got a little tapestry. It's so beautiful.

TE: It's better than the lamb in a box.

DB: The irony of course is that it's made in wool. I mean it's so delightful. All the cold context gone. It's just this pretty little picture, in wool.

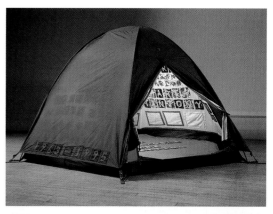

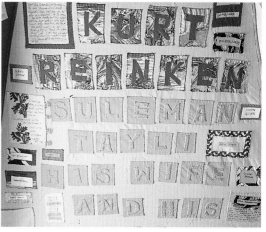

Top: Everyone I have Ever Slept With 1963/1995, *1995, appliquéd tent, mattress, and light, 48 x 97 x 85 in/ 122 x 245 x 215 cm. Courtesy Jay Jopling/White Cube, London.*
Above: Everyone I have Ever Slept With 1963/1995, *detail.*

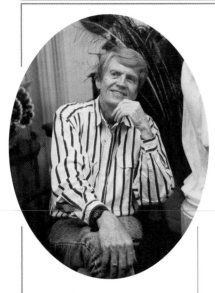

DUANE HANSON

His hyper-realism now recognized throughout the world, Hanson's interest in the realistic presentation of human form was evident early on. He was born in Minnesota in 1925, and at the age of 13 he created a three dimensional wooden version of Gainsborough's The Blue Boy *using his mother's butcher knife as a tool.*

During the time he studied at the Cranbrook Academy of Art, the trend in art schools was toward abstraction; Hanson said of his experience, "I went to school and heard you had to be modern… I didn't really warm up until Pop Art made Realism legitimate again."

Moving to Florida in 1965, he sculpted Abortion, *a two-foot long mixed-media rendering of a dead pregnant woman, a piece which provoked strong public reaction. He began creating sculpture by casting molds taken directly from his models' bodies which he then embellished with hair, clothes, and props. Moving to New York in 1969, his work inspired critics and began to be widely exhibited. He returned to Florida in 1973 where he worked until his death in 1996.*

Duane Hanson

by Andrew Motion

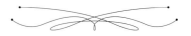

LIFE IS LIKE THAT

No, life is like this – one moment outside, the next: a white hush and people inside drifting. Just glancing round it's not clear who is alive and who is only pretending.

My God, they look tired, these ones no one can quite decide about. Tired is not the word. Take this one here, the gallery stooge. He is leaning so hard against that wall at the end of the day his shoulder has almost melted. Or take that jogger. He lost his shirt on something and now has one foot bare, one red hand rubbing his sole. His finger ends look scarred. The black treads of his trainers (sneakers) are worn

to a smoothness against the law. And a fly-explorer is scouring the jungle of his hair, desperate for a mouthful of sugary sweat. But no, there is no moisture of any kind. Life is not like that, you see; it's like this.

One reason why they might be so tired is: they have died and used all their energy trying to work back towards life. The life where their old clothes and jobs are still waiting. And they have so nearly made it!

Look: here is a tourist fallen out of thin air and getting his breath back before flying on, head heavy but wedged among reliable luggage.
He has assembled a smooth body full of food,
well-bitten nails, bruises, even, as he loomed

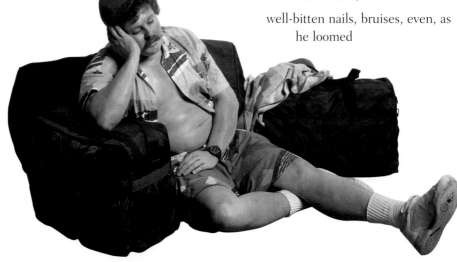

large again in what he had lost.
　　It is a miracle,

almost. How much he must hate
　　staying dead.

Then again: what about his body
　　which trundled

all the way here from the grave wheeling

her cleaning trolley (cart), and took care to
　　fill up

and align every one of its detergent bottles,

just so, rinky-dink in their plastic
　　yellow apron.

Or this poor man, so spent by the
　　hot boredom

of a paper-bag-lunch alone in a
　　nameless place,

he would ignore anything you cared
　　to tell him.

His arms are thin but their sheer
　　weight is such

his elbow-skin has crumpled
　　like an elephant's.

Salvation. You could say that to him,
　　for instance,

though that is not the word either.
　　SAL-VAY-SHUN.

More like that. Bigger. When a mind
　　feels its way

exhaustedly along the whole length
　　of its body

and knows that it can no longer
　　continue alone.

When travelers are stuck between
　　their homes

and wherever they're going,
　　and threatening

to enjoy it. Or when they are lost
　　in their journey

and admit the better logic is to decide
　　not to know

what happens next. Salvation. Not
　　like that, like this:

SAL-VAY-SHUN.

And until then: just staring off.
　　The glass eyes

which never blink and are in fact
　　not eyes at all,

but have seen what it is like to die
　　and stay dead,

and stare levelly back from the
　　other side full

of knowledge they cannot speak. Knowledge

I inherit merely by looking but
　　now understand

I must keep to myself. And of course I shall.

When I eventually leave here, I shall keep it

to myself. Life is like this. What else
　　did you think?

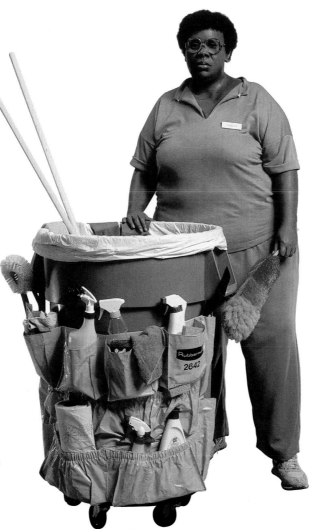

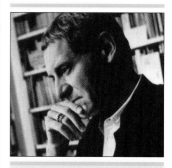

ANDREW MOTION

As Britain's Poet laureate, Andrew Motion has advocated bringing poetry to a wider audience, especially to young people.

Born in 1952, Motion studied at Oxford with the poet John Fuller and taught at the universities of Hull and East Anglia, taking time between the two positions to edit the journal Poetry Review.

Motion's recurrent themes of isolation and loss appear in his first collection of verse, The Pleasure Steamers, in 1978. The collection includes the poem Inland, which describes 17th-century villagers in the wake of a devastating flood. The poem received the Newdigate Prize in 1975.

Motion's critical works and biographies are often portraits of those whose work influenced him, such as Edward Thomas and Philip Larkin – poets he believed to have been undervalued. He has written the biographies Philip Larkin: A Writer's Life, and The Lamberts: George, Constant & Kit, for which he won the Somerset Maugham Award.

Far left: Traveler, *1988, autobody filler, fiberglass & mixed media, life size. Saatchi Gallery, London.*

left: Queenie II, *1988, polychromed bronze, with accessories, life size. Saatchi Gallery, London.*

Richard Billingham

by Nick Hornby

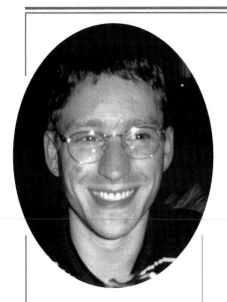

RICHARD BILLINGHAM
*Born in 1970 and brought
up in the public housing
projects of Birmingham,
England, Billingham began
to use a cheap camera to
gather material for his
undergraduate paintings.
His family and the banality
of everyday existence were
the subjects of this work.
Michael Collins, the
photo editor of London's
Sunday Telegraph,
discovered these powerful
photographs and instigated
the publishing of
Billingham's celebrated
book,* Ray's a Laugh.
*In this dark family album,
nothing is concealed —
not the violence,
hopelessness, or the mess.*

*Almost every rule of
photography is broken in the
photographs. Images are
blurred, overexposed, and
grainy; the human subjects
are marred by a red-eyed
glare. He takes some shots
lying on the floor. There's a
bizarre humor to it all.*

*Never intending to be a
photographer, Billingham
states, "I had a very elitist
viewpoint when I was young.
I thought that painting and
sculpture were the best." But
the power of this series of
photographs, many of which
were shown at the Museum
of Modern Art in 1997,
is obvious.*

HOWEVER ENTHUSIASTIC YOU FELT about Charles Saatchi's traveling exhibition "Sensation," much of it was unlikely to detain you for long. I don't mean that in any pejorative sense, or at least, I don't think I do: presumably there are critics who would argue that any successful work of art should provoke at least a break in a gallery visitor's stride, and that therefore works such as Sarah Lucas's *Au naturel* (the one with the dirty mattress, and his'n'hers melons, bucket, banana, and oranges) are comprehensive failures. You see it coming, as it were, from the other side of the room; you snort – with existential and aesthetic despair, if you are Brian Sewell, or with amusement, if you are a normal person – and you move on. I don't have a problem with that. For a few seconds I loved *Au naturel*, which means that I loved it more than I have loved other works that demanded much more of me and turned out not to repay the effort.

Even if they do nothing else – although actually they do plenty else – the photographs of Richard Billingham do detain you. You might not want to be detained; you might think, when you see his pictures of his battered, bewildered, distressed, and alcoholic father Raymond, and of Elizabeth, his enormous, tattooed mother, that you'd rather wander off and look at something funnier, or more beautiful, or less real (and despite the proliferation of blood and pudenda and intestines elsewhere in "Sensation," nobody could describe the show as sober). But you can't. Wandering off is simply not an option, not if you have any curiosity at all: there is too much to think about, too much going on, too much narrative.

The first thing to think about is the rights and wrongs of these pictures, because anyone who has ever had parents of any kind, let alone parents like Billingham's, would wonder whether it were possible to justify snapping their moments of distress and plastering them all over the walls of the Royal Academy. You could argue that Billingham is unfortunate that he is a photographer: the immediacy of his medium seems to expose people in a way that writing never can. Tobias Woolf, Mary Karr, Blake Morrison, Tim Lott, and Katherine Harrison, among many others, have all displayed and analyzed their parents' crises and failings in recent years, but prose mediates and transforms, creates a distance even while trying to tell you things about a character's innermost soul. It's only writing, in other words, whereas photography is real life. But of course that is one of the

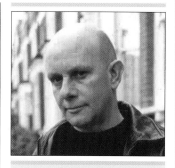

tricks Billingham plays on you, because part of his art is to strip distances away, to convince you that this is life unmediated – an artistic device in itself.

Spend enough time with these pictures and eventually you realize that their complexity and empathy answers any of the questions you might ask of them and their creator: there's nothing exploitative going on here. Empathy is not to be confused with

"MY FATHER RAY IS A CHRONIC ALCOHOLIC. HE DOESN'T GO OUTSIDE AND MOSTLY DRINKS HOMEBREW."

sentimentality, however: whatever else it is, Billingham's work is not sentimental. One of the most striking photographs in the "Sensation" exhibition shows Raymond sitting on the floor by the lavatory, his eyes cast down so that he seems to be in a state of philosophical and weary self-acceptance. His fly is undone, the soles of his sneakers are facing the lens; the toilet seat is broken, and some indistinct bodily waste – puke? blood? – is trickling down the outside of the bowl. It was never going to be a pretty picture, but Billingham's pitiless, neutral gaze doesn't overweight it, and consequently it is allowed to take its place in the ongoing narrative of his parents' life together.

It takes some talent, and some nerve, to be able to do this, and it is Billingham's impeccable judgement that impresses one first of all. It would have been easy for the artist

NICK HORNBY

Capturing the voice of a generation, Hornby is a writer who deals with the theme of obsession. He was born in England in 1957, and became a teacher and a journalist before turning to literary writing.

~

His 1992 childhood memoir, Fever Pitch, a study of obsession, families, identity, and class, revolves around soccer. Some critics compare his first work of fiction, High Fidelity, to the work of J.D. Salinger; the novel was made into a movie in 2000. Among other works is the 1999 novel About a Boy, and his latest release How To Be Good.

~

Hornby also writes for British journals – The Sunday Times, Times Literary Supplement, and Literary Review.

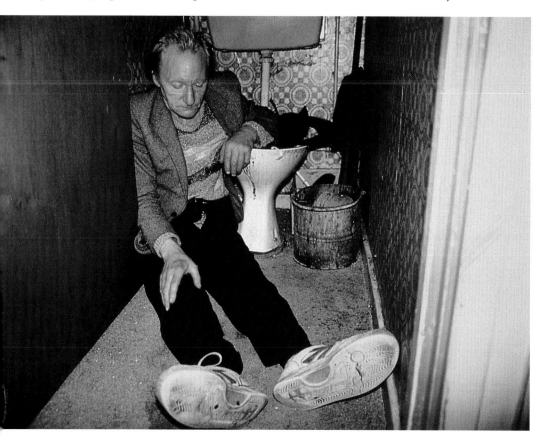

Untitled, *1994, SFA4 color photograph mounted on aluminum, 20 x 30 in/50 x 75 cm. Courtesy of Anthony Reynolds Gallery, London.*

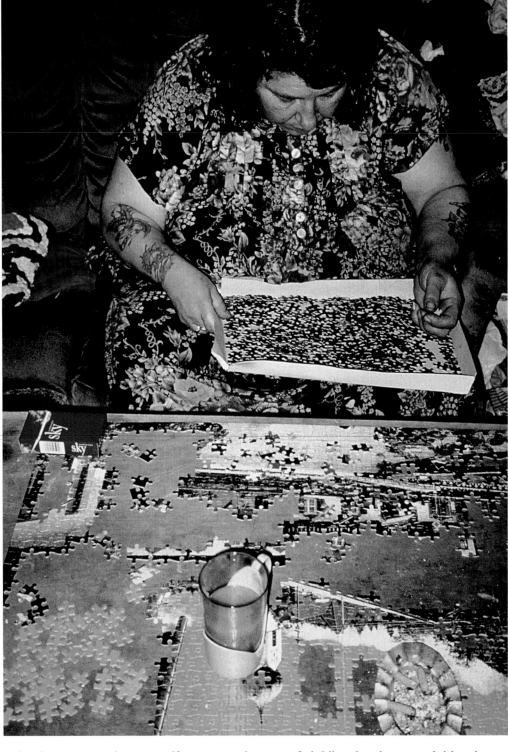

"FLASH INTO THE FACE OF MOM AND DAD. A BRITISH FAMILY ALBUM SO COOL THAT I CAN SEE AND HEAR WHAT GOES ON BETWEEN THE FRAMES."

—*Robert Frank*

Untitled, *1995, SFA4 color photograph on aluminum, 47 x 31 in/120 x 80 cm. Courtesy of Anthony Reynolds Gallery, London.*

to let these pictures become self-pitying — what sort of childhood and young adulthood is possible in this domestic climate? — but they are not: there is too much tolerance. Nor are they angry, hectoring, or loud. Even the pictures depicting violence, a violence born, presumably, out of alcohol and despair, don't succeed in turning the collection into a campaign about this or a plea to the government for that.

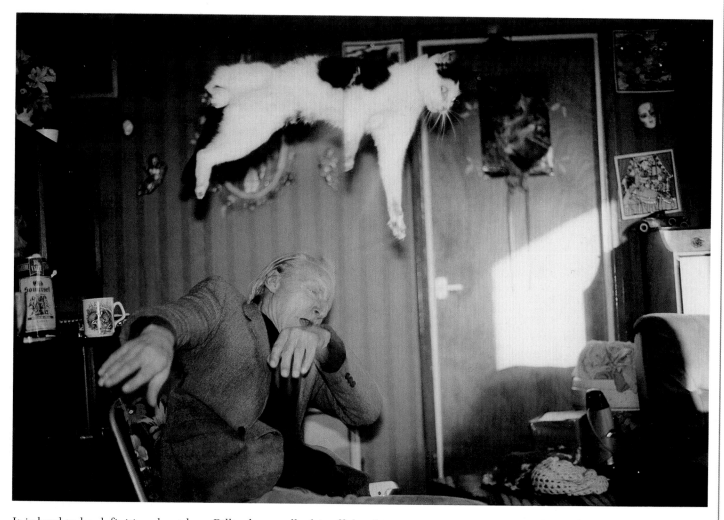

Untitled, *1995, SFA4 color photograph mounted on aluminum, 41 x 62 in/105 x 158 cm. Courtesy of Anthony Reynolds Gallery, London.*

It is hard to be definitive about how Billingham pulls this off, but his insistence on giving Raymond and Elizabeth, his two leads, equal attention is certainly wise, because then these pictures become the portrait of a marriage as much as an analysis of social despair or urban alienation, and the artist is at pains to show that this marriage has its moments of calm domesticity and evidently peaceable companionship, as well as all the other stuff. Elizabeth sitting over a jigsaw (a brilliantly realized shot, this, with the jigsaw pieces, Elizabeth's floral print dress, and her tattoos coming together in an orchestrated riot of synthetic color); Raymond and Elizabeth sitting watching TV on the sofa, a roast dinner on their laps, gravy down their fronts, the family pets in between them; even the spectacular shot of Ray hurling the cat violently through the air is a strangely matter-of-fact, life-goes-on moment. Given their context, these photos are rich and strange.

But there is blood on the walls in this household, and Billingham shows it to us – quite literally, in the case of one photograph, which depicts a thin claret trickle apparently emerging from one of those cutesy mass-produced portraits of a mannequin that you used to be able to buy in Boots. There is more action here than one might expect to find in a selection of family snapshots: three of the pictures in Billingham's "Sensation" selection deal with violence or its immediate aftermath, and the changes of clothes alert you to the fact

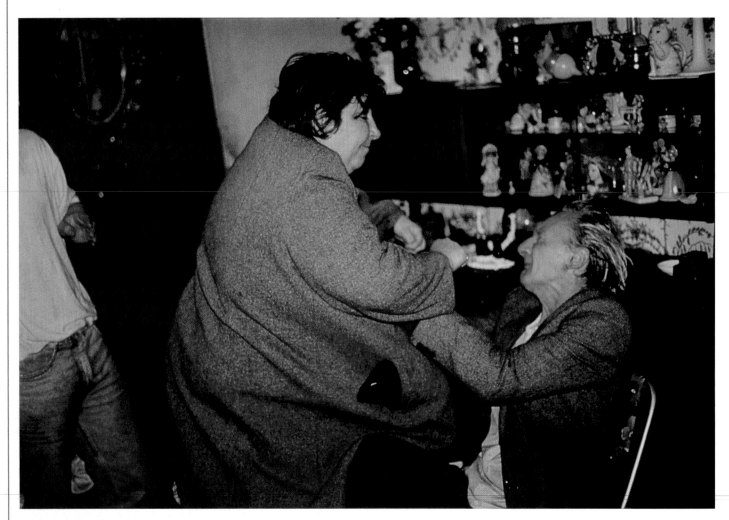

*Untitled, 1994, SFA4 color
photograph on aluminum,
31 x 47 in/80 x 120 cm.
Courtesy of Anthony Reynolds
Gallery, London.*

that this is not a sequence, but simply part of an ongoing domestic pattern. That Billingham
was able to take the pictures at all is a clear indication that physical abuse is an organic part
of the day; Raymond and Elizabeth would, presumably, have preferred their spats to take
place away from their son's lens, but in the end were unable to stop themselves.

There is an inherent and perverse fascination, of course, in seeing grown people knock

"MY MOTHER ELIZABETH HARDLY DRINKS BUT SHE DOES SMOKE A LOT."

lumps off each other, and the fascination in this case is intensified by Elizabeth's obviously
immense physical power. In one picture the couple are resting after what must have been a
particularly vehement disagreement. Elizabeth has a bloody nose. Ray's scars are around his
eye, and there is a sense that this match has ended in a score draw – Elizabeth even
appears to be offering Raymond a paper hankie in a gesture of concern and reconciliation.
In the rest, however, there is no doubt who the victor has been or will be. Perhaps the
saddest photo of the lot is of an angry Elizabeth, fist raised, threatening her utterly defeated
and understandably trepidatious partner: it is the closest Billingham comes to direct

articulation of despair, if only because Raymond's expression has, for once, not been neutralized by the blank mask of drink, and we can see him clearly. Even when he is out of his head and toppling head first towards the floor, there is no indication of feeling, and maybe, you can't help reflecting, it's better that way.

"This book is about my close family," Billingham writes on the dustjacket of his book *Ray's a Laugh*. "My father Raymond is a chronic alcoholic... My mother Elizabeth hardly drinks but she does smoke a lot. She likes pets and things that are decorative. My younger brother Jason was taken into care when he was 11 but is now back with Ray and Liz again."

There is a tone to these words that could be mistaken for blankness, just as the photographs could seem blank if one couldn't be bothered to look at them hard enough, but actually this collection is much, much warmer than that: it is clearly about love. Richard Billingham, one would hazard, loves his parents, but they are not loveable, not in the most straightforward sense of the term. Hence the careful neutrality of tone, the refusal to allow his lens to become clouded with pity or anger or disgust: he knows that enough of his audience will feel those things anyway, and that actually the truth is a lot more complicated. The last picture in the "Sensation" exhibition shows Raymond and Elizabeth cuddling on the bed, and it's a kind of optimistic ending to an unsettling, extraordinary show – until you see Raymond's eyes, focusing somewhere in the middle distance, and you wonder what he has seen.

Below: Untitled, *1995, SFA4 color photograph on aluminum, 41 x 62 in/105 x 158 cm. Courtesy of Anthony Reynolds Gallery, London.*

Bottom: Untitled, *1994, SFA4 color photograph on aluminum, 20 x 30 in/50 x 75 cm. Courtesy of Anthony Reynolds Gallery, London.*

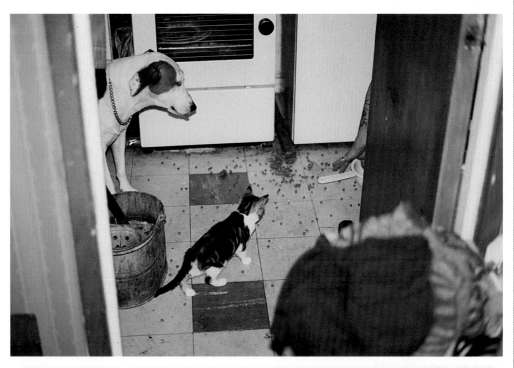

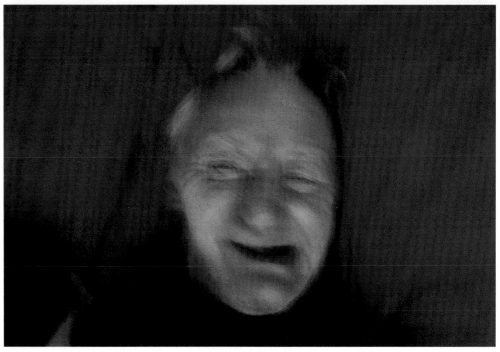

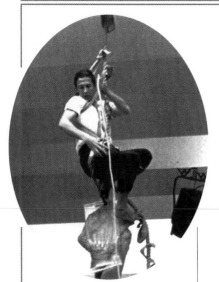

ROBERT RAUSCHENBERG
Born in Texas in 1925, Rauschenberg studied art at Academie Julien in Paris, the Kansas City Art Institute, and at Black Mountain College in North Carolina. In 1949, he moved to New York and worked on window displays for Bonwit Teller and Tiffany while attending the Art Students League.

Although he played an important role in the transition of Abstract Expressionism to Pop Art, Rauschenberg's art defies categorization. His first works in the '50s were collages overlaid with textiles, photographs, and torn newspaper clippings. A few years later he produced "combine paintings" – assemblages of painted surfaces and found materials such as light bulbs and coke bottles – which are ironic in theme. Monogram (1955-1959), a stuffed goat with a tire around its middle, is a well-known example.

In the early '60s, Rauschenberg produced silk-screen prints in black and white and in color. During the '70s and '80s he worked on lithographs and other graphic arts with a focus on collage and on new ways to transfer photographs.

In 1998, The Guggenheim Museum put on its largest exhibition ever with four hundred works by Rauschenberg.

Robert Rauschenberg

by Bryan Robertson

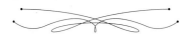

FOR ME, RAUSCHENBERG IS HIGHLY PLACED among the most enjoyable and admirable of those American artists who achieved prominence internationally in the second half of the 20th century. To place him in time, Ellsworth Kelly and Jasper Johns, for example, are his contemporaries. An imaginative energy, generosity of vision, and breadth of handling through the uninhibited execution of ideas in different dimensions and media activate all of his work. There is nobody quite like Rauschenberg in twentieth-century art; apart from his originality he has, for me, more than touched greatness many times. As I have recorded before, when Rauschenberg's first big retrospective show opened at Whitechapel (London) – an augmented version of his 1964 Venice Biennale exhibition, which won the Grand Prize for painting – we had to ask the local police to help control

"I REFUSE TO BE IN THIS WORLD BY MYSELF. I WANT AN OPEN COMMITMENT FROM THE REST OF THE PEOPLE."

the crowds waiting to get into the gallery every day and jamming the pavement outside. The show caused a sensation, packed with people reacting with warm enthusiasm to the paintings and the newly invented *Combines*, that bristling mixture of painting with free-standing or interlinking solid objects. Among other exhibits, the show contained the notorious *Bed*, in which the pillow, sheets, and folk-art cover of a neatly made single bed had been drenched in paint, and the whole up-ended on the wall; and *Monogram*, in which a stuffed ram tightly encircled by a black tire was placed on a painting that covered a mobile wooden trolley. The show was particularly appreciated by younger artists seeking a sufficiently broad opening between the Scylla of Abstract Expressionism and the Charybdis of Pop Art.

Back then in the '60s, after a close relationship through the '50s when they worked for a short period in adjoining studios, Rauschenberg and Johns were invariably bracketed together, like Colquhoun and MacBryde or Minton and Vaughan in England in an earlier, post-war, decade, or as Newman and Rothko were linked, meaninglessly and confusingly, later on. Both Rauschenberg and Johns appeared to touch a new nerve, to invoke fresh territory in art. But it seemed, also, that the hard-won connoisseur's art of Johns tended to close things off for a younger generation, however much they might admire those delectably painted early maps and targets, while Rauschenberg's work created a more extrovert and open situation, with loose ends still alive with possibilities.

Much later, a rather depleted traveling exhibition of Rauschenberg's work arriving at the Tate Gallery in 1981 fell flat because too many of the richest key exhibits had been extracted one by one as the show toured European venues, on grounds of fragility, or for more urgent deployment elsewhere. What was left for London was a thin show, unimaginatively hung, indifferently lit – a depressing situation for those of us asked by a new

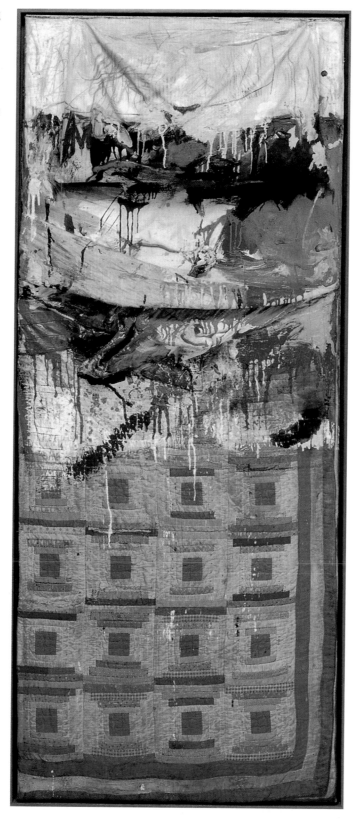

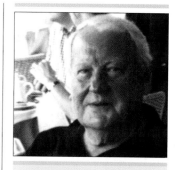

BRYAN ROBERTSON
One of the most important figures on the London art scene, Bryan Robertson was born in 1925, son of a wool agent who was a compulsive gambler. As an asthmatic child, he spent long periods in bed studying art books and reproductions.

Robertson became a junior-editor, at the age of 19, for the magazine The Studio, leaving in 1947 to spend a year in Paris. Upon his return to London, Robertson worked briefly at the Lefevre Gallery before moving to Cambridge, England, in 1949, to run the Heffner Gallery where he presented the first exhibition of modern French painting in Cambridge.

In 1952 at the age of 27, Robertson was appointed Director of the Whitechapel Gallery. There, he presented a sequence of exhibitions alternating younger British artists with the work of celebrated older and more established figures.

In 1969 Robertson left Whitechapel to become the director of the Roy R. Neuberger Museum, State University of New York at Purchase, remaining in the position for five years before returning to the UK where he currently lives and writes.

generation to explain what all the fuss had been about a decade back at Whitechapel. Art is intensely vulnerable to indifferent handling: you cannot make a third-rate artist look first-class, but you can make a first-class artist look second-rate through frowzy presentation. Artists don't like to hear this, with their basic mistrust of middlemen, but it's true.

BED, *1955, combine painting: oil and pencil on pillow, quilt, and sheet, mounted on wood 75 x 32 x 7 in/191 x 80 x 17 cm. Museum of Modern Art, New York.*

"NO DOUBT ABOUT IT, RAUSCHENBERG KNOWS HOW TO GET THE PUBLIC ALL HOT AND BOTHERED"

—Jed Perl

Chain Reaction (Anagram), 1996, *vegetable-dye transfer on paper, 60 x 120 in/153 x 304 cm. Courtesy of PaceWildenstein.*

When Rauschenberg first came to London in the '60s for his Whitechapel show, we recorded an interview for *Monitor*, Huw Weldon's TV arts program, and installed the show together. Breaking for lunch, we wandered along Brick Lane in search of food – a rougher district then, not the bourgeois Banglatown it is today. Rauschenberg's *Combines*, with a chair or a steel window-frame or a light-plug and chord attached to a canvas, had impressed me with their freedom of handling and rich, gutsy play with dimensions, but they were still quite new in idiom and sometimes seemed a bit wild, like the stuffed goat and car tire. While I was brooding on all this, we were suddenly confronted in the street with the spectacle of a vast and hideously decorated wardrobe slowly being lowered on a rope down the front of a tall, multi-story building, itself painted in hectic colors and plastered all over with lurid posters. Here was a *Combine* in action, in life. It was pure Rauschenberg and it taught me how intensely an artist's work can appear to spread into life and permeate the world around us if we steep ourselves in it and believe in it sufficiently.

Since that stirring first exposure, it hasn't always been easy to keep in touch with Rauschenberg's widely dispersed work and multi-faceted exploits in the '70s, '80s, and early '90s. But I met him by chance in the crowd at the MOMA New York Gala opening of the Jasper Johns retrospective in the fall of 1996. He reminded me of his own show, which I saw the next day and which moved me intensely, and at a new depth, by its originality – all over again – and in its strength of feeling. Seeing such a heart-warming show meant a lot to me at that moment, because my admiration for Rauschenberg's art had been slightly shaken by an elegantly executed but rather tame, cut-and-dried exhibition of recent work at the Fondation Maeght at St. Paul de Vence in 1984. That show of tidily presented printed

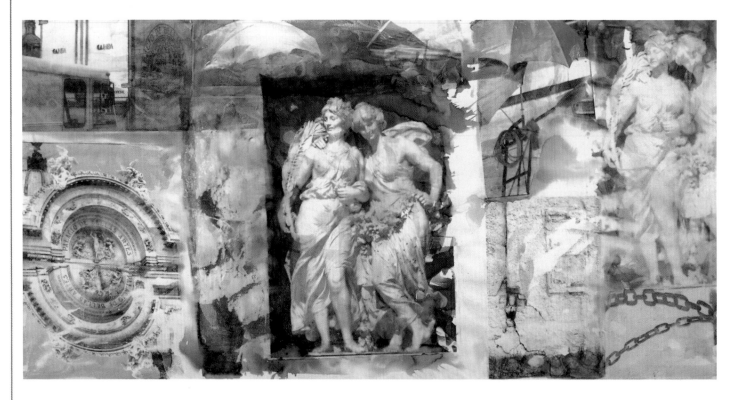

images, collaged onto vertical canvases and schematically colored en série, gave me the feeling that Rauschenberg had perhaps gone into manufacture – a dangerous assumption, like any other hasty verdict based on a single show.

The Pace exhibition of 1996 exploded that notion with a vengeance: Rauschenberg's *Anagrams* set extraordinary images from across the world in fresh juxtaposition, with an intensely moving eloquence felt by everyone who saw the exhibition. The big, individually complex batteries of mood, scene, and event – a new fusion of painting, drawing, staining,

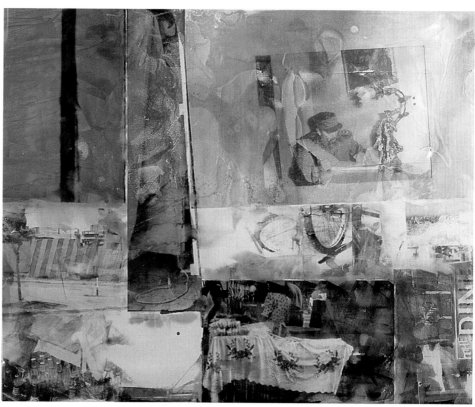

Fusion (Anagram), *(detail), 1996,*
vegetable dye transfer on paper,
61 x 145 in/154 x 368 cm.
Whitney Museum of American Art,
New York

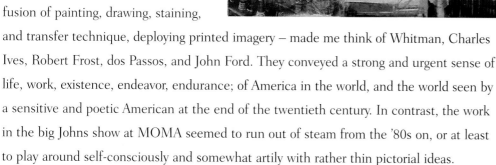

and transfer technique, deploying printed imagery – made me think of Whitman, Charles Ives, Robert Frost, dos Passos, and John Ford. They conveyed a strong and urgent sense of life, work, existence, endeavor, endurance; of America in the world, and the world seen by a sensitive and poetic American at the end of the twentieth century. In contrast, the work in the big Johns show at MOMA seemed to run out of steam from the '80s on, or at least to play around self-consciously and somewhat artily with rather thin pictorial ideas.

I set this dispiriting thought down because it's been fashionable for years to extol Johns at the expense of Rauschenberg, whereas I believe it should have been the other way around: Johns is marking time, always intelligently, and with good will everywhere still for his earlier work – we live in hopes – while Rauschenberg has forged dramatically ahead. His energy was evident not only in the 1995–56 *Anagrams*, but also in a wide range of exceptionally strong work made through the last decade, as so forcefully set out in the uptown and downtown Guggenheim shows of 1997. This exhaustive and exhausting retrospective was not easy to digest: too big, of course, but something about Rauschenberg's essential bigness of heart, sheer nerve, and generosity of spirit – at one level his willingness to take risks all the time – seemed to need this vast exposure. As an artist, Rauschenberg himself runs to excess on occasion, or at least to a super-abundance of energy and ideas, and the show supported that idea. It was a salutary lesson to experience the immense weight and range of his achievement, and depressing to find how very little of it we had seen in Europe during the past three decades. Rauschenberg has exhibited in China, Japan, all over South America, occasionally in Europe, but not in London or Paris.

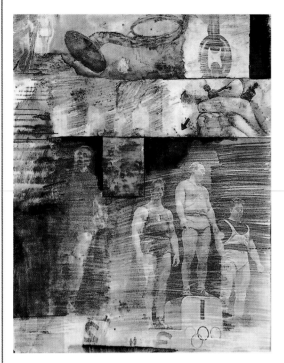

Canto xxxi: The Central Pit of Malebolge, The Giants, *1959–60, for Dante's Inferno, solvent transfer on paper, with colored pencil, gouache and pencil, 15 x 12 in/37 x 29 cm. Museum of Modern Art, New York.*

Barge, (detail, right side)
1962–63, oil and silkscreened ink on canvas, 80 x 386 in/203 x 980 cm. Collection of the artist.

Although the work uptown suffered, as all serious art does at the Guggenheim, from the spiraling and sloping viewing conditions, a number of major pieces more than held their own. A large number of the magnificent *Dante drawings*, for instance, made in 1959–60, were clearly set out in a side gallery and looked as magical as ever, images as delicate as moths' wings breathed onto the paper – taken together, among Rauschenberg's grandest works. The 32-foot long *Barge* of 1962–63 was also decently presented, in the isolation that this masterpiece demands, in a separate gallery just above the entrance lobby of the museum. This sequential work of joined panels has never looked better: an intensely dramatic, tightly structured gamut of incident and scene explodes, implodes, and hangs suspended in a deep blue, gray, black, and white space of printed imagery set against painted sections. The way that violent brush-marks seem to unfurl and expand in contrast to the tighter, more condensed, printed images, reflects the unfailing balance achieved by Rauschenberg in his selected photographic material, which always switches from the large-scale scene to the small and particular figure or incident. In its mixture of associations, references, and painted and printed imagery, *Barge* seems to me a key work for the '60s, as *Night Fishing at Antibes* was for the '40s, and *Blue Poles* became for the '50s.

But it was the range and wholly individual nature of work shown in the downtown Guggenheim that seemed to take on a special energy and eloquence of its own. It is a pleasure to add that a good deal of this enlivening work was also the latest in date, a

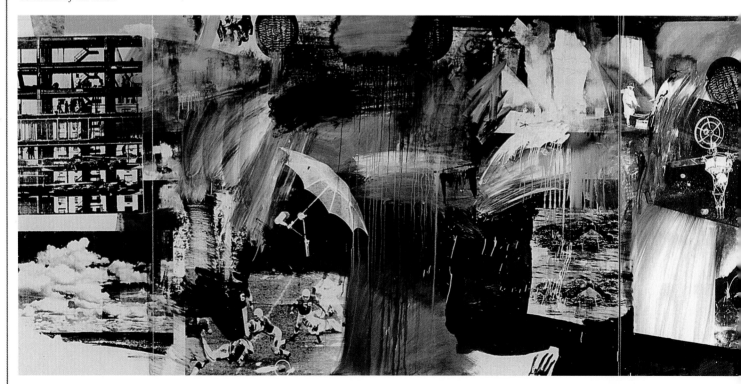

revelation for everyone in terms of vitality, color, light, and scale. Many big transfer paintings had been made on gleamingly reflective surfaces, like copper or stainless steel, and these – apart from the reflective spatial ambiguity – had a buoyancy and the specific brilliance of high-keyed very fresh color. Seen in the context of the theater pieces, shown nearby on film and photograph – Rauschenberg as a performer, choreographer, and designer of sets, costumes, and lighting – the recent work took on another dimension which seemed to illuminate his oeuvre as a whole. What emerged very clearly from the downtown installation – and referred us back in memory to some uptown works – is that Rauschenberg is, preeminently, from first to last, *a performer*, and that the whole of his art springs from the essential character of performance, its directness, apparent spontaneity, swiftness – *speed* – animation, and lightness of touch.

The idea of the artist as a performer is probably, in some ways, as old as the concept of patronage and commissioned murals, ceiling decorations, or altarpieces – some aspects of Michelangelo's labor for Pope Julius in the Sistine Chapel meet some of the conditions and requirements of performance. But with the decline of that inspired level of patronage, we arrived at a situation in the first half of the twentieth century when, on the whole, we preferred our artists to be confined to studios, with their creations separated from their untidy begetters and neatly corralled into the neutral terrain of an art gallery. An artist working in public, performing in public, was a highly suspect, flashy notion. On the other hand we still enjoyed the stirring spectacle of the composer as performer, from Paganini and Liszt, through to Rachmaninov in the '30s, interpreting his own piano music with unmatched virtuosity. Ravel played his *Piano*

> "HE HAS ALWAYS SEEN HIS WORK AS AN ACTIVE PARTICIPANT IN ITS OWN ENVIRONMENT, AND THE VIEWER AS AN ACTIVE PARTICIPANT IN THE WORK"
> —*Billy Klüver*

Concerto in G all over Europe around the same time, and Stravinsky conducted *Le Sacré du Printemps* and *Les Noces* everywhere – but these examples really do no more than extend into our own time the examples set by Mozart and Haydn as self-interpreters.

More recently, David Tudor and John Cage brought another dimension to the notion of the artist or composer as performer, with only half a piano, or the piano wires taped, or in a recital consisting of absolute silence, so that the concept of "a performance" by the composer was extended into a neo-Dada territory of anarchic or absurdist theater.

At the same time, Happenings and Events materialized in New York and elsewhere, and finally the rather less engaging sequences began of conceptual performance works and installation pieces, rehearsing or presenting conceptual arguments, formal, social, or political, but still a kind of performance.

I believe that it was Picasso's startling appearance on camera in Clouzot's terrific film *Le Mystère Picasso* in 1951, when he made drawings with colored light in a darkened room and then painted a big picture behind glass, also on camera, which most dramatically brought to everyone's attention the idea, freshly delivered, of the artist as performer – which, until that breathtaking moment, had been extremely suspect. Around the same time, Jackson Pollock was improvising with paint, mesh, cord, and assorted bits and pieces, a collage behind glass – also functioning steadily within the camera's gaze as the work developed – for Hans Namuth's film that used also a collage-like, very spatial score by Morton Feldman. This was the essence of inspired improvization at work by an artist in a

"RAUSCHENBERG WANTS HIS WORKS TO BE THE MEANS FOR STIMULATING THINKING AND DOING, ENCOUNTERS THAT LEAVE THE VIEWER CHANGED."

—*Billy Klüver*

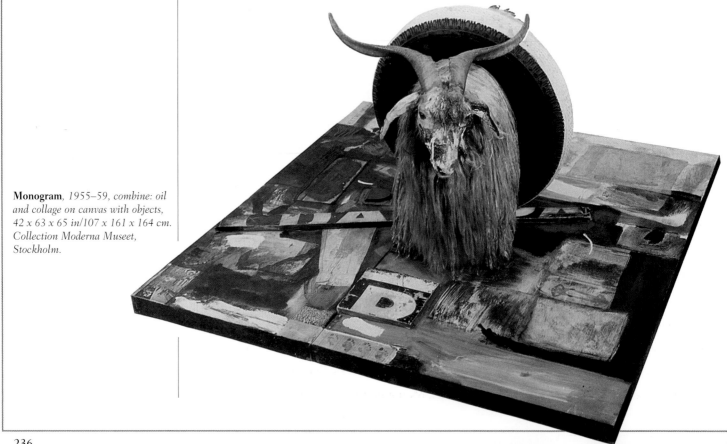

Monogram, *1955–59, combine: oil and collage on canvas with objects, 42 x 63 x 65 in/107 x 161 x 164 cm. Collection Moderna Museet, Stockholm.*

performance which disclosed a radically new technical and spiritual approach to art that also invoked ancient usages. A little later, and rather differently, as an imaginative extension of the ancient idea of follies – but brought out of the private estate and private patronage into the participatory world of public performance and state sponsorship – came Christo and his team of workers with the floating islands, fences straddling a continent, and wrapped bridges and buildings.

Rauschenberg came out of all this, not in any sense of obligation or adherence to direct lineage, but simply through being a highly sophisticated, exceptionally gifted young artist working in Manhattan in the '50s and then the '60s, with an imagination sympathetic to the notion of spontaneity. Abstract Expressionism had helped clear the air. If his art was unprecedented from the beginning in its range, attack, energy, and character, then the water had at least been partially tested. In the late '40s, he had studied at Black Mountain College in North Carolina under Josef Albers. (Rauschenberg once gave me a jokey

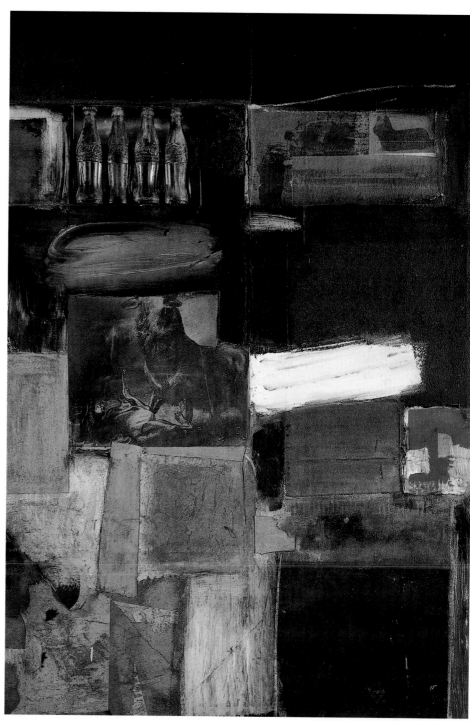

Curfew, 1958, combine painting: oil, paper, fabric, wood, engraving, printed reproductions, and printed paper on canvas and wood, with four Coca-Cola bottles, bottle cap, and unidentified debris, 57 x 40 x 3 in / 144 x 100 x 7 cm. Private collection.

explanation for his early "White" paintings: "After months of Albers's color theory, I couldn't even think about color any more and I made the 'White' paintings." But then he went on to make the "Black" and the "Red" paintings… In this sense, Rauschenberg's paintings, even when less directly conceptual than these early works, may also be seen as performance pieces.) At that time he began a potent friendship with the choreographer Merce Cunningham, the composer John Cage, and with David Tudor, who was busily putting music, and notably piano music, through the wringer. This group of friends, inspired by Cage, precipitated and staged at Black Mountain the first Happening.

Rauschenberg has of course been an integral part for long periods of the Cage, Cunningham, Tudor, Johns axis, which has played such a vital role in dance, stage design, and performance in the US, as well as serving as a fund-raising agency over the years for all kinds of artists fallen on bad times.

The central impulse and identity of all Rauschenberg's work is improvisation and performance. No other artist in the twentieth century has also been a dancer and an experienced performer on stage and a choreographer. It's an odd concept as well as unique:

"MY ART IS ABOUT PAYING ATTENTION — ABOUT THE EXTREMELY DANGEROUS POSSIBLITY THAT YOU MIGHT BE ART."

Right: Robert Rauschenberg & Susan Weil, Untitled (double Rauschenberg), *c 1950, exposed blueprint paper, 83 x 36 in/210 x 92 cm. Private collection.*

Below: Pelican, *detail of Rauschenberg's costume. Judson Dance Theater: Concert of Dance 5, America on Wheels roller-skating rink, Washington, D.C., May 9, 1963.*

can you imagine considering, in addition to their paintings, the performances of Léger or Matisse as *dancers*? Such a new kind of hybrid being could only have surfaced in the '60s, and in the US. Of course Rauschenberg was not a great dancer or even a particularly good one, but he had enough physical grace, control, and stage presence to hold his own, and he knew how to move or stand in relation to other dancers on stage. Like other Americans, Rauschenberg had absorbed some of the instinctive feeling for casual, inconsequential gesture and movement in dance which Martha Graham had been the first to set against her more formalized and hieratic use of stylised movement. And most of his stage appearances come under the heading of performance rather than dance, often involving nothing more complicated than standing up and sitting down in a kind of musical chairs sequence – which is one memory I retain of a semi-danced Happening at the New York Armory, with Rauschenberg

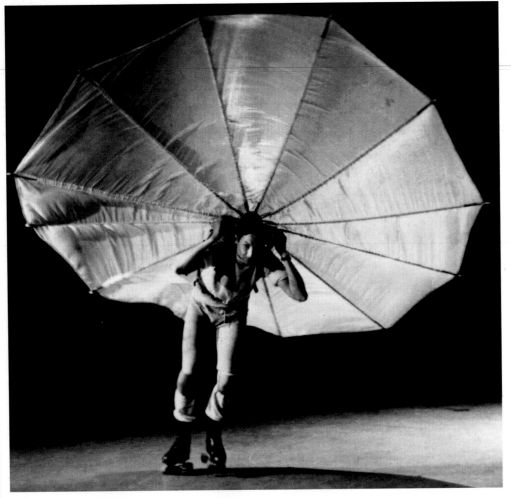

and the marvelous dancers Yvonne Rainer and Steve
Paxton walking from one group of dancers to another,
or climbing up and down ropes. Physically demanding
perhaps, but not really dance. But he certainly danced
well enough on occasion, notably in his poetic
extravaganza of 1963, *Pelican*, in which with other
dancers he appeared on rollerskates and wearing a
parachute. More weightily and resoundingly,
Rauschenberg has also designed sets and costumes
and all the lighting for dozens of stage works, some of
them pure dance choreographed by himself, but
mostly for the choreography of Paul Taylor, Merce
Cunningham, Viola Farber, or Tricia Brown, with
other works presented as performance pieces for
himself in association with various dancers, or on
stage with fellow artists – such as Tinguely, Niki de
Saint Phalle, or Frank Stella.

If Rauschenberg always brought an inspired
element of play into his stage work as a performer,
alone or with others, or as a designer of sets and
lighting, this element was more tightly focused and
extended in his concern for assemblage: in the big
Oracle of 1962–65, for example, the grand "five-part
assemblage with five concealed radios; ventilation
duct; automobile door on typewriter table with
crushed metal; ventilation duct in washtub and water
with wire baskets; constructed staircase control unit
housing batteries and electronic components; and
wood window frame with ventilation duct." A few of
these assemblages seem now rather marooned in their
time and place, but others transcend their moment
with undimmed verve, notably those constructions
involving neon and other light forms. Those which
don't quite pass the test of time perhaps fall under
Wallace Stevens's verdict on free, unbridled
aestheticism: "The essential fault of surrealism is that
it invents without discovering."

Always animated by Rauschenberg's instinct for

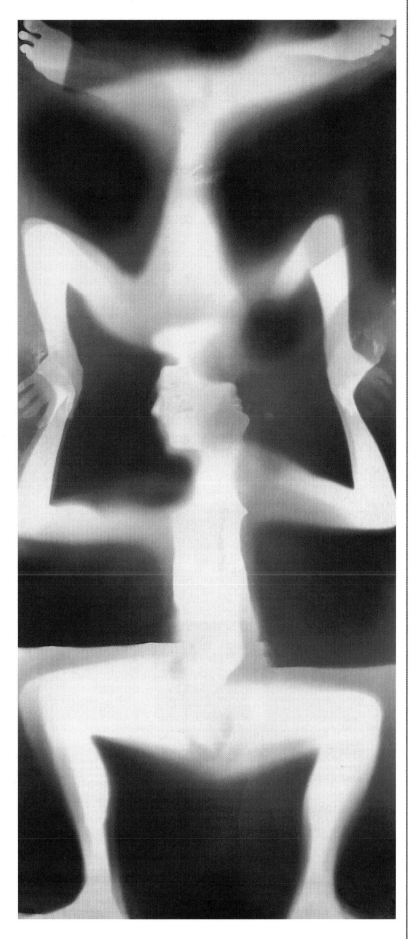

spontaneity is his lifelong use of photography and the printed image. He experimented at Black Mountain in 1949 with photographic blueprints, and some of his own early photography was like Walker Evans without the people; but since those early excursions nobody in this century has used printed images – our daily, visual world currency – as Rauschenberg has presented and re-deployed them over such a wide range of references, from harbors and markets and shantytowns to moon landings, from images of JFK to anonymous athletes and dancers. Nobody has worked harder to pioneer innovative techniques in printmaking itself. Nobody has used collage so grandly or sumptuously, setting printed imagery and painting in tense relationship, and nobody else can touch Rauschenberg's sharply instinctive placement.

Events occur at different speeds in Rauschenberg's work, but are composed, counterpointed, reconciled, within variable spaces: the blank, anonymous space of white paper, inhabited and therefore atmospherically or psychologically nuanced space, neutral space, space as color. His unerring flair for placement and structure combine to give a

Master Pasture (Urban Bourbon),
*1989, acrylic on mirrored
and enameled aluminum,
97 x 121 in/246 x 307 cm.
Private collection.*

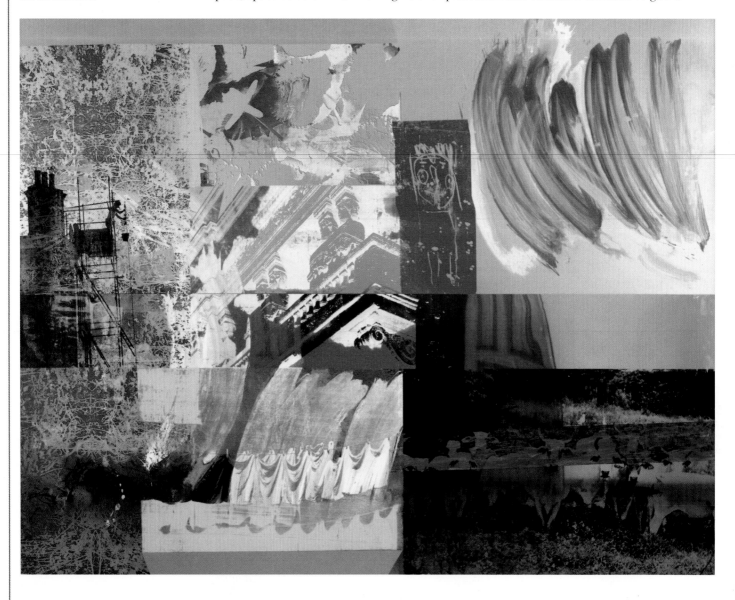

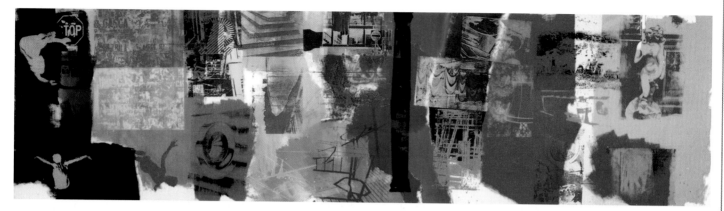

Immerse, *1994, acrylic on canvas, 121 x 436 in/307 x 1,107 cm. Created as set for Merce Cunningham Dance Company's Joyce Event; subsequently used as set for Merce Cunningham Dance Company's Events. Collection of the artist (diver images courtesty of Aaron Siskind Foundation).*

highly personal dimension to each composition. The writer, Grace Paley, has spoken of her refusal to use a single plot line in her stories because "the absolute line between two points… takes all hope away. Everyone, real or invented, deserves *the open destiny of life.*" The open destiny of life – that's Rauschenberg, despite his early disclaimer about wanting to work in the space somewhere between art and life.

He has also a distinctly American sense of placement, with its own authoritative presence – found in nineteenth-century American art in the paintings of Peto and Harnett, and extending all the way through to Motherwell's collages. This highly individual sense of placement is also happily at work in American folk-art and has nothing to do with the essentially cubist-derived sense of placement and space in the work of collagists like Schwitters, for instance, or other European artists.

If the clue to all Rauschenberg's work is performance and spontaneity, he must also be seen as a supreme animator. He can bring to new life disparate objects and elements and leave them freshly revealed in edgy coexistence. Are all the printed images – which he has always either photographed himself or collected personally over the decades – some kind of an eye on the world? A report on mankind? Another plea for the better use of our damaged planet? An eye on the world certainly, but without any time or use for propaganda, or any narrow position. What Rauschenberg communicates is something deeper in himself.

In referring to Whitman, Robert Frost, Charles Ives, dos Passos, and John Ford, I have particular attributes in mind which I sense very strongly in Rauschenberg's Combines and transfer paintings, from *Barge* through to the new *Anagrams* or the 1989 *Urban Bourbon* acrylic paintings on mirrored and enameled aluminium. Whitman comes to mind because of the global reach of Rauschenberg's imagery and its underlying stress on people and the interdependence of human activity; Robert Frost, because there are in Frost's poetry sharp, single images of landscape or place – a few trees, a back yard, or a chair and a porch – which are natural images but still have some built-in feeling of an ethical reference, of a virtue, a life lived and endured, a permanence, and a vulnerability that stretch beyond their own physical presence. Dos Passos comes to mind because of his pioneering use in his magnum opus of the *Camera Eye* actualities, like newsreels, which punctuate the long fictional narratives of the US – many years before Doctorow's *Ragtime* also brought the interactions of history, with its anonymous workers and famous personages, into a continuous present.

Rauschenberg fractures and dissolves our sense of time by presenting us with a continuum of simultaneity, not unlike the nonlinear structuring and development of musical phrases with their equal emphases that you find in Messiaen's *Chronochromos*. An even more distinct parallel exists, I believe, between some aspects of Rauschenberg's art and the music of that other authentic American genius, Charles Ives, who made his own musical

"A PAIR OF SOCKS IS NO LESS SUITABLE TO MAKE A PAINTING WITH THAN WOOD, NAILS, TURPENTINE, OIL AND FABRIC."

collages to parallel, in simultaneity, the multiple impressions, sensations, and memories of sound heard in everyday life. The innovative use of multilayered soundtrack based on a continuous present in Robert Altman's early masterpiece, *California Split*, is another example of this eager but also quite coolly rigorous reaching-out to record a multiplicity of sound and sensation. It is very American: the radio call-ins were an American invention and so are the products of Bill Gates.

The official Rauschenberg biography in recent catalogs reminds us of a number of events, organizations, and foundations which have perhaps passed England by, all of them impressive and personal to this artist, in addition to a lifetime of steady production, travel, setting up of studios, and very hard improvisatory work on tour with impoverished dance companies, involving transcontinental travel. The Rauschenberg Overseas Culture Interchange (ROCI), begun in 1984, was an evolving exhibition of over 200 works by the artist, based on his visits and collaborations with artists and artisans in many countries. This "global peace-seeking odyssey of art and information," as it has been called, included sculptures, paintings, video tapes, prints, and photographs that "reflect the artist's respect for the qualities which mark the differences among the various cultures of the world." The eight-year tour included exhibitions in Mexico, Chile, Venezuela, China, Tibet, Japan, Cuba, Moscow, the former USSR, Germany, Malaysia, and Washington's National Gallery of Art.

Before this, in 1966, to coordinate and clarify his experiments with electronics, Rauschenberg co-founded, with the electronics engineer Billy Klüver, Experiments in Art and Technology (EAT), to promote cooperation between artists and engineers. The five-part construction *Oracle* (owned by the Centre Pompidou, Paris) materialized, with other works,

"HE OPENED ART TO ENTRY BY A MOTLEY CREW: ENGINEERS, SOCIALITES, ALL-ABOUT-EVE ASSISTANTS, POLITICIANS, TRADE UNIONISTS, DANCERS, INSTANT COLLECTORS, UTOPIANS, SCIENTISTS, FOUNDATION SWINGERS, ART GROUPIES, AND HEAVEN KNOWS WHAT ELSE; ALL RUBBED SHOULDERS WITH LESS SUCCESS THAN THE INCONGRUOUS ELEMENTS IN HIS ART."

—*Brian O'Doherty*

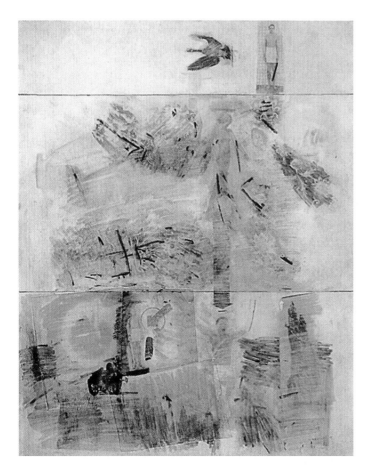 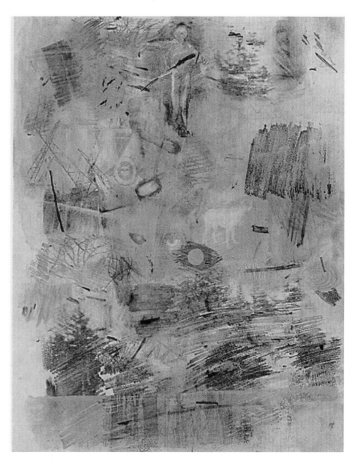

from this collaboration. Rauschenberg also founded and directs Change Inc., a nonprofit organization, now in its twenty-seventh year, which provides emergency funds for artists. And there is a Robert Rauschenberg Foundation, started in 1990, also a nonprofit entity, devoted to projects that will increase public awareness about subjects of vital interest to the artist: medical research, education, world hunger, global enhancement of the arts....

Rauschenberg has of course helped to subsidise dance companies and choreographers over the years, and donated a formidable number of outstandingly beautiful posters, none of them slight or merely turned out for the occasion, for innumerable good causes, apart from dance, and including the work of the United Nations. From what he has done and made and backed and promoted, Rauschenberg seems a protean figure with a global reach and commitment at a time of increasing narrowness and tight specialization, and yet he retains, always, his sense of intimacy, personal discovery, liveliness, and a distinctly individual touch and energizing flourish for everything that he handles.

The *Anagrams* tell me that as he gets older, he may also perhaps have moved out of that space between art and life, to embrace another viewpoint of Wallace Stevens: "The relation of art to life is of the first importance especially in a sceptical age since, in the absence of a belief in God, the mind turns to its own creations and examines them, not alone from the aesthetic point of view, but for what they reveal, for what they validate and invalidate, for the support that they give."

Above Left: Illustrations for Dante's Inferno, Canto I: The Dark Wood of Error, *1958, solvent transfer on paper, with gouache, wash, pencil, and watercolor. 15 x 12 in/37 x 29 cm. Museum of Modern Art, New York.*

Above Right: Illustrations for Dante's Inferno, Canto II: The Descent, *1958, solvent transfer on paper, with cut-and-pasted paper, watercolor, wash, and pencil. 14 x 11 in/37 x 29 cm. Museum of Modern Art, New York.*

Patrick Heron

by A.S. Byatt

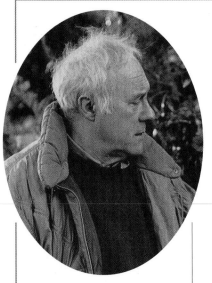

PATRICK HERON
*Born in Leeds in 1920,
Heron became one of
Britain's most prominent
abstract painters and art
critics before his
death in 1999.*

*Studying at the Slade School,
he began painting in the* Art
Informel *style – luminous still
lifes and interiors that show
the influence of Matisse and
of the Abstract Expressionists,
especially Rothko. An
innovator of the concept of
denial of the picture plane,
Heron used simple shapes and
floating color to emphasize the
flatness of the picture surface.*

*In the late 1940s, he
expanded his horizons,
becoming a leader in the St.
Ives community of abstract
painters and revealing talent
as an art critic. From 1947 to
1950, he wrote art reviews for
the* New Statesman *in which
he argued against the
emphasis on pure abstraction
in modern art.*

*Heron continued to paint,
using horizontal bands of
color with reference to the
traditional landscape. Simple
forms dense with color
appeared, and, later, large
color surfaces, as in the
painting* Long Cadmium
with Ceruleum in Violet.
*During the '80s, Heron's
color became even more
expansive and organic.*

THERE WAS AN ELEMENT OF CHANCE, OR GOOD FORTUNE, about the choice of Patrick Heron to paint my portrait. Claire Tomalin had invited me to lunch and I was early, so I went into the National Portrait Gallery to browse, and bought some postcards of Heron's portrait of T. S. Eliot, which is one of the modern portraits I most admire. Over lunch Claire asked if I would be painted, and we discussed possible painters. I felt doubtful; I feel that whereas film has changed and enlivened the novel in many ways, photography has had a sad effect on the art of the representative portrait. We looked at several examples of more or less realistic portraits, and felt unsure. I said that what I would really like would be an abstract portrait, a modern work, like the Heron. What I meant was that I would like a Heron. The English painters I most admire are the colorists, Heron and Hodgkin, the elegant, the flamboyant, those who reject the native suspicion of brightness, and delight in Matisse's revelation of color as form. I love them partly because what they do is the opposite of verbal narrative, an art-form that can't be reduced to, or adequately described in, words. I knew that Heron had painted two portraits: the Eliot (1948), which is a somber cubist construction – Braque-like – and a very good likeness both of the man and his work, and a beautiful yellow and blue Jo Grimond, giving a sense of the man in two clear colors and a minimal amount of visual information perfectly deployed. I didn't know

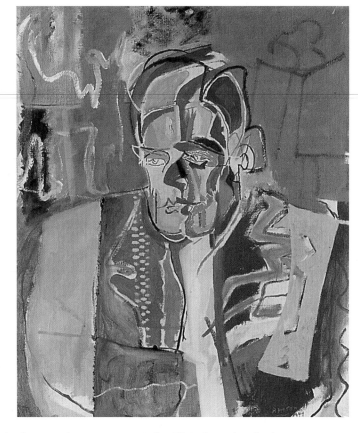

then about the Herbert Read which hangs in the director's office in the National Portrait Gallery (London). Both the Eliot and the Grimond seemed appropriate to their subjects, and visually inventive. Claire, rather to my surprise, said that it would be worth asking Patrick Heron, and Charles Saumarez Smith (the director) was enthusiastic. I was nevertheless startled and delighted when Patrick Heron agreed to have lunch to discuss the idea. The lunch went well. "You do want an abstract portrait," he said. I said that that was exactly what I wanted. I have come to hate being photographed, and to hate the existing photographs that reappear in my life from time to time. When I first read about primitive people who thought photographs were theft, I thought that was an elegant fancy,

> ## "I DO NOT FIND MYSELF 'DESIGNING' A CANVAS: I DO NOT 'DRAW' THE LOZENGE-SHAPED AREAS OR THE SOFT SQUARES. AND THESE FORMS ARE NOT REALLY 'FORMS' AT ALL, ANYWAY, BUT SIMPLY AREAS UNDER MY BRUSH WHEN I START TO TRY TO SATURATE THE SURFACE OF THE CANVAS WITH, SO TO SPEAK, VARYING QUANTITIES OF THIS COLOR OR THAT."

an interesting observation. I now feel it is an exact description of my experience. I wanted the opposite of a photograph. Patrick Heron said that he preferred to work in the absence of the subject, and from memory. That suited me too.

I went to visit Patrick at Eagles Nest, his house on the Penwith peninsula in the far reaches of Cornwall, in March 1995, for him to make some preliminary drawings. I slept in a white room with a red Heron and a howling gale outside, visited the Tate, learned a great deal about St. Ives, and the St. Ives artists, saw the sea and the stones and the garden. Being at Eagles Nest turns the visitor into a primarily visual creature. It is a very English house, but the spaces and the white walls are inhabited by brilliance. There is a striped painting at the head of the stairs; in one room a non-functional television sits next to a painting whose rounded rectangles echo its screen.

I found myself thinking about the exact color of that screen, as I found myself, as the Atlantic dark descended, holding my wine glass under the light and studying the ellipses, the transparency, the bubbles. The many-colored sea, seen from the bedroom window, and

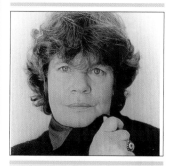

A.S. BYATT

One of England's foremost contemporary writers, A.S. Byatt was born Antonia Susan Drabble in 1936, in Sheffield. Known for her erudite novels, Byatt is also a distinguished critic, essayist, and lecturer.

Often bedridden as a child, Byatt fed her hunger for fiction with the novels of Dickens, Austen, and Scott. She went on to study literature at Cambridge and later attended Bryn Mawr and Oxford.

In the 1960s, Byatt taught at the Central School of Art and Design and, later, literature at University College, London, before becoming a full-time writer in 1983. The Virgin in the Garden (1978), added "acclaimed novelist" to her reputation as scholar and critic.

Byatt's novel Possession (1990), a bestseller in England and the US, won the Booker Prize in 1990, and Angels & Insects, her 1991 novella, was made into a film in 1995.

Among Byatt's many critical works are Degrees of Freedom, a study of the novels of Iris Murdoch, and Passions of the Mind, a selection of essays.

Left: Portrait of T.S. Eliot, *1949, oil on canvas, 30 x 25 in/76 x 64 cm. National Portrait Gallery, London.*

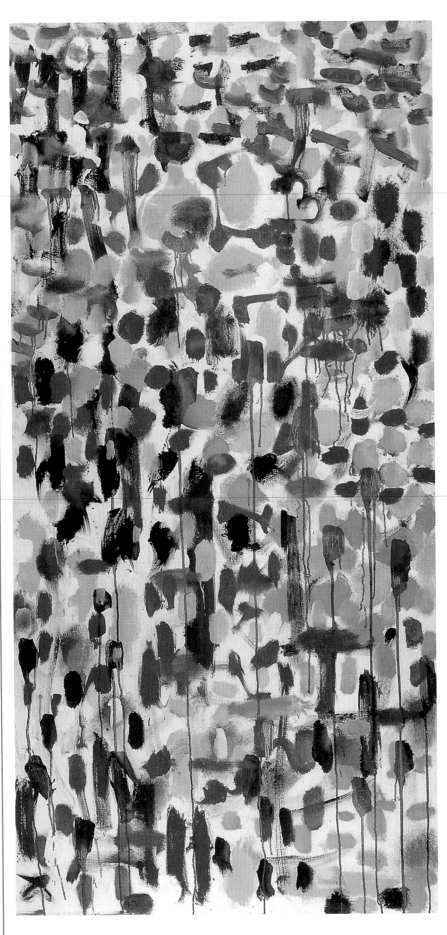

the huge stones in the windblown garden, are not parts of landscapes or seascapes. They are forms, spaces, relations of light, dark, and color. The world is solid and dissolving there.

Finally, on the last evening, both of us reluctant, I sat to be drawn. I recognized an anxiety before the blank paper which corresponds to the writer's anxiety before the blank page – only in the case of a portrait this anxiety is doubled; both sitter and artist are anxious. I like to watch, to take mental notes, not to be observed watching. I felt like an object, large and heavy. I sat. Patrick suddenly began to scribble furiously, with charcoal, made two or three sketches, and then a more prolonged one, drawn, rubbed out, drawn, rubbed out, drawn, rubbed out. And there, from nowhere, was a presence, a shadowy solid person with a blank face, but recognizably myself. It looked, I said, like a portrait of what it felt to look out of my head, from inside. He had somehow drawn the body as it feels from inside looking out. The watcher watched.

After that visit there was a long gap, and then Patrick wrote and said he had made progress and felt he should work "in the presence of the subject." So I went back to Land's End in June 1996 and spent two days sitting in the studio. I put on a green shirt, because I like the way it makes my eyes green. Patrick lost a purple scarf, and kept mislaying a most brilliant purple glasses case. The canvas had to be moved frequently along the studio wall because Patrick's eye was distracted by marks left by Ben Nicholson years earlier.

I recognized the delaying of work. I saw that a blank white canvas is much more intimidating than blank writing paper. Patrick mixed paints – a delicate shadowy mauve, a scarlet, a rich blue, a pale sharp green. He told me about Ben Nicholson, brush in hand, staring at the blank canvas. The paintings, when they arrived, were done suddenly and *fast*. I watched, from inside my head. Patrick would always smile apologetically, and both of us

would laugh nervously, and then his face would set into a detached, slightly furious look, and he would take a stab at the canvas, and then a rush. A square head appeared, and a decorative trellis of flowers. Various faces, shadowed in delicate mauve, existed for a moment, and then were wiped away. I was fascinated by how the ghosts of the expunged forms continued to exist and to make the subsequent versions more complex and substantial. Purple is Patrick's favorite color. It is not mine. But I became entranced by the shadowy half-depths of that particular mauve running across the canvas. It is unfortunate that I am allergic to spirit (solvent), so that as the canvas became swimmy, so did my head. I had supposed that an abstract portrait would at least make me less anxious about small vanities; Patrick noticed, and reproduced unerringly the way my hair bulks above my head, which I don't like, my square jaw, and the mascara I put on because I don't like my eyes without it. He devised a rapid twirl of spiky paint to represent this, in various versions. The prettiest small oil

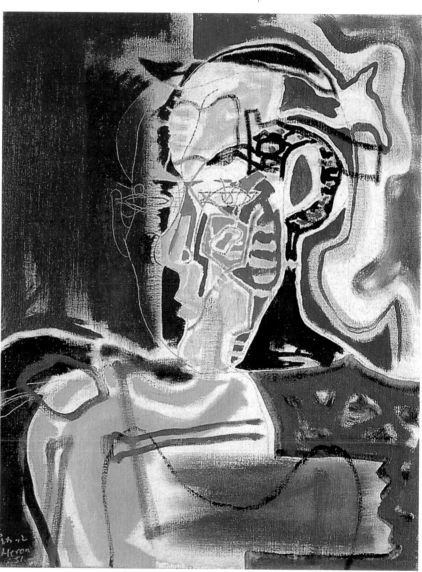

sketch he pronounced (rightly) to be not very like. It's like what I was as a student, I protested sadly. His gaze is mild but accurate. He looked doubtful.

I did not go back to Eagles Nest for over a year. This visit was made with Charles Saumarez Smith in benign weather. When we went into the studio everything had changed: various new portraits were hanging on the walls and newsprint photographs of me – one from the *The Observer*, holding a St. George's flag at an England-Germany football (soccer) match, one by a Frenchwoman, one of the very few I like, muffled in hat and scarf, were attached to Patrick's pinboard. There was a new, elegant small portrait, in Matisse-like colors, which made something decorative of the square jaw in a square canvas, and had a

Self-Portrait, *1951, oil on canvas, 20 x 16 in/51 x 41 cm). National Potrait Gallery, London.*

Opposite page: Autumn Garden, *1956, oil on canvas, 72 x 36 in/183 x 92 cm. Collection of the artist's family.*

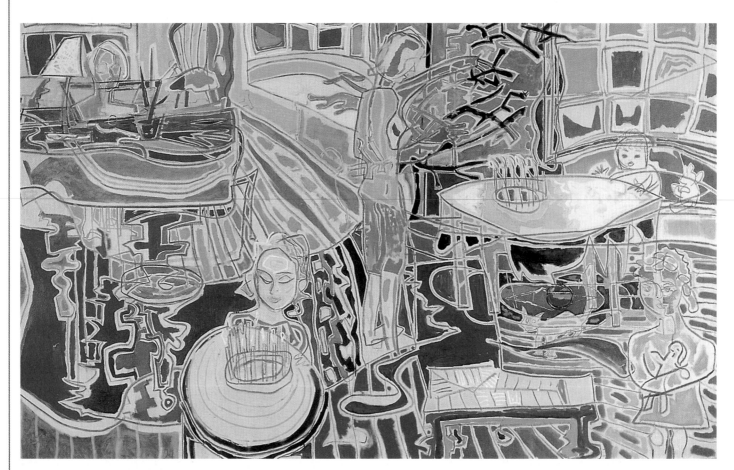

Christmas Eve, *1951,*
oil on canvas,
72 x 120 in/183 x 305 cm.
Courtesy Waddington Gallery,
London.

"HERON WAS
TEMPERAMENTALLY
ON THE SIDE OF
BEAUTY, NOT THE
SUBLIME."

—*David Cohen*

shape of the brow and eyes, done in a simple line and two dots, that was nevertheless a good likeness. There was a much larger, paler painting, with a quite different version of myself, with animated talking hands next to an animated plant, a minimal pretty presence. There was the original charcoal drawing, which seemed to have increased in authority. It is curious how a featureless face can be such a good likeness.

Over the next three days a lot of work was done, in quick fierce rushes between long conversational considerations. A substantial seated figure became more and more solid. Patrick and his daughter became excited by the way solid forms spaced themselves in an illusory perspective. I was worried, as the figure, in so far as she was representative and not abstract, represented a person I didn't like and didn't recognize. I could see that the way color created mass was interesting, but I didn't like the creature the masses made up. I felt that that was an illegitimate objection. I was encouraged by Charles' feeling that it was not enough of a likeness. There is a short story to be written about being haunted by an unacknowledged and unloved emanation of oneself. I found myself making notes in a red notebook about redness. I was feeling just about enough at home in the studio to become a writer again and not just a watcher who wanted to be unobserved but was being looked at. Patrick was more at home, too, and stared more concentratedly and intently at my features. He asked me what color I thought my eyes were, and I said green. He said that my eyes were unusual because when I was interested in something the whole of the iris was visible.

He said, quite suddenly and decisively, it is time to try strong primary colors. He made a sitting figure in cobalt blue, and painted in and out a series of complex blue patterns and scribbles and zigzags on the body. Many faces, many heaps of hair, appeared briefly, were wiped away, were redone, again with the odd impression that their ghosts added substance to what went over them. Trailing green leaves and trellises, red sills and zigzags were traced

and filled in. This is a very expensive red, said Patrick, applying it from the tube, one you can't buy any more. He made extravagant swoops and sweeps, undoing much of the allover patterning he had started out with. He dances at the canvas with poised brush like a dart thrower – I want to write a toreador placing a sword-stroke but feel both he and I don't belong with that metaphor. What was happening was a making solid, and at the same time brilliant, of what had been a wild pattern with a figure in the left-hand half of it. He made hair, like mud, adding color after color. It was a little like watching order out of chaos being deliberately stirred back into chaos again. I found myself reciting over and over in my head a line from Wallace Stevens' *Notes Towards a Supreme Fiction*, "the real must from its crude compoundings come / Warmed by a desperate milk."

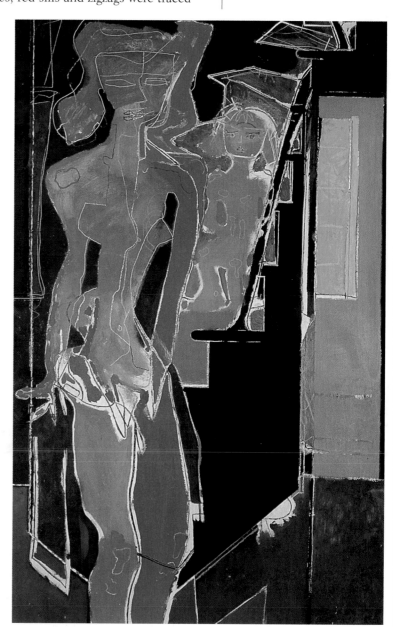

When it was finished, I did not know what to think for a moment. It had not been there, and now was. We both stared. Patrick moved it to a different wall of the studio, and we went backward and forward, looking at it from a distance and close up. I had a curious experience of it settling into shape, becoming itself, as I looked at it. I began to read the fierce expanses of color as masses, saw that the pink of the face of the figure was dark because it was *contre-jour*, with a yellow blaze of light behind it. The energy, the brashness, the uncompromising splashes of primary color represented what I had wanted in an abstract portrait by a great colorist. But they represented something else as well. They were a painting of the writer, of how I feel when I start work, a vanishing, watching body in a sea of light and brilliance. The raw, churned color is like the primary chaos of Wallace Stevens' muddy center that existed before we breathed. Stevens' *Notes Towards a Supreme Fiction* comes to mind often when I look at Heron's work, and did so more precisely in the world of Land's End.

The Staircase, 1954,
oil on hardboard,
72 x 48 in/183 x 122 cm.
Private collection.

There was a muddy center before we breathed.

There was a myth before the myth began.

Venerable and articulate and complete.

Mostly I associate Heron with Stevens for the elegance of their reds and greens, for the "coulisse bright-dark, tragic chiaroscuro / And comic color of the rose," for the "yellow, yellow thins our northern blue." But the muddy center is there too.

I have always felt that Heron's work was *about the act of seeing*. He wrote in 1969: "When you open your eyes, the entire visual field (which opening them reveals to you)

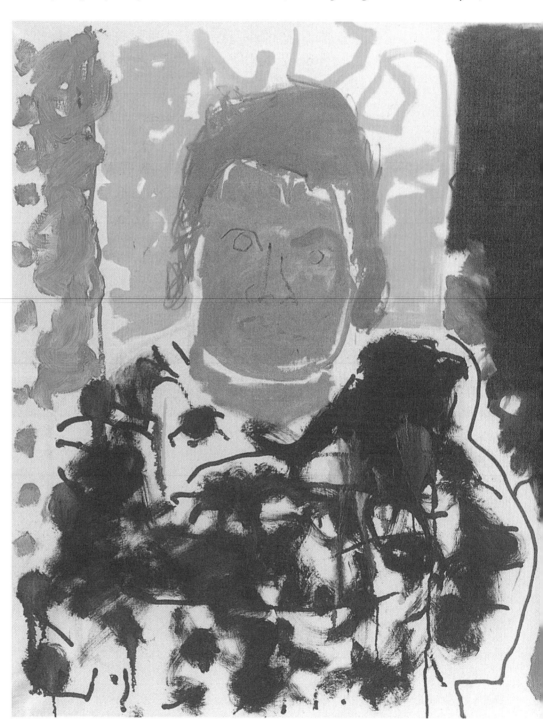

> "JUDGED ALONGSIDE
> TRANSATLANTIC
> RIVALS LIKE KENNETH
> NOLAND, JULES
> OLITSKI, AND
> ELLSWORTH KELLY,
> HERON'S STYLE
> SEEMED ORGANIC
> AND VULNERABLE."
>
> —*David Anfam*

Portrait of A.S. Byatt: Red, Yellow, Green, and Blue, *24 September 1997, oil on canvas, 38 x 48 in/97 x 122 cm. National Portrait Gallery, London.*

consists of one thing; and that thing is color." His paintings are about how we construct the world we see out of this flood of color. In his essay on Bernard Leach, he gives one of the best descriptions I know of the desire to begin work on a painting.

"As a painter, I can testify to the following sequence of sensations: the sudden apprehension of the form of a new picture is first registered, in my own case at any rate, as a distinct feeling of hollowness: and to locate this sensation somewhere in the region of the diaphragm is not to indulge in a pretentious whim: it is merely to acknowledge physical fact. I am noting possible subjects all day long, every day, quite involuntarily.

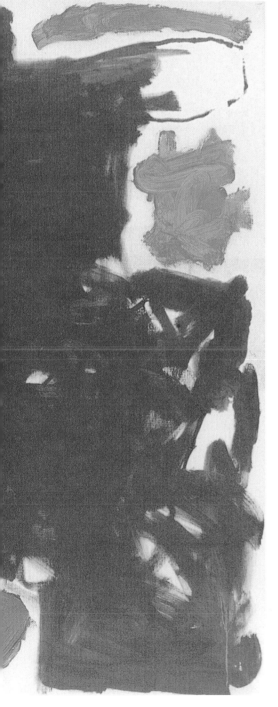

Thus it is not a question of painting when I see a subject: it is a question of calling up a subject (or to be more precise, of calling up an immense variety of remembered subjects simultaneously) when I am ready for action with my brush and palette. So I begin with this hollow feeling. Next, this uncomfortable sensation in one's middle grows into a sort of palpitation, which, in turn, seems rapidly to spread upward and outward until the muscles of one's right arm (if one is right-handed!) become agitated by a flow of electric energy. This energy in one's arm is the prelude to painting because it can only be released by grabbing a brush and starting to paint."

The almost anonymous but recognizable figure of the "primary-colored painting" is related to the first charcoal drawing, and gives me the same feeling, with its sketched features and dark presence, of something painted with a sense of what it is like to be inside my head.

When Charles came back to the studio I watched him go through the process of registering the painting as a kind of unfinished chaos, and then begin to see it as a form, a representation, of a writer in a sea of light.

"YOUR TACTICAL MISTAKE WAS TO WRITE SO INTELLIGENTLY ABOUT PAINTING...IT IS NOT DONE BY THE REAL PAINTERS — IT DOES NOT FIT IN WITH THE PUBLIC'S CONCEPTION OF THE PAINTER AS A DUMB OX."
—*Herbert Read*

Henry Darger

by John Ashbery

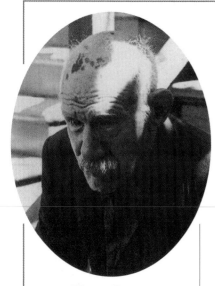

GIRLS ON THE RUN

I

A great plane flew across the sun,

And the girls ran along the ground.

The sun shone on Mr. McPlaster's face, it was green like an elephant's.

Let's get out of here, Judy said.

They're getting closer, I can't stand it.

But you know, our fashions are in fashion

Only briefly, then they go out

And stay that way for a long time. Then
    they come back in

For a while. Then, in maybe a million
    years, they go out of fashion

And stay there.

Laure and Tidbit agreed,

With the proviso that after that everyone
    would become fashion

Again for a few hours. Write it now,
    Tidbit said,

Before they get back. And, quivering, I
    took the pen.

Drink the beautiful tea

Before you slop sewage over the horizon,
    the Principal directed.

OK, it's calm now, but it wasn't two

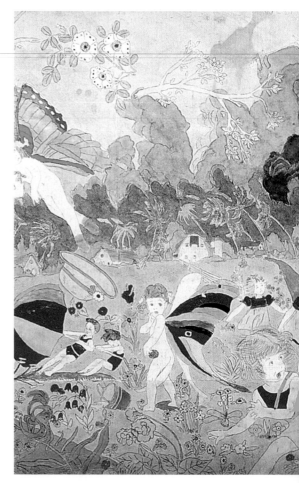

minutes ago. What do you want me to do, said Henry,

I am no longer your serf,

And if I was I wouldn't do your bidding. That is enough, sir.

You think you can lord it over every last dish of oatmeal

On this planet, Henry said. But wait till my ambition

Comes a cropper, whatever that means, or bursts into feathered bloom

And burns on the shore. Then the kiddies dancing sidewise

Declared it a treat, and the ice-cream gnomes slurped their last that day.

Inside, in the twilit nest of evening,

Something was coming undone. Dimples could feel it,

Surging over her shoulder like a wave of energy. And then –

It was gone. No one had witnessed it but herself.

And so Dimples took off for the city, which was near and wholesome.

There, with her sister Larissa, she planned the big blue boat

That future generations will live in, and thank us for. It twitched

At its steely moorings, and seemed to say: Live, like life, with me.

Let the birds wash over them, Laure said, for what use are earmuffs

In a snowstorm, except to call attention to distant tots

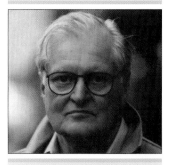

JOHN ASHBERY

Perhaps the most widely honored American poet of his generation, John Ashbery was born in Rochester, New York, in 1927. He began to write in the 1950s – work that was considered avant-garde. Educated at Harvard, Columbia, and New York University, he has worked as a poet, a critic, and an editor.

His 1976 poetry collection Self-Portrait in a Convex Mirror *won him the Pulitzer Prize, the National Book Award, and the National Book Critics Circle Prize. His more recent collection,* Houseboat Days, *has been called "the most original book of poems of the 1970s." His poetry is often compared to other art forms, specifically to abstract expressionist painting. Like an expressionist painter, Ashbery's poetic images convey a sense of movement.*

Ashbery's influence on poetry has been vast, as evidenced by the multitude of those embracing his style. He has won numerous awards and honors, including two Guggenheim fellowships, a National Institute of Arts and Letters Award, the Pulitzer Prize, a McArthur Foundation fellowship, and the Robert Frost medal from the Poetry Society of America.

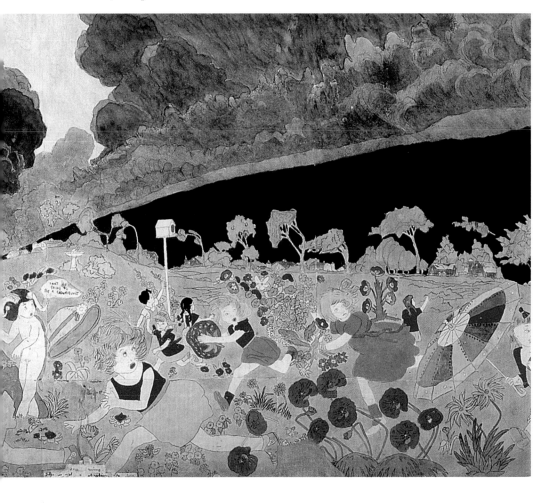

The storm is coming. This is not a strawberry the little girl is carrying in her hand, *decal and watercolor, detail (left hand) 30 x 125 in/77 x 317 cm. Collection Art Brut, Lausanne, Switzerland.*

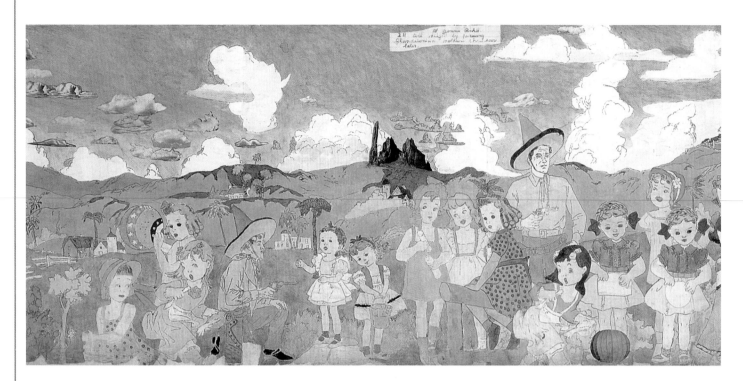

At Jennie Richie. They mingle with the child prisoners and in the absence of the guards they overcome to get them to quit work and follow them next morning, *decal and watercolor, detail (right half)*
24 x 108 in/60 x 275 cm.
Courtesy Kioyko Lerner.

Who have strayed. And now the big Mother warms them,

Accepts them, for the nervous predicates they are. Far from the beach-fiend's

Howling, their adventure nurses itself back

To something like health. On the fifth day it takes a little blancmange

And stands up, only to fall back into a hammock.

I told you it was coming, cried Dimples, but look out,

Another big one is on the way!

And they all ran, and got out, and that was that for that day.

V

Just as a good pianist will adjust the piano stool

Before his recital, by turning the knobs on either side of it

Until he feels he is at a proper distance from the keyboard,

So did our friends plan their day. Sometimes, after a leisurely breakfast,

They would get to work immediately, cutting, gluing, stitching

As the model came entrancingly into view. Other days it was more of a pain,

Or more elaborate. Persnickety Peggy was frequently at the heart of things,

Her strength often an inspiration to the others, though offset by her tendency to brawl

And generally make a nuisance of herself. The other girls took this in stride,

Though. Little by little the house was rising

Where only sky had hung before, and it seemed like good news,

A good berth. That was before Tommy took over

And ruined everything. But I am getting ahead of my story.

Sometimes to wake up in the morning was enough. They began feeling better.

Lecture plans were discussed, and a gleaming white envelope, shocking in its purity

As the dawn, would be sealed by two or three of them. There,

That's better, no one would say, and that's how they got down to business.

On rainy days they would stay indoors

Watching the chase of drops on the pane, realizing, a little half-frugally,

How it would be impossible to ever go outside. Moss drips on moss;

The more interesting-smelling exhibits have been packed away.

Or was there a terminus, sadly, deep underground? This, only children can know,

And some adults who have turned the steep corner into childhood.

Plums are ripening.

The pitcher of sangria darkens and deepens. So it was ever this way,

Until it was past time to become "normal" again. Tell it to the neutered pets

That day! Already the verandas are awash with trouble, and color, the darts seldom miss
　　their mark.

Heidi and Peter dissolve in the crystal furnace;

Something says it's too late to change, now better to let it come toward

Us, then we will see what it is made of.

To have had a son back there...

But the unthinkable is common knowledge now. We must let down a ladder

So the others may attach their boats to it, and in that way we shall be saved.

Only I think we're... It's all coming nearer.

At Jennie Richie. Out in the open they view the clouds of a storm coming, *decal, watercolor and collage, detail (left half) 24 x 109 in/60 x 278 cm. Collection Art Brut, Lausanne, Switzerland.*

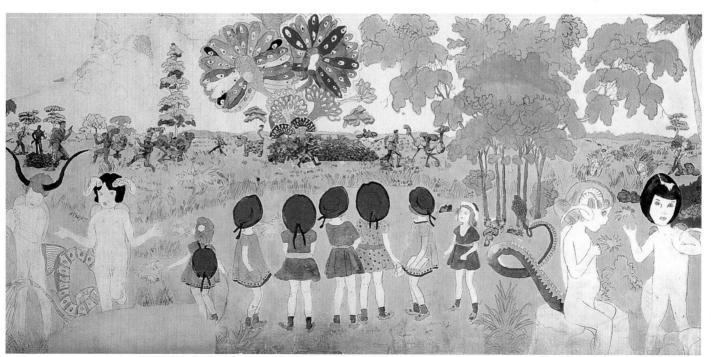

Constantin Brancusi

by Paul Bailey

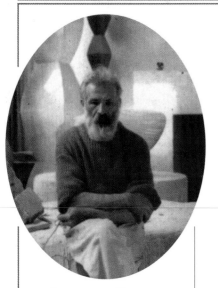

CONSTANTIN BRANCUSI
*Born in a small village in
Romania in 1876, Brancusi
was schooled in sculpture in
Bucharest before settling
in Paris in 1904.*

*There, he was influenced by
the contemporary Parisian
"primitives" Picasso and
Gauguin, and he soon
discarded his technique of
modeling in clay to begin
chiseling in stone. His first
major commissions during
this period were funerary
monuments – The Prayer at
Dumbrava Cemetery,
Bouzau, Romania, and
The Kiss, Montparnasse
Cemetery, Paris.*

*Like other artists of his time,
Brancusi rejected the realism
and embellishment of
sculptors of the nineteenth
century. Reducing his forms
by eliminating ornament and
superfluous detail, he created
streamlined birds and fish
that manifest purity of form
and appeal to the senses.*

*In 1937, the National
Women's League of Gorj
commissioned Brancusi to
produce a monument in
honor of Romanian troops
who fought in World War I.
The work Brancusi produced
for the Tirgu, Romania, site
consists of three sculptures,
and was called a "climax of
the sculptor's career."*

*Brancusi died in
Paris in 1957.*

THERE'S HIS NAME, TO BEGIN WITH. Hearing it spoken for the first time outside his native Romania, you would probably assume him to be of Italian origin: *Bran-cu-si*. At least three generations of art critics and curators have either ignored or been unaware of the circumflex above the "a" and the cedilla beneath the "s" (which is not even available on most fonts in this country).

The great sculptor we persist in calling Brancusi is known in the country of his birth as Brâncuşi, which is pronounced *Bruncoosh*. That final "i" is never voiced. In Paris, where he spent most of his long life, Constantin Brancusi was deprived of his distinguishing accents several decades ago.

I make this pedantic point because it was once made to me, by a professor of English in Bucharest. She expressed mild irritation on hearing me refer to Brancusi, and went on to observe that the majority of intelligent people have no trouble with French

"THERE HASN'T BEEN ANY ART YET. ART IS JUST BEGINNING."

names, which are often accented. It's a simple matter of education, of course, and sophisticated Romanians, of whom my friend is one, are saddened – to use no stronger word – by the fact that we in the West have little knowledge of their cultural inheritance. Our Italianizing of a national genius is a small, but telling, indication of a larger unfamiliarity with the roots of his subtle, and profoundly spiritual, art.

Unlike Eugène Ionesco and the maverick philosopher Emil Cioran, both of whom wrote in French, Brancusi was always a slightly reluctant Parisian. It was customary for Ionesco and Cioran to dismiss the Romanian peasant as a "savage," though Cioran – whose brilliant musings are full of contradictions – liked to remark that he preferred the company of a Carpathian shepherd to that of a novelist or intellectual. The chances of his bumping into a Carpathian shepherd on the Champs Élysées were pretty remote, as he was well aware, but the conceit is typical of his mordant nature. Ionesco and Cioran were just two gifted Romanians who deliberately turned their backs on a heritage they came to regard as primitive. Brancusi did no such drastic thing, as his finest works testify. His *Endless Column*, in its various manifestations, owes nothing to the sculpture of the Renaissance and everything to the anonymous art of generations of peasantry. It is possible to see, in those remaining village graveyards that escaped Nicolae Ceausescu's bulldozers, the eerily beautiful "death poles" that rise out of the earth heavenwards. Brancusi would have watched artisans carving and shaping them in Hobitza in his childhood, and he would certainly have understood what the poles signified – the soul of the dead person embarking on its last journey.

Hobitza, where Brancusi was born in 1876, is in the region of Wallachia called Oltenia. The Oltenians were accustomed to building their own wooden houses, designing and making the furniture they needed. The local genius for carving elaborate door frames, gates, and columns – a talent nurtured and developed over centuries – was still finding expression during Brancusi's formative years. His great-grandfather Ion had been responsible for many of the wooden churches in and around Hobitza, while his father worked as a carpenter before taking possession of a small piece of land. Brancusi's ancestors produced tapestries and exquisite works of embroidery with which to decorate their cottages, but it is the Oltenian carpet that even now attracts collectors and antique dealers. One, or perhaps more than one, of these carpets must have hung on the wall in the living room of his family's house. The designs are of birds (the hoopoe is a constant), flowers, and beasts, but there are abstract patterns, too. Brancusi was obsessed with birds throughout his career, refining the *Bird in Space* into a shining bronze that seems to be already

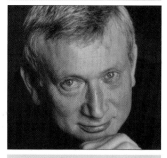

PAUL BAILEY
Critics describe Bailey's fiction as exhibiting sensitivity without sentimentality. He writes about isolation and personal catastrophe in a minimalist style that is austere and pure.

Bailey was born in London in 1937. In 1967 he published his first novel, At the Jerusalem, about a woman's life at an institution for the elderly. Subsequent novels, Trespasses, A Distant Likeness, Gabriel's Lament, and Sugar Cane, deal with breakups, isolation, mental illness, and suicide without making absolute moral judgements.

Bailey has also written short stories, plays, essays, and biographies, including a memoir – An Immaculate Mistake: Scenes from Childhood and Beyond. In 1995, he edited of a collection of fiction and nonfiction, The Oxford Book of London.

Among many honors for his work, Bailey has received an Arts Council of Great Britain Award and an E.M. Forster Award. He writes regularly for the New Statesman, The Observer, the London Sunday Times, and the Daily Telegraph. He lives in London.

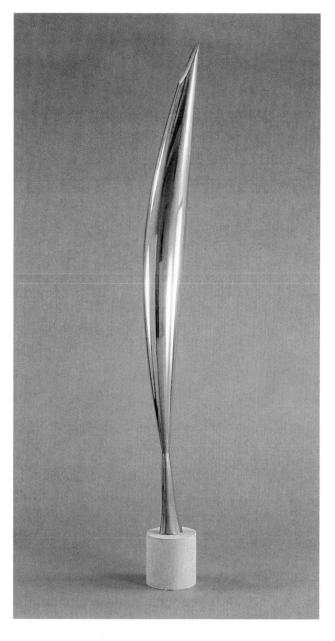

The Bird in Space, *1925, bronze, bird: 72 x 18 in/184 x 45 cm. base: 7 in/18 cm. National Gallery of Art, Washington, D.C.*

liberated from the pedestal on which it is permanently poised for flight. On some of the "death poles" a bird is perched at the very peak, its head leaning forwards, ready to depart.

The early life of Constantin Brancusi is the stuff of a certain kind of Romantic literature. It might have been penned by Panait Istrati, whose chronicles of love and brigandry among the Romanian peasants were very popular in France in the '20s and '30s. Istrati taught himself French and then taught himself to write fiction in it, yet there is nothing Gallic about his style. The best passages in his books are totally unaffected, perfectly natural. He believed, as did Brancusi, in goodness and innocence, and sustained that belief, for a while, in the most cynical city in Europe. Istrati could have described Brancusi's two-year trek, much of it on foot, from Romania to the French capital, where he earned money by washing dishes in a restaurant. And he would have written with a delicate understanding and appreciation of the boy who "came to sculpture" by a charmed accident:

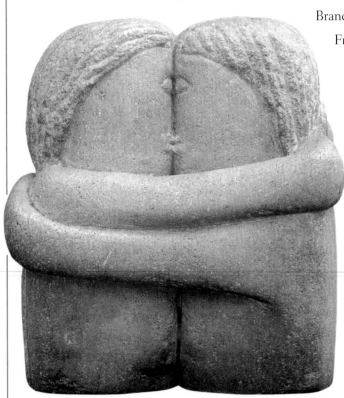

The Kiss, 1907, stone,
height: 11 in/28 cm.
Muzeul de Arta, Craiova, Romania.

I was eleven years old (Brancusi recalled), working in a cleaning and dyeing shop. I had straightened out and arranged everything so well in the shop that the owner said to me, "I know something you will not be able to do – make a violin!" I started working and made a violin. I discovered the secret of Stradivarius. I hollowed out the wood. I boiled it. The violin made a wonderful sound. After I made the violin, the owner said, "You must be a sculptor."

And so it had to be. Every monograph on Brancusi reveals that he studied at the School of Arts and Crafts in Craiova, then at the School of Fine Arts in Bucharest, where he won many prizes. In Paris, his work impressed Rodin, and the young Romanian was briefly the great man's pupil. But only briefly: he felt confined in Rodin's studio; he needed to get out from under the shadow of a huge tree. The sculpture that was to emerge in the next few years, in particular *The Kiss* of 1908 which crowns the headstone of the grave of Yanosa Sasevscaia in the Cimetière Montparnasse, shows him returning to the sights and shapes of Oltenia. *The Kiss* is as ethereal as it is sensuous, for the man and woman are conjoined spiritually and physically. The carving of the rough stone, it has been noted by critics, is coarse, yet the effect is of an extraordinary sensitivity. The fact that it adorns a grave has inspired much speculation, but I favor the notion that Brancusi, given his upbringing in the Orthodox faith, looked on death as a part of life, as a fact not to be shunned or sentimentalized. In later (1912) and earlier (1907) versions, the lovers are virtually indistinguishable in their state of oneness, with a single eye between them.

Giacometti accused him of creating "objects," and Henry Moore pronounced that he was overrated; the latter's judgement can now be taken with an ocean's worth of salt. Giacometti was right, to an extent: Brancusi did fashion objects, but they are objects of surpassing beauty. In his old age, he wanted his objects to be viewed alongside each other in his *atelier*,

"SIMPLICITY IS NOT AN OBJECTIVE IN ART, BUT ONE ACHIEVES SIMPLICITY DESPITE ONE'S SELF BY ENTERING INTO THE REAL SENSE OF THINGS."

his workplace. Thirty years after his death, that studio – "reconstituted," as the brochure says, by Renzo Piano – is open to the public, who can study or contemplate those objects of a lifetime almost as he would have wished them to. "Almost" is appropriate, since his studio at No.11 Impasse Ronsin has been reconstituted behind glass in the bunker-like building close to the Centre Georges Pompidou. Initially, the spectator is confused by the sheer mass of sculptures, and by the necessity to consult the charts that identify them. What's more, everything looks so clean, so preserved, so safely kept away from contaminating hands. There is no dust, no real disorder. But then, gradually, one forgets the dividing glass, and sees the famous objects – the *Cock*, *Bird in Space*, *Endless Column* (not as endless here), *Mlle Pogany*, *The Kiss*, *Leda*, *et al* – in happy unity. They represent Brancusi's achievement in all its purity, which is in itself a reflection of the anonymity of the art that inspired and moved him as a child. He bequeathed them to the French nation, together with his library, his records, the Guaneri violin on which he played Romanian folk tunes, and the tools with which he made not only the sculptures but the furniture he used daily. He constructed that limestone fireplace, the chairs and stools, the bed, the wooden pots. Room 3 affords his admirers the spectacle of hammers, saws, adzes, the entire array of equipment he

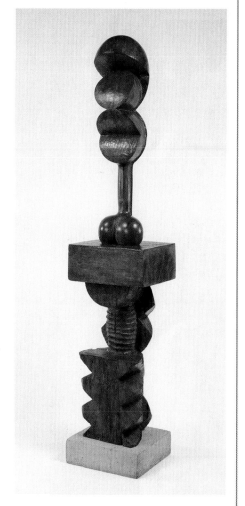

Left: **Little French Girl**, *1914–18, oak, 60 x 13 x 15 in/152 x 33 x 37 cm. including base. Solomon R. Guggenheim Museum, New York.*

Right: **Adam and Eve**, *1916–21, wood, height: 89 in/227 cm. Solomon R. Guggenheim Museum, New York.*

employed as a working artist. It ought to be messier than it is, but the imagination can provide the missing creative chaos.

Brancusi left Romania in 1903, and paid eight short visits to the country before the Second World War. In Paris, he cooked Romanian dishes in the two studios he occupied on Impasse Ronsin, and frequently wore an approximation of peasant dress. It would be

"Nude men in sculpture are not as beautiful as toads."

tempting to picture him as a naif son of the soil, because he did not discourage such a picture, but he was infinitely more complex. He is Romania's greatest visual artist by reason of the passion and intellect (a quality he was too modest to dwell on in conversation) he brought to the business of reshaping and revivifying the images of rural Romania – the Byzantine icons (think of the bronze Sleeping Muse), the wayside crosses and altars, the "death poles," the ornately carved gates and columns. To visit the Village Museum in Bucharest, with its rugs from Oltenia, its religious paintings, its pots and pans and other utensils, is to appreciate out of what everyday beauty and simplicity Brancusi carved and molded with his own peculiar vision works of universal meaning and importance. In exile, he kept those artefacts in mind, and never saw fit to demean them with words like "primitive" or other terms signifying artlessness.

"WHEREVER HE WAS, EVERYTHING HAD TO BE ALL WHITE. HE WORE WHITE, HIS BEARD WAS THEN ALREADY WHITE. HE HAD TWO WHITE DOGS THAT HE FED WITH LETTUCE FLOATING IN MILK. MY MEMORY OF BRANCUSI IS ALWAYS OF WHITENESS AND OF HIS BRIGHT AND SMILING EYES."

—Isamu Noguchi

Sleeping Muse, 1910,
polished bronze,
6 x 11 x 7 in/16 x 27 x 19 cm.
Centre Georges Pompidou, Musée National d'art Moderne, Paris.

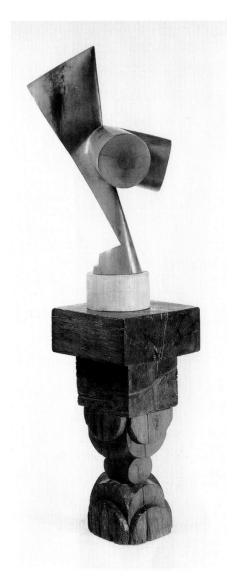

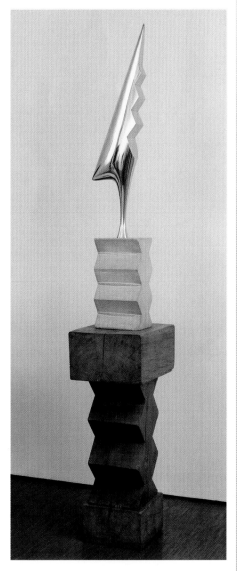

Yet he was not a nationalist. His decision to remain in Paris is evidence enough. He was friends with the poets Tudor Arghezi and Lucian Blaga, but could not endorse Blaga's sanctification of the Romanian peasant. In the years between the wars, Romanian intellectuals began to worry that the influence of French literature and art was robbing writers and painters of a national identity. Blaga spoke and wrote of the wisdom of the peasant, which had endured since the Roman invasion of Dacia. It is hard, now, to understand precisely what the poet was envisaging – a return to some type of Edenic idyll, maybe. Brancusi, conversely, looked to the future. He used peasant art as his source material, to be expanded, reinvented. The past is to be examined and considered, not to be recreated to the letter. He also acknowledged the truth behind Ionesco's wariness of those aspects of Romanian culture that glorify savage events in her long and chartered history.

Ionesco was fond of Brancusi, and amused by his lack of worldliness. He liked to recount how little use Brancusi had for the telephone, even when the sculptor was ill and in need of help. Rather than pick up the dreaded instrument, he chose to fling stones at the windows of friends in order to receive their assistance. He hobbled out into the street with his leg in plaster on one occasion, instead of doing what every other sensible invalid would have done. There was no calculation in his perversity, just as his indifference to colossal wealth was genuine. He did not end up as his detractor, Henry Moore, ended up, manufacturing squat figure upon squat figure for international businesses and banks. How pleasing it is for me to write of an artist who loved his work, and working, above every other distraction or temptation. The loss of integrity, the desire for praise and fame, were matters for lesser spirits to cope with or combat. It is common in Romania for people to talk of the soul – *suflet* is a word you will hear on the janitor's lips – and Brancusi's soul is there, undoubtedly there, in the lyrical, soaring, aspiring objects he has given to the world beyond Romania, the country he escaped from in the flesh but did not desert in the spirit.

Above right: The Cock, *1935, polished bronze, 41 x 5 x 12 in/103 x 12 x 30 cm. on wood and stone base. Solomon R. Guggenheim Museum, New York.*

Above left: The Sorceress, *1916–24, walnut, 39 x 25 x 19 in/100 x 64 x 48 cm. limestone base: height: 6 in/5 cm. diameter: 11 in/28 cm. Shown on* **Oak Base**, *1920, oak, height: 15 x 39 in/38 x 98 cm. Solomon R. Guggenheim Museum, New York.*

Giorgio Morandi

by Siri Hustvedt

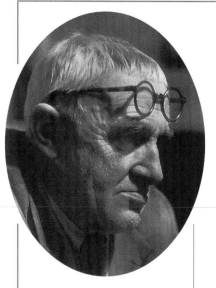

GIORGIO MORANDI
*Italian painter, draftsman,
and printmaker, Giorgio
Morandi was born in 1890
in Bologna, where he lived
most of his life. In 1909
he began studies at the
Academy of Fine Arts in
Bologna, and while there, he
discovered reproductions of
Cezanne's work, which
were to influence him
throughout his life.*

*Although Morandi was not
closely aligned with a
particular art movement, his
first paintings were exhibited
with the Futurists and, in
the 1920s, with artists of the
Metaphysical school. From
1930 onward, the motifs of
his paintings and etchings
were still lifes in a muted
range of colors consisting
of a few objects arranged
in subtle relationships.
Gradually increasing in
abstraction, his paintings
became increasingly
simple depictions of
geometric shapes.*

*Morandi taught drawing in
Bologna, and from 1930 to
1956, was a professor of
printmaking at the Academy
of Fine Arts. His reputation
as an artist grew, and his
fame began to spread abroad
after he won the Grand Prix
for painting at the 1948
Venice Biennale. In the
late '50s he retired from
public life to devote his
time to painting until
his death in 1964.*

I HAD JUST ARRIVED AT THE PEGGY GUGGENHEIM GALLERY IN VENICE. My eleven-year-old daughter Sophie, who accompanied me, settled herself on the floor of the first room with her sketch book and pencil. We had come to look at the exhibition of Giorgio Morandi's late work, from 1950 to 1964 (the year of the artist's death), and Sophie knew that we were going to be there a very long time. The Gallery wasn't crowded, but it wasn't empty either, and as I stood in that first room, trying to digest what I was seeing, I heard an exchange between an American couple. The husband, who apparently had entered the Gallery through the other door and come to the first paintings last, looked around him with a somewhat bewildered expression on his face and called to his wife, "More bottles!" From the other room, I heard her answer him in an accusatory voice, "I told you. They're all the same!"

"WHAT INTERESTS ME THE MOST IS EXPRESSING WHAT'S IN NATURE, IN THE VISIBLE WORLD, THAT IS."

I don't quote this couple to make fun of them, but rather to begin with what they so succinctly pointed out. In his last years, Morandi mostly painted the same things, and he did paint a lot of bottles. He did not, however, paint only bottles, and yet the man's comment resonates with the experience of seeing the work, because the most recognizable objects in these canvases are often bottles. Almost every work includes at least one bottle, although there are paintings that feature a pitcher or some other quickly identifiable object. Near the paintings were small texts that included the names of some of the other things – a cigar box, for example. But the boxes and cylinders that accompany the bottles in these paintings do not scream cigars or matches or salt. It is impossible to know what they are without being told.

The first question when you look at Morandi, which may also be the last question, is: "What exactly am I looking at?" This question brings up the further questions, "How should I look?" and "Where should I look?" One could argue that nearly every painting, both representational and abstract, elicits these questions, but I think with Morandi, they go to the heart of the work. The identities of the artist's bottles, vases, cups, and boxes are recessive, by which I mean that as you look at the objects before you on the canvas, the sense of them as ordinary named things diminishes over time. The objects seem to pull away from you into another spatial dimension, a second world that you recognize, but its content has changed.

This impression of otherness continued to grow as I looked. I kept asking myself where I should rest my eyes. It turned out that as quiet as these paintings are and as beautiful as a whole, there is something restless about them, too, and they challenge the spectator to work at unpacking the curious relations between the objects in front of him. Among the first works in the show (catalog no.1, 1948–50) is a configuration of bottles, vases, and a pitcher. (The canvas includes the fluted white bottle that recurs in a number of paintings and is featured in the show's single early painting, one from 1916, which despite the similarity of content demonstrates starkly the distances Morandi traveled during his career.) The white bottle is flanked from behind by a yellow bottle on the left and a rusty red or terracotta-colored vase on the right. Directly beside it on the right is a small white vase, and between the yellow and the red object is a dark gray pitcher that has been turned away from the viewer and is barely recognizable. Except for a small open space of light near the mouth of the red vase, its darkness fills up the entire space between the adjacent things.

In the gallery, I sketched the shapes in a notebook, a simple act which brings out very clearly the relations between the neighboring forms. The pitcher's handle follows closely but

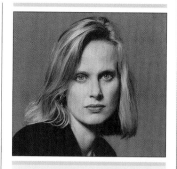

SIRI HUSTVEDT
Born in Minnesota in 1955, Hustvedt was educated at St. Olaf College and at Columbia University.

She published a collection of poetry, Reading to You, *in 1983, and in 1992, her first work of fiction,* The Blindfold. *Hustvedt's 1996 novel,* The Enchantment of Lily Dahl, *presents the coming of age story of a Marilyn Monroe-like aspiring actress in an exploration of the mysteries of identity.*

The title piece of her 1998 book of essays, Yonder, *explores the spaces between "here and there," which, for Hustvedt, are Minnesota where she was raised, the Norway of her parents' youth, and her home today in New York City.*

Hustvedt's poetry has appeared in The Paris Review Anthology, *her stories in* Ontario Review, Fiction, *and* Best American Short Stories, *and her essays in* The Art of the Essay: The Best of 1999, *among others.*

She currently lives and writes in New York City. She is married to the writer Paul Auster.

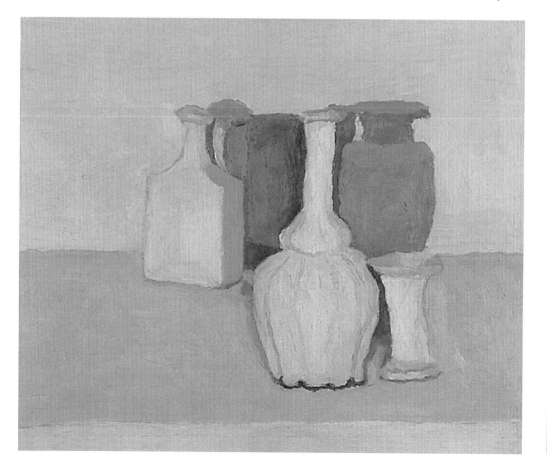

Still Life, *1948–50, oil on canvas, 15 x 18 in/38 x 45 cm. (cat.1) Private collection, Venice.*

not exactly the line of the yellow bottle's neck; the small white vase imperfectly echoes the curve of the fluted bottle. The lower side of the red vase moves along the neck of the white bottle. Furthermore, adjustments in the shapes of the bottles have been made for their neighbors. What is undoubtedly a symmetrical object in the studio becomes asymmetrical on the canvas. When you look closely at the lower bulbous section of the white fluted bottle, you see that the side which borders the small vase has been shorn of its fullness and a blackened area marks the space between them. It is very dark. The light and shadow of real perception cannot account for it. This is not an imitation of sensory experience. The diffuse gray light that illuminates these paintings would never produce such blackness. Morandi has invented it, and the recurring black and deep gray places in the paintings accentuate what the artist is after, which is not only to render the things themselves but the spaces between them – the drama of their relations. Although normal perception tells us that the pitcher stands behind the white bottle, the paint tells us that they touch, that these things are closely bound in a space where separations and distances are muted at best. The fluted white bottle is pulled close to the object that appears furthest from it by an inexplicable long gray shadow, which ends in a darker gray shape that nearly touches the rear of the yellow bottle: it flirts with proximity.

It can be argued that these objects create a formal arrangement that plays with abstraction, that mimesis is secondary to the space of the canvas itself. Links have been made between Morandi and abstract artists, including Rothko, Albers, Judd, and Mondrian. While it is easy to see these connections, particularly to Rothko's luminous canvases and to Mondrian's development from his architectural trees to his famous rhythms of primary grids, I think that the project Morandi undertook for himself is finally very different from that of painters who ended up in a thoroughly abstract space. Morandi stubbornly resisted the debate about abstraction that raged around him during the years when he painted these canvases. He stuck to his bottles.

Still Life, *1953–54, oil on canvas, 14 x 16 in/36 x 40 cm. (cat. 25) Private collection, Venice.*

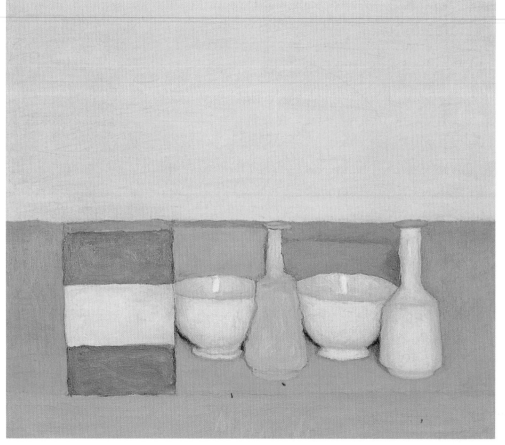

In a radio interview in 1957, he said, "For me nothing is abstract. In fact, I believe there is nothing more surreal, nothing more abstract than reality." This curious statement contains a paradox. Morandi first says that nothing is abstract and then he says that reality itself is abstract: everything is abstract. So which is it? I think it is not either/or, but both – an almost mystical statement about the problem of seeing. What I see and paint is real. I paint the real and that reality looks like this – abstracted. Morandi did not hold himself back from the Abstract Expressionists out of some conservative urge to resist temptation. He simply did not see the world in their terms, and he wanted to paint what he experienced as a truth about what he saw. But what was he seeing?

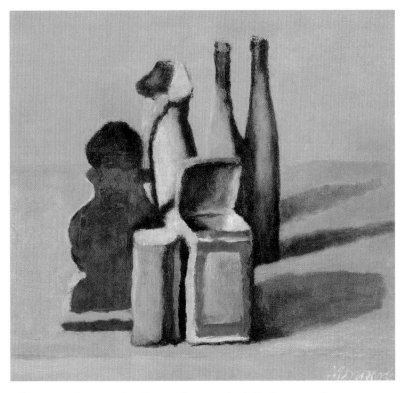

Still Life, *1959, oil on canvas, 10 x 11 in/25 x 28 cm. (cat. 37) Private collection, Venice.*

The overall visual effect of the paintings is one of a refinement that nearly aches with subtlety. The colors, the light, the little things on a vanishing table or shelf create an impression of an exquisite, cerebral distance, but the fact is that when you get close to the paint, when you stick your nose right up to a canvas, there is something rough and suggestive about the way the objects are painted. The canvas shows through. The lines that delineate the objects wobble and wave. These things do not compose geometries or systems. In a painting from 1953–54 (cat. 25), Morandi essentially divided his canvas in half, although the upper gray portion of the painting is in fact longer than its gray-brown counterpart at the bottom. The group of objects is entirely located in the painting's lower half. Three boxes, two bottles, and two cups are grouped together. The tops of the bottles actually touch the line of division. Again, when you look closely at the row of objects, you see how one thing accommodates the other, how the line of the blue bottle is pushed by the cup which ordinary vision suggests should be behind it. It is as if the cup were a soft, not a solid, body. The blue bottle's lines are sketchy, as if its outlines have been drawn, not painted. The bottom rim of the white cup to the left is rumpled, its proportions squeezed by the things on either side of it. It, too, is a hard object that is not hard. The illusion of depth is undermined in the canvas by the three boxes, shown as pure flat rectangles that repeat the two large rectangular spaces which divide the painting itself. The red box to the right is so blurred that it appears to vanish into the table, occupying a zone between thing and shadow.

Before I went to Venice, Karen Wright, the editor of *Modern Painters*, told me something that originated in the mouth of David Sylvester, the art critic, whose book on Giacometti I greatly admire. Mr. Sylvester is reported to have said that he thought

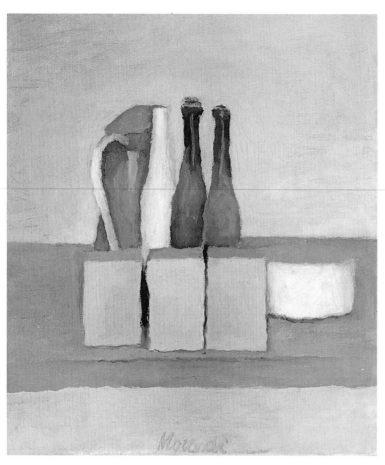

Still Life, *1956, oil on canvas, 40.5 x 35.5 cm. (cat. 33) Trento, Museo d'Arte Moderna e contemporanea di Trenot e Roveveto.*

Morandi's late paintings were more closely related to the cityscape of Bologna than to still life. I carried this astute comment with me to Venice. The division in the painting with the three boxes does seem more closely linked to a horizon than to any table top. It is like the line between sky and ground, even in its coloring. The boxes and bottles have an architectural feeling to them, as do the objects in many of the canvases. The painting with three boxes in front of three bottles and a pitcher (cat.33), for example, might be of towers behind squat buildings. Apparently Sylvester was not alone in this insight, for in the catalog's introduction, the critic Carlo Ludovico Ragghianti is quoted as saying that Morandi's interest in still life is "…wholly architectural, so much so that it should prompt us to think of cathedrals rather than of bottles." And to illustrate this point, the catalog shows us a black-and-white reproduction from the Pinacoteca Nationale in Bologna of the city held in the hands of St Petronius. It is a powerful image, for in the hands of the saint the city is miniaturized – reduced to a still life.

The colors in all the paintings are colors you see when you walk the streets of almost any Italian town, hues baked and lightened by the sun – green and blue shutters, yellow walls, old terracotta turned pink, and stone, lots of stone, varying in shade from a pale white-gray to sooty black. And there is the changing sky, too, its blues and grays and cloudy alterations. These are the colors Morandi uses, and he did paint many landscapes. But the question then becomes, if it is really landscape you are interested in, why paint so many still lifes? Why paint objects instead of what you see out your window? Why paint a city as bottles? Weather alters everything you see. Buildings vanish behind clouds. The sun makes a hill rise up in clarity while on other days its glare makes it disappear. There is morning light and evening light and the light of high noon. Morandi's still lifes are haunted by weather, by the forms and colors of earth and city. The mutable landscape Morandi saw from his window every day was part, but not the end, of an idea he had about reality. The little bottles and objects he worked with and carefully tended by allowing them to get dustier and dustier until a heavy film blurred their outlines became the obsessive focus of a man's quest for the real. In these still lifes, we are neither outside nor inside, but both inside and outside. Just as the mysterious light that shines on these objects is influenced by the effects of natural light on things but is not natural light. Morandi used a system of veils on his window to cut, alter, and change sunlight, to produce in the studio a strange, eternal illumination for his dusty little things. He manipulated light for his own purposes.

That Morandi looked at and loved the outlines and architecture of his own city seems obvious, but the ghostly cities that lie suggestively behind his paintings are also cities of paint. Before we left Venice, Sophie and I visited the Accademia. Even in August when tourists crowd the streets, this museum that contains some of the world's greatest paintings is strangely empty of people. I have been there four times, always at peak season, and each time the Accademia has felt curiously abandoned. In most of its rooms Sophie and I were alone. We had little time, and I rushed to look again at what is perhaps my favorite painting in the world, Giorgione's *The Tempest*. After spending hours with Morandi, I found myself looking at the dead city in the background of that canvas and at the strange wall, topped by two curious cylinders further to the foreground, with new eyes. Giorgione's columns and rectangles brought Morandi's still lifes into clearer focus. The city of *The Tempest* is not a real city but a mixture of classical towers and Venetian rural buildings. Looking at the Giorgione painting again did not make me believe that Morandi was referring directly to it, but rather that the weird city in *The Tempest* is a particularly mysterious example of countless little cities that appear in the background of Renaissance Italian painting. For example, in Giovanni Bellini's *The Madonna of the Meadow*, at the National Gallery in Washington, the city in the distance creates a harmony of spatial forms which is both mimetic and abstract, of the world and not of it. After my visit to the Accademia, I read in the catalog that John Berger felt the presence of the Renaissance in Morandi and made general comparisons between him and Bellini, as well as Piero della Francesca, in his catalog essay for the Italian show at the Museum of Modern Art in 1949.

Architecture in Renaissance painting was of course increasingly influenced by the actual vision of the painter. Bellini was asked to put Paris in the background of a painting and said he couldn't do it because he had never seen it. But architectural forms in Renaissance painting, particularly early Renaissance painting, nevertheless served a spiritual idea of harmony and order that went beyond the merely seen. And in this lies the deep affinity between Morandi and the formal abstractions of Renaissance painting. Looking at these late canvases of Morandi, I kept thinking of the words behind, under, beyond. These are not bottles and vases and cups, and although they may suggest a city, they are not cities either. After a while, they did not even seem like still lifes any more. It is as if I were seeing forms that evoked idea rather than thing. The object – bottle, cup, cloth, vase – recedes into some larger mystery.

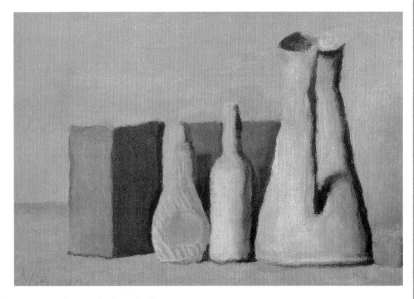

Still Life, *1958, oil on canvas, 8 x 12 in/21 x 31 cm. (cat. 36) Private collection, Milan.*

"AT FIRST GLANCE, MORANDI'S OBJECTS APPEAR TO BE THE DETRITUS OF DOMESTICITY, A COLLECTION OF THINGS ONCE IN DAILY USE, BUT DISCARDED EITHER BECAUSE THEY HAVE SUFFERED SOME KIND OF DAMAGE OR BECAUSE THEIR CONTENTS HAVE BEEN EXHAUSTED."

—*Karen Wilkin*

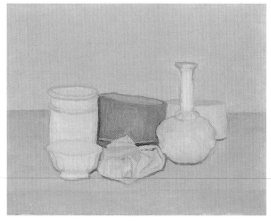

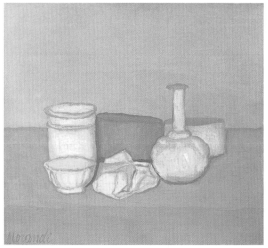

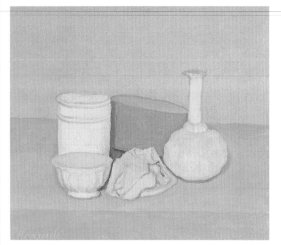

Above, top to bottom:
Still Life, 1952, oil on canvas,
14 x 18 in/36 x 46 cm.
(cat. 14) Private collection.
Still Life, 1952, oil on canvas,
16 x 18 in/41 x 46 cm.
(cat. 15) Mattioli Rossi collection,
Milan.
Still Life, 1952, oil on canvas,
14 x 16 in/35 x 40 cm.
(cat. 16) Civiche Raccolte d'Arte,
Milan.

When I looked at the series of six paintings from 1952, which all include a yellow cloth and were hung together in one room, I felt as if the canvases were having a mute conversation with one another. The white fluted bottle, its ridges less evident in this series than in some of the other paintings, remains as an anchor on the right in all of them. The striking yellow cloth remains front center. The cup and cylindrical vase are constant anchors on the left. What changes is the object between the flanking white bottle and vase. A brown form, described as a basket, is replaced by a green bowl in others, the hue of which changes dramatically between two canvases, from dark green in one to a much yellower tone in the other (cat.14 and 15). In these two canvases there is an additional object, an extended cylindrical white form that appears behind the white bottle. In the series, the shifting happens in the space between white objects, from one brown to another, from one green to another. It made me think that Morandi was exploring "between-ness" itself, asking what constitutes a border? In the canvas with the paler green bowl (cat.16), the bowl seems to tip upward. Its edge behind the white cylinder is outlined in a deep gray, which continues downward to divide the yellow cloth and white cup, a fine dark line of distinction that is nearly erotic in its closeness. After looking for a while, I found this darkness between cup and cloth obsessively interesting, more interesting than the objects themselves.

Nevertheless, the yellow cloth announces itself in the show, because these six paintings are the only ones which include it as an element. I asked myself whether the cloth was folded identically from one painting to the next? Had the folds changed or had Morandi merely shifted the angle of the cloth as a whole? I'm not sure. The sensibility of the painter suggests that every change would have been made both deliberately and carefully. Significantly, the cloth itself – its creases, shadows, interstices – does not contrast sharply with the other objects. It is not a soft body next to hard ones. The material of the brown basket (cat.17) appears to fold slightly in harmony with the cloth. Again I was drawn back to Renaissance painting, to the countless examples of drapery and clothing that fall, fold and knot over architecture, but especially over bodies. The small rounded knot of cloth appears and reappears in canvas after canvas during high Renaissance painting. Even the most cursory look at Pontormo's *Deposition*, for example, shows countless examples of folded cloth draped sinuously over heads and shoulders and arms, and then there is the roselike tie or knot of material looped around Christ's hips. This rose of cloth hides Christ's genitals in innumerable pietàs, entombments, and Crucifixions. An example of this knot in a painting with a classical theme may be seen in

Titian's *Rape of Lucretia* (Tarquin and Lucretia). A rose of pale cloth lies between her legs, surrounded by the deep shadow where her thighs meet. While it would be far-fetched to say that Morandi is referring directly to any of these paintings, the cloth evokes these other cloths in the delicacy of the painting, as well as in the sensual pleasures of looking at fabric. In Morandi the spectator is invited to consider the nature of threshold itself, the boundaries between one body and another – all bodies – both inanimate and animate. Just as Morandi is not painting cities as bottles, he is not painting the human body as objects either, but the world of the flesh is not as far from these paintings as one might at first think. In the strange give and take between and among forms in the canvases, in the often barely perceptible wrinkling or folding inward, in the deep shadowed crevices and the mysterious softness of their material, these things make us think about the physical world, and from that meditation we begin to think about "thingness" and about what is there and what is not there.

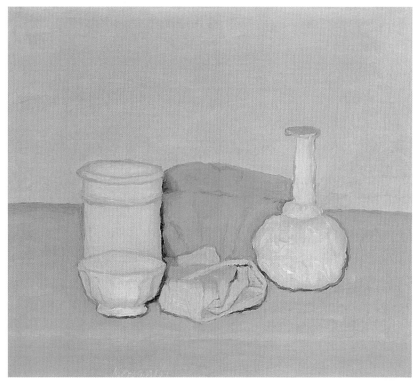

Still Life, 1952, oil on canvas,
16 x 18 in/41 x 46 cm.
(cat. 17) Private collection.

The simplest examples of a thing that is at once present and absent occur in two paintings from 1957. They both include the shadow of an object beyond the borders of the canvas. In one (not reproduced in the catalog), two bottles and a cylinder stand in the center of the painting. All cast shadows backwards and to the right, but then, at the edge of the canvas, just below the line of the table, is a shadow from something else that we can't see. Exactly how this object could cast a shadow in that direction, considering the illusion

Below Left: Still Life, *1952, oil on canvas,*
17 x 22 in/43 x 56 cm.
(cat. 18) Private collection, Bologna.
Below Right: Still Life, *1953, oil on canvas,*
12 x 14 in/30 x 35 cm.
(cat. 19) Private collection, Cuneo.

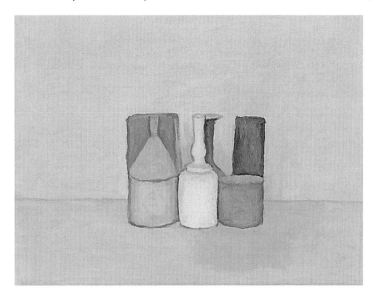

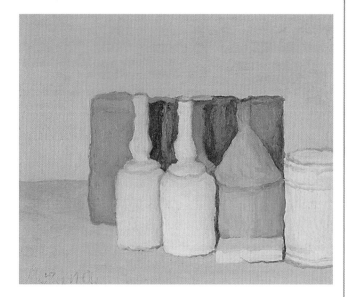

"THIS DIALOGUE - OR TUG OF WAR - BETWEEN THE SPECIFIC AND THE ELEMENTAL LIES AT THE HEART OF MORANDI'S WORK."

—*Karen Wilkin*

created in the painting about the angle of light, is a mystery. The second example (cat.30) is more subtle, but to the far right is a gray triangular shadow that implies the presence of another thing we cannot see. A canvas from 1959 (cat.41) shows two similar pale bottles, the small white vase viewed in earlier paintings, and a smoky gray-black rectangular form that appears to float out of the side of the bottle on the left. It is impossible to identify this form, and impossible to penetrate its position in terms of conventional vision. A drawing and a watercolor, from 1958 and 1959 respectively, show the same two bottles. The space between them is differently shaded, but is the site of intense focus in both. The black rectangle of the painting is a sober occupant of space but not a thing as the bottles are things. It is neither shadow nor object. Indeed, the difference between the objects and the space that separates them increasingly loses its significance as you look at that dark form in relation to what is around it. The growing focus on the spaces between objects is a philosophical one. The lines we draw between the objects we see and live with are the product of our vision, a vision determined by the living language we use, a language that has profound and changing cultural meanings. To simplify this statement in terms of painting, one can say that a cup in a painting done in 1390 is different from a cup in a painting done in 1998. The conventions, the language of looking, the perspective we use to decipher meaning, have changed.

Giorgio Morandi is in the business of subverting the conventions of seeing. It makes perfect sense that he loved Cézanne who had a related desire to strip things down, to see them again as if for the first time. Morandi shares Cézanne's acute attentiveness and desire to lift off the veil of convention from visual experience, but there is in Morandi something belated, something beyond the present moment that is not found in Cézanne. The very last paintings in this show are almost like after-images: those blots of shape and color and

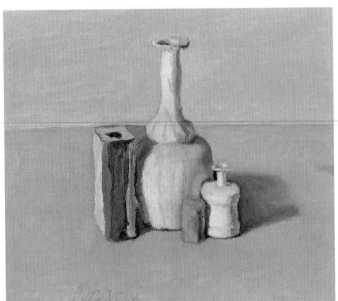

Still Life, *1957, oil on canvas,*
12 x 14 in/31 x 36 cm.
(cat. 30) Private collection.

light that remain even after you have closed your eyes to the things themselves. In the last paintings, the relations between objects and empty space, between solid form and air, between the edge of one thing and another is persistently questioned. Where does one thing begin and another end? In the exhibition's remarkable last painting, one wonders if the ghostly white bottle is actually coming out of the dark one that stands beneath it. Looking at Morandi's work, I felt a lingering Platonism that may well come from the overwhelming power of the painterly past, that great translation of Pauline Christianity into art, which reinvented Platonic thought through the events of the life of Jesus. The ideas in these paintings feel more real than the things themselves: "For me nothing is abstract. In fact, I believe nothing is more surreal, more abstract than reality."

The legacy of Christian thought is far-reaching. Among the deep marks it has left on the Western soul is a feeling among many people that what we see is not everything – that there is something more lurking behind the merely physical – a spiritual dimension to life. But the thought may be turned around as well: whatever one may believe about spirituality, it seems undeniably true that the idea of an object creates its reality to a large extent. The physical world is mysterious, and the longer and harder you look at it the stranger it becomes. Of this much I am certain: Morandi felt that he was painting the world in those bottles. He did not feel that by reducing the numbers of the objects he painted he reduced the range of his vision. On the contrary, the very narrowness of the field became the vehicle of his liberation. This is a modernist position. As for Giacometti, as for Beckett (to give a literary example), reduction opened up possibilities that inclusiveness did not have. From a few things, you get everything.

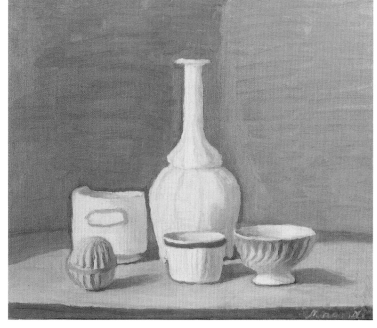

Still Life, *1944, Oil on canvas, 12 x 21 in/30 x 53 cm. Center Pompidou, Paris.*

Freedom, however, remains a relative term. A friend of mine, Bill Corbett, reported to me yet another second-hand story which comes from Nick Carone, an American painter who lives in both America and Italy. Carone was with Morandi at the Venice Biennale in 1948, and de Kooning's work prompted this comment from Morandi: "He just jumps in before he knows how to swim." The utterance was apparently not made without admiration, but it speaks directly to the artist's aesthetic. He may have found his path to freedom, but that path was one of restraint, patience, repression, and suggestion. His canvases are controlled and masterly. Looking at the actual paintings is important, because the light that seems to come out of them reproduces very poorly. These canvases reveal themselves slowly and reward the spectator who bothers to look long and hard. In the end, they create a surprising tension between thought and the senses.

The paintings in this exhibition are also the works of a man's maturity and require a certain maturity in the spectator. Sophie didn't know what to make of Morandi, and for an eleven-year-old she has a very good eye. In the Accademia, she pulled me away from Giorgione to the room filled with Tintoretto's huge canvases. She remembered them from an earlier visit, and I watched as she stood spellbound before them. "I like this museum better than the other one, Mom," she confided to me later. I did not argue with her. And yet, if there's one thing I've understood about art in general it is that there are thousands of different ways of getting at the world and what we experience as its truths. In Morandi's case, the path to that truth was by the way of "more bottles."

MORANDI'S INTEREST IN STILL LIFE IS "..WHOLLY ARCHITECTURAL, SO MUCH SO THAT IT SHOULD PROMPT US TO THINK OF CATHEDRALS RATHER THAN OF BOTTLES."

—*Carlo Ludovico Ragglianti*

Jackson Pollock

by Martin Gayford

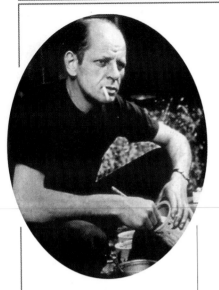

JACKSON POLLOCK
Creating a unique visual language, Pollock explored the expressive process of painting using trowels, knives, and dripping paint to create intricate, intertwined lines.

He was born in 1912 in Wyoming, and grew up in California. In 1929 he moved to New York to study at the Art Students League with the regionalist painter Thomas Hart Benton who influenced Pollock with a rhythmic, dynamic composition. In the '30s, Pollock was inspired by epic, large-scale murals of the Mexican painters Siqueiros, Orozco, and Rivera. Pollock's themes became mythic, focusing on gesture and emotional content. He was also influenced by Surrealism, and became interested in the role of the unconscious in the painting process. The work he produced in the early '40s eliminated all recognizable imagery and focused on ever-larger canvases with interwoven, fluid lines that extended into infinity. Pollock gained public recognition when Peggy Guggenheim gave him a one-man exhibition at the Guggenheim Museum in 1943.

Pollock's struggle with alcoholism and depression fueled a turbulent relationship with his artist-wife Lee Krasner. In 1956 he died in a car crash.

IN THE EARLY 1950S, ABOUT THE TIME JACKSON POLLOCK WAS PAINTING *BLUE POLES*, the architect Tony Smith asked him what he thought was the greatest work of art in North America. By that stage, the Museum of Modern Art in New York was already rich in masterpieces by Picasso, Miró, Matisse – artists who meant a lot to Pollock. At the Met and the Frick there were correspondingly magnificent old masters. Then there were numerous American paintings that he might have considered – not least the first great abstracts by his contemporaries Willem de Kooning and Mark Rothko. But he didn't mention any of those. Without hesitation, he replied "the Orozco mural at Pomona College." Now, why on earth should he have chosen that?

Well, clearly it was a painting that had made a big impact at a formative moment, before he could have seen any of those other things. In the summer of 1930, before he first set out for New York, Pollock had driven out from Los Angeles to the little town of Claremont, 30 miles away, to see the painting, *Prometheus*, that the Mexican painter Jose Clemente Orozco had recently completed at Pomona College. It was huge, the main figure over twenty feet high, filling a gothic arch at the end of the refectory. Prometheus seems to be launching himself into space, pushing with his arms at the confining edges of the arch.

It is a powerful image, though not one that many people would drive 30 miles to see these days. From photographs, it looks like a rough and ready pastiche of El Greco, with a dash of Tintoretto thrown in. It would not have much, you might think, to interest the intuitive master of gestural abstraction, already hailed by *Life* magazine as the successor of Picasso. It is an awkward, out-of-date-looking image, a byway from the mainstream of the history of art (the Mexicans Orozco, Siqueiros, and Rivera are perhaps the most attractive representatives of the socialist painting of the '30s, though most people today wouldn't think that was saying much). But then, Pollock's own life and experience of art did not follow the orthodox path.

His training, such as it was, was mainly as a student of the bombastic regionalist Thomas Hart Benton, whose style, in the words of Robert Hughes, "was bad in the way that popular art can sometimes be … flat-out, lapel-grabbing vulgar, unable to touch a pictorial sensation without pumping it up" (and pumped up is exactly what many of Benton's male figures look, half way between Michelangelo and Tom of Finland). Benton's most substantial surviving work, in the House Lounge of the State Legislature of Missouri, Hughes feels, gives a sense of Benton the man, "his worship of the late Renaissance and his cornball humor, his self confidence and the anxiety that's written all over these huge posturing figures in their buckling space."

In addition to admiring the work of Orozco, and sitting at the feet of this strange Huck Finn-meets-Schwarzenegger of a master, Pollock also spent some time working with, and for a while was influenced by, another, wackier Mexican socialist realist, David Alfaro Siqueiros. It wasn't a standard route into the modernist avant-garde; nonetheless there were those who wondered whether this odd background might be part of Pollock's secret. "What is interesting about Pollock," observed George McNeil, a fellow artist, "is that he came from very bad influences like Benton and the Mexican muralists and other

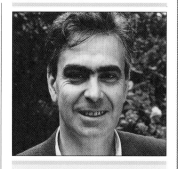

MARTIN GAYFORD
Martin Gayford is a critic, author, and editor. He studied philosophy at Cambridge, and art history at the Courtauld Institute of London University. Writing prolifically about art and music, he contributes regularly to London's Daily Telegraph *and the* Sunday Telegraph, *the* Independent, *and also to exhibition catalogues for the Tate Gallery and other art galleries. Since 1994, he has been the art critic for* The Spectator. *With his co-editor Karen Wright, he edited the* Grove Book of Art Writing.

He currently lives and writes in Cambridge, England.

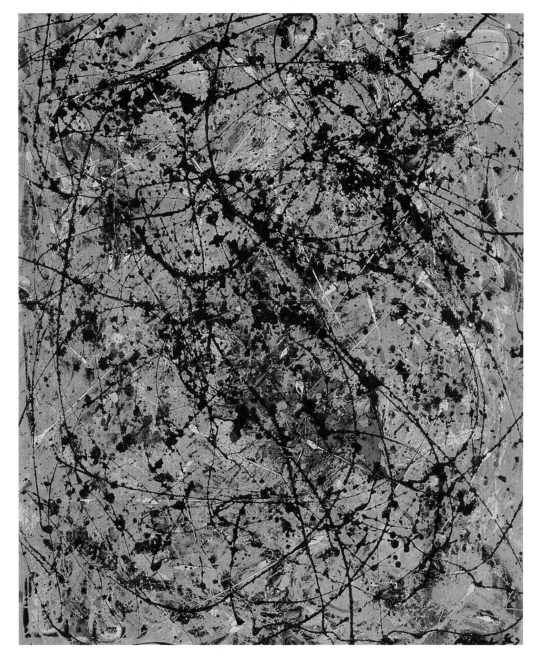

Reflection of the Big Dipper, *1947, oil on Canvas, 44 x 36 in/111 x 92 cm. Stedelijk Museum, Amsterdam.*

anti-painterly influences, and yet, somehow, in a kind of alchemy, he took all the negatives and made them into a positive. It's a mystery. The rest of us were following the right path, and therefore the magic didn't issue."

So what rare alchemical ingredients could Pollock have picked up from Orozco, Benton, and co.? First, simply that they painted murals, covering huge areas with bounding, vigorous, if – as it now seems to us – somewhat crass designs. A mural is the alternative to an easel painting: not a portable, frame-bound piece of furniture, but an image so big and powerful that – if it is good – it dominates the space it occupies. Michelangelo, Tiepolo, and Tintoretto painted murals, some of the time at least, and so did Pollock. The easel painting, it was frequently proclaimed at this time by the critic Clement Greenberg, was a

"BUT HOWEVER STRONGLY INFLUENCED POLLOCK WAS BY SURREALIST IDEAS OR BY BENTON'S HARDY EXPRESSIONIST STYLE, HE NEVER WHOLLY ENTERED INTO THE DISCUSSIONS AND CONTROVERSIES WHICH OCCUPIED SO MANY OF THE OTHER ARTISTS. HE ALWAYS RETAINED HIS LOVE FOR THE VAST EXPANSES OF THE FAR WEST, WHICH HE LIKED TO TRAVERSE IN AN OLD AUTOMOBILE AS HE HAD DONE AS A YOUTH."

—Herschel B. Chipp

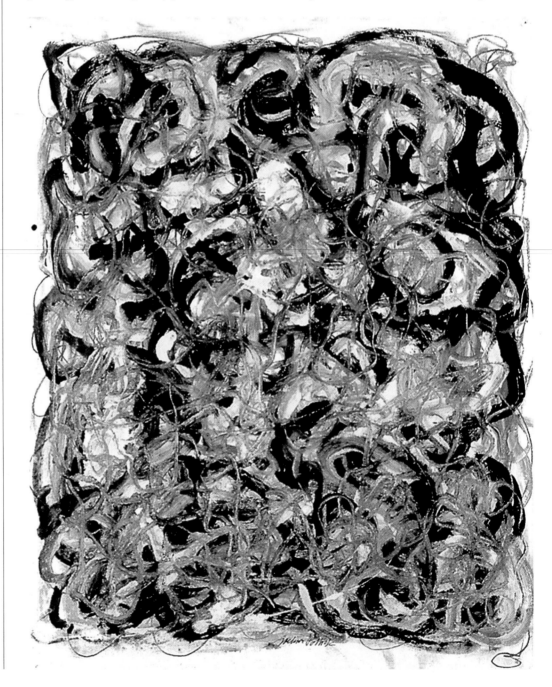

Untitled. *c 1945, pastel and enamel on paper, 26 x 21 in/65 x 52 cm. Thyssen-Bornemisza collection, Lugano.*

dying form – and Greenberg, of course, was the critic who more than any other championed the work of Pollock, indeed built his career on doing so.

That does not, of course, necessarily mean that he knew how and why it came about – though his judgements of quality were unerring. Asked whether Greenberg had understood his work, Pollock replied, "Not a thing" (expletives deleted). But on the question of large-scale mural painting Pollock and Greenberg were at one. Interviewed on a radio program in 1950, Pollock took a similar, though less messianically prophetic, line. "Painting today seems very vital, very alive, very exciting. Five or six of my contemporaries around New York are doing very vital work, and the direction that painting seems to be taking here is – away from the easel – into some sort, some kind of wall – wall painting."

At this point the interviewer, William Wright, remarked that some of Pollock's own works were of "unusual dimensions," to which Pollock answered that they were in fact of "an impractical size – nine by eighteen feet," for example. "But," he continued, "I enjoy working big and – whenever I have a chance, I do it whether it's practical or not." "Can you explain," Wright then asked, "why you enjoy working on a big canvas more than a small one?" But actually Pollock couldn't. "I'm just more at ease in a big area than I am on something two by two; I feel more at home in a big area."

An interesting point emerges from this: it is an artistic imperative, an inner urge, this desire to paint on the scale of a wall. There is nothing practical about it. On the contrary, in practical terms the easel painting wasn't dying at all – it was exactly what collectors wanted to buy, and still do, for that matter. So when Pollock painted huge pieces such as *Autumn Rhythm* or *One: Number 31*, he was doing so in the full knowledge that they would be hard to sell, that what he should have been painting to generate sales was lots of little canvases two by two or smaller (in fact, at one point Pollock was persuaded to do just that, which helps explain the large quantity of small Pollocks around).

Pollock was right to trust his impulse to work on a huge scale. It is the biggest paintings, *One: Number 31*, *Number 32* (1950), and *Autumn Rhythm*, which lift you off your feet and form the climax of his work. No photographs can duplicate the effect of scale, the almost physiological effect of a painting so large it fills your visual field, so big it seems to envelop you. There is a difference in kind from an easel-sized picture, a difference

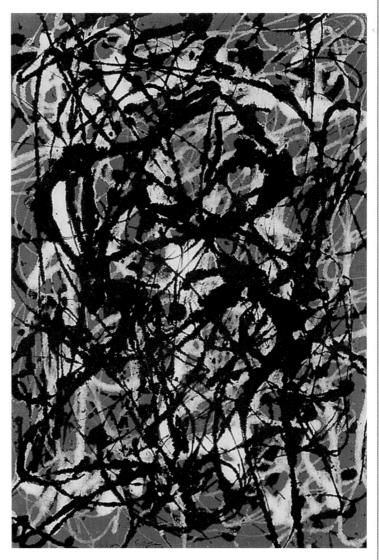

Free Form, *1946, oil on canvas, 19 x 14in/49 x 36 cm. Museum of Modern Art, New York, The Sidney and Harriet Janis Collection.*

that Mark Rothko put his finger on (though his largest paintings don't measure up to the great Pollocks). "Small paintings since the Renaissance," Rothko announced in a lecture at the Pratt Institute, "are like novels; large pictures are like dramas in which one participates in a direct way." Looking at Pollock's big paintings, one understands exactly what he meant.

"On the floor I am more at ease. I feel nearer, more a part of the painting, since this way I can walk around it, work from the four sides and literally be in the painting."

You look at a small painting as at a tableau, a toy theater; if a painting is big enough, it starts to act on you; you may even get the impression you might enter it.

Writing of Rothko, David Sylvester remarks that his paintings create "a kind of confrontation … we are faced with a highly ambiguous presence which seems, on the one hand, ethereal, empty, on the other, solid and imposing, like a megalith. It is a presence that alternates between seeming to be receptive, intimate, enveloping, and seeming to be menacing, repelling. It plays with us as the weather does, for it is a landscape, looming up over us, recalling the imagery of the first verses of Genesis." (A Barnett Newman, on the other hand, Sylvester finds, "gives us a sense of being where we are which somehow

Lavender Mist: Number 1, *1950, oil, enamel and aluminum paint on canvas, 87 x 118 in/221 x 300 cm. National Gallery of Art, Washington, DC.*

> "(Pollock's works are) exciting and unusual… I don't understand them, but something very important is happening here."
> —*Piet Mondrian*

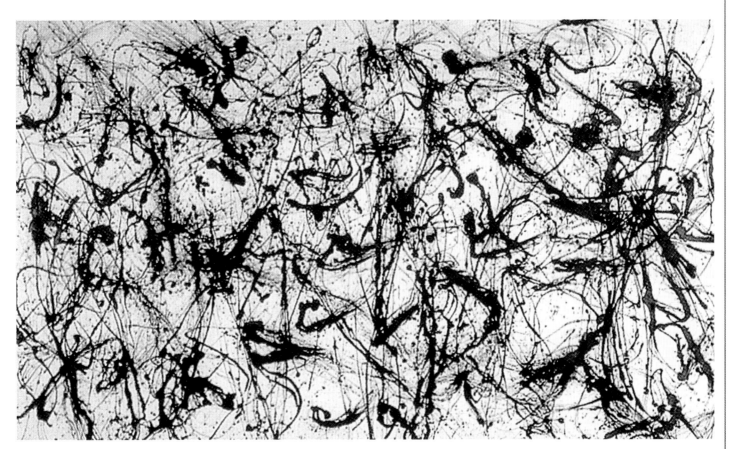

Number 32, *1950, enamel on canvas,*
106 x 180 in/269 x 458 cm.
Kunstsammlung Nordrhein-Westfalen, Düsseldorf.

makes us rejoice in being there," "it heightens, through the intensity of the presence of its verticals, our sense of standing there.")

What sensations, then, does a big Pollock have to offer? You are confronted not with a megalith as with Rothko, or a vertical "zip" cleaving the painting apart, as in Newman – but with a space pulsing with energy, made up of endless filaments, tentacles, and flecks of paint, all springing and flying together. We might be confronting a star map, the nerve-paths of the brain, a tangled primeval forest. These paintings don't seem to confront you or fix you in your place; the feeling is uplifting, elating, a release into space.

When I talked to Frank Stella last year, he described the experience of looking at *One: Number 31* like this: "like most of Pollock's paintings, it just sings. There's a lot of space in it, and it vibrates and everything, but when you see it, you're basically still overwhelmed by the feeling – the tactile and optical sensations being so rich and so straightforward and so simple, and in the end on top of that you know how it was done, and you know how straightforward a physical release it was. You are overwhelmed by the fact that it's possible just to do it like that. It's impossible not to be affected by it. You are absorbed by it. And you're taken maybe deep down with the metaphor, the dream of freedom. When you look at it you feel free. You just feel free in a way that you'll almost never be."

The epic Pollocks offer a mountain top high, but with a dangerous undertone. If *One: Number 31* is the point of balance, in the others, especially *Number 32*, there is violence and frenzy, also traditional accompaniments of a bacchanalia, as well as euphoria. Beautiful

"JACKSON BROKE THE ICE."
—*Willem deKooning*

277

as the smaller paintings are, they are not so overwhelming – though *Lavender Mist*, at seven feet by almost ten comes close. *Autumn Rhythm*, in particular, seems to move in front of your eyes, the tentacles of paint, flickering, swirling, and shooting across the canvas. *One: Number 31*, in comparison, is denser, less dynamic, a galaxy in which one goes wandering, a single, endlessly intricate unity – hence the fitness of the title, which was cooked up long after the execution of the painting, because a prospective buyer wanted a better handle than

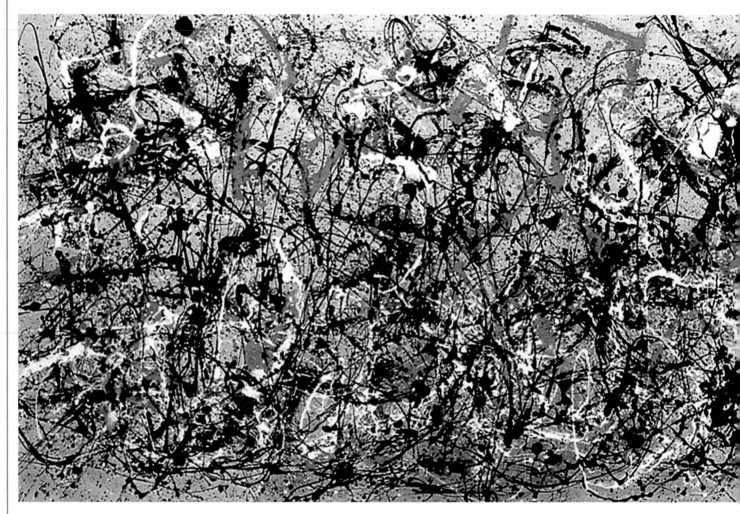

Autumn Rhythm: Number 30, *1950, oil on canvas, 105 x 207 in/267 x 526 cm. Metropolitan Museum of Art, New York.*

one of Pollock's unmemorable, randomly assigned numbers. The stark, monochrome *Number 32* brings to mind much more clearly a dance – a euphoric affair of leaping figures rather than the slow ballet we see Pollock himself executing as he paints in the films of Hans Namuth. Those figures really do seem to have been in Pollock's imagination – the bacchanalian chorus more or less materializes in other works, such as *Untitled (Cut Out Figure)*, *Summertime* and *Out of the Web*.

Like the late Monet *Waterlilies*, these big Pollocks can also strike one as cosmological paintings. Their blend of extreme complexity and sheer happenstance corresponds to the twentieth-century view of the universe post-Einstein, post chaos theory: not a macrocosm contained in a microcosm – everything there is reflected in a stretch of water – but the macrocosm itself. (Whether Pollock had anything like that in mind is impossible to say; chaos theory was not formulated until several years after he died.)

The surprise of the Pollock show, however, isn't the three great paintings from 1950 (*One: Number 31* in particular is among his best known pictures, hanging in the permanent display at MOMA). The revelation is the mural that he painted at the very beginning of 1944 for Peggy Guggenheim's New York apartment – a canvas which has remained at the University of Iowa more or less since Miss Guggenheim decamped to Venice in 1947, unseen by any except those who journeyed to Iowa.

This, just as much as his first drip paintings, was his break-through work (indeed, the exhibition demonstrates that he had been doing the occasional drip and "all over" picture for some years before the main drip period of the late '40s and early '50s). The Guggenheim *Mural* was painted with a brush, not dripped, except for the odd accidental spatter – apparently it was done in one frantic, inspired night and day session – but it has a great deal of the dancing energy, the visceral force of the largest drip paintings. In reality – again this is something one just can't get from reproductions – it is astonishing, a dionysiac release, a thrilling change of gear, as one stepped out of the rooms containing Pollock's earlier work when the show was at MOMA.

It not only looks like a change of gear; for the artist it represented an amazing leap forward. Pollock was not an artist whose work, or life, proceeded in orderly stages. It consisted of rushes of manic productivity, interspersed with long periods of block when little or nothing was done, and the artist spent much of his time drunk. *Mural* was the cause of one of his most agonizing, drawn out periods of total creative inertia, followed by his most extraordinary eleventh-hour escape. It was also the only occasion when someone actually asked him to paint a huge painting. There were a few attempts later on to arrange for a mural commission for Pollock, but this was Peggy Guggenheim's idea.

Or rather, it was the idea of her prescient and luckless adviser Howard Putzel, who, even more than Greenberg, was responsible for discovering and fostering Pollock's talent. He it was, who persuaded Peggy Guggenheim, very much against her better judgement, to look at his work, and finally – aided by a famous accolade from Mondrian – to take him on as a gallery artist on a retainer of $150 a month. As an additional part of the deal, she commissioned the mural for her new apartment, because Putzel wanted to discover

"THE MOST POWERFUL PAINTER IN CONTEMPORARY AMERICA AND THE ONLY ONE WHO PROMISES TO BE A MAJOR ONE IS A GOTHIC, MORBID, AND EXTREME DISCIPLE OF PICASSO'S CUBISM AND MIRÓ'S POST-CUBISM, TINCTURED ALSO WITH KANDINSKY AND SURREALIST INSPIRATION. HIS NAME IS JACKSON POLLOCK."

—*Clement Greenberg*

"whether a larger scale would release the force contained in Pollock's smaller paintings."

Initially, it did nothing of the sort. The canvas, nine feet by twenty, was delivered to his studio in July, 1943. He mounted it on a stretcher, and for month after month did nothing but look at it (there is a photograph of him doing so). Meanwhile, many other paintings were produced, on the absolute verge of complete abstraction, but not quite there (arguably, of course, that goal is never reached by Pollock or anyone else): *The Moon Woman Cuts the Circle*, *Guardians of the Secret*, *Pasiphae*. November, when the mural was supposed to be delivered, came and went. Nothing happened, or rather, Pollock struggled, made studies and sketches, but nothing "made the leap" into the grand scale. Lee Krasner, Pollock's mistress and wife to be, came home frequently to find him staring at the white expanse, "getting more and more depressed."

Peggy Guggenheim became displeased. She set a deadline: the mural must be ready by the day in January on which a party was to be held in the apartment, or else that $150 might disappear. Still nothing happened. The day approached, Krasner began to panic. Then at the very last moment – so the story goes, and it is a story according to the catalog to this exhibition that is supported by the evidence – Pollock began to paint, and worked all night, finishing at nine the following morning. "I had a vision," he explained much later. "It was a stampede ... cows and horses and antelopes and buffaloes.

Mural, *1943–4 (dated 1943), oil on canvas,*
96 x 238 in/243 x 603 cm.
University of Iowa Museum of Art, Iowa City. Gift of Peggy Guggenheim.

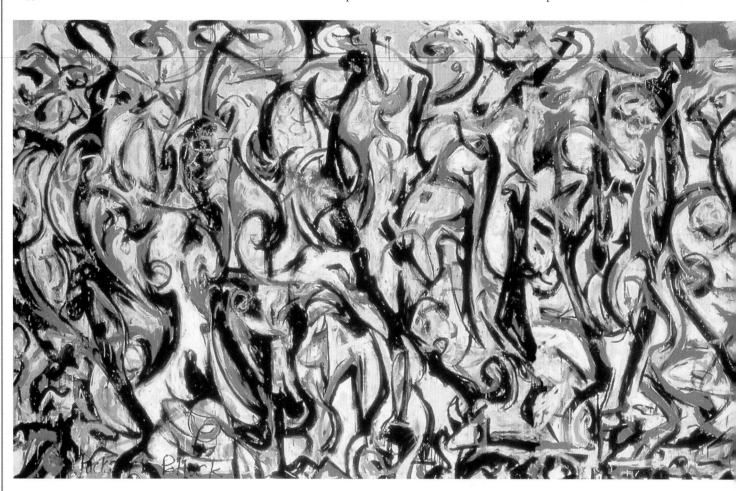

Everything is charging across that goddamn surface."

But that isn't at all obvious when you look at *Mural* (though given the clue, it is possible to find, or think one has found, a rearing stallion here, a bull's head there). What Pollock has painted is not the stampede, but the frenetic energy of it, the rhythmic turmoil. That's what's there on Peggy Guggenheim's twenty-foot canvas, and it is an overwhelming sight – Pollock's art raised at one bound to a far higher power than ever before.

After that, he did nothing nearly as strong for two more years. There followed, as happened cyclically in Pollock's career, a period of depression, inertia, drunkenness, degradation, long periods of doing little painting at all, followed by others of feeling around. In retrospect, it seems clear than he needed one more ingredient. *Mural* has the volcanic energy, of, say, *Number 32*, but not the musical grace or Olympian power. For that, he needed to find a new way of working. He discovered it, of course, or rediscovered it, in the drip technique.

But to understand what he was searching for, and why, it is helpful to go back to the

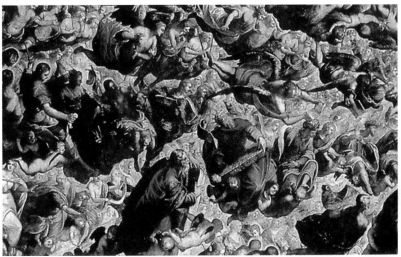

Tintoretto, Paradise (*detail*), *1446. Hall of the Great Council in the Palazzo Ducale, Venice.*

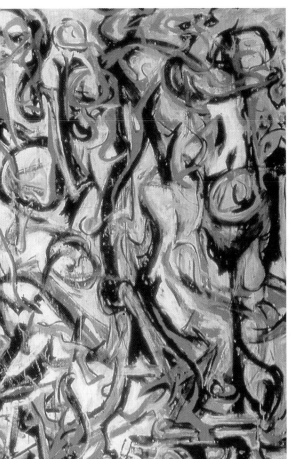

Mexican muralists. One thing Pollock could have got from Orozco's *Prometheus* was a sense of heroic visual scale. The other, in a word, was the Renaissance. There were Renaissance paintings galore in American collections, many of which Pollock certainly saw, and in some cases – Signorelli, Tintoretto, and El Greco, for example – copied during the time he studied with Thomas Hart Benton. But what he couldn't see much of in America, because it is impossible to transport, was Renaissance painting on a huge scale. He wouldn't even have seen much of the largest Rubens, or Delacroix – Delacroix's late *Lion Hunt in Bordeaux* offers an analogy to the ferocious vitality of *Mural*. But the Mexicans were working, in a rather crude, secondary fashion, in that tradition. So too was Benton.

"HE IS THE FIRST PAINTER I KNOW OF TO HAVE GOT SOMETHING POSITIVE FROM THE MUDDINESS OF COLOR THAT SO PROFOUNDLY CHARACTERIZES A GREAT DEAL OF AMERICAN PAINTING."

—Clement Greenberg

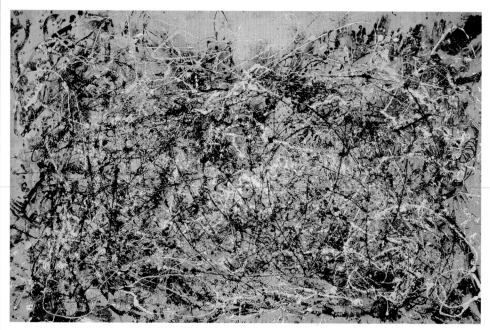

Number 1, 1948, oil and enamel on unprimed canvas, 68 x 104 in/173 x 264 cm. Museum of Modern Art, New York.

"HARD DRINKING TOUGH GUY THOUGH HE WAS, POLLOCK HARBORED – IN ADDITION TO GENUINE PSYCHOLOGICAL DIFFICULTIES – A SOFT SPOT FOR MUMBO JUMBO."

—*Kirk Varnedoe*

If one thinks about it for a moment, however, there were obvious analogies between the Renaissance – or more precisely, the post-Renaissance and baroque – mural tradition, and what Pollock was to do. We tend, casually, to think of Renaissance painting in terms of the perspective box, a stage with orthogonal tramlines shooting off to a point. But that is much truer of easel paintings than of the great succession of murals that begins with Michelangelo's *Last Judgement*, and wall-sized Tintorettos such as those in the Palazzo Ducale in Venice, and continues through Veronese, Rubens, Pietro da Cortona, Tiepolo, and so down to Delacroix.

Those paintings often inhabit something much more akin to an "all-over design" – famously an attribute of Pollock and some other Abstract-Expressionists – an arrangement of figures, and perhaps animals, floating or swirling through the sky, plummeting or soaring, piled up precipitously in tangled heaps on the ground. In the case of the ceilings of Veronese, Da Cortona, or Tiepolo, they rise or circle above our heads (Francis Bacon once remarked on how much painters had lost through the disappearance of angels; they made it so much easier to fill the upper halves of pictures). Such late Renaissance and Baroque

"EVERY GOOD PAINTER PAINTS WHAT HE IS."

paintings, naturally, make virtuoso use of foreshortening, but the other necessary technique is the ability to transform the human body into a rhythmic, gesturing entity that can take its part in a grander design, a rhythmic whole.

To do this one had, as Delacroix once put it, to be able to draw a man falling from a high window before he hit the ground. In other words, the figure had to be analyzed into its dynamic essence, in a flowing line or two. Otherwise, the whole design would never flow. The anatomical details could be added later. Jackson Pollock was taught drawing somewhat in this tradition by Benton, who was, as Hughes notes, obsessed by the late Renaissance. To the end, Pollock was fascinated by all that. At the height of this triumph, in the late '40s, a protégé, Harry Jackson, remembered him talking "my goddamn ear off." He "analyzed Tintoretto in great detail, explaining the composition of this and that; what he was doing was bringing me pure Tom Benton: Venetian Renaissance to Tom. Tom to Jack. Jack to Harry." But if Benton was highly, if unpleasantly, accomplished in this mannerist style, Jackson Pollock just wasn't very good at it. He couldn't quite get it, try as he might. His figure drawing is effortful, clumsy, crudely vigorous. And, in the end, the fact that he wasn't very good at it probably turned out to be a boon.

It is not true, as is sometimes claimed – I'm afraid I've made the claim myself – that the masters of abstraction had been, before they reached that phase, masters of figurative art. It might have been the case with Mondrian and Malevich, but wasn't particularly true of Kandinsky. Of the great American abstract painters, only de Kooning and Ellsworth Kelly could be considered brilliant draftsmen in the conventional sense. What strikes one, looking at the early work of both Rothko and Pollock, is how cack-handed (awkward) it is – though in both cases having considerable power.

Particularly in the case of Pollock, that was probably a spur. He was oppressed by the fact that he "could not draw" – one of innumerable anxieties that hung over him. But, just as the young Matisse simply could not turn himself into a salon artist, somehow couldn't get the hang of it, Jackson Pollock couldn't be a Thomas Hart Benton. Instead, he built up a huge head of frustration, a frustration that perhaps helped fuel his terrible drunken rages and three-day binges.

Untitled (Naked Man with Knife) from 1938–40 is a horrifying picture because it is so crammed with violence and anger. It could be the painting of a madman, and perhaps it was. Pollock was regarded as unhinged by many people who met him, and ended up in an asylum taking a cure for alcoholism a couple of years before this painting was done. More disturbingly, he was known to threaten friends with knives and, in one case, an axe; he ended up killing not only himself, but also an innocent passenger in a car accident that might well have been deliberately induced.

But *Naked Man With Knife* also shows Pollock on the way to solving his graphic problems. It is actually quite difficult to work out exactly what is happening in the picture – except that it is something nasty and aggressive – or how many figures are involved. That is because El Greco-oid musclemen of Benton's world are in the process of turning into a system of arcs and

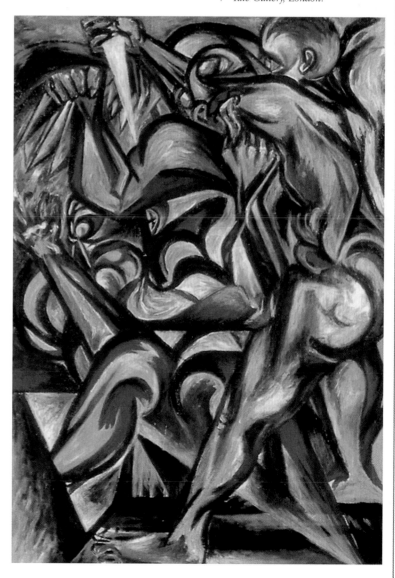

Untitled (Naked Man with Knife), *c. 1938–40, oil on canvas, 50 x 36 in/127 x 91 cm. Tate Gallery, London.*

vectors of force. To work this transformation, of course, he needed hints and help from the masters of orthodox Modernism, Miró and Picasso particularly.

There are one or two pictures from the early '40s – *Untitled (Blue (Moby Dick))*, and *Red and Blue* – that almost look like pastiches of Miró. From him, Pollock learned how a wandering, apparently random line – a doodle, to all appearances – can take on personality and float on a flat background of color. *Guernica*, which Pollock saw in 1939, was his introduction to Picasso, and an important painting to him in several obvious ways – in its hugeness (eleven feet by 25), its black and whiteness (echoed by many later Pollocks) and its intense dynamic drama, expressed by a tangle of curving lines. Its effect is very clear in a painting such as the *She-Wolf* (1943). When Pollock, on one of many trips to stand in front of *Guernica*, heard an artist make a rude remark about it, characteristically, he asked him "to step outside and fight."

Pollock's stylistic progression, like that of most artists, was not a neat step by step affair. He was doing drip paintings, small ones, in 1943, before the Guggenheim *Mural* (*Compositions with Pouring I and II*, for instance). But the *Mural* itself, for all its churning force, still has the laborious, congested feeling of pictures such as *She-Wolf* or *Pasiphae*.

It took another three years for him to make the crucial leap. In the interim, figures come and go – making a slightly absurd appearance in *War*, for example, more impressive in the Matissey *Accabonac Creek* series. These alternate with all over abstractions such as *Sounds in the Grass* of 1946.

But it was not until the first days of 1947, in a clear, cold light just after New Year's Day that Pollock put it all together and began to pour and drip

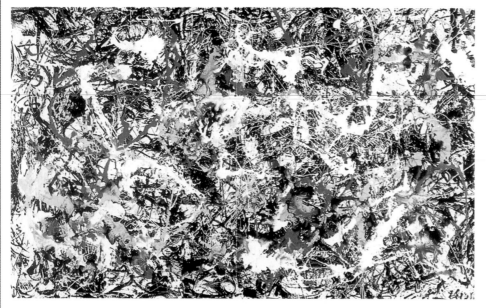

Convergence: Number 10, *1952, oil on canvas, 94 x 155 in/238 x 394 cm. Albright-Knox Art Gallery, Buffalo.*

paint, on a larger and larger scale, from sticks and brushes and chicken-basters. It is one of the most amazing ugly-duckling-into-swan-performances in art. All the effortfulness, laboriousness, the sense of congestion that hang over his early work disappear. He becomes graceful, air-borne. Suddenly he is flying.

A great deal of investigation has gone into the possible imagery that underlies these classic Pollock abstractions. In their monumental biography *Jackson Pollock: An American Saga*, Naifeh and White-Smith argue that, hidden behind those skeins of paint lie the primal scenes of Pollock's early life – the occasion on which Pollock and his mother in their horse and buggy were threatened by a bull, and so forth. Pollock himself told Lee Krasner that, just before he started the drip paintings, he would paint images, "heads, parts of the body, fantastic creatures," then cover them up, "veil the imagery."

In the drip paintings, he told a friend, he was not "just throwing the paint," he was delineating some object, some real thing, from a distance above the canvas." That

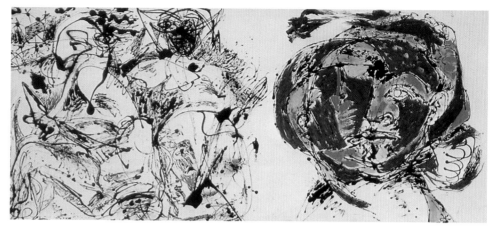

Portrait and a Dream, *1953,*
oil on canvas,
59 x 135 in/149 x 342 cm.
Dallas Museum of Art.

image might suggest another and another. "He painted like a machine," according to Nick Carone, a fellow Long Island artist, "but the machine was clicking away on another level. It was a conscious, unconscious dialogue." Lee Krasner insisted that he never ceased to be a figurative painter, but his figuration was drawn in the air, "aerial forms that then landed." He himself called his paintings "memories arrested in space." Computer imaging of the paintings he carries out in the Hans Namuth films confirms that, in those cases at least, he began with recognizable human forms.

"MOST OF THE PAINT I USE IS A LIQUID, FLOWING KIND OF PAINT, THE BRUSHES I USE ARE USED MORE AS STICKS RATHER THAN BRUSHES – THE BRUSH DOESN'T TOUCH THE SURFACE OF THE CANVAS, IT'S JUST ABOVE."

But surely the point is that the imagery was veiled, that it isn't easy to make out – though the paintings are hugely suggestive of this and that, as I describe above. In effect, Pollock had found a way to depict the bounding vitality of a certain kind of figurative painting, without the figures. In parallel, Rothko found a way to recapitulate the simplicity, frontality and presence of classical art and architecture in abstract terms. Pollock developed at several removes from mannerism and the baroque; Rothko recognized himself in the frescoes of Pompeii and the doric temples of Paestum.

The essence of Pollock's method in the drip paintings was that it was an extended improvisation. "I don't know where my paintings come from," he told Clement Greenberg, "they just come." He may have used those figures as a starting point – as a jazz musician might use a song or blues – but where did he get to? Well, to an enormously more ambiguous, freer place, neither inside nor outside, not merely landscape – which, by the

"IF THIS WORK WERE UNDERSTOOD, CAPITALISM AND OPPRESSION WOULD DISAPPEAR."
—*Barnett Newman*

way, he loved – nor just psychic self-expression. (Pollock said "painting is self-discovery. Every good artist paints what he is," but then he also said, "I am nature.")

In this improvisatory method – and also in his absolute originality and self-destructive dissipation – Pollock resembles his contemporary, the jazz musician Charlie Parker. In both cases, the impossible behavior and amazing debauchery were perhaps related to the extraordinary levels of concentration required by their work ("I have seen him," said Barnett Newman of Pollock, "come out of the studio like a wet rag"). It is difficult to say which, of Parker and Pollock, was the more erratic, cantankerous, or prone to pass out at unexpected moments; but Pollock was the more unsettlingly nutty, the more filled with aggression. Invite him to dinner, and he would, probably after a long period of gloomy silence, upset the table, insult the other guests, destroy the crockery and drive off dangerously into the night shouting obscenities.

Artistically, both Parker – known as Bird – and Pollock flew and flew until they crashed. But Pollock's artistic crash happened before his actual one. It occurred on November 25, 1950, the day that Hans Namuth's color film of the artist at work was

> "THERE WAS A REVIEWER A WHILE BACK WHO WROTE THAT MY PICTURES DIDN'T HAVE ANY BEGINNING OR ANY END. HE DIDN'T MEAN IT AS A COMPLIMENT, BUT IT WAS. IT WAS A FINE COMPLIMENT."

completed, and he fell off the wagon. For a couple of years he had been more or less off the booze, and on tranquillisers. That night, he went back to the bottle, and upturned the table (a favorite trick). After that, it was more or less downhill to the end.

You can see the trajectory in his work. Up and up, higher and higher through '47, '48,'49, '50, as the work becomes more expansive and exultant. Then crash. The black paintings of '51 are figurative again, and smaller – dark, bitter, but still impressive. After that, he was back to finding his way as in '44. One style alternates with another haphazardly. *Blue Poles* is a drip painting – apart from the poles – but one that was forced to work through endless repainting, rather than smoothly unfurling as Pollock's conscious and unconscious worked in synch. It has the encrusted, congested feel of the early '40s paintings, not the lyric flow of *One: Number 31* or *Autumn Rhythm*.

In other paintings, it is back to Picasso – as in *Portrait and a Dream*. *Ocean Grayness* is a return to a compulsive image – eyes metamorphosing into whirlpools – that cropped up before in his career, in *Head* from 1938–40, and *Eyes In The Heat* from 1946. *The Deep* looks more like a fresh beginning; it looks like an all white Ryman from a decade later with a black chasm in it. Clement Greenberg thought he was "on to something in *The Deep*, but just missed it."

Did Pollock's art decline because he drank so much, or did he drink so much because he had lost the thread of the painting? It is hard to say, and no doubt Kirk Varnedoe is right to say that psychoanalyzing the dead is a fool's game. But at least it is obvious that Pollock was on some sort of manic depressive cycle, and that everything he did was intuitive, visual, non-verbal. According to his Jungian analyst, Joseph Henderson, he was "basically uneducated ... [though] highly intelligent, much more so than he appeared, but it was all intuitive. His inability to express ideas went both ways – he couldn't absorb words, and he couldn't use them, but he picked up the subtlest nonverbal signals."

Pollock seems to have been regarded as a bit of a bumpkin in Abstract Expressionist circles, but we might ask how Caravaggio would have functioned in that hyper-articulate milieu. One wonders whether, as much as in his multitudinous hang-ups, the clue to Pollock's great paintings is to be found in that nonverbal awareness. "When Jackson looked at something," his friend Nick Carone remembered, "it was as if he were getting into the pores of it, the most minute molecular structure of it; the level at which even the most insignificant thing, like an ashtray, has life and is constantly moving."

At any rate, whatever the vision was, in the early '50s he lost it. Perhaps it would have returned, as it did after previous periods of searching. But by then, Pollock was too drunk, too ill, and too depressed to make another leap. Many people tried to get him to do so. Very near the end, at the beginning of '56, the painter Conrad Marca-Relli urged him to paint an even bigger painting, bigger than the biggest he'd done before. "Why don't you paint a really big one? What about forty by sixty?" For a moment Pollock was fired by the idea: "I'm gonna do it. I'm gonna paint a big one." But the next time Marca-Relli saw him, he was drunk and had forgotten all about it. It would have been marvelous to see that painting.

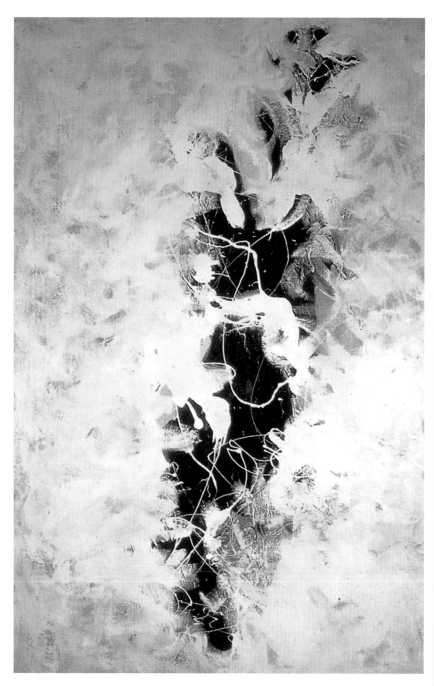

The Deep, *1953, oil and enamel on canvas,*
87 x 59 in/220 x 150 cm.
Musée National d'art Moderne
Georges Pompidou, Paris.

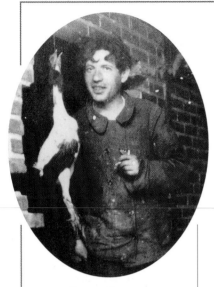

CHAÏM SOUTINE

Born into an Orthodox Jewish community in Lithuania, in 1893, Chaim Sutin, (gallicized to "Soutine") wanted to be an artist despite his family's objections. He managed to attend the Vilna School of Fine Arts and then left for Paris, where he lived in poverty, working in Georges Rouault's studio and digging ditches to support himself while studying at the Ecole des Beaux-Arts.

Soutine painted with a manic intensity related in style to Van Gogh and to German Expressionism. His abstract landscapes and still lifes appear to be expressions of his ethnic background, but he never referred directly to his roots in his paintings.

In 1923, a wealthy American, Albert Barnes, bought several of Soutine's paintings, establishing him among collectors and pulling him out of poverty. His work was included in the 1937 Paris Exposition des Artists Independants.

Soutine served in the French army during World War I. When the Germans occupied France, life became dangerous for him and other Jews. Soutine managed to hide with the help of friends, but Gerda Groth, his lover, was deported to a concentration camp, and he never saw her again. He died from an illness in 1943.

Chaïm Soutine

by Tom Paulin

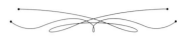

MAN WALKING THE STAIRS – but the stairs are outside in a stormy garden
where they seem as wild and as bent as the trees
trees van Gogh or Kokoschka would've recognized
which isn't to say it's at all a secondhand garden
only these trees are ecstatic dionysiac deeply unsettled
oily and ocher and deadened raw
yellowgreen – dingy deliberately dingy is the look and
texture they have
– remember Faulkner's *The Wild Palms*? well these
are wild poplars or beeches or chestnuts
– but maybe the poplar that rubbery tree is most likely?
and from poplar to populace is only a short step
so the crowd or the mob have elbowed their way in
which turns all those swirls into street action dustups
which isn't perhaps as farfetched as you might think
for as Canetti points out the crowd has many symbols
– fire the sea rain rivers forests corn wind sandheaps
and treasure
so the trees are flames that'll either attract a crowd
or represent already the crowd they attract
which means that the cobbled foamfleece in
Hopkins's *Wreck*
is a street or a square where halfbricks cobbles
bottles and stones
as well as petrol bombs and metal bolts are flying
for Hopkins attended monster meetings in
Phoenix Park
and knew a fellow priest who watched the
Communards
rise up like the rooks in Rimbaud's *Les Corbeaux* –

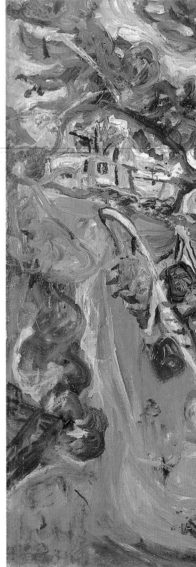

that *armée étrange aux cris sévères*

but if the trees are a crowd in action why are these steps called stairs?

maybe *l'escalier* means inside/outside? maybe it means both? and why

is it *man walking* which I read first as man climbing?

I suppose in both cases it's just a mistranslation – *Man Walking the Stairs* is definitely odd

the *ting tang tonk tunk* of two slightly wrong notes

– like *do a tobacco* for *faire un tabac* that is *have a hit* or *I you ask* for *je vous en prie*

but because I'm in the National Gallery in Merrion Square

I've no means of knowing till I get back home

and check it in the book on Soutine that my pal Jamie has

– book? well the huge *Catalogue Raisonné* maybe then I'll find out if it's the climbing the

walking man's back and his face I can see and if he's coming or going over

what might be a bridge or an air bright thoroughfare crossing a stream or a pond

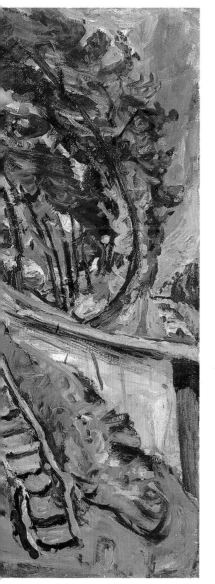

– maybe a pontifex or pontoon but whatever it is it

makes me uneasy

because this stormtossed this in a way nautical garden

has such a closed in such a claustrophobic feeling

and the climbing man is hunched or contorted in

some way

– has he his hands tied behind his back like a prisoner?

so he may be taking a last look over his shoulder?

– it could be the Bridge of Sighs then transposed

to nature?

though of course a garden is more than nature

just as the Bridge of Sighs is more than a stone opera

just as the man climbing the steps or the stairs is more

than a man climbing

in the year nineteen hundred and twentytwo

– like a prisoner or a refugee this man's been told – *walk!*

and everything – stormy trees oily shapes colors

everything in the painting is unhappy is coerced

or coercive

except within it the spirit of the painter that represents

the man

almost as though he's the Wandering Jew who has been

ordered to act the part of a felon

desperately treading a treadmill in a circus tent

that a big wind has blown into rips and tatters

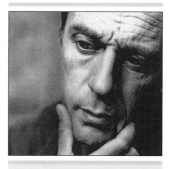

TOM PAULIN
Although he was born in Leeds, England, in 1949, Tom Paulin grew up in Belfast and considers himself Northern Irish. Educated at Oxford, he went on to teach in the US at the University of Virginia and at the universities of Reading and Nottingham in the UK. Known as one of the "Ulster School" of poets, he currently teaches literature at Oxford.

Paulin's first collection of poetry, A State of Justice, *in 1977, was a Poetry Book Society Choice and the winner of a Somerset Maugham award. He received the Geoffrey Faber Memorial Prize for his second collection,* The Strange Museum. *Other works include* Fivemiletown, *his fourth volume of poetry, and a play,* The Riot Act: A Version of Sophocles' Antigone, *staged in Ireland in 1984.* Seize the Fire, *a version of* Prometheus Bound, *was produced for television. His most recent book of poetry is* The Wind Dog.

Paulin currently directs the Derry-based Field Day Theater, and appears as a regular guest on the BBC television program The Late Show. *His next poetry collection,* The Invasion Handbook, *will be published in the fall of 2001.*

Man Walking the Stairs, *1919–22, oil on canvas, 32 x 26 in/82 x 65 cm. National Gallery of Ireland.*

Jean-Michel Basquiat

by Harland Miller

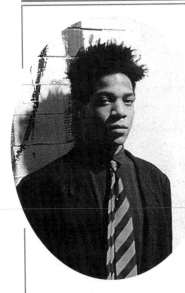

JEAN-MICHEL BASQUIAT
*Basquiat was born in
Brooklyn in 1960 into a
Puerto Rican-Haitian family
who encouraged his early
interest in art. While in high
school, he and a classmate,
Al Diaz, used New York
City's D train as a canvas for
their graffiti art. They signed
the paintings with the
acronym "SAMO," and this
character, along with short
poetic phrases, became their
recurring theme, receiving
attention in a* Village Voice
*article in 1978. The next
year, Basquiat's collaboration
with Al Diaz ended.*

*In the early 1980s, Basquiat
became prominent in the
New York club circuit.
During this period, the
penniless artist painted on
any available surface until
he achieved his first solo
exhibition, held at the
Annina Nosei Gallery. The
result was a commercial
and critical success that
catapulted Basquiat into
the worldwide art scene.*

*In 1983, his work was
chosen for the Whitney
Biennial. In the eight-year
span of his mature work,
Basquiat's subject matter
dealt with black and
Hispanic identity, blending
words and images in
expressionistic drama. After
he died in 1988, the
Whitney Museum organized
a major retrospective.*

I CAN'T RECALL JUST EXACTLY HOW LONG AGO IT WAS that I made my first visit out to old New York, but it must have been over a decade ago now, because I know I turned twenty-one while I was out there.

The New York that I arrived in back in say 1986 was a different New York from the one you arrive in nowadays, and, equally, the London I left from was also a pretty different place from the one you leave now. (Though the differences in New York are probably greater, due to mayor Giuliani's clean-up campaign, than any of the major changes London has undergone in the last couple of years – not least of which, of course, is getting our own mayor, and it seems unlikely that Ken Livingstone's going to have the same sanitary effect here.) So while people in London openly wonder where all the sparrows have gone, so people in New York must secretly wonder where all the bums have gone. I do.

Anyway, I was at Chelsea art school at the time of this first visit. I'd managed to get some dough from the art history department for my ticket. This was on the understanding

> ## "SINCE I WAS SEVENTEEN, I THOUGHT I MIGHT BE A STAR. I'D THINK ABOUT ALL MY HEROES, CHARLIE PARKER, JIMI HENDRIX... I HAD A ROMANTIC FEELING OF HOW PEOPLE HAD BECOME FAMOUS."

that while I was there – or rather it was the sole purpose of my being there – I would research my thesis. The subject was the transition of graffiti art from the street – figuratively speaking – into the gallery. I think I got the dough because back then – even though the phenomenon had been and gone – there was still very little information available in England on the subject. I had a few books: *Subway Art*, *Rap Attack* by David Toop, and a *New York Times Magazine* article with Jean-Michel Basquiat on the cover. He was sitting midst his studio scene, rocking back in a chair and looking straight at camera. His elbows were resting on his knees and his hands came together, fingers touching to make a steeple. He was wearing a *Comme des Garçons* black suit, white shirt, and black tie; he wasn't wearing any shoes or socks. I've still got the photo somewhere, though I don't really need it, as I retain a strangely vivid impression of it in my mind. I was given the magazine by a mature student on our course whose name I'll never forget was Christopher de Lotbiniere. As his name suggested, he was a reasonably international character who'd just got back from the States. He handed me the mag with great gravity as if to say, take a look what's going on over there. At that time in England the idea of a young artist being on the cover of a Sunday was… well, it wasn't an idea even, not as far as I'm aware anyway. Basquiat was in fact the main focus of my own thesis, and I suppose, looking back on it, the idea was to go out there, meet him somehow and ultimately maybe see if I could ask him a few questions. In truth, I hadn't really worked it out.

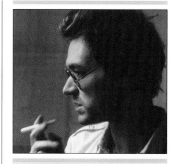

HARLAND MILLER

Born in Yorkshire, England, in 1964, Miller studied at the Chelsea College of Art before moving to New York and, subsequently, living in New Orleans, Paris, Berlin, and now London.

Miller's novel Slow Down Arthur, Stick To Thirty *established him as one of the great comic novelists of his generation. An unconventional rite of passage novel set in working-class northern England in the early 1980s, it captures the climate of the era and the region. Miller's latest book* First I Was Afraid, I Was Petrified *deals with an acute case of obsessive-compulsive disorder.*

In his various jobs, he has been a T-shirt printer for rock bands, a model, and an escort. Miller now pursues life as an artist and continues to write.

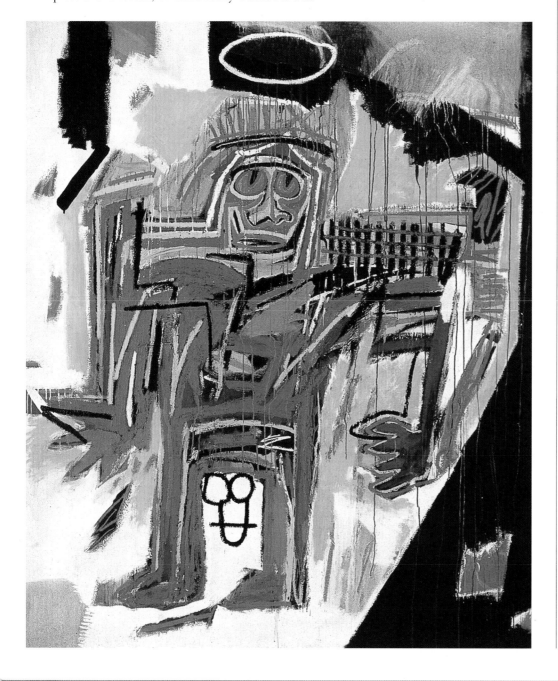

Pater, *1982, acrylic and oil paintstick on canvas, 84 x 72 in/213 x 183 cm. Private collection.*

"IF CY TWOMBLY
AND JEAN DUBUFFET
HAD A BABY,
AND GAVE IT UP
FOR ADOPTION,
IT WOULD BE
JEAN-MICHEL."

—*Rene Ricard*

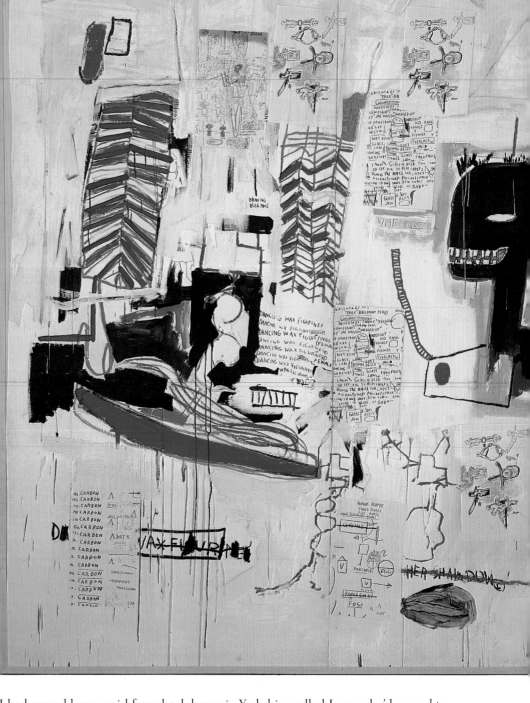

Untitled (Diptych), *1984–85,
acrylic and Xerox collage on paper
mounted on plastic panel,
90 x 93 in/229 x 237 cm.
Courtesy Cheim and Read.*

I had one address: a girl from back home in Yorkshire called Lucy who'd moved to
Williamsburg to become an artist. She'd said I'd be very welcome to sleep on her floor.
To get the keys for her apartment I was first to go to the restaurant where she worked
checking coats. The restaurant was the then – the then, mind you – extremely fashionable
Odeon. It was downtown on West Broadway and Duane.

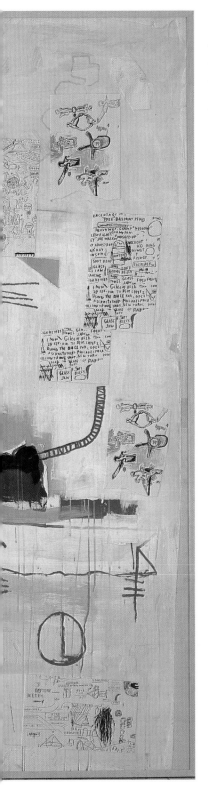

Inside it was another world. Outside it was another world, graffiti everywhere, streets in a bad state of repair, old trash cans characterized by late night crashings and bangings and scuttling rats. A juxtaposition you never saw in London at that time. It was a glass-fronted restaurant, so the two worlds interconnected in some way that managed some extra flattery to both. To describe this spot to you now, well… I could actually refer you to any number of similarish spaces in London, but at the time there was nothing in the way of it. It was strange, then, to

"I WANTED TO BE A STAR NOT A GALLERY MASCOT."

see Lucy making her way toward me, and for a moment I was totally disorientated. "Harland," she greeted me warmly enough, but had little time to chat as she was busy setting up for the evening.

Though the place was still relatively empty, emphasizing its great size, she guided me over to some bench-seating that ran along the length of the shining fenestration, and there she left me in the corner. Before returning to her station she got me a beer, hailing the handsome barman. "Hey Anselm, this is my friend from England. Anselm'll get you a drink," she said. "What do you want?"

"Uhmmm"

"Why don't you have one of these Dos Equis?"

I nodded. I'd never heard of them but I nodded.

Anselm, the handsome barman, opened it for me. "You're from England?" He smiled and nodded down at the idea as he inserted a lime into the bottle neck. Again, fourteen years on, I don't see him nodding and smiling any more at the idea of someone being from England.

As I waited I resumed an article I was reading in the English newspaper I'd been given on the plane. I was reading from the middle pages, holding it out in front of me in the manner of a distant father at the meal table, when a black man's finger appeared over

"HIS **STUFF** IS THE CONTINUALLY DIVIDING CELL OF OUR FUTURE-PAST. EMBRYOS WITH ALL THE CROSS-REFERENCED FEATURES IN PLACE. BUT THE STASH WAS TERMINATED BEFORE MATURITY. I SHOULD LIKE TO HAVE SEEN IT ALL GROWN-UP."

—*David Bowie*

> "HE HAD TO LIVE UP
> TO BEING A YOUNG
> PRODIGY, WHICH IS
> A KIND OF FALSE
> SAINTHOOD."
>
> —*Keith Haring*

the top of it, and, hooking into the spine, gently pulled down the paper. I looked up into the face of a smiling man looking down on me from high up on his bar stool. He was a smart-suited guy of about … fifty? – fifty-five? "Are you English?" he asked me straight out. "Yeah," I said. He swiveled on his bar stool, clicking his fingers up high. "Hey Anselm! get this guy a drink will you – he's from England." He swiveled back round to me and we began an easy conversation.

I was about half way through my second Dos Equis when a good-looking blonde woman arrived. Waving over at my host, she came right up and kissing him eased herself onto the next barstool along. We were introduced, and although I detected a slight accent in her I couldn't place, she had mine immediately. "Yorkshire?"

"Yeah, how did you – ?"

"I'm from Manchester," she cut in.

"I AM NOT A BLACK ARTIST, I AM AN ARTIST."

As she'd looked so American, almost like Rhoda as she'd crossed the bar, this came as a surprise, more so when it turned out her sister lived round the corner from my sister, in Prestwich, I seem to recall.

We talked on, galvanized into what I'd call chat by this new discovery, and then – and this is really the main point of my narrative – the man asked me what I was doing over in New York. I shrugged and said I was over to try and do an interview with a young artist whose work I liked, for my college thesis, I added. I remember clearly how I didn't bother to mention the artist's name, because, coming from England as I was, I felt there was no likelihood of anybody I'd just met in a bar back home knowing the name of any young artist – or any artist at all, barring Picasso and Leonardo da Vinci, or maybe possibly Hockney or Rolf Harris.

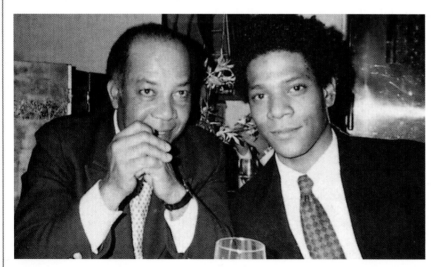

Gerard and Jean-Michel Basquiat, *New York, 1985.*

The couple looked at me for more, and then asked the name of the artist.

"Oh, well, it's a guy called Jean-Michel Basquiat," I pronounced it slowly for them, still unhopeful. The couple exchanged glances and nodded knowingly then began smiling.

"You've heard of him then?" I asked.

"Yes," said the smartly dressed black guy, "I'm his Dad!"

For a moment I couldn't take in, then I think I must have broken into some vaguely disbelieving laughter, which he picked up on and, swiveling round on his stool, called out to the barman "Hey, Anselm. What's my name?"

"What?"

"What's my name?" he repeated.

Anselm, polishing a glass or something, paused and answered, "Er – Gerard."

"No," said the man, "What's my second name?"

"Oh …" he seemed to swat at a passing fly as if to say, "Oh that," then answered, "Basquiat."

Gerard swiveled back round to me, organizing his hands into a series of genial movements as if to say, "Well, what did I tell you!"

I can't help it but I'm obliged to say that I was flabbergasted. It wasn't that I didn't believe him, but seeing in my posture – arrested in what was really amazement – something of doubt, he sought to dispel it by adding, "Look us up in the phone book, we're the only two Basquiats in Manhattan." In my memory of him saying this, it seemed to follow on straight away that suddenly his attention was caught, and he pointed past me out of the window. "Look! there's Jean-Michel now!" He lifted the words over my head and I followed round just in time to see the unmistakable figure of Basquiat speeding by on a racing bike. I remember very well that he was wearing a royal blue v-neck jumper (sweater), and took one hand from the handlebars to wave in at us, then he was gone.

JUST TO CONCLUDE THIS STORY – though it's no longer relevant to my point – the Basquiats invited me to go round for dinner at their place the next night, saying that "Jean-Michel was coming too and I could ask him all the questions I wanted then."

I got pretty drunk that night and ended up back at some girl's place way out in chuffing Brooklyn. When I woke up it was already dark again, I was jet lagged, I'd lost the card with the Basquiats' address on and I had no money, just Thomas Cook travelers' cheques. I never made it round for dinner and I never got another chance to meet Basquiat.

Untitled, 1983–84, acrylic and color Photocopy paper mounted on canvas, 47 x 30 in/118 x 71 cm. Courtesy Cheim and Read.

"BASQUIAT'S GREAT STRENGTH IS HIS ABILITY TO MERGE HIS ABSORPTION OF IMAGERY FROM THE STREETS, THE NEWSPAPERS, AND TV WITH THE SPIRITUALISM OF HIS HAITIAN HERITAGE, INJECTING BOTH INTO A MARVELOUSLY INTUITIVE UNDERSTANDING OF THE LANGUAGE OF MODERN PAINTING."

—Jeffrey Deitch

Willem de Kooning

by Bill Berkson

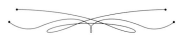

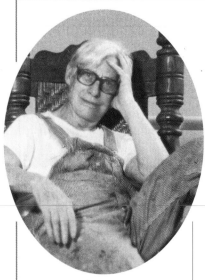

WILLEM DE KOONING
One of the leading figures of Abstract Expressionism, de Kooning arrived in New York as a stowaway in 1926 from Rotterdam, where he was born in 1904. He worked as a house painter and then painted murals on public buildings for the WPA.

De Kooning's themes of the '30s focused on both human figures and abstraction. His semi-realistic figures were distorted and ragged-edged. After his first one man show in 1946 – a series of black and white abstractions notable for their torn edges, splashes of paint, and seemingly spontaneous markings – he became recognized in the avant-garde art scene.

After exhibiting in the Venice Biennale of 1950, de Kooning turned his attention to expressionistic paintings of women, focusing on their roles as sexual partners, as maternal figures, and as destructive forces.

In 1968, de Kooning returned to the Netherlands for the opening of his retrospective at the Stedelijk Museum of Amsterdam. When he died in 1996, he left behind four decades of work held in private collections and respected museums around the world.

Right: Photographs by Rudy Burckhardt of Six States of **Woman I,** *1950-52.*

L OOKING AT AN EARLY DE KOONING CALLED *SUMMER COUCH* IN THE EARLY '60S, Edwin Denby told how, in the '40s when the painting was done, de Kooning had intended "a wind blowing across the surface" to keep the parts of his pictures off kilter while their overall compositions settled in. The painting's furniture scheme admitted an undertow – there were sharks in that wind! – and a finely tethered, wobbly balloon. Similarly, in the teeming *Woman I*, an eventful composure seems the whole point of the image's arrival; Rudy Burckhardt's documentary photographs of the painting at different stages show that the objective was to get the elusive figure to declare herself, to sit still in an otherwise uncertain space. (Not to be tiresomely iconological, but if you know your chairbound Madonnas by Duccio, Cimabue, Giotto et alia, you know what de Kooning was wrestling with.) Once she had plunked herself down, the woman's eyes and smile flared accordingly.

"IF YOU'RE AN ARTIST, THE PROBLEM IS TO MAKE A PICTURE WORK WHETHER YOU ARE HAPPY OR NOT."

Woman I got down without style. The goddesses we know from Western culture don't, as de Kooning said he wouldn't want to, "sit in style." Instead, they take up attitudes. De Kooning said of himself: "I have to have an attitude."

Throughout his career, in writing and talking, de Kooning can be spotted using this word, one of his multi-purpose words (others are "marvelous," "space," "light," "ordinary," "absurd"), and this word "attitude" changes in his usage in much the same way certain

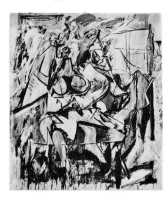
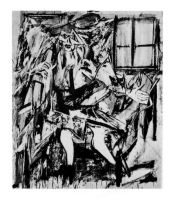
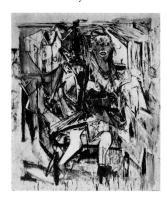

shapes change according to how he tilts them or the colors they wear. In 1949, in a talk about movements in modern art as distinct from his own feelings for tradition and the professional life of painting, de Kooning said: "An artist is someone who makes art too. He didn't invent it. How it started – 'the hell with it,' it is obvious that has no progress. The idea of space is given to him to change if he can. The subject matter in the abstract is space. He fills it with an attitude. The attitude never comes from himself alone."

Here it should be obvious that de Kooning didn't intend "attitude" in the more recent, negative sense of affecting a nastily argumentative stance. De Kooning's sense, I believe, is closer to the one in classical dance vocabulary, having to do with how parts of the body are arranged: for example, lifting the body from the toes of one foot, up and outward, with one leg out behind and bent – a balancing act, like Mercury's classic one, that lasts only a couple of seconds or it has to be regained. Or else, and more to the point (from Webster's Tenth): "a … state of readiness to respond in a characteristic way to a stimulus (an object, concept, or situation)." Here is de Kooning on how he works, mercurially, from scratch: "I see the canvas and I begin." And for the affective part, as he told a TV interviewer: "It's a necessary evil to get into the work, and it's pretty marvelous to be able to get out of it."

De Kooning's great old friend was Edwin Denby, the poet and dance critic who met the artist in the '30s when his kitten wandered off the fire escape into Edwin's loft on West 21st Street, and Edwin then found out who had been playing Louis Armstrong, flamenco, and Stravinsky's *Symphony of Psalms* on a phonograph with the volume turned

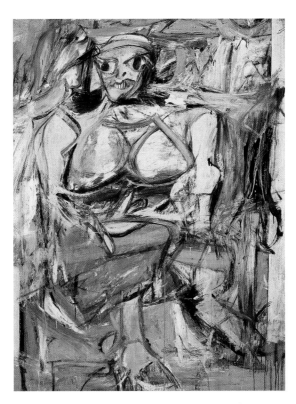

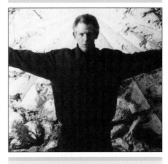

BILL BERKSON
Poet, critic, teacher, and sometime curator, Berkson has been active in art and literary worlds throughout his career. The author of fourteen books of poetry, including Saturday Night: Poems 1960-61, Shining Leaves, Enigma Variations, Blue Is the Hero, *and* Lush Life, *he was born in New York City in 1939. He studied at Brown and Columbia Universities and at the New York University Institute of Fine Arts.*

During the '60s, Berkson wrote poetry, edited, and taught literature workshops at The New School in New York and at Yale. In 1970 he moved west to California where he edited the magazine Big Sky. *In the '80s, he returned to writing, and contributed to many journals and anthologies including* Artforum, Modern Painters, Art on Paper, *and* American Craft. *Since 1988 he has been the corresponding editor for* Art in America.

Berkson's many awards include the Dylan Thomas Memorial Award for Poetry and grants from the Poets Foundation, the National Endowment for the Arts, and the Artspace Award for Art Criticism. He has taught and directed public lectures at the San Francisco Art Institute since 1994.

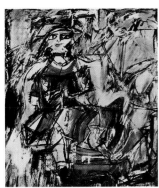

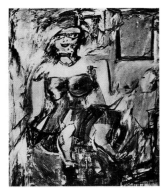

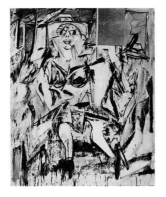

Above: Woman, I, *1950–52, Oil on canvas, 64 x 58 in/193 x 147 cm. Museum of Modern Art, New York.*

way up in the next-door building. Nowadays, the idea of art as a form of social behavior seems lost in the mists of time. Denby's memoir of de Kooning in the '30s, written in 1957, conveys the feeling of simultaneously making and inhabiting a hometown New York culture during the depression years; it conveys the understanding that attitude matters, not as the stuff of manifestos but as something extending from what Baudelaire called "*tempérament*" – an everyday sensibility manifest in the work.

It's my impression that Denby's writings on de Kooning are too little known, or else too little observed, although for many writers of my generation they long ago settled into the category of basic texts. A couple of excerpts should give you the flavor of them:

In the presence of New York at the end of the '30s, the paranoia of surrealism looked parlor-sized or arch. But during the war Bill told me he had been walking uptown

"IF I STRETCH MY ARMS AND WONDER WHERE MY FINGERS ARE - THAT IS ALL THE SPACE I NEED AS A PAINTER."

one afternoon and at the corner of 53rd and 7th; he had noticed a man who was making peculiar gestures in front of his face. It was Breton and he was fighting off a butterfly. A butterfly had attacked the Parisian poet in the middle of New York. So hospitable nature is to a man of genius.

Talking to Bill and to Rudy for many years, I found I did not see with a painter's eye. For me the after-image (as Elaine de Kooning has called it) became one of the ways people behave together, that is, a moral image. The beauty Bill's depression pictures have kept reminds me of the beauty that instinctive behavior in a complex situation can have, mutual actions one has noticed that do not make one ashamed of oneself, or others, or of one's surroundings either. I am assuming that one knows what it is to be ashamed. The joke of art in this sense is a magnanimity more steady than one notices in everyday life, and no better justified. Bill's early pictures resemble the later ones in that the expression of character the picture has seems to me of the same kind in early and later ones, though the scope of it and the performance in later ones becomes prodigious.

In 1951, de Kooning gave his talk at the Museum of Modern Art in New York on "What Abstract Art means to me," in the course of which he famously said: "Spiritually I am wherever my spirit allows me to be, and that is not necessarily in the future... Art never seems to make me peaceful or pure. I always seem to be wrapped in the melodrama of vulgarity." The force of those sentences came home to me afresh thanks to a talk given a few years ago by T. J. Clark in Berkeley on Hans Hofmann and abstract expressionism. Clark shrewdly pinpointed vulgarity as a positive factor in Hofmann's art. He had a lot of fun with it, and he didn't mention de Kooning's "melodrama." It struck me how correct he was about some degree of vulgarity being crucial to Abstract Expressionism – especially to de Kooning and Hofmann as ex-Europeans, and in another way to Clyfford Still, and maybe to early Rothko, as well. In fact, the intrusion of vulgarity divided the New York School down the middle, or more literally at the midtown mark: "uptown" artists like Newman (whose trouble, Clark says, was that he was "never vulgar enough") or Rothko, and most especially Motherwell, were never in the same league vulgarity-wise with "downtown" (or "Tenth Street") artists like de Kooning, Krasner, Kline, or even Pollock (although Pollock was supposed be aligned with the former "uptown" group).

Be all that as it may, the word "vulgar" means one thing to the keen little Dutchman aswim in American slang, and something else to an astute English art historian who quotes liberally on the topic not from de Kooning but from Jane Austen, John Ruskin, Matthew Arnold, and George Eliot. Strictly speaking, "vulgarity" – or call it simply any rude sampling of vernacular energy wafting in from street level – has been a constant sign in Western art of where the action is. It is what everybody knows, as against the cloistered, protectionist assumptions of official taste. Oil paint – behaving as it does – is, or can be, "vulgar enough." As de Kooning sensibly recalled, "Flesh was the reason oil paint was invented." Frank

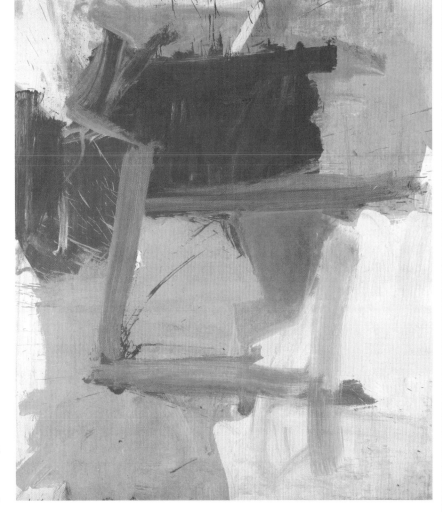

Untitled, *1961, oil on canvas, 80 x 70 in/203 x 178 cm. Daros Collection.*

O'Hara's poems speak of "love's life-giving vulgarity" and argue for a poetry "at least as alive as the vulgar." O'Hara once met de Kooning hurrying back to his studio on Tenth Street with a blue box of Kleenex under his arm: "I've been out buying some environment," de Kooning said.

It was part of de Kooning's genius to invent a kind of English as well as a vocal pitch perfectly suited to communicate the attitude he had at any particular moment. This "beautiful lingo" (as Robert Rauschenberg calls it), a kind of urban American Mandarin emitted in stubby staccato bursts, allowed for gorgeous malapropisms like "I'm no country dumpling" – for "country bumpkin," I guess, but conflating "Humpty Dumpty" and "ugly duckling" – and some wonderfully accurate redoubling. He once told Rudy Burckhardt: "What you do when you paint, you take a brush full of paint, get paint on the picture, and you have fate" (that is, "faith" with a Dutch accent).

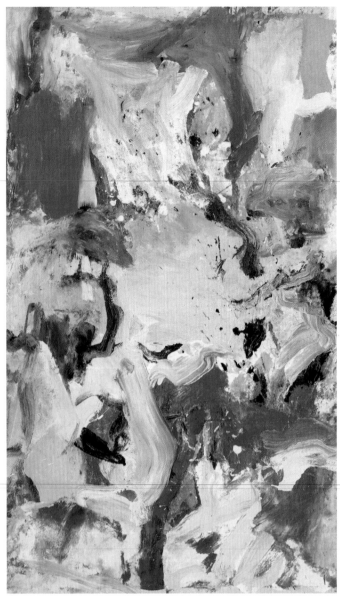

Untitled, *1970, oil on vellum mounted on canvas, 72 x 43 in/183 x 108 cm. Daros Collection.*

It makes sense that George Balanchine, the other artist closest to Denby's heart, would share not just de Kooning's tastes in music and long-legged American women but what Denby called "a love of style" and "force of expression" that could not be divided and that just got more limber with age. Balanchine's neo-classical court dance in *Agon*, set to Stravinsky's score, premiered in 1957, the same year as de Kooning's "highway" pictures. As Denby described it, "*Agon* shifts traditional actions to an off-balance balance on which they swiftly veer. But each move large or small, is extended at top pitch. Nothing is retracted. The ardent exposure is that of grace way out on a limb."

"The subject of *Agon*, as … O'Hara remarked, is pride" – a character trait noted early on in the de Kooning literature. In 1955, Clement Greenberg identified de Kooning's "Luciferian pride" with an ambition that "were he to realize it, all other ambitious painting would have to stop for a while because he would have set its forward as well as its backward limits for a generation to come." Were he to realize it, de Kooning/Lucifer, the fallen rebel archangel – and let's not forget that the name Lucifer means "bearer of light" – would upset the tidy cosmic order of Greenberg's dialectical "modernism," which is pretty much what happened in the ultra-modernity of de Kooning's wayward art.

As the years went by, Greenberg was more and more at pains to qualify and corner de Kooning's achievement. This titanic struggle (for such it was) is paralleled by anyone's attempt to nail down the ultimate quality, yes or no, of de Kooning's individual phases or works. Without abjuring for an instant whatever critical powers I might possess, I would argue that de Kooning's paintings both oddly and regularly

"Flesh was the reason oil paint was invented."

work to defer or render achingly provisional any such judgement. The paintings just won't sit still for it. When the tallies were in on the 1994–5 retrospective, no two critics agreed on which were de Kooning's best years, best paintings, or where his level had, if ever, fallen off. There was much less agreement, in fact a kind of across-the-board stalemate, in discussion of the late pictures shown a year later. A de Kooning can be just as vulnerable as any other painting to context and disposition. It's as if the "slipping glimpse" of his process transfers to the viewer. Your principles just hit the skids.

Susan Rothenberg recently told of having similar troubles with Matisse: "The problem with Matisse is that I can't ever figure out when he's done a good painting or a bad painting because I don't know how to analyze him. I just know that I like the way he put it on and I like his airs and forms." Analyzing a de Kooning puts you up against a certain tenuousness – not of critical standards exactly (he doesn't trouble my standards the way Hofmann, for instance, does) – but of critical timing, or even necessity, and certainly, consistency. Just as de Kooning's pictures contradict themselves internally, favoring the opening out rather than the closing down of what they might show or become, one is exposed to the contrary tugs of one's own sensational logic.

Some artists fill the airs of their eras so utterly that you feel lucky to be contemporary with them. When Balanchine died in 1983, one admirer took the news as proof positive of "the end of civilization"; certainly some phase had come and gone, the remnants of which would never be that full any more. With the end of de Kooning's able-minded life as a painter, one painting culture, perhaps Western-style painting itself as accumulated and sustained in de Kooning's hands, runs out. Unless, of course, you take the attitude that it doesn't. At the San Francisco Art Institute, a few years back, Alex Katz told a group of students: "Painting seems an old man's business. After a certain time you're out of it, and you just paint masterpieces." The sense of "masterpiece" here is professional and precise; it focuses on artistic activity in a condition of impersonal mastery, not on the object as having any value other than as evidence of that condition. De Kooning showed what easel painting has been, can be, and simply is: "Here is the song, it goes like this." Or like one of Denby's sonnets:

> Alex Katz paints his north window
> A bed and across the street, glare
> City day that I within know
> Like wide as high and near as far
> New York School friends, you paint glory
> Itself crowding closer further
> Lose your marbles making it
> What's in a name – it regathers
> From within, a painting's silence
> Resplendent, the silent roommate
> Watch him, not a pet, long listen
> Before glory, the stone heartbeat
> When he's painted himself out of it
> De Kooning says his picture's finished.

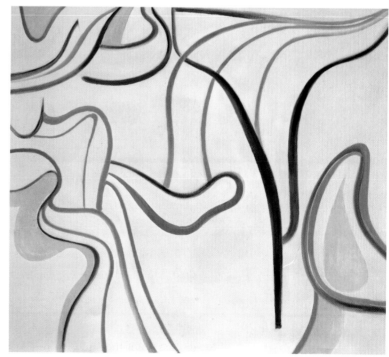

Untitled XIX, 1985, oil on canvas, 77 x 88 in/20 x 224 cm. Daros Collection.

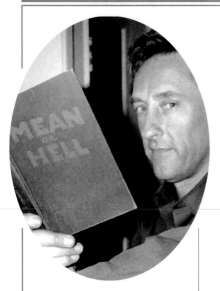

ED RUSCHA
Born in Nebraska in 1937, Ruscha's early interest was cartooning; as he matured, he was intrigued with Surrealism and the Dadaists. After studying at the Chouinard Art Institute and at the school for Walt Disney illustrators, he eventually settled in Los Angeles, where he taught printmaking at the University of California.

After achieving prominence with collages similar to those of Jasper Johns and Robert Rauschenberg, Ruscha later produced paintings consisting of words and images that were simultaneously obvious and ambiguous. During the '60s and '70s, he used unorthodox materials – blood, medicine, chocolate, and gunpowder – to create silk-screen prints. In the '60s, he also published his unique book projects, Some Los Angeles Apartments *and* Thirty-four Parking Lots in Los Angeles.

A retrospective of Ruscha's work was arranged by the San Francisco Museum of Modern Art in 1982. A traveling exhibition, beginning in 2000, went to the Hirshorn Museum in Washington, D.C., the Museum of Contemporary Art, Chicago, and the Museum of Modern Art, Oxford.

Ed Ruscha

by Julian Mitchell

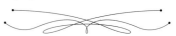

SOMETIME IN THE '70S, knowing how much I liked the work of Ed Ruscha, a film-producer friend brought me back from Los Angeles a copy of *Every Building on The Sunset Strip*. It's 27-foot long when unfolded, a montage of black-and-white photos of both sides of the street, even numbers on top, odd numbers upside-down below. There is no written commentary, it is simply the Strip in all its sun-soaked melancholy, the houses, shops, bars, hotels, filling stations, car showrooms, restaurants, banks, parking lots, billboards. Ruscha must have taken his pictures in the early morning, because there are few cars about and even fewer people. What he was after, he has said, "was that storefront plane. It's like a Western town in a way. A storefront plane of a Western town is just paper, and everything behind it is just nothing." The famous heart of Hollywood, then, is no more than a film set itself.

> "WHEN I BEGAN PAINTING, ALL MY PAINTINGS WERE OF WORDS WHICH WERE GUTTERAL UTTERANCES LIKE SMASH, BOSS, EAT. THOSE WORDS WERE LIKE FLOWERS IN A VASE"

Between two empty lots, and above a car rental agency, is a huge sign advertising Stanley Donen's movie *Arabesque*. It was my first film, and with a microscope you might just be able to find my name, though I doubt it; writers famously don't count for much in Hollywood. But Ed Ruscha is the artist who has best captured the aching thinness of Californian city life. To have my movie in one of his books delights me more than I can say. I feel it gives me real LA street cred, for all its empty worth.

Ruscha was born in Omaha, Nebraska, in 1937, and grew up in Oklahoma City. In 1956, aged nineteen, he and a writer friend drove to LA from Oklahoma along Route 66, later celebrated in song and a TV series. The journey took them through Texas, New Mexico, Arizona, and California. It was the most important thing that had ever happened to him and, according to most critics, probably still is.

In one of three excellent articles in the catalogue of the big Ruscha exhibition that traveled America before going to the Oxford MOMA in 2001–02, Kerry Brougher says Route 66 is now a ghost of its former self. I'm sorry to hear it. Making more or less the same journey as Ruscha four years later, I was awed by its astonishing desolate beauty. The sheer size of the landscape was overwhelming. The light was pure, the heat violent, the colors amazing. It was easy to imagine oneself back a hundred years, a frontiersman pushing as fast as he could through the barren wilderness; or, just 30 years earlier, as one of John Steinbeck's Okies, desperately struggling towards the promised land of California.

There was nothing soft or European here, no sense of a world that had been tamed by thousands of years of human occupation. On the contrary, the landscape was often hostile, the climate unforgiving. But I loved it, I loved the sheer inhumanity, the sense that human

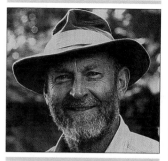

JULIAN MITCHELL
Born in England in 1935, Mitchell was educated at Winchester College and at Oxford, where he began his writing career in 1961 with the novel Imaginary Toys.

Best known as a playright, the prolific writer has succeeded in many forms, including novels, the theater, television, film, and radio. He achieved success in 1977 with the play Half-Life, *but it was the 1981 drama* Another Country *that brought him critical acclaim, including the Society of West End Theatre "Play of the Year" Award. He later adapted the play for film and went on to write screenplays, including* Vincent and Theo, August, *and* Wilde. *He continues to write for the screen and stage.*

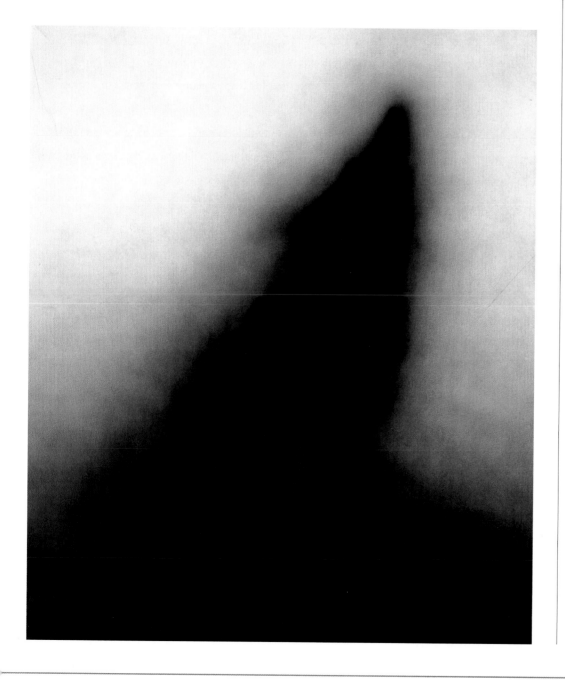

Howl, *1986, acrylic on canvas, 78 x 64 in/198 x 163 cm. Private collection.*

life – and there wasn't much beyond truck stops and gas stations and diners and Mormon-run motels – was extremely precarious. There was a thin layer of concrete on the desert floor, a few flimsy structures above it, it only needed one good tornado – or something worse – and the whole lot would vanish. In the main street of Globe, Arizona, not far from Los Alamos, where horribly apocalyptic things were being done, a sign flashed on and off all night: GLOBE MORTUARY – 24 HOUR SERVICE. And yet I found it intensely exhilarating. I felt free of class, upbringing, culture. My Britishness was vanishing away in the rear mirror with every Burmashave billboard. I arrived in LA ready to begin an altogether new life.

Most painters, faced with the cinemascopic grandeur of that landscape, simply wilt, though David Hockney brought his individual interpretation to *Rocky Mountains and Tired Indians*. (There are also his later photo-montages of desert roads.) And in the '60s Alan d'Arcangelo did some powerful paintings of empty highways seen from inside cars, sometimes through rearview mirrors. But Ed Ruscha is the only artist who has captured the experience of driving what he calls the "continuously moving, mindless miles," the idiot banality of billboards rushing toward you, the

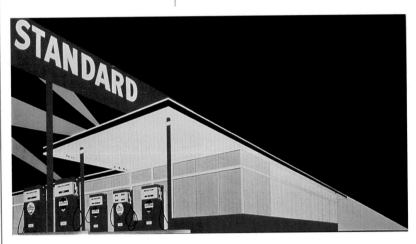

Standard Station, Amarillo, Texas,
1963, oil on canvas,
65 x 124 in/165 x 315 cm.
Hood Museum of Art, Dartmouth
College, Hanover.

spiritual emptiness of the paper towns, the anonymous comfort of almost identical gas stations. He did it through his emblematic paintings and prints of Standard stations, and their companion piece, his first photo-book, *Twenty-six Gasoline Stations*. These have become almost too famous, for little of his later work refers directly to the journey along Route 66. It is far more about what he found when he arrived in the land where the promises usually turn out empty.

Ruscha had seen very few paintings before he went to LA, except in reproduction, and painting itself seemed "an almost obsolete, archaic form of communication." "Newspapers, magazines, books, words [were] more meaningful than what some damn oil painter was doing." Studying fine and commercial art at the Chouinard Art Institute in LA, it was the latter which at first most interested him. He felt frustrated by Abstract Expressionism, then the dominant genre; there seemed nothing more to be done with it. And then he saw his first Jasper Johns, *Target with Four Faces*. It was only a one-inch by two-inch black-and-white reproduction in *Print Magazine* but it showed him the way forward. As Neal Benezra puts it, "In Johns, Ruscha found an artist who had mastered the processes of painting but who had turned that mastery against the soul-baring ethos of the Abstract Expressionists." Ruscha's only other art encounter of equal importance seems to have been with Duchamp, when he met the artist at a show in Pasadena in 1963. He very much liked the ready-mades. Duchamp was "a non-painterly person in a painterly world." After Johns, Rauschenberg, and

"RUSCHA'S WORK
IS NOT BEYOND
A BIT OF
MYSTICISM."

—Kerry Brougher

Duchamp, he felt free from all tradition, free to be his own artist.

The liberation took various forms. As well as the *Standard Stations* series, some with searchlights, some with torn Western pulp novels, some with stuffed olives, he did the 20th Century Fox logo, equally large, equally commercial in design, also with searchlights. As with his versions of the Hollywood sign, it gives off the air of having nothing behind it. Meanwhile he was also doing his photo-books. He claims that he thought of the title of *Twenty-six Gasoline Stations*, and imagined the cover, before he went out and took the photos. (He draws his books, before or after making them, and he draws their contents, the apartment buildings etc., as well as photographing them. There is no sense of one form of recording being more important than another.) This first book can be read most simply as a record of a journey from LA back to Oklahoma, with the gas stations as plot points on a road map. Someone has worked out that Ruscha must have been driving 400 to 500 miles a day, which is about right. But there are other ways to read it, and the deadpan presentation leaves you to find your own. Is it conceptual? Was the driving the work of art, of which the book is a record? Neville Wakefield suggests it may be a secular form of the Stations of the Cross, a

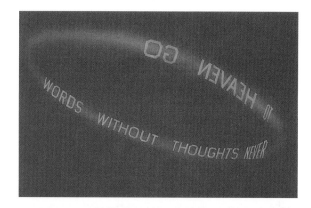

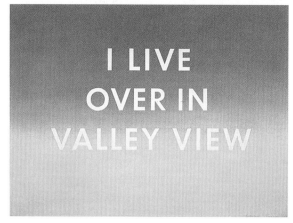

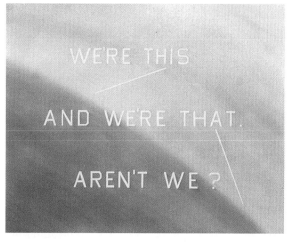

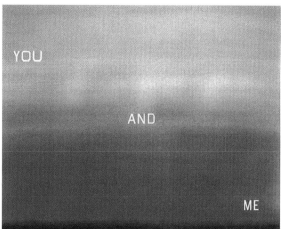

Above, top to bottom:

Golden Words, *1985, dry pigment and acrylic on paper, 40 x 60 in/102 x 153 cm. Collection of Frito Lay Corporation.*

I Live Over In Valley View, *1975, pastel on paper, 21 x 29 in/54 x 73 cm. Private collection.*

We're This and We're That. Aren't We?, *1982, pastel on paper, 23 x 29 in/54 x 73 cm. Private collection.*

You and Me, *1985, dry pigment on paper, 23 x 29 in/59 x 74 cm. Private collection.*

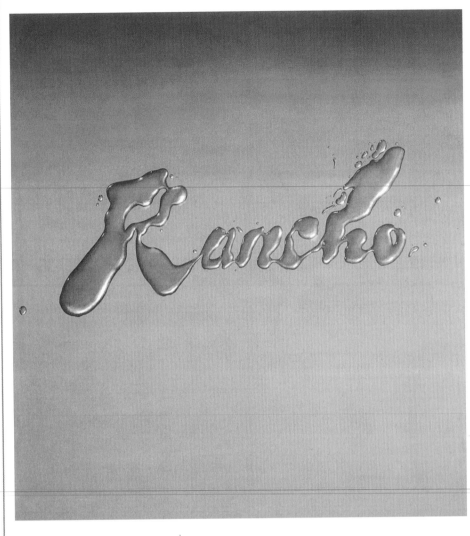

*Rancho, 1968, oil on canvas,
60 x 54 in/152 x 137 cm.
Collection of the Artist.*

symbolic Calvary of a lapsed Catholic. I don't buy that myself, but Ruscha has certainly used religious ideas and images.

Political ones, too – perhaps. For the book *Royal Road Test*, he threw an old Royal typewriter out of a car traveling at 90 mph, then solemnly photographed and recorded the result as if it had been an important scientific experiment. A joke? Yes, of course. But wait a minute, why a Royal, not some other make? Throwing a Royal out of a car window, defenestrating him or her? Is Ruscha saying, this is California, we make our own history here, we don't want any of that old European baggage – out the window with it? Or is this just me, with my own old European baggage? Either way, the book is typically enigmatic.

Thirty-four Parking Lots in Los Angeles, Real Estate Opportunities, Some Los Angeles Apartments, and the other photo-books contain apparently random, apparently artless, usually black-and-white photos of utterly banal subjects. Together they encapsulate the whole spirit of that sweaty, gasoline-tainted, unmanageably large and lonely, but still magical, city.

Magical? Yes. One of Ruscha's teachers was Robert Irwin, who once said he'd almost rather ride around in a car in LA than do anything else. I understand that completely, and whenever I go back I still drive around the endless anonymous streets simply for the sake of it. There's nowhere to go, nothing to see, the driving is *it*. Hockney caught some of this feeling when he first got there in 1964–65 and drew street signs and apartment blocks not unlike the ones Ruscha was then drawing and photographing.

However commercial his training, Ruscha quickly mastered the techniques of fine art, and the first thing to strike one is how much he was still influenced by the Abstract Expressionists in his early work. *Boss*, for instance, seems to be challenging Rothko, with its bars of somber color. The influence of New York, though, quickly evaporates, painterliness becomes less important, the words and their typography more so. People called him a Pop artist, because he sometimes used imagery from comic books, though when he took on *Little Orphan Annie*, it was the "Annie" and its typography that interested him, not the little girl or her plight. (There are very few people in his work, and those mostly shadows.) The Pop label also came from his exceptional skill at illusion. *City* and *Rancho*, for instance, are traditional oil on canvas but look as though they're painted in globs of goo. The celebrated *Los Angeles County Museum on Fire* is like a Renaissance exercise in perspective. Move to either side, and the buildings begin to leap and rear. (I wonder whether Ruscha was aware of Edward Albee's play *Tiny Alice*, in which a scale model of the building where the characters are living catches fire at the same time as the building itself?)

He didn't like being called a Pop artist. It made him "nervous and ambivalent," and he seems regularly and genuinely to have distrusted his own gifts. Just when he seemed to have achieved success as an oil painter he gave up painting altogether for two years. When he came back it was not to oil and canvas but to peculiar stains on unusual surfaces. His rueful joke about beach sex, *Sand in the Vaseline*, is equalized egg yolk on satin; *Very Angry People* is in cherry stain on moiré. Are the materials relevant to the subject? I suspect he wouldn't like to be pinned down. No sooner does he master one form, than he abandons it for another. He even whited out his words for a while, and they had seemed absolutely essential to his art, free-floating images, suggestive but troublingly imprecise in meaning. As one writer has pointed out, they are like words in film credits, huge on the screen, detached from ordinary use. (Ruscha attended lectures by the famous Saul Bass, who reinvented film titling in the '50s and '60s.)

His liking for film, his love of the myth of the movies, can be found everywhere. Critics have pointed out a debt to Robert Franks' *The Americans*, which contains a picture of the tatty back of the H of the Hollywood sign. But Ruscha made the sign his own, invoking nineteenth-century sublimity by giving it a totally Hollywood sunset backdrop, ironical and loving at the same time. The sunset is even more Hollywood when the sign is painted from behind. He uses grainy cinematic effect in pictures such as the *End* series or *9,8,7,6*, which takes its image from countdown film leader, or *Western*, where a pair of wigwams are reproduced as though in a badly worn print of a silent Western.

But words have usually mattered more than cinema images. Commissioned by Miami-

> "HE CAN TAKE AN IMAGE AND, THROUGH CHANGES OF COLOR AND SUBTLE ADDITIONS OF IMAGERY, CREATE A SERIES THAT FURTHERS HIS PARTICULAR BRAND OF POP, SURREAL, AND CONCEPTUAL ART."
>
> —*Laura Janku*

The Back of Hollywood, 1977, *oil on canvas, 22 x 80 in/56 x 203 cm. Musée d'art Contemporain, Lyon.*

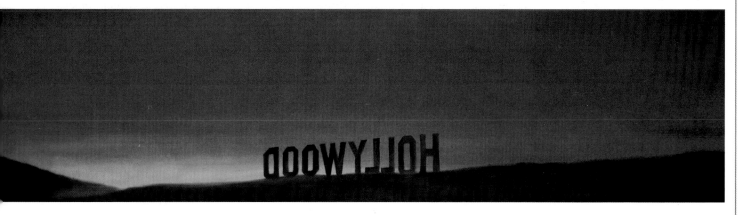

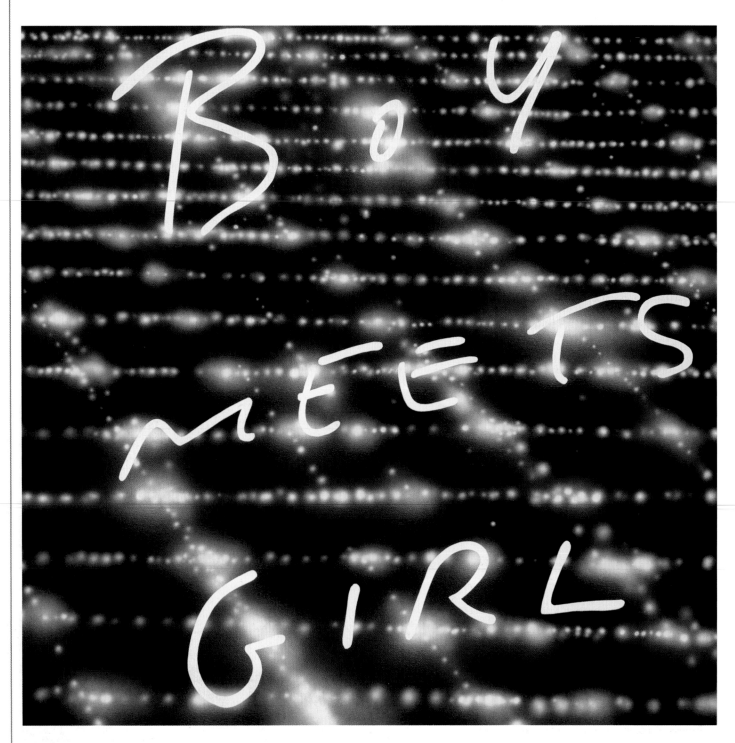

Boy Meets Girl, *1987, acrylic on canvas, 72 x 72 in/183 x 183 cm. Private collection.*

Dade Public Library, Ruscha came up with a quote from Hamlet: "Words Without Thoughts Never to Heaven Go." The words now circle inside the dome of the library, and float through many paintings and drawings, like the belt of Jupiter. They look simple enough, but the context in which they're said is not. They are spoken by Claudius, murderer of Hamlet's father, as he rises from failed prayer. He had wanted to be forgiven, but couldn't bring himself to genuine repentance. Hamlet, watching and not knowing this, afraid God may have pardoned Claudius, and wanting him to go to hell, has just – dramatic irony! – refrained from killing him. The citizens of Miami-Dade will no doubt take the words as they receive them, but I'm sure Ruscha, the ex-Catholic, means them in as many ways as possible.

The black-and-white acrylic pictures he did in the 1980s were another change of tack. They are often wordless, or have the words whited out. They're as skillfully painted as everything he does, very somber and sometimes directly religious. (*Sin* has a cloud covering the sun in what for Ruscha is a very traditional metaphor.) I find these less interesting than his other work, and am glad the man he says comes and looks over his shoulder and tells him when it's time to move on, moved him on to *Boy Meets Girl*. It is a blue night scene, the grid pattern of LA seen from above, defined by street and car lights. The title is scribbled over the grid in white, and you feel all that electricity challenging the stars is just an excuse for car-borne romance and celebratory graffiti. When Ruscha reverted to black and white he came up with *Five to Eleven*, an astonishing airbrushed clock with a long cane, like a fishing rod, apparently floating in front of it. What it means I have no idea, but it's a terrific picture.

The last room in the exhibition has three of his recent mountain peak paintings. They look like large postcards, only there are white words written across them. One just says "The"; another has "Blast Curtain"; the third has the LA street grid superimposed, with "Sunset" just where the setting sun is lighting the top of the mountain. Is it a challenge? Is he saying, the old notion of sublime beauty is dead, we have a new one in LA? I don't know. Enigma is all. Across the room are two very large spray paintings of what could be desert sand, both crisscrossed with other versions of the Los Angeles grid. These *Metro Plots* seem much easier to interpret – a wonderful new version of what Ruscha has been painting for nearly 40 years – the joy of driving, the aridity of the journey, the thinness of the culture when you arrive, the lovely tawdry romance of LA.

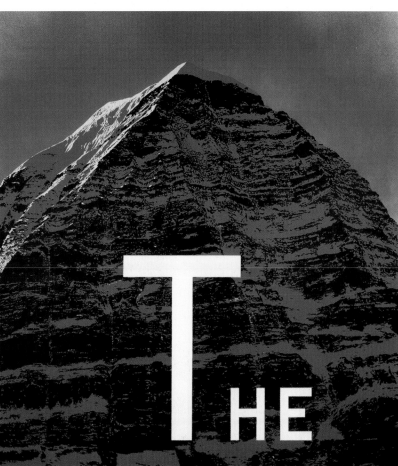

The Mountain, *1998, acrylic on shaped canvas, 76 x 72 in/193 x 183 cm. Private collection.*

Ruscha can draw like an angel, lost or otherwise, in graphite or gunpowder or anything else that comes to hand, and there are many beautiful drawings in the show. But he's ambivalent about drawing, as about everything. Pencils appear in several early works, often broken, as though the artist wants to break with fine art, or is dissatisfied with his dealings with it. An example is the early *Noise*. But the true noises of Ruscha's world are of a car door slamming, an engine starting, a man on his way to somewhere new.

Jules Olitski

by Jules Olitski

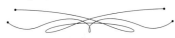

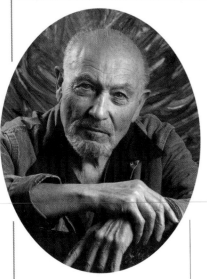

JULES OLITSKI

Olitski was born in Russia in 1922, a few months before his father was executed by the Soviet government. Olitski's mother and grandmother soon emigrated with the child to the US, settling in Brooklyn. Encouraged in art as a child, he eventually studied at the National Academy of Design and the Beaux Arts Institute; he earned an M.A. from New York University.

Now considered one of America's leading color field painters, Olitski's early work was expressionist, but soon he began to experiment with stained paintings, leaving large areas of canvas bare and saturating shapes with dense color. He soon abandoned shape altogether and used rollers and spray guns to create what have been called the first entirely abstract versions of Impressionism.

Throughout the '60s and '70s, Olitski was one of America's most influential painters. His work was chosen for the 1964 Venice Biennale. The Metropolitan Museum of Art mounted a one-man exhibition in 1969, and in 1973, the Boston Museum of Fine Arts produced a full retrospective.

Olitski continues to paint in his Florida studio and exhibits internationally.

WHEN I WAS YOUNG I LONGED FOR KAHNWEILER: MY KAHNWEILER, the one who would be for me what the legendary one had been for Picasso, Gris, Braque, and the others. What a Kahnweiler! He would understand my art, and he would love me – oh, my Kahnweiler could bring tears to my eyes.

Starting out in 1940 it never occurred to me that I would make money out of my art. How I would make my living was a scary question: I didn't feel, apart from making art, that I was much good at anything. Times are different now; given our current art scene, an aspiring artist might well expect a quick mix of fame and fortune arriving around the same time as his or her pubic hair.

For myself, I foresaw tough times, even martyrdom. Like a sponge, I soaked up angst. I saw myself in Rembrandtesque light, while in surrounding shadow art critics skulked, impatient to feed. But Kahnweiler stood by me, and when my art triumphed, as it was destined to do, and finally, finally, fame and fortune and an adoring Jean Harlow were mine, he was there, old and bald as a saint. I imagined Paul Muni in the part.

What I did not foresee was what it would feel like time after time, year after year, for my art to be turned down. In a piece I wrote for Partisan Review in 1978, I said: "There is value in long years of obscurity, if one doesn't go insane or become suicidal, in that, simply because nobody is looking, the habit of fooling around and trying things out gets

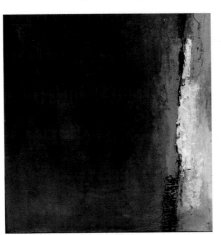

ingrained…" True, but there must be a better way.

As for Kahnweiler, he never came. I've known (and still know) some absolutely first-rate art dealers – my friend André Emmerich, for example – but I learned along the way that there never is, or likely will be, a Kahnweiler. Even the real Daniel Henry Kahnweiler, I suspect, was not a Kahnweiler.

Many years ago I heard someone say: "The greatest cause of human misery lies in confusing expectations with reality." I am a slow learner. My childish fantasy lasted well into middle age – and even now in my mid-sixties, every now and then, I am haunted by its ghost.

I was in my early thirties when I began looking in earnest for my Kahnweiler. I told myself I wasn't necessarily aiming for a one-man show; one or two paintings in a group show now and then would be enough for the time being. I just wanted a foot inside a door. That's what I told myself, between dreams.

I had come back to New York after two years in Paris, on the GI Bill (and had had my first one-man show in a tiny gallery on the rue St. Julien le Pauvre, called Galerie Huit). I was divorced. I had brought my infant daughter to my parents in Brooklyn to be taken care of until, euphemistically, as they put it, "You could get back on your feet." I was close to broke and living in a cold-water flat in Hell's Kitchen. I don't imagine that anyone I knew believed I had much of a future; I sure as hell didn't.

Somewhere I'd read that peanuts could provide most, if not all, of the nutrients anyone needed to stay reasonably healthy. I lived on peanuts and coffee. As I said, I was close to broke. I had an army disability pension, but most of it went to my parents for the care of my daughter. Much as

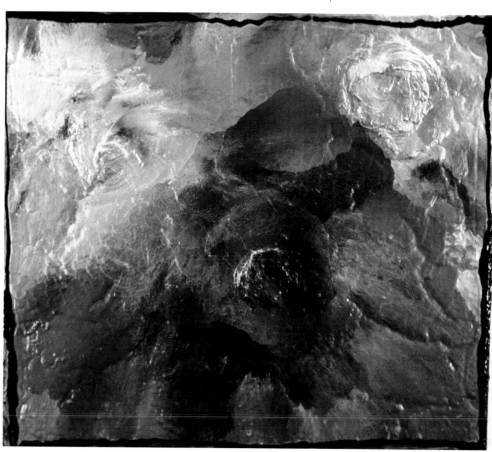

Above: Embarking, *2001, acrylic on canvas, 34 x 40 in/102 x 86 cm. Collection of the artist.*

I liked peanuts and coffee, sooner or later I would get hankerings after meat, drink, and cigarettes. I stole. I stole art supplies. I filled the deep pockets of my army overcoat with tubes of oil paint. I stole canvas. I stole books. I fancied myself a sort of Robin Hood, stealing from the rich and giving to the poor: me. I was scared all the time, even when filching a five-cent Baby Ruth. While I planned bank robberies down to the most exquisite details in my mind's eye, I always saw myself, right in the middle of everything, pistol in hand, fainting away from terror on a cold marble floor.

None of this was fun. Why didn't I climb out of the hole I was in? I don't know why. I was numb. There was a cafeteria on 42nd Street where I would sit at a table all night nursing a coffee; I couldn't sleep in the cold-water flat. At night rats took over; my mattress was on the floor. I'd find book bindings chewed and wet when I came home at daybreak.

I did make a stab at honest work. I got a job as a "barker" standing outside the Victoria movie theatre in Times Square, in a uniform a Libyan general might envy, chanting,

Left: Demikov – One, *1957, spackle, acrylic resin, and dry pigment on canvas, 37 x 37 in/94 x 94 cm. Private collection.*

311

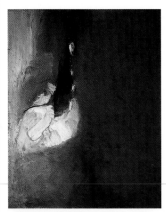

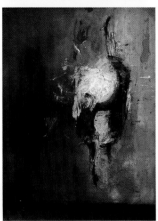

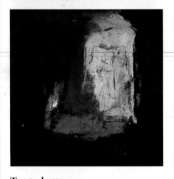

Top to bottom:
Late Madness of Wentworth,
*1958, spackle, acrylic resin, and
dry pigment on canvas,
60 x 47in/152 x 122 cm.
Collection of the artist.*

Whore of Babylon, *1958,
spackle, acrylic resin, and dry
pigment on canvas,
73 x 59 in/185 x 150 cm.
Collection of the artist.*

Molière's Chair – Three, *1959,
spackle, acrylic resin, and dry
pigment on canvas,
71 x 74 in/182 x 187 cm.
Collection of the artist.*

"Feature begins in five minutes … going in now … immediate seating … feature begins in …" I was so good at this that the manager set me to work inside answering the phone. When callers asked what movie was on and what it was about, I made up fake plots: usually about a starving artist in love with Jean Harlow; sentenced to die in the electric chair for killing a bank guard – the gun went off accidentally as the hero fainted – he is rescued by an art dealer named Kahnweiler, played by Paul Muni. People complained that the movie they'd paid for was not the one described on the phone. I was fired.

The time had come to begin my career as a professional artist. I chose four paintings that I could just about manage to carry – two under each arm. Off I went to 57th Street, to try my luck with the lesser-known galleries where I thought I might have more of a chance. I drew a blank, a monotonous blank. "We don't need you, we don't need you, we don't need you." Or the refrain was varied with, "You're good, but we don't need you." I decided to try an important gallery. Why not?

My appointment at the Charles Egan Gallery on East 57th Street was for a bit after ten. No one was around until Mr. Egan appeared, drink in hand. He offered me one. I

"THE TIME HAD COME TO BEGIN MY CAREER AS A PROFESSIONAL ARTIST."

figured this was the sort of thing Kahnweiler might have done. A good beginning that got even better when he looked at my paintings and said, "Not bad, not bad – as good as any of these guys." He waved a hand at the paintings on the walls. A group show was on; I remember a de Kooning and a Franz Kline among others. But that was as good as it got, because he went on to say, "I'm not gonna take you on." When I asked why not since I was as good as "these guys," his reply was as cheery as the sliver of ice shrinking to nothing in his drink. "Who needs you when I've got them?" Again that wave at the walls.

I said something about how I could use some encouragement, that I wasn't a kid, that I'd been around "and just knowing my paintings are here, in a gallery – all I'm asking is to be in a group show," but nothing doing. He wasn't taking on any artists that year.

"How about next year?"

"No."

"Two years, three years – five years. I don't care how long it takes, just so I know."

"Sorry."

"Well, that's just goddamn discouraging."

Poor Charles Egan. I must have exasperated him. Maybe he was dying for another drink and just wanted me the hell out of there. He looked like he hadn't slept much. He took a weary step back and closed one eye, as if to measure me – to measure me for what?

The tomb of the unknown artist?

"Don't bullshit me," he half grinned. "You'll quit painting if I don't show you? You won't quit. I can tell just looking at you."

Sure, I thought, the son of a bitch is right. So what? I'll keep painting but that's only the half of it – where's the other half if no one sees the work? The power of the art dealer was coming home to me; it seemed awesome. I left feeling a bit more alone, more vulnerable than I had just a dozen minutes earlier.

My future took a promising turn at the Tibor de Nagy Gallery on West 57th Street. There I met John Bernard Myers. He was working with Tibor at that time. He did something none of the others had, and I remain grateful to him. Not that he was going to let me be one of the artists in that gallery. Far from it; he said much of the same I'd been getting all along. What he did do, while I was standing there, was to get on the phone and call Elinor Poindexter: "There's a young artist here. I think he's very good. As you know, Tibor isn't taking on any new artists, and since you're planning to open your own gallery, you must be looking for good new painters." He made a date for Mrs. Poindexter to visit my studio. He told me Mrs. Poindexter had been the money behind the Egan gallery but that she'd become impatient with Egan's drinking habits.

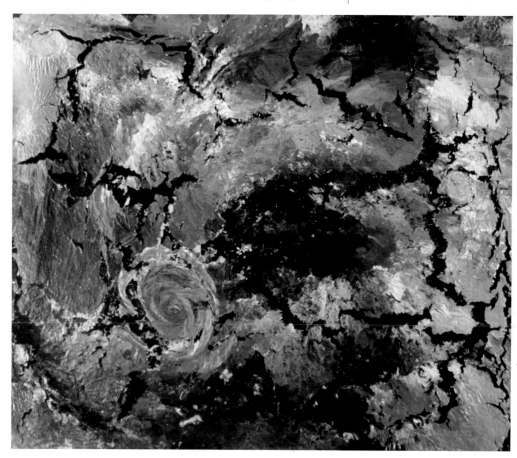

Third Day, *2000, acrylic on canvas, 40 x 48 in/102 x 122 cm. Private collection.*

It turned out that she herself was no advertisement for the Temperance League, which was fine by me. She was a handsome woman with the look and feel of upper-class money in her background. We drank a hell of a lot while she looked at my work. She seemed fluttery, nervous. After all, she didn't know me, and the neighborhood was scary. She looked and looked and finally said she didn't understand any of my paintings.

"I'm frightened. I'm afraid to make a mistake. I'll come back in the summer and take another look. I'll decide then."

Dismaying, but there was still hope. The summer was five or six months away. I could do a lot of painting, terrific painting, between now and then. And who knows, she might turn out to be the Bride of Kahnweiler.

I worked like a crazy man. I worked day and night, often days and nights at a time – without sleep. Gallons of coffee kept me awake; the paintings kept me fired up. Between bouts of work I fancied my future with the Bride.

This time she would really see my work. Enraptured, she would fall to her knees. Finally my art would be seen. I, too, would be seen. Bishop Berkeley had it right: "To be is to be perceived" – or something to that effect. I learned there was a Mr. Poindexter, Elinor's husband. Maybe he would be, for me, a loving older brother, or maybe a devoted uncle; I could see the two of us pursuing exotic creatures in

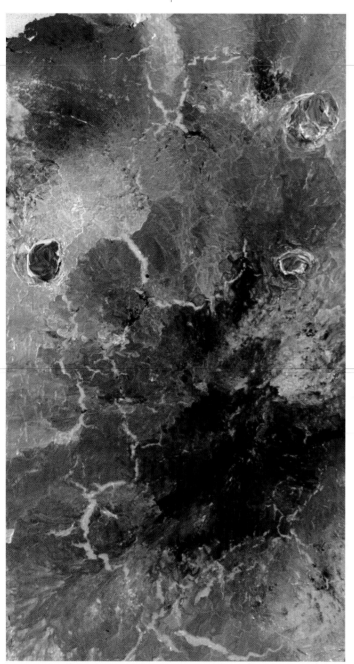

Celebrations: Pink and Blue,
2000, acrylic on canvas,
44 x 24 in/112 x 61 cm.
Private collection.

> ## "I WORKED LIKE A CRAZY MAN. I WORKED DAY AND NIGHT, OFTEN DAYS AND NIGHTS AT A TIME – WITHOUT SLEEP. GALLONS OF COFFEE KEPT ME AWAKE; THE PAINTINGS KEPT ME FIRED UP."

Mongolia. One day, far in the future, the Bride and me and Mr. Poindexter – we would journey to Snovsk and find the house where I was born. All in all, it was a terrific six months until, one afternoon on a boiling summer day, Elinor Poindexter returned. To be or not to be, indeed. I was not to be. She looked at everything and this time she was certain. "Now I know it for sure," she said. "I won't risk showing you."

She tried to be kind. She wanted to help. Did I know anyone? Who were the artists I hung out with? I told her I didn't know anyone. Her face lit up. My not knowing anyone had to be the reason my work didn't look quite right. Now she knew how to help me. "You must go to the Cedar Bar! That's where they hang out – Jackson, Bill, Franz, the boys. Go there as often as you can. Get to know the boys. Become part of the scene. That's how it's done. And your paintings will change."

I knew about the Cedar Street Bar. I had long ago decided not to go there – for much the same reasons she was now urging me to.

As things turned out, about five or six years later, Ellie Poindexter did become my dealer. I was with her gallery for seven years. She became dear to me and always will be, but watching her go down the steps that day and out of the building, I cursed silently. The letdown of that day stayed with me a long time. I pretty much gave up. I left the flat only to go to the movies along Times Square. In and out, one movie after another; three got me through the night. I drank a lot of booze. I slept in my army overcoat, my legs and feet inside the sleeves of my field jacket. I put newspaper inside my shoes to cover the holes. A dismal enough state, capped as it was by the Bride of Kahnweiler fiasco. There were times in that apartment when I might have gone out the window if I hadn't lived on the second floor.

One day a boyhood friend named Hal Dareff turned up. He had an idea. Why not use the two years I had left on the GI Bill by going to New York University. "Get a degree, become a college professor." I could then reclaim my kid, maybe remarry, and have more kids, at the least I could live better. The idea that I could become a college professor was a laugh. Me? As a kid I was regarded as the family dummy, the moron; my future, they told me, was the Bowery or death in the electric chair. Sometimes both.

Even so, the idea of escaping my lot for two years by going to school and getting the GI Bill money was attractive. Incredibly enough, all that Hal Dareff had proposed became real: Master's degree, new wife, reclaimed daughter, college professor. It was a new life. I sat among the professors at faculty meetings that seemed insane and endless, and thought of suicide. I drank myself silly.

I became chairman of the art department at a liberal arts college out on Long Island called C. W. Post, and we, my wife, reclaimed kid, and a new baby daughter, were living in a handsome old stone house in Northport. I was pushing thirty-six.

I had but one experience with an art dealer during the time I was taking courses at New York University. To save time and subway fares, I had moved into an attic on Greene Street, a stone's throw from the downtown NYU campus. I loved going to school. I painted at night. Reginald Pollack, an artist I had met in Paris, brought his brother Lou to my attic. Lou was the director of the Peridot Gallery, a very good gallery. I liked Lou. A slow-speaking, sensitive, meditative type, he definitely had the Kahnweiler stamp about him. His gallery had New Talent shows from time to time. He said something of mine would be featured in his next New Talent show. After he left, I waltzed around the attic, but Lou never put on another New Talent show. A few years later he died.

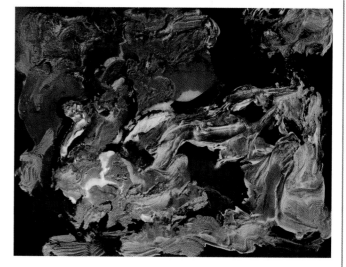

Deep Socket, *1999, wb acrylic on canvas, 30 x 40 in/76 x 102 cm. Collection of the artist.*

"WHAT HE REALLY BELIEVED WAS THAT DRAWING WAS EVERYWHERE, IN EVERY FLECK AND SPATTER AND LOOP AND DRIP OF THE PAINTING."

—*Matthew Collings*

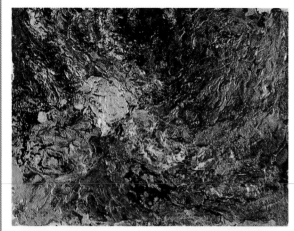

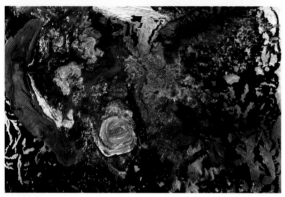

Top: **Charge of Angels**, 2000,
acrylic on canvas,
20 x 26 in/51 x 66 cm.
Collection of the artist.

Above: **Origins Snovsk**, 2000,
acrylic on canvas,
45 x 71 in/114 x 180 cm.
Collection of the artist.

I grew a thick skin. Maybe it was a defence, a kind of protective device. No one gave a damn – I wouldn't give a damn. It would not matter to me if you did or didn't go for my work. I had nothing to lose. Not that I gave up on my future; like a horse with blinders, I would keep going. I imagined a dedicated handful of collectors, types like the Cone sisters, Gertrude and Leo Stein, Shchukine and Morosov, Barnes, Quinn, etcetera. I imagined Clement Greenberg writing about me in Partisan Review.

With a suddenness I had not foreseen, I had become respectable. More to the point, I had a studio and money for art materials. I felt I was painting better than ever. Why not give Kahnweiler another shot? Back to 57th Street and the galleries on Madison Avenue. Once again the same old thing. Nothing. One day I had an appointment with Betty Parsons. She wasn't in. Her secretary looked at a pad. "Gee, I'm sorry. Miss Parsons must have forgotten. She's gone for the day."

Not the end of the world, I said to myself as I waited at the elevator.

At that time the Parsons Gallery was on the same floor as Sidney Janis's. The door opened and Sidney Janis stepped out. Maybe I would get lucky. I told him how I happened to be there and said, "If you have a minute, Mr. Janis, would you look at my paintings?"

"I haven't looked at my mail yet," he said and kept going.

On the elevator down, I thought he could have said: "Why don't you make an appointment?"

On the sidewalk I swore I would never put myself in that position again. Never again would I ask an art dealer to look at my work. Terrific! I felt lifted up. Free. I drove home to Northport. In my studio that night, looking around, I said to myself: so what do you do now?

I thought about that a lot. How come I'm always turned down, even when they say I'm good? Is it something in my art? In me? What would convince them? So many years of trying and nothing had worked.

I figured it had to be me. Somehow I was in my own way. Yes, that was it. It wasn't the dealers: they lacked conviction, they couldn't necessarily tell good from bad. They operated on some other level; it would take more than art to convince them. None of this would apply to my Kahnweiler – but where was the elusive son of a bitch? Unconventional measures were called for – but what?

Was there something I could have done – something I could not do? That was it! I could not put my work before an art dealer and say: "Hey! Look at these paintings. This is great art. You have to show my work." No, I could not say such things. I'd rather boil a goat. But if I wasn't talking about myself – if I was talking about someone else …? I had my answer.

What I had arrived at was a crazy answer, bizarre – though it seemed profoundly reasonable at the time. I had tried the straight and usual, the conventional ways. I had a stomach full of sour No's. I would fight the dealers in my own way and I would win. I hardly thought of anything else. I had to have my one man show: one shot at it was all I asked.

I would invent an artist; the more dramatic his history, the better. A kind of ghost artist: no one could ever see him in the flesh but me. I was probably certifiably mad at that time; I hardly recognize myself.

So then: Jevel Demikov, a talented young Soviet artist whose socialist realist canvases had attracted the attention of Joseph Stalin. He became Stalin's protégé. Thanks to Stalin, Demikov had been permitted to spend the year of 1950 in Paris to further refine his skills at the Académie des Beaux Arts. We happened to meet. We became friends. I took him around to the galleries that showed modern art. Demikov was enthralled and seduced. His paintings turned abstract.

Back home in Moscow he painted his pictures of tractors, buxom maidens, stalwart workers, Red Army heroes; at night in secret he made forbidden art. Demikov showed his abstract paintings to some of his fellow artists. Soon there were underground cells of artists

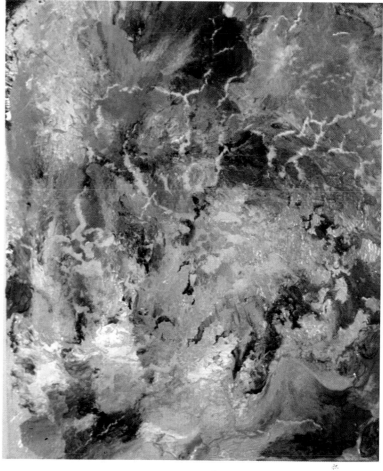

On the First Day, *2000, acrylic on canvas, 48 x 40 in/122 x 102 cm. Private collection.*

making what they took to be Modern Art. Like a rampant cancer the cells spread all over the USSR. The OGPU sniffed and scowled. They went looking for Demikov, enemy of the people. He fled. Hidden in a barrel, he was put ashore in Brooklyn. He had no one to help him but me. I had to help. The Soviet secret police were on his trail. If they got him, Demikov said, they would kill him on the spot. Stalin himself was demanding the head of Demikov. I hid my friend in a cellar. Once a week I drove to Brooklyn and brought him food and drink and paint and canvas. He was painting away like a man obsessed. I could hardly believe what I saw. Here was a breakthrough that would make the New York art scene spit.

My plan developed; there were a couple of offshoots. One involved Alfred Barr, the director of the Museum of Modern Art. I wrote him about the plight of Demikov. Mr. Barr wrote back, saying he was interested and asked for photographs of the work. I sent photographs. He wrote and said he was now very interested and would I please bring some of the paintings to his office, and the artist himself. As things turned out, I didn't need to follow through. When I finally did get a gallery to give me a show I wrote Mr. Barr that Demikov had disappeared, probably murdered. A last-resort plan called for hiring an actor, fluent in Russian. He would be interviewed by Time and Life magazine reporters. He would wear a paper bag over his head with holes cut out for his eyes and mouth. Through an interpreter he would tell his story. Demikov's paintings would be reproduced. Maybe something would happen.

I didn't have to use the back-up plan.

This is what I did: at the college I scheduled an exhibition called "L'Ecole de Paris Aujourd''hui." I borrowed paintings for the exhibition from some of the galleries in New York, any one of which would suit my purpose just fine. In the late 1950s in New York City it was amazingly easy to arrange such a show. None of these dealers knew me; the college was out of town, new, barely known. As far as I know they took me at my word. I could have walked off with all that treasure. It was a lovely show. And there, cheek by jowl with the stars of Paris, was my Russian. I had an announcement of the exhibition printed, listing all the artists.

"WITH A SUDDENNESS I HAD NOT FORESEEN, I HAD BECOME RESPECTABLE."

When the show ended I drove to the city to return the paintings. My first stop, as it happened, was the Alexander Iolas Gallery. Mr. Iolas was expecting me. I handed him his paintings; I think one was a Mathieu and one a Dubuffet. He asked about the exhibition. I said it had been a beautiful show and would he like a copy of the announcement for his files? Yes, he would.

"Ah," he says, reeling off the list of artists, "Matisse, Picasso, Miró, Léger, Dubuffet, de Stael…" He stops short and looks at me. "Who is this Demikov?"

"Ah," I say, "of course you don't know him. He's unknown in America." I tell Mr. Iolas Demikov's story: how he had been seduced by abstract art, his return to the USSR, Stalin's tantrum, and the barrel ending up in Brooklyn and, "At this moment, Mr. Iolas, a great artist is hiding in a cellar in Brooklyn. You must look at his work."

"Well," he says, "I'm sympathetic. I'd like to help. Could you bring some paintings?"

I tell him I have four Demikovs from the exhibition in my Microbus. "I'm on my way to Brooklyn to return them. I'll bring them in."

"Bring them in."

I bring the paintings in and lean them against a wall.

He looks closely at each painting. He looks and looks. I'm standing behind him. Why is he taking so long? What does he see? What is he thinking? I'm prepared for a No. I'm telling myself: this is just the first stop. There are still other galleries … sure. And if they all turn me down? Then what? Then I'll get the masked Russian and Time and Life… Jesus I'm getting old standing here.

Finally he stands, straightens up, turns around, looks me in the eye, and says: "You're right. He's a genius. We must have a show."

I'm stunned. Can it be? This slim, dark, olive-skinned Greek dressed in a black, elegantly-cut Italian suit – my Kahnweiler? I want to throw my arms around his neck. I want to kiss him. All I can manage to say is: "Demikov will be ecstatic. Ecstatic." I keep saying it: "Ecstatic. Ecstatic."

Mr. Iolas is businesslike. "To have an exhibit, I will need more paintings."

I tell him Demikov paints day and night. "I'll bring a truckful of paintings. Big ones. Even better than these. You'll see. Masterpieces. I can't wait to tell Demikov. He'll be ecstatic, ecstatic. What a wonderful thing..." I'm going on, out of control.

"When can I meet the artist?"

I'm stopped in my tracks. "Good God," I say, "don't you understand?" I'm talking fast about Stalin and his thugs. "They're out there. They never give up. Demikov won't come out. He won't come out. Impossible. You want to get him killed?"

Mr. Iolas is looking a bit uneasy, a bit goggle-eyed. He's giving me a funny look. "I must meet the artist," he says.

"All you need are the paintings," I say. "I will bring the paintings. I will be the go-between."

"What do you want out of this?" I don't like the edge in his voice.

"Me? Nothing. I'm a professor. I'm not even an artist. I teach art history. You think I want money?" I try a disdainful chuckle, but it gets away from me and comes out sounding like the bray of a donkey.

He's looking at me the way you'd look at someone selling fake Persian rugs. I suggest a PO box in Demikov's name (though how Demikov can use it if he never leaves the cellar, I hope Mr. Iolas won't ask). "If there are any paintings sold, you can send him the money. I," I say solemnly, "am only trying to help my friend, a great artist."

Mr. Iolas has had enough. "No!" he says. "No! I've never dealt with a living artist that I did not know personally. I won't deal with you! Tell your friend I am not political. He has nothing to fear from me. Tell him I will meet him anywhere he chooses – in the middle of the Brooklyn Bridge at midnight, if he wishes – but without our meeting, fine artist though he is, there will be no show."

It's all slipping away. My head feels like a popcorn machine operating at highest speed. What to do? Tell the truth. There's no other way. But I can't say it in English. I give a sigh and say, "Alors, Demikov, c'est moi." Mr. Iolas answers with a shake of his shoulders and his palms up, and a sound, something like "Pouuuuf." I think at that moment Mr. Iolas was not sure as to who I was: an escaped Russian or a lunatic American.

About eight months later Mr. Iolas gave me my first New York show.

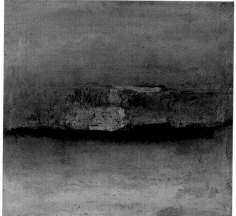

Demikov – Two, *1957, spackle, acrylic resin, and dry pigment on canvas, 22 x 24 in/56 x 61 cm. Collection of the artist.*

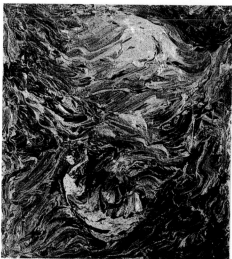

Rude Passage, *2000, wb acrylic on matboard, 22 x 21in/57 x 52 cm. Collection of the artist.*

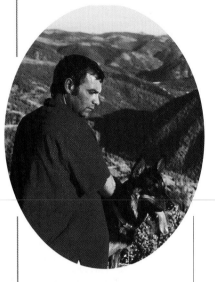

WES MILLS

Born in Tucson, Arizona, in 1960, Mills spent much of his youth in eastern Oregon on his family's orchard. His family later moved to Montana where Mills, encouraged by his junior and senior high school art teachers, began to draw, as he remembers, a lot of trees.

Mills moved to New York City in 1982 with the intention of pursuing an art career but, discouraged with the New York gallery scene, he ceased making art, working instead as a cabinetmaker and carpenter. After moving to Taos, New Mexico, in 1993, Mills began to draw again.

His work has been compared to the evocative work of Agnes Martin and to the gestural quality of Cy Twombly's. Mills' minimalist, densely drawn, small-scale works contain notations that only suggest the real world. The drawings seem to be personal meditations, that are a blend of what one critic described as "ethereal delicacy and authoritative presence," presented without title or explanation.

Mills' work has shown widely in the US and abroad. He now lives and works in Missoula, Montana.

Wes Mills

by Lance Esplund

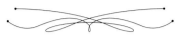

MAKING ART IS ESSENTIALLY A SOLITARY ACTIVITY. The isolation of the studio forces that difficult interaction between the self and possibility. The reward is that each decision, if weighed honestly, can bring an artist closer to a personal truth, whatever that might be. Freud believed that the process transforms aspects of the artist's unconscious (the psyche, or soul) into physical form, form that has the power to reveal truths and relieve anxieties in both the artist and viewer. Kafka likened making art to prayer: "[Both] are passionate acts of will. ... Art like prayer is a hand outstretched in the darkness, seeking for some touch of grace which will transform it into a hand that bestows gifts." In ancient Egypt, where an artist was working under the strictest of canons, all rules

> **"I LIKE THINKING ABOUT THE STATE OF NOT KNOWING AND HOW IT IS MOST NEAR TO THAT OF KNOWING. DRAWING CAN BE THE MOMENT BETWEEN THE TWO."**

were useless if the carver could not summon the depths of his own conflicted experience in the world. Only then could he both fully articulate and bring into harmony the extreme tensions of frontal, profile, and aerial views within the same composition. Even in the grand studio of Rubens, after his assistants had busied his canvases with a multitude of figures, flora, and fauna, it was Rubens, the singularly sensitive and knowing artist, who with his brush alone brought them all to life.

Making art is also about paring down, getting at essentials. Each choice an artist makes, though it may bring him closer to a purer state, also illuminates what will never be. In the drawings of Wes Mills, one is constantly aware of what has been lost — so much so that the initial feeling of the work is a kind of palpable emptiness or sorrow. A Mills drawing slows one down. Each unique, wispy image is imbued with a weight larger than its very small scale and lightness first suggest. The works vary greatly in their look and feel, but each piece conveys the one-to-one intimacy of a handwritten letter. As I stood with Mills last July in his Missoula, Montana, studio, going through stacks of drawings, I felt a surrender to, and from, the work, as if I were made privy to someone's personal secrets.

In his drawings of the early 1990s, Mills was including words and recognizable objects that move back and forth between personal symbol, pictograph, and sign. These obsessively built-up surfaces resemble ancient wall carvings, children's scratchboards, and the drawings of the insane. The pictures have a haunting playfulness and are compelling enough to hold one's attention, but they remain vague narratives impossible to decipher, that is, unless the viewer is aware of the traumatic stories they tell. In the work of the last five years, Mills has been divining forms as much as he has been making pictures, drawing with his gut intuition, as he attempts to open up ever-smaller, internal doors. It is as if he has distilled the essences of, or feelings evoked by, those earlier images, and abstracted them into vapors and meandering lines.

In these recent drawings, Mills has been working on small, mostly square sheets of white or off-white paper. All of the drawings I have seen have been a foot or under in any direction, and the tiniest of pieces seem most at home when held in the palm of your hand, where one feels the need to treat them delicately. Some of the drawing surfaces look porous, like gray stone; others have a bluish-silver cast, like metal; some have a built-up, soft-white density, resembling shell or plaster.

The drawings are spare. Most are made with layers of graphite and white powdered pigment. At times, Mills draws with water and gum arabic or by cutting into the paper. The cuts, which he makes to better unite the space between him, the drawing and the viewer, can have a painful directness. Often, one is first aware of the emptiness of the white field, and then of the simple,

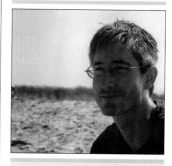

LANCE ESPLUND
Writer Lance Esplund was born in Dodge City, Kansas, in 1962. He was educated at the Kansas City Art Institute and, after moving to New York in 1985, at Queens College. He studied to be a painter and, indeed, painted for a time before turning his attention to writing full time.

He is a critic for Art in America *and writes the New York Letter for* Modern Painters. *His subjects are diverse, ranging from the pyramids to the graphic arts. Esplund has written for* The Threepenny Review, *the* Yale Review, *and Condé Nast's* House and Garden, *among other publications, and for* The New Republic Online.

Since 1990, Esplund has taught at the Parsons School of Design. He currently lives in Brooklyn, New York, with the painter Evelyn Twitchell, and still draws.

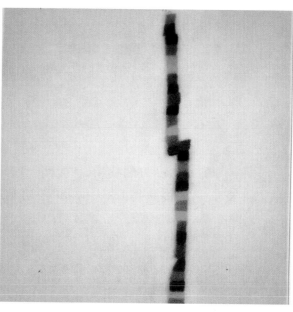

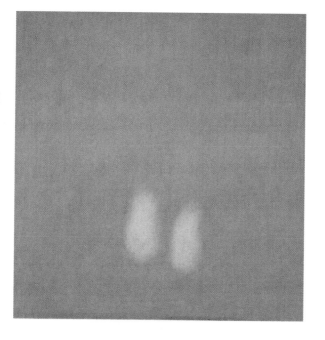

Top: Untitled, *1998, graphite and pigment on paper, 5 x 5 in/12 x 12 cm. Courtesy Joseph Helman Gallery, New York.*
Bottom: Untitled, *1997, graphite and pigment on paper, 7 x 7 in/17 x 17 cm. Courtesy Joseph Helman Gallery, New York.*

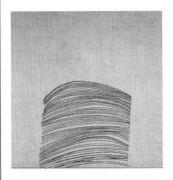

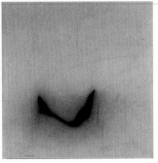

Top: White, *2000, etching,*
7 x 7 in/18 x 18 cm.
Private collection.
Above: Untitled, *1995, graphite on*
paper, 6 x 6 in/16 x 17 cm.
Private Collection.

isolated shape or shapes, line or lines. These forms are drawn with hairline exactitude or built up slowly into dark masses that are as much volume as void. Some of the shapes have the frank immediacy of stencils or cattle brands, but most of Mills' forms and lines move with a start-and-stop hesitancy that suggests complex, conflicting intentions. Lines intersect, separate, and then join forces again. A sheaf of lines rises like mountain peaks; other forms crawl like snails. Mills' forms, at times, look so tentative as to seem to be afraid to alight on the page. Occasionally, one senses the displaced or the disembodied: a gray shape shadows a form like a shed skin; a tangle of lines lingers next to a form like a skeleton separated from its host. These free-floating, tenuous lines and forms uncomfortably twist in the plane in an attempt, seemingly, to lodge, or dislodge, themselves, as each one acts as a passageway or bridge that extends and opens up the space.

Wes Mills, who just turned forty, is not afraid to pare down his life either. In 1981 he abandoned making art altogether for nearly ten years, two of which he spent roughing it in a Maine cabin without running water or electricity. A bit of a nomad, Mills, who was born in Tucson, Arizona, spent his childhood in Montana, and has lived in Kentucky, New Mexico, California, Boston, and New York. While in New Mexico, he was represented by the prestigious Laura Carpenter Gallery, now the Georgia O'Keeffe Museum, in Santa Fe, where he met and exhibited with Richard Tuttle and Agnes Martin, among others. Currently, Mills is represented by the Joseph Helman Gallery in New York but, since 1998, he has chosen to relocate in Montana, where he lives with his wife, Tina, an artist and writer, and their daughter Ava.

Although Mills collects the work of older, die-hard minimalists, he shies away from categorization and groups, and talks little of other artists. When asked about his influences or loves, Mills will talk of the difficulty and necessity of ridding preciousness from his work or of attaining subtle truths in a drawing, truths that are "felt" rather than understood. He

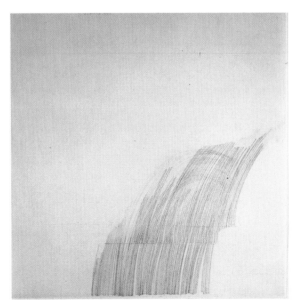

Duchamp, *1999, graphite on*
paper,
8 x 8 in/20 x 20 cm.
Private Collection.

will discuss the universality of the circle, a form he has "discovered" in his own work, and he will repeatedly touch upon the circular interaction between the line of an artist's memory and the lines in a drawing and the experience of the viewer. Mills will read aloud from books on Buddhism or bring to my attention objects that he owns: a carved spiral and an artist's fingerprint in a Sung Dynasty bowl; Neolithic jade burial amulets found in the mouths of the deceased;

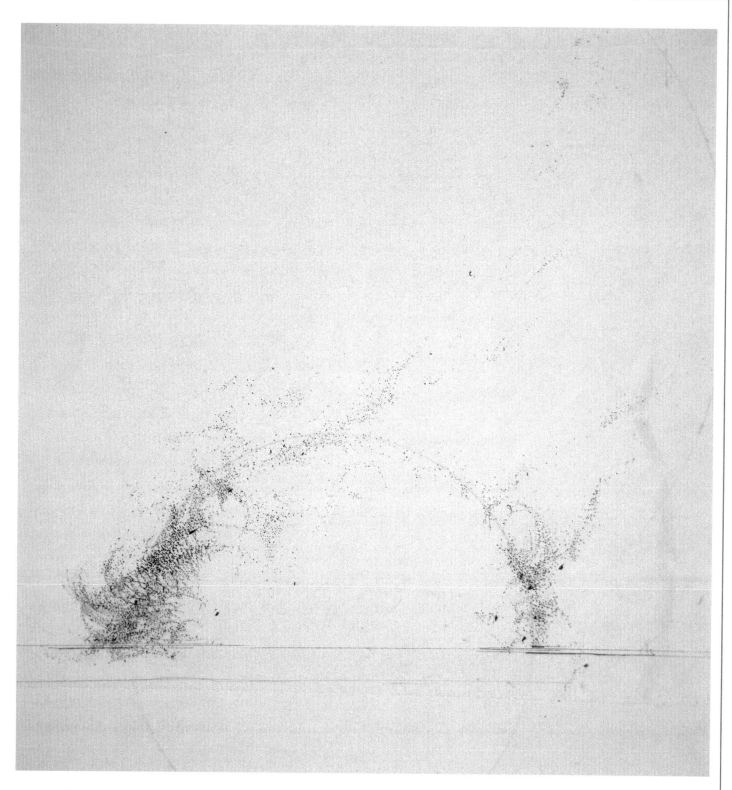

Untitled (detail), 2001, graphite on paper, 8 x 8 in/20 x 20 cm. Courtesy Joseph Helman Gallery, New York.

nineteenth-century photographs of Egypt; rocks picked up while he was hiking. Mills held up one translucent stone, the color of lapis, and said that it was exactly the color of Oregon's Crater Lake; and of another stone, after soaking it in water; he remarked that it looked just like "the wet skin of an elephant." And amazingly, it did.

A Mills drawing is a bit of a tease. His mnemonic drawings, the Memory Line groups, excite in us our desire to compare. Two very similar lines or forms, almost identical, are kept at just the right distance from one another, so that they seem to be tethered to one another by the viewer's own visual memory and the tension between the forms' need to reunite and to separate, both in appearance and in space. The forms are so small that to fully comprehend each of them individually (and in order to compare one form to its

> ## "LIKE THE DARKNESS OF NIGHT CREEPING IN AND OUT AT THE EDGES OF A CAMPFIRE, THE SPACE BETWEEN REMINDS ME OF DRAWING."

brother), the viewer must get in so close to one, as to lose the twin in the periphery. Even Mills' tiny signature and the hundreds of minutely written words that expand into mountainous shapes in his earlier work are best seen with the aid of a magnifying glass. After spending time with Mills' drawings, one begins to think about things on a much smaller level. Like a latter-day Thoreau, one may find oneself contemplating varieties of sprouts or musing over the shadows of insects.

Three Bridges, *2000, graphite and white pigment on paper, 7 x 7 in/18 x 18 cm. Courtesy Joseph Helman Gallery, New York.*

Looking at Mills' drawings, one is hit, not with questions about their meaning but with the immediate tensions of felt relationships. There is not the dynamic equilibrium of a Mondrian in Mills' work, nor is there the metaphoric range of an Arp, but Mills takes us to quiet little vistas of his own. The abstract forms in his current pieces invite analogies – bones, footprints, the phases of the moon. But the drawings eschew these readings just as easily as they welcome them. In Mills' drawings, we never know where we began, no more than we know where we are going. Part of their power lies in the tension felt between our need to identify and the ever-evasive quality of the works. This ambiguity, like the Zen journey, is the purpose of the trip, not the destination.

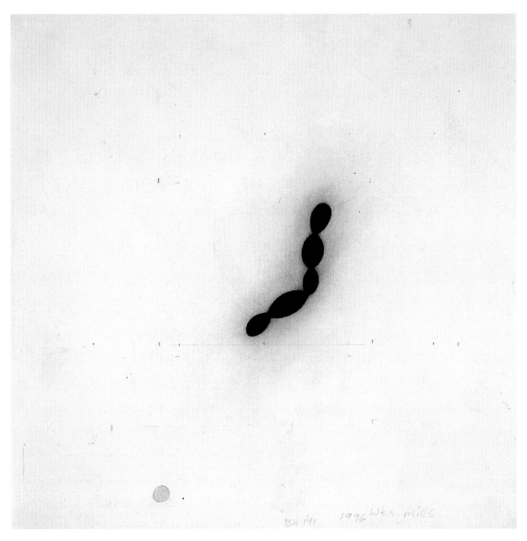

Untitled, *1997, graphite and ink on paper, 6 x 6 in/15 x 15 cm. Courtesy Joseph Helman Gallery, New York.*

Mills, whose work comes out of an inner need to learn and find solace, could be making his drawings almost anywhere. In Missoula, he has pared down his life to something of a neutral ground, one where the divisions between landscape, self-contemplation, and art are becoming less distinct. But if an artist is aware, both of himself and of his surroundings, he will inevitably produce work that speaks not only about who he is but also where he is. Unlike Gauguin, who attempted to "shake off ... filthy Europe" in the paradise of Tahiti, Mills is pushing ever inward to find form, as if through self-discovery one is destined ultimately to explore the world. But what better place to search for one's "significant form" than in the soil where one first took root? Mills' forms come first from a personal necessity, but you cannot take the Montana out of Mills. In his drawings, I am always aware of that particular quality of the small event suspended under a Big Sky.

In Missoula, Mills is surrounded by mountains, rivers, and grand vistas. But rather than dwarfing him, all this expansiveness only reaffirms and extends his reach. Mills cannot easily visit a gothic cathedral or explore the halls of the Louvre. But he has a spectacular view of the landscape – a mix of golden-rose, lime-green, and black rock. And he has those long, Montana sunsets: chorus after chorus of intense color changes, fiery oranges, deep

"MILLS' DRAWINGS TRACE OUT THE WAY TO THE (NO)PLACE WHERE FEELING AND THINKING, ALIKE, WILL NEVER REACH AN END; WILL NEVER HIT THE MARK."

—*Mark van de Walle*

violets, and massive, white clouds set off against blue-black mountain silhouettes.

Those who choose to live closer to nature learn to find the most efficient solutions to the problems of everyday life. People often equate living in the country with retreat from progress and technology. In fact, with the wilderness as a guide, form never followed function better. American pioneers have always been modernists: the bare-essential designs of the famous McCormick reaper and the Colt revolver, both invented in the 1830s, had as much to do with "significant form" as they had to do with how the West was won. We think of artists as being, like scientists, farmers, and explorers, through necessity, very aware of their surroundings. They are problem-solvers in search of the most direct routes.

Mills is basically a self-taught artist. He is the first to say that he does not really know how to look at artworks. But his work has a formal resolution and power because his drawings remain for him unresolved until they recreate, and speak to, his own internal tensions. There is an extreme, hands-on practicality to this way of building form. Mills, who collects Chinese ceramics, said that he never really understood Chinese art until he held a few objects in his hands, and then it all made sense. This is a sculptor's or

> "FOR MILLS,
> DRAWING IS A
> KIND OF REMOTE
> MICROSURGERY IN
> WHICH A CHILD
> SUTURES HIS
> WOUNDS, STITCHING
> CLOSED THEIR LIPS
> IN PATTERNS THAT
> RETRACE, AND SO
> SPEAK, THE SHAPE
> AND CHARACTER OF
> THEIR ORIGIN IN
> THE FAMILY."
> —Thad Ziolkowski

Untitled (detail), 2001, graphite on paper, 8 x 8in/20 x 20 cm. Courtesy Joseph Helman Gallery, New York.

an architect's sensibility, a little-by-little touching and building-up of forms that provide entry for viewers and safe seclusion for the artist.

Being connected is very important to Mills: connected to the landscape, to his work, to his experience of the world. But if one tries too hard, all is lost. Things must flow naturally between hand, eye and paper. Mills talks of this experience in a Duchamp etching, a restrike, from Mills' own collection. In the Duchamp print, it is impossible to tell the difference between the lines in the original image and those that Duchamp added to mark-out the plate. Mills believes that this confusion was Duchamp's intention, but, more importantly, Mills is interested in the freedom of those restrike marks, the straightforward, unpretentious place from which those marks came. It is this place, the making of a drawing without the intention of "making a drawing," for which Mills strives. He works toward obliterating sacredness and preciousness before ever the drawing is begun.

Untitled, 1996, graphite and ink on paper, 11 x 11 in/28 x 28 cm. Courtesy Joseph Helman Gallery, New York.

Ultimately, he is attempting to make art as it was made before "intention": to go back to a time when art as a concept did not exist, when objects and pictures were purely practical, outer extensions of inner life, when metamorphosis was part of a cyclical interchange, rather than an artist's game. Ironically enough, it was ready-made pieces like Duchamp's *Fountain* (the urinal out of context) that changed all that. I believe that Picasso was closer to finding that quality of interaction in his own transformations of life into art and art into life, with pieces like his Bull's Head, which he described:

"One day I took a bicycle saddle and handlebars, put one on top of the other and had a bull's head. That was fine. But what should have happened then was that I should have thrown out the bull's head, out into the street, into a stream, anywhere, but just thrown it out. Then a workman would have come by and picked it up."

And he'd think that maybe with that bull's head, he could make a bicycle saddle and handlebars, and then do it … that would have been really wonderful. That's the gift of metamorphosis.

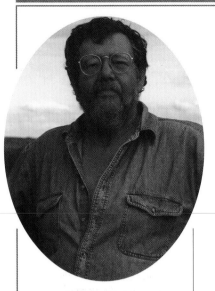

Barrie Cooke

by Seamus Heaney

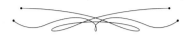

BARRIE COOKE
Cooke was born in 1931 in England and moved to the US as a teenager. After studying art history at Harvard, he studied painting in Salzburg with Kokoschka. He has lived in Ireland since 1954, and associates himself most closely with the country's landscape.

Often semi-abstract and expressionist in style, Cooke's landscapes are influenced by the perspective of Ireland, his adopted home. Beyond landscapes, Cooke's subject matter includes nudes seen through what Nobel laureate Seamus Heaney has called "Cooke's aqueous vision."

Working in other media over a ten year period in the '70s, Cooke produced a series of "bone boxes" made of an acrylic material containing real and artificial bone fragments. He also collaborated on projects with poets including Heaney and Ted Hughes.

Exhibited throughout Europe and North America, his paintings belong to various private and public collections, including the Irish Museum of Modern Art, the Hague and the Stedelijk museums in the Netherlands, and the Municipal Gallery of Modern Art, Dublin. The Haags Gemeentemuseum in the Netherlands has presented a major retrospective.

BARRIE COOKE WAS BORN IN CHESHIRE, EDUCATED AT HARVARD, and has lived in Ireland since the mid-1950s. For the past four decades he has been an independent and greatly admired presence among Irish artists, painting rivers and riverbanks, roots, rain, flesh, bones, nudes, woods, bodies in bogs, fish in (and out of) water, elk horns, algae – everything, in fact, that a hunter and gatherer might encounter or prospect for. And all of this is done with a characteristically muddy if opulent palette, as if *la boue* and *la beauté* swam together in the pigment and strove against each other for control. He is a painter in earnest, up to his eyes in the elements and the medium.

From the start, Cooke's life and work have paid into each other. During his first years in Ireland, he did in fact live off the land and an aura of the aboriginal has surrounded him ever since. The period he spent on his own in a cottage in the Burren in Co. Clare, a more or less self-sufficient fisherman and gamehunter, turned out to be definitive: in one way or another, he has never stopped being out on his own, at a saving distance from what W. B. Yeats used to call "the coteries," as much a Ben Gunn as a Paul Gauguin.

No wonder a mutual friend put him in touch early on with Ted Hughes, another patrolman of the marches who was to become a companion on the salmon rivers of the north-west and the pike lakes of the Irish midlands every year until he died. Each was a complete angler, and their primary aim was to catch fish, but a bonus of these expeditions was their collaboration on an extraordinarily bold set of lithographs. In each print, Hughes' longhand version of his fishing poems and Cooke's big black trawl of loaded landing nets and miscellaneous tackle present themselves so simply and starkly you can almost feel a wind on the back of your neck as you look at them.

But even before we get to the years of his Irish domicile, the curriculum vitae is promising. Here, for example, is an extract from an old catalogue: "1951: An impoverished summer in Martinique, including a brief unhappy spell working in a slaughterhouse, redeemed only by a first reading of Rabelais." The information there may be sparse enough, but the suggestion of intellectual eagerness in the context of offal and the tropics gives you a sense of a man already on some sort of quest, prepared to dirty his hands but unprepared to surrender his intelligence – all consistent with the impression a viewer still gets from the paintings 50 years on.

A susceptibility to what we might call the Martinique factor – to lucid air, lucid waters, an encroaching fetor, a reek of corrupting matter – continues to be felt in his most recent work. There has been no dulling of response, the drama of fresh encounters with the world and with the medium is as vital as ever. What is being registered is an original, creaturely delight in rivers and rocks, or a corresponding sense of affront at algae and pollutants of all sorts in lakes and seas; and what keeps the feeling of first-timeness alive is, paradoxically, a lifetime of action in front of the easel, an action where the painter's well-schooled sense of his predecessors in the art has accommodated itself to his need to proceed without calculation, surrender himself to the work in hand.

The demands of art work, after all, are strictly contradictory: the practitioner has to know what's called for and yet has to be able to forget himself, and it seems to me that Barrie Cooke's achievement rests upon an ability to be true to the doubleness of that rule. Not for him the knowingness of travesty and vandalism: he has been equidistant from the ironies of belatedness and ignorances of the come-lately. And yet in his practice, an internalized knowledge of the art of the past probably does count for as much as the actuality of the subject. As he makes his mark, the Rubens he forgets he knows is as important as the river he knows he is remembering.

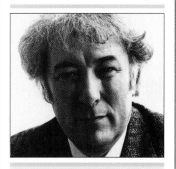

SEAMUS HEANEY
Heaney was born at Mossbawn, his family's farm near Belfast, in 1939, the eldest of nine children. After growing up in the countryside, he attended St. Joseph's College, where he was inspired to write by the poetry of Robert Frost and Ted Hughes. He published his work in the college journal under the pseudonym "Incertus."

Heaney garnered public attention in the mid-'60s, when he was linked to poets in the "Northern School" of Irish writing. The early poems tie him to his rural childhood at Mossbawn – especially in his first two volumes Death of a Naturalist *and* Door into the Dark. *He also confronts Northern Ireland's conflicts in works like* Casualty, *a poem about a Catholic friend murdered by a bomb set by the Provisional Irish Republican Army.*

Heaney won the Nobel Prize in Literature in 1995 and was made a Commandeur de L'Ordre des Arts et Lettres *by the French Ministry of Culture in 1996. He is a member of Aosdana, the Irish academy of artists and writers, and a Foreign Member of the American Academy of Arts and Letters. Heaney's translation of Beowulf was published in 2000 to great critical acclaim. Electric Light is his latest volume of poetry.*

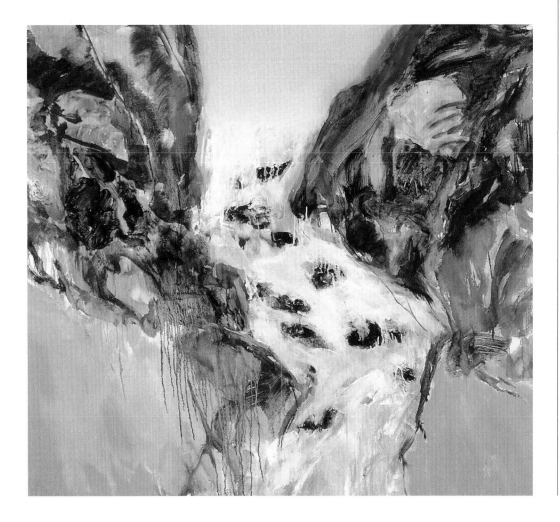

Roaring Billy's Falls, *2000, oil on canvas, 54 x 60 in/137 x 152 cm. Courtesy Kerlin Gallery, Dublin.*

Knocknarea I, *2001, oil on canvas,*
73 x 85 in/185 x 215 cm.
Courtesy Kerlin Gallery, Dublin.

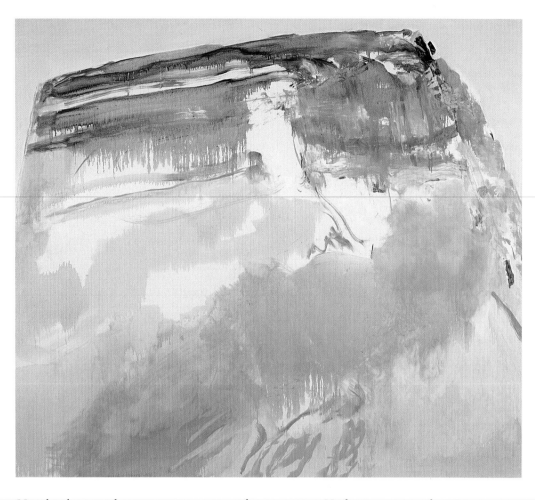

Not that he is in the remotest way an academic painter. He loves to quote the sarcastic praise given by Kokoschka (with whom he worked in Salzburg in 1955). "You could frame that," the master said of one student's particularly skillful picture, "and hang it in an exhibition." And only recently I got from him in the mail, without covering note – the scrawl on the envelope was the recognizable spoor – an extract from an interview with Picasso, where Picasso described his process of repeated humiliation of anything in the image that looked as if it were the slightest bit satisfied with itself or inviting of admiration.

Phytophthera Infestans III,
1996, oil on canvas,
60 x 84 in/152 x 213 cm.
Courtesy Kerlin Gallery, Dublin.

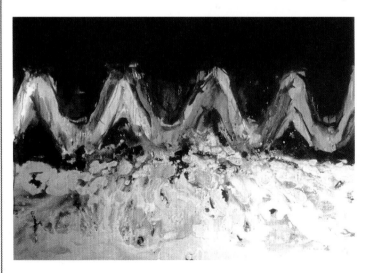

A pursuit of the true thing through a discipline of abnegation shows not only in Barrie Cooke's conduct at the easel, but in his near indifference to the business of exhibiting. Already in the Martinique moment, the inclination to go walkabout is in evidence, and the impression of somebody not particularly interested in positioning himself for career purposes has been born out by his demeanor and commitments ever since.

There have been marvelous one-man exhibitions, of course, in Dublin and The Hague, in France and the United States, and he has figured significantly in many group shows of Irish painting that have been toured in Britain and Europe. Even so, his chosen habitat continues to be far from the gallery and gossip circuit, and his talk is more likely to get excited when he is reporting the weight of a big salmon than when he is reacting to the latest overprice paid for Irish art by the cub millionaires of the Celtic tiger.

None of this should be read as indifference to what goes on in the world, or lack of conviction about the crucial work that art can and should perform in it. There is nothing quietist in his stand-off. In fact, there is great activism in his concentration, and years of silent brushwork and rodwork have only served to deepen his awareness of something crucial at stake, something to which and for which he is answerable.

If I had to describe that "something," I would say it is a vision of the inter-connectedness of all life, its vulnerability and its deliciousness. On the wall of his studio, for example, Barrie Cooke has inscribed in Greek Heraclitus' declaration that "Everything flows," but he also has newspaper reports of chemical poisoning of local rivers and lakes, and press photographs of fish-kills and oil-slicks. And the concerns that are obvious on the walls of his workroom inform the images that have figured – often radiantly, occasionally indignantly – on the canvases that constitute his by now richly coherent oeuvre.

The Heraclitus quote is only to be expected from a man who spends his time stepping

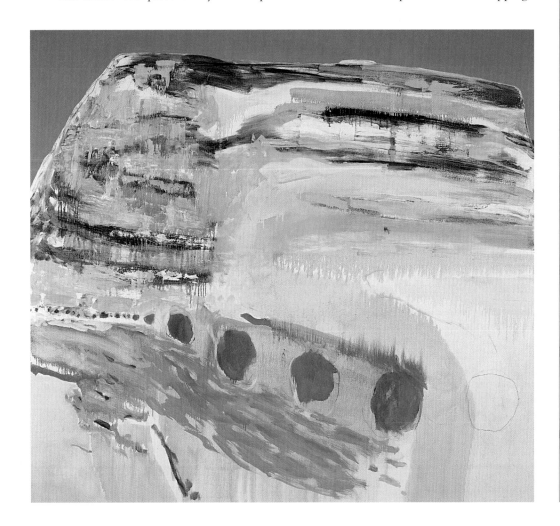

Knocknarea II, *2001, oil on canvas, 73 x 81 in/185 x 205 cm. Courtesy Kerlin Gallery, Dublin.*

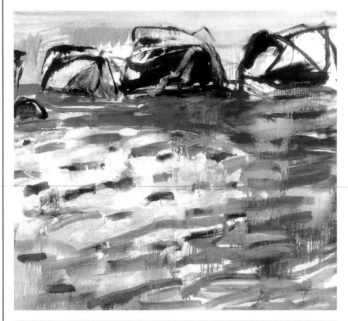

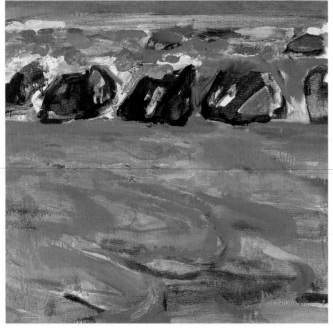

Top: Black Stones, 1999, oil on canvas, 54 x 60 in/137 x 152 cm. *Private collection.*

Above: Brown Stones I, 1999, oil on canvas, 38 x 40 in/97 x 102 cm. *Courtesy Kerlin Gallery, Dublin.*

into rivers. But Barrie Cooke also spends much time poring over books – in his freshman year at Harvard, for example, he studied Chinese Poetry as well as Biology and Art History – and one book which may be worth mentioning in connection with his work is *Sensitive Chaos*, a translation of an "alternative" scientific text by Theodor Schwenk, published in 1965.

This has been described as belonging to a tradition "based on visionary insights bolstered by sustained observation and a fundamental belief in an underlying natural unity." Schwenk is as liable to talk about the way bones "flow" into one another across the particular space of joints as to study the dynamics of river-water pouring over a stone, and however skeptical the official scientific community might have been about the anthropomorphic elements in his discourse, there was great attraction for Cooke in the book's central insight that a watery principle lay behind all processes, something fundamentally rhythmical and fluid.

So the bones and blood of the Martinique slaughterhouse begin to tie up with other things observed on other expeditions undertaken by Cooke in the years that followed. In the mid-1970s he headed for Borneo, where the downpours sluicing through creepers and slicking the tree-trunks of the rainforest brought him to his painterly senses in a new way; and again in the '80s, his jubilation at discovering an environmentalist's (and fisherman's) paradiso in the rivers of New Zealand led to a rhapsodic reawakening of something celebratory in his impulse and his art.

During the 1980s, in fact, he permitted himself a kind of epical joy: images of the Great Irish Elk with its incandescent horns lifted towards the galaxies like receiving stations, nudes whose sensuality was as drowsy as a seal's and as cultivated as an odalisque's; flesh-colored mandalas of mating that could be read as takes on a how-to sex manual or aids to meditation in a sacred text. There was an element of proclamation about it all, as if he were waving the banners of nature's kingdom and mustering its forces for the battle against pollution and destruction which life on the planet has now turned into.

To put it like that, of course, makes it all sound too rhetorical and preachy. Many of the recent paintings take up the theme at a point where the relish of pigment and the recognition of corruption intersect: the seductive glitter and slither at the mouth of a pipe in a waste disposal system is seen as a phenomenon that is both fascinating and deplorable; the blisters and soft infestations that attend the process of potato blight are rendered in all their sinister beauty. And yet in *Phytophthera Infestans III*, the undulations that represent potato drills could be an allusion to the zig-zag hieroglyph for life itself; so it might not be too far out to read the stones that figure in some paintings in the current exhibition as a kind of Yeatsian affirmation that "the stone's in the midst of all" – the stone of geological and psychological obstinacy, of creative, even sacred, resistance.

Something I wrote in the early 1990s about Cooke still applies to this recent work:

> His wariness about being co-opted as the celebrator of a given, pristine, pre-economic, extra-political nature has occasionally come to the fore in images of pollution … But his belief in the necessity of reestablishing clean personal contact between each individual and the planet … a belief rooted in his countryman's hand-to-hand, hour-by-hour contact with flora and fauna … gets painterly expression in, for example, images which proclaim a solidarity with Sweeney, the "green man" of the Middle Irish saga.

The actual image of Sweeney may not figure in the new show, but his spirit presides. Sweeney's story tells of a king who was cursed by a saint and banished to the woods and hills, turned into a panicky, birdlike creature, somebody as intimate with wind and rain as Poor Tom was on King Lear's storm-lashed heath. As a result of this exposure, he became a mouthpiece for some of the most enduring and intense nature poetry in the Irish language, and I don't think it too fanciful to see Barrie Cooke's sojourn on the wild side of the Irish landscape as the endeavor of a green man redivivus, a kind of Sweeney come-back whose canvases possess the same unmediated quality as the poetry of the original:

> Sainted cliff at Alternan,
> nut-grove, hazel wood!
> Cold quick sweeps of water
> fall down the cliff-side.
> Ivies green and thicken there,
> its oak mast is precious.
> Fruited branches nod and bend
> from heavy-headed apple trees.

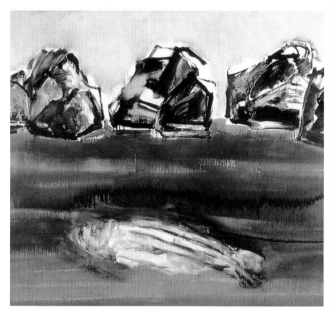

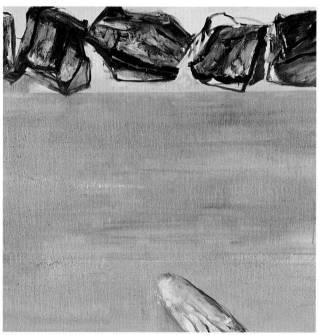

Top: Black Stones and Striper, *2000, oil on canvas, 73 x 85 in/185 x 215 cm. Private collection.*

Above: Black Stones and Striper II, *2001, oil on canvas, 73 x 73 in/185 x 185 cm. Courtesy Kerlin Gallery, Dublin.*

Donald Judd

by Charles Darwent

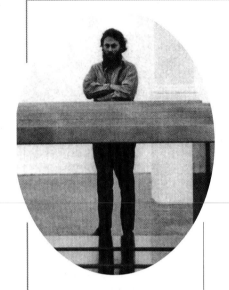

DONALD JUDD

Sculptor, painter, and writer, Donald Judd was born in Missouri, in 1928. As a young man, he came to New York to study at the Art Student's League during the late '40s and early '50s. He also studied art theory, painting, and sculpture at Columbia University.

Rejecting the strong force of Abstract Expressionism, his intent in his paintings was to simplify composition and to instill a sense of order. He began to concentrate on sculpture which championed this same minimalism and simplicity. He placed his wood, metal, and plexiglass forms directly on the ground rather than on bases, and used industrial materials to construct boxlike geometric modules. These "stacks" were installed with the spaces between the units precisely equal to the dimension of the units themselves.

From 1959 to 1965, Judd wrote art criticism for Arts *Magazine and other American journals. During the same period, he exhibited his abstract work, such as the painted wooden* Cadmium Red Oil on Wood, *at the Green Gallery in New York.*

Judd's work expanded the boundaries of art, architecture, and design. He died in 1994, one of the most influential artists of his time.

SOMEWHERE IN WESTERNMOST WEST TEXAS, in the kind of country that puts you in mind of famines and plagues of locusts and other of the stricter moments in the Old Testament, is a little piece of New York. You know you've come across it when you drive down its Main Street. Instead of flatbed trucks there are Volvo estates; car bumpers are noticeably devoid of stickers proclaiming their owners' allegiance to George W. Bush, or (a common thing in West Texas) to Charlton Heston. There is a bookshop (an uncommon thing in West Texas), and a bookshop that sells – get this – cappucinos: possibly the only frothed coffee to be had between San Antonio and the Rio Grande. At the time of writing, the shop's windows advertise two sorts of works: the *Dean & Delucca Cookbook* (an inordinately uncommon thing in West Texas), and monographs on Donald Judd.

The place, of course, is Marfa. As contemporary art myth now records, Judd was passing through the half-horse cow town in 1971 when he was struck by its charms and decided to stay. Like the town bookshop, owned by Houstonians and patronized by New Yorkers, Judd was in Marfa but not of it. His first action on moving into an ex-light industrial building down by the railway yard – a moment of TriBeCa in the Texan desert –

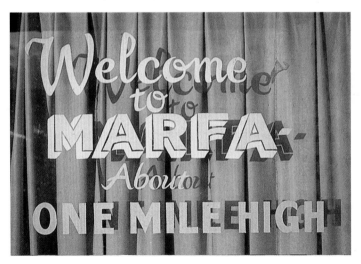

was to build a ten foot adobe wall around it to keep locals out. He then set about buying up a slew of properties, including ranches and the town's mohair factory, from impoverished townsfolk on the other side of it. Walk around Marfa today and you'll see Judd's ghost everywhere: in the dozen or so buildings labeled "Judd Foundation," a trust that looks after the artist's private estate and is managed by his son, Flavin; in the excellent art section of the Marfa Bookshop; and in the faint but perceptible resentment directed by locals at people who drive Volvos, vote Democrat, and drink funny coffee.

Most obviously, you'll find Judd's shade just outside of town, in a one-time army base called Fort D.A. Russell. During the mid-1970s, Judd bought the base with the help of the Dia Art Foundation and the oil millions of its co-founder, Philippa de Menil. When Schlumberger stock dipped in the early 1980s oil crisis and Dia funding for the project dried up, Judd characteristically sued the Foundation. Just as characteristically, he won. Fort D.A. Russell, re-christened the Chinati Foundation in 1976, became Judd's personal fiefdom.

So what would Judd's ghost make of Marfa now? On one level, it would be delighted. Judd began life not as an artist but as a critic. Trained at Columbia by Rudolf Wittkower and Meyer Schapiro, he took a predictably high-minded view of American museology. Museums like MOMA were crowded, uncomfortable, and forced the art shown inside them to fit in with their off-the-peg architecture. Worse, they favored anthology hangs – displays

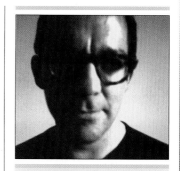

CHARLES DARWENT
Born in Trinidad in 1958, Charles Darwent studied English literature at Cambridge University and art history at the University of London. He has been art critic of The Independent on Sunday *newspaper since 1998. He also is a book reviewer for the* Times Literary Supplement. *His principal interest is in French 18th-century art, particularly painting in the revolutionary period.*

Darwent lives and writes in London.

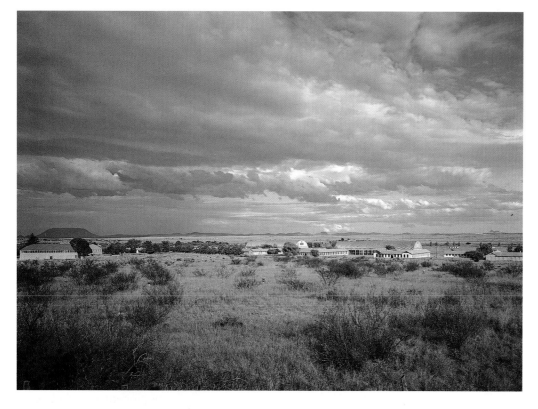

Marfa, Texas, overview.
The Chinati Foundation.
Photograph by Todd Eberle.

that put the works of several artists together in the same space with the aim of suggesting some kind of art historical likeness. To Judd, this reduced the experience of American museum-visiting to an eternity of "freshman English." What he wanted – and what he wanted particularly for his own work – was a tailor-made building in which art and architecture could interract contrapuntally, where discrete spaces would be given over to individual artists, and installations would be permanent.

And so it was that his eye fell on the redundant artillery sheds of Fort D.A. Russell. Step into them from the stinging heat of a Texan afternoon and you'll see why. There is just no questioning the sublimity of the hundred untitled milled aluminium boxes that Judd installed there between 1982 and 1986, nor their beauty. Cut to tolerances of a few

A Sign in Marfa, Texas.
Photograph by Ian McMillan.

thousandths of an inch, the boxes – each roughly 3 x 4 x 6 ft/1 x 1 x 2 m– look at first like identical modernist menhirs. As the desert light filtering through the glass walls of the sheds shifts, though, so the invisible differences between the cuboids (a front panel recessed at a slight angle, a surface that stands marginally clear of the structure beneath it) make themselves felt. One box turns into bronze, another into perspex (an acrylic material); some exude an internal, Manet-ish light, others swallow light up like black holes. It's hard not to look at them as religious works, altars to a particularly austere vision of the world and its art.

> "IT TAKES A GREAT DEAL OF TIME AND THOUGHT TO INSTALL WORK CAREFULLY. THIS SHOULD NOT ALWAYS BE THROWN AWAY. MOST ART IS FRAGILE AND SOME SHOULD BE PLACED AND NEVER MOVED AGAIN."

And to the ego. The artillery sheds were used to house German prisoners during World War II: Judd insisted that the minatory notices intended for them – *Den kopf benutzen ist besser als ihm verlieren!* – should be left where they were. The effect is oddly unsettling. Look at a shed full of glinting metal boxes and it may put you in mind of an assembly line, or maybe even of a church. See the same boxes contained within walls decorated with Teutonic warning signs and you think of something more sinister: serried ranks, the microscopic

15 untitled works in concrete,
1980-84, 100 x 100 x 200 in/
250 x 250 x 500 cm.
Chinati Foundation, Marfa, Texas.

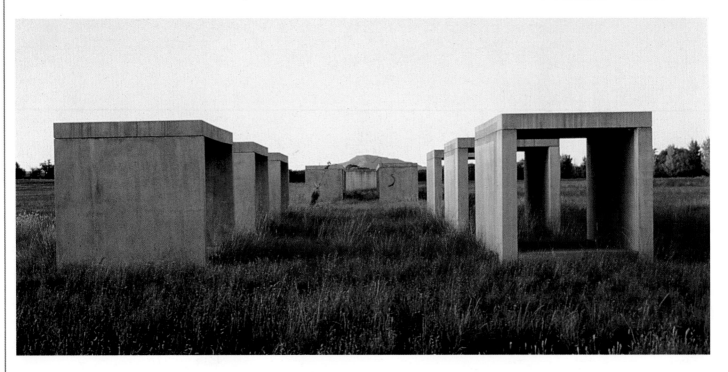

tolerances of war, ideology run amok. And you think of the kind of egotism that believes in absolutes, and in leaving the imperfect world to find them.

Which makes what is happening around Judd's sheds all the more interesting. In early October, the unseasonally icebound streets of Marfa were filled with the strumming of a mariachi band and the smell of frying burritos. These emanated from the Chinati Foundation's annual open house, a tradition founded by Judd himself back in the 'Eighties. This year, though, things were different. The refried beans may have been the same, but there

> ## "SOMEWHERE A PORTION OF CONTEMPORARY ART HAS TO EXIST AS AN EXAMPLE OF WHAT THE ART AND ITS CONTEXT WERE MEANT TO BE."

were far more people than usual, some two thousand of them. Many had flown in from New York and Los Angeles. Nicholas Serota, director of the Tate Galleries, had come from London.

The reason for this was that the bash coincided with the unveiling of a major new work at Fort Russell – a neon installation by Dan Flavin, entitled *Untitled (Marfa project)* (1996). Occupying a row of six one-time doughboy mess huts, Flavin's Marfa project is an extraordinary piece of work. Each U-shaped hut has had its center section walled off to form a kind of cave, passage through which is barred by either one or a pair of rhomboidal gates made out of Flavinish neon tubing, blue and yellow strips in the first two huts, pink and

North Artillery shed interior with permanent installation of 100 works in aluminium, *1982–84, each work 41 x 51 x 72 in/ 104 x 130 x 183 cm. Chinati Foundation, Marfa, Texas. Photograph: Todd Eberle.*

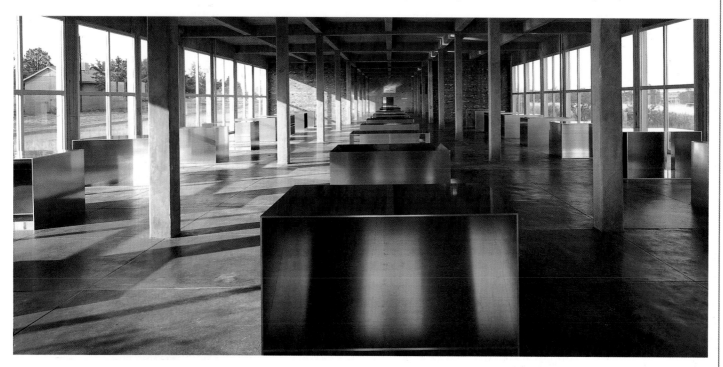

green in the second, a mix of all four colors in the third. To get from one hut to the next, you are forced to emerge from the aqueous gloom of Flavin's artificially lit interiors into the white glare of a West Texas day. Among other things, this inside-outside progression raises questions about the role of memory in the way we see things. By the end of the sequence, you have forgotten which is the real light and which is not: a fiat lux rendered in a few dollars worth of neon tubing.

It all makes a good fit with Judd's sacerdotal boxes. Both sets of work manipulate architecture to explore ambient light; both use small-scale things – recessed planes, obtuse angles – to produce large-scale effects. Although Judd disliked the term "minimalism," both sets of work fit roughly into its remit. And both bear Judd's own imprimatur. Although the date of Flavin's Marfa project is given as 1996, this is misleading: its bare bones were approved by Judd for inclusion in the Chinati Foundation before his death in 1994. So, too, was an installation of twenty-three variously titled works by John Chamberlain, housed off-site in a converted mohair warehouse in downtown Marfa.

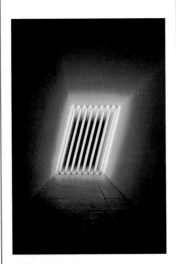

Dan Flavin, Untitled,
(Marfa project), 1996, detail,
building four.
Chinati Foundation, Marfa, Texas.

"OLD MASTER PAINTING HAS A GREAT REPUTATION FOR BEING PROFOUND, UNIVERSAL, AND ALL THAT, AND IT ISN'T NECESSARILY."

All this makes a kind of sense. Three artists do not make an anthology show, especially when they are housed in separate spaces and in different kinds of buildings. But Flavin's Marfa project is not the only piece to have seen the light of day at Fort Russell since the death of Donald Judd. Wander elsewhere on the site and you will see huts filled with permanent work by other artists: Carl Andre, John Wesley, and Ilya Kabakov, for example, all of them Judd-approved. Between these are land sculptures by Richard Long and a vast, teetering horseshoe by Claes Oldenburg and Roni Horn. A project to make over a pair of nearby aircraft hangars as showing spaces is also in the pipeline. Then there are the Foundation's temporary installations, usually of works produced by the various Chinati artists in residence and thus post Judd's mortem. Among other artists to have taken part in the program are Kate Shepherd, Daniel Göttin, and Andreas Karl Schulze, some of whom Judd would never have heard of.

A recent piece in Jack Pierson's *Issue 4* by ex-Chinati director, Jeff Kopie, suggests that "the Foundation steadfastly upholds the modernist belief in art for art's sake. Nearly all of the work made in Marfa rejects postmodernist ideas about appropriation, the impossibility of originality, and the irrelevance of the artist/author." Nonetheless, it is difficult to see these vague philosophical similarities as manifested in both, say, Kabakov's *School No. 6* – a recreated Soviet schoolhouse – and the geometric abstraction of Schulze's paper works as being more important than the differences between them. Nor, given the messianic motives of Chinati's founding, is it easy to overlook the fact that some of the works on show at the Foundation are pre-Judd and some post- him. (This is especially true of the paintings, Judd having declared the medium "pretty much finished" back in the 1960s.)

Does any of this matter? Were the Chinati Foundation to have been set up as a regular contemporary art museum, the answer would probably have been no; change is a given in gallery curating, and never more so than today. The fact is, though, that Chinati was set up to be precisely the opposite of a regular contemporary art museum. Like Judd's boxes, its large-scale effects derived from its smallness – not many artists, not much curation, tiny visitor numbers, little material change. Given Judd's antipathy to crowds in art venues, it seems likely that a large part of Marfa's appeal for him lay in its remoteness. Even today, the four-hour schlep on desert roads from El Paso, the nearest town with an airport, is enough to give all but the keenest Juddites pause for thought.

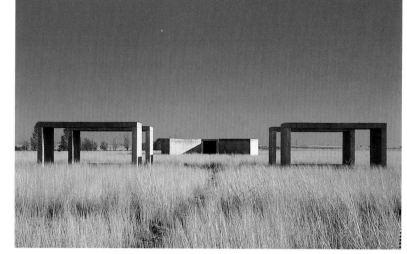

Untitled, 1980–84, four units,
each unit
8 x 8 x 16 ft/2.5 x 2.5 x 5 m.
Chinati Foundation, Marfa, Texas.
Photograph: Todd Eberle.

But Judd's reticence (or elitism, as you will) has left Marianne Stockebrand, the Foundation's director, with a problem. On the one hand, Marfa is a space for showing art. On the other, it isn't. Fort Russell is not just a collection of mixed works in an unusually arid setting. It is a monument to one man and his ideas on museology, an artefact in its own right.

And there's the rub. When Judd died, he famously left his Foundation teetering on the edge of bankruptcy. (The figure given for the Chinati's bank balance at its founder's death varies between $240 or $400, depending on who you speak to.) That two thousand people attended its October guacamolefest and more than five times that number will visit its artworks this year suggests the ingenuity that has gone into saving Marfa. Had the Foundation been left as it was at the time of Judd's death, there's next to no chance that it would still be in existence.

The trouble is that, to keep Marfa alive, Stockebrand has had to attract financial backing; and to do that, she has had to offer potential investers new (or at least old-new) things to back. She has also had to be able to point to rising attendance figures. As time goes by, the Chinati Foundation is coming to resemble the very thing that Donald Judd hated most – an anthology showing space with a large number of visitors. The survival of Judd's anti-museological baby may no longer be in doubt, but its survival in a form that Judd would have approved of is a different matter. There is more than one way of dying.

Harmony Korine

by Ian MacMillan

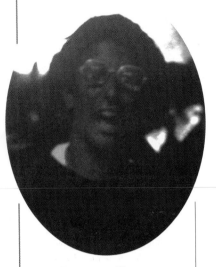

Dear Harmony, Hello from London. You're probably wondering what I'm doing writing to you, and I bet you get shit like this all the time. In fact, I checked out a few of the posts on the message board on one of the internet sites devoted to your films and it's full of incomprehensible notes from people with weird names sending trite stuff labeled "anal cunt" and "I drink piss not you," so you almost certainly attract your fair share of junk mail from lunatics.

Well, rest easy. For a start I'm a bit older than you and probably far more boring and sedate than most of those people, and I'm doing this for a reason. I was asked to help edit an issue of an art magazine discussing how film and video have entered into the art world, and the first person I thought of was you. To be honest, I'm a bit bored by the plague of video-based artworks I keep on coming across, scuttling around otherwise respectable museums like the bugs swarming out from underneath the falsely glossy family portrait which that kid keeps trying to re-hang in a scene from your first movie. How much of the pixilated-Renaissance posturings of Bill Viola, say, can one person take? Anyhow, what I'm

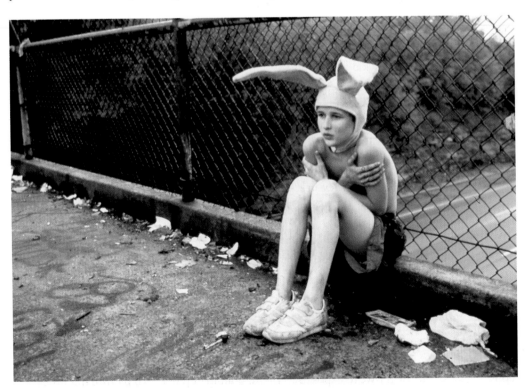

trying to say is that I think what you do with film, and photography and the writing and all the other stuff you do, is of far greater interest than anything the majority of these poseurs get up to, and so this letter is my attempt at justifying that, to myself as much as anything.

It's odd I should be doing this at all, for do you know what, Harmony? For the longest time I really couldn't stand you. I think my venom was at its strongest when you were interviewed in the Saturday magazine section of the *Guardian* newspaper over here. You seemed so cocky and self-assured, with your imagistic novel that was about to be published and which was bound to be drivel (another attempt at the non-narrative novel, oh please), waxing lyrical and sometimes splenetic, posing on the cover in your Lower Eastside drag like the skateboarding cat that got the cream. My friend's girlfriend suggested I was jealous, and maybe I was, a little, but I don't really think that was it. It was more that my bullshit detector was going into overdrive and I had taken quite enough of the rags-to-riches little boy genius myth that threatened to engulf you.

I realize right now that the problem with writing about you, Harmony Korine, is that words cannot convey what it is you do with images. A few months after I vowed never to go near another magazine piece about you I went to see *Gummo*, the feature film you had directed, and from about the first few minutes I was transfixed. Do you know that clichéd put down, "He can walk the walk but he can't talk the talk"? Christ, can you talk. The scenes just keep on coming like an animated photo album from a warped amateur

"A MISTRESS IS SOMETHING BETWEEN A MASTER AND A MATTRESS."

—*from* A Crackup at the Race Riots—

photographer. The skinny kid flexing his muscles, the boy in the bunny ears spitting through the mesh fence, the dark scurrying speckled maggots and flies on the dead white cat. For sure there was still an element of the dislikable preening egomaniac about you (I couldn't help but notice that your name was in a dramatically bigger type in the opening credits than any of the cast's or even the film's title), but the sheer beauty and pictorial elegance of these shots alone won me over. And they just keep on unfolding and developing, and for me at least it's unbelievably stimulating. You sure know your Fassbinder and your Godard, but you know how to make them your own, and how to depict a unique milieu. If the Gap ever wants to go for the speedball and crack-pipe market, they've got to get you to do the ads. (Oh I forgot; you don't do commercial work – principles.)

What is it with these critics who say you've got no plot and storyline? Do they need a bouncing ball at the bottom of the screen helping them through it, or what? Don't they see that they're like a pinhole camera into your mind, these scenarios etched into our consciousness the longer we're exposed to them, building up our own picture from the

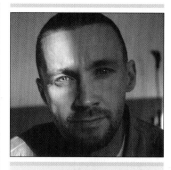

IAN MACMILLAN
A documentary filmmaker, writer, and photographer, MacMillan's many films on culture and the arts have been shown on the BBC and in museums and film centers around the world. They include Skinhead Farewell, *about the pulp novelist Richard Allen, and the award-winning* Big Art in a One Horse Town *about the sculptor Donald Judd. He also made the film recently broadcast on British television,* The Scholte Affair, *an exploration of the bombing of Dutch painter Rob Scholte.*

MacMillan was the photographer for Matthew Collings book Blimey! From Bohemia To Britpop: The London Artworld From Francis Bacon To Damien Hirst, *and he has just finished producing* Hello Culture, *a television series featuring Matthew Collings.*

Left: *Gummo,* 1997, *film.*

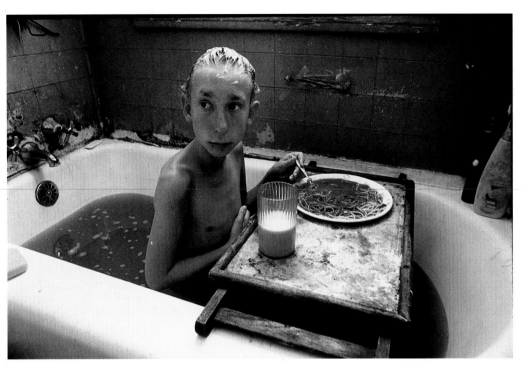

blocks you arrange and rearrange as you edit. And it's all so beautiful, even through the gloom. The kid in the bath eating spaghetti, the way you linger on the foaming peak of his hair as his mother washes it for him, the wide-eyed innocence of the child surrounded by his methane-sniffing parents. You're not really a bratty nihilist at all, are you? You really do care about these people. It's no wonder you get angry when people talk about surrealism in relation to you, it's just a world they don't, or rather can't, believe exists.

Right and below: Gummo,
1997, film.

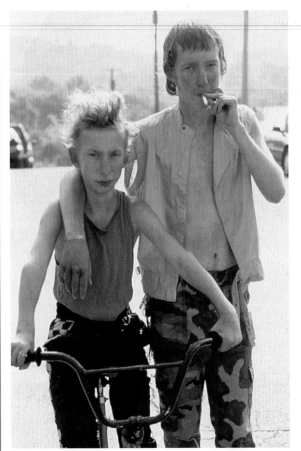

I particularly like the scene with the high school jock brothers in the kitchen, which I think best illustrates my point. Whereas someone like Bruce Weber would sexualize them in sepia, all middle-aged homoerotic gaze and American Dream, or a '60s photojournalist would pour his "true grit" all over them, you present rather than represent them. They're just themselves, and we know *they're* larking about for the camera, but it's their larking, not one you've imposed on them. Your trick is to know exactly which is the right bit, and where to place it, and with what to surround it. (I know you shoot a lot, and that loads of it ends up on the cutting-room floor.) I can almost picture you directing. "Okay, now wrestle that chair." No wonder you hardly ever use professional actors, they'd wet themselves on day one. I take that back – you would probably use that as a direction in itself.

Anyhow, as I say, one viewing of *Gummo* was all I needed to realize that you're not merely good copy. Actually, you're lousy copy sometimes. Don't you think it's just a little pretentious to come out with quotes like

"After the scene was completed I vomited in a bucket to show my appreciation"? Also, a contrived or constructed enigma is fine up to a point but it can backfire. It's what irritated me most about you in the first place. Your father was a fur trader, you told Werner Herzog in a famous interview. Now we learn your father was a documentary director for PBS in the 1970s, often chronicling poor characters in the South just as you have done in your own work. We know you're smart, so don't ruin it by being an asshole.

Being a renaissance man (I'm sorry, Harmony, but I couldn't think of a better term) is a delicate trick to pull off and I still can't make up my mind on how successful you are in your non-cinema

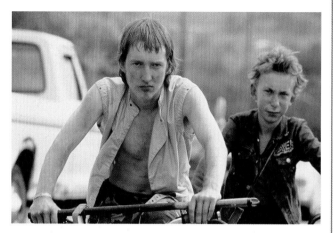

"JACKSON POLLOCK HAD A FOOT FETISH."

—*from* A Crackup at the Race Riots—

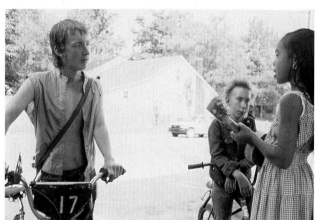

endeavors. I can see that there is, as you are aiming for, a pure singularity of vision streaming through everything you turn your hand to, and I thought your fake suicide notes exhibition was simultaneously witty, alarming, and almost an insidious joke on the very gallery it was held in. However, I can't really judge your most recent photographic book because £75 for a tome devoted entirely to pictures of the aging child star Macaulay Culkin is just a bit too much even for a fan like me, and I'm yet to "get" the ironic reinvention of this former hideous little show-off as a credible downtown scene figure. But if you send me a copy I'm willing to give it the benefit of the doubt. Your symphonic musical piece composed entirely on three black keys from the lower end of the piano I can probably do without, ditto the record of banjo music,

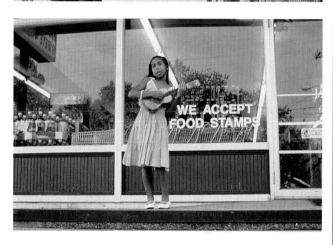

though I don't doubt your sincerity in either, nor your unflappable belief that you may one day reinvent the tap dance in an avant-garde form.

All the above: Gummo, *1997, film.*

I got round at last to reading your novel, A Crackup at the Race Riots, *and I can* thankfully confirm that it's more than just a great title and not at all the drivel you will have seen I was previously expecting. The handwritten bits remind me a lot of Basquiat's use of text, and it's got that freeform riffing thing that makes his paintings so incredible. I admire the way you can deliver a whole scene in just one sentence ("Kevin slept with his ex-girlfriend's mother"), and that combination of half-truths, paranoid scribblings, and bizarre scenes given a blank twist of banal normality really echoes your last film *Julien Donkey-Boy.*

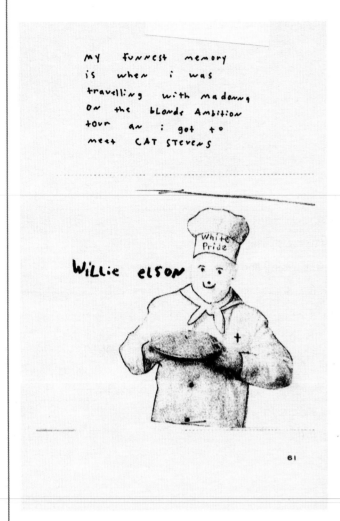

my funnest memory
is when i was
travelling with madonna
on the blonde Ambition
tour an i got to
meet CAT STEVENS

Willie elson

White
Pride

61

Above: Page from *A Crackup at the Race Riots*, 1998, novel.

It was a Saturday afternoon when I saw *Julien* so there were only about eight people in the theater with me, but I can confirm that they all seemed to have been both moved and shell-shocked by the experience, like we'd all just shared some intense psychotropic drug. It has to be about the dirtiest film I've ever seen, in the literal sense of the word. You really took that Dogma dictate of filmmaking and made it your own, didn't you? Trust you to take a set of rules and then make a movie that seemed as if you'd invented them. I found that cloying and oppressive grain of the image really drew me into the screen instead of seeming like a barrier; I suppose you re-transferred and blew up and messed about with the original digitally shot footage, though I know you filmed with a variety of cameras and even went to the extreme of having the actors wear miniature cameras on their own bodies. And I'm glad you didn't explicitly suggest that the central character was schizophrenic but just placed him in a haphazard Venn diagram of similarly elusive anti-archetypes and waited to see what would happen. I think I read somewhere that you were imagining a cinema of chance or of chaos, and I celebrate your espousal of "mistake-ist" filmmaking. Let's face it, any movie starring a psychotic Ewan Bremner, an alluring Chloe Sevigny, and Werner Herzog drinking cough syrup out of a shoe had to have something going for it, but take it from me when I say that it is truly the most visually startling and inventive mainstream distributed film I have ever seen.

"THIS IS ABSOLUTELY THE WORST TIME OF MY LIFE."

—from Suicide Note, A Crackup at the Race Riots—

Well, Harmony, I guess you're probably not going to give a fuck what I think, because you don't seem to care what anyone does, but I hope I don't sound like some sycophantic acolyte, and it's only because the precise visual poetry of your framing of the world has made me look so closely at the moving image again that I care enough to write this in the first place. I'm sure you would hate me if you met me, I've no doubt *I* would hate *you* if I met you. You'd probably want to kick the very life out of me, which is funny given that your legendary *Fight Harm* project involves you going up to people in the street, preferably much bigger than little guys like you and me, provoking them until they start to beat you up and then having a companion shoot it on a concealed camera. It's said you were hospitalized as a result of one of these encounters, or is that just another bit of five cent bubble gum from the Korine myth machine? I have a lingering hope that *Fight Harm* remains what it currently is, an unseen legend, rather than what it could be, a misconstrued ultimate-attention-seeking empty exercise. But I may be wrong about you here. I have been before.

I'm going to have to go now because they would only let me have so many words to send you, but a few things before I sign off. I found a postcard in Paris the other week of Godard with a quote from him underneath that reads, "Counter vague ideas with sharp images." I wanted to send it to you as I thought it appropriate, but having eventually found your official website (www.o'salvation.com – what a name!) I see that it's still under construction. I hope this doesn't mean you're too strung out to get on with spreading the word in yet another medium. And I don't know how this happened but putting your name into the search engine gave me a listing for a site called TripleNipple.com, wherein lie the most alarming and semi-pornographic images of women with three nipples that would certainly out-gross you to even your most judgemental of critics. I couldn't go far enough to find out what was the connection to you, it was too horrid. And to think they say you peddle ugliness.

Finally, I watched *Gummo* again late last night before finishing this, and half way through it snowed outside and there was a halo of gently drifting snow around my television for the remainder. Assuming you'd appreciate this image yourself, I finally came to realize that you have your own anti-archetype: the romantic misanthrope. Keep it up.

All the best,
Ian.

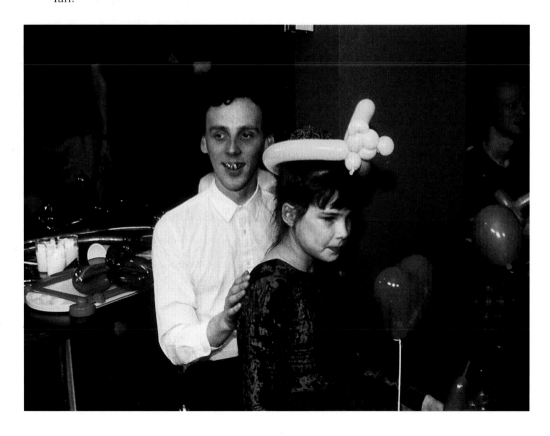

Julien Donkey-boy, *2000, film.*

Index

Picture Credits

Quotation Credits

p. 13, Russel Ward, *A Nation For a Continent: The History of Australia, 1901-1975* (London: Heinemann, 1978). p. 14, Lou Klepac (ed), *Australian Painters of the Twentieth Century* (Sydney: The Beagle Press, 2000). p. 16, John Richardson, *A Life of Picasso, 1907-1917: The Painter of Modern Life* (London: Jonathan Cape, 1996). p. 21, Ibid. p. 27, David Hockney, *Hockney On Photography* (London: Jonathan Cape, 1988). p. 35, William Feaver (London: Modern Painters, Volume 12, no.1). p. 30, Nikos Stangos (ed), *That's the Way I See It* (London: Thames and Hudson, 1993). p. 35, William Feaver (London: Modern Painters, Volume 12, no.1, 1999). p. 38, David Hockney, *Hockney On Photography* (London: Jonathan Cape, 1988). p. 39, *R.B. Kitaj: A Retrospective* (London: Tate Gallery Publications, 1984). p. 40, Robert Hughes, "The Princeling" (Time Magazine, February 8, 1993). p. 43, Jeff Koons, *The Jeff Koons Handbook* (London: Thames and Hudson, 1992). p. 45, Ibid. p. 50, Andy Warhol and Pat Hackett (ed), *Andy Warhol Diaries* (New York: Rizzoli, 1989). p. 58, Ibid. p. 60, "Andy Warhol," (U.S. News and World Report, 1987). p. 60, Andy Warhol and Pat Hackett (ed), *Andy Warhol Diaries* (New York: Rizzoli, 1989). p. 65, Victor Willing, *Paula Rego* (London: Tate Gallery Publishing, 1997). p. 65, John McEwen, "Exhibition Reviews," (London: Modern Painters, Volume 7, No. 4, 1994). p. 70, Victor Willing, *Paula Rego* (London: Tate Gallery Publishing, 1997). p. 72, Frank O'Hara, *City Poet: The Life and Times of Frank O'Hara* (New York: Alfred A. Knopf, 1993). p. 75, Ibid. p. 77, Ibid. p. 81, Bill Berkson, "A New York Beginner," (Modern Painters Vol. 11, No. 3, 1998). p. 82, Eva Karcher, *Dix* (Benedikt Taschen, 1988). p. 82, Sarah O'Brien Twohig and Frank Whitford, *Otto Dix* (London: The Tate Gallery, 1992). p. 85, Frank Witford, *The "Revolutionary Reactionary" in Otto Dix* (London: Tate Gallery, 1992). p. 87, Sarah O'Brien Twohig and Frank Whitford, *Otto Dix* (London: The Tate Gallery, 1992). p. 88, Jill Lloyd, German *Expressionism: Privitism and Modernity* (New Haven: Yale University Press, 1991). p. 94, John Elderfield, *Henti Matisse,: A Retrospective* (New York: Museum of Modern Art, 1992). p. 96, Robert Hughes, "A Domaine of Light and Color" (Time Magazine, July 2, 1990). p. 99, Wayne Thiebaud, "Matisse at MOMA" (London: Modern Painters, Vol. 6, No. 3, 1993). p. 102, Herschell B. Chipp, *Theories of Modern Art: A Source Book by Artists and Critics* (Berkeley: University of California Press, 1971). p. 104, Charles Harrison and Paul Wood (editors), *Art in Theory, 1900 – 1990: An Anthology of Changing Ideas* (Oxford: Blackwell Publishers, 1992). p. 104, Herschell B. Chipp, *Theories of Modern Art: A Source Book by Artists and Critics* (Berkeley: University of California Press, 1971). p. 109, Ibid. p. 109, Hilton Kramer, "Duchamp's Progeny" (London: Modern Painters, Volume 6, No. 3). p. 111, Stuart Davis, "Is There a Revolution in the Arts?" Bulletin of America's Town Meeting of the Air (Volume 5, No. 19, Feb. 19, 1940). p. 115, Philip Rylands (curator), "Stuart Davis–A European Memoir," Stuart Davis (Milan: Electra, 1997). p. 116, Dawn Ades and Fiona Bradley, *Salvador Dali, A Mythology* (London: Tate Gallery Publications, 1998). p. 118, Jose Maria Faerna (ed), *Dali* (Barcelona: Abrams, 1994). p. 119, Dawn Ades and Fiona Bradley, *Salvador Dali, A Mythology* (London: Tate Gallery Publications, 1998). p. 120, Ibid. p. 124, Rudolph Giuliani, "This Week," (New York: ABC News, October, 1999). p. 133, Jed Perl, *Eyewitness–Reports from an Art World in Crisis* (New York: Basic Books, 2000). p. 137, Martin Gayford (London: Modern Painters, Volume 7, no.4, 1994). p. 138, Jane Watkins, *Cezanne* (London: Tate Gallery Publishing, 1996). p. 142, John Elderfield, "Henri Matisse: A Retrospective" (New York: The Museum of Modern Art, 1992). p. 145, Marsden Hartley, "Art and the Personal Life, 1928" (New York: Creative Art, June 1928). p. 147, Jane Watkins (ed) *Cézanne* (London: Tate Publishing, 1996). p. 149, Andrew Graham-Dixon, *Howard Hodgkin* (London: Thames and Hudson, 1994). p. 149, David Sylvester, "Howard Hodgkin: Forty Paintings: 1973-84" (The Whitechapel Art Gallery, London, 1984). p. 150, Ibid. p. 155, Ibid. p. 149, Timothy Hyman, "Howard Hodgkin: Making a Riddle out of the Solution," (Art and Design Vol. 1, No. 8). p. 150, Ibid. p. 151, Julian Mitchell, (London: Modern Painters, Volume 14, no.2, 2001). p. 155, Timothy Hyman, "Howard Hodgkin: Making a Riddle out of the Solution," (Art and Design Vol. 1, No. 8). p. 159, Richard Kendall (ed), *Degas By Himself* (New York: Little, Brown and Company, 1987). p. 160, Ibid. p. 153, Ibid. p. 163, Stephen Phillips and Karen Wilkin, *Degas To Matisse: Impressionists and Modernists Masterpieces* (New York: Universe, 2000). p. 165, Ibid. p. 166, Nan Rosenthal, *The Drawings of Jasper Johns* (Washington: The National Gallery of Art, 1990). p. 170, Ibid. p. 171, Ibid. p. 173, Ibid. p. 174, Stephanie Terenzi (ed) *The Collected Writings of Robert Motherwell* (Los Angeles: University of California Press, 1999). p. 177, H.H. Aranson,, "Robert Motherwell" (New York: Abrams, 1977). p. 177, Ibid. p. 179, Ibid. p. 182, Ibid. p. 183, Arthur Danto, *The Collected Works of Robert Motherwell* (Oxford University Press, 1992). p. 184, Piet Mondrian, Harry Holtzman, Martin James, (editors), *The New Art and the New Life: The Collected Wrtings of Piet Mondrian* (London: Thames and Hudson, 1986). p. 188, Tom Lubbock (London: Modern Painters, Volume 8, no. 1, 1995). p. 188, Piet Mondrian and Harry Holtzman and Martin James (editors), *The New Art and the New Life: The Collected Wrtings of Piet Mondrian* (London: Thames and Hudson, 1986). p. 194, Ibid. p. 195, Matthew Collings, (London: Modern Painters, Volume 8, no. 3, 1995). p. 197, William I. Homer, *Seurat and the Science of Painting* (Cambridge, Mass, 1964). p. 199, John Leighton and Richard Tompson, *Seurat and the Bathers* (London: National Gallery of London, 1997). p. 199, William I. Homer, *Seurat and the Science of Painting* (Cambridge, Mass, 1964). p. 200, John Leighton and Richard Thomson, *Seurat and the Bathers* (London: National Gallery of London, 1997). p. 202, Ibid. p. 208, David Bowie, "Tracey Emin" (London: Modern Painters, Volume 11, no.1, 1998). p. 209, Gary Hume, Tracey Emin–I need Art like I need God (London: Emin, Brown, Kent, Collings, and Jopling, 1998). p. 212, David Bowie, "Tracey Emin" (London: Modern Painters, Volume 10, no.3, 1997). p. 214, David Bowie, "Tracey Emin" (London: Modern Painters, Volume 9, no.1, 1996). p. 225, Richard Billingham, "Ray's a Laugh" (New York: Scalo, 1996). p. 228, Richard Billingham, "Ray's a Laugh" (New York: Scalo, 1996). p. 230, "Robert Rauschenberg" (Art Journal, #48, 1989). p. 235, Billy Kluver with Julie Martin, Robert Rauschenberg: A Retrospective (New York: The Soloman R. Guggenheim Foundation, 1997). p. 237, Ibid. p. 238, "Robert Rauschenberg" (Art Journal, #48, 1989). p. 242, Brian O'Doherty, American Masters: The Voice and the Myth (London: Thames and Hudson, 1988). p. 242, "Robert Rauschenberg" (Art Journal, #48, 1989). p. 245, A.S. Byatt, A.S. (London: Modern Painters, Volume 14, no.1, 2001). p. 248, David Cohen, (London: Modern Painters, Volume 9, no.2, 1996). p. 250, Mel Gooding, Patrick Heron (London: Phaidon Press Ltd., 1994). p. 256, Eric Shanes, Brancusi (Abbeville, 1989). p. 258, Ibid. p. 260, Ibid. p. 262, Emily Braun, Speaking Volumes: Giorgio Morandi's Stll Lifes and the Cultural Politics of Strapaese (Baltimore: Johns Hopkins University Press, 1999). p. 264, Ibid. p. 267, Karen Wilkin and Giorgio Morandi, Giorgio Morandi: Twentieth Century Master Series (New York: Rizzoli, 1999). p. 270, Ibid. p. 271, Ibid. p. 274, Herschell B. Chipp, Theories of Modern Art: A Source Book by Artists and Critics (Berkeley: University of California Press, 1971). p. 276, Piet Mondrian, Harry Holtzman, Martin James, (editors), The New Art and the New Life: The Collected Wrtings of Piet Mondrian (London: Thames and Hudson, 1986). p. 276, Herschell B. Chipp, Theories of Modern Art: A Source Book by Artists and Critics (Berkeley: University of California Press, 1971). p. 277, Joan Ullman, "Willem de Kooning: An Appreciation" (The Independent Online, www.peconic.net). p. 279, Clement Greenberg, Horizon (London: #16, no. 93-94) October 1947. p. 281, Ibid. p. 282, Kirk Varnedoe, Essay: "Comet: Jackson Pollock's Life and Work" p. 283, Brian O'Doherty, American Masters: The Voice and the Myth (London: Thames and Hudson, 1988). p. 285, Kristine Styles and and Peter Seltz (editors), Theories and Documents of Contemporary Art: A Sourcebook of Artists' Writings (Berkeley: University of California Press, 1996). p. 286, Phillip Hensher, (London: Modern Painters, Volume 12, no.1, 1999). p. 286, Brian O'Doherty, American Masters: The Voice and the Myth (London: Thames and Hudson, 1988). p. 290, Phoebe Habon, "Samo© is Dead: The Fall of Jean-Michel Basquiat" (New York, September 26, 1988). p. 292, Rene Ricard, "The Radiant Child," (Artforum #20, December 1981). p. 293, Phoebe Habon, "Samo© is Dead: The Fall of Jean-Michel Basquiat" (New York, September 26, 1988). p. 294, Jeffrey Deitch, "Jean-Michel Basquiat: Annina Nosei," (Flash Art #16, May 1982). p. 294, Phoebe Habon, "Samo© is Dead: The Fall of Jean-Michel Basquiat" (New York, September 26, 1988). p. 295, Jeffrey Deitch, "Jean-Michel Basquiat: Annina Nosei," (Flash Art #16, 1982). p. 296, Herschell B. Chipp, Theories of Modern Art: A Source Book by Artists and Critics (Berkeley: University of California Press, 1968). p. 297, Hilton Kramer, "The Ghost of Willem de Kooning" (London: Modern Painters, Volume 7, no.2, 1994). p. 301, Robert Rauschenberg (Art Journal, #48, 1989). p. 302, Neal Benezra and Kerry Brougher, "Ed Ruscha" (Smithsonian Institution and Museum of Modern Art, 2000). p. 304, Neal Benezra and Kerry Brougher, "Ed Ruscha" (Smithsonian Institution and Museum of Modern Art, 2000). p. 307, Laura Janku, "Acquisition of an Archive: The Graphic Work of Ed Ruscha," (Internet: ArtResources.com). p. 312, Jules Olitski, (London: Modern Painters, Volume 13, no.3, 2000). p. 314, Ibid. p. 315, Matthew Collings (London: Modern Painters, Volume 11, no.3). p. 318, Robert Rosenblum p. 318, Jules Olitski, (London: Modern Painters, Volume 13, no.3). p. 320, Wes Mills, Drawing Notes, 2000 p. 324, Ibid. p. 331, Aidan Dunne, "Cooke's Voyage," (The Irish Times, July, 1999).≥ p. 336, Donald Judd, Chinati Foundation p. 337, Donald Judd, Chinati Foundation p. 338, Donald Judd, Chinati Foundation p. 341, Harmony Korine, A Crackup at the Race Riots (Faber and Faber, 1998). p. 343, Ibid. p. 344, Ibid.

Acknowledgements

Karen Wright would like to thank the following people: First, Craig Burnett. Without his fortitude, this book would not have happened, and he seemed to find the humor in every awful situation. There were many people within the *Modern Painters* group who rolled up their sleeves, including Julie Bettridge, Anthony Jay, Litia Perta, Kate Barrette, Shane Waltener, Sarah Luddy, Tara Richards, and Maria David. For design, gratitude to Akio Morishima and Herman Lelie. Enormous thanks must go to *Modern Painters* Associate Editor Linda Saunders for her patient and skillful editing of the pieces prior to their appearance in this book. This is not to overlook the team in DK New York, and in particular Sean Moore, Barbara Minton, Megan Clayton, Tina Vaughan, Chris Avgherinos, and Todd Fries, whose input has been invaluable in planning, shaping, and producing the book. And thanks also to Sophie Raynor, Gabriella Hallas, and designer Steve Hawes at Cambridge Publishing Management, who helped combine *Modern Painters* and DK style into a fantastic finished product. Finally, I'd like to thank Patrick Walsh of Conville and Walsh, UK, for his support and enthusiasm.

DK Publishing would like to thank Gus Yoo for additional design and Crystal Coble for editorial assistance.